T&T CLARK HANDBOOK OF THEOLOGICAL ANTHROPOLOGY

T&T Clark Handbooks

Forthcoming titles in this series include:

T&T Clark Handbook of Analytic Theology,
edited by James M. Arcadi and James T. Turner, Jr.

T&T Clark Handbook of Colin Gunton,
edited by Andrew Picard, Myk Habets, and Murray Rae

T&T Clark Handbook of Theological Anthropology,
edited by Mary Ann Hinsdale and Stephen Okey

T&T Clark Handbook of Christology,
edited by Darren O. Sumner and Chris Tilling

T&T Clark Handbook of Christian Prayer,
edited by Ashley Cocksworth and John C. McDowell

Titles already published include:

T&T Clark Handbook of Pneumatology,
edited by Daniel Castelo and Kenneth M. Loyer

T&T Clark Handbook of Ecclesiology,
edited by Kimlyn J. Bender and D. Stephen Long

T&T Clark Handbook of Christian Theology and the Modern Sciences,
edited by John P. Slattery

T&T Clark Handbook of Christian Ethics,
edited by Tobias Winright

T&T Clark Handbook of Thomas. F. Torrance,
edited by Paul D. Molnar and Myk Habets

T&T Clark Handbook of Christian Theology and Climate Change,
edited by Ernst M. Conradie and Hilda P. Koster

T&T Clark Handbook of Edward Schillebeeckx,
edited by Stephan van Erp and Daniel Minch

T&T Clark Handbook of Political Theology,
edited by Rubén Rosario Rodríguez

T&T Clark Companion to the Theology of Kierkegaard,
edited by Aaron P. Edwards and David J. Gouwens

T&T Clark Handbook of African American Theology,
edited by Antonia Michelle Daymond, Frederick L. Ware, and Eric Lewis Williams

T&T Clark Handbook of Asian American Biblical Hermeneutics,
edited by Uriah Y. Kim and Seung Ai Yang

T&T Clark Handbook to Early Christian Meals in the Greco-Roman World,
edited by Soham Al-Suadi and Peter-Ben Smit

T&T CLARK HANDBOOK OF THEOLOGICAL ANTHROPOLOGY

Edited by
Mary Ann Hinsdale, I.H.M.
and Stephen Okey

t&tclark

LONDON • NEW YORK • OXFORD • NEW DELHI • SYDNEY

T&T CLARK
Bloomsbury Publishing Plc
50 Bedford Square, London, WC1B 3DP, UK
1385 Broadway, New York, NY 10018, USA
29 Earlsfort Terrace, Dublin 2, Ireland

BLOOMSBURY, T&T CLARK and the T&T Clark logo are trademarks
of Bloomsbury Publishing Plc

First published in Great Britain 2021
Paperback edition published 2023

Cover design: Terry Woodley
Cover image: Gandee Vasan/Getty Images

A catalogue record for this book is available from the British Library.

A catalog record for this book is available from the Library of Congress.

ISBN: HB: 978-0-5676-7832-4
PB: 978-0-5676-9903-9
ePDF: 978-0-5676-7833-1
eBook: 978-0-5676-7834-8

Series: T&T Clark Handbooks

Typeset by Newgen KnowledgeWorks Pvt. Ltd., Chennai, India

To find out more about our authors and books visit www.bloomsbury.com
and sign up for our newsletters.

CONTENTS

ACKNOWLEDGMENTS

The *T&T Clark Handbook of Theological Anthropology* is a book born of collaboration, and we would be remiss not to open the text by expressing our gratitude to all those who contributed to its creation. We wish first to thank the staff at Bloomsbury, especially Anna Turton, Sarah Blake and Veerle Van Steenhuyse. We hope this volume is a valuable contribution to the *Handbook* series, and we thank you for all you've done to bring it into existence. Thanks also to M. Shawn Copeland, Susan A. Ross and the anonymous reviewers of our proposal for this book. Their feedback was very valuable at the beginning stages of the project as we sorted out the issues and major figures that the text has focused on. We also wish to thank the many contributors to this volume, who wrote excellent essays, were responsive with feedback and have been patient throughout the whole process.

Unless indicated otherwise, scripture quotations are from New Revised Standard Version Bible, copyright © 1989 National Council of the Churches of Christ in the United States of America. Used by permission. All rights reserved worldwide.

Mary Ann Hinsdale would like to thank the graduate students in her Theological Anthropology seminars over the past twenty years at Boston College, as well as those she taught earlier at St. John's Provincial Seminary. Their questions and contributions have provided much of the "fertilizer" for the terrain of this volume and continue to prune the landscape of my theological reflection. Finally, I am indebted to the theological mentors, colleagues and friends who have supported me in this project: Joann Wolksi Conn, M. Shawn Copeland, Mary E. Hines, Mary Ellen Sheehan, I.H.M. and Suzanne Sattler, I.H.M.

Stephen Okey would like to thank his colleagues and students at Saint Leo University for their always helpful conversation, questions, suggestions and insights. I am also grateful for the fellowship and prayers of my parish community at Saint Joseph Catholic Church. Finally, I am most grateful for my wife, Paige, and our daughter, Dorothy, for their support and their patience as this project came to conclusion.

Mary Ann Hinsdale, I.H.M.

Stephen Okey

Introduction

MARY ANN HINSDALE, I.H.M., AND STEPHEN OKEY

Theological (or Christian) anthropology is a relatively recent subdiscipline within systematic/constructive theology. The goal of this book is to serve as a handbook for those seeking to understand the various approaches (classical, modern, postmodern) that present-day Christian theologians have taken to present and interpret the doctrines of creation, the human person as *imago Dei*, sin, grace and the relationships that humans have with other creatures. We also attempt to address some of the more critical challenges facing theological anthropology in a postmodern (or post-postmodern?) age.

Our volume assembles the insights of both veteran theologians and emerging scholars who write in the field of theological anthropology in order to "companion" inquiring readers who want to make sense of what becoming "human" means in an increasingly violent and threatened world. How is it still possible to savor the beauty and joy of this great adventure? In presenting theological anthropology, our volume is primarily from an ecumenically aware Roman Catholic perspective. We have striven for a "small c" catholic outlook that includes often neglected voices and perspectives (women, African American, Asian, Latino/a, disability, class and LGBTQ). We revisit authors from the "Great Tradition" (early church, medieval, modern) and offer theological perspectives that are critical and liberationist (feminist, decolonial, intersectional and critical race theory). We are conscious, however, that our book (with some exceptions) reflects mostly North Atlantic viewpoints (the United States, Canada, UK). At the same time, we are pleased that the vast majority of our authors are in dialogue with a broad range of voices from other social locations.

The handbook is divided into four parts: I. "Methodology" (Chapters 1–3); II. "Key Themes" (Chapters 4–10); III. "Key Figures" (Chapters 11–25) and IV. "Contemporary Constructive Concerns" (Chapters 26–32).

PART I: METHODOLOGY

In Chapter 1, Veli-Matti Kärkkäinen first traces and analyzes classical approaches to theological anthropology in the history of Christian theology up to the dawn of modernity. The main lens he uses is the concept of "soul," an essential feature of the dominant dualistic account of human nature throughout the history of Christian theology. After having located the anthropological question within theology as a whole, including its relation to the concept of the *imago Dei*, Kärkkäinen traces the main historical "turns" in the understanding of soul and ends with a critical assessment of the liabilities and challenges of anthropological dualisms.

Kevin M. Vander Schel, in Chapter 2, considers the "modern method" approach to theological anthropology, with its emphasis on "the turn to the subject." During this period, theological understandings of anthropology underwent a notable shift, in which reflection upon human persons and experience no longer indicated one specific area of theological study but became the touchstone of theological inquiry overall. Vander Schel inquires into this methodological shift by examining the "turn to the subject" in the writings of two foundational figures: Immanuel Kant and Friedrich Schleiermacher. Kant's critical philosophy raised enduring questions about the possibility and limits of theological knowledge claims. Schleiermacher outlined both a pioneering understanding of Christian self-consciousness and a reorganization of theological method that redefined the modern academic study of theology.

In Chapter 3, Anthony J. Godzieba argues that rather than a "method," the postmodern condition emphasizes patterns of "difference," the always-already-present structuring condition of all historical and cultural realities. With roots in twentieth-century philosophy, this opposition to the modern rational quest for unity quickly morphed into cultural critique and exposed the historical contingency of the principles that Western modernity assumed to be absolute (or at least well-founded) about human persons. Is it possible to recuperate "person" and human agency? For Godzieba, this is the challenge posed to any contemporary theological anthropology: how to look to an ethical retrieval of "difference" grounded in belief in creation, the Incarnation and Christ's resurrection.

PART II: KEY THEMES

Part II considers seven themes that have typically been considerations focal points for theological anthropology: creation, *imago Dei*, relationality, finitude, sin, grace and freedom.

Daniel P. Horan, OFM, tackles the theme of "creation" in Chapter 4, reminding us that any adequate reflection on the human person within the Christian tradition today must begin with consideration of the broader reality of creation. Horan explores (1) the recent discussions about the Christian doctrine of *creatio ex nihilo*; (2) renewed interpretations of scripture that emphasize the community of creation and challenge earlier presuppositions about the doctrine of *imago Dei*; and (3) insights from the theory of evolution for a theology of creation in general and the human person in particular. Horan illustrates how these themes lay the foundation for the kind of "integral ecological" approach to theological reflection adopted by Pope Francis in his encyclical, *Laudato Sí*. Whereas creation has long been treated as a subfield within theological anthropology, this chapter suggests that any responsible theological anthropology must begin with creation.

In Chapter 5, Michelle A. Gonzalez sees creation of humanity in the image of God as one of the most captivating, vague and significant theological concepts in Christian thought. Whether via more abstract formulations of human nature, or concrete on-the-ground reflections, theologians throughout the centuries have interpreted and reinterpreted both human and divine nature in light of the *imago Dei*. For Christians, the image of God reveals who we were, who we are and what we will become through the life of faith. The notion of creation in the image of God may be highly abstract, so theological reflections on that image must always be grounded in concrete everyday lives.

The "relational turn" in theological anthropology is the subject explored by Rosemary P. Carbine in Chapter 6. Carbine explores different women's liberation theologies to creatively chart new directions in a relational anthropology, illustrated by such key concepts as interrelationality, intersectionality, interculturality, interstitiality and interreligiosity. These theologies take the experiences of women from very different social locations as their starting points for theological reflections on humanity. Whether these theologies reflect on God, creation in the image of God or living into that divine image in Christ, they present a shared understanding of the human person as embodied in multiple, dynamic and future-oriented relations, which are perennially negotiated, and occasionally integrated, in shaping a more just and solidaristic sense of self and world.

Chapter 7 addresses the topic of finitude. Linn Marie Tonstad draws our attention to the concrete existence of creation, arguing that in theology, finitude indicates both dependence and limitation. While many theologians have turned to the affirmation of finitude as a panacea for unlimited human desire, that turn often draws attention away from the very particularities and conditions of existence that finitude picks out. Rather than thinking finitude in abstraction, her chapter examines dependence, death and desire in recent theology in order to push theological anthropology toward a concrete reckoning with history, differentially distributed vulnerability and the questions of death and loss.

In Chapter 8, Darlene Fozard Weaver maintains that sin, when properly understood, complicates our understanding of moral agency and challenges the enterprise of ethics. Sin shows us that ethics can be a vehicle for sin, by legitimating what is sinful in our status quo or narrowing our moral concern to our own goodness or badness. For these reasons, the discourse of sin benefits Christian ethics and Christian theological anthropology, showing the viability of that anthropology and leveraging its value for advancing our understanding of human persons. Sin is a valuable and underutilized language for grappling with human agency and the malformation of the world.

Shawn Colberg offers an overview of "grace" in Chapter 9, emphasizing grace as a concept for naming and systematizing the diverse effects of God's love in the economy of salvation, especially its anthropological dimensions. He retrieves the biblical language used for grace, explores its development in apostolic and ancient Christian sources, and observes its varied inflections in the Christian East and West. Colberg traces the increasingly systematic implications of grace for human nature through Latin theologies of the high scholastic and Reformation eras, noting diverse emphases on the intrinsic and extrinsic effects of grace. He plots the developments in nature/grace questions through the modern period and argues that no one theology of grace can fully capture the breadth and creative power of God's love so that grace ultimately operates as a polyvalent symbol that names God who loves, and so graces, the world.

Chapter 10 considers the last theme in this part: "freedom." Here, Philip Rossi, SJ, provides a theological articulation of the intelligibility of human freedom, referenced to the Christian proclamation of the triune God as Creator, Redeemer and Sanctifier of humanity and of the cosmos. As Creator, God is gracious originator and sustainer of human freedom and the world of its exercise; as Redeemer, God is transformative healer of the self-incurred brokenness of human freedom and its consequences; as Sanctifying Spirit, God is enlivener of the fullness of communion with God to which human freedom is oriented for its eschatological completion. This construal is offered in contrast to prevailing accounts of freedom that, referencing it to the subjectivity of individual human agency, underlie important strands of the culture of Western secularity.

PART III: KEY FIGURES

Part III comprises the bulk of the handbook by introducing fifteen "key figures" who have made substantive contributions to theological anthropology, ranging chronologically from Irenaeus of Lyon to Orlando Espín.

In Chapter 11, Francine Cardman notes that, in the five books of *Against Heresies*, Irenaeus defends material creation, the fleshly and spiritual human being, and the Word made flesh while refuting various "gnostic" views of these same fundamental elements of the "apostolic tradition." Irenaeus frames his argument within the construct of "recapitulation," a scriptural and cosmic perspective on the coherence of beginning and end, creation and eschatology, held together in the making and remaking of human being by the Word, who sums up in human flesh God's merciful love for humankind, made in the image of God. In Irenaeus' recapitulative Word are the beginnings and ends of theological anthropology.

Gregory of Nyssa is the figure examined in Chapter 12. J. Warren Smith observes that Gregory of Nyssa, in *On the Making of Man* and in the deathbed dialogue *On the Soul and Resurrection*, uses the consummation of all things in the Resurrection as the lens through which one can rightly view human nature and understand both what God intended humanity to be in the beginning as well as how sin has caused such a corruption of human nature. In later works, Gregory builds upon the idea that rational creatures are continually growing in likeness to God through ceaseless participation in God to define human perfection as *epektasis*, the soul's eternal movement.

Douglas Finn takes up the doctor of the Church, Augustine of Hippo, in Chapter 13. Finn situates Augustine's theological anthropology in a broader reflection on theological language. He highlights the centrality of the unity-in-difference of the human person—an integral whole of soul and body—in Augustine's understanding of the mystery of the human being, who is a creature of God made in his Trinitarian image. In particular, he shows how, for Augustine, the human mystery does not leave one utterly speechless but rather enables the type of language appropriate to the revelation of divine transcendence and the excess of God's love. It is this love that then extends into the finite world through the acts of creation, salvation and eschatological perfection.

Chapter 14, by Dominic Doyle, explores the theocentric and Trinitarian nature of Thomas Aquinas' theological anthropology in four parts: (1) creation, (2) *imago Dei*, (3) sin and (4) grace. The human person, as created in the *imago Dei*, is *capax Dei*. As a result, divine grace heals and perfects fallen human nature. Aquinas casts this transformation in Trinitarian terms in his account of how the two temporal missions of the Word (Incarnation) and Spirit (grace) gather human understanding and loving into God's eternal Wisdom and Love.

The reformer Martin Luther is the subject of Chapter 15. Luther scholar Candace L. Kohli notes that a challenge for theological anthropology is to give a robust theological account of the human person as she is in herself while also doing justice to the human person as she exists in relation to God in Christ. She examines Luther's theological anthropology in order to identify a theological approach for investigating the person as person and also vis-à-vis God. Luther utilized the conceptual apparatus of justification to reconsider the person in relation to the Holy Spirit. This allowed him to parse temporal anthropological features using Aristotelian categories supplied by medieval philosophical anthropologies and moral theology. He was then able to consider how human noetic faculties may be temporally altered as a result of the person's new relation to Christ and the Spirit.

Chapter 16 discusses John Calvin's Trinitarian Theological Anthropology. Arnold Huijgen regards the distinction between human beings before and after the Fall as crucial for Calvin's anthropology. As such, human beings exist before God (*coram deo*). An awareness of God is therefore fundamental to Calvin's anthropology. In the hierarchy of being, humans are positioned between angels and animals. Humans are created in the image of God, which is found primarily in the immortal soul. In his context, Calvin shows a tendency toward equality between man and woman. With respect to human beings after the Fall, Calvin emphasizes the corruption of human nature. Through the work of the Holy Spirit, believers learn to love the life to come. Enjoyment is only allowed with caution.

In Chapter 17, Tim Hartman considers Karl Barth's approach to Theological Anthropology. "Being human means being with God" is Swiss-German theologian Karl Barth's (1886–1968) definition of what it means to be human. Human existence is never an existence in isolation or independence but always already an existence in relation to God and to one's fellow creatures. We cannot know what it means to be human without considering human beings in relationship with God and with one another. Hartman critically examines Barth's definition of humanity, including his understanding of race, gender and sexuality, with an eye toward potential implications of Barth's theological anthropology for contemporary theological scholarship.

Chapter 18 by Susan Abraham has the intriguing title, "Karl Rahner for Twenty-First-Century Cyborgs." Abraham observes that present-day "cyborgs"—persons who have enhanced themselves through technological additions and prosthetics—often seem as if they do not need theology or a theological imagination. Thus, she asks, whether Karl Rahner's theological anthropology could still be relevant for them. Believing that many cyborgs also seek spiritual transcendence, she aims to make the case that the theological anthropology of this twentieth-century Roman Catholic German theologian is a great source for spiritually seeking cyborgs. Rahner's understanding of the human creature and of Jesus Christ as seeking each other in a mutually enhancing relationship offers a creative resource for cyborgs. However, where Rahner challenges cyborgs is in the assumption that transcendence can be bought or consumed as another thing in the world. Thus, Abraham argues the cyborg can actively seek transcendence as she creatively engages with it to transform herself and her world.

In Chapter 19, Carolyn Chau examines the theological anthropology of Hans Urs von Balthasar, finding it grounded in a poignant kenotic Christology and a notion that all humans are invited, through Christ, to participate in the *theodrama* of life in God. One's receptivity to the divine invitation to take up one's mission, and to live one's life as and through ceaseless prayer to God, enables one to reflect divine love in the world and reveal divine glory. Chau's chapter discusses these features of Balthasar's account of the human person, along with his spirituality of childhood and notion of ecclesial personhood. She also considers Balthasar's controversial understanding of sexual difference.

Chapter 20 examines the theological anthropology of another twentieth-century Catholic theologian, Edward Schillebeeckx. Edmund Kee-Fook Chia observes that Schillebeeckx did not write a specific volume dedicated to theological anthropology, but through his writings one can easily discern his understandings of God and God's relationship with humans, the nature of human experience and the very mystery of humanity itself. Kee-Fook Chia's chapter discusses all this, beginning with Schillebeeckx's understanding of creation faith, the limitations of human finitude and God's graciousness.

It then addresses the quest for salvation, Jesus as paradigm for humanity and the significance of Christian praxis in the pursuit of the *humanum*.

Bernard Lonergan's theological anthropology is investigated by Jeremy D. Wilkins in Chapter 21. According to Wilkins, the center of Lonergan's work is self-appropriation, a personal exploration of the dynamic structures of inquiry and love, culminating in a decision to faithfully observe their requirements. This program grounds Lonergan's theological anthropology. Wilkins goes on to offer a summary description of Lonergan's project and the positions it led him to take on consciousness and self-transcendence, inquiry and bias, love and conversion, progress and decline in the historical unfolding of the human good, and the possibility of redemption through the law of the cross.

Chapter 22 examines the theological anthropology of "the philosopher pope," John Paul II (Karol Wojtyła). Jennifer Bader summarizes John Paul II's life and historical context, articulating the questions that preoccupied him: How does one ground an absolute claim to human dignity? In light of this, how does one understand the human body, gender and/ or sexual difference? Bader demonstrates that his definition of human nature is motivated by his desire to defend human dignity from the philosophical materialisms of his time. She explores key aspects of the pope's understanding of the human body-person and critiques John Paul II's methodology in light of both his own original project and contemporary questions of human sexuality.

In Chapter 23, Susan A. Ross presents Rosemary Radford Ruether as offering a liberationist, feminist critique of hierarchical and dualistic structures that dominate and oppress not only women but also racial-ethnic minorities and the Earth. Ross argues that Ruether's view of humanity can best be understood through the various lenses that she has used throughout her work to analyze relevant topics involving the human person. Long before the term "intersectionality" became a buzzword in academia, Ruether saw the connections among various forms of oppression and has consistently argued against dualistic conceptions of the person in favor of a holistic approach that encompasses different, but also complementary, "lenses." She uses the lenses of history, theology, ecology and global awareness to understand what it means to be human, how the various theological subtopics in anthropology are informed by these lenses and how current crises affect her understanding of the human person. The combination of a critical understanding of history, a passion for justice and a deep faith in the possibilities of the human person mark the deeply significant contribution of Rosemary Radford Ruether to contemporary theological anthropology.

In Chapter 24, "Salving the Wound of Race: Racialized Bodies as Sacrament in the Theology of M. Shawn Copland," Karen Teel discusses Copeland's contribution to theological anthropology. Teel reads Copeland as probing the corporeality of US imperialism in the late twentieth and early twenty-first centuries. In her writing, Copeland calls the United States and US Catholic Church to come to terms with its historic and ongoing subjugation of nonwhite bodies. Copeland has clarified that, under white supremacy, black women's striving for freedom constitutes an affirmation of human dignity that is nothing less than sacramental. This theological insight compels us to confront the concrete and spiritual realities of other bodies. If struggling black women's bodies reveal God's presence, what do relatively easeful white bodies reveal? Under white supremacy, can white bodies ever constitute a sacrament? Copeland pushes us to confront the concrete and spiritual realities of bodies and their fates, to see their meanings illuminated in the eschatological context of death and resurrection, of Christ's body and other bodies. In the US context, racism implicates all of our bodies, such that theologians investigating theological anthropology cannot responsibly defer difficult questions about it to others.

The final key figure considered in Part Three is Latino theologian Orlando Espín. In Chapter 25, Néstor Medina teases out Espín's anthropology by highlighting his Latina/o/x contextual considerations as part of a "theo-ethical" endeavor to explore what it means to be human and how to understand the varying ways people live their humanness. Attention is given to Espín's interdisciplinary scholarship through which he affirms the inherent theo-ethical, revelatory character of Latinas/os/xs lived experiences. Medina proposes that Espín's theo-ethical anthropology and methodology reorient prevailing understandings of humanity and humanness; his work provides critical tools for accounting for the different ways different people live their humanness and celebrate their religious traditions.

PART IV: CONTEMPORARY CONCERNS

In Chapter 26, Stephen Okey looks at how the understanding of the human person has shaped research into artificial intelligence (AI). Okey examines the concepts of *imago Dei* and of personhood as frames for investigating AI in terms of intelligence, affectivity, embodiment and agency. While AI research has delved into all four of these areas, there remain both technological limitations and metaphysical questions about where such research might go. The chapter concludes by considering a Thomistic approach to personhood and highlighting the significant questions a "technological" person would raise for theological anthropology.

Lorraine Cuddeback-Gedeon looks at "disability" in Chapter 27 and raises challenges to "rationality" and "embodiment" in theological anthropology. Her consideration begins with a brief overview of how disability as a concept and theory developed, moves on to explore how disability (despite being a modern concept) has been theologically treated and, finally, considers the most common challenges raised by these treatments, namely, to the role of rationality plays in understanding the human soul and to the unity of body and soul against dualism. By engaging the experience of disability, in all its varieties, Christian theological anthropology has the opportunity to deepen its intersectional analysis, as well as gain a greater awareness of voices that have been ignored in doing theology.

Chapter 28, "A Theological Anthropology of Racism" by Amey Victoria Adkins-Jones, considers the import of holding theological anthropology accountable for contributing not only to the idea of race and superiority but also to the racism latent in both church doctrine and practice. Highlighting the historical context of Black theologians living and writing in the United States, the article cites Jewish supercession and Christian-colonial enterprise as important theological loci for responding to contemporary realities of anti-blackness and racial violence. Adkins-Jones builds her argument around the confessional character of race and turns to the legacy of Black churches in America to consider a way forward.

In Chapter 29, Mary Ann Hinsdale, I.H.M., examines the concept of "gender" as it has played out in feminist, intersectional attempts to discern the meaning of sex, gender and sexuality in the context of reclaiming a theological anthropology that takes embodiment seriously. Focusing particularly on gender issues in the Catholic Church, Hinsdale looks at official Roman Catholic magisterial statements that endorse the equality of the sexes, yet maintain an essentialist understanding of gender complementarity. Because these statements do not attend to the intersectional reality of sex, gender and sexuality, they ultimately exclude certain groups from full participation in human personhood. In conclusion, the chapter looks at some recent attempts by contemporary theologians to propose alternatives to gender complementarity.

In Chapter 30, Heidi Russell looks at how we understand the human person in the light of neuroscience. She examines particularly the ways neuroscience has developed in the subfields of affective neuroscience, social neuroscience and interpersonal neurobiology. The chapter then explores the contribution of neuroscience to questions about the role of the brain in religious/mystical experience and the relationship between body/soul, before concluding with some questions that neuroscience raises for a contemporary theological anthropology.

In Chapter 31, "Neoliberalism and Theological Anthropology: The Hidden Formation of Student Loan and Dating Apps," Vincent J. Miller considers how neoliberalism—a twentieth-century movement of activist economists—informs the contemporary understanding of the human person. Its influence is not the result of a cultural consensus rooted in ideas but comes from the movement's influence on policy. By replacing the communitarian policies of postwar social democracy with market-based policies emphasizing individual choice and risk, neoliberalism has made a world in which the common good has become difficult to imagine. Various dimensions of the neoliberal self are outlined and contrasted with Catholic notions of the human person. The chapter concludes by considering resources for an ecclesial response.

Finally, in Chapter 32, Oliver Davies considers the impact of recent scientific research on theological anthropology. A wide range of fields, including quantum theory, evolutionary anthropology and neuroscience contribute to complex questions about the human person. This is especially the case with the human capacity for free will. Davies draws on the work of theologian Henri de Lubac on "mystery" in order to claim that new scientific discoveries offer new possibilities for non-reductive, non-transcendental and non-metaphysical readings of space and time.

PART I

Methodology

CHAPTER ONE

Classical Approaches to Theological Anthropology

VELI-MATTI KÄRKKÄINEN

INTRODUCTION: THE DOCTRINE OF HUMANITY VIS-À-VIS THE DOCTRINE OF CREATION

The purpose of this essay is to trace and analyze theologically the "method" of and "approaches to" (doing) theological anthropology in the history of Christian theology until the dawn of modernity. The main lens through which this is attempted has to do with the concept of "soul," an essential feature of the dominant dualistic account of the human nature throughout the history of Christian theology. Other lenses also could have been chosen, particularly the *image of God*, but for that topic a separate article is devoted in this *Handbook*. Before delving into the main topic, a brief look at the relationship between the doctrine of creation at large and the doctrine of humanity will be taken, to be followed by a consideration of the place and locus of theological anthropology in Christian theology prior to modernity.

A defining feature of traditional theology was to make a fairly categorical distinction between "nature" (creation at large) and human person as a creature. Indeed, traditionally Christian theology used to consider the transition from the discussion of nature to humanity as a disjuncture with the intention to underscore the importance of the difference between humanity and the rest of creation. In other words: it was important for theology to elevate and highlight the unique nature of humanity as the image of God, a special handiwork of the Creator, vis-à-vis other creatures that—notwithstanding their capacity to reflect their Maker—did not enjoy this privileged status. Herein is a dramatic difference from contemporary (to us) theology, which considers the transition from the doctrine of creation to the doctrine of humanity just that—namely, a *transition* rather than a disjuncture, starting with the question of "what links human beings with animals and all other creatures."[1]

This essay is based on and draws directly from my *Creation and Humanity: A Constructive Christian Theology for the Pluralistic World*, vol. 3 (Grand Rapids, MI: Eerdmans, 2015), especially chapter 12, but also chapters 9 and 11 to a smaller measure.

[1] Jürgen Moltmann, *God in Creation: A New Theology of Creation and the Spirit of God*, trans. Margaret Kohl (Minneapolis, MN: Fortress, 1993), 185.

The classic disjuncture is not in keeping with the creation theology of the Old Testament. Indeed, the biblical data seems to be pointing to an integral connection between "nature" and humanity. The two creation narratives in the beginning of the Old Testament point to a dynamic mutuality, fellowship, and unity in diversity among creatures. The emergence of a sequence of forms—or "generations [*toledoth*] of the heavens and the earth when they were created" (Gen. 2:4a)—culminating in the creation of humanity, makes creation an interrelated web, a network. The Yahwist narrative makes the creation of human beings a matter of having been "formed ... of dust from the ground" and having had "breathed into his nostrils the breath of life," as a result of which "man became a living being" (Gen. 2:7). This "spirited," living being, formed of *ha adama* (earth), is called *Adam*. Similar to all other creatures, the one created "in the image of God" (Gen. 1:27) depends for her livelihood on the "green plant for food" (Gen. 1:30; cf. 29).[2] Jürgen Moltmann rightly concludes, "It is only when we become aware of the things which human beings have in common with other creatures, and the things that differentiate them, that we can understand what the human being's designation as the image of God really means (Gen. 1:26)."[3]

Another defining shift has taken place in theology with regard to the doctrine of creation and the doctrine of humanity. It has to do with the source and means for knowledge of God. In patristic and subsequent theology before modernity the knowledge of God was envisioned to be possible through the observation of the cosmos and its operations. Just think of Thomas Aquinas' ways for attaining knowledge of God. While this tactic was not necessarily left behind at modernity, the focus shifted to human nature as the key to knowing God. More precisely, for modern theologians, "human experience of the world and of the individual's existence in it repeatedly supplied the point of departure for discussing the reality of God."[4] The reticence in early theology for making the human being the lens for knowledge of God most probably stems from its taking seriously the exceedingly great power and wisdom of God as the Creator; the human being and human nature in comparison with this infinite Creator can hardly supply the access to that knowledge. The cosmos as something mysterious and often times scary to mortal man and woman, on the contrary, could be "big" enough to provide such a platform. Be that as it may, there is no denying the tendency to "anthropologize" theology in modernity.

LOCATING THEOLOGICAL ANTHROPOLOGY IN CHRISTIAN TRADITION PRIOR TO MODERNITY

One of the changing factors with regard to theological anthropology is its location in systematic and doctrinal theology. Rather than forming their own locus ("place," i.e., chapter), anthropological questions were scattered among other doctrinal themes. Typically, premodern theology discussed theological anthropology in four loci:[5]

---

[2]For comments, see ibid., 187.

[3]Ibid., 188; see further 189.

[4]Wolfhart Pannenberg, *Anthropology in Theological Perspective*, trans. Matthew J. O'Connell (Philadelphia, PA: Westminster Press, 1985), 11; see also his "Anthropology and the Question of God," in Pannenberg, *The Idea of God and Human Freedom*, trans. R. A. Wilson (Philadelphia, PA: Fortress, 1973), 80–98.

[5]See David H. Kelsey, *Eccentric Existence: A Theological Anthropology*, 2 vols. (Louisville, KY: Westminster John Knox, 2009), 1:27–41. For an interesting discussion of how views and foci of theological anthropology have shifted throughout theological history among the main Christian traditions and in the context of new theological breakthroughs, see Stephen B. Bevans and Roger P. Schroder, *Constants in Context: A Theology for Mission for Today* (Maryknoll, NY: Orbis, 2004), chapter 1 (for a summary table, see 37).

In the doctrine of creation, in distinction from the rest of the creatures, the uniqueness of humanity and human nature was considered through the defining concept of the *imago Dei*. This concept claimed to provide a foundational account of the human person and humanity in relation to the Creator, other creatures and the cosmos as a whole. Notwithstanding the scarcity of direct references to the concept in the biblical canon—after three occurrences in the beginning (Gen. 1:26-27; 5:1; 9:6), the concept disappears until it is picked up in a couple of NT passages (1 Cor. 11:7; Jas 3:9)—from early on theological tradition made it an umbrella term. Everywhere in the Fathers, Gen. 1:26 plays a significant role when commenting on humanity and human destiny. Part of the discussion included long-standing debates about how to frame the dualist understanding of human nature, whether as spirit-soul-body (trichotomist) or as spirit/ soul-body (dichotomist), as well as the question of the origins of the soul of which there were a number of theories: preexistence (a view soon abandoned because of its pagan connections); traducianism according to which both soul and body come from the union between the parents; and creationism that teaches that God "directly" brings about each individual soul at the moment of conception.

In the doctrine of sin and salvation, the emphasis was placed on the salvation of the "soul." A literal understanding of the Gen. 2–4 narrative was assumed with historical Adam and discussed a literal "intermediate state." While belief in the resurrection of the body pointed to the "material" nature of the Christian eschatological vision, a holistic, cosmic vision of the new creation was often missed because of a predominantly "spiritual" hope. The doctrine of revelation considered the conditions for the reception of divine revelation, under the rubrics "general revelation" and "natural theology"; however, the main platform for access to the knowledge of God was the cosmos rather than human nature.

THE IMAGE OF GOD AND THE SOUL

As mentioned, the most central concept of theological anthropology from the beginning of Christian theology was the *imago Dei*. Understandably, it has entertained a number of interpretations throughout history as discussed by Michelle Gonzalez in this *Handbook*. For the purposes of this essay, it will suffice to consider the concept's significance in relation to the "soul" as the way of explaining the uniqueness and God-towardness of the human being.

A major reason why soul, the God-given immaterial part of human nature as something "above" the physical, and the image of God seem to couple so well had to do with the linking of the image with reason[6] and will[7] (in the so-called structural view, that is, an interpretation of image of God according to which there is something within the

---

[6]This came to culmination in Augustine; see, e.g., *Confessions*, 13.32; Philip Schaff and Henry Wace, eds., *A Select Library of the Nicene and Post-Nicene Fathers of the Christian Church*, 1st ser., 14 vols. (Edinburgh: T&T Clark, 1880–6), public domain, available at www.ccel.org, vol. 1, 201–2; *City of God*, 12.23; ibid., vol. 1, 241–2; *On Christian Doctrine*, 1.22; ibid., vol. 2; 527–8; for detailed discussion, see Stanley J. Grenz, *The Social God and Relational Self: A Trinitarian Theology of the Imago Dei* (Louisville, KY: Westminster John Knox, 2001), 152–7.

[7]Representative is Justin Martyr, *The First Apology*, 28; Alexander Roberts et al., eds., *The Ante-Nicene Fathers: Translations of the Writings of the Fathers down to A.D. 325*, 9 vols. (Edinburgh: T&T Clark, 1885–97), public domain, available at www.ccel.org, vol. 1, 172 (ANF[1], hereafter); Justin Martyr, *Dialogue with Trypho*, 141; ibid., 269–70.

structure of the human being which constitutes the image). It seemed like what really makes the human beings absolutely unique among the creatures had to do not only with the presence of the soul but also with the possession of superb mental powers of reason and will. A related factor contributing to this interpretation had to do with the fact that that the biblical concept of "spirit" (*ruach* in Hebrew; *pneuma* in Greek) was linked with reason and rationality, rather than with what current (to us) biblical scholarship rightly argues—namely, the principle of life (as, e.g., in Ps. 104:29-30).

Modern critical scholarship has rightly noted that while both rationality and will obviously belong among the central features of the human being, there is very little, if any linking, between the image of God and these two mental features (even the mandate of the Creator to humanity to name the creatures may be just that: a *mandate*, a task, rather than an analysis of the content of the image God). Similarly—and perhaps surprisingly to many—there is absolutely no connection between the "soul" and the image of God, as far as the soul is taken in its face value—namely, a separate constitutive part of human nature separate from the body. The linking of reason (and will) aligns itself more easily with Hellenistic philosophy than with the Bible, particularly the holistic-embodied Old Testament anthropology.[8] In the Bible, it is not rationality or will, but rather the placement of the whole of the human person, and indeed the whole of the humanity, in relation to God that is central. That said, the linking of reason and will with the image is, of course, not completely mistaken. Reason and will are necessary for the establishment of freedom, including moral freedom, the potentiality of becoming what God intended the human being to be.[9]

Only slowly and gradually did patristic and subsequent theology begin to correct itself and move toward a more holistic vision of humanity in which, rather than any single feature or property, it is the whole human person that is the *imago*.[10] Thus, the physical side of the human person also belongs to the image. Indeed, the Fathers rightly intuited that the final, eschatological vision of God cannot be had without the body, if the bodily resurrection is the final goal.[11] Although body–soul dualism still continued, the linking of the image with embodiment was an important benefit.

Now to the main focus of this essay: Why is it that dualism of body and soul (or a dualistic trichotomy of body, soul and spirit) gained ascendancy and even dominance in premodern Christian theological anthropology? What are the implications of this

---

[8]The background to the centrality of reason lies in the Aristotelian idea of the human person as "rational animal." See Aristotle, *De Anima (On the Soul)*, 3.3, trans. E. M. Edghill and Daniel Kolak, 37–9, at https://pdfs. semanticscholar.org/a359/828a1c8c0c5ecaf1eab67c98f79dffbbafff.pdf, accessed September 8, 2020.

[9]Gregory of Nyssa, *On the Making of Man*, 16.9–11; Schaff and Wace, eds., *Select Library of the Nicene and Post-Nicene Fathers*, 2nd ser., 14 vols., vol. 5, 404; Irenaeus, *Against Heresies*, 4.37.1, 4; ANF[1], vol. 1, 519. Consider the comment by Joel B. Green (private e-mail, September 28, 2013): "It isn't that patristic interpreters focus on 'reason'. It is that many patristic interpreters focus on 'the soul', which they define as a 'reasonable soul', and this 'reasonable soul' would then be equated with the immortal soul (over against the 'animal soul' shared with other creatures)." For further details, see Joel B. Green, *Practicing Theological Interpretation: Engaging Biblical Texts for Faith and Formation* (Grand Rapids, MI: Baker Academic, 2011), chapter 3, particularly. While I endorse Green's critique of the patristic focus on reason, I also give more credit to the rational capacity in humanity, as the subsequent discussion reveals.

[10]Irenaeus, *Against Heresies*, 5.6.1; ANF[1], 531–2; Gregory of Nyssa, *On the Making of Man*, 29; NPNF[2], vol. 5, 419–21; for examples from Maximus the Confessor, see Robert Louis Wilken, "Biblical Humanism: The Patristic Convictions," in *Personal Identity in Theological Perspective*, ed. Richard Lints, Michael S. Horton and Mark R. Talbot (Grand Rapids, MI: Eerdmans, 2006), 25–6.

[11]Irenaeus, *Against Heresies*, 5.7.1; ANF[1], vol. 1, 532–3.

development? And how is all of this indicative of the "method" or approach of classical theological anthropology?

THE APPEAL OF ANTHROPOLOGICAL DUALISM(S)

The roots of the body–soul dualism[12] can be traced back to Hellenistic philosophy (which in itself was not a unified tradition but rather a constellation of many).[13] Typically in that tradition, *soma* (body) denoted something alien.[14] It is significant that Plato's idea of death as "the separation of the soul from the body" is contrasted with the immortality of the soul.[15] Soul is eternal and remains while the body is decaying and fleeting.[16] Soul is the higher aspect of humanity: soul directs, rules and masters, and body serves and is ruled.[17] Platonism significantly influenced the earliest Christian anthropologies, although not uniformly, nor uncritically. Take for example Tertullian. The Platonic-type dualistic account, influenced by the Stoics, interestingly enough, argued for the corporeality of the soul[18]—whatever that may mean precisely! But while gleaning from Hellenistic philosophers, Tertullian also combated their errors such as the preexistence of the soul: because "soul originates in the breath of God, it follows that we attribute a beginning to it."[19] While distinguished from each other, soul and body also belong together as they are brought about simultaneously at birth.[20]

Plato's pupil, Aristotle's conception of the soul is markedly different from his teacher's. For him, the soul is the "form" (or actuality) of the body.[21] Rather than an entity, soul is more like a life principle, "that aspect of the person which provides the powers or attributes characteristic of the human being," but not only the human being but also all other living entities, such as animals and plants.[22] Unlike in Plato, where it seems like soul and body can "live" separately, for Aristotle "the soul is inseparable from its body."[23] To properly understand this hylomorphic account of reality, one has to leave behind the contemporary (to us) notion of "form" as something secondary and "thin." Instead, for Aristotle, form denotes something like actuality-having-reached-potentiality. "Form is an

---

[12]Not surprisingly, dualisms come in many forms. Hence, to speak of dualism in the singular is a bit misleading. Yet, for the sake of convenience and economy—and following established theological practice—this essay will continue to do so, but with the caveat that in the course of my discussion, differences among dualisms will hopefully become evident.

[13]See Jan N. Bremmer, *The Early Greek Concept of the Soul* (Princeton, NJ: Princeton University Press, 1983), 13–69 particularly; Raymond Martin and John Barresi, *The Rise and Fall of Soul and Self: An Intellectual History of Personal Identity* (New York: Columbia University Press, 2006), 9–38.

[14]Eduard Schweizer, "Soma," in *Theological Dictionary of the New Testament Theology*, 10 vols., ed. Gerhard Friedrich, trans. and ed. Geoffrey W. Bromiley (Grand Rapids, MI: Eerdmans, 1971), vol. 7, 1024–94.

[15]Plato, *Phaedo*, trans. David Gallop (New York: Oxford University Press, 2009), 64c.

[16]Hence, Plato considers highly *meditatio mortis* of the body, mindfulness of the mortality of the body; e.g., Plato, *Phaedo* 80e–81a.

[17]Plato, *Phaedo*, 79e–80a.

[18]Tertullian, *A Treatise on the Soul*, chapter 7; ANF[1], vol. 3, 186–7; in chapter 5, 184–5, he acknowledges the Stoic background of the view; see chapter 6 for rebuttal of the Platonic view of the incorporeality of the soul, 185–6.

[19]Tertullian, *On the Soul*, chapter 4; ANF[1], vol. 3, 184.

[20]Ibid., chapter 27; ANF[1], vol. 3, 207–8.

[21]Aristotle, *On the Soul*, 2.1–3, 14–19; here "actuality" is used for "form." On the importance for Christian tradition, see J. N. D. Kelly, *Early Christian Doctrines*, rev. ed. (New York: Harper & Row, 1978), 171.

[22]Nancey Murphy, *Bodies and Souls, or Spirited Bodies?* (Cambridge: Cambridge University Press, 2006), 13.

[23]Aristotle, *On the Soul*, 2.1, 16.

immanent principle that gives things their essential characteristics and powers."[24] Hence, it is doubtful whether Aristotelian anthropology (later adopted by medieval Thomism) is essentially dualist at all;[25] if named as such, it is markedly different from other dualisms.

What is common to all ancient Greek notions of humanity is the

> recognition that human beings have some remarkable capabilities all their own (such as doing mathematics and philosophy) and others that they share with animals (sensation). It did not seem possible to attribute these powers to matter—to the body—and so philosophers developed theories about an additional component of the person to account for them. Since living persons have all these powers and corpses do not, the soul is also taken to be the life principle.[26]

This intuition was by and large shared by Christian tradition.[27]

By the time of Augustine, the shift toward a more robust dualism, along with the stronger hierarchic view of soul and body (the former higher than the latter),[28] had taken the upper hand. In his psychological analogy, Augustine focused on the "soul" as the seat of the image of God.[29] The key aspect of the soul is rationality; indeed, "the image of God is to be sought in the immortality of the rational soul."[30] The mature Augustine, however, began to correct himself, mentioning that the "soul having body does not make two persons, but one man."[31]

Jumping from the patristic to medieval theology, St. Thomas Aquinas followed Augustine in locating likeness to God in rationality,[32] but with the help of Aristotelianism, he also took important steps toward rediscovering key aspects of the original biblical unity of human nature. His baptizing of Aristotle's idea of the soul as the "form" of the body[33] became church dogma at the Council of Vienna (1312).[34] "On this view the soul is not just a partial principle but that which makes us human in our bodily reality. Conversely, the body is the concrete form in which our humanity, the soul, finds appropriate expression."[35] No doubt, this hylomorphic interpretation, while still dualist, points toward the dominant holistic twentieth-century view in its defeat of such dualism that makes soul and body separate substances.[36]

---

[24]Murphy, *Bodies and Souls*, 13.

[25]So also ibid., 13.

[26]Nancey Murphy, "Human Nature: Historical, Scientific, and Religious Issues," in *Whatever Happened to the Soul? Scientific and Theological Portraits of Human Nature*, ed. Warren S. Brown, Nancey C. Murphy and H. Newton Malony (Minneapolis, MN: Fortress, 1998), 4.

[27]See Tertullian, *On the Flesh of Christ*, chapter 12; ANF[1], vol. 3, 538–9.

[28]The idea of the supremacy of the soul over the body was already present in Tertullian (*A Treatise on the Soul*, chapter 13; NPNF[1], vol. 3, 192–3), but he also emphasized their interrelatedness, as discussed above.

[29]Moltmann, *God in Creation*, 236. There is no citation from the *Trinity* on this page.

[30]Augustine, *Trinity*, 14.4, chapter title; NPNF[1], vol. 3, 185. Augustine, however, qualifies the talk about "immortality," reminding us that the souls of those who do not enter blessedness will die (14.4.6, 186); hence, his idea of immortality is not that of Plato.

[31]Augustine, *Tractates on the Gospel According to John* 19.15 (on John 5:19-30); NPNF[1], vol. 7, 129; so also, Augustine, *Trinity*, 15.7.11; NPNF[1], vol. 3, 204–5.

[32]*The Summa Theologica of St. Thomas Aquinas*, 2nd and rev. ed., trans. Fathers of the English Dominican Province (1920), accessed July 13, 2018, http://www.newadvent.org/summa/, 1.93.4, 6.

[33]Aquinas, *Summa Theologica*, 1.76.1; indeed, in art. 4, he clarifies that it is the only essential form of the body.

[34]*Council of Vienne (1311–1312)*, Decree 1, accessed September 8, 2020, https://www.ewtn.com/catholicism/library/council-of-vienne-1542.

[35]Wolfhart Pannenberg, *Systematic Theology*, trans. Geoffrey W. Bromiley (Grand Rapids, MI: Eerdmans, 1994), vol. 2:184.

[36]For contemporary hylomorphistic accounts, see Brian Leftow, "Souls Dipped in Dust," in *Soul, Body, and Survival: Essays on the Metaphysics of Human Persons*, ed. Kevin Corcoran (Ithaca, NY: Cornell University Press,

Completing this sweeping historical survey takes us to a critical turning point in Christian—and secular—thinking on human nature, the dawn of modernity and modern science. Modern science introduced an atomist-corpuscular conception of matter with the replacement of the Aristotelian hylomorphism (and teleology, i.e., purposefulness) for mechanistic explanations.[37] Since another entry discusses the anthropology of modernity, there is no need to go into any details—suffices it to merely highlight a feature that helps put the patristic dualism and Medieval hylomorphism in a wider historical context. As Moltmann explains, building on the Platonic heritage, the modern French philosopher Rene Descartes also significantly transformed it. Whereas in

> Plato, the anthropological dualism of body and soul belonged within the framework of the ontological dualism of non-transient Being and transient existing things[,] … [f]ollowing the Christian tradition in its Augustinian form, Descartes no longer understands the soul as a higher substance: he sees it as the true subject, both in the human body and in the world of things. He translates the old body-soul dualism into the modern subject-object dichotomy.[38]

However, Descartes goes further into dualism than Christian tradition in the mainline, further even than Augustine had been willing to go:

> And although I may, or rather, as I will shortly say, although I certainly do possess a body with which I am very closely conjoined; nevertheless, because, on the one hand, I have a clear and distinct idea of myself, in as far as I am only a thinking and unextended thing, and as, on the other hand, I possess a distinct idea of body, in as far as it is only an extended and unthinking thing, it is certain that I [that is, my mind, by which I am what I am] [am] entirely and truly distinct from my body, and may exist without it.[39]

This "nonthinking thing," the body, is to be compared to a machine.[40] Unlike the Aristotelian-Thomist view in which the soul served a number of purposes, including the "vegetative and nutritive," that is, life-sustaining task, the Cartesian body needs no soul to animate it.[41] Furthermore, herein soul's only task is cognitive (inclusively understood, and hence "mind" and "soul" became synonymous).[42]

Having now traced briefly the rise and diversification of anthropological dualisms all the way to the advent of modernity, let us take an evaluative look in light of biblical and theological considerations.

2001), 120–38; John Haldane, *Reasonable Faith* (Abingdon: Routledge, 2010); Eleonore Stump, "Non-Cartesian Substance Dualism and Materialism without Reductionism," *Faith and Philosophy* 12, no. 4 (1995): 505–31.

[37] See chapter 8 in Martin and Barresi, *The Rise and Fall of Soul and Self*.

[38] Moltmann, *God in Creation*, 250.

[39] René Descartes, *Meditations on First Philosophy: Sixth Meditation, Meditations on the First Philosophy* [1641], 195, in *The Method, Meditations and Philosophy of Descartes*, trans. from the Original Texts, with a new introductory Essay, Historical and Critical, by John Veitch, and a Special Introduction by Frank Sewall (Washington, DC: M. Walter Dunne, 1901); accessed September 8, 2020, http://oll.libertyfund.org/titles/1698.

[40] E.g., Descartes, *Sixth Meditation*, 198; for comments, see John R. Searle, *The Rediscovery of the Mind* (Cambridge: MIT Press, 1992), 25.

[41] Aquinas, *Summa Theologica*, 1.78.1; see Murphy, *Bodies and Souls*, 56–69.

[42] See Nancey Murphy and Warren S. Brown, *Did My Neurons Make Me Do It?: Philosophical and Neurobiological Perspectives on Moral Responsibility and Free Will* (Oxford: Oxford University Press, 2007), 15–16.

CHRISTIAN ANTHROPOLOGICAL DUALISM(S) IN A THEOLOGICAL ASSESSMENT

Between a Unified, Holistic Vision and the Rise of Dualisms

While the gradual shift in Christian theology away from a (Platonic) dualism, which made a sharp distinction between the body and soul, toward a unified and holistic view is usually attributed to changes in contemporary philosophy and particularly (neuro)sciences, Wolfhart Pannenberg reminds us that the shift is "in line with the intentions of the earliest Christian anthropology." Too often the investigation into the history of the body–soul relationship, he contends, ignores the fact that, unlike Platonism (which by the end of the second century had become the dominant philosophy), important early patristic thinkers defended the psychosomatic unity even when they continued distinguishing between body and soul (spirit). However, this attempt to hold on to the idea of body–soul unity soon gave way to dualism for the simple reason that, in keeping with the times, even those theologians who championed the psychosomatic unity did not thereby reject the idea of soul as an independent entity.[43] Pannenberg's judgment is that "this process illustrates the acceptance by early Christian thinking of ideas that the Hellenistic culture of the age took for granted," and hence "is not an interpretation that has any essential place in Christian anthropology."[44] (Consider that Pannenberg himself is not a physicalist but rather represents an integral holistic property—dualist type of view.)

That said, even with their dualism, early theologians critiqued key aspects of pagan philosophy, as already mentioned. A case in point is the belief in the immortality of soul. Although it was affirmed by some early theologians,[45] the preexistence of the soul (and corollary idea of transmigration of the soul) was rejected,[46] as well as the soul's divinity.[47] Furthermore, the belief in the resurrection of the body[48]—an anathema to Hellenistic thought—trumped the immortality of the soul; hence, the body was not the prison of the soul as in Plato, neither was death liberation.[49]

Dualisms under a Biblical Assessment

A popular biblical passage even today to support anthropological dualism is from the second creation account: "And the Lord God formed man of the dust of the ground, and breathed into his nostrils the breath of life; and man became a living *soul*" (Gen. 2:7 King James Version; my emphasis). But as is well-known among the scholars, the

---

[43]Tertullian is an illustrative case in point.

[44]Pannenberg, *Systematic Theology*, vol. 2:182; for "The Triumph of Dualism" in early theology, see Martin and Barresi, *Rise and Fall of Soul and Self*, 61–74.

[45]Tertullian, *A Treatise on the Soul*, 22, 200–2; Irenaeus, *Against Heresies*, 2.34; NPNF[1], vol. 1, 411–12.

[46]With the exception of Origen, for whose view see *De principiis*, 2.9.6–7; NPNF[1], vol. 4, 291–2; for a more detailed exposition of the topic of "soul," see 2.8, 286–9.

[47]See Justin, *Dialogue with Trypho*, 5, 6; NPNF[1], vol. 1, 197–8.

[48]According to Athenagoras (*Embassy for the Christians, On the Resurrection of the Dead*, trans. Joseph Hugh Crehan, SJ; Ancient Christian Writers, vol. 23 (New York: Paulist Press, rev. ed., 1956), 15), resurrection of the body is necessary because eternal life is meant for the whole person.

[49]In this section, I am indebted to Pannenberg, *Systematic Theology*, vol. 2:183–4.

Hebrew term *nephes* means rather "being," as Revised Standard Version rightly renders it ("man became a living being") rather than to "soul" as opposed to the rest of the human nature.[50] At times it simply means "person" (Lev. 2:1; 4:20; 7:20). What is striking is that it can also be used to denote animals (Gen. 1:24; 2:7; 9:10). A related Hebrew term, *basar* ("flesh[ly]"; Ps. 119:73; Isa. 45:11-12), may be used in parallel to (but not in contrast to) *nephes*. These two terms "are to be understood as different aspects of man's existence as a twofold unity."[51] The same applies by and large to other terms used in the OT (*gewiyya*, *leb*, even *ruach*); they "speak of humans from the perspective of their varying functions."[52]

Regarding the New Testament, it was a commonplace to claim that whereas the Old Testament is holistic, the New Testament is dualist. This generalization is just that, a *generalization*, and thus in need of a careful reshaping. First, the monist orientation of the Old Testament does not rule out duality or plurality in its presentation of the human being, as even a casual reader notes. Second, more importantly, we know now that the Hellenism of the New Testament times was far from uniform. Third, the version of Hellenism that was also influential on early Christianity was linked with Judaism—Hellenistic Judaism that gleaned from both Hebrew and Greek sources; its influence on Saint Paul was considerable, rabbi as he was by training.[53] With all of that in mind, I find the biblical scholar James D. G. Dunn's suggestion of "aspective" and "partitive" New Testament accounts regarding human nature quite instructive:

> While Greek thought tended to regard the human being as made up of distinct parts, Hebrew thought saw the human being more as a whole person existing on different dimensions. As we might say, it was more characteristically Greek to conceive of the human person "partitively", whereas it was more characteristically Hebrew to conceive of the human person "aspectively", That is to say, we speak of a school *having* a gym (the gym is part of the school); but we say I *am* a Scot (my Scottishness is an aspect of my whole being).[54]

Using linguistic philosophy's sources, Keith Ward's way of referring to "soul" and "body" (not as substances but) as a way of employing differing language and their functions in human life makes a similar point.[55]

---

[50]The term occurs about 800 times in the OT and has as its etymology the meaning of "throat" or "gullet"; hence, it denotes human need (as a thirsty throat) and physicality; see further Joel B. Green, *Body, Soul, and Human Life: The Nature of Humanity in the Bible* (Grand Rapids, MI: Baker Academic, 2008), 57.

[51]N. P. Bratsiotis, "*Basar*," in *Theological Dictionary of the Old Testament*, ed. G. Johannes Botterweck and Helmer Ringgren (Grand Rapids, MI: Eerdmans, 1975), vol. 2:326, quoted in Joel B. Green, "'Bodies—That Is, Human Lives': A Re-Examination of Human Nature in the Bible," in *Whatever Happened to the Soul?* ed. W. Brown et al. (Minneapolis, MN: Augsburg Fortress, 1988), 157–8. This paragraph is indebted to Green.

[52]Green, "Bodies," 158. Note Moltmann's subheading: "Thinking with the Body in the Old Testament" (*God in Creation*, 256).

[53]For the complexity of Hellenistic anthropologies, see Green, "Bodies," 159–63, on which this paragraph is based.

[54]James D. G. Dunn, *The Theology of Paul the Apostle* (Grand Rapids, MI: Eerdmans, 1998), 54, emphasis in original.

[55]Keith Ward, *Defending the Soul* (Oxford: Oneworld, 1992).

IN CONCLUSION: THE LIABILITIES AND CHALLENGES
OF ANTHROPOLOGICAL DUALISMS

So, what might be the problems and liabilities of classical anthropological dualism in light of the critical biblical scholarship[56] and philosophical-theological reflection attempted in this essay? First, dualisms (as much as they also differ from each other, particularly Platonic-Cartesian and Aristotelian-Thomist versions) locate humanity (human uniqueness) in the soul rather than in the human person as a whole. This goes against the biblical vision and is problematic theologically, as argued. Second, dualisms tend to speak of soul in terms of intellect (*anima intellective*), which elevates rationality as the vital principle, hence ignoring the basic meaning of *nephes* as the whole human being or person.

Third, contrary to the Bible, where the divine Spirit (*ruach*) is the principle of life, life-force,[57] even the Aristotelian-Thomist account relegates that to soul. On the contrary, in Gen. 2:7, "the soul is not merely the vital principle of the body but the ensouled body itself, the living being as a whole. Hence, it does not have the autonomy expressed by the Aristotelian-Thomistic concept of substance."[58] The existence of human life (Job 34:14-15)—along with all life of all creation (Ps. 104:29, 30)—is the function of the life-giving force of the divine Spirit. Hence, human life is eccentric, referred to beyond itself; it is a life of dependence on the Creator.[59] In contrast to the Hellenistic philosophy and occasional tendencies in early theology, even reason/rationality is contingent on divine breath and has no autonomy.[60]

Fourth, the dualisms suffer from the downplaying of the body, emotions and passions. It may lead—and has led—at times to an isolationist spirituality and Christian life. A related critical question then is, "If the body does not belong to the *imago Dei*, how can the body become 'a temple of the Holy Spirit'?"[61] Finally, dualisms seem to run against much of current neuroscientific knowledge (see Chapter 30 in this *Handbook*).

So then, why possibly have dualisms persisted in Christian theology—and still do, particularly among conservative traditions and in popular Christian imagination? The reasons are many and worthwhile, including the following:

- That there is "more" to human life than just the material;[62]

- That there is something "more" than merely material processes that explain the uniqueness and dignity of human life;[63]

---

[56]See N. T. Wright, "Mind, Spirit, Soul and Body: All for One and One for All; Reflections on Paul's Anthropology in his Complex Contexts," paper presented at Society of Christian Philosophers Eastern Meeting, March 18, 2011, accessed May 14, 2018, http://ntwrightpage.com/2016/07/12/mind-spirit-soul-and-body/.

[57]See Hans Walter Wolff, *Anthropology of the Old Testament*, trans. Margaret Kohl (Philadelphia, PA: Augsburg/Fortress, 1974), 22.

[58]Pannenberg, *Systematic Theology*, vol. 2:185.

[59]See Pannenberg, *Systematic Theology*, vol. 2:186 particularly.

[60]See Pannenberg, *Systematic Theology*, vol. 2:190–1.

[61]Moltmann, *God in Creation*, 239. This problem did not go unnoticed by the Reformation theologians, as can be seen in John Calvin, *Institutes of the Christian Religion*, 1.3, trans. Henry Beveridge (Philadelphia, PA: Westminster Press, 1845), 1.15.3.

[62]See Keith Ward, *More Than Matter: Is There More to Life Than Molecules?* (Grand Rapids, MI: Eerdmans, 2011).

[63]In his classic history of European morality throughout ages, William E. H. Lecky, *The History of European Morals from Augustus to Charlemagne*, vol. 2 (New York: George Braziller, [1869], 1955), 18, 34, argues strongly that there is an essential link between Christianity's establishment of the dignity of each human person and belief in the soul. This is of course not limited to Christian tradition, as discussed with regard to Hindu and Jewish views in Stephen G. Post, "A Moral Case for Nonreductive Physicalism," in *Whatever Happened to the Soul?*, ed. W. Brown et al. (Minneapolis, MN: Fortress Press, 1998), 199–201.

- That affirming morality and an ethical base calls for "more" than material explanation; and[64]
- That there is hope for life eternal, and therefore, even at the moment of my personal death, I am not forgotten by God.

That most Christian theologians would affirm the maintenance of these kinds of values seems to be uncontested. But that it (the maintenance) would require classical dualism (in any form) has become a deep and wide issue of contention in modern and postmodern theologies. Thus, they are providing other ways of imagining the nature of human nature.

SUGGESTED FURTHER READING

Brown, Warren S., Nancey C. Murphy, and H. Newton Malony (eds.), *Whatever Happened to the Soul? Scientific and Theological Portraits of Human Nature* (Minneapolis, MN: Fortress, 1998).

Green, Joel B., *Body, Soul, and Human Life: The Nature of Humanity in the Bible* (Grand Rapids, MI: Baker Academic, 2008).

Kärkkäinen, Veli-Matti, *Creation and Humanity: A Constructive Christian Theology for the Pluralistic World*, vol. 3 (Grand Rapids, MI: Eerdmans, 2015).

Kelsey, David H., *Eccentric Existence: A Theological Anthropology*, 2 vols. (Louisville, KY: Westminster John Knox, 2009).

Murphy, Nancey, *Bodies and Souls, or Spirited Bodies?* (Cambridge: Cambridge University Press, 2006).

Pannenberg, Wolfhart, *Anthropology in Theological Perspective*, trans. Matthew J. O'Connell. (Philadelphia, PA: Westminster Press, 1985).

---

[64]E.g., Brandon L. Rickabaugh, "Responding to N. T. Wright's Rejection of the Soul: A Defense of Substance Dualism." An unpublished presentation at the Society of Vineyard Scholars Conference, Minnesota, accessed April 28, 2012, http://www.academia.edu/1966881/; so also J. P. Moreland and Scott B. Rae, *Body and Soul: Human Nature and the Crisis in Ethics* (Downers Grove, IL: InterVarsity, 2000).

CHAPTER TWO

Modern Method in Theological Anthropology: The Turn to the Subject

KEVIN M. VANDER SCHEL

In the more than four hundred years spanning from the close of the late Middle Ages to the beginning of the twentieth century, theological anthropology has occupied an increasingly foundational role in theological reflection. While creation in the image of God, human nature and the relation of body and soul formed central topics of theological study in the classical and postclassical eras, in the modern period theological reflection on human personhood underwent a marked change of direction. Earlier doctrinal systems had carefully attended to the nature or substance of human being, drawing from propositions given in Scripture, the heritage of Greco-Roman philosophy and the rich theological categories developed in Patristic thought. Yet the dawn of the modern period brought a new set of intellectual challenges, through changing assumptions regarding the individual in European society and the proliferation of new scientific, historical and philosophical disciplines devoted to the task of understanding what it means to be human.[1]

Within this new intellectual situation, theological understandings of anthropology experienced a notable shift of focus, turning from an emphasis on the substance or nature of human being as one specific area of theological reflection to a foundational analysis of the human person as subject. In contrast to the relatively static conceptions of human personhood in classical and medieval thought, in which the individual human being was still treated as an instance of a universal idea of humanity, theologians in the modern period begin to examine the human subject as conscious, present to oneself and developing within a particular cultural and historical context.[2] This anthropological turn, or turn to the subject, consequently involved a growing concern with theological method.

---

[1] On this increasing recognition of the individual and the growth of scholarly disciplines, see J. Greenaway, *The Differentiation of Authority: The Medieval Turn toward Existence* (Washington, DC: Catholic University of America Press, 2012), especially at 51–82; and Neil Ormerod, *Re-Visioning the Church: An Experiment in Systematic-Historical Ecclesiology* (Minneapolis: Fortress, 2014), 241–352.

[2] See Karl Rahner, "Man (Anthropology), III. Theological," in *Encyclopedia of Theology: The Concise* Sacramentum Mundi, ed. K. Rahner (New York: Crossroad, 1984), 887–93 (889). The central distinction between substance and subject is a recurring theme in the work of the Jesuit theologian Bernard Lonergan. See his essays "*Existenz* and *Aggiornamento*" and "Christ as Subject: A Reply," in Lonergan, *Collection* (Collected Works of Bernard Lonergan), vol. 4 (New York: University of Toronto Press, 1993), 153–84 and 222–31.

The new focus on personhood ushers in a decisive transition from the classical conception of theology as fixed, normative and unchanging to historically minded approaches that view theological understanding as an ongoing process open to development, critique and change.[3]

Of itself, this focus on human personhood is not an exclusively modern development. Anthropological elements can be found throughout the biblical writings, in emphases on personal faith, moral conversion and individual responsibility before God. A concern with human interiority also appears in central patristic and medieval writings, such as Gregory of Nyssa's *Life of Moses*, Augustine's *Confessions* and *De Trinitate*, and Thomas Aquinas' reevaluation of faith and reason in the *Summa Theologiae*. And it comes to the fore in the Reformation period, in the debates surrounding faith, good works and Christian liberty.[4] However, beginning in the late eighteenth century, a further self-critical posture developed around the study of theology, raising questions about the possibility of theological knowledge claims, the limits of human autonomy, the role of historical and empirical research and the status of divine revelation. In this period, theological reflection thus finds itself in a new intellectual context. A new climate of thought emerges in which the understanding of the human person no longer indicates a particular area of study set alongside other theological topics but the touchstone of theological inquiry overall. Modern theology is marked by the realization that it is not possible to speak of God without at the same time speaking of human beings, for each question of the content of theological knowledge, doctrine or interpretation raises the prior question of the human knower. In this sense, the question of the human person pervades and shapes the entirety of theological inquiry. Within this new horizon, as Karl Rahner notes, theological anthropology "is also the whole of theology," for "there is no domain of reality which does not formally enter into theological anthropology."[5]

This chapter attends to this foundational methodological shift in modern theology through the growing recognition of the role of the human subject in theological inquiry. The treatment here proceeds by considering two figures in particular, each of whom is associated with a pivotal development in the modern study of theology: Friedrich Schleiermacher, hailed by admirers and critics alike as the father of modern liberal theology; and Immanuel Kant, whose critical philosophy stands at the close of the European Enlightenment.

IMMANUEL KANT AND THE RISE OF INTERIORITY

Though the trend toward a greater anthropological orientation in theology has roots already in patristic, medieval and Reformation thought, it ripens fully in the modern era. The scientific, political and philosophical revolutions of the Renaissance and Enlightenment of the seventeenth and eighteenth centuries paved the way for a refashioned understanding of human reason, as an independent, authoritative criterion grounded in the individual. This shifting conception of human rationality overturned older understandings of the individual's place in the broader social order and yielded a changed relationship to the natural world, which appeared no longer as a fixed and

---

[3]See Bernard Lonergan, *Method in Theology*, 2nd ed. (New York: University of Toronto, 1994), xi–xii.
[4]On the gradual rise of this anthropological orientation within Christianity, see Ormerod, *Re-Visioning the Church*, 228–38, 241–77 and 313–23.
[5]Rahner, "Man (Anthropology), III. Theological," 887–93 (888).

unchanging order but a developing, elastic reality given shape and purpose by human reason.[6]

Kant's groundbreaking critical philosophy articulates a foundation for this new conception of human reason. Following upon the philosophical skepticism of David Hume's empiricism, Kant established a far-reaching inquiry into the scope, structure and limits of human understanding and knowing. His *Critique of Pure Reason* (1781), *Critique of Practical Reason* (1788) and *Critique of Judgment* (1790) offered an exacting analysis of human understanding, reason and moral agency, sharply restricting claims to metaphysical knowledge and establishing a new and notably restrained framework for religious belief.

Kant's critical project centers on examining the essential elements of human personhood and thereby recognizing the tasks and limits of human rationality and moral agency. His analysis offers a pointed rebuke of any system of metaphysics that would claim to transcend human experience and heralds a second Copernican revolution that grounds the study of philosophy in the human knower rather than the objects known.[7] His philosophy effects a turn to interiority, a painstaking exploration of the inner world of consciousness that constitutes the human "I," reorienting philosophy away from metaphysical inquiries into supersensible or heavenly realities and toward the terrestrial questions constitutive of human living: "What can I know? What ought I to do? What may I hope for?"[8]

The explicit aim of this analysis was constructive. Kant hoped to strike an intermediate path between dogmatic rationalism and skeptical empiricism, and so provide a foundation for more adequate and fruitful investigations of the natural world and human morality.[9] His work sought to bridge the "bottomless abyss" of metaphysics by examining the limits and grounding principles of the faculties of human cognition.[10] His proposed solution focused on properly relating the *a priori* forms and categories of human understanding to the *a posteriori* data given in sensation, in order to provide a solid basis for ongoing studies of the natural world. Yet in so doing, his approach also imposed strict limits upon the speculative exercise of reason. As human reason apprehends objects only as given in experience, its reach extends only as far as the phenomenal world of sensible appearances. Whatever might belong to the supersensible, or noumenal, realm of intelligible objects exists beyond the grasp of the human mind. Accordingly, while Kant maintained that his critical philosophy provided positive guidelines for further scholarship, he also recognized its main significance consists in what it negates. It signals an epistemic self-discipline of the human mind, which does not expand the powers of human knowing but fixes its

---

[6]See Ormerod, *Re-Visioning the Church*, 313–20.

[7]See Immanuel Kant, "Preface to the Second Edition," in *Critique of Pure Reason*, trans. and ed. Paul Guyer and Allen W. Wood (New York: Cambridge University, 1998), 106–24 (110).

[8]Kant, *Critique of Pure Reason*, 677. Kant's three *Critiques*—on Pure Reason, Practical Reason, and Judgment— take up these questions respectively. On the specific relation of Kant to theological anthropology, see Philip J. Rossi, "Reading Kant from a Catholic Horizon: Ethics and the Anthropology of Grace," *Theological Studies*, 71 (2010): 79–100; and Jaqueline Mariña, "Kant on Grace: A Reply to his Critics," *Religious Studies* 33 (1997): 379–400.

[9]See Kant, *Critique of Pure Reason*, 702–4.

[10]Kant refers to metaphysics as a "bottomless abyss" and "a dark and shoreless ocean, marked by no beacons." See Kant, "The Only Possible Argument in Support of a Demonstration of the Existence of God," in *Theoretical Philosophy 1755–1770*, ed. D. Walford and R. Meerbote (Cambridge: Cambridge University, 2002), 107–201 (111). His later *Critique of Pure Reason* similarly describes metaphysics as a path that must be retraced "countless times," "a battlefield" and "a groping among mere concepts" (109–10).

proper limits: "instead of discovering truth it has only the silent merit of guarding against errors."[11]

Such a restriction holds clear consequences for propositions of religious belief. Affirmations such as the existence of God, personal freedom and the immortality of the soul, however indispensable they may be for guiding moral action, cannot be firmly established through speculative reason. They instead form "postulates" that guide and point practical reason to its noblest end of bringing about a moral world. And though these postulates do not offer the comfort of theoretical certainty, Kant nonetheless maintains that they allow for a species of "rational faith," directing human action towards a moral kingdom without falling back upon the speculative extravagance and overreach that marred earlier thought.[12]

Christianity within the Bounds of Mere Reason

With this critical analysis of religious belief, Kant's philosophy posed an enduring challenge for modern theological scholarship. Kant's *Critiques* marked a turning point, as theologians saw in his work the limitations of their own thought and the need to ground their work in an analysis of interiority.[13] Yet the significance of Kant's philosophical legacy for theology and theological anthropology relates especially to two of his later works: *Religion within the Limits of Reason Alone* (1793) and *The Conflict of the Faculties* (1798).

Kant's *Religion within the Limits of Reason Alone* examines the relationship between revealed and natural religion. While his *Critiques* proceeded through close, painstaking conceptual analysis, this work draws out implications of this critically delimited rational faith through a comparison of this natural religion with the revealed teachings of Christianity. Natural religion consists in the "pure moral disposition of the heart," coupled with rational faith in the postulates of practical reason. It is the one universal religion incumbent upon all human beings, which is "free from every dogma" and "engraved in all [human] hearts."[14] This true religion is invisible; its servants are not public officials adorned with the trappings of an ecclesiastical institution but those rare teachers whose lives embody these moral demands. Even the greatest of these teachers should deserve praise not for establishing any particular religious faith but for witnessing to the true religion of reason that from a small beginning "like a grain of seed in good soil, or a ferment of goodness, would gradually, through its inner power, grow into a kingdom of God."[15] Kant describes revealed and learned religion, conversely, as a faith that demands belief in dogmas inaccessible to reason, which are preserved in holy writings and authoritatively communicated by a cadre of authoritative interpreters. Such learned faith has its foundation not in universal human reason but in "revealed credal doctrine,"

---

[11]Kant, *Critique of Pure Reason*, 672.

[12]See Kant, *Critique of Pure Reason*, 113, 117. On this anticipated moral kingdom, see, 680–82; and Dieter Henrich, "The Moral Image of the World," in *Aesthetic Judgment and the Moral Image of the World: Studies in Kant*, ed. Eckart Förster (Stanford: Stanford University Press, 1994), 3–28.

[13]On Kant's influence within nineteenth-century theology, see Karl Barth, *Protestant Theology in the Nineteenth Century* (Valley Forge: Judson, 1973), 266–312.

[14]Immanuel Kant, *Religion within the Limits of Reason Alone*, trans. T.M. Greene and H.H. Hudson (New York: Harper & Row, 1960), 147.

[15]The "wise Teacher" Kant offers as an example here clearly alludes to Jesus of Nazareth, though he remains unnamed in the text (see ibid., 147–51).

which is historically given and closely guarded by a small class of textual experts.[16] In place of an internally binding moral claim, then, it rests on supposed historical facts that are expanded by later tradition, interpretations and regulations.

Kant further develops this contrast through distinguishing the "rationalist" from the "supernaturalist" in matters of belief. The "rationalist" is the one who "interprets the natural religion alone as morally necessary" and, while not denying the possibility of supernatural revelation outright, refrains from affirming "works of grace" or anything in the "inscrutable realm of the supernatural."[17] The "supernaturalist," by contrast, "holds that belief in [revelation] is necessary to universal religion" and that such divine revelation provides an indispensable precondition for the growth of genuine faith.[18]

The terms of this discussion would echo throughout the next generation of philosophers and theologians.[19] Yet, the significance of Kant's focus on the subject extends beyond the specific question of religious faith as rational or revealed. His critical philosophy points to the deeper and more fundamental issue that all human knowledge, even that which might lay claim to a divine and supernatural origin, is contingent upon human experience and thus restricted to the realm of appearances. Any revelation received by the human mind, however miraculously and immediately it is given, remains subject to the same limitations that face any other operation of human reason. His philosophy offers a modest practical faith," which rests on genuine moral principles and brings "comfort and hope (though not certainty)."[20]

The Conflict with Theology

This contrast between natural and revealed religion is deepened in Kant's subsequent 1798 work *The Conflict of the Faculties*. One of Kant's most personal works, written amidst fierce backlash against his *Religion within the Limits of Reason Alone* and a threat of government censorship, this text examines the organization of university study and centers on the conflict between the "higher" faculty of theology and the "lower" philosophical faculties.[21] Conflict between these faculties is, for Kant, unavoidable since they rest on two opposing principles: rational critique and supernatural revelation. The call to pure, natural religion is accessible to human reason alone and thus falls within the province of philosophy. Yet the revealed, "ecclesiastical faith" is based on holy Scriptures and the sacred doctrines pronounced by clergymen.[22]

Kant's argument in this short volume unfolds against the background of a broader discussion of university reform in the late eighteenth century and a widespread dissatisfaction with the primacy of the theological faculty in the university. This growing criticism led many to argue that further progress in scholarship would require a

---

[16]Ibid., 152.

[17]Ibid., 143, 148.

[18]Ibid., 143.

[19]On the opposition of the post-Kantian theological schools of rationalism and supernaturalism in nineteenth-century German theology, see K. Vander Schel, *Embedded Grace: Christ, History, and the Reign of God in Schleiermacher's Dogmatics* (Minneapolis, Fortress, 2013), 17–44.

[20]Kant, *Religion within the Limits of Reason Alone*, 55, 70.

[21]Kant outlines the circumstances surrounding this publication in the work's preface. See Kant, *The Conflict of the Faculties*, trans. M. J. Gregor (Lincoln: University of Nebraska, 1992), 9–21; and Thomas A. Howard, *Protestant Theology and the Making of the Modern German University* (New York: Oxford University, 2006), 121–9.

[22]Kant, *The Conflict of the Faculties*, 63.

fundamental restructuring of university disciplines away from the medieval or "scholastic division," which saw the lower philosophical faculty as merely preparatory for studies in the three higher faculties of theology, medicine or law.[23]

In a properly modern university, Kant argues, these traditional roles should be reversed. Philosophy, as the disinterested and truth-seeking faculty in the university, alone has the capacity to monitor and critique other university disciplines when they fall short of demands of rationality.[24] In contrast to faculties of theology, medicine and law, whose members operate as "businessmen" and "tools of the government" in serving a societal interest, the philosophy faculty marks an autonomous, independent field of inquiry that answers only to the demands of truth and scholarly inquiry and should remain free of external regulation.[25] It is thus equipped to judge the standards and limits of scholarship in any field, even that of religion. This critical role of philosophy, for Kant, is not only justified but also necessary to prevent religious faith from growing ever more estranged from reason. Here, then, the traditional hierarchical relations among university faculties are upended, undercutting theology's traditional claim to be "queen" of the sciences. If philosophy is to remain the "handmaid" of theology, its service is closer to that of a "torchbearer" that courageously forges ahead rather than a "trainbearer" who obediently trails behind.[26]

From this vantage point, Kant argues that "biblical theologians" overreach the authority of their discipline when making claims that exceed the limits of human reason, as when discussing the inner workings of God, insisting on the rational certainty of supernaturally revealed dogmas or asserting as fact the claim that God speaks through the Bible in literal fashion.[27] In this critical perspective, religion is better judged on the strength of its moral teachings rather than its speculative doctrinal formulas. Indeed, Kant asserts that the traditional doctrines of the Trinity, Incarnation, resurrection and ascension, as affirmed in the language of ecclesiastical creeds, hold no rational or moral content in themselves. "The doctrine of the Trinity, taken literally," he writes, "*has no practical relevance at all*, even if we think we understand it."[28] Rather, when set within its proper bounds, the doctrine represents three distinct aspects of the moral idea of the relation of God to humanity: as lawgiver, sustainer and judge.[29] Likewise, he argues, it would be a mistake to conceive of the Incarnation as a miracle of "the Divinity 'dwelling incarnate'" in a real "God-Man," as "we can draw nothing practical from this mystery."[30] This teaching instead indicates for us an archetype of moral purity, pointing to the "idea of humanity in its full moral perfection."[31] In both cases, Kant maintains, the genuine moral relation to God needs to be cleansed of anthropomorphic elements.

In relation to theology, then, philosophy has the role of overseer, a necessary check on the superstitious view of theologians' "magic power" to operate as "soothsayers and magicians, with knowledge of supernatural things."[32] And theology, in turn, must answer

---

[23]Howard, *Protestant Theology and the Making of the Modern German University*, 122.
[24]Ibid., 127.
[25]Kant, *The Conflict of the Faculties*, 51, 25.
[26]Ibid., 45; see also Howard, *Protestant Theology and the Making of the Modern German University*, 127.
[27]See Kant, *The Conflict of the Faculties*, 65–77.
[28]Ibid., 65; emphasis in original.
[29]On Kant's treatment of the doctrine of the Trinity, see his *Religion within the Limits of Reason Alone*, 130–3.
[30]Kant, *The Conflict of the Faculties*, 67.
[31]Ibid.
[32]Ibid., 51, 49.

to the authority of critical philosophy and submit itself to the proper tasks and limits of human reason.

The momentous theological implications of Kant's thought, in both its promise and challenge, were not lost on his contemporaries or scholars in the generation that followed. While many found themselves unsatisfied by his conclusions, his analysis of interiority exercised a formative influence on both philosophers and theologians throughout the nineteenth and twentieth centuries, disclosing both the basis and limitations of religious knowledge claims. Friedrich Hölderlin put the matter more succinctly. In navigating the new terrain of this modern and critical understanding of religious faith, he writes, "Kant is our Moses."[33]

SCHLEIERMACHER AND MODERN THEOLOGICAL METHOD

Schleiermacher's pioneering analysis of pious Christian self-consciousness both reflects and resists the critical limitations outlined in Kant's philosophy. His theological writings offer careful reflections on human consciousness and the distinctive character of Christian piety. Yet in place of speculative analysis of conceptions of God and transcendence, his writings reframe the study of theology as a historically minded discipline that reflects upon the thought and practice of existing Christian communities.

The task of unpacking Schleiermacher's contribution to modern theological anthropology and theological method is complicated by the ambiguous legacy of his thought. On the one hand, Schleiermacher is rightly understood as standing at the forefront of a new era in theological inquiry that privileges the role of the conscious human subject.[34] His theological writings combined an innovative and comprehensive treatment of Christian doctrine with careful examination of the depth and richness of the interior conscious life of the human person. His 1799 work *On Religion: Speeches to Its Cultured Despisers* describes the open, "pious heart [*Gemüthe*]" that is attuned to the higher life of faith.[35] Likewise, his 1811 *Brief Outline of Theology as a Field of Study* depicts that Christian faith is a "particular way of being conscious of God."[36] And his signature theological work *Christian Faith* (1822; 1830) turns on a novel conception of "Feeling" (*Gefühl*), a term that designates no particular emotion or sensory experience but the "immediate self-consciousness" and the presence to self that grounds both thinking and acting.[37] At the highest level of this immediate self-consciousness, Schleiermacher posits the "feeling of absolute dependence," a general consciousness of finitude and createdness that reflects a fundamental albeit indirect relation to God.[38]

---

[33]See James J. Sheehan, *German History, 1770–1866* (New York: Oxford University, 1989), 342.

[34]Barth, despite his deep reservations about Schleiermacher's theology, lauds him as the *Kirchenvater* of the nineteenth century. See Barth, *Protestant Theology in the Nineteenth Century*, 425.

[35]F. D. E. Schleiermacher, "The Second Speech: 'On the Essence of Religion' (1806)," in *Schleiermacher: Christmas Dialogue, The Second Speech, and Other Selections*, ed. and trans. Julia A. Lamm (New York: Paulist, 2014), 152–223 (183).

[36]F. D. E. Schleiermacher, *Brief Outline of Theology as a Field of Study*, trans. Terrence N. Tice, 3rd ed. (Louisville: Westminster John Knox, 2011), §1.

[37]See F. D. E. Schleiermacher, *Christian Faith: A New Translation and Critical Edition*, ed. Catherine L. Kelsey and Terrence N. Tice, trans. Terrence N. Tice, Catherine L. Kelsey, and Edwina Lawler (Louisville: Westminster John Knox, 2016), §3.

[38]Ibid., §4.

This analysis of piety presents a sober awareness of the limits of religious knowledge. Though positing this "consciousness of God" (*Gottesbewußtsein*) as an inherent feature of human living, Schleiermacher acknowledges that "we cannot frame a real concept of the highest being."[39] The content of theological affirmations is instead restricted to states of human interiority. While appealing to the authority of Scripture and ecclesiastical confessions, theological propositions do not convey direct knowledge of God but fundamentally relate to the "facts [*Thatsachen*] of religious self-consciousness," as descriptions of religious affections or distinct states of mind and heart (*Gemüthzustände*) taken from the realm of inner experience.[40] In this respect, Schleiermacher largely remains within the bounds set by Kant's critical project. Theological analysis describes faith and the developing awareness of God but falls short of knowledge of God in God's self.[41]

On the other hand, Schleiermacher expressly rules out any position that would enshrine a particular conception of philosophy or anthropology as the basis of his theological system. He was suspicious of attempts to develop a theory of pure natural religion, general doctrine of God or apologetics that would serve as a foundation for theological reflection.[42] Accordingly, in the introduction to his *Christian Faith*, he writes that his own approach "wholly disassociates itself from the task" of establishing theology on the foundation of a general doctrine of God or anthropology.[43] The structure and content of his theological system are instead founded on the fundamental relation to Jesus Christ.

In contrast to the two dominant post-Kantian options of rationalism and supernaturalism, then, Schleiermacher sought to orient his own theological reflections toward the new and decisive character of Christ's influence amid the ongoing development of human history. His approach departed both from attempts to separate "the pure truth of a universal rational faith" from historical Christianity and from positions that would reduce Christian thought to a collection of immediately revealed supernatural truths.[44] Instead, he focuses his treatment on the redemptive activity of Christ as it develops and takes shape in human history, the "great mystery of God's revelation in the flesh."[45] The entrance of Christ into human living inaugurates the gradual emergence and becoming of the reign of God, which he describes as "the supernatural-becoming-natural."[46] This appearance of the Redeemer and his enlivening influence in history form the "one true miracle" upon which Christianity stands, signaling the "development ... of the one great fact: that God is love."[47]

---

[39]See Schleiermacher's letter, "To F.H. Jacobi. Berlin, March 30, 1818," in *Schleiermacher*, 264.

[40]Schleiermacher, *Christian Faith*, §29, 220; see also §31, and §30.2.

[41]On Schleiermacher's indebtedness to Kant's religious epistemology, despite their significant conceptual differences, see Theodore Vial, *Modern Religion, Modern Race* (New York: Oxford University, 2016), 55–92.

[42]See F. D. E. Schleiermacher, *On the Glaubenslehre: Two Letters to Dr. Lücke*, trans. J. Duke and F. Fiorenza (Atlanta: Scholars, 1981), 55–73.

[43]Schleiermacher, *Christian Faith*, §2.1, 43.

[44]See Schleiermacher, *Two Letters to Dr. Lücke*, 42, 78; and Schleiermacher, *Christian Faith*, §10, p.s. and §13, p.s.

[45]See Schleiermacher's sermon, "Pentecost Sunday (May 1825), 1 Corinthians 2:10–12," in *Schleiermacher*, 224–40 (238).

[46]See Schleiermacher, *Christian Faith*, §88.4 and §89.4. On the theme of the "supernatural-becoming-natural," see also Vander Schel, *Embedded Grace*, 83–86, 176–79.

[47]Schleiermacher, "Pentecost Sunday (May 1825)," 224–40 (239); and see Schleiermacher, *Christian Faith*, §103.4, and §127.

Theology at the University of Berlin

Alongside these considerations, however, is another aspect of Schleiermacher's thought that has exercised a decisive influence on modern theology and theological anthropology: the reordering of theological method at the University of Berlin. After the publication of his *Speeches* and amid his early teaching at the University of Halle in 1804–6, Schleiermacher began turning his attention to the role of theology in the university and the task of outlining a specific program for modern theological study.[48]

This methodological focus is evident in Schleiermacher's 1808 work *Occasional Thoughts on Universities in the German Sense*. The contentious publication of Kant's *The Conflict of the Faculties* had been followed in quick succession by proposals for university reform from other leading thinkers of the day. Schleiermacher's treatise joined essays by Johann Gottlieb Fichte, Friedrich Schelling, Heinrich Steffens and Alexander von Humboldt in taking up the pressing question of the proper organization of the university, and the place of theology within it, with an eye toward establishing a distinctively modern university in Berlin.[49] In the end, Humboldt's essay with its emphasis on the "pure idea of *Wissenschaft*" most closely aligned with the structure the new University of Berlin would take at its founding in 1810. Yet it was Schleiermacher's treatise, with its constructive vision of theology in the university, that gave lasting shape to the University's new faculty of theology.

Schleiermacher envisioned this new theological faculty as combining the university's *wissenschaftlich* spirit with Christianity's distinctive religious sensibility. Like other disciplines in the new university, theology would be animated by the drive to critical inquiry: here, as elsewhere, the first and primary task of students is "to learn how to learn."[50] Yet, it integrates this impulse with a practical awareness that binds this scholarly inquiry with a concern to cultivate the thought and practice of existing Christian communities. In organizing the theological faculty at the University of Berlin, Schleiermacher thus sought to bring in thinkers that neither represented the rigidity and polemics of the older confessionalism nor were mired in abstract speculative disputes about reason and supernatural revelation. Theological study in Berlin, by consequence, would reflect a character that differed markedly from prior modes of theological study, leading to a new, historically inclined and self-consciously modern course of theological scholarship.[51]

Brief Outline of Theology

Schleiermacher's conception of theology's place in the university reflected his careful understanding of theological method. His *Brief Outline of Theology*, initially published during the first official semester of the University of Berlin in 1811, outlines a significantly revised understanding of theological study. This work reframed the multiple aspects of theological study into an integrative and interdisciplinary method, a positive discipline grounded in the historical life of the church that draws from other disciplines in order

---

[48]See Kurt Nowak, *Schleiermacher: Leben, Werk und Wirkung* (Göttingen: Vandenhoeck & Ruprecht, 2001), 147–51.

[49]For a discussion of these five treatises for university reform, see Howard, *Protestant Theology and the Making of the Modern University*, 155–77.

[50]Ibid., 167.

[51]See ibid., 193–9.

to fulfill its specific task. Thus conceived, theology is not the abstract science of God or an account of revelation but a heuristic discipline that appropriates procedures and conceptual tools borrowed from other scholarly disciplines in order to further its inquiry into faith and the place of church in society.

The *Brief Outline of Theology* retained many of the traditional designations of the theological subdisciplines of the late eighteenth century, such as exegetical, dogmatic, historical and practical theology. Yet it refashioned these to better meet the exigencies of modern historical investigation. Schleiermacher's revision subsumed exegesis and dogmatics under historical theology and added a further subdiscipline of philosophical theology that inquires into the distinctiveness and uniqueness of Christian faith. By consequence, this new program had a decidedly historical orientation. The modern study of theology, he writes, requires a "genuine historical apprehension" of Christianity and this historical knowledge forms "the indispensable condition of all intelligent effort toward the further cultivation of Christianity" and the basis for understanding Christian life and thought.[52] Dogmatic, or systematic, theology, then, presents no final or complete understanding of Christian faith but is limited to the "systematic representation of doctrine" current at the present time.[53]

In this manner, Schleiermacher conceived the modern study of theology as inescapably related to human interiority, yet proceeding in substantially historical terms, with an openness to ongoing scholarship and an enduring connection to the concrete life of Christian communities. His unique vision of theological method laid the groundwork for the "scientization" (*Verwissenschaftlichung*) of the study of theology in the nineteenth-century university.[54] Following his novel approach, the study of theology would proceed in new fashion, taking up fundamental questions of the conscious human subject and the historically contingent character of Christian teaching.

CONCLUSION: THEOLOGY OF THE SUBJECT

This brief summary of the influence of Kant and Schleiermacher within theological anthropology illustrates several important aspects of the turn to the subject in the modern study of theology. Despite noteworthy differences in approach, both Kant and Schleiermacher highlight the fundamental role of the knowing subject in theology. A critical understanding of the human person is implicated in any claims about knowledge of God or the reality of religious experience. Further, both recognize that this analysis of the subject necessarily entails further questions of the organization, coherence and limits of theology overall, in its relation to other academic disciplines and its connection to historical inquiry.

These reflections from Kant and Schleiermacher thus serve to underscore the inseparability of modern theological anthropology and modern theological method. What sets modern theological anthropology apart is its inescapably foundational role in shaping and delimiting theological discourse. The significant debates and advances in modern theology turn on the understanding of the conscious human subject, both in relation to God and to broader lines of historical development. The form, tasks and limits

---

[52]Schleiermacher, *Brief Outline*, §§40, 70.
[53]Ibid., §97.
[54]Howard, *Protestant Theology and the Making of the Modern University*, 133.

of theological reflection, as well as the shape of modern theological proposals, all derive from this underlying consideration. As Karl Rahner writes, "Dogmatic theology today must be theological anthropology."[55]

This modern focus on the subject provides both distinct advantages and recurring challenges. It raises possibilities for renewed theological reflection that retrieves and deepens insights into traditional theological doctrines concerning sin and grace, Christology, the doctrine of the Trinity and the understanding of the church's role in society. In both Protestant and Catholic circles, it has also given rise to constructive and insightful lines of theological inquiry on questions of nature and the supernatural, revelation and history, and theological method, developments which have shaped Christian thought and practice from the nineteenth century onward.[56]

This emphasis on interiority also heralds the transition from classicist to historically minded models of theology. Where theologians in previous eras strove to derive certain and universal conclusions from fixed principles given in Scripture and Tradition, modern theology has become a substantially critical and historically minded discipline. It engages in the ongoing task of gathering information, refining its concepts and images, and striving for ever more adequate modes of understanding. Theological reflection in the modern period has thus transitioned from the static to the dynamic, from the abstract and universal to the concrete and historically situated, and from a fixed and invariant structure to adaptive forms of inquiry. Moving beyond abstract and ahistorical notions of human nature, it regards the human person as a "historical being" and "incarnate subject" and one who is able to "listen to God in history."[57]

Yet this anthropological turn, even when taken within its own scope, has also introduced persistent difficulties. Many theologians argued that this focus undermines central tenets of faith and object to liberal or modernist traditions that would deduce all theological content from human experience, as if theological assertions were merely symbolizing or making explicit experiential aspects of human living.[58] This emphasis on interiority also experiences limits in another direction. In focusing on the knowing subject, the normative structures of human consciousness and rationality are often conceived on the model of a particular class of persons: those who are white, male and inheritors of the European intellectual tradition. Indeed, Kant's own contributions to philosophical anthropology were bound up with his writings on the superiority of the European race, a position he maintained until the end of this life. And for Schleiermacher too, notions of religious and historical progress are racially inflected.[59]

These limitations would leave modern theology ill-equipped to respond to the pressing social and political crises of the twentieth century, in questions of mass suffering, systematic economic injustice, the recurring oppression of marginalized and vulnerable communities, and the ongoing human involvement in the devastation of the environment.[60] Meeting these new challenges would call for new modes of reflection on

---

[55]Karl Rahner, "Theology and Anthropology," in *Theological Investigations*, vol. IX, trans. Graham Harrison (New York: Herder and Herder, 1972), 28–45 [28].
[56]See J. C. Livingston and F.S. Fiorenza, eds., *Modern Christian Thought*, vol. II: The Twentieth Century (Saddle River, NJ: Prentice Hall, 2000), 1–9.
[57]Bernard Lonergan, 'Theology in its New Context', in *A Second Collection*, eds. W.F.J. Ryan and B.J. Tyrrell (Philadelphia: Westminster, 1974), 55–68 [60–61]; and Rahner, 'Theology and Anthropology', 28–45 [42].
[58]See *Modern Christian Thought*, vol. II, 1–9; and S. A. Ross, *Anthropology: Seeking Light and Beauty* (Collegeville: Liturgical Press, 2012), 47–65.
[59]See Vial, *Modern Religion, Modern Race*, 21–36, 189–220.
[60]See Ross, *Anthropology*, 65–9.

human living that more closely attend to questions of pluralism, dynamics of power and the embodied, contextualized and fragmented character of the human self.

Despite these lingering challenges, however, this modern anthropological orientation signals an enduring theological legacy. It has set theology on a new footing, both establishing a lasting basis for future theological reflection and outlining its unfinished task. Theological reflection continues to shift and evolve as it grapples with the still-developing understanding of the human person, what Nietzsche calls the "as yet undetermined animal."[61]

SUGGESTED FURTHER READING

Immanuel Kant, *The Conflict of the Faculties* (trans. M. J. Gregor; Lincoln: University of Nebraska, 1992).

Lonergan, Bernard, "Theology in Its New Context," in *A Second Collection* (ed. W. F. J. Ryan and B.J. Tyrrell; Philadelphia: Westminster, 1974), 55–68.

Rahner, Karl, 'Theology and Anthropology', in *Theological Investigations*, Vol. *IX* (trans. Graham Harrison; New York: Herder and Herder, 1972), 28–45.

Schleiermacher, Friedrich, *Brief Outline of Theology as a Field of Study* (trans. Terrence N. Tice; Louisville: Westminster John Knox, 2011).

---

[61]F. Nietzsche, *Beyond Good and Evil*, trans. Walter Kaufmann (New York: Random House, 1966), 74.

CHAPTER THREE

Postmodern Method?
Begging to Differ

ANTHONY J. GODZIEBA

Postmodern method—isn't that an oxymoron, a performative contradiction? If a method is a way of unifying and sequencing diverse activities for the purpose of reaching a definitive result or conclusion, and if the heyday of rational method is the modern era, stretching from Descartes' *Discourse on Method* (1637) to the hegemony of scientific method into the 1970s, then the usual understanding of "postmodern" is surely the exact opposite of this—it is anti-method, polemicizing against both the unifying intent and the mastery that it implies. Already in the early 1980s, in what has become (quite ironically) this polemic's classic statement, Jean-François Lyotard condemned this search for a methodical unification of differences as the "transcendental illusion" of totalization, bequeathed to us by the Enlightenment and German Idealism, and that "the price to pay for such an illusion is terror."

> The nineteenth and twentieth centuries have given us as much terror as we can take. We have paid a high enough price for the nostalgia of the whole and the one, for the reconciliation of the concept and the sensible, of the transparent and the communicable experience. Under the general demand for slackening and for appeasement, we can hear the mutterings of the desire for a return of terror, for the realization of the fantasy to seize reality. The answer is: Let us wage a war on totality; let us be witnesses to the unpresentable; let us activate the differences and save the honor of the name.[1]

Here the key elements of a postmodern attitude are brought to the fore: the opposition to philosophical and scientific attempts to represent and thereby control ("seize") reality, as well as the assertion of the primacy of difference over against attempts to reduce experiences to "the same." The hegemony of rational domination aiming to reconcile "the many" into a one-size-fits-all concept marks the modernity that "postmodernity" allegedly surpasses. "Post-" thus takes on a double meaning: as a periodization ("coming after" modernity as a chronological era) and as a critique ("going after" modernity as a social imaginary and as a culture in order to oppose and dismantle it).

---

[1] Jean-François Lyotard, "Answering the Question: What Is Postmodernism?" (Fr. orig. 1982; trans. Régis Durand), in Jean-François Lyotard, *The Postmodern Condition: A Report on Knowledge*, trans. Geoff Bennington and Brian Massumi, Theory and History of Literature, vol. 10 (Minneapolis: University of Minnesota Press, 1984), 71–82 (81–2).

MODERNITY AND ITS CRITIQUES

Can we more clearly describe the "modernity" that we are said to be "post-"? It is not the early modernity of the sixteenth and seventeenth centuries with their varied and inventive approaches to human agency and human affections, to which Counter-Reformation and Baroque spirituality made notable contributions.[2] Nor is it the early nineteenth-century sense of "modern" celebrated by poets and social thinkers as a time of exhilarating, rapid and indeed chaotic change, of fragmentation, experimentation and creative destruction. Nor is it the modernity of Schleiermacher, Herder or the Romantics, who emphasized the depth and richness of diverse perspectives of human experience. Rather, it is the modern objective rational project stemming from the Enlightenment and expressed in "grand narratives of truth, reason, science, progress and universal emancipation,"[3] a project that ran parallel to celebratory modernity, eventually engulfed it and persists today tightly bound to late capitalism. It is important to note that this project was never merely philosophical but also encompassed the arts, social life and industry—it became a cultural project. "The development of rational forms of social organization and rational modes of thought promised liberation from the irrationalities of myth, religion, superstition, release from the arbitrary use of power as well as from the dark side of our own human natures. Only through such a project could the universal, eternal, and the immutable qualities of all of humanity be revealed."[4]

By the end of the nineteenth century, though, the claim that "the world could be controlled and rationally ordered" if reason could discover "a single correct mode or representation" of the underlying universal truth of humanity was already being exposed as an illusion.[5] Critics such as Max Weber (modern instrumental reason leads to the "iron cage") and Friedrich Nietzsche ("truths are illusions which we have forgotten are illusions") had laid bare the inherent instabilities of the modern myth of a unified field of knowledge and the progress and power that flow from it.[6] Despite these critiques, however, between the two world wars a belief in progress, rational order and technological efficiency returned. This belief functioned both as a way of reconstructing society and for combating the despair and restlessness that persisted since before the turn of the twentieth century. And after the Second World War, a "high" modernism devoted to sleek architectural lines, rationally efficient social organization, absolute truths and linear progress became standard fare, even more so now that it was easily intertwined with the logic of capitalism. "The legitimacy of the modern world thereafter anchored itself in the promise of 'will as infinite enrichment', on the one hand, and the promise of justice for

---

[2]For the various "modernities" in play during this period, see Anthony J. Godzieba, " 'Refuge of Sinners, Pray for Us': Augustine, Aquinas, and the Salvation of Modernity," in *Augustine and Postmodern Thought: A New Alliance against Modernity?*, ed. Lieven Boeve, Frederick Depoortere and Martin Wisse, BETL 219 (Leuven: Peeters, 2009), 147–65.

[3]Terry Eagleton, *Literary Theory: An Introduction*, 2nd ed. (Minneapolis: University of Minnesota Press, 1996), 200.

[4]David Harvey, *The Condition of Postmodernity: An Enquiry into the Origins of Cultural Change* (Oxford: Basil Blackwell, 1989), 12.

[5]Ibid., 15, 27, 29–30.

[6]Max Weber, *The Protestant Ethic and the Spirit of Capitalism*, trans. Talcott Parsons (New York: Routledge, 2001 (orig. 1930)), 123–4; Friedrich Nietzsche, *On Truth and Lies in the Nonmoral Sense*, in *Philosophy and Truth: Selections from Nietzsche's Notebooks of the Early 1870's*, ed. and trans. Daniel Breazeale (Atlantic Highlands, NJ: Humanities Press International, 1979), 79–97 (84).

the individual in the liberal state, on the other."[7] This, in a nutshell, is the "modernity" that the postmodern opposes, with either less intensity (say, in architecture, where there are numerous rivals alongside the default high modernism) or more (in philosophy and social science, whose "perpetual criticism" intends to undermine modern presuppositions of rational mastery of reality).[8]

At this point, we should be careful to distinguish between "postmodernity" and "postmodernism": the former can be seen as a more historical-philosophical term referring to the end of the era of grand narratives of truth and reason, while the latter refers to "the form of culture which corresponds to this world view."[9] And, in all fairness, there are those interpreters who contest any sort of sharp break and argue that postmodernity and postmodernism are not the "end" of anything. Instead, "the recent critique of modernity by postmodern theorists may be regarded as a contemporary manifestation of a much longer set of oppositional movements against the rationalising tendency of the modern project."[10] In other words, the contemporary oppositional critique can be viewed as a power that was already constitutive of what it meant to be "modern." This modern critique could be directed at previous traditions (e.g., early modernity's dismissal of the myriad distinctions of medieval scholasticism or the convolutions of late medieval polyphony) or even at modernity's own foundations (as with the "radical Enlightenment" and its supposed roots in Spinoza's thought), a reflexive critique that created fissures in the modern rational project despite attempts to cover them over. One interpretation sees the postmodern already prefigured in both the seventeenth-century Catholic Counter-Reformation and in the Baroque with the development of "a mass culture of emotionality," which pushed back against "modern forms of individuality, rationalism and asceticism" that have their roots in Calvinism.[11] Another sees postmodernism as merely working out the fundamental logic of consumer capitalism, the latest form of the modern commodification of culture.[12]

PATTERNS, NOT METHOD: SOME PHILOSOPHICAL BACKGROUND

In any event, opposition is the key element. However, the oppositions deemed "postmodern" are not carried out by any sort of determinate method *per se*. Rather, there are certain recurring patterns, most stemming from a persistent emphasis on *difference* and *otherness*. One important source for this emphasis is Martin Heidegger's critique of metaphysics and ontotheology in light of the "ontological difference," the always-already-operative condition—the process of differentiation—that precedes human reflection and allows it to distinguish between Being and beings. This is the "difference" that classical metaphysics, while claiming an all-encompassing worldview, left unthought because it

---

[7]Stephen K. White, *Political Theory and Postmodernism*, Modern European Philosophy (Cambridge: Cambridge University Press, 1991), 3.

[8]Ibid., 2.

[9]Eagleton, *Literary Theory*, 201. He comments that "postmodernity is a kind of extended footnote to the philosophy of Friedrich Nietzsche, who anticipated almost every one of [its] positions in nineteenth-century Europe" (ibid.).

[10]Bryan S. Turner, *Religion and Social Theory*, 2nd ed. (London: Sage, 1991), xviii.

[11]Ibid., xvii.

[12]Fredric Jameson, *Postmodernism, or, the Cultural Logic of Late Capitalism* (Durham, NC: Duke University Press, 1991).

could only conceive of reality in terms of two elements in hierarchical opposition (e.g., the Ground/grounded distinction).[13]

Another source is Jacques Derrida's notion of *différance*. He intensifies Heidegger's insight by making it linguistic. Derrida reacted to Ferdinand de Saussure's earlier structuralist view of language as a closed, stable system (*langue*), an underlying structure of differences and negations that we negotiate in everyday use (*parole*; e.g., "cat" is not "cap" or "bat"). Saussure viewed language as a system of signs (composed of a graphic or aural "signifier" and a "signified," the meaning) where meanings are generated from "within" the linguistic system, rather than by the sign pointing to a reality "outside" the system (the "referent"). That is, the system of signs functions within itself differentially: " 'In the linguistic system,' says Saussure, 'there are only differences': meaning is not mysteriously immanent in a sign but is functional, the result of its difference from other signs."[14] The relation between any sign and referent is culturally constructed and conventional and thereby arbitrary, as arbitrary as the relation between the signifier and the signified.

Derrida took Saussure's argument and blew it open by foregrounding its covert insight: the deconstruction of any claim to represent timeless truths in language. "Since the meaning of a sign is a matter of what the sign is *not*, its meaning is always in some sense absent from it too. Meaning, if you like, is scattered or dispersed along the whole chain of signifiers," and any settled meaning or reference is infinitely suspended, since every linguistic sign is conditioned by the signs around it, and so on endlessly.[15] Nor is there an extralinguistic ultimate meaning that grounds all other meanings (the "transcendental signified," such as Being, Idea or God), for "there is no concept which is not embroiled in an open-ended play of signification, shot through with the traces and fragments of other ideas" and other signs.[16] "Difference"—or in Derrida's neologism, *différance*—is operative always and everywhere (the aural undecidability in French between *-ence* and *-ance* is suggestive); one might call it a quasi-transcendental. For Derrida and his followers there is no thought or behavior that is not somehow "discourse," that is, a differential play of signs whose meanings depend on other signs, and so forth. "What is written as *différance*, then, will be the playing movement that 'produces'—by means of something that is not simply an activity—these differences, these effects of difference. ... *Différance* is the non-full, non-simple, structured and differentiating origin of differences. Thus, the name 'origin' no longer suits it."[17] This deconstruction of linguistic meaning and reference is about as close as one might get to highlighting any sort of postmodern "method" (although due to its wider agenda "postmodern" should not be simply conflated with Derrida's "deconstruction").

Derrida emphasized the destabilization that this emphasis on difference causes in cherished Western narratives about timeless metaphysical essences, the desire for a fixed center beyond the arbitrariness of signs or the search (going back to Plato) for a transcendental standpoint that would serve to anchor the shifting meanings of time-bound

---

[13]Martin Heidegger, "The Onto-Theo-Logical Constitution of Metaphysics," in *Identity and Difference*, trans. Joan Stambaugh (New York: Harper and Row, 1969 (Ger. orig. 1957)), 42–74, esp. 69–72.
[14]Eagleton, *Literary Theory*, 84.
[15]Ibid., 111.
[16]Ibid., 114.
[17]Jacques Derrida, "Différance", in *Margins of Philosophy*, trans. Alan Bass (Chicago: University of Chicago Press, 1982 (Fr. orig. 1968)), 3–27 (11).

experience. But instead of relying on "a fundamental immobility and a reassuring certitude," one must

> begin thinking that there was no center, that the center could not be thought in the form of a present-being, that the center had no natural site, that it was not a fixed locus but a function, a sort of nonlocus in which an infinite number of sign-substitutions come into play. This was the moment when language invaded the universal problematic, the moment when, in the absence of a center or origin, everything became discourse.[18]

It is also the moment when the power of rational systems and their narratives to define "the truth" in ways that include and exclude (from *definire*, to draw a limit or boundary)—that is, to take account of what fits into a conceptual system and call that "true" and to suppress what does not fit and call it "false" or unthinkable—came undone, and when the excluded "other" began to regain its voice and place in the cultural mix.

CRITIQUES OF CULTURE

The combined force of the critique of metaphysics and the deconstruction of the stability of linguistic reference eventually opens out into a series of postmodern oppositional movements that deploy the priority of difference in different ways, not as any particular "method" but as a varied set of strategies for reading and critiquing culture.

There is, for example, Lyotard's famous opening gambit in *The Postmodern Condition*. "Modern," he argues, refers to a culture that has justified the truth of its view of reality and its moral value by appealing to certain overarching, objectively certain, theoretical explanations ("metanarratives"). These are used to legitimate the basic principles and projects of modern life "by making an explicit appeal to some grand narrative, such as dialectics of Spirit, the hermeneutics of meaning, the emancipation of the rational or working subject, or the creation of wealth." This legitimation constructs a system of inclusions and exclusions geared toward efficiency that works through power and "a certain level of terror, whether soft or hard: be operational (that is, commensurable) or disappear."[19] But contemporary culture is no longer "modern," he reports, but "postmodern"—suspicious of all such overarching explanations and fragmented into various "language particles" and heterogeneous communities that have no common thread and thus defy any overarching explanation.

> Simplifying to the extreme, I define *postmodernism* as incredulity toward metanarratives. ... The narrative function is losing its functors, its great hero, its great dangers, its great voyages, its great goal. It is being dispersed in clouds of narrative language elements. ... Conveyed within each cloud are pragmatic valencies specific to its kind. Each of us lives at the intersection of many of these. However, we do not necessarily establish stable language combinations, and the properties of the ones we do establish are not necessarily communicable.[20]

---

[18]Jacques Derrida, "Structure, Sign, and Play in the Discourse of the Human Sciences", in *Writing and Difference*, trans. Alan Bass (Chicago: University of Chicago Press, 1978 (Fr. orig. 1966)), 278–93 (279).
[19]Lyotard, *The Postmodern Condition*, xxiii (grand narratives), xxiv (terror).
[20]Ibid., xxiv.

Modern narratives claimed to present an absolute truth or schema, but they have been exposed as unable to perform as promised; the difference between the narrative and the absolute it claimed to (re)present is unbridgeable. "The incredulity of the master narratives goes hand-in-hand with the discovery of their real nature as exaggerated *hegemonic discourses of an Idea* that adheres to illegitimate universal and cognitive presentations."[21] For Lyotard, ideas such as "the world (the totality of what is)," "the simple," "the infinitely powerful" and so on "are Ideas of which no presentation is possible. Therefore they impart no knowledge about reality (experience). ... They can be said to be unpresentable."[22] The difference between a totalizing narrative and the unpresentable is compounded by the fact that narratives themselves are linguistic structures that occur in a discourse universe made up of diverse phrases and genres whose linkages are contingent, not necessary. Lyotard calls this situation a differend (*le différend*), a linguistic conflict where particular contingent linkages that occur in communication, by their very nature, simultaneously exclude all the other communicative possibilities at that moment. "There is no genre of discourse that has the ultimate power to determine what phrase is to follow any given phrase. It follows that every phrase poses its own differend: the question, unresolvable by any genre of discourse, of what should follow it."[23] The differend is Lyotard's version of the dispersal of meaning among shifting signifiers; he considers it intimately connected to justice and politics.[24]

Another deployment of difference can be seen in Fredric Jameson's diagnosis of postmodern culture as marked by pastiche and schizophrenia, along with his claim that cultural practices of all kinds reveal that something new is afoot that pushes back against the deeply held assumptions of modern social and economic life.

Pastiche, like parody, involves imitation. Parody is modern: its satirical imitation involves "some secret sympathy for the original," a continuity of understanding between the parodist and who or what is being parodied. It presupposes there is a deeper essence or self "behind the scenes," so to speak—a unique individual whose idiosyncratic tendencies can be understood, imitated and communicated by means of a common language; parodist and parodied share the same world. With pastiche, however, the imitator is no longer "inside" the same world as the imitated; there is no assumed underlying norm or deeper unique self to which one can appeal. What is imitated is only the surface, a style: postmodern pastiche is "a neutral practice of such mimicry ... without that still latent feeling that there exists something *normal* compared to which what is being imitated is rather comic." It is the random use of symbols and language with no investment in their meaning: "All that is left is to imitate dead styles, to speak through the masks and with the voices of the styles in the imaginary museum."[25] This is the structuralist vision of language projected onto culture: cultural codes and styles function in a differential play like linguistic signs.

---

[21]Lieven Boeve, *Lyotard and Theology* (London: Bloomsbury, 2014), 25 (emphasis original).

[22]Lyotard, *The Postmodern Condition*, 78.

[23]Gary Gutting, *French Philosophy in the Twentieth Century* (Cambridge: Cambridge University Press, 2001), 327.

[24]For helpful analyses of Lyotard's complex notion of the differend, see Boeve, *Lyotard and Theology*, 14–28; and Gutting, *French Philosophy*, 321–31.

[25]Fredric Jameson, "Postmodernism and Consumer Society," in *The Anti-Aesthetic: Essays on Postmodern Culture*, ed. Hal Foster (1983; repr. New York: The New Press, 1998), 111–25 (113; secret sympathy), (114; neutral practice), (115; dead styles). An expanded version of this argument can be found in Jameson, *Postmodernism*, chapter 1, "The Cultural Logic of Late Capitalism."

For Jameson, the parody/pastiche distinction describes more than an aesthetic shift. It signals the end of "the conception of a unique self and private identity, a unique personality and individuality, which can be expected to generate its own unique vision of the world and to forge its own unique, unmistakable style." It is the announcement that "that kind of individualism and personal identity is a thing of the past; that the old individual or individualist subject is 'dead.'" This announcement of the postmodern "death of the subject" can be taken in either of two ways: either that "the older bourgeois individual subject" once existed but has been erased by the signs of corporate capitalism or, more radically, that this autonomous modern self *never* really existed in the first place" but was "merely a philosophical and cultural mystification."[26] This is supported by Jameson's claim that postmodern culture is also schizophrenic. If "the self" is fundamentally a story I tell myself about myself, then the narrated self functions precisely as structuralism claims all narratives do: it is constituted out of a differential play of signifiers whose "meanings" are made up of flickering presences and absences, ungrounded by any outside referent. Borrowing from the psychoanalyst Jacques Lacan, Jameson argues that our experiences of past, present and future, and "the persistence of personal identity over months and years," are "an effect of language." Schizophrenia is "the breakdown of the relationship between signifiers" and the loss of their time-markers. "The schizophrenic thus does not know personal identity in our sense, since our feeling of identity depends on our sense of the persistence of the 'I' and the 'me' over time."[27] This, for Jameson, is also the diagnosis of contemporary social life driven by the logic of late capitalist consumerism: our forgetfulness of the past, our inability to conceive of a future and our fixation on the present as disconnected from anything else. The modern humanist subject doesn't stand a chance.

Jameson's take on postmodern culture shows how the primordial issue of difference migrated easily from semiotics to cultural critique. When "language invaded the universal problematic" (Derrida), it became easy to believe "that everything behaves like language. Body language, garment language, the silent expression of gesture, the layout of a city or a fashion magazine or a university: all of these are complex, coded systems of meaning and value. … Language thus conceived is a model of organization that is both powerful and finite."[28] And as Jameson shows (via Lacan), this affects notions of the self as well. For if language as a network of differences and negations means, as Terry Eagleton puts it, that "it is an illusion for me to believe that I can ever be fully present to you in what I say or write," then I can never know myself as a unified self—or really know myself at all.

> Since language is something I am made out of, rather than merely a convenient tool I use, the whole idea that I am a stable, unified entity must also be a fiction. Not only can I never be fully present to you, but I can never be fully present to myself either. I still need to use signs when I look into my mind or search my soul, and this means that I will never experience any "full communion" with myself.[29]

---

[26]Jameson, "Postmodernism," 114–15.
[27]Ibid., 119.
[28]Elizabeth Deeds Ermarth, "Postmodernism: 2. The Role of Language," in *Routledge Encyclopedia of Philosophy* (New York: Taylor and Francis, 2011), https://www.rep.routledge.com/articles/thematic/postmodernism/v-2/sections/the-role-of-language.
[29]Eagleton, *Literary Theory*, 112.

POSTMODERNISM AND THE CHALLENGE
TO THE HUMAN PERSON

Right here the postmodern assertion of difference as primordial intersects with the subject of this volume. One of the residual effects of this assertion is the strong postmodern opposition to one of modernity's most cherished claims, namely the humanism that for centuries has sought to define a universal human essence and has used this to argue for the dignity, freedom and power of the individual subject both autonomously and in community. Michel Foucault, whose early "archaeology of knowledge" projected the structuralist claim across the human sciences, was able to show the instability of the historical and social construction of the supposedly "silent and immobile" presuppositions of Western humanism and claim that "man is an invention of recent date. And one perhaps nearing its end."[30] What kind of a "person," "self," or "subject," then, is left for theological anthropology to talk about? Opposition-based-in-difference has exposed the historical contingency of the ideals and principles that Western modernity assumed to be absolute (or at least well-founded) about human persons. Is it possible, in the postmodern condition, to retrieve and recuperate human subjectivity and agency?

One attempt to show how difference not only deconstructs but also offers a constructive engagement with the notion of the self is Richard Kearney's advocacy for the postmodern imagination.[31] He agrees with Jameson and others that the postmodern condition is already one of commodified imagery and "pseudoevents" where image is reality. Even more to the point, "image and reality have dissolved into a play of mutual parody—to the point where we can no longer say which is which." The postmodern image "parodies itself" and "exposes its status as an *imitation without original*, which draws attention to its own artificiality—whether mediatized, technologized, fetishized, or commodified."[32]

This situation calls for new arguments on behalf of human agency. We have an "ethical duty" to respond to the "call of the other" in the wake of the postmodern dismantling of the modern humanist imagination that presupposed historical progress and "the almost messianic role of the idealist subject in such progress." This does not mean, however, that we should deny "the creative human subject any role whatsoever in the shaping of meaning," as do those postmodern arguments that view difference as a sort of transcendental condition or net in which human beings are caught. To do so would run the risk of slipping into "a corrosive rhetoric of apocalyptic pessimism" or a paralyzing and impotent nihilism. "While accepting that the 'humanist imagination' does indeed require decentering ... we must insist on the possibility, in the wake of deconstruction, of affirming some notion of a properly *human* imagination."[33] This imagination will view the other not as a mirror image or a commodity, but as an image with a referent: the particular person who demands a response from me, one "whose very *otherness* refuses to be reduced to an empty mimicry of *sameness*. Beyond the mask, there is a face."[34]

Kearney's new interpretation of imagination, by way of a phenomenology of the image, is expressed in two typologies. The first describes the Western imagination in

---

[30]Michel Foucault, *The Order of Things: An Archaeology of the Human Sciences* (New York: Vintage/Random House, 1973), xxiv (silent and immobile), 387 (invention).
[31]Richard Kearney, "Ethics and the Postmodern Imagination," *Thought* 62 (1987): 39–58; Richard Kearney, *The Wake of Imagination: Towards a Postmodern Culture* (Minneapolis: University of Minnesota Press, 1988).
[32]Kearney, "Ethics," 39–40.
[33]Ibid., 42–3.
[34]Ibid. (emphases original).

terms of chronologically ordered paradigms. The *premodern* imagination is fundamentally theocentric and mimetic, mirroring reality and especially its divine source in images that are essentially an act of creative *hommage* (the Byzantine icon is a prime example). The *modern* imagination is anthropocentric and productive, more lamp than mirror, devoted to autonomous self-expression, crafting images that are always "a portrait of the artist." The *postmodern* imagination is parodic and eccentric, dethroning the theocentric and the anthropocentric in acts of *bricolage*, juxtaposing fragments of meaning that it has not created and turning image into reality.[35] The second typology outlines the imagination's operations. First it is called to be *critical*, demystifying both ontotheological and anthropocentric claims to be the sole origin of meaning, and discriminating between authentic and inauthentic aspects of the postmodern context. Second, and most importantly, the imagination is called to be *poetic* in the sense of *poiêsis*, "inventive," challenging the status quo of endless imitation by daring to invent new possibilities of social existence that break free of the technological and ethical quagmire of the postmodern context. Kearney's definition is pivotal: "Renouncing the pervasive sense of social paralysis, the poetic imagination would attempt to restore man's faith in history and to nourish the belief that things can be changed. The first and most effective step in this direction is to begin to *imagine* that the world as it is could be *otherwise*."[36] Here, difference is projected across time, denying that temporality is merely a linguistic effect and helping to restore historical consciousness and produce social change.

Although roughly three decades old, this argument's formal outlines are still viable, especially its ethical demand for a response to persons as persons rather than as commodified images.[37] No aspect is more valuable than Kearney's theory of the "otherwise." How precisely does the poetic imagination "restore [our] faith in history" and "nourish the belief that things can be changed"? It is both a realistic response to contemporary situations and a direct probing of the new possibilities for existence, which those situations present. This invests difference with ethical and utopian value. Thinking otherwise asks "what if ...?" What if the present were different and better? The poetic imagination is thus critical in its own right: it judges the "business-as-usual" context of the present as inadequate or even oppressive, not humanizing enough, incapable of fulfilling human desires for happiness. By thinking otherwise than the modern status quo, the poetic imagination reactivates historical consciousness and allows for the different, the new, the unprecedented to break into contemporary consciousness. Historical consciousness threatens the status quo by disclosing that the present situation is not absolute and that "the real" is not simply repetition or a mirror image. What the poetic imagination suggests is a refiguration of reality that can act as a catalyst for change: *thinking* otherwise (i.e., entertaining new possibilities that could be made real and appear to be within range of human happiness) can serve as a catalyst for *acting* otherwise (i.e., the actualization of new possibilities, changing the situation for the better). *Thinking otherwise* as the retrieval of historical consciousness restores both a belief that the present context is neither circular nor absolute, and a hope in newly imagined possibilities for a different and better future

---

[35]Kearney, *Wake of Imagination*, 1–18.
[36]Kearney, "Ethics and the Postmodern Imagination," 44 (his emphasis).
[37]Indeed, Kearney's argument may be even more appropriate for the image-driven and media-saturated "post-truth" era in which we find ourselves. For an appreciative critique, see Anthony J. Godzieba, "Knowing Differently: Incarnation, Imagination, and the Body," *Louvain Studies* 32 (2007): 361–82.

that can exceed our abilities and expectations, possibilities that *acting otherwise* can put into play.

An argument such as this is crucial: it gives us a wider view of the effects of postmodern oppositional culture because it inverts our expectations. What we might ironically call a "canonical" type of postmodernism dismisses the modern metanarrative, in whatever form, in favor of reading the contemporary as a welcome *mélange* of unreconcilable cultural fragments. It views "difference" as the always-already-present structuring condition of all historical and cultural behavior, a condition ignored or suppressed by the modern drive to unify knowledge that in turn excluded any thought or activity that could be considered "other" and did not "fit" the unifying scheme. The result, though, as Jameson, Kearney, and others have noticed, is a logjam of sameness that the signs commodified by late consumer capitalism almost mechanically impose on the human condition. No matter to what degree signs differ from other signs, all consumer images/commodified realities are simply that: commodified images obeying the same universal logic.

Difference does indeed lead to the unreconcilable, but also to more of the same, a system. Terry Eagleton has noted this contradiction of postmodernism as being akin to that of the simultaneously radical and conservative nature of structuralism: "It is as though by pressing a sort of technological determinism all the way through to the mind itself, treating individuals as the mere empty locus of impersonal codes, it imitated the way modern society actually treats them but pretends it does not, thus endorsing its logic while unmasking its ideals." Postmodernism reflects this contradiction by presenting itself as "a resourceful subversion of the dominant value-system, at least at the level of theory." At the level of practice, though, it "scoops up something of the material logic of advanced capitalism,"[38] turning it into a metaphysics that substitutes for the classical metaphysics it jettisoned.

A surprising contemporary example of this is the postmodern digital economy on which social media floats. Social media's various forms are praised as avenues for freedom of expression and exchange of information, including the free flow of diverse opinions in public discourse. But, as the philosopher and cultural theorist Byung-Chul Han argues, the digital economy is a neoliberal economy: it demands a transparency that transforms everything into usable data, and sees "secrecy, foreignness, and otherness" as "obstacles" to efficient communication that must be eliminated. "Transparency makes the human being glassy. Therein lies its violence. Unrestricted freedom and communication switch into total control and surveillance."[39] In a society of transparent positivity where people willingly bare (i.e., "posit") their souls, their political choices and their music preferences, individuality, suffering and otherness are negativities that stall efficient communication and cannot be economically exploited, and thus resist the political-economic status quo.[40] On this reading, the digital platform—where image truly equals reality—promises a humanizing difference that surpasses the modern humanist ideal, but eventually (and almost inevitably) delivers dehumanization and more of "the same."

---

[38]Terry Eagleton, *The Illusions of Postmodernism* (Oxford: Blackwell, 1996), 131 (determinism), 132 (subversion), 133 (logic of capitalism).

[39]Byung-Chul Han, *The Transparency Society*, trans. Erik Butler (Stanford, CA: Stanford University Press, 2015), viii.

[40]Ibid., 7–8. See also Byung-Chul Han, *Psychopolitics: Neoliberalism and New Technologies of Power*, trans. Erik Butler (London: Verso, 2017), 3: "Neoliberalism represents a highly efficient, indeed an intelligent, system for exploiting freedom. ... It is inefficient to exploit people against their will. ... Only when freedom is exploited are returns maximized."

CONSEQUENCES FOR THEOLOGY

What are the theological consequences of digitally mediated space that is already positioned by an economically colonized meta-culture that, as Han puts it, is now in "the process of organizing the human psyche in an entirely new way"[41] while also manipulating us? How does the theologian deal with a digital culture that levels out all experiences and turns all data into exploitable commodities? This is the new postmodern condition that Christian theology confronts, an unexpected twist in a narrative that claimed to out-narrate the modern narrative.

Is there, then, a postmodern method? No, only an emphasis on difference, which is recognized and put into play in different ways in opposition to the modern rational project. An ethical focus such as Kearney's attempts to crack the kind of reductionist logic that contemporary deployments of difference seem to have fallen into. An ethical retrieval of postmodern difference, when considered truly anthropologically and temporally, can foster the "otherness" of the other person, as well as my own "difference" from any code, to disrupt a rigid system of signs and codes by revealing both the other who appeals to us to recognize their unique dignity and a way to activate and participate in that shared happiness for which we long. A theological anthropology that develops out of a strong creation theology, recognizes the importance of the Incarnation for the material and historical particularity of grace and affirms the Resurrection as God's view of the potential of human life should be robust enough to take on these challenges and take on the task to "activate the differences and save the honor of the name."

SUGGESTED FURTHER READING

Eagleton, Terry, *The Illusions of* Postmodernism (Oxford: Blackwell, 1996).

Godzieba, Anthony J., "Knowing Differently: Incarnation, Imagination, and the Body," *Louvain Studies* 32 (2007): 361–82.

Hart, Kevin, *Postmodernism: A Beginner's Guide* (Oxford: Oneworld, 2004).

Jameson, Frederic, *Postmodernism, or, the Cultural Logic of Late Capitalism* (Durham, NC: Duke University Press, 1991).

Lyotard, Jean-François, *The Postmodern Condition: A Report on Knowledge*, Theory and History of Literature, vol. 10, trans. Geoff Bennington and Brian Massumi (Minneapolis: University of Minnesota Press, 1984).

---

[41]Han, *Transparency Society*, 5.

PART II

Key Themes

CHAPTER FOUR

Creation

DANIEL P. HORAN, OFM

The relationship between theological reflection on creation as such and theological anthropology has varied over the course of Christian history. Oftentimes, consideration of that which God has brought into existence collectively has been subordinated to focus on the particularity and specialness of humanity within the created order (*oikonomia*). This sense of what God has created collectively is what David Kelsey describes in terms of the object of "first theology," by which he means "the distinctive ways in which God relates to all that is not God."[1] In what we may generally call the premodern era, theologians and scriptural exegetes frequently relegated the notion of nonhuman creation to a cosmic backdrop for the unfolding of the history of human salvation. In the modern era, the Western Enlightenment's "turn to the subject" reified a theological anthropocentrism, which situated consideration of nonhuman creation to a place of secondary concern at best but more often led to a dualistic view of the created world as containing rational human creatures on the one hand and irrational corporeal animals on the other.[2]

Today, with ready access to superabundant natural and social scientific knowledge, we can no longer presuppose a naïve understanding of our place within the broader cosmos. Whereas theological anthropology has often treated theologies of creation as a subset or afterthought, any credible consideration of the human person from a theological perspective today must take seriously the broader community of creation as its rightful starting point. To this point, while there are numerous ways one might approach the topic of creation in a handbook to theological anthropology, I have elected to focus this chapter on three key themes in contemporary discussions about creation that are relevant for theological reflection on the human person. Though these sections are in no way exhaustive, the themes are: (1) recent discussions about the Christian doctrine of *creatio ex nihilo*; (2) renewed interpretations of scripture that emphasize the community of creation and challenge hitherto presuppositions about the doctrine of *imago Dei*; and (3) insights from the theory of evolution for a theology of creation in general and the human person in particular.

---

[1] See David H. Kelsey, *Eccentric Existence: A Theological Anthropology*, 2 vols. (Louisville: Westminster John Knox Press, 2009) 1: 12–45.

[2] In recent decades, continental philosophers have deconstructed this anthropocentric enlightenment bias, which has provided theologians with much to consider concerning the human person. For example, see Jacques Derrida, *The Animal That Therefore I Am*, ed. Marie-Louise Mallet, trans. David Wills (New York: Fordham University Press, 2008); Jacques Derrida, *The Beast & The Sovereign*, ed. Michel Lisse, Marie-Louise Mallet and Ginette Michaud, trans. Geoffrey Bennington, 2 vols. (Chicago: University of Chicago Press, 2009—11); and Giorgio Agamben, *The Open: Man and Animal*, trans. Kevin Attell (Stanford: Stanford University Press, 2004); among others.

THE DOCTRINE OF *CREATIO EX NIHILO*

As David Burrell has observed, the era of Western modernity ushered in a period during which the doctrine of creation from nothing waned in visibility and its apparent usefulness came under attack.[3] In addition to the recognized intellectual challenges brought about by modern philosophy, postmodern thinkers in our contemporary era have raised further concerns about the doctrine in terms of both its origins and implications.[4] Burrell's call is to recover this ancient—if admittedly contested in biblical origins—theological claim.[5] The major criticism leveled against the contemporary value of the doctrine is that it is a metaphysical claim that has been imposed on an otherwise biblically rooted theological tradition. On this point, the critics are *prima facie* correct. As Carlo Cogliati rightly notes, it is true that *"creatio ex nihilo* is a metaphysical concept, not a physical event."[6] Furthermore, the earliest recorded appearance of a doctrine of *creatio ex nihilo* appears late in the second century C.E. in the writings of Theophilus of Antioch: "God brought everything into being out of what does not exist, so that his greatness might be known and understood through his works."[7] Indeed, *creatio ex nihilo* is a metaphysical concept that cannot be found explicitly articulated in the canonical scripture.[8]

Critics of the doctrine suggest further that the implications that arise from this doctrine contribute to distorted and non-Christian images of God as Creator, emphasizing divine sovereignty and power that too often mirrors human actions and views of domination and subjugation—especially within a patriarchal context. The real if rare problems of a distorted image of the Creator in some theological reflection on God and creation notwithstanding, proponents of *creatio ex nihilo* argue that the metaphysical nature and late-second-century emergence of the doctrine do not immediately preclude it from usefulness and orthodoxy. Additionally, just because a Christian doctrine is emergent—it develops over centuries as opposed to being contained comprehensively in

---

[3]David B. Burrell, "*Creatio ex Nihilo* Recovered," *Modern Theology* 29 (2013): 5–21.

[4]For example, see David Ray Griffin, "Creation Out of Nothing, Creation Out of Chaos, and the Problem of Evil," in *Encountering Evil: Live Options in Theodicy*, ed. Stephen T. Davis (Louisville: Westminster John Knox Press, 2001), 101–36; Catherine Keller, *Face of the Deep: A Theology of Becoming* (London: Routledge, 2003); John D. Caputo, *The Weakness of God: A Theology of the Event* (Bloomington: Indiana University Press, 2005); and Mary-Jane Rubenstein, "Cosmic Singularities: On the Nothing and the Sovereign," *Journal of the American Academy of Religion* 80 (2012): 485–517; among others.

[5]Among those in support of a contemporary recovery of *creatio ex nihilo* are Kathryn Tanner, *God and Creation in Christian Theology* (Minneapolis: Fortress Press, 1988); Rowan Williams, "On Being Creatures," in *On Christian Theology* (Oxford: Blackwell, 2000), 63–78; Brian D. Robinette, "The Difference Nothing Makes: *Creatio Ex Nihilo*, Resurrection, and Divine Gratuity," *Theological Studies* 72 (2011): 525–57; Ian A. McFarland, *From Nothing: A Theology of Creation* (Louisville: Westminster John Knox Press, 2014); and Janet Soskice, "Why *Creatio ex Nihilo* for Theology Today?," in *Creation ex Nihilo: Origins, Development, Contemporary Challenges*, ed. Gary A. Anderson and Markus Bockmuehl (Notre Dame: University of Notre Dame Press, 2018), 37–54; among others.

[6]Carlo Cogliati, "Introduction," in *Creation and the God of Abraham*, ed. David B. Burrell, Carlo Cogliati, Janet M. Soskice and William R. Stoeger (New York: Cambridge University Press, 2010), 8.

[7]Theophilus of Antioch, *To Autolycus*, 1.4, in *The Ante-Nicene Fathers*, ed. Alexander Roberts and James Donaldson, 10 vols. (Peabody: Hendrickson Publishers, 1994), 2: 90. For more on the history of the early development of the doctrine, including intimations of it in preceding thinkers, see Gehard May, *Creatio Ex Nihilo: The Doctrine of 'Creation out of Nothing' in Early Christian Thought*, trans. A. S. Worrall (Edinburgh: T&T Clark, 1994).

[8]For a sampling of recent scholarship on *creatio ex nihilo* and scripture, see Richard J. Clifford, "*Creatio ex nihilo* in the Old Testament/Hebrew Bible," in *Creation ex Nihilo: Origins, Development, Contemporary Challenges*, 55–76; and Sean M. McDonough, "Being and Nothingness in the Book of Revelation," in *Creation ex Nihilo: Origins, Development, Contemporary Challenges*, 77–98.

scripture—does not mean that it is unorthodox or unhelpful.[9] There has been a notable effort to provide a contemporary *apologia* for the doctrine with arguments highlighting the constructive ways it supports theologies of creation and of the human person. Brian Robinette has argued convincingly that the doctrine actually contributes to a holistic understanding of three essential dimensions of Christian faith: namely, the affirmation of both divine transcendence and immanence, the distinction between God and creatures, and the universal significance of the resurrection, which joins together both protology and eschatology in the spirit of Irenaeus of Lyons and other early theologians.[10] It is worth examining each of these dimensions in turn.

First, the doctrine of *creatio ex nihilo* says something significant about both the transcendence and immanence of God. Critics of the doctrine have suggested that affirmation of *ex nihilo* disproportionately emphasizes divine omnipotence and therefore unhelpfully distances God from creation. In turn, such critics have argued for a radical embrace of divine immanence or emphasis on the vulnerability of God to counter any divine indifference or oppressive paternalism implied by a strong transcendence. Drawing on the work of Henri de Lubac and Kathryn Tanner, Robinette argues that defense of divine transcendence does not necessarily imply denial of divine immanence. In fact, when it comes to God as Creator, in maintaining transcendence one necessarily implies divine immanence. To assert that God is transcendent—wholly other—is to affirm that nothing stands in opposition to God, nothing can be compared to God and nothing can limit God. Robinette explains, "To declare God as 'wholly other' is to issue a denial of a thoroughgoing sort. God and world are not 'one,' yet neither are they 'two.' God and world cannot be identified, yet neither are they two beings constituted by a zero-sum relationship. They are 'not-two'—nonconstrastive and noncompetitive, as Tanner puts it."[11] In creating all that exists from nothing, God establishes God's self as wholly other and therefore capable of drawing infinitely close to that which is brought into existence and remains dependent on the Creator for being. The doctrine of *creatio ex nihilo* protects the utter gratuity of the divine creative act, while also supporting "a vision of the God-world relationship that sees no 'opposition' between them."[12]

Second, the doctrine of *creatio ex nihilo* says something about our creatureliness. To assert that God creates from nothing, without prior constraints or limits, is to also contend that we are *not* God. As obvious as that statement might appear, it bears an important theological ramification. As human beings we are not of a special class or composed in a manner apart from the other manifold and various aspects of creation. Instead, we share an ontological identity with all other creatures precisely as creatures, which have been brought into existence by God from nothing. This has both vertical and horizontal implications. Vertically, the doctrine challenges our anthropocentric worldviews that foster a distorted sense of importance, uniqueness and independence. Alterity rests with the Creator who alone is "wholly other" from creation; it is not of our making or determination. Horizontally, the doctrine calls us in the species *Homo sapiens*

---

[9]Janet Soskice, who has written frequently about the doctrine of *creatio ex nihilo*, compares it to the doctrine of the Trinity, which itself emerged over the course of many centuries. See Soskice, "Why *Creatio ex Nihilo* for Theology Today?," 37–8.
[10]Robinette, 'The Difference Nothing Makes,' 532–57.
[11]Ibid., 533.
[12]Ibid., 535.

to recognize an inherent kinship we share with all creation from the largest and most impressive creature to the smallest quanta seen only in mathematical representation.

Finally, the doctrine of *creatio ex nihilo* says something about the unity of protology and eschatology, of creation and salvation. Robinette and other supporters of the doctrine insist that we take seriously the theological valence of *creatio ex nihilo* rather than misunderstand it to represent some kind of speculation about the first instant of creation. On this point, we do well to recall the Pauline notion of recapitulation (*anakephalaiosis*) that sets the stage for Irenaeus and others in the centuries that follow. Rather than understand creation and salvation as separate acts of the divine will, we should see them joined together: protology and eschatology as two sides of the same coin. It follows that if God creates all that exists *ex nihilo* and therefore as an *exitus* from God's self, salvation is best understood as the complementary *reditus* back to the Creator. Irenaeus, in his second-century *apologia* against the anti-materialist Gnostics of his age, framed this singular soteriological movement in terms of God's action by Word and Spirit—famously described as the two "hands" of the creator God. Robinette argues

> that *creatio ex nihilo* is best thought of as a doctrine of hope for creation, not a doctrine that provides an explanation for the world. It is a soteriologically motivated doctrine that declares the penultimacy of evil, sin and innocent suffering: because they do not have the "final" word—this is its "eschatological vision"—neither are they "original" or anterior to creation.[13]

This doctrine of hope for creation is capacious enough to include human and nonhuman creatures alike, thereby further affirming the inherent kinship or community of creation established by God. Elizabeth Johnson has argued in her recent work that if we can speak of the "Deep Incarnation," meaning that the Word becoming flesh (*sarx*) has significance for *all creation* and not simply humanity alone, then we can also speak about "Deep Resurrection" in this same vein.[14]

Despite the understandable contention surrounding the doctrine of *creatio ex nihilo* at times, recent work provides insight about and highlights the relevance of the doctrine for today. For the purposes of theological anthropology, the doctrine is especially helpful in resituating the human person from a "human-separatist"[15] context into a "community of creation" context that is truer to both science and scripture.

REREADING GENESIS AND RECONSIDERING THE *IMAGO DEI*

The book of Genesis has often been the target of understandable criticism for its role as a source of proof-texting by those who defend dominion models of creation, which situate humanity over and against nonhuman creation in terms of absolute sovereignty

---

[13]Ibid., 555.

[14]See Elizabeth A. Johnson, *Creation and the Cross: The Mercy of God for a Planet in Peril* (Maryknoll: Orbis Books, 2018); and Elizabeth A. Johnson, *Ask the Beasts: Darwin and the God of Love* (London: Bloomsbury, 2014). For more on "Deep Incarnation," see Niels Henrik Gregersen, ed., *Incarnation: On the Scope and Depth of Christology* (Minneapolis: Fortress Press, 2015); and Matthew Eaton, "Theology and An-Archy: Deep Incarnation Christology Following Emmanuel Lévinas and the New Materialism," *Toronto Journal of Theology* 32 (2016): 3–15.

[15]I borrow this term from David Clough, *On Animals: Systematic Theology*, vol. 1 (New York: T&T Clark, 2012).

and dominance.[16] However, as recent scholarship has shown, the account in Genesis 1, rather than presenting a divine mandate for domination and the shoring up of human sovereignty, presents a creation designed from the beginning "to be an interconnecting and interdependent whole, and so the refrain is varied at the end of the work of the sixth day: 'God saw everything that he had made, and behold, it was very good' (1:31). The value of the whole is more than the value of the sum of its parts."[17] Even before the exclamation of goodness God offers in light of the completed creation, we see parallels and continuity between human beings and nonhuman creation. Just as God blesses and commands human beings to "be fruitful and multiply, and fill the earth" in Gen. 1:28, God also blessed and commanded the water and air creatures to do likewise in Gen. 1:22: "God blessed them, saying, 'Be fruitful and multiply and fill the waters in the seas, and let birds multiply on the earth.'" Mark Brett has commented that this parallel between humanity and nonhuman creatures (including the Earth, which God commands to "grow vegetation" [Gen. 1:11]) can be read as the divine bestowal of creative agency to all living things. Instead of being an object for manipulation by God or humanity, nonhuman creation is viewed also as cocreators with God, something Brett sees bolstered by God's universal covenant with all creation (as opposed to humanity alone) later in Gen. 9:8-17.[18] That the earth is later commanded again to "bring forth living creatures of every kind' in Gen. 1:24-25 suggests that "the creation of these land animals is the result of the combined activity of the earth and the Deity," which connotes the cocreativity traditionally reserved for humanity.[19]

While the apparent commands of God to humanity in Gen. 1:26 ("have dominion") and Gen. 1:28 ("subdue") have seemingly contributed to the justification and proliferation of various iterations of the dominion model of creation, the second creation account in Genesis offers a scriptural challenge quite distinct from its textual, if not historical, mythological-narrative predecessor.[20] In the second creation account we read that "the Lord God formed man from the dust of the ground [adama], and breathed into his nostrils the breath of life; and the man became a living being" (Gen 2:7).[21] The formation of human beings out of the ground (ha-adama) is the same process by which God forms all the animals and other creatures: "So out of the ground [ha-adama] the Lord God formed every animal of the field and every bird of the air" (Gen. 2:19). There is an explicit semantic parallel in this creation account that bespeaks a richly theological observation,

---

[16]The most famous example of such criticism is Lynn White Jr., "The Historical Roots of our Ecologic Crisis," *Science* 155 (1968): 1203–7.

[17]Richard Bauckham, *The Bible and Ecology: Rediscovering the Community of Creation* (Waco: Baylor University Press, 2011), 15.

[18]Mark G. Brett, "Earthing the Human in Genesis 1–3," in *The Earth Story in Genesis*, ed. Norman C. Habel and Shirley Wurst (Sheffield: Sheffield Academic Press, 2000), 77. Also, see William P. Brown, *The Seven Pillars of Creation: The Bible, Science, and the Ecology of Wonder* (New York: Oxford University Press, 2010), 44–6.

[19]William P. Brown, *The Ethos of the Cosmos: The Genesis of Moral Imagination in the Bible* (Grand Rapids: Eerdmans, 1999), 40–1.

[20]For more context of the Genesis accounts, see Nahum Sarna, *Genesis*, JPS Torah Commentary (Philadelphia: Jewish Publication Society, 1989), xi–xix; and Gerhard Von Rad, *Genesis*, trans. John H. Marks, Old Testament Library, rev. ed. (Louisville: Westminster John Knox Press, 1973), 13–44.

[21]Though the NRSV and most English translations gender the *adam* ("human") as male (in both the sense of "Adam" as proper noun from the opening of Genesis 2 and the pronoun usage), the Hebrew is best rendered "humanity" in general. The word *adam* is in the original masculine, but the word *'iš* meaning "biological male" does not appear until after YHWH builds the woman. For more, see Phyllis Trible, *God and the Rhetoric of Sexuality* (Minneapolis: Fortress Press, 1978), 72–165; and David W. Cotter, *Genesis*, Berit Olam series (Collegeville: Liturgical Press, 2003), 29–31.

which is echoed elsewhere in the Hebrew Scriptures including in the book of Job: "Your hands fashioned and made me; and now you turn and destroy me. Remember that you fashioned me like clay [*adama*]; and will you turn me to dust [*adama*] again?" (Job 10:8-9).[22] The relational dimension of this act of creation reveals an intimacy between the Creator and creation. The Creator molds or shapes the created world in a way akin to a potter whose hands actualize the intentional design of God with the material of the earth.

Additionally, human beings and the rest of creation are, according to this account, made from the same material and have the same origin. The same dust or clay of the ground physically constitutes humanity as well as other animals, plant life and so on. This originating source and material are reiterated in Gen. 3:19 when God declares the punishment for the man stating, "By the sweat of your face you shall eat bread until you return to the ground [*adama*], for out of it you were taken; you are dust [*adama*], and to dust [*adama*] you shall return." Beyond the two creation narratives in Genesis, we see later in primeval history (Genesis 1–11) the way in which the authors and redactors of the biblical text recount the covenant made by God after the great flood. While Christians often *think* the covenant is made between God and Noah, or even between God and Noah's family more broadly, the covenant is in fact made explicitly between God and "all flesh" (*kol-basar*) and alternatively "every living creature." This is something repeated more than five times in the famous divine speech announcing the covenant (Gen. 9:8-17), and it further strengthens readings of Genesis 1 and 2 that recognize a degree of agency and even subjectivity in nonhuman creation. Furthermore, these texts reaffirm a vision of inherent creaturely kinship between human and nonhuman creatures that is often lost in otherwise anthropocentric accountings of creation in general and the human person in particular.

These reconsiderations of the Genesis creation accounts more broadly have led theologians to reexamine the Christian doctrine of the *imago Dei* as well, which is such a significant dimension of classical theological anthropology. Traditionally, the emergence of the dominion model of creation was inextricably tied to the view that human beings were absolutely unique and therefore categorically distinct from the rest of creation. This anthropocentrism and "human separatism" was encapsulated in the doctrine of humanity having been created *imago Dei* as witnessed in Gen. 1:26-27.[23] And yet, it is striking that an expression that appears in the Hebrew Bible only three times, and each time only in the book of Genesis (1:26-27, 5:1 and 9:6), would serve such a definitive purpose in the course of theological reflection on the human person and her relationship to the rest of creation. J. Richard Middleton has noted that the long-standing inattention to the context of the Hebrew Bible, generally, and of the book of Genesis, specifically, has led many interpreters of scripture to "turn to extrabiblical, usually philosophical, sources to interpret the image and end up reading contemporaneous conceptions of being human back into the Genesis text."[24] Middleton goes to great lengths to survey the semantic tensions and ambiguities present in the Hebrew and similar Ancient Near Eastern usages of "image of God," noting that there is no absolutely clear or conclusive meaning that can be tied to the Christian doctrine of *imago Dei* from the biblical texts alone, which is why Christian thinkers and exegetes have for centuries relied on anthropocentric philosophical

---

[22]For more, see Daniel P. Horan, *All God's Creatures: A Theology of Creation* (Latham: Lexington Books/Fortress Academic, 2018), 90–6; and Johnson, *Ask the Beasts*, 269–73.
[23]See David Fergusson, *Creation* (Grand Rapids: Eerdmans, 2014), 11–13.
[24]J. Richard Middleton, *The Liberating Image: The* Imago Dei *in Genesis 1* (Grand Rapids: Brazos Press, 2005), 17.

presuppositions in applying meaning not found in the scripture to the Hebrew terms *selem* (image) and *demut* (likeness).[25]

In addition to the scriptural issues beyond an anthropocentric reading of *imago Dei*, evolutionary biology, contemporary ethology, psychology and other social sciences have all bolstered a more complex vision of the creaturely family within which the human species is found rather than affirming an absolute distinction that has been long presumed. For centuries theologians and philosophers have proposed numerous characteristics thought to be unique to *Homo sapiens* as a species: rationality, language, emotion, relational capacity, tool usage and moral agency, among others. We know now that we cannot maintain such rigid distinctions and take the natural sciences seriously. In response, theologians have been offering tentative proposals to help us reconsider what we might mean in our theological affirmation of the *imago Dei*. One such proposal worth considering is what Leslie Muray has argued for in terms of the way we talk about human and nonhuman creatures. He argues for "human *distinctiveness*" as opposed to "human *uniqueness*," given that science has shown that there is not an absolute difference between human and nonhuman animals. "While humans are different from non-humans and have a 'special' role to play (as do all species), we are firmly implanted in non-human nature … humans and non-humans alike are part of the natural world. The difference between humans and non-humans is a matter of degree and not of kind."[26] Muray's aim is for theologians to recognize that the *imago Dei* is not best understood as a threshold point that separates humanity from other creatures but instead could be understood as an expression of the "individual-in-community." Muray explains,

> Describing the individual, human and non-human, as an individual-in-community is to claim that the self is a relational self, internally related to its environment, human and non-human. The word "community" includes the whole of the environment, human and non-human, of any individual event. The individuated event is part of the whole of that community, and the community is a part of the individuated event.[27]

Perhaps human beings are not the only ones who bear the *imago Dei*, but that all God's creatures are created *imago Dei* in some sense (if not always in the same sense). There is room for distinction amid relationship, diversity within the community of creation. While this is but one attempt to rethink the doctrine of *imago Dei*, its meaning remains far from resolved. However, contemporary theological anthropologies must take into consideration what science tells us about who we are and how we belong and not merely echo uncritically anthropocentric presuppositions about human uniqueness.

---

[25]Middleton is not the only one to note this. In addition to Middleton's *The Liberating Image*, see David Fergusson, "Humans Created According to the *Imago Dei*: An Alternative Proposal," *Zygon* 48 (2013): 439–53; Ian McFarland, *The Divine Image: Envisioning the Invisible God* (Minneapolis: Fortress Press, 2005), 1–6; David Clough, "All God's Creatures: Reading Genesis on Human and Nonhuman Animals," in *Reading Genesis After Darwin*, ed. Stephen C. Barton and David Wilkinson (New York: Oxford University Press, 2009), 145–61; and David S. Cunningham, "The Way of All Flesh: Rethinking the *Imago Dei*," in *Creaturely Theology: On God, Humans, and Other Animals*, ed. Celia Deane-Drummond and David Clough (London: SCM Press, 2009), 100–17.

[26]Leslie Muray, "Human Uniqueness vs. Human Distinctiveness: The *Imago Dei* in the Kinship of All Creatures," *American Journal of Theology and Philosophy* 28 (2007): 306. Additionally, although she is not as uncomfortable with the emphasis on rationality as a dimension of humanity's expression of the *Imago Dei* as others, Kathryn Tanner nevertheless also allows for a continuum or system of degree in assessing the whole of creation's ability to, in some way, bear the divine image. See *Christ the Key* (New York: Cambridge University Press, 2010), 9–17.

[27]Muray, "Human Uniqueness vs. Human Distinctiveness," 308.

CREATION AND HUMANITY IN AN EVOLUTIONARY VIEW OF THE WORLD

In recent decades, theologians have paid increasing attention to what the natural sciences in general and the theory of evolution in particular might have to say for a Christian theology of creation.[28] While every particular mechanism and detail of how evolutionary biology works as the slow process of development and differentiation remains the source of ongoing study and discovery, a scientific consensus has formed around the theory of evolution as such. To consider creation from a theological vantage point requires that we also accept as axiomatic this scientific process. In time, organisms that once shared a common source, perhaps many millions of years earlier, become so differentiated that they are no longer recognizable as belonging to the same species. This is what evolutionary biologists refer to as "speciation" and the result is an incredible diversity of creatures.[29] What we see evolve over the course of billions of years is poetically described by Darwin in the conclusion of his 1859 book *On the Origin of Species by Means of Natural Selection.* He invites us contemporaries to consider the "entangled bank" of the world, "clothed with many plants of many kinds, with birds singing on the bushes, with various insects flitting about, and with worms crawling through the damp earth, and to reflect that these elaborately constructed forms, so different from each other, and dependent on each other in so complex a manner, have all been produced by laws acting around us."[30]

One of the promises for theology we can recognize immediately in this brief summary of evolution is the recognition of a common source and an intrinsic interrelatedness shared among all creatures. Indeed, as seen in the last section of this chapter, alongside all other creatures—sentient and otherwise—found within Darwin's "entangled bank," we humans are *ha-adamah*, made "from the earth." And yet, while the seeming scientific affirmation of the second Genesis creation narrative presumed by evolution may be a comfort to many believers, a challenge concurrently arises for those committed to a strict teleological worldview.

Evolution does not account for the possibility of what is sometimes called "intelligent design."[31] This concept, proposed by those who hold a literal or fundamentalist reading of Genesis, holds that even modern theories of evolution cannot account for every detail of the complexity of species, let alone the self-appropriated superiority of humanity, which therefore illustrates the existence of "design" (as opposed to the ostensible randomness of evolutionary theory). Proponents of this view describe the current state of advance species,

---

[28]E.g., see Johnson, *Ask the Beasts*; Cynthia Crysdale and Neil Ormerod, *Creator God, Evolving World* (Minneapolis: Fortress Press, 2013); Denis Edwards, *How God Acts: Creation, Redemption, and Special Divine Action* (Minneapolis: Fortress Press, 2010); Celia Deane-Drummond, *Christ and Evolution: Wonder and Wisdom* (Minneapolis: Fortress Press, 2008); John F. Haught, *God after Darwin: A Theology of Evolution*, 2nd ed. (Boulder: Westview Press, 2008); and Jürgen Moltmann, *God in Creation: A New Theology of Creation and the Spirit of God*, trans. Margaret Kohl (Minneapolis: Fortress Press, 1993); among many others.

[29]Francisco J. Ayala notes that there are "more than two million existing species of plants and animals" that have been named and described, while there remain even more—perhaps as many as ten million—that have not yet been identified or classified (to say nothing of those species that have gone extinct). See his essay, "The Evolution of Life: An Overview," in *God and Evolution: A Reader*, ed. Mary Kathleen Cunningham (London: Routledge, 2007), 59.

[30]Charles Darwin, *On the Origin of Species by Means of Natural Selection* (New York: Bantam Books, 2008), 478.

[31]For more on "intelligent design," see Michael J. Behe, *Darwin's Black Box: The Biochemical Challenge to Evolution* (New York: The Free Press, 1996). For a strong rebuttal, see Kenneth R. Miller, "Answering the Biochemical Argument from Design," in *God and Evolution: A Reader*, 159–74.

such as *Homo sapiens*, as necessitating a supplemental actor—an *intelligent designer*—whom, in the case of many evangelical and fundamentalist Christians, is obviously the God of the Christian faith. The pseudoscientific and inadequately theological hypothesis of "intelligent design" is really an effort to rebrand creationism for those who cannot square the overwhelming scientific evidence for biological evolution—including for the human species—with faith in a providential God.

What evolution requires of Christians is to hold two seemingly contradictory or paradoxical claims in creative tension: that God is the "Creator of heaven and earth, of all things visible and invisible" and that biological evolution operates according to what we might generally describe as *chance*. Such a tensive dynamic should not be unfamiliar to Christians who profess faith in numerous seemingly paradoxical doctrines: the hypostatic union of Christ's fully human and divine natures; a God who is singular in divine being or substance yet Triune; and the reality of life after death, to name just a few examples. Still, for some self-professed Christians the simultaneity of biological evolution and God-as-Creator is too much to accept.

It may be worth a brief mention of at least one response to this supposed impasse. It is here that Elizabeth Johnson's 1996 article, "Does God Play Dice? Divine Providence and Chance," illumines at least a preliminary path beyond the perceived evolution–Creator divide.[32] Reiterating the issue at hand, Johnson summarizes, "Taken together, scientific understandings of the indeterminism of physical systems at the quantum level, the unpredictability of chaotic systems at the macro level, and the random emergence of new forms of life through the evolutionary process itself undermines the idea that there is a detailed blueprint or unfolding plan according to which the world was designed and now operates."[33] While creation does not come into existence in a singular, static manner as proposed by so-called creationists or proponents of intelligent design, it is also not entirely arbitrary or chaotic. Johnson, drawing on the insight found in centuries of scientific research, reminds us that there are such things as scientific laws. What evolutionary theory on the macro level and quantum mechanics on the micro level reveal are the dynamics or interchange between "chance and law," it is a truly "both/and" approach to reality.

Admittedly, nature is mysterious and the ultimate working of the laws of nature are never comprehensible in their entirety. Still we can say that there are some principles of reality that remain in some kind of consistency, but, as Johnson contends, "the laws of nature require the workings of chance if matter is to explore its full range of possibilities and emerge toward richness and complexity. Without chance, the potentialities of this universe would go unactualized."[34] Rather than think of dichotomous possibilities, Johnson argues that there is merit—scientific and theological—to thinking of God creating the universe precisely with the capacity for chance and possibility, an unfolding of evolution and the actualization of potential (to borrow a traditional Hellenistic formulation). In other words, what if it was not God's plan to work out each and every aspect of the universe and its activity for all time, as so many conceive divine providence to entail, but

---

[32]Elizabeth A. Johnson, "Does God Play Dice? Divine Providence and Chance," *Theological Studies* 57 (1996): 3–18. For another contemporary engagement with this tension, see Gordon D. Kaufman, *In the Beginning...Creativity* (Minneapolis: Fortress Press, 2004), in which he proposes the concept of "serendipitous creativity" as the means by which God operates vis-à-vis creation.
[33]Johnson, "Does God Play Dice?," 7.
[34]Ibid.

rather to empower creation to unfold within a contingent frame guided and enabled by the working of the Holy Spirit, as the Christian doctrine of *creatio continua* entails?[35]

Johnson affirms this creational framework and draws from Thomas Aquinas' theory of divine causality (delineated in terms of primary and secondary causality) to provide a robust theological grounding:

> As God is the primary cause of the world as a whole and in every detail, endowing all created beings with their own participation in divine being (enabling them to exist), in divine agency (empowering them to act), and in divine goodness (drawing them to their goal), so too God graciously guides the world toward its end in and through the natural workings of the processes found in creation as a whole. Immanent in these processes, divine providential purposes come to fruition by means of purposes inherent in the creatures themselves.[36]

Put simply, that the universe exists and unfolds within an evolutionary frame is precisely the way God creates and reflects the Creator's divine intention. God is truly the "Creator of Heaven and Earth," but is so on God's own terms. As Creator, God remains the primary cause of the evolving universe but, as Aquinas says, God acts through secondary causes, including the apparent randomness of evolution and the dynamic that plays out between chance and law over billions of years.

The good news of evolution here is that God is not a micromanager, despite how much some people would love God to be such according to their own image and likeness. Rather than torpedo the Creator God of Christianity, the meaning of evolution offers the promise of a more holistic understanding of the human person situated within an evolving universe, connected to all other aspects of creation and participating in an awe-inspiring history of becoming that is anything but antithetical to Christian faith. In fact, evolution is precisely the manner by which God desires to create all creatures, including us human beings.

CONCLUSION

In the opening chapter of his encyclical letter *Laudato Sí*, Pope Francis suggests that one of the primary reasons we face such ecological crises in our day is that "we have forgotten that we ourselves are dust of the earth (cf. Gn 2:7); our very bodies are made up of her elements, we breathe her air and we receive life and refreshment from her waters."[37] With the promulgation of this widely anticipated text, Francis drew attention to the intersection of theological reflection on creation and theological anthropology in his call for the development of an "integral ecology." This chapter introduced three key themes in the theological area of creation that helps lay the foundation for such an integral ecological approach to theological reflection on the human person. The at times

---

[35]For more on the doctrine of *creatio continua*, see Arthur Peacocke, "Biological Evolution—A Positive Theological Appraisal," in *God and Evolution: A Reader*, ed. Mary Kathleen Cunningham (London: Routledge, 2007), 251–72; Herbert McCabe, *God, Christ, and Us*, ed. Brian Davies (New York: Continuum, 2003); and John C. Polkinghorne, "*Creatio Continua* and Divine Action," *Science and Christian Belief* 7 (1995): 101–8; among others.

[36]Johnson, "Does God Play Dice?," 13–14.

[37]Pope Francis, *Laudato Sí*, On Care for Our Common Home (Vatican City: Libreria Editrice Vaticana, 2015), no. 2.

contentious doctrine of *creatio ex nihilo* presents underappreciated implications for our understanding of human creatureliness and interrelationship within the broader community of creation. The renewed approaches to and interpretations of the book of Genesis—and scripture more broadly—offer new insight into the Christian understanding of creation and humanity's place within it, while also challenging longstanding presuppositions about the potential meaning of the doctrine of *imago Dei*. And the theory of evolution, alongside other discoveries from the natural and social sciences, offers theologians new opportunities for considering the place of humanity within the community of creation. Whereas creation has long been treated as a subfield within theological anthropology, these three foci explored in this chapter suggest instead that theological anthropology cannot begin without first starting with creation.

SUGGESTED FURTHER READING

Edwards, Denis, *Christian Understandings of Creation: The Historical Trajectory* (Minneapolis: Fortress Press, 2017).

Horan, Daniel P., *All God's Creatures: A Theology of Creation* (Lanham: Lexington Books/ Fortress Academic, 2018).

Johnson, Elizabeth A., *Ask the Beasts: Darwin and the God of Love* (New York: Bloomsbury, 2014).

Middleton, J. Richard, *The Liberating Image: The* Imago Dei *in Genesis 1* (Grand Rapids, MI: Brazos Press, 2005).

Tanner, Kathryn, *God and Creation in Christian Theology* (Minneapolis: Fortress Press, 2005).

CHAPTER FIVE

Created for God and for Each Other: Our *Imago Dei*

MICHELLE A. GONZALEZ

The creation of humanity in the image of God is one of the most captivating, vague and significant theological concepts found within Christian thought. Located in the first chapter of the book of Genesis, Christians draw from this notion that opens the Hebrew Scriptures in profound and varied manners throughout the history of Christianity. The *imago Dei* reveals aspects of the nature of humanity; however, for Christians, it also simultaneously reveals something about the nature of God. The two creation stories found in Genesis 1–3 are fundamental sources for uncovering human nature and also God's nature. Intimately linked to the manner in which we express our creation in the divine image is our notion of the divine. In other words, *imago Dei* theological anthropology has strong implications for our concept of God, Jesus Christ, and the Trinity. The way we envision our God as Creator, Savior and Trinity deeply impacts how we understand ourselves as human beings. The two feed off of each other, especially in the context of the *imago Dei*. Creation in the image of God has also served as the foundation for anthropological exceptionalism within the Christian tradition, too often manipulated to highlight humanity as distinctive from, rather than interconnected with, God's broader creation.

CREATED

The creation story found in chapter 1 of the book of Genesis offers a theological interpretation of the nature of God's creation that is distinctive from the second creation account found in Genesis 2–3. The very notion of creation by God implies order, structure and purpose. Creation was not an accident, and the account describes a movement from chaos to order. Multiple times in Genesis God proclaims that creation is good. There is an order to creation. Different living creatures and the natural world are created on different days. Humanity is the only group within creation that is given the designation "in the image of God." In Genesis 1 God creates in six days. The seventh day is labeled as holy, the Sabbath, making a clear distinction between everyday life and sacred or holy time.

The foundation of the Christian understanding of humanity's relationship with God and Jesus' universal salvation is found in the doctrine of creation, the Christian teachings that focus on the creation of this universe by God as based in the Genesis accounts in the Hebrew Scriptures. The two Genesis creation stories have captured religious and popular imagination for centuries. Whether it is in the writings of the earliest Christian thinkers, contemporary debates on gender roles or popular images of Adam and Eve, perhaps no other section of the Hebrew Scriptures and Christian Bible has provoked as much creativity and debate as the first three chapters of Genesis.

Creation in the image of God implies that we human beings have a supernatural orientation toward the sacred and that all of humanity shares in this common human nature. We are created to be with God. This is our destiny as human beings and until we accept this we will be unsatisfied. In twentieth-century Roman Catholic theology this was described by Karl Rahner as the "supernatural existential," the human orientation to God's intended transformation through grace. As Rahner scholar William Dych describes it,

> If God created human beings in the first place so that there would be creatures with whom God could share his own divine life in knowledge and love, that is, if God created human beings precisely for the life of grace, then the offer and the possibility of grace is given with human nature itself as this nature has been historically constituted. Creation is intrinsically ordered to the supernatural life of grace as its deepest dynamism and final goal. The offer of this grace, then, is an existential, an intrinsic component of human existence and part of the very definition of the human in its historical existence.[1]

Implied in this concept is that at the core of human nature lies the ability for self-transcendence. We are created to be in relationship with the sacred.

GENDER

Genesis 1 emphasizes the idea of a purposeful and ordered cosmos created by God from chaos. As God creates the many elements of this universe and the days go by, the narrative culminates with the creation of humanity and the pivotal line in the story found in verse 27: "So God created humankind in his image, in the image of God he created them; male and female he created them." This statement has been a central point of contention and a foundation for Christian understandings of men and women for centuries. The notion that humanity is created in the image of God, distinguishing us from the rest of creation, and the exact meaning of that image, continues to mystify and challenge the religious imagination of Christians. Contrary to the spirit of the passage, male Christian authors have argued for centuries that creation in the image of God as male and female does not necessarily lead to an egalitarian relationship between men and women. Women are seen as possessing the image deficiently, for example, or only in relationship with men. Interpretations such as these have falsely denied the full image of God in women, equated her with the body and elevated man as the ultimate representation of rationality and spirituality, the expression of the image in its fullness.

Genesis 1:27 is central not only for Christian understandings of the human but also for feminist claims regarding an egalitarian anthropology. Because of her association with the body, woman is often interpreted within the Christian tradition as reflecting the image of God in a flawed or lesser manner. These false interpretations of the text discredit the significance of the Incarnation, of God taking human flesh in Jesus of Nazareth. The body

---

[1]William V. Dych, SJ, *Karl Rahner* (Collegeville, MN: Liturgical Press, 1992), 36.

is too often interpreted as that which impedes us from true union with God or reaching our full potentiality as faithful Christians. This is ironic, for Christians often use the Incarnation to legitimize humanity's privileged relationship with God above the rest of creation. After their creation humans receive dominion over the earth. In the end, like the rest of creation, God claims that this creation is good.

The patristic era is one in which reflection on the divine image flourished; and writings on the *imago Dei* were extensive in this time period. For many of the church fathers, the notion of the *imago Dei* was intimately linked to their understanding of the soul and spirituality. The image was most fully realized in the act of contemplation of God. The human being does not truly realize him or herself unless he or she goes beyond their selves and returns to the Being in whose image they are created. This is the most profound sense of the patristic theology of the *imago*.[2] The church fathers contend that the *imago Dei* is a dimension of our soul and mind. For the majority of these thinkers the body does not reflect the image, and thus, for woman, it comes to be a factor that hinders the image's expression.

OUR ALIENATION

While the textual location of the *imago Dei* account of creation is found within chapter 1 of the book of Genesis, later Christian interpretations of the image of God rely heavily on Genesis 2–3. Genesis 2–3 tells us the story of Adam and Eve, their betrayal of God and consequent expulsion from paradise. A pressing concern for theological anthropology is the relationship between humanity as described in the opening chapters of Genesis (which falls from God's original creation, and consequently becomes deficient) and the new creation that Christians claim is found in Christ. The classic formulation of this new creation is found in Paul's letter to the Galatians when he writes, "There is no longer Jew or Greek, there is no longer slave or free, there is no longer male and female; for all of you are one in Jesus Christ" (Gal. 3:28). How one constructs the relationship between the old and the new remains a central question for theological anthropology, one that has plagued Christians since New Testament times.

> If the emphasis is placed on the contrast between the new humanity in Christ and the old, it becomes easy to wonder whether the differences of (for example) gender and race that are overcome in Christ are part of God's good creation or signs of some defect in the created order. On the other hand, if abiding significance of these differences is affirmed, then it might seem to follow that social practices designed to reinforce them should be preserved.[3]

The creation story found in chapters 2 and 3 of Genesis offers a radically different account of humanity and the cosmos' creation. Unlike the earlier narrative, where humanity appears on the sixth day, this account places humanity at the front and center of creation. The human being is formed from the dust in the ground, is placed in the Garden of Eden to care for it and warned against eating from the tree of knowledge of good and evil. God

---

[2]P. Th. Camelot, OP, " La Théologie de L'Image de Dieu," *Revue des Sciences Philosophiques et Théologiques* 40 (1956): 471.

[3]M. Shawn Copeland, Dwight N. Hopkins, Charles T. Mathewes, Joy Ann McDougall, Ian A. McFarland and Michele Saracino, "Human Being," in *Constructive Theology: A Contemporary Approach to Classical Themes*, ed. Serene Jones and Paul Lakeland (Minneapolis, MN: Fortress Press, 2005), 84.

determines that the human being needs companionship, so God puts the human to sleep, removes a rib and from that rib creates another human being, Thus, male and female are created. With the opening of chapter 3 a new actor enters the narrative, the serpent. The serpent convinces the woman to sample from the tree of knowledge, and she in turn gives some to her partner. God enters the Garden, finds the two hiding and realizes what they have done. As a result of their actions, God banishes them from the Garden and the nature of their relationship is forever transformed, with woman destined to be subordinate to man. Due to their transgression the egalitarian relationship between man and woman is destroyed, and the man becomes the master of the woman. The Fall results in the end of the intended model of companionship and instead leads to dominion. This was not the intended order of creation. This is a consequence of their actions. Thus, the domination of women was not how God intended the relationship between the sexes to be. In addition, this second creation story presents a God that is unforgiving and swift to punish. God does not give them a second chance.

The account of humanity's fall from grace will become the foundation for the Christian teaching on original sin. The doctrine of original sin is central to Christian beliefs. Original sin is the basis of the belief and need for Jesus Christ's redemptive works. Jesus takes away our original sin. As highlighted by Paul in Rom. 5:10, "We were reconciled to God through the death of his Son." Christian teachings on original sin explain the origin of evil and the need for salvation. It also explains the need for the church as mediator of Christ's healing. At the core of the teaching is the question, "Why do we alienate ourselves from God?" Because of our first parents, Adam and Eve, and their sin and disobedience, we are all born in a state of sin. It is as if their sin is passed on to us in our DNA.

Because of Adam and Eve's sin of disobedience we are all born defective in a sinful state. This is an important point. If Christians are going to claim that Jesus came to save all humans, all of us need to be saved from something. We all have a shared defect that needs to be redeemed. The correction of that flawed state is through Jesus' salvation achieved on the cross. The state in which we are born is not how God intended us to be. Adam and Eve prior to their sin is how God created us. However, due to their disobedience we are all in a fallen state. In 1 Cor. 15:45-49 Paul writes,

> Thus it is written, "The first man, Adam, became a living being"; the last Adam became a life-giving spirit. But it is not the spiritual that is first, but the physical, and then the spiritual. The first man was from the earth, a man of dust; the second man is from heaven. As was the man of dust, so are those who are of the dust; and as is the man of heaven, so are those who are of heaven. Just as we have borne the image of the man of dust, we will also bear the image of the man of heaven.

Without the salvific work of Jesus we continue to resemble the flawed earthly Adam. This is why Jesus is referred to as the New Adam, or heavenly man, whose obedience corrects the disobedience of the Garden of Eden. One day we will bear that heavenly image instead of being in the image of the earthly human.

ORIGINAL SIN

While the doctrine of original sin developed gradually, the fourth-century church father Augustine of Hippo is considered its classical author. Prior to Augustine there was no consensus or comprehensive approach to original sin. Augustine does not resolve the question of Adam being created as wholly oriented toward God and the source of his sin that led to fallen humanity—in other words, why Adam sinned. Sin damages the image of God within us, and only grace can heal us. Wickedness is why we sin (a result of Adam's sin); it is the result of a change in human nature. Christians believe that Adam and Eve's sin was transferred biologically via procreation. The human was created in a state of original blessedness—where humans did not have the ability to sin. Augustine never gives us "the why" of humanity's first sin. For many Christians humanity's sin is pride, our desire to be like God. We are now disordered in a state of concupiscence (disordered desire). This disorder is what remains after baptism; it inclines us toward sin. We are now predisposed to sin, though the image of God within us is not destroyed. Grace (God's freely given love), for Christians, heals human nature and we are redeemed through participation in the church and consequently participation in God. Grace redirects our will toward God. Jesus' crucifixion and resurrection become the fundamental moment within Christian salvation history and our redemption from original sin.

Christianity teaches that humans were created in an original state of blessedness. However, due to our free will human beings are all now fallen. We are in a disordered state of misdirected desire where we try to find satisfaction in all of the wrong things instead of our true path in God. This disorder is what remains within humanity after baptism, leaving humans with the inclination toward sinfulness. We are now predisposed to sin. Though the image of God within us is not destroyed it is clouded. The only way that we can be redeemed is through God's grace. Jesus' dying on the cross was the ultimate sacrifice on our behalf and is rooted in the sacrificial system of ancient Judaism. The Jewish sacrifice in the temple is the basis for the Christian belief in Jesus as sacrifice, Jesus is "Offered once to bear the sins of many" (Heb. 9:26). Some Christians interpret this sacrifice as an atonement. Since Adam insulted God, this sin requires repayment. Jesus, as human and divine, could repay the enormous debt to God. The Incarnation of Jesus is repayment for our original sin. These understandings of Jesus as atoning for humanity, as a sacrifice for humanity and as the final offering in the face of our sinfulness, in addition to the heavy reliance on the book of Genesis, demonstrate the ways in which ancient Judaism truly shaped how Christians understood not only human nature but also how they came to understand God's salvific work within the context of the Trinity.

DIFFERENCE

A fundamental dimension of theological anthropology is "difference." The category of difference refers to not only the differences and diversity that exist between different human groups but also the difference that challenges constructions of pure identity. Difference refers to the manner in which we are different from each other and the manner in which our identity challenges the often-rigid categories in which we place human beings. We are not only different from others, we also embody difference within the complexity of our identity. Too often discussions of our identity are dominated by binary categories: black/white, male/female, rich/poor. Similarly, our identity is often reduced to one component of who we are, for example, race or gender, denying the fullness of our identity.

In her book, *Being about Borders: A Christian Anthropology of Difference*, Michele Saracino highlights the significance of difference for contemporary theological anthropologies in our globalized world. She warns us of the dangers of erasing borders through globalization, for in that process the complexity of human difference is wiped out. We must overcome the notion that difference somehow undermines unity. This is of special concern for Christians, she emphasizes, for Jesus' ministry was always at the border. Fundamental to Saracino's text is the notion that we must honor the hybridity of who we are. She highlights that the border marks our encounter with difference.

A theological anthropology that takes the encounter with difference seriously must acknowledge the affective dimension of humanity. An affective understanding of theological anthropology does not allow emotion to be subordinate to reason. Just because today we are encountering difference at exponential rates does not mean that individuals are not having negative reactions to it. Too often, we celebrate out newly interconnected and globalized world without recognizing the complexity and sometimes negativity associated with this interconnectedness. As Saracino points out, "The conflation of globalization with openness to others obscures the practical reality of living with those who are different in the midst of hybrid experience."[4] Christians are called to acknowledge the interconnectedness of human life and our feelings toward it. We must avoid a sense of narcissism in these encounters, a false notion of the superiority of one group over other. Likewise, we must be aware of the politics of identity and power that are at play in these encounters.

However, difference cannot just be reduced to "embodied" difference. It also refers to the differences we have between us as human beings beyond embodied identity, such as political and intellectual diversity. We are living in a political climate of name-calling and division and in world that is increasingly incapable of speaking across differences and reduces entire peoples as "other," based on one aspect of their beliefs, ideologies and identities. We must move beyond these superficial polarizations of difference and find ways to communicate with and through and not just in spite of difference. Difference is at the core of how God created humanity.

DYNAMIC ANTHROPOLOGY

Difference also highlights the distinctiveness between Creator and creature. The twentieth-century Roman Catholic theologian Hans Urs von Balthasar emphasized this in his theological method, where he constantly reminded us of the inadequacy of human words and concepts to express the sacred. The analogy of being plays a key role in both von Balthasar's anthropology and theological method. The analogy of being affirms that we can make true references to God, however analogous they may be; as God's creation the universe must be somehow connected to God, but as creation it cannot be identical with God. While von Balthasar maintains the analogy of being, he emphasizes the greater dissimilarity between Creator and creature. Much of von Balthasar's work in this area is influenced by two figures: theologians Erich Przywara and Karl Barth. From Przywara, von Balthasar learned to emphasize this greater dissimilarity. Crucial for Przywara, as highlighted by Edward Oakes, is his understanding of "analogy": "What analogy really means is that the self-manifestation of God in his creation is never an exhaustive one: although there is some similarity between the world and God, in this very

---

[4]Michele Saracino, *Being about Borders: A Christian Anthropology of Difference* (Collegeville, MN: Liturgical Press, 2011), 14.

likeness there is even greater dissimilarity."[5] The analogy is "dynamic" and arises out of the act of faith.

Both Barth and von Balthasar have a Christocentric theology that emphasizes the objective content of theology as revelation. Barth does not speak of an analogy of being but instead of faith: because God created us and has established our relationship there is analogy, not because of shared being. In other words, only through belief in God's saving message do we achieve a relationship with God. For Barth, analogy is grounded in Christology exclusively. Balthasar, one the other hand, wants to speak of a distance between Creator and creature that allows us to grow in grace. "Balthasar believed that the *analogia fidei* which he also accepted, based on revelation, did not exclude but involved an *analogia entis*."[6] Instead of collapsing Creator and creature, as Oakes notes, "analogy of being is meant to put into conceptual terms the distance that inheres in the relationship between God and creature."[7] Balthasar wants to maintain the drama of Creator and creature in history. Through a dynamic analogy of being that grows in faith, this dramatic encounter can grow and flourish. The image of God within us is not stagnant. It is dynamic and alive. Our growth in the image of God is part of our self-discovery of who we are as created by God. This leads to a dramatic anthropology where the human is in a process of becoming. We are always moving toward God.

The border is also the marker of our experience of the sacred, where the line between natural and supernatural converge. Through the incarnation of Jesus as the Christ those lines are erased. An awareness of hybridity does not have to always provoke a negative response and in fact can promote empathy. This hybridity of difference is fundamental to the Christian understanding of the incarnation. The incarnation reminds us of the porous nature of the border between the sacred and the profane. Jesus himself was a hybrid: man, Jew, friend, son; his hybridity is theological in its salvific import to all. Jesus is, after all, on the border of God and humanity. This awareness of difference and hybridity as constituting our humanity also opens the door to the complexity and diversity of Christian faith life. Flesh and the body matter. The created world is a reflection of God's glory, and one must celebrate it while not being overly consumed by the material and the physical.

SUFFERING AND THE BODY

Throughout the centuries speculation on the nature of our humanity has often ignored concrete, lived human life. As noted by Michelle Voss Roberts, "A view of the human person that centers upon and privileges a single power, the mind, has impoverished Christian theological anthropology."[8] Decontextualized and abstract reflections on the nature of all humanity have dominated theological anthropologies of the past. In addition, as Voss Roberts argues, if one superior faculty is attributed to the image of God, a hierarchical structure of humanity is created based on who possesses this attribute

---

[5]Edward T. Oakes, *Pattern of Redemption: The Theology of Hans Urs von Balthasar* (New York: Continuum, 1997), 34–5.

[6]John Thompson, "Barth and Balthasar: An Ecumenical Dialogue," in *The Beauty of Christ: An Introduction to the Theology of Hans Urs von Balthasar*, ed. Bede McGregor, OP and Thomas Norris (Edinburgh: T & T Clark, 1994), 177.

[7]Oakes, *Pattern of Redemption*, 68.

[8]Michelle Voss Roberts, *Body Parts: A Theological Anthropology* (Minneapolis, MN: Fortress Press, 2017), vxii.

more than others. More and more today we find critical, constructive theological voices that explore the nature of humanity in all its concrete messiness. The human as abstract essence is slowly unraveling. Instead, everyday lived religion becomes the starting point of contemporary theological anthropologies. Classic theological anthropologies have often emphasized our spiritual relationship with the divine and downplayed its implications for our concrete existence. Otherwise put, "The main focus of theological anthropology has tended to be the supernatural orientation of humankind as beings created (in the words of Gen. 1:27) 'in the image of God' (*imago Dei*). As a result of this focus, the other, more material side of existence has been overshadowed, even obscured."[9] Theological anthropology must remain firmly grounded in the contemporary situation and not fall into abstract speculation that ignores the very materiality of human life.

What does the body mean for being human? After all, suffering bodies reveal the suffering that is at the heart of Christianity. In her most recent theological anthropology, black Catholic theologian M. Shawn Copeland outlines five convictions that ground her anthropology: (1) an understanding of the body as mediator of divine revelation; (2) the significance of the body for shaping human existence as relational and social; (3) an emphasis on the creativity of the Triune God as revealed through differences in identity; (4) an embodied understanding of solidarity; and (5) the role of the Eucharist in ordering and transforming bodies. Thus, she writes provocatively, "The body provokes theology."[10]

Basing her anthropological reflections on suffering black women's bodies, Copeland argues, "No Christian teaching has been more desecrated by slavery than the doctrine of the human person or theological anthropology."[11] Copeland's starting point of black women's bodies not only reminds us of the suffering these women endured but also that no theological reflection on the body can begin in abstraction. Hers is a Eucharistic meditation on the body, for both the Eucharist and racism imply bodies. The Eucharist embodies Jesus' sacrificial gift of his life in order to bring his Father's mercy and love. Eucharistic solidarity is a countersign to violence toward bodies; we are Jesus' body, and this calls for an embodied praxis of discipleship. Jesus' suffering body also reminds us of the crucified peoples who have suffered throughout history and who do not suffer alone.

An emphasis on suffering as central to a contemporary theological anthropology is found in the constructive work of Latino theologian Roberto S. Goizueta. With his haunting description of the Good Friday reenactment at San Fernando Cathedral in San Antonio, Texas, Goizueta enters into the popular rituals surrounding one of the most powerful images in Latino/a religiosity, the Crucified Jesus. The Jesus of Good Friday is a central Christological symbol within Latino/a theology. This stems from a theological worldview that strongly emphasizes Jesus' humble origins, his prophetic message and his active presence in the present-day lives of Christians, in particular his solidarity with the oppressed and marginalized. This strong emphasis on Jesus' suffering and passion distinguishes Latino/as from other Catholic ethnic groups in the United States. As noted by Goizueta, the theological significance of this distinctive Latino/a understanding of Jesus is the subject of Latino/a Christologies. Goizueta holds that the foundation of the Crucified Christ of Latino/a popular Catholicism is found in a relational anthropology

---

[9]Copeland et al., "Human Being," 79.

[10]M. Shawn Copeland, *Enfleshing Freedom: Body, Race, and Being* (Minneapolis, MN: Fortress Press, 2009), 7.

[11]Ibid., 67.

that sees the human, and consequently Jesus, as essentially social in nature. The image of the *Via Crucis* is exemplary on this point.

At the foundation of Goizueta's communal anthropology is an understanding of the human as relational. We are intrinsically relational and our relationships are constitutive of who we are. Relationships come prior to the individual. This is affirmed by the Genesis 2–3 creation story that shows us that humanity needs companionship. These relationships include our ancestors and the institutions that are a part of, or perpetuate, our identity; language also highlights the communal nature of human being. Goizueta contrasts this relational understanding of the human to modern liberal anthropologies, where the individual comes before the community. Community is also often placed in opposition to institutions, and instead of a constitutive idea of community, there is a "sentimental" one. This modern liberal anthropology leads to a dichotomy between the particular and the universal, with an option for the individual.

In the anthropology of Latino/a popular Catholicism, Goizueta argues, community is seen as preexistent and constitutive. Evoking the image of the *Via Crucis* in Good Friday processions, Goizueta notes that "it is in our common accompaniment of Jesus on the cross that *he* constitutes *us* as individuals and a community."[12] Popular devotion to Mary is yet another example of this communal, relational anthropology. Mary is also defined by her relationships; she too accompanies and is accompanied. Relationship, however, is not some stagnant essence of the human, but is instead dynamic. Human relationality is found in our actively engaging each other, in our interactions with other human beings. The dynamic character of relationship brings forth the interactive and interdependent nature of humanity.

This relational community is not only characteristic of interhuman communities, it also marks humanity's relationship with the divine. For Goizueta, worship expresses this concretely. The human person is not solely constituted by human relationships; one's relationship with the divine as giver of life is foundational. As Goizueta emphasizes, our relationship with the God who gives us life—and I would add, the God in whose image we are created—is the foundation of all our other relationships. Using Latino/a fiestas as an entry point, Goizueta puts forth a theological anthropology that "understands the human person as *constituted* by relationships, not only relationship to the human community which precedes and forms the person, but especially by relationship to the primordial, triune Community whose love *is* life."[13] The caricature of the modern autonomous self is shattered when the giftedness of life is revealed. Similarly, the isolated individual is unmasked to reveal the relational human community. This relationality is one that is characterized by hybridity and mixture.

CONCLUSION

Whether it is more abstract formulations of human nature or concrete on-the-ground reflections, theologians throughout the centuries have interpreted and reinterpreted the nature of our humanity and God's nature in light of the image of God. For Christians the

---

[12]Roberto S. Goizueta, *Caminemos con Jesús: A Hispanic/Latino Theology of Accompaniment* (Maryknoll, NY: Orbis Books, 1995), 68.

[13]Roberto S. Goizueta, "Fiesta: Life in the Subjunctive," in *From the Heart of Our People: Latino/a Explorations in Catholic Systematic Theology*, ed. Orlando O. Espin and Miguel H. Diaz (Maryknoll, NY: Orbis Books, 1999), 96.

image of God reveals who we were, who we are and what we will become through the life of faith. Christians often vacillate between this notion that we are like God, yet at the same time fragile, broken and mortal. Christian understandings of the image of God have been manipulated to uplift and marginalize particular groups at different moments in human history. The notion of creation in the image of God is highly abstract; however, theological reflections on that image must always be grounded in concrete everyday lives with an awareness of how power, prejudice and privilege can distort what Christians claim is one of God's greatest blessings upon humanity.

SUGGESTED FURTHER READING

Copeland, M. Shawn, *Enfleshing Freedom: Body, Race, and Being* (Minneapolis, MN: Fortress Press, 2009).

Jonas, Beth Felker (ed.), *The Image of God in an Image Driven Age: Explorations in Theological Anthropology* (Downers Grove, IL: Intervarsity Press, 2016).

Saracino, Michelle, *Christian Anthropology: An Introduction to the Human Person* (Mahwah, NY: Paulist Press, 2015).

Voss Roberts, Michelle, *Body Parts: A Theological Anthropology* (Minneapolis, MN: Fortress Press, 2017).

CHAPTER SIX

The Relational Turn in Theological Anthropology

ROSEMARY P. CARBINE

Theological anthropology consists of religious understandings of the human person that emerge from a religious tradition's claims about the divine, cosmology, soteriology, eschatology and so on. Within Christian theological anthropology, human beings express and embody "the dynamic unfolding of created spirit in the struggle to exercise freedom in history and society."[1] In that dynamic, we are fundamentally relational, not ruggedly individualist, self-asserting, self-aggrandizing, self-made or self-sufficient beings. Rather, we are (1) divinely created in and for relationship with God, ourselves, others and the Earth, even unto the cosmos; (2) broken and damaged in those relationships by original sin; (3) actively and perpetually distorting and de-creating those relationships through structural and personal sin; (4) continually healed in those relationships through the divine gift of grace as self-love, love of others and love of God; (5) creatively, cooperatively and constantly living into reclaimed and reconciled relationships through grace-filled and empowered personal, liturgical, social and political praxis; and (6) ultimately open to and reaching for the full potential and flourishing of those relationships, of being and becoming human together, in a perennially not-yet realized eschatological future.[2]

What feminist theological anthropologies contribute to a relational anthropology is a critically reappropriated and reconstructed understanding of relationality itself, beyond what Elisabeth Schüssler Fiorenza calls kyriarchal paradigms of personhood, explained further below, which negatively portray and essentialize our differences and assimilate us to dominant-subordinate relational norms of human identity.[3] These negative relations such as racism, hetero/sexism, poverty, neo/colonialism, militarism and imperialism, and

---

[1] M. Shawn Copeland, *Enfleshing Freedom: Body, Race, and Being* (Minneapolis, MN: Fortress Press, 2008), 8; see also 24, 46–50.

[2] Both Mary Catherine Hilkert and Peter Phan offer a future-oriented view of our full humanity, an identity project which we undertake in the present and most fully realize in an eschatological future horizon that always lies ahead of us, both historically and spiritually. Hilkert, "Cry Beloved Image: Rethinking the Image of God," and Phan, " 'Woman and the Last Things: A Feminist Eschatology," in *In the Embrace of God: Feminist Approaches to Theological Anthropology*, ed. Ann O'Hara Graff (Maryknoll, NY: Orbis Books, 1995).

[3] Ada María Isasi-Díaz, *Mujerista Theology: A Theology for the Twenty-First Century* (Maryknoll, NY: Orbis Books, 1996), 79–81. Michelle Gonzalez treats egalitarianism, relationship and community, the body and the *imago Dei* as four different themes in feminist theological anthropology, whereas this essay views these themes through the lens of relationality. Gonzalez, *Created in God's Image: An Introduction to Feminist Theological Anthropology* (Maryknoll, NY: Orbis Books, 2007), 109.

globalization are usually couched in an allegedly divinely created or intended hierarchical order as well as founded on dualistic anthropologies that dignify the ideal image of God in some and degrade or outright deny it in *others* (e.g., white vs. nonwhite, men vs. women, straight vs. LGBTQIA+, privileged vs. poor, colonizer vs. colonized, developed vs. under/maldeveloped, Global North vs. Global South). These ideological interpretations of Genesis 1–3 create polar opposite and agonistic ways of being human in in the world; they place and reposition us in abusive, exploitative, dehumanizing relationships, whether personal, social, sexual, economic, political or geographic. However, relationality need not signify division, domination, degradation or dehumanization. As explored and expressed in different women's liberation theologies, relationality offers opportunities for egalitarian connections and inclusive solidarity. These theologies take women's experiences in very different social locations as their starting points for theological reflection on being human. Nonetheless, the feminist, womanist, Latina/*mujerista* and Asian American feminist theologies examined in this essay reflect on God, creation in the image of God and living into that divine image in Christ in order to present a shared understanding of the human person that is grounded in embodied and future-oriented relations of equality, mutuality and solidarity.

FEMINIST THEOLOGICAL ANTHROPOLOGIES: INTERRELATIONALITY

"In the Beginning was the Word, and the Word was consciousness—understanding that women can and should be whole human beings ...—is, was, and always will be the soul of feminism."[4] Feminist consciousness emerges in community and lays the foundation for justice-based activism because it sheds light on how religious and social institutions, norms and practices shape our very selves and society, whether in oppressive or transformative ways. Reflecting on our inherently interrelated experiences with one another (for good or ill) within religious and sociopolitical structures holds revolutionary potential for becoming whole human beings, personally and collectively. Conscientization, the raising of one's own and others' awareness about how oppression and justice operate at micro-individual and macro-structural levels, helps forge new relationships for full human flourishing and for broader global and eco-justice to arise.

Feminism has undergone at least three waves in the United States: the first was associated with suffragist movements of the late nineteenth to the early twentieth centuries for women's equal political participation; the second emerged during Civil Rights and anti-war movements of the mid-to-late twentieth century and focused on women's educational, economic, and racial equality; and the third involved global women's liberation movements from the late twentieth century onward and emphasized differences among global women's experiences of oppression, as well as fostered transnational solidarity in women's struggles for empowerment. Each of these waves has critically extended and broadened the scope of human relationality beyond sex/gender.

This movement is concerned not simply with the social, political, and economic equality of women with men but with a fundamental re-imagination of the whole of humanity in relation to the whole of reality, including non-human creation. In other

---

[4]Jennifer Baumgardner and Amy Richards, *Manifesta: Young Women, Feminism, and the Future* (New York: Farrar, Straus and Giroux, 2010), 11.

words the feminist consciousness has gradually deepened, the feminist agenda has widened, from a concern to right a particular structural wrong, namely, the exclusion of women from the voting booth, to a demand for full participation of women in society and culture, to an ideal of re-creating humanity itself according to patterns of eco-justice, that is, of right relations at every level and in relation to all of reality.[5]

Global feminism resists essentializing or reducing women's experience to any one factor and thus challenges any unifying story about being human. Instead global feminism holds that different women's experiences in different historical, social and cultural contexts require different women's movements—as well as theologies and theories—which increasingly feature the multiplicative effects of gender, race, class, sexuality, ability, nationality and religion on women's struggles for justice in a kyriarchal world characterized not by a sex/gender system but by power relations. The term "kyriarchy" better captures how men and women are relatively advantaged and marginated in different social locations through the interlocking, mutually reinforcing relations of gender, race, class, culture, religion, sexual identity and other marks of identity. It also illustrates how such relations construct and justify some men's and women's privileged status over most men's and women's marginal and disempowered status.[6] Global feminism thus undercuts any totalizing definition or praxis of feminism, since women identify and pursue struggles against oppression and for justice and liberation in different social locations (and even within the same shared social location) differently.[7]

Feminist consciousness in religion can be described as ambivalence, as the ability, or better agility, to live simultaneously inside and outside religious traditions and to cultivate the virtues of critical vigilance and ongoing openness to new insights and possibilities about them. Religions both subordinate and liberate women; thus, feminist theologians both belong to and are alienated from their religious traditions as they engage in the "triple task" of "critical distance from one's community, conservation of its deepest insights, and innovation."[8] Within Christianity, feminist theological anthropology can be considered critical and constructive reflection about the impact of lived experiences on interpreting Christian scripture and tradition, beliefs and practices regarding the meaning of being human. Feminist theologians have examined central Christian texts, doctrines and symbols, and practices in order to interpret how they shape and mold our worldviews and our self-understandings as persons. Feminist approaches utilize "imaginative lenses" and "performative directives," creating an ethical framework within which to understand and act in the world. Feminist theologians point out that religious

---

[5]Sandra M. Schneiders, *With Oil in Their Lamps: Faith, Feminism, and the Future* (New York: Paulist Press, 2000), 8.

[6]Elisabeth Schüssler Fiorenza, *But She Said: Feminist Practices of Biblical Interpretation* (Boston: Beacon Press, 1992).

[7]However, the UN Women's campaign called Planet 50-50 by 2030: Step It Up for Gender Equality still, at least statistically speaking, analyzes global women's realities from a gender egalitarian rather than multifaceted justice perspective. Its infographic attends to women's unequal access to politics, fair wages, senior management, media coverage (of "gender (in)equality issues") and education as well as women's disproportionate labor and vulnerability to violence and war. See UN Women, "Gender Equality: Where Are We Today?," September 2020. Available online: http://www.unwomen.org/en/digital-library/multimedia/2015/9/infographic-gender-equality-where-are-we-today (accessed September 12, 2020).

[8]Mary Farrell Bednarowski, *The Religious Imagination of American Women* (Bloomington: Indiana University Press, 1999), 17–20, quote at 20.

traditions exert a "person-shaping" power that seeks to reimagine an alternative future personal identity and collective social order.[9]

In keeping with the third wave, global feminist perspective, feminist theology is now pluralized into various feminist theologies. For example, the US context has produced white feminist theologies, African American womanist theologies, Latina/*mujerista* theologies, Asian American feminist theologies and so on. Yet, these theologies often share the triple task or method mentioned previously: (1) to take women's experiences of struggle and hope as the starting point for critical reflection on religious and social norms and structures that legitimate and justify kyriarchy; (2) to recover possible liberative resources from scripture, tradition, history and practices; and (3) to construct alternative theological and ethical worldviews and praxis that support full human flourishing in just and solidarity-based relationships.[10] Feminist theologians are particularly attuned to Christian symbols for God and their implications for theological anthropology. Godtalk shapes and influences other Christian claims about the world and the understanding and action of humanity in it. Moreover, human beings are regarded as created in the image and likeness of God (Gen. 1:26-27), and Godtalk can often be channeled literally and prescriptively, rather than metaphorically or figuratively, to sacralize and reinforce unjust religious and kyriarchal power relations, such as hetero/sexism, racism, poverty, colonialism/imperialism or globalization.[11]

White feminist theologians wrestle with exclusively enshrined monarchical, masculinized and racialized scriptural and theological language and images for God (as father, king, lord and Trinitarian names of Father, Son and Spirit reinforced by Jesus the Christ as the incarnate often whitewashed male image of God). This kind of Godtalk limits the Christian imagination of God's incomprehensible mystery by forging an allegedly divinely ordained and thus naturalized connection between these titles and images for God and Godself, which dehumanizes nondominant, nonwhite women and men by marginalizing them from embodying the image of God and of God in Christ. Instead, to denounce the kyriarchal effective histories of this Godtalk, to affirm the full humanity of all women and men formed in the image of God and transformed into the image of Christ (Gal. 3:27-28; 2 Cor. 3:18), and to promote right relations along gender, racial and ecological lines, Elizabeth Johnson recovers the female personification of God as Wisdom from biblical texts and traditions because it highlights images of God and of Christ that convey God's empowering and vivifying activities of creation, liberation, and sustainability. Appearing in Proverbs 1–9 as well as in the books of Sirach and the Wisdom of Solomon, the prophetic street preacher Wisdom has divine status or origin (Prov. 1:20-33, 8:22-26), serves as a cocreator with God (Prov. 3:18-19, 4:13; 8:27-30), and continues to delight in and sustain daily life (Prov. 8:31).[12] Likewise, Jesus the Christ proclaimed by early Christian communities as incarnate Wisdom, Sophia, has less to do with the metaphysical makeup of Jesus' human and divine natures codified in the Christological councils and more to do with his deeds, his performative praxis of empowering right relations.[13] Expressing

---

[9]Serene Jones, *Feminist Theory and Christian Theology: Cartographies of Grace* (Minneapolis, MN: Fortress Press, 2000), 16–17.

[10]Rosemary Radford Ruether, *Sexism and God-Talk: Toward a Feminist Theology* (Boston: Beacon Press, 1993).

[11]Hilkert, "Cry Beloved Image."

[12]Elizabeth A. Johnson, *She Who Is: The Mystery of God in Feminist Theological Discourse* (New York: Crossroad, 1992).

[13]Elizabeth A. Johnson, "The Maleness of Christ," in *The Power of Naming: A Concilium Reader in Feminist Liberation Theology*, ed. Elisabeth Schüssler Fiorenza (Maryknoll, NY: Orbis Books, 1996), 311–13, and, "Redeeming the Name of Christ: Christology," in *Freeing Theology: The Essentials of Theology in Feminist*

the *imago Dei* and *Christi* then involves creatively and cooperatively participating in, or re-citing not necessarily replicating or imitating, this ministry to build just and life-giving, transforming and sustaining community—solidarity—with others, including the Earth.[14]

To further show how Christian Godtalk opposes kyriarchal power relations and bolsters the subjectivity of persons-in-relation and in-community, the late Catherine LaCugna reclaimed the equal, mutual and inextricably intertwined love relations of the triune God, highlighted by the early Eastern Christian notion of *perichoresis* or mutual indwelling of the three persons in the one divine substance. From a perichoretic perspective, the Trinity symbolizes an ongoing communion of coequal persons in mutual love relations within God that overflows in creative, salvific and sustaining acts between God and the world. These perichoretic relations carry religio-political implications for non-kyriarchal relations in personal and social life. The intrinsic dynamic relations of three persons co-constitute the one God, and the relational equality and solidarity within God and between God and the world patterns albeit indirectly and imperfectly our personal, social, religious and political arrangements in God's image.[15] Since relationality characterizes God's nature, relationality or self-in-relation typifies being human in the image of a Trinitarian God. All persons, all life, is thus made for egalitarian, mutual, interpersonal relationships of solidarity, through which we continually create ourselves and our world.[16] Humanity reflects the *imago Dei* as *imago Trinitatis* or *imago Christi* an icon of the Trinity or Christ through sociopolitical praxis that enlivens and empowers all life in inclusive and just (i.e., right) relationships.

WOMANIST THEOLOGIES: INTERSECTIONALITY

Unlike feminist theologies, womanist theological anthropology does not start with critical reflection on doctrines of God, creation in the image of God, or conformity to the divine image in the Trinity, or in Christ. Rather, womanist theology offers theological reflection on being human, on subjectification, based on the lived experiences of Black women within the Black community, which in US society is affected by the interconnected objectifying realities of racism, hetero/sexism and poverty.[17] Womanist theological reflection on being human also highlights encounters with God in narrative, in witness found in Christian scriptures and in the resources of African American cultures, such as slave narratives,

---

Perspective, ed. Catherine Mowry LaCugna (San Francisco: HarperSanFrancisco, 1993), 120–7. Womanist theologies, discussed later in this essay, complexify this singular focus on Jesus' emancipatory ministry to entail a ministry of mutual accompaniment and struggle with suffering peoples. See Jacquelyn Grant, " 'Come to My Help, Lord, For I'm In Trouble': Womanist Jesus as the Mutual Struggle for Liberation," in *Reconstructing the Christ Symbol: Essays in Feminist Christology*, ed. Maryanne Stevens (New York: Paulist Press, 1993), 66–9, and Kelly Brown Douglas, *The Black Christ* (Maryknoll, NY: Orbis, 1994), 108–10.

[14]Johnson, "Redeeming the Name of Christ," 128–9, 132–4, Laura Taylor, "Redeeming Christ: Imitation or (Re)citation?," in *Frontiers in Catholic Feminist Theology: Shoulder to Shoulder*, ed. Susan Abraham and Elena Procario-Foley (Minneapolis, MN: Fortress Press, 2009), 131–6, and Douglas, *The Black Christ*, 113.

[15]Catherine Mowry LaCugna, "God in Communion with Us: The Trinity," in *Freeing Theology*, ed. Catherine Mowry LaCugna (San Francisco: HarperSanFrancisco, 1993); also Kathryn Tanner, *Jesus, Humanity, and the Trinity: A Brief Systematic Theology* (Minneapolis, MN: Fortress Press, 2001).

[16]Hilkert, "Cry Beloved Image," and also Ann O'Hara Graff, 'Struggle to Name Women's Experience', in *In the Embrace of God: Feminist Approaches to Theological Anthropology*, ed. Ann O'Hara Graff (Maryknoll, NY: Orbis Books, 1995).

[17]Jacquelyn Grant, "Subjectification as a Requirement for Christological Construction," in *Lift Every Voice: Constructing Christian Theologies From the Underside*, ed. Susan Brooks Thistlethwaite and Mary Potter Engel (Maryknoll, NY: Orbis Books, 1998), and Copeland, *Enfleshing Freedom*, 15–22.

autobiographies, novels, music, poetry and plays. In this way, womanist theology draws its self-understanding from historical, political, literary and religious sources.[18] Womanism emerged in response to the white racism of first- and second-wave US feminist movements and the lack of a multidimensional analysis of oppression in the US Civil Rights movement as well as in early Black liberation theologies (which coincided with second wave feminist movements). This marginalization rendered invisible Black women's concerns regarding the intersectionality[19] of religion with race, gender, sexuality and class. Rather than a solely reactionary theology to racism, hetero/sexism and poverty, Black women stake out their own critical contextual and constructive theological standpoint to advocate for the full humanity of Black women and the Black community, confronted by the disenfranchising and dehumanizing legacies of slavery, Jim Crow segregation, the new Jim Crow of hyper-racialized incarceration, police brutality and the recent rise of white nationalist populist movements in the era of US President Donald Trump that foment and legitimate all kinds of xenophobia. Indeed, the contemporary Black Lives Matter movement galvanizes and mobilizes prophetic witness to and struggle for the full humanity of the Black community, "to prove our humanity over and over again to a legal and administrative system that doesn't believe it."[20] US society operates with and reifies kyriarchal norms and definitions of being human, for example, white, Western, middle class and aged, heterosexual, able-bodied men, which alienates the Black community and in particular Black women. Kelly Brown Douglas also draws key principles from Alice Walker's innovative definition of the term: a Black feminist of color whose strong self-love and love of the community, regardless, prompts audacious, courageous, Spirit-inspired struggle for the agency, survival, and wholeness of an entire people.

> A social-political analysis of wholeness will confront, racism, sexism, classism, and heterosexism not only as they impinge upon the Black community, but also as they are nurtured within that community. ... A social-political analysis of wholeness urges womanist scholars to remain in solidarity with their oppressed sisters around the world. It seeks a world where all women, indeed all humanity, live together in relationships of mutuality. ... Finally, and perhaps most fundamentally, a social-political analysis of wholeness recognizes the importance of wholeness for the individual as well as the community. This analysis urges Black people, but especially Black women, to confront the ways in which societal oppression has left them less than whole beings – spiritually, emotionally, psychologically, and so forth.[21]

Finally, Delores Williams's trailblazing work in womanist Godtalk firmly founded womanist theology on Black women's intertwined experiences of race, gender, sexuality and class and on Black's women's experiences of "struggle for survival and for the development of a positive, productive quality of life" en route to liberation, a liberation

---

[18]Stephanie Y. Mitchem, *Introducing Womanist Theology* (Maryknoll, NY: Orbis Books, 2002), 55–64, 87–91.
[19]Although womanist theologians employed this analysis for some time, the term "intersectionality" was coined by legal scholar Kimberlé Crenshaw, "Demarginalizing the Intersection of Race and Sex: A Black Feminist Critique of Antidiscrimination Doctrine, Feminist Theory and Antiracist Politics," *University of Chicago Legal Forum* (1989): 139–67.
[20]Kashana Cauley, "rica Garner and How America Destroys Black Families," *New York Times*, January 2, 2018. Available online: https://www.nytimes.com/2018/01/02/opinion/erica-garner-black-families.html (accessed May 10, 2020).
[21]Douglas, *The Black Christ*, 98–9, 102, 104.

that involves divine accompaniment and divinely empowered human actions for well-being and freedom.[22]

Womanist theologies "as an opportunity to state the meanings of God in the real time of Black women's lives"[23] impact theological anthropology. In alignment with the triple task of feminist theologies, womanist theology prioritizes Black women's lived realities of the troubling intersections of race, gender, class and sexuality within the Black community and within Christian-supported racist and elitist ideologies of white supremacy and privilege. Womanist theologians then critically recover and reconstruct Christian scripture, tradition, beliefs and practices to support the full humanity of all persons in relation, in community. [24] M. Shawn Copeland employs this trifold method to explore the postmodern theological turn to the subject—to the marginalized subject, not the Enlightenment's nationally, culturally and racially privileged subject of individuality, autonomy and rationality[25]—with implications for a social Trinitarian theology and ethics rooted in Christology. Copeland's womanist theological anthropology prioritizes the embodied subjectivity of poor women of color to challenge how "we have all betrayed the very meaning of humanity—our own, the humanity of exploited, despised women of color, and the humanity of our God."[26] Exemplified by the subjugated body of Jesus under Roman imperial rule and colonial culture, all our bodies are regulated, negatively marked and thereby fragmented from ourselves, one another and the Earth, and ultimately from God by contemporary forms of imperialism, such as racism, hetero/sexism, xenophobic backlash against immigrants and refugees, war, poverty and so on.[27] Situating subjectivity in an incarnational frame of the inclusive solidaristic ministry of Jesus in relation to God and others in the quest for God's reign of love and justice,[28] being human for Copeland can oppose such de-creation and instead can interpret body marks positively. A theological anthropology is needed in which "we all may recognize, love, and realize our bodyselves as Jesus' own flesh, as the body of Christ."[29]

> These bodily marks ground intelligence, discovery, beauty, and joy; enable apprehension and response to sensible experiences; and shape culture, society, and religion. ... The body's marks complexify through creolization, *mestizaje*, and hybridity; just as often, these marks render self-disclosure confusing and frustrating, invigorating and alchemizing.[30]

---

[22]Delores S. Williams, *Sisters in the Wilderness: The Challenge of Womanist God-talk* (Maryknoll, NY: Orbis Books, 1993), xii, 6–7, 33.

[23]Mitchem, *Introducing Womanist Theology*, 60.

[24]Grant, "'Come to My Help, Lord, For I'm In Trouble'," 54–66. Kelly Brown Douglas expanded beyond a womanist race, gender, class analysis of Black women's troubles and advocated for a sexual analysis of heterosexism and homophobia in the Black community. She articulated a sexual discourse of resistance as a survival strategy amid the dehumanization of LGBTQIA+ Blacks. She developed this discourse in anthropological terms about all of our equally good and embodied creation in the image of a loving God whose image is exemplified in the incarnate love of God in Jesus' "liberating, healing, empowering, and life-sustaining ministry" and whose image we reflect in all kinds of loving relationships, whether physical, social or political. See Douglas, *Sexuality and the Black Church: A Womanist Perspective* (Maryknoll, NY: Orbis, 1999), 87–108, 112–19.

[25]Copeland, *Enfleshing Freedom*, 9–12.

[26]Ibid., 88, 90.

[27]Ibid., 55–61, 65–78.

[28]Ibid., 61–5, 80–1.

[29]Ibid., 78.

[30]Ibid., 56.

Consequently, for Copeland, being human in the *imago Christi* consists of being

(1) a creature made by God; (2) person-in-community, living in flexible, resilient, just relationships with others; (3) an incarnate spirit; (4) capable of working out essential freedom through personal responsibility in time and space; (5) a social being; (6) unafraid of difference and interdependence; and (7) willing daily to struggle against 'bad faith' and *ressentiment* for the survival, creation, and future of all life.[31]

Recovering the incarnation helps reconstruct theological anthropology beyond kyriarchal power relations toward solidarity: "If personhood is now understood to flow from formative living in community, rather individualism, from the embrace of difference and interdependence rather than their exclusion, then we can realize our personhood only in solidarity with the exploited, despised, poor 'other'."[32] Copeland states that participating in and realizing the body of Christ through solidarity introduces us to and foreshadows our participation in the Trinitarian relations. Similar to feminist theologies, solidarity in light of Trinitarian theology stresses the full realization of personhood through the present communal praxis of social justice-oriented relations as an eschatological foretaste of our already but not yet fully realized future participation in Trinitarian relations. As Copeland shows, perichoretic mutual love relations of the divine persons within God and between God and humanity in the body of Christ "reminds us of our inalienable relation to one another in God, and steadies our efforts on that absolute future that only God can give."[33] Realizing more just communal relations, albeit partially and imperfectly, is the goal of feminist and womanist theologies focused on a theologically grounded and socio-politically-oriented praxis of solidarity.

LATINA AND *MUJERISTA* THEOLOGIES: INTERCULTURALITY

Latina and *mujerista* theological anthropologies prioritize primarily but not exclusively grassroots Latinas' social location of living at the borders of and/or between different worlds, of living in intercultural communities—characterized by racial, cultural, and sociohistorical mingling and integration—as a result of conquest, colonialism and immigration (*mestizaje/mulatez*) as well globalization. Similar to womanist theologies, Latina and *mujerista* theologies also emphasize women's praxis in daily life (*lo cotidiano*) and in social movements for personal and communal liberation—for "justice, equality, human rights, true democracy and greater equality of life for all,"[34] rather than doctrines, in order to elaborate an understanding of being human. Latina feminist theology itself enables and enacts a new theological anthropology. As María Pilar Aquino argues,

Latina feminist theology as reflective religious language, as conceptual elaboration, as cognitive space, as intellective process, as critical reflection on our faith experiences, and as systematic articulation of our socioreligious practices seeking justice, becomes

---

[31]Ibid., 92.

[32]Ibid., 89; see also 92–5, 99–101.

[33]Ibid., 102–3, quote at 103; see also 104.

[34]María Pilar Aquino, "Latina Feminist Theology: Central Features," in *A Reader in Latina Feminist Theology: Religion and Justice*, ed. María Pilar Aquino, Daisy L. Machado, Jeanette Rodríguez (Austin: University of Texas Press, 2002), 134.

for us a key language with which we say who we are and how we seek to affect the present and future direction of society, culture, academy, and the churches.[35]

Women's rightful claim to be subjects, to "the search for one's own identity" as sociopolitical actors in struggles and movements for religious and social change and transformation, signifies a subjectivity that Aquino articulates as: egalitarian based on equal creation in the image of God; centered on the multidimensionality of human existence (including the body and sexuality[36]), social and communal relations, and destiny within history; and, historically realist but yet freely, creatively, sacramentally and hope-fully oriented toward concrete praxis, movements and struggles for resistance, solidarity and justice that reveal both God and a new alternative more just world.[37]

As the late Ada Maria Isasi-Díaz explains, *mujerista* theological method aligns with the triple task of feminist theological method, broadly understood. It criticizes racism, ethnic prejudice, sexism and poverty in Latinas' personal and communal lives; recovers religious sources from Christian scripture and tradition as those sources are tapped and emerge from the lived religious experiences of God in the daily life of the community, especially its popular religious traditions and practices; and creates a new religious understanding of humanity and of the future through interconnected personal and communal well-being, which Isasi-Díaz theologically depicts as "bring[ing] to birth new women and new men" in the kin-dom of God.[38] Isasi-Díaz further clarifies this future humanity and just world in her theological anthropology.

For Isasi-Díaz, struggle (*la lucha*), voice (*permitanme hablar*) and community (*la comunidad*) act as the starting points for a Latina/*mujerista* theological anthropology,[39] through which Christian doctrines may be critically recovered and reconstructed for liberation, particularly Christology and creation. *La lucha* refers to the "daily ordinary struggle ... to survive and to live fully," to claim moral, religious and sociohistorical and political agency through active resistance to daily oppressive realities and through celebrations of everyday joys in the midst of those realities. Rather than a Christology of "idealized suffering" that women are called to imitate in order to realize full humanity, struggle places the suffering both of Jesus and of women in a larger sociopolitical context, without totally determining their humanity.[40] *Permitanme hablar* illustrates the importance of speaking for Latinas' historical subjectivity and agency, for claiming public voice and making history, rather than enduring marginalization from established dominant sociopolitical histories of nations, social movements, religions and so on.[41]

---

[35]Ibid., 148.

[36]Teresa Delgado investigates how Latino/a religio-cultural norms and practices both perpetuate and counteract the exploitation or the giving up of women's bodies to meet the needs—familial, economic or sexual—of others. Identifying women with self-gift and self-sacrifice, whether culturally or Christologically, jeopardizes women's sexual subjectivity. By contrast, reconstructing the *imago Dei* through Trinitarian (rather than spousal) relations restores women's sexual subjectivity because all humans enjoy freedom in mutual co-equal relations with others. See "This is My Body...Given for You: Theological Anthropology *Latina/mente*," in *Frontiers in Catholic Feminist Theology: Shoulder to Shoulder*, ed. Susan Abraham and Elena Procario-Foley (Minneapolis, MN: Fortress Press, 2009), 25–47.

[37]María Pilar Aquino, *Our Cry for Life: Feminist Theology from Latin America* (Maryknoll, NY: Orbis Books, 1993), 18–25, 81–108; quote at 92; Aquino elaborates on some of these same characteristics of being human in "Latina Feminist Theology: Central Features," 149–50.

[38]Isasi-Díaz, *Mujerista Theology*, 64–74, quote at 62.

[39]Ibid., 128, 144–5.

[40]Ibid., 129–32.

[41]Ibid., 132–4.

Rather than seek religious or political authority to legitimate their voices and histories, "speak[ing] our own word," states Isasi-Díaz, is closely linked with Latinas' personal affirmation and recognition of human dignity, of ethical and political subjectivity, of participation in cocreating their own lives and the larger society.[42] Politically, this phrase facilitates reclaiming Latino/a history and the roles of Latinas in constructing that history. Theologically, this phrase also involves sharing individual and communal narratives of resistance to suffering and of prophetic hope in justice—a social, political and religiously rooted praxis that is concretely connected with public theology, with the role of religion in enhancing the public good.[43] *La comunidad* underscores Latinas' participation in struggles as social, historical and political actors in relation to various communities and vast network of relationships that condition and co-constitute us. We belong to and become fully human through belonging to this community of relations, of origin, affinity and solidarity. Although related to *la familia, la comunidad* is not construed as the kyriarchal family but more broadly understood as far-reaching networks of kin and community relationships, of "we others," that expands well beyond the nuclear and extended family into the *familia de Dios*. It also emphasizes Latinas' praxis of mediating a Christologically inspired vision of an anti-imperial, this-worldly just society, namely the kin-dom of God.[44]

> Each of us also mediates the kingdom of God in an essential way and in a way that would not happen without us. This is so because each and every one of us is an image of God, an *imago Dei*: each and every one of us carries seeds of divinity that make who we are capable of being and what we are capable of doing essential to the unfolding of the kingdom of God. This is precisely one of the key reasons why we can rescue the kingdom from the other world and incarnate it once again in our midst. This is one of the most important reasons why we see our struggles in this world as part of the overall work of God's creation. It continues in us and with us.[45]

The praxis of the kin-dom's relations flows from a renewed and reconstructed sense of humanity's creation in the *imago Dei* and thus theologically shapes, forms and characterizes the meaning of human being in *mujerista* theology.

ASIAN AMERICAN FEMINIST THEOLOGIES: INTERSTITIALITY

Akin to *mujerista* theology's emphasis on *mestizaje/multaez*, Asian American feminist theologies, or theologies articulated by Pacific, Asian, North American Asian Women in Theology and Ministry (PANAAWTM), reflect on human being and God in light of Asian women's experiences of colonialism, imperialism and globalization, illustrated by the term "Asian" itself. "Asian" often refers to an imaginary, static and geographical or continental concept for the academic purpose of regional or area studies. Likewise, "Asian" recalls a binary dualist, or better Orientalist, stereotype of either underdeveloped

[42]Ibid., 135–7.
[43]Rosemary P. Carbine, "Turning to Narrative: Toward a Feminist Theological Understanding of Political Participation and Personhood," *Journal of the American Academy of Religion* 78, no. 2 (June 2010): 375–412.
[44]Isasi-Díaz, *Mujerista Theology*, 137–41, 143–4; Isasi-Díaz, *La Lucha Continues: Mujerista Theology* (Maryknoll, NY: Orbis Books, 2004), 243–51.
[45]Isasi-Díaz, *La Lucha Continues: Mujerista Theology*, 247.

poorer nations or of exceptional nations as economic influencers and rising superpowers (e.g., India, China), portrayed in contrast with but to the benefit of Euro-American ideals and interests. It thus signifies US colonialist, nationalist and economic constructions of Asians in racist ways as either perpetual foreigners or model minorities.[46] Although there is no one singular or unitary way of being Asian or being an Asian woman due to diverse cultures, languages, religions and so on, PANAAWTM theologies use the term "Asian" strategically as an identity political concept that evokes a common history of oppression and joint coalitional struggles for justice, both in Asia and in the United States.[47]

In keeping with a critical transnational rather than regional analysis, Kwok Pui-lan observes that Asian and Asian American women's experiences are intersected by race, labor, state and gender in our current globalized economy that controls and benefits from women's unsafe and underpaid labor. This multidimensionality of being human—based on race, ethnicity, culture, religion, gender, class, state and other identity markers—requires a process of becoming human at these intersections, at these in-between spaces at the borders of and even within social locations.[48] Rita Nakashima Brock describes interstitial integrity as the ongoing improvisational performance of self-identity and knowledge at the negative and positive intersections of diverse social and communal ingredients found within us and impinging on us. Interstitiality challenges the binary or polarity of dual nature anthropologies that feed into racism, sexism and ethnic/cultural prejudices, including American myths of elect/chosen people versus conquered/colonized people that then map onto political anthropologies, such as citizen versus slave, patriot versus terrorist.[49] Moreover, interstitiality fosters recognizing and residing at the nexus of multiple worlds connected to the histories of racism, sexism, colonialism and imperialism that simultaneously inhabit us (as "layers" or "others who live in us" engaged in fluid "constant conversation" among different social locations, cultures, histories, religions, etc.) and which we partly but never totally inhabit but nevertheless reshape.[50] For Brock, interstitiality resonates with being an incarnated spirit, "refusing to split ourselves" and struggling to bring together multiple layered worlds both in one person and into a new more just world.[51] Being human, thus, means being intersected by our personal and social identity markers in a web of kyriarchal power, reintegrating at times deeply dissonant relations within our self-identities and likewise becoming interconnected through personal and by implication transnational solidarity in shared struggles for justice.

Kwok's transnational analysis of Asian and Asian American's women's experience and of being and becoming human entails the critique, recovery and reconstruction of Christian Godtalk, especially divine power. She challenges "from above" images of God as father, warrior and king, which enshrine monarchical power and reinforce Orientalist as well as global consumer cultures. Rather than feminist and womanist turns to Trinitarian theologies of equal, mutual, solidaristic relations that she considers "too utopian" and "hard to put into practice,"[52] she innovates instead "from below" images of God as a

---

[46]Gale A. Yee, "'She Stood in Tears amid the Alien Corn': Ruth, the Perpetual Foreigner and Model Minority," in *Off the Menu: Asian and Asian North American Women's Religion and Theology*, ed. Rita Nakashima Brock et al. (Louisville, KY: Westminster John Knox Press, 2007), 45–52.
[47]"Introduction," *Off the Menu,*, xiv–xix; in that same volume, see also Kwok Pui-lan, "Fishing the Asia Pacific: Transnationalism and Feminist Theology," 4–5, and Nami Kim, "The 'Indigestible' Asian," 23–6, 34–9.
[48]Kwok, 'Fishing the Asia Pacific', 5–7, 16–17.
[49]Rita Nakashima Brock, "Cooking without Recipes: Interstitial Integrity," in *Off the Menu*, 126–8, 132–3.
[50]Ibid., 133–7.
[51]Ibid., 139–40.
[52]Kwok, "Fishing the Asia Pacific," 13–14.

"God of the interstices," of the in-between spaces and social locations where different peoples, cultures and ideas converge and compete in order to rethink kyriarchal norms of race, gender, culture and citizenship. Similar to feminist and womanist Trinitarian theologies, God is envisioned here not as a hierarchical power but as a matrix of power:

> If we imagine divine power not as hierarchical, unilateral, and unidirectional but rather in the form of a matrix, then the interstices are the nodal power connections where something clever and creative can occur ... divine interstitial power ... is energizing and enabling, because it rejoices in creating "synergistic relations", readjusts and shifts to find new strength, and discovers hope in the densely woven web of life that sustains us all.[53]

Human beings embody the image of a God of the intersections by embracing interstitiality, by collaborating in networks, in relations of transnational solidarity that enable creative ways of seeking women's empowerment and liberation.

TOWARD SOLIDARITY IN DIFFERENCE: INTERRELIGIOSITY

Different models or typologies of being human are engaged by and emerge from women's engagements with a variety of Christian theological anthropologies: dual, single, justice or transformation and multipolar.[54] The feminist, womanist, Latina/*mujerista* and Asian American feminist theologies of human nature described above tend to oppose a dualistic anthropology, in which idealized human beings (families, communities and even nations) versus others are structured and stratified as polar opposites and possess complementary forms, different degrees or defective or deficient forms of humanity. Dual anthropologies emphasize polarity, while single anthropologies stress similarity; however, these can be reductionistic, thereby neglecting the concrete complexity and multidimensionality of humanity. Women's ways of doing theological anthropology do not restrict being human to any one single factor, such as sex/gender duality or difference; thereby, they resist an intransigent heteronormativity in Christian theologies. Instead, they suggest an anthropology that repositions sex/gender among a wide variety of other characteristics that co-constitute what it means to be human, creating a praxis of sociopolitical participation, transformation and justice. Elizabeth Johnson, for example, describes a multipolar anthropology that offers a kaleidoscopic, multifaceted view of human identity that illuminates insights from the feminist, womanist, Latina/*mujerista* and Asian American feminist theologies of being human explored above. Johnson reworks single nature anthropology from within a multipolar approach: her single nature anthropology embraces and integrates multiple features that coincide and consequently shape both the similarity and the diversity of what it means to be human.

> A way beyond the impasse is emerging beyond those options: one human nature celebrated in an interdependence of multiple differences. Not a binary view of two male and female natures, predetermined forever, nor abbreviation to a single ideal, but a diversity of ways of being human: a multi–polar set of combinations of essential human elements, of which sexuality is but one. ... The goal is to reorder the two–term

---

[53]Ibid., 19.
[54]Gonzalez, *Created in God's Image*, 109–12.

and one–term systems into a multiple–term schema, one which allows connection in difference rather than constantly guaranteeing identity through opposition or uniformity. ... Difference itself ... can function as a creative community-shaping force.[55]

In a multipolar anthropology, "essential human elements" or "anthropological constants" form the common matrix of human identity that is then conditioned and expressed in diverse ways. As Johnson explains, these constants include relationship to our bodies, to sexuality, to other persons, to the Earth, to the sociohistorical, economic and political structures of our environment, to the process of culture-making and to the future. These constants avoid any essentialist ideal of humanity and instead emphasize the concrete materiality of relationships in which human identity is conditioned and construed in different social locations.[56]

The feminist, womanist, Latina and *mujerista*, and Asian American feminist theologies discussed above offer innovative approaches to being human-in-relation, with respect to key themes such as interrelationality, intersectionality, interculturality and interstitiality. Being human—or becoming human, eschatologically speaking—entails being embedded in multiple dynamic relationships that influence us via the social and religious norms of sex/gender, race, class, embodiment, sexuality and nationality. Nonetheless, we must critically and creatively negotiate and occasionally integrate these different relationships in shaping a more just sense of self and world. Women's liberation theologies continue to creatively chart new directions in relationality by considering interreligious differences, along with their political implications.

Feminist theologian Michele Saracino combines theology, ethics and psychology to attend to the cognitive, affective and corporeal dimensions of being human-in-relation. Her concept of "being about borders" captures an empathetic engagement across differences. Saracino blends postcolonial theories of hybridity, the plural stories that configure our personal identities, with postmodern ethical and feminist theories of "coming undone," the ability of another to uncreate and redefine us. In doing so, she highlights the range of negative emotional responses—fear, entitlement and numbness—that shape the inescapably "enmeshed nature of human existence."[57] For Saracino, creation and Christology, along with women's experiences, catalyze our hybridity. Reinterpreting the Genesis creation stories shows that human beings are inherently hybrid, carrying both the divine and other humans within their very nature. Reinterpreting gospel literature underscores the many-storied identity of Jesus, illustrated by the hypostatic union of divine and human natures in his person, by his navigation of multiple social identities and by his other-oriented and bodily based healing ministry.[58] Maternity or bearing another's story affords a non-idealized and highly contextualized metaphor from women's experience for incarnating hybridity in our contemporary pluralistic and globalized society.[59]

By attending to creation, Christology and women's experience, Saracino presents three features of an affective anthropology rooted in relational difference: (1) alterity, exemplified by constructive conflict modeled in Jesus' encounter with the Syro-Phoenician woman in Mark; (2) emotional exposure based on the entire kenotic life, ministry and

---

[55]Johnson, "The Maleness of Christ," 309, 310–11.
[56]Ibid., 310.
[57]Michele Saracino, *Being about Borders: A Christian Anthropology of Difference* (Collegeville, MN: Liturgical Press, 2011), 15.
[58]Ibid., 29–34, 49–51.
[59]Ibid., 53–7.

death of Jesus in which "asymmetrical relationships of dependence are rendered positive, sacramental, and salvific"; and (3) mourning the loss of "a privileged and singular sense of self, story, or place in relation to another."[60] Saracino concludes this anthropology of borders with "rules of engagement" denuded of militarist meanings and instead derived from a hybridized Christology that yield practical implications for negotiating interreligious and international encounters. Her five rules of engagement include attending to affect and to the sin of blindness to others' needs, feelings and stories in our daily life; utilizing storytelling as a praxis of mourning; accepting vulnerability as living in and into the *imago Dei*; and balancing self-care and care for others.[61] These rules both emerge from and are applied to creative case studies of Jewish-Catholic relations, Israeli-Palestinian relations and post-9/11 US international relations. "Being about borders" thus involves "creating safe spaces for encounter to unfold, becoming adept at naming [our] emotions and those of others, becoming more aware of the role that body language plays in border encounters, and actively working toward building intimacy, Christians can begin to live out an anthropology of difference."[62]

Feminist comparative theologian Jeannine Hill Fletcher also explores historical and contemporary case studies of women's lived religious experiences from interfaith social locations as a starting point for fresh insights into interreligious dialogue and theological anthropology. Hill Fletcher engages each case to examine new insights into a relational theological anthropology: "relationality precedes the individual, constraint challenges our freedom, and interreligious knowing is recognized as a new form of sacred knowledge."[63] For example, the Maryknoll Missionary Sisters in early-twentieth-century China may have established friendships with Chinese women as a mission tactic. Yet, such friendships contested and changed the Sisters' traditional notions of catechesis and divine presence. From a feminist theological perspective, Hill Fletcher emphasizes the Sisters' emerging understandings of God as an infinite horizon of love enabling multiple types of human love and of Christ's life and ministry as "embedded in relationships, called in care for the least, shaped across the divides of difference, and fulfilling a vision of human being and becoming together."[64] Second, she examines leading lights in various waves of feminist movements who pursued interreligious encounters and forged alliances across such differences in order to support women's resistance and well-being. Christian, Jewish, Muslim, Hindu, Buddhist, Native American and many other women created "interreligious solidarity in the secular movement of women's rights," which in turn "transform[ed] their religious traditions."[65] By analyzing religion as both oppressive and liberating, these interreligious alliances in women's movements highlight "constraint as constitutive of our human existence [in which] we find courage to employ our human creativity."[66] Third, and finally, Hill Fletcher's ethnographic studies of the Philadelphia Area Women's Interfaith Group showcase women's practices of interfaith dialogue for peace through their spiritual autobiographies. Practices of personal storytelling underscore alternative ways and sites for encountering the sacred. These dialogical practices do not

---

[60]Ibid., 36, 39, 44–6, 66–7.
[61]Ibid., 137–41.
[62]Ibid., 137; see also 126 and 128.
[63]Jeannine Hill Fletcher, *Motherhood as Metaphor: Engendering Interreligious Dialogue* (New York: Fordham University Press, 2013), 6; see also 196–7.
[64]Ibid., 65.
[65]Ibid., 96.
[66]Ibid., 109.

feature religious officials or academic experts discussing doctrines and texts; rather, they forefront lived religion within women's everyday lives and events.[67] Hill Fletcher situates these insights within her main argument for motherhood as a lens through which to view "many, diverse, intersecting, conflicting, and complicated relationships that characterize the experience of being human," relationships that are conditioned and problematized by inequality relative to race, gender, class, sexuality, religion, culture, nationality and so on, but through which we nonetheless sustain the search for solidarity. [68]

SUGGESTED FURTHER READING

Gandolfo, Elizabeth O'Donnell, *The Power and Vulnerability of Love: A Theological Anthropology* (Minneapolis, MN: Fortress Press, 2015).

Hill Fletcher, Jeannine, *Motherhood as Metaphor: Engendering Interreligious Dialogue* (New York: Fordham University Press, 2013).

Ross, Susan A., *Anthropology: Seeking Light and Beauty*, Exploring Theology: Catholic Perspectives (Collegeville, MN: Liturgical Press, 2012).

Saracino, Michele, *Being about Borders: A Christian Anthropology of Difference* (Collegeville, MN: Liturgical Press, 2011).

Teel, Karen, *Racism and the Image of God* (New York: Palgrave Macmillan, 2010).

---

[67]Ibid., 148–9, 160–2, 181–3.
[68]Ibid., 47, 49–58.

CHAPTER SEVEN

Finitude

LINN MARIE TONSTAD

There are at least two questions to address when taking up the subject of finitude for theological anthropology: one, what work finitude as a theme does—what does it illuminate, make apparent, draw attention to, stipulate or the like? And two, why does finitude as such become a theme for theological anthropology, and indeed for theology in general? The first question is arguably descriptive or programmatic, while the second draws attention to the larger contexts within which a particular theme becomes prominent in a scholarly or cultural discussion at a given time. Finitude, as a description of the (de)limitation characteristic of created existence, is shorthand for "all that exists is limited and particular, and not self-standing." As a theme, it becomes prominent as well as problematized in the period that represents itself to itself as modernity: the possible incompatibility of finitude as lived and experienced with classical Christian understandings of God's presence to and activity in the world becomes a pressing concern for many.

Discussions of finitude thus serve multiple functions in theological discourse: they may illuminate the condition of being created by an infinite God, or they might equally well challenge certain conceptions of infinity on grounds of the nature of the reality finitude discloses. Exploring *how* an infinite God enters into engagement with the finite might equally serve as a defense of the idea *that* an infinite God so does. But finitude also becomes a theme in relation to the cultural and economic developments that threaten the current state of the whole Earth, including the existence of humanity and its companion species. Here, finitude typically emerges as a lens focusing attention on the brokenness of human existence. While Augustine might read the openness and indeterminacy of human desire as a reflection of its ultimate orientation toward God, that openness and indeterminacy—especially as reflected and intensified by money's fungibility—can also take shape as greediness and futility. Incapable of adapting our wants to our needs (to the limited extent that such a distinction makes sense), some of us want and take far more than our fair share of finite resources. Desire's restlessness and discontent renders its satisfaction impossible, for desire moves beyond any particular object or state, driving human beings onward toward no particular goal. The very condition of finitude is such that it is a state of futility and self-contradiction, or so many have argued.[1] Finitude (not always under that moniker) also emerges as an important theme within theological and theoretical developments that center the differences among people and that seek to

---

[1] These diagnoses are typical among theologians hoping to offer theological responses to global capitalism. See, e.g., Daniel Bell, *Liberation Theology after the End of History: The Refusal to Cease Suffering* (New York: Routledge, 2001); and William T. Cavanaugh, *Being Consumed: Economics and Christian Desire* (Grand Rapids: Eerdmans, 2008).

decenter the human (especially in its autonomous and self-determining form), such as feminists, critical race theorists, and queer theorists.

How, then, should finitude be approached within theological anthropology? There is a risk that any theme that spans so wide an array of meanings and contexts rather elides than illuminates anything of particular importance. A reference to finitude can sometimes presume more meaning and specificity than the term really has, becoming an associative or performative way to signal certain attachments and concerns without specifying them in any great detail. At the same time, the concept of finitude, if it means anything at all, is such that it cannot and should not be rendered schematic. That to which finitude refers, the condition of existence as a limited, contingent and dependent being, is just so a realm of existents, not species, of particulars, not universals, of events, not substances.

Because that is so—and that is both a constative and contestable statement—there are three themes that theological anthropology might find particularly helpful in approaching and illuminating finitude: dependence, death and desire (though I will raise questions about the role desire plays).

DEPENDENCE

Dependence allows us to approach finitude from two directions at once: describing both the relation finite existence is taken to have to God and the condition of finite existence itself, its "inward" or actual state. These two aspects are perhaps most effectively brought together in the thinking of Friedrich Schleiermacher, who distinguishes between the absolute dependence of all of creation on God and the relative dependence exhibited within the world-system. In conversation with Schleiermacher, it becomes apparent why it might be worth distinguishing those two meanings of dependence.

For Schleiermacher, absolute dependence describes the relation that creation is.[2] To be created is to be absolutely dependent, to exist because of something that lies outside existence in its ordinary meanings. Theologians have long wrestled with the difficulty of describing what creation means, since all terms for creation derive from within creation but refer to some "thing" (not a thing[3]) beyond or outside it. As a concept, creation implies a "before" and an "after," but of course before and after, time and causality are all concepts that arise within and with creation; to speak of a "before" creation is already to speak improperly. In popular discourse, creation is often taken to mean that "once upon a time God created," but time, scientifically as well as theologically, is an aspect of material existence; creation does not take place *in* time. So creation is not something that happened once and was subsequently followed by other happenings. Creation describes or encompasses the idea that the world-system, the cosmos, all that exists—the universe and other universes—is dependent on a God who cannot be identified with anything within the world, neither with an all-powerful Father ruling in the sky nor with the cause of the Big Bang (which is causeless, in a certain sense, for a similar reason as is creation).

Put differently, to be finite is to be dependent on the infinite, to exist (at every moment and in every way) as dependent rather than self-causing. But this dependence, importantly, is not identical with the relation finite existents or events have with each other. Within the

---

[2]This implies that creation is not the relation of one thing (God) to another thing (creation), but a relation in which creation comes into being.

[3]If God exists (and even the term existence doesn't apply to God in any ordinary sense), God is not a being among other beings or a thing among other things.

world-system, there is another kind of dependence, a relative dependence, that expresses both the interconnection of all that is and the specific ways in which finite existents depend upon each other. In the human case, theologians often illuminate that dependence in cis-centric and sometimes patriarchal ways by emphasizing the dual dependence an infant has on its mother: the mother is both the one who bears the child, thus, the condition of possibility of its physical coming into existence at all, and the one who smiles at and interacts with the child, eliciting the child's response, which is what begins the process of bringing the child into the reciprocity of human interaction.[4]

The relative dependence characteristic of the interconnected world-system has causal (or, better, contingent[5]), material, geographical, sociopolitical and personal aspects. Who and what a human being is—the particularity of a human's finite existence—takes shape in engagement with and dependence on other particularities. These include whoever gives it birth and cares for it, what passports (if any) it has, what landscape feels familiar to it, the food and drink it is given, the state of the public transportation system (if any) in the geographical region in which it lives and the prevalence of guns in its environment. The human being is shaped by the form racialization takes in its cultural and national context, the cell growth that takes place in the body that the human is, the election system that shapes the local and national policies where it lives, the state of the stock market as it enters the workforce (if it does so), its height, appearance, body shape (and the reactions of others to such features). The human being is affected by the friendliness or hostility of its built environment to humans or cars, its susceptibility to police or military violence and the knowledge it receives from ancestors, teachers, parents, mentors and friends. Features that form the human also include the noise, pollution, trees, drone strikes, fields, airports, unexploded mines, playgrounds (and so on) in its environment, the degree of intimacy it has with nonhuman animals (rats, ants, pigs, water buffalo, hippos, lions, kittens, foxes), nonhuman organisms (gut flora, parasites) and insects (e.g., mosquitoes)—and, of course, the incredibly complex and interconnected patterns that make up the world-system as a whole and the individually unpredictable but simultaneously global and hyperlocalized effects of climate change. This selective and very partial list is intended to spark the imagination into considering far more broadly and carefully the *degree* and *extent* of relative or partial dependence that contributes to giving each human life its particular form.

Schleiermacher's discussion of relative dependence is connected with his discussion of the relative freedom the human also experiences in relation to the world.[6] While the human is affected, determined and partially dependent in all the ways we've surveyed and more, it stands also in reciprocal relations to those determining environments (to use a word that gestures at, but also perhaps erases, the depth and specificity of the factors canvassed in the previous paragraph). Schleiermacher's notion of freedom here ties together two elements that are often presumed apart: what we might (somewhat reluctantly) call choice or action and something more like responsivity, or acting without

---

[4]Feminists often draw attention to the neglect of the maternal or natal (not all who give birth are women) body in theological reflection, with the exception of the body of Mary, which is often abstracted into a theological locus turned to ecclesial use.

[5]Causality may seem to imply something like a world-system that operates according to abstractable and absolute rules in the old billiard-ball sense, rather than the real world of emergence, unpredictability and probability.

[6]See Friedrich Schleiermacher, *The Christian Faith*, ed. H. R. Mackintosh and J. S. Stewart (Edinburgh: T&T Clark, 1999), §4.3.

necessarily being an actor who chooses. My environment affects me; I also affect my environment in how I respond to it. Philosophical, theological and theoretical discussions tend to consider the nature and extent of human freedom (and so, presumptively, responsibility) or else to work toward dismantling ideas of the human as free and self-determining (autonomous). Schleiermacher emphasizes that whatever freedom we may have, it is always only partial, responsive and codetermined by that on which we are relatively dependent. I am an actant[7] in my environment in ways that far exceed any capacity I have to make choices, both because much of bodied being is nonvolitional and because being a living body is also always to be active, in some sense, as long as life continues (and perhaps even after, in the effects on the environment of the materials that make up the body that I am). My choices and their consequences also escape my understanding and control, for the system within which I act is neither closed nor total.[8] Even when I make choices in what I experience as free and intentional ways, I cannot foresee the consequences of those choices. The very notion of choice as a free, intentional act that takes place at a certain point in time presumes something like a snapshot, frozen or momentary quality to the lived life that it doesn't actually have. Still, it is a widespread human activity to represent ourselves to ourselves as choice-makers and, maybe more broadly, as actors, whether or not such action is construed or experienced as free.

The point of this section, for the purpose of a theological consideration of finitude, is this: one of the elements of human existence that finitude picks out is dependence, in its concrete and material form. That concrete and material form is all-embracing: there is no *in*dependent existence within creation or the world-system. But that all-embracing form of intra-creation dependence also makes room for and exhibits whatever freedom and possibilities for action that creatures have. Dependence within creation is thus partially contrasted with finite possibility, but it is also the condition of such possibility. Dependence here—within the world-system, as it were—is not the same as dependence on God, nor can the partial contrasts within the world-system be read into the relation between God and creation. Dependence on God is the condition of existence as such in classical Christian thought, a way to elucidate what it means to be created and to emphasize just the difference between the complex differential forms of dependence within which reciprocity finds its place and the God-relationship that excludes that kind of differentiation.[9]

Theologians are prone to approach finitude in quite general and sometimes abstract terms, rather than through the concretions that finite existence is. Thinking finitude from a theological perspective means approaching finitude both as a general condition of limitation, bodied being and susceptibility to death (more about that in a moment), *and* as a specific condition of being differently conditioned, that is as codetermined by the contingent and highly particular dependencies and interactions on which this section focuses. These kinds of dependence make up the history, materiality and politics of finitude. They have been far less prominent in theological discussion than the idea of

---

[7]Actant might be a better word than actor because it avoids the implication of full self-determination or autonomy.
[8]This may be a partial departure from Schleiermacher. Arguably, his theology presumes a kind of closure of the world-system as a totality and that the world is a whole in terms of the interconnected causal nexus that gives it shape.
[9]The God-relationship may include many types of relation. But creation's dependence on God is, in classical Christian thought, absolute and undifferentiated: all that is depends on God, totally; all that is depends on God, equally; all that is relates to God, fully. See, e.g., Thomas Aquinas, *Summa Contra Gentiles*, book two, qq. 16–18.

finitude as a general condition illuminated and emphatically punctuated by death. It is, thus, to death that we now turn.

DEATH

Finitude as subjection to death is perhaps the most challenging topic to approach. We will touch on three ways in which death plays a significant role in theological discussions of finitude: (1) as something humans seek to avoid recognizing; (2) as the—in a sense—central act and question of human life; and (3) as a question of the nature, plausibility and effect of Christian beliefs. These are aspects of death that operate on different personal, structural and theological levels, touching on questions of meaning in individual lives, on the systematic social effects of cultural practices and what many consider to be the heart of theological discussions of finitude, that is, what it would mean to affirm finitude rather than seek to escape it.

First, let us consider the desire to avoid recognizing the role of death in life. Many theologians and cultural theorists, albeit with different concerns in mind, argue that fleeing the recognition of human subjection to death plays a substantial role in the generation of discriminatory and dominating social, cultural and perhaps also economic practices. Feminist theologians, about whom more anon, have suggested that the association of men with culture, rationality, transcendence and self-making is often the effect of the denial and refusal of death, which is then projected onto women through their association with nature and the body, and perhaps even an effect of male envy of women's capacity to give birth to new life.[10] The sort of person economic theories imagine exists—the autonomous, self-making, rational decision-maker whose decisions are fully reflective of his preferences—is very much the sort of person whose life is envisioned as attentive to opportunities and possibilities for self-making, not to the possible ultimate futility of all striving in the face of death. Or, put differently, it is perhaps such a person's fear of recognizing the possible ultimate futility of all striving that generates the frantic effort to expand one's possibilities and one's power—by way of money—past all limitations. When those enriched, beyond imagination's capacity to comprehend, by the accumulative and extractive logics of contemporary capitalism turn their disproportionate power and resources to escaping the confines of the earth, quite literally, it is difficult not to recognize the power of an analysis of this kind.

Critical race theorists have also demonstrated that one meaning of racialization, especially anti-blackness, is the disproportionate enforcement of vulnerability to death on minoritized, particularly black and enslaved, populations. For example, Ruth Wilson Gilmore famously defines racism as "the state-sanctioned or extralegal production and exploitation of group-differentiated vulnerability to premature death."[11] The transatlantic slave trade—a genetic and fundamental component of modern capitalism—involved the intentional and indiscriminate subjection of black people to premature and gruesome forms of death. But it also involved what theorist Orlando Patterson has famously called "social death," in which the enslaved were forcibly robbed of symbols of belonging and social recognition: symbols (including ancestry and ritual) that marked them in other

---

[10]Typically, these discussions are not structurally sensitive to the nonidentity of being a birth-giver and being a woman.
[11]Ruth Wilson Gilmore, *Golden Gulag: Prisons, Surplus, Crisis, and Opposition in Globalizing California* (Berkeley: University of California Press, 2007), 28.

bodily and ritualistic ways (e.g., clothing and hair) and reduced them by physical violence into those excluded from the realm of the human.

It need not be the case that these dynamics of what it is too mild to call injustice depend on any particular individual's desire to flee recognition of their own death. On an individual level, it might even be the case that recognition of death's inevitability permits and reinforces practices of accumulation and subjugation, since the fleetingness of this life might invite taking and holding as much as possible while it lasts. But even within the inevitability of death for all people, accumulation of goods, money and power over others allows for whatever relative security it is possible to have. Incredibly wealthy people may die prematurely of cancer, for instance, but they are vanishingly unlikely to die of violence, especially of the state-sanctioned kind. Even less wealthy groups of people—here, the 1 percent instead of the 0.1 percent—live longer than others by every measure; white people (especially white Europeans and North Americans), who benefit transnationally from the inheritance of literal and social accumulation of capital[12] by way of colonial extraction, are a clear example of these dynamics.[13]

To be the sort of finite creature that can represent itself to itself and extend its vision of itself into the future is, then, to be the sort of finite creature that knows that it will die.[14] Knowing that one will die, that one is vulnerable to death, may generate a desire to reduce that vulnerability as much as possible, to secure oneself as much as possible against the inevitable, to delay it or to enjoy as much power and opportunity as one can in the interim. While many theorists and theologians analyze these dynamics as the fleeing of death, they may also be considered as a recognition of death, without acceptance or *rapprochement*. In both ways of approaching the question, fear of death plays a role in the generation of concrete political and economic injustices.

More commonly, theological anthropology approaches death in the second way, as the central act and question of human life. Within the logic of Christian beliefs, it seems almost inevitable that this would be so. God's victory over death in Christ was taken early on (by Paul most significantly, but also in the later gospel narratives and elsewhere) to be the decisive reason to become a follower of Jesus, one who was eventually termed a "Christian." A theological consideration of finitude must involve attention to death's significance to any evaluation of, or approach to, human life. We will consider, in the third part of our discussion of death, what, exactly, different theological approaches mean by God's victory over death.

In modern theology, the Jesuit theologian Karl Rahner (1904–1984) offers perhaps the most compelling description of what it might mean to consider death as an act and event embracing all of human life. In his classic *On the Theology of Death*, he says, "Death is an event which strikes man in his totality [*den ganzen Menschen*[15]]." Because human

---

[12]Individual inheritance as well as state provision of a broader array of social goods.

[13]To be clear: the argument is *not* that these dynamics explain all forms of social injustice, nor that they account for the complexities of local and global forms of racialization in every case. However, in the most concrete ways imaginable, the wealthier—and wealth is always entangled with exploitative relations—*have more life*, live longer, than the less wealthy. The lengthening of their lives depends, in part, on the shortening of the lives of others. Length is not the only, nor even the most significant, measure of life, by any stretch of the imagination, but it is certainly an aspect of life that matters. At least some parts of the Bible reflect a view of death as an evil only when it arrives early, before someone becomes full of years, replete with the measure of life allotted to the human.

[14]Leaving aside here the question of whether such knowledge is restricted to humans, or what form it takes in nonhuman creatures.

[15]Karl Rahner, "Zur Theologie des Todes," *Zeitschrift für katholische Theologie* 79, no. 1 (1957): 4.

existence is both natural (biological, in a nonreductive sense) and personal, death must combine a necessary and a free aspect, an aspect in which the human being "disposes freely of [itself]."[16] Rahner's distinction however, is not between a purely biological-inevitable aspect of death, by virtue of being a living, material being, and a purely spiritual aspect. Rather, the inevitability of our subjection to death is the result of sin, since death, as a merely biological event, might be no more than accidental, lacking its actual significance to human life.[17] Death is not just "something without purpose simply undergone [*ein a-teleologisches "Leiden"*[18]]," nor a "destructive fate striking [the human being] from without"; death is rather "the accomplishment of the end towards which man positively strives," avers Rahner.[19]

How might that be? For many, Christian approaches to death are assumed to render this life unimportant, at best a prelude to something else (whether heaven or hell). For Rahner, just the opposite is the case. Death gives weight and significance to life: it means "taking this earthly life with radical seriousness. It is truly historical, that is, unique, unrepeatable, of inalienable and irrevocable significance. ... [T]here is only a history, happening once and for all."[20] This historical life is where the decision for or against God is made,[21] and death is where that decision is completed, enacted, finalized. Does this mean that the only significance of this life is that it is the stage *where* that decision is made? Decidedly not, Rahner thinks, for it is precisely the concrete, historical particularity of an existence that gives content and shape to such a decision, that prevents it being an external verdict or an abstract yes/no and instead makes the decision into the unified totality of a particular personal existence. Importantly, then, death is not simply "an occurrence which is passively undergone"; it is also "an act that [the human being] interiorly performs. Moreover, ... it must be death itself which is the act, and not simply an attitude the human being adopts towards death."[22] How can death be an *act*, not merely an event—or the end of all action and event?

Rahner interprets death "both as act and fate, as end and fulfilment, as willed and as suffered, as plenitude and emptiness."[23] Death is the act in which a person achieves full self-possession, and the event in which a person is robbed of self, destroyed and lost. "Humanly speaking," as Rahner puts it, it cannot be known which of these is the case.

The language of self-possession may rightly cause alarm. Isn't the self-possessive human being precisely the autonomous human that consideration of finitude seeks to undo, the model of the free human contrasted with the slave that lies at the ground of modernity's dialectic? Rahner's theology overall may not be completely free of these elements, but it's important to note how he understands self-possession, or what he means in considering death as a fully self-possessed act. Death, rightly approached, is "an act in which [the human being] surrenders [itself and its reality[24]] fully and with unconditional openness

---

[16]Karl Rahner, *On the Theology of Death*, trans. C. H. Henkey (New York: Seabury Press, 1973), 13. The translation here is slightly modified to reflect that the German refers to *das Wesen* as "that which disposes of itself."

[17]Rahner, *Theology of Death*, 14–15.

[18]Rahner, "Theologie des Todes," 11.

[19]Rahner, *Theology of Death*, 25.

[20]Ibid., 27.

[21]Ibid., 26.

[22]Ibid., 30. The German is "*Tat des Menschen von innen*," *Theologie des Todes*, 15.

[23]Rahner, *Theology of Death*, 41.

[24]The English translation substitutes "fully" for "*seine Wirklichkeit*."

to the disposal of the incomprehensible decision of God, because, in the darkness of death, [the human being] is not in a position to dispose of [itself] unambiguously."[25] Put differently: the only self-possession or act of self-completion a person might have, according to Rahner, is to give oneself trustingly to God, to accept one's own death, without either despairing or assuming that death is an escape from material confinement or finitude's ambiguity.

There is more than can be said here about the soteriology involved in Rahner's approach to death.[26] Giving oneself over trustingly to God is, he thinks, participation in the death of Christ, the death in which human emptiness is transformed by plenitudinous divine grace.[27] Reaching out for the grace offered by God in faith, hope and love, without escaping, denying or pretending not to experience the threat of meaninglessness and emptiness that death entails, "makes death itself the highest act of believing, hoping, loving."[28] For our purposes, the crucial element is that Rahner understands the embrace of death *in its ambiguity and real threat*, but not in despair, as the act that brings finite existence to completion. To be finite is to be vulnerable to death. To be a sinful finite being is to be subjected to death as judgment. To embrace one's finitude in light of death and one's own sinfulness is to give oneself over, trustingly, to death in light of divine transformation of death in Christ.

Which brings us, then, to the third element of this discussion of death. Just what happens to death in light of Christ? What effects do Christian beliefs about the transformation of death in Christ have? Critics of Christianity and theologians working from womanist, feminist, process and ecological directions have argued that Christian belief that death is overcome in Christ—that death is not the end, but the event of or prelude to bodily resurrection, entry into heaven or whatever form of postmortem existence one envisions—is a major contributor to Christian exploitation of the earth and carelessness about the lives of other human beings.[29] These charges are not without foundation. I once stormed out of a room in which well-known, mainline Christian ethicists were having a serious discussion of much torture God may be presumed to forgive in the life to come.

In response to problems like this, some theologians intensify what it might mean to accept finitude and death's role in finitude. Fear of death alone, not death itself, is the problem death presents to human existence. All that lives, dies. If and to the extent that Christianity denies death's inevitability, Christianity must be given up. Alternatively, it must be reinterpreted, especially since a human person is not something separable from the material body that it is. To accept one's finite existence just means to accept one's death as the natural completion of existence. Death itself is not ambiguous, in the sense that Rahner approaches it. Indeed, death is not a problem, except insofar as premature death is inequitably distributed through social, political and economic processes (processes that, as we have seen, are arguably intensified by the denial of death). At death, the matter the human is returns to the earth from which it came, and contributes to ever new cycles of birthing, becoming and dying as world-processes continue. Within this life, there are

---

[25]Rahner, *Theology of Death*, 44.
[26]As well as about the role of sin!
[27]Rahner, *Theology of Death*, 70.
[28]Ibid., 71.
[29]See, e.g., Rosemary Radford Ruether, *Introducing Redemption in Christian Feminism* (Sheffield: Sheffield Academic Press, 1998); Delores Williams, *Sisters in the Wilderness: The Challenge of Womanist God-Talk* (Maryknoll, NY: Orbis, 1993); and Catherine Keller, *On the Mystery: Discerning Divinity in Process* (Minneapolis, MN: Fortress Press, 2008).

what Ivone Gebara calls "daily acts of salvation and resurrection" that take place within the horizon of an affirmed mortality.[30] Eventually, cosmic death will mean also the end of the world. The work of theological anthropology, from this perspective, is in part to sift through the detritus of Christian traditions to bring out whatever elements may be found in it that assist in the reconciliation with finitude that acceptance of death entails.

It's hard to imagine the reconciliation of Christian hopes for bodily resurrection and cosmic transformation with acceptance of death's inevitability and unambiguity. Even though one might distinguish between death as a punishment for sin and death as a natural end to bodily existence (as theologians like Rahner do), Rahner will insist that death, in its concrete reality, is ambiguous in that sin and judgment hang over death as a question. A divide may remain between those who argue that acceptance of finitude just means acceptance of death as the end of personal existence and those who argue that acceptance of finitude means risking the embrace of death in all its ambiguity but with hope of resurrection by way of participation in the death and resurrection of Christ.

DESIRE

Finitude is often thematized in contemporary theology in connection with desire.[31] Desire, in practice, becomes one of the main ways in which finitude is discussed. It is not immediately apparent why this would be the case. Isn't finitude more closely connected to the sorts of themes we've already canvassed—creation, death and materiality—than to general considerations of desire? Many contemporary theologies approach finitude as a condition that, rightly approached, reigns in desire's potential illimitation with respect to the world. That finitude cannot satisfy desire requires that desire be limited and redirected toward God.

Christian theology continues to relate to cultural contexts in the West within which it has lost much of its reason for being. The reasons for that are complex and beyond the scope of this essay. However, one aspect of that loss of influence is a pervasive sense that Christianity is at a minimum co-responsible for the destruction that modernity has wrought. Theologians typically respond to that assignation of blame either by arguing that Christianity is the solution to, not the source of, modernity's problems or by arguing that there are nonetheless resources within Christianity that can assist in addressing the large-scale social and economic problems confronting humankind as a whole. Interestingly, these very different responses often converge in seeing the mismatch between desire's illimitation and finitude as limitation, as a driving dynamic of human existence.

The large-scale problems of modernity—issues like sex, sexuality, gender, consumerism, capitalism and ecocide—appear to many to be consequences of the combination of plasticity with openness that human finitude entails. Human finitude includes the capacity to orient oneself, or to be oriented, toward a variety of ends. Yet those ends are not themselves necessarily commensurate with the capacity of any particular being: the ends themselves can be pursued beyond any notion of satiation. Human beings need and want shelter, food, security. Yet human desire doesn't match want to need: instead of securing a minimum level of shelter, food and security for all, some accumulate mansions

---

[30]Ivone Gebara, *Out of the Depths: Women's Experience of Evil and Salvation*, trans. Ann Patrick Ware (Minneapolis, MN: Fortress Press, 2002), 130. See also Ruether, *Introducing Redemption*, 117–20.
[31]This theme has been especially prominent in recent Anglican theology in the work of Rowan Williams, Graham Ward, and Sarah Coakley.

and yachts while others go without the basic necessities of existence. Desire doesn't rest content with enough; instead, it always pushes beyond any particular satisfaction. Or, put differently, at the moment at which desire is satisfied, desire has already outstripped itself and moved on to something else. Desire's capacity to orient the human being becomes both the problem and the solution to fundamental distortions of human coexistence in this type of account.

The analysis often runs—greatly simplified, of course—along something like the following lines. To be a human being is to desire. Desire may be rightly or wrongly ordered. Rightly ordered desire is, in typically Augustinian fashion, oriented toward God. All other desires are to be ruled and transformed by the fundamental desire for God—cue "our hearts are restless until they rest in Thee" quotation. The restlessness of human hearts—the plasticity and fungibility of human desires—means that humans seek fulfillment in ends and objects that cannot finally fulfill the desires oriented toward them. Human desires are, thus, fruitless and self-destructive unless a fundamental reorientation of the heart takes place. A reoriented heart and a cleansed desire learns to value, or not value, rightly, in such a way that its practices lose their excessive character and instead are directed and moderated away from destruction, greed and consumption.

This very general account of human desire can be played out in relation to each issue mentioned above. Consumerism, especially when it is wrongly presumed to be the motor of capitalism (whether capitalism is considered intrinsically evil or simply excessive in practice), seems so evidently to be a matter of desire's disorder. Similarly, human desires run rampant—desires for domination rather than cooperation, for instance—permit the disregard for creation characteristic of the exploitative and extractive practices that cause global warming and species extinction. The theme of desire also appears as a corrective to historical theological anthropologies that have focused excessively on the capacity of reason to direct the will. To see the human being as desiring sidelines the "Man of Reason" in both medieval and early modern versions, it is thought.

Giving the mismatch between desire's illimitation and finitude's limitations the central role it often has in theological anthropology allows the theologian to offer an almost infinitely adaptable nostrum for individual and social problems. If the problem is that desire is potentially insatiable, the solution must be to transform and redirect that insatiability in some way, typically through ascetic practices, participation in the Eucharist, learning Christ-like sacrifice or the like.

Such accounts are difficult to connect with life as it is actually lived, both individually and socially. They also turn attention away from the concrete determinants and interdependencies of finite existence toward an abstract account of the formation of the person within an ecclesial order that presumes a coherence to personhood, and a coherence to the ecclesia, that neither actually has. Giving desire the centrality it has in contemporary accounts of finitude keeps attention firmly on the orientation of the will as the condition of human action, but leaves mostly unaddressed the many ways in which humans are actants without the involvement of an oriented will. Turning to desire is, in a sense, too easy. The prescription of ascetic or liturgical practices assumes that they involve lifelong struggles to enact, but the answer they offer to human problems doesn't address those problems in their real complexity, nor is it falsifiable by any actual events, including the perpetration of tremendous horrors and ongoing injustices by those most engaged in those very ascetic and liturgical practices. Approaching finitude through desire may thus be another way to escape the concrete histories and events that make up the existence that finitude is.

CONCLUSION

While that to which finitude refers—the concrete particularities of created existence—is of crucial significance for theological anthropology, finitude, as thematized, is too often made into an abstract site of reflection that has little capacity to illuminate its putative subject. As a way to focus attention on the condition of being created and the interdependence of creation, finitude can, however, help theologians to notice the processes and concrete realities about which they hope to think and speak. Finitude also invites consideration of death as a political as well as individual event. The question of death is crucial for a tradition of reflection in which the destruction of death stands at its genesis and at its heart. Approaching finitude mainly through its mismatch with desire may, however, repeat the abstractive practice that turning to finitude is supposed to prevent.

Whether and to what extent finitude can be transformed or reformed is perhaps at the heart of religious and existential reflection on the conditions of existence. Does Christianity depend on the hope that death has been *overcome*, or that it has been *defanged*? Can the conditions of production and distribution that make up finite (political) arrangements be changed to make finitude, with all its lived ambiguity, somewhat less destructive and violent? What self-understanding, and which practices of self-making, will allow humans to live together as well as we might? The answers one offers to questions such as these are where the abstraction "finitude" meets the realities to which it attempts to be responsible.

SUGGESTED FURTHER READING

Boyer, Ann, *The Undying: Pain, Vulnerability, Mortality, Medicine, Art, Time, Dreams, Data, Exhaustion, Cancer, and Care* (New York: Farrar, Straus and Giroux, 2019).

Rahner, Karl, *On the Theology of Death*, trans. C. H. Henkey (New York: Seabury Press, 1973).

Schleiermacher, Friedrich, *The Christian Faith*, ed. H. R. Mackintosh and J. S. Stewart (Edinburgh: T&T Clark, 1999).

Williams, Delores, *Sisters in the Wilderness: The Challenge of Womanist God-Talk* (Maryknoll, NY: Orbis, 1993).

CHAPTER EIGHT

Sin and the Subversion of Ethics: Why the Discourse of Sin Is Good for Theological Anthropology

DARLENE FOZARD WEAVER

Sin is a key feature in Christian cosmology and Christian theological anthropology. Sin "came into the world" (Rom. 5:12) and had disruptive consequences for divine-human relations, for human relationships with one another and with the created world. A Christian theological anthropology would be incomplete without some account of sin. While sin is neither the first nor the last word about human persons, it is ingredient to the truth Christianity wants to tell about us.

Although sin is key to a Christian understanding of human persons, explicit talk about sin in American churches and in Christian theological scholarship declined dramatically in the latter half of the twentieth century in both mainline Protestant theology and in Catholic theology after the Second Vatican Council (1962–5). Sin has remained a marginal theme in much of Christian theology.[1] The marginalization of sin reflects various worries and aversions about the discourse of sin. It appears to traffic in dogmatism and moralism and foster excessive degrees of guilt and shame. Moreover, the discourse of sin too often operates as a weapon in polarized and deeply unequal communities. There is something scandalous about the discourse of sin as well, when it is selectively applied. Historically churches have disproportionately focused on sexual sins versus the sinfulness of economic and political choices or structures, or sins in ordinary life beyond the bedroom. Talk of sin increasingly seems unhelpful or even imprudent in a cultural context marked by polarization as well as rising rates of religious disaffiliation. In such an environment, sin seems an unlikely vocabulary for bridging divides or undertaking evangelical outreach. For these and other reasons, sin may seem like an aspect of Christian theological anthropology to mute or pass over quickly.

It does not follow that Christian thinking about sin has been stagnant. Some recent work on original sin has engaged philosophical discussions of responsibility and

---

[1] This observation is echoed by many. See, e.g., Beverly Roberts Gaventa, "The Cosmic Power of Sin in Paul's Letter to the Romans: Toward a Widescreen Edition," *Interpretation* 58, no. 3 (2004): 229–40. See also Karl Menninger, *Whatever Became of Sin?* (New York: Hawthorn Books, 1973).

freedom. Most contemporary scholarly contributions to sin, however, concern social sin. Liberation theologies in particular have shown the limits of some traditional accounts of sin and have led to fruitful reflection on the sinfulness of social structures and cultural mores. If Christian theologies of sin used to emphasize an individual's sinful actions, liberation theologies enlarge our focus to the structures, machinery and mores of systemic oppression. Social forms of sin are important for understanding human action, moral priorities and theological questions about the scope of human responsibility to set things right in the world.

This chapter argues that sin is properly understood in relational terms and that doing so can navigate emphases on personal and social dimensions of sin. It discusses several types of sin, then describes the contributions liberation theologies have made. This discussion shows that the discourse of sin challenges several assumptions built into modern moral discourse, helpfully complicating our understanding of moral agency. Finally, the chapter explores the interrelation and difference between sin and immorality. The chapter argues that sin, properly understood, subverts the enterprise of ethics. Understanding this is important for appreciating the exercise of human moral agency amidst dynamics of sin and grace. In its complicating and subversive work, the discourse of sin benefits Christian ethics and Christian theological anthropology, showing the viability of that anthropology and leveraging its value for advancing our understanding of human persons. Sin is a valuable and underutilized language for grappling with human agency and the malformation of the world.

SIN IS RELATIONAL

A juridical or forensic understanding of sin is too narrow. Sin is not first and foremost the violation of some law. The violation of laws matters only insofar as laws are morally adequate expressions that certain behaviors and structures are enjoined or prohibited. The laws do not make those behaviors or structures good or sinful but express communal wisdom (or the lack thereof, in the case of unjust laws) about how we should live together. Nor is sin best understood through paradigmatic vices, like selfishness or pride, or through purity codes or taboos, though each of these rubrics can convey something about the lived experience of sin, or capture theological or moral aspects of sin. Sin is irreducibly relational. It names the variety of ways our relationships with God, ourselves and others go wrong. In short, sin is the disruption of proper relationship with God, self and others.

Indeed, part of the value of sin as a theological concept is that it can capture the interpenetration of our relationships and the migration of dysfunction across them.[2] Sin against God, say, in the form of idolatry, is not hermetically sealed from the rest of my relationships, including my own self-relation. Idolatry already signals an improper regard for some finite thing or person. If I inordinately value money, for example, that disordered love will impact the way I value and comport myself in relation to other persons, such as undervaluing my family members or instrumentalizing my neighbors. My devotion to money may express itself in vicious character traits like a callous indifference to the needy, or snobbery. Dysfunction in the "vertical" relationship between me and God therefore has consequences for my "horizontal" relationships with other persons and

[2]Jesse Couenhoven, *Stricken by Sin, Cured by Christ: Agency, Necessity, and Culpability in Augustinian Theology* (Oxford: Oxford University Press, 2013).

for my own selfhood. Sin therefore presupposes that there is a proper ordering for our multiple relationships.

A relational account of sin is consistent with Hebrew and Christian scriptures. The Hebrew word *hata* and the Greek word *hamartia* both mean "missing the mark" and come from the context of archery or spear throwing. Hebrew and Christian scriptures describe the ways we "miss the mark" through a diverse set of tropes. Sin is pride and rebellion (1 Sam. 15:23), falsehood (Isa. 28:15-18, Rom. 3:13), corruption (Tit 1:15-16; Eph 4:22) and so much else. These examples evoke different aspects of disordered relationships. Idolatry is the worship of something finite as divine and a betrayal of the devotion that is due only to God. Pride is a misapprehension of oneself or one's value, enacted in rebellion against one's place in a larger ecology of relationships with God and neighbor. Falsehood is not simply wrong belief but estrangement from God who is the Truth. Conceiving of sin as corruption helps to capture one's malformation by sin, which signals departures from what ought to be the case. Corruption means I am ill-equipped to be in relationship with others. The fact that scripture conceptualizes sin in different ways is valuable. While all sin involves a disruption of proper relationship, that disruption occurs, unfolds, looks and feels in different ways. Moreover, these diverse ways of conceptualizing sin suggest that sin includes both concrete behaviors as well a general disposition against God. An adequate understanding of sin needs to do justice to both.

A relational account of sin is faithful to the best insights of Christian theological anthropology: our status as creatures made in the image of God, our relationality, our finitude, our freedom and our dependence on grace.[3] As creatures of God we are made to know and love God and to be in loving community with others. Sin disrupts this created order. God not only made us but also created us in the divine image. Sin does not eradicate our dignity in the disregard of our *imago Dei*, but the full gravity of sin becomes clearer in contrast. Christian views of the person, particularly in Catholic theology, affirm our profound relationality. Indeed, one way of interpreting the Christian claim that persons are created in the image of God (*imago Dei*) is to point toward our sociality. Human persons image God, who we recognize as a Trinity of persons, by virtue of our capacity for and our fulfillment within relationships with others. Sin makes human finitude a problem. Sin renders human biological death as a manifestation of and punishment for sinfulness.[4] Sin compromises human freedom. In particular, insight into the import of sin for human freedom is a key contribution Christian theological anthropology offers for contemporary understanding of the person. Finally, sin is crucial for understanding human dependence on divine grace. It is because of sin and from sin that we need deliverance by grace. Even in theological anthropologies that emphasize the importance of human cooperation with grace, insistence that the exercise of human agency depends on grace is essential to a truthful Christian description of persons.

The relational character of sin and these preliminary insights into sin become clearer as we consider types of sin.

---

[3]Note that these insights correspond to the other key themes in theological anthropology explored in this volume.
[4]Darlene Fozard Weaver, "Death," in *Oxford Handbook of Theological Ethics*, ed. Gilbert Meilaender and William Werpehowski (Oxford: Oxford University Press, 2005), 254–70.

TYPES OF SIN

Christians identify several types of sin, each of which have important implications for theological anthropology and each of which raise questions about moral agency. These types of sin include original sin, personal sin and social sin. Catholics further distinguish personal sin into venial and mortal forms of sin.

However, before discussing types of sin, it is worthwhile to note that Catholic and Protestant thinking about sin displays some characteristic differences. Catholic accounts of sin have tended to focus more on individual actions and belong to broader theological and moral anthropologies that are informed by natural law.[5] Protestant theologians have argued that Catholic theology tends to minimize or trivialize sin.[6] There are two reasons for this charge. First, by focusing on sins (that is, individual sinful actions), Catholic theology has underappreciated sin as a power, principality or force.[7] Second, Catholic theological anthropology displays a persistent optimism about human persons. It claims we are capable of using reason to discern the moral law, that we are made for relationship and therefore are open to collaboration and good will. Such optimism is another way of underestimating the depth of human captivity to sin (Rom. 6:6, 16) and the scope of sin as a power from which we need to be liberated (6:17-18, 20-22). Characteristic differences among Christian traditions can generate constructive tensions within which contemporary reflection on sin can develop. The following typology of sin, along with recent work in liberation theology, illustrates such tensions.

Original Sin

Original sin refers both to the original disruption of the divine-human relation—the entrance of moral evil into the world—and the religious and moral inheritance of that sin. The book of Genesis depicts original sin through the story of Adam and Eve eating the fruit of the tree of the knowledge of good and evil. The story is a nonliteral account of how the fallen world we experience came to be. It also describes the relational consequences of sin that we inherit, detailing our estrangement from one another, our bodies and the created world. In this regard, original sin is a discourse for describing and grappling with the human predicament.

Traditional doctrines of original sin represent a challenge for theological anthropology, because they consider individuals guilty for a situation they did not freely effect. Yet, Alistair McFadyen and Jesse Couenhoven have persuasively argued that a traditional doctrine of original sin has value for precisely these reasons. McFadyen looks specifically at child sexual abuse and at the Holocaust as fields for testing whether original sin has explanatory power.[8] He shows that original sin helps explain aspects of pathological dynamics that non-theological discourse cannot convey. Moreover, the explanatory power of original sin lies precisely at the point at which it chafes against our modern understanding of moral responsibility. A modern understanding of responsibility is one in

---

[5]Charles Curran, *The Catholic Moral Tradition Today: A Synthesis* (Washington, DC: Georgetown University Press, 1999), 144–6.
[6]J. R. Daniel Kirk, 'Principalities and Powers', in *T&T Clark Companion to the Doctrine of Sin*, ed. Keith L. Johnson and David Lauber (New York: Bloomsbury, 2016). See also, James M. Gustafson, *Protestant and Roman Catholic Ethics* (Chicago: University of Chicago, Press 1978), 8–11.
[7]Gaventa, "The Cosmic Power of Sin," 229–40, 232–6.
[8]McFadyen stresses that child sexual abuse and the Holocaust are not examples of sin: "I am not trying to exemplify an understanding of sin which has been (or could be) worked out independently of the consideration

which we can only be found culpable for actions we originate when we have the freedom to do otherwise. Traditional doctrines of original sin claim we are responsible for and incur guilt for a situation that originated long before us. For McFadyen, part of the horror of pathological dynamics like child sexual abuse and the Holocaust are the ways they co-opt their victims' wills, involving them as active contributors to the pathologies and therefore as sharing responsibility for the dynamics. Importantly, McFadyen is not blaming victims. He is arguing that original sin helps to explain features of these pathologies that modern secular moral analysis misses, specifically the incorporation, cloistering and bondage of victims' own wills within these dynamics. Understanding the full reality and moral atrocity of these pathologies requires understanding that these pathologies effect "a manifold confusion (in practice as well as in cognition) about reality—the limits, nature and possibilities of agency, the nature of causality, what is true and false, valuable and pathogenic, good and bad, right and wrong and why."[9]

Couenhoven argues that original sin helps us to make sense of our fundamental dependence on others in dynamics of both sin and grace. He concurs with McFadyen that doctrines of original sin offend modern moral sensibilities because they hold us accountable and blameworthy for the sins of others. For both thinkers, original sin is not an inheritance that is activated only through personal choice. Rather, it describes the preconditioning of our agency. Couenhoven, like McFadyen, argues that we are born into a bondage of sin and that as we develop into responsible creatures we are already beings whose beliefs and loves are fundamentally disordered.[10] Our disordered beliefs and loves are in themselves sinful. They also lead us to engage in personal sins, what Couenhoven calls "secondary sins." Original sin gives the lie to any account of human agency that views freedom, reason or will as intact, or depicts the field of human action as a neutral space into which we project our intentions. We become free and responsible persons within a sinful ecology that has already warped us within. Original sin is key to understanding the character and limits of human freedom and the depth of our dependence on divine grace.

Personal Sin

Personal sin refers to the sinful choices, vices and omissions that mark our daily lives. Catholic thinking about personal sin originates, of course, in Judaism and is therefore framed by experiences of being a people oppressed by occupying forces, liberated by God, covenanted with God, gifted with a law that structured this covenantal relation and subsequently responding to this covenantal relationship in successive generations marked by infidelity and fidelity. Early Christian thinking about sin was shaped decisively during the sixth to the ninth centuries, when the practice of confessing sins changed from a single, public experience to a practice that was repeated and done privately. During this transition Irish monks developed handbooks to assist priests with hearing confessions and assigning appropriate penances. The handbooks left an indelible mark on Catholic

---

of these concrete situations. Rather, I am trying to understand and to test the doctrine of sin in and through a consideration of these two situations, which draws theology into conversation with secular forms of discernment and description" (Alistair I. McFadyen, *Bound to Sin: Abuse, Holocaust and the Christian Doctrine of Sin*, Cambridge Studies in Christian Doctrine 6 (Cambridge: Cambridge University Press, 2000), 48).
[9]Ibid., 195.
[10]Like McFadyen, Couenhoven works principally with an Augustinian notion of original sin. Couenhoven, *Stricken by Sin*, 15.

moral reasoning. They prompted confessors to question the circumstances surrounding particular actions, consider differences in a penitent's motives and intentions, and to think analogically about sins, that is, to consider how types of sins are related to or different from one another. John Mahoney's important book *The Making of Moral Theology* describes the importance of these penitential handbooks for Catholic moral thought. They inaugurated patterns of moral reasoning about moral actions that persist to this day and thereby created strengths in casuistry (analysis of moral cases), robust conceptual frameworks for practical moral reflection and a fertile method of analogical reasoning that assists Catholic ethics in grappling with new and emerging issues in ethics (consider technological developments that create new moral possibilities for human beings). There is a downside to these strengths. Sometimes Catholic moral assessment of specific actions leads to an emphasis on actions at the expense of focusing on persons, though the opposite is also sometimes true.[11]

Catholic theology further distinguishes personal sin by degrees of gravity. Venial sin represents relatively minor injuries to one's relationships with God, neighbor and self. Venial sins reflect the brokenness and concupiscence of the human person. Venial sins do not cause irreparable damage to our relationships, but they do weaken them. Moreover, they can accumulate in patterns of habituation and moral formation so that their impact is more significant. Mortal sin refers to sins that comprise a decisive rejection of God's grace. They are "mortal" because they break our relationship. For a sin to qualify as mortal it must meet several conditions. It must be undertaken with full knowledge (an agent must know it is a sin) and consent (an agent must choose to commit the sin anyway), and it must involve "grave matter." The meaning of "grave matter" is a subject of considerable debate among Catholic moral theologians.[12] Suffice it to say that the distinction between venial and mortal sin is helpful inasmuch as it encourages us to consider a number of issues regarding sins and sinning. Personal responsibility usually requires some degree of knowledge (one is not acting in ignorance) and freedom (one is not coerced). Can we identify some actions as always and unavoidably sinful, even as so sinful as to amount to a decisive rupture between a person and God? Or is it necessary to know an agent's intentions? Some recognition of circumstances is obviously important. An act of sexual intercourse is morally different between a married couple than between an adult and a child, for example.

One limitation of viewing personal sin in terms of venial versus mortal sins lies in the presumption that sins are simply actions we commit. While we certainly do commit sins, that is, freely and knowingly engage in behaviors that injure our multiple relationships with God, neighbors and ourselves, this emphasis on discrete action omits other significant aspects of sin. Sin includes character traits that are sinful. If I am greedy person, I do greedy things—consuming more than my fair share of Thanksgiving pie, for instance. But the sin of greed is not confined to a discrete instance of pie-eating. It describes an enduring quality of me as a person, my anxiety about not having enough, my tendency to horde, my persistently competitive approach to resources, my focus on myself and neglect of others' needs and wants. The sinfulness of greed lies in my affects, my thinking and in my willing. The vice of greed prompts me to engage in behaviors or perform actions that are greedy.

---

[11]Darlene Fozard Weaver, *The Acting Person and Christian Moral Life* (Washington, DC: Georgetown University Press, 2011).
[12]Ibid., 107–10.

Sin also often involves *in*action, or omission. As Andrew Flescher puts it, "From the moment we are born, evil is something with which we have to contend. By doing nothing, our proximity to evil increases. ... Evil is the upshot of inaction just as much if not more than it is the upshot of action. It is the *is not* for which human beings are distinctively accountable".[13] When forms of violence are often explored only in terms of a victim/perpetrator binary, we fail to grapple with the ways that the inaction of bystanders permits violence to continue.[14] Charles Pinches points out that omissions imply a shared moral world.[15] To judge a parent or a health care provider as negligent, for example, presumes a shared understanding of what that parent or health care provider is reasonably expected to know and do. Sins of omission, then, provide fruitful avenues to grappling with personal formation and responsibility in relation to larger sinful social structures and cultural dynamics. They prompt us to acknowledge that sin is more pervasive and more powerful than isolated bad choices or foibles. According to Pinches, "it is a mistake to think of actions as self-creations, as moral self-expressions by a self who, at various points, chooses to do this or that in or to the world by moving it about with his action. Rather, actions, like omissions, take place in an already moral world."[16]

Social Sin

The act analysis fostered in Catholic moral tradition explains a relative neglect of social sin in much of Christian tradition. For other reasons, mainline Protestant discussion of sin has tended to construe sin in terms of individual bondage to the power of sin and a disposition against God rather than consider sin in terms of institutions or structures. To be sure, both Catholic and Protestant thinkers have recognized social dimensions to sin and collective or corporate participation in sin. Moreover, both Catholic and Protestant moral traditions provide examples in which sin is conceptualized in a manner that is somewhat analogous to the concept of social sin, for example, Walter Rauschenbusch's structures of evil. In some sense, all sin is social. As noted above, original sin has cosmic consequences that disrupt human interpersonal relations. Personal sins impact others even when they do not directly qualify as sins against our neighbors. The more selfish I become, for example, the more disposed I am to disregard your interests.

Social sin, however, designates more than the inevitably social dimensions of original or personal sin. Sin consists in more than a common human predicament, on one hand, and the particular vices, choices and omissions of individuals, on the other hand. Institutions, social structures and cultural mores can be sinful as well. According to Kristin Heyer, "in its broadest sense social sin encompasses the unjust structures, distorted consciousness, and collective actions and inaction that facilitate injustice and dehumanization."[17] Examples of social sin include racism, sexism and ableism. The category of social sin allows us to grapple with the reality that the sinfulness we encounter in the world is not limited to an inherited condition or individual actions, but is also institutionalized and

---

[13]Andrew Michael Flescher, *Moral Evil* (Washington, DC: Georgetown University Press, 2013), 196.
[14]Elisabeth Vasko, *Beyond Apathy: A Theology for Bystanders* (Minneapolis, MN: Fortress, 2015).
[15]Charles Pinches, *Theology and Action: After Theory in Christian Ethics* (Grand Rapids, MI: Eerdmans, 2002), 170–82.
[16]Ibid., 184.
[17]Kristin E. Heyer, "Social Sin and Immigration: Good Fences Make Bad Neighbors," *Theological Studies* 71 (2010): 410–36, 413.

enculturated. Moreover, social sin names more than a quality of our structures, policies and customs. It captures the import of systemic sinfulness for individual and collective consciousness, which in turn impacts our prospect for moral action. The sin of racism encompasses individual racist actions as well as racist laws and legacies of economic and health disparities. But it also includes the unreflective, often unconscious racism of white supremacist culture. As a white person, my personal complicity with racism ranges from the systemic privilege I experience vis-à-vis persons of color to my history of inaction and limited action against racism, to the deeply rooted bias and prejudice I cannot help but have acquired in a white supremacist society. The latter is manifest in my unthinking reversion to white social norms, for example, or involuntary and shameful experiences of fear I have felt when encountering black men while walking alone.

Social sin both contributes to and complicates our thinking about personal responsibility. On the one hand, social sin seems to attenuate personal responsibility. Global food systems hide from me many of the consequences of my economic choices. In many cases I do not know the origins of my food, the labor practices involved or the environmental impact of its production. How can I be responsible when such ignorance attends my action and, moreover, when I have so little power to correct what is morally wrong with global systems? On the other hand, social sin increases my personal responsibility. Social structures do not appear out of thin air. They are fashioned through the accumulation of personal choices—in the form of action and inaction. As the Catholic Church's Congregation for the Doctrine of the Faith puts it, "Structures, whether they are good or bad, are the result of man's actions. ... The root of evil, then, lies in free and responsible persons."[18] Notice that this description seems to portray social sin as the accumulated consequences of personal sins, which themselves spring from an intact individual moral agency, rather than (or in addition to) a context in which we are already embedded as moral agents and by which our moral agency is already distorted. It would be difficult to muster hope that social structures can be changed if we could not admit that they are in some real sense products of choice in addition to being contexts for choice. And yet social sin should reckon with "pervasive, internalized ideologies [that]make us susceptible to myths; operative understandings [that] influence our actions of inaction. When bias hides or skews values, it becomes more difficult to choose authentic values over those that prevail in society, a tendency already present because of original sin."[19]

LIBERATION THEOLOGY AND SIN

There is value in delineating types or forms of sin insofar as a typology expresses aspects of human existence within dynamics of sin and grace. Sin complicates modern moral notions of responsibility. It "concerns relationship with God much more broadly and as such exceeds the kind of answerability at stake in moral responsibility."[20] Reflection on sin enriches our understanding of human agency and provides a discourse that not only is capacious enough for capturing features of human experience but also has explanatory power in capturing the reality of pathological dynamics. Christian progress

---

[18]Congregation for the Doctrine of the Faith, "Instruction on Certain Aspects of the Theology of Liberation," *Origins* 14, no. 15 (1984): 194–204.
[19]Heyer, "Social Sin and Immigration," 429.
[20]Ryan Darr, "Social Sin and Social Wrongs: Moral Responsibility in a Structurally Disordered World," *Journal of the Society of Christian Ethics* 37, no. 2 (2017): 21–37, 31.

in understanding sin, particularly social sin, is due largely to the contributions from liberation theologies. They deepen our understanding of the pervasive scope and radical depth of sinful dynamics. Liberation theologies raise important questions regarding the scale of moral evil that should draw our focus and the proper understanding of human agency in relation to larger social and cultural struggles.

Liberation theologies also provide critical insight into the basic categories through which we understand sin. For example, feminist accounts of sin challenge long-standing tendencies to view sin in terms of self-interest or self-assertion. Feminists like Barbara Hilkert Andolsen argue that these accounts of sin reflect men's experience. The corrective to such sin is self-sacrifice understood paradigmatically in terms of Jesus' sacrifice on the cross. Women, feminists argued, struggle less with self-interest and more with forms of self-effacement. Excessive self-sacrifice is not an antidote. As Andolsen puts it, "Women have too often found in practice that Christian self-sacrifice means the sacrifice of women for the sake of men. ... Men have espoused an ethic which they did not practice; women have practiced it to their own detriment."[21] Moreover, while feminist theologies inaugurated important corrections in Christian thinking about sin, womanist and mujerista theologies show that these corrections are themselves in need of further correction. White feminist theology too often neglects the intersection of various forms of oppression and too often has claimed to speak for all women while failing to recognize the very different experiences, needs and assets of women of color.[22]

Liberation theologies show that human beings become selves within fundamentally dysfunctional and vicious ecologies of relationship. There is no "me" that exists apart from my formation within gendered, racist and class dynamics and subsequently chooses whether or how to engage these phenomena. My consciousness and will are already contaminated. In her discussion of white supremacy as a corporate vice, Katie Grimes argues that "the average white person's lack of conscious awareness of their racial actions renders them not innocent but perfectly habituated and entirely culpable."[23] Grimes goes on to say, "The embodied character of both racial habituation and moral actions further underscores the difficulty of reforming the world within without simultaneously reforming the world outside of us."[24]

As our understanding of sin develops in these directions, significant questions arise for other key themes in Christian theology and anthropology. Understanding that we are thrown into a world that malforms us so deeply, what do we make of divine providence? What are our prospects for affirming the goodness of creation when our knowledge of creation is skewed and accounts of creation—particularly human nature—are themselves subject to sin? How does sin thus understood affect our understanding of grace, redemption and sanctification? What does it mean for interpreting Jesus' suffering and death? In general, an account of sin ought not to drive what we may say about other themes and aspects of Christian life. But because liberation theologies are challenging us to rethink the adequacy and acknowledge the complicity of traditional theological categories and

---

[21]Barbara Hilkert Andolsen, "Agape in Feminist Ethics," *Journal of Religious Ethics* 9 (Spring 1981): 69–83, 75.
[22]See Ada María Isasi-Díaz, "Defining Our *Proyecto Histórico: Mujerista* Strategies for Liberation," in *Feminist Ethics and the Catholic Moral tradition*, Readings in Moral Theology 9, ed. Charles E. Curran, Margaret A. Farley and Richard A. McCormick, S.J. (New York: Paulist Press, 1996), 120–35. See also, Traci C. West, *Disruptive Christian Ethics: When Racism and Women's Lives Matter* (Louisville, KY: Westminster John Knox Press, 2006).
[23]Katie Walker Grimes, *Christ Divided: Antiblackness as Corporate Vice* (Minneapolis, MN: Fortress Press, 2017), 101.
[24]Ibid.

claims, we may note that a better understanding of sin can tell us something useful about what redeemed human life looks like.

For instance, in the contemporary theological classic *A Black Theology of Liberation*, James Cone argues that because God has revealed that liberation is the essence of the divine self, it is true to say that God is black.[25] Human redemption therefore involves becoming black like God. Cone's description of redemption disabuses us of any idea that salvation is individual or private. Becoming black like God is surely a *personal* conversion, but it is one of being converted into radical solidarity. However, if it appears that redemption then takes the form of being an ally to black neighbors, caution is in order. Timothy McGee argues that for Cone, white attempts to be in solidarity can simply reinscribe efforts to control and redeem white identity.[26] In the face of Cone's searing disruption of white theology, how should white theologians and predominantly white congregations respond? There may be little theological or ethical recourse left but fresh cries of "Lord, have mercy."

SIN AND THE SUBVERSION OF ETHICS

Christian accounts of sin complement Christian ethics by providing a capacious language for conveying the religious depths of moral failure. But accounts of sin also subvert the work of Christian ethics. As McGee essentially noted in his reading of Cone, ethics tempts us into a concern over our own goodness. When we construe the cultivation of our own goodness as the point of Christian life we neglect or instrumentalize our neighbors in that cause. We also live out a form of bad faith, relying more on our good works than on the grace of God. Scholarship on social sin, and in liberation theology more generally, suggests that concern over the morality of my individual choices is misplaced given the scale of the crises we face, or at least premature if we have failed to reckon with the way individuals are deeply entrenched in and often unreflectively complicit in systems of oppression. It does not follow that personal sins are unimportant and undeserving of moral and religious attention. Advances in our understanding of social sin do, however, make us more accountable for the ways we frame the range of moral concerns and the attention we devote to them in our faith communities and in scholarship.

Sin subverts the work of ethics in a second sense. McFadyen observes that original sin means "our very sense of what is good, right, true—and why—itself participates in and is distorted and disoriented by sin. ... Moral discernment and action may themselves become vehicles and expressions of spiritual disorientation."[27] Theologies of sin centered around the vice of pride or selfishness that reflect men's experience not only exclude and silence the experience of women, but those same theologies are used to legitimate a sexist status quo by encouraging women to interiorize and cooperate with their own subjugation in a patriarchal order. Theologies of sin predicated on an implicit whiteness efface the experiences of black persons and legitimize white supremacist culture. In short, discourse about sin can itself be sinful. Womanist and mujerista theologies of liberation show that ethically motivated endeavors for justice, as in the case of white feminist theology, can replicate and sustain forms of injustice. Put differently, they can be sinfully complicit.

---

[25]James Cone, *A Black Theology of Liberation: Fortieth Anniversary Edition* (Maryknoll, NY: Orbis Books, 2010).
[26]Timothy McGee, "Against (White) Redemption: James Cone and the Christological Disruption of Racial Discourse and White Solidarity," *Political Theology* 18, no. 7 (2017): 542–59.
[27]McFadyen, *Bound to Sin*, 198.

The twofold subversion of ethics is paradoxically good for Christian ethics. A pronounced doctrine of sin can keep us honest about certain aspects of theology and ethics and provides an important way to show the value and viability of Christian theological anthropology. Sin helps us grapple with dimensions of human experience that modern moral discourse cannot adequately capture. It also calls us to critically assess and repent of problematic aspects of traditional theological discourse. Finally, as liberation theologians make explicit, reckoning with sin enlivens and corrects our understanding of redeemed life.

GRACE AND FORGIVENESS

Grace, not sin, is the last word on human persons. Moreover, given the disorientation and confusion about the reality that sin entails, we come to recognize sin *as* sin as God draws us into the dynamics of grace.[28] Like sin, grace is best understood in relational terms. It is not some divine largesse that is earned and stockpiled but a share in God's own life. Grace redeems and sanctifies us by drawing us into and reforming us within the divine life. If sin binds us in an inheritance we do not choose, grace makes freedom truly possible for us. It frees us to love what is truly good.

Christians need to reclaim the discourse of sin as a language of solidarity that is integral to the conditions for and practice of forgiveness.

The knowledge that personal sins are powered by deep-seated, inherited and involuntary faults motivates compassion, helping us to see sinners as the weak and poor and misguided and vainly grasping creatures that sinners actually are. It may even mitigate (without necessarily entirely removing) the desire for punishment or the ways in which we do actually punish—not least by reminding us that sin often functions as its own punishment.[29]

Beyond motivating compassion, the discourse of sin can be deployed in ways that make forgiveness possible. Naming sin *as* sin is essential to telling the truth about the havoc and harm in which we find ourselves entangled, by which we discover ourselves to be corrupted and to which we admittedly contribute through our action and inaction. Such truth-telling is a condition for acknowledge the scope of what needs to be forgiven and the depths of our dependence on grace.

CONCLUSION

Sin complicates our understanding of moral agency and subverts the very enterprise of ethics. It shows us that ethics is too often a vehicle for sin, both as a resource for legitimating what is sinful in our status quo and at times narrowing our moral concern to our own goodness or badness. Paradoxically, the very reasons why a robust doctrine of sin vexes ethical thinking are reasons why sin is good for Christian ethics. Sin is a discourse we can use to foster solidarity rather than division. Reflection on sin is therefore important for larger projects of showing the viability and value of Christian theological anthropology.

---

[28]James Alison, *The Joy of Being Wrong: Original Sin Through Easter Eyes* (New York: Crossroad, 1998).

[29]Couenhoven, *Stricken by Sin*, 223.

SUGGESTED FURTHER READING

Fredriksen, Paula, *Sin: The Early History of an Idea* (Princeton: Princeton University Press, 2012).

Nelson, Derek R., *What's Wrong with Sin: Sin in Individual and Social Perspective from Schleiermacher to Theologies of Liberation* (London: T&T Clark, 2009).

O'Keefe, Mark, *What Are They Saying About Social Sin?* (New York: Paulist Press, 1990).

Rubio, Julie Hanlon, "Moral Cooperation with Evil and Social Ethics," *Journal of the Society of Christian Ethics* 31, no. 1 (Spring/Summer 2011): 103–22.

CHAPTER NINE

The Gift of Grace and the Perfection of Human Nature

SHAWN COLBERG

The Christian notion of grace conveys nothing other than God's love expressed for creation and, especially, humankind. It rests on doctrines of God and Christology, which understand the Trinity as source of all that exists and who, particularly in the Incarnation of the Son, shares God's very self in love with the world. Grace thus expresses God's reality; indeed, one of the most paradigmatic uses of the word of "grace" in scripture is Paul's frequent epistolary greetings: "Grace to you and peace from God our Father and the Lord Jesus Christ" (Rom. 1:7, Gal. 1:3, 2 Cor. 1:2, Phil. 1:2, etc.). Grace flows from the Triune God and the Lordship of Jesus, and it connects persons and communities to God. Just as one cannot therefore speak of grace apart from speaking of Trinity and Christology, one cannot speak of the effects of God's grace apart from human beings as recipients. Theologically, grace acts as connective tissue, integrating the classic topics of systematic theology and expressing through them the human encounter with God.

GRACE IN THE SCRIPTURES

Grace conceptually is diffused throughout the scriptural witness. The bible uses a variety of terms to describe the effect of God's gratuitous love as well as a surfeit of images, narratives and literary genres to convey its effects. In narrower terms, grace in Old Testament is connected to the terms *hēn*/*hānan* and *hesed*, which convey a sense of God's gracious action.[1] *Hānan* connotes kindness or love given freely to another, and it appears some sixty times in the Old Testament with a plurality of instances in the psalms (e.g., Pss. 6:9, 27:7 and 37:21). God as subject shows gracious care to another, frequently someone in significant distress. The psalmist points to God's solidarity with those in need or harm's way (Pss. 9:13 or 51:1). *Hānan* moreover underscores God's sovereign freedom to show favor beyond the confines of human justice; take, for example, God's response to Moses: "I give grace (*hānan*) to whom I please, and I show mercy (*raham*) to whom I please" (Ex. 33:19). Closely related, *hēn* regularly connotes the disposition of graciousness, typically by that of a superior, which is expressed in relationship to another

---

[1] Other less direct but important terms include *rahamim* (tenderness), *'emet* (truth or fidelity) and *sedeq* (justice related to peace).

(1 Sam. 16:22 or 2 Sam. 15:25). *Hēn* thus expresses the quality of love or grace that moves one to be gracious while *hānan* indicates the action of being gracious itself.

If *hānan* and *hēn* convey the quality of gracious love, particularly in reference to the giver, *hesed* captures communal dimensions of grace. Often associated and translated as "mercy," *hesed* also acts as substantive for *hānan*. *Hesed* generally conveys a kind of shared community or covenant in which people show kindness and mercy toward other members (e.g., Gen. 21:23 or 24:29). It is both the cause and the effect of persons being in community; that is, God's *hesed* as gift binds people together, particularly Israel as a chosen people in a covenantal relationship. It cannot be missed, then, that the Torah itself is an expression of God's grace inasmuch as it both binds Israel to God and provides the conditions by which to recognize God's loving kindness. God's *hesed* reveals a steadfast kindness that goes beyond what can be imagined as just within the confines of community or covenant (e.g., 1 Kgs. 20:13, Josh. 2:13 and 1 Sam. 15:6). In response, Israel also uses the language of *hesed* in praise of God: "God's *hesed* endures forever" (Ex. 34:36). Last, those who experience *hesed* must respond; they must remember it, meditate on it and offer praise to God. The gratuity of divine *hesed* thus sets the foundation for a way of life, a life of grace, in which love of God and neighbor constitutes an authentic response to God's kindness.

The New Testament's presentation of grace is varied and rich. The Greek term *charis* is typically translated as grace. *Charis* is not used, however, in Mark's or Matthew's gospels even as both proclaim messages of God's love and mercy. *Charis* enters the Christian lexicon primarily through Paul and those writings attributed to the apostle; of the roughly 150 uses of *charis* in the New Testament, just over 100 of those come from the Pauline corpus. *Charis* in the secular Greek of Paul's time connotes charm, favor or thanks, and while the Septuagint translates *hesed* as *eleos* (mercy) and *hēn* as *charis*, Paul inflects *charis* with new meanings. *Charis* is fundamentally the favor and love of God, which is manifested definitively in Jesus. It reflects forgiveness of sin—the central problematic of salvation history—as well as bestowal of gifts or charisms on its recipients. Paul takes sin seriously both in juridical and anthropological senses. Sin as an act of disobedience brings condemnation and punishment under the law; it is pandemic and universal: "All have sinned and fall short of the glory of God" (Rom. 3:23). God's grace as undeserved favor, made available through the incarnation, life, death and resurrection of Jesus, reconciles the sinner to God. Paul sometimes sets grace as against (1) the power of the law and (2) the power of death (Rom. 3:25 and 6:23), and he highlights such forgiveness as gratuitous, something that cannot possibly be given as a reward for human effort (Rom. 4:4, 11:16 and Gal. 2:31). Ultimately, the "grace and peace" of Jesus liberates its recipients from bondage and death (2 Cor. 3:17), thus opening a new and decisive chapter in salvation history. While God's grace, realized in faith (Rom. 3:22), makes forgiveness of sins possible, it also transforms the believer's outlook and very being. God's *charis* instills a knowledge of Jesus and his riches (Eph. 3:8); it effects "communion" with the Son (1 Cor. 1:9) and the Holy Spirit who endows believers with varied charisms (Gal. 3:3 and Rom. 4:6), especially the gift of charity (Rom. 5:6 and 2 Cor. 8:4). Grace ultimately makes believers adopted sons and daughters of God (Rom. 18:15 and Gal. 4:4). Baptism initiates the life of grace, which is not only a reception of divine favor and gifts but also a commissioning to discipleship or a "new way of living" (Rom. 6:3). Adopted daughters and sons do works of justice (Rom. 8:4) and bear the fruits of the Spirit (Gal. 5:22).

The language of *charis* is more muted outside of Pauline literature. Luke's gospel uses it six times, referring to God's favor in the Hebrew sense of *hēn*. Acts associates *charis* with preaching the gospel (Acts 14:3, 20:24) and believing it (Acts 4:33 and 13:43). The term is used four times in John's gospel, all in the prologue (1:14-17) where grace, as fullness of life, is set against works of the law. The rich synoptic and Johannine traditions of parables in which people are shown mercy, forgiven, healed, empowered to do something or rewarded with further gifts might be fairly said to convey the richness of God's grace in Christ. Take for instance, the gift of talents given to the servants, which empowers them to prepare for the master's return (Mt. 25:14-30/Lk. 19:12-28) or God's free sharing of gifts to the laborers in the vineyard, many of whom are undeserving of the full day's wage (Mt. 20:1-16). Images of Jesus as shepherd, vine and friend indicate the horizon of God's grace as nothing short communion between God and humankind. Finally, if one starts to unpack how the language of love is used throughout the New Testament, one may begin to sense the breadth of grace in its polyvalent meaning and effect.

ANCIENT CHRISTIANITY AND GRACE

Early Christian notions of grace find most fertile soil in the lived praxis of the early church: in discussions of mission; the practices of prayer, baptism and Eucharist; as well as its confrontations with persecution and martyrdom. Ignatius of Antioch uses the language of grace to describe how God equips or disposes Christians for discipleship: "But let me charge you to press on even more strenuously in your course, in all the grace with which you are clothed and to call your people to salvation."[2] In other places, Ignatius will speak of his approaching martyrdom as a grace and one that requires further graces from God to bring it to its end. Grace also has corporate effects, and many early Christians identify the church (*ecclesia*) as the primary locus for sharing in God's grace—whether by hearing the gospel proclaimed, practicing baptism and Eucharist or gathering for social action. Drawing on Paul's sense of grace as charisms for a particular office, writers like Ignatius saw the local bishop as one through whom God's grace flowed to others, uniting them in community.[3] At other points, Ignatius makes important connections between "breaking bread" and the medicine of grace, which makes those who share the meal "immortal." Grace is used to speak of new life with God, and it underwrites the Christian mission, its prayer and worship and its sense of unity in the church.

Early Christological and Trinitarian controversies expanded conceptions of grace. Gnostic Christian movements in the second century challenge Jesus' humanity as well as the fundamental value of material things. Defenses of Christ's full humanity, grounded in language of Incarnation, not only affirm the fundamental goodness of creation and God as creator; they insist that Jesus' humanity graces and thus transforms humankind so that the denial of an incarnate savior imperils the salvation and transformation of humanity. Arguing in favor of Christ's full humanity and against Valentinian Gnosticism, Irenaeus of Lyons reasons that God creates and orders the entire economy as an effect of God's gracious love with the *telos* of human participation in God's own life. The fall complicates this order by introducing corruption of human nature as well as disorder into the economy. Fallen humanity cannot rise of itself in order to pursue the ends that God intends for it. The Word's taking on flesh establishes an "ontological bridge" or

---

[2] Ignatius of Antioch, "Letter to Polycarp," in *Early Christian Writings*, ed. Andrew Louth (London: Penguin, 1968), 109.
[3] See Ignatius, "Letter to the Ephesians," 20.

communication between divinity and humanity that recapitulates human nature and capacitates it for participating in God's life. Irenaeus writes, "The Logos of God became a human being, and the son of God was made Son of man, so that humanity, having received the Logos and accepted adoption, might become Son of God."[4] The Incarnation communicates God's grace as something internal, uncreated and participatory in God's own nature.

The Arian denial of the Son's equality with the Father draws Christians to explore how the Son's full divinity is consequential for salvation and Christian life. Athanasius of Alexandria argues for consonance between God's creation of human nature and its salvation through the Word's Incarnation. God creates *ex nihilo* and through the Word. By virtue of coming from nothing, all things have a natural orientation of return to nothing, and by virtue of coming into being through the Word, all created things share a natural relationship with the agent of their existence. This is especially true of human beings to whom God "bestowed a special grace which other creatures lacked—namely, the impress of his own image, a share in the reasonable being of the very Word Himself."[5] Human beings are created in grace to participate in God's divine life and become increasingly deiform through the right use of their *imago Verbi*. Sin has disastrous effects on human nature. It corrupts the image of the Word in human nature, damaging its capacity to know and love God, and it ultimately turns humanity back toward *nihilo* as its end. Sin also violates divine justice so that sinners deserve punishment. The twofold outcome of progressive corruption and punishment can only be resolved by God, and Athanasius argues that the Word's Incarnation, life, death and resurrection fittingly recreate humanity: "He, indeed, assumed humanity that we might become God. He manifested himself by means of a body in order that we might perceive the Mind of the unseen Father. He endured shame from [human beings] that we might inherit immortality."[6] The grace of the Incarnation exercises an intrinsic and capacitating effect on human nature as well as an extrinsic remission of sin and restoration of justice that establish anew the conditions for a proper relationship between God and human beings.

This historical context of the Christian east and west gives distinctive shape to discussions of grace. In the Christian east, the language of grace is especially linked to that of the Trinity by theologians like the Cappadocians. Receiving grace means experiencing the Trinity—God's very self. Yet if God is fundamentally triune—a communion of persons sharing one dynamic, perichoretic mode of existence—then the human experience of grace is one that flows from the divine persons, beginning in the Father and proceeding through the Son and through the Holy Spirit. Speaking, for example, of Baptism, Basil writes, "How are we saved? Clearly we are regenerated through the grace of baptism. How else? So then knowing that this salvation is established through the Father, and the Son, and the Holy Spirit, should we cast away the 'standard of teaching' we have received"?[7] The experience of the Spirit's power in sacramental action, for Basil, attests to the Spirit's divinity in the Trinity. Gregory of Nyssa similarly stresses the Trinitarian

---

[4]Irenaeus, *Against Heresies*, III, 19, 1, in *The Christological Controversy*, ed. Richard A. Norris (Minneapolis, MN: Fortress, 1980), 55.

[5]Athanasius, *On the Incarnation of the Word*, trans. A Religious of C.S.M.V. (Crestwood, NY: Saint Vladimir's Seminary Press, 1996), 28.

[6]Athanasius, *On the Incarnation*, 93.

[7]Basil the Great, *On the Holy Spirit*, trans. Stephen Hildebrand (Yonkers, NY: St. Vladimir's Seminary Press, 2011), 56.

movement of grace: "But God, who is overall, becomes the Savior of all, while the Son effects salvation by the grace of the Holy Spirit. On account of this they are not named three saviors by Scripture, although salvation is confessed from the holy Trinity."[8] Grace as a sharing in the Trinitarian life is communicated through the sacraments and the liturgy; it capacitates recipients to imitate the incarnate Word, and it culminates in full participation in the divine life, eternal *theosis*.

Latin-speaking Christianity grapples with the sinner's personal liberation from sin against questions raised by Donatism and Pelagianism. Donatism questions the conditions under which sinners might be forgiven and who may participate in the life of the church where grace is mediated. Pelagianism attempts to safeguard God's reliable gift of radical human freedom even from the corruption of sin. Pelagius writes, "We merely try to protect [human nature] from an unjust charge, so that we may not seem to be forced to do evil through a fault in our nature, when, in fact, we do neither good nor evil without the exercise of our will and always have the freedom to do one of the two, being always able to do either."[9] From the Pelagian perspective, grace is auxiliary as opposed to indispensable to human nature. Sources of grace like the gospel or the sacraments fortify nature, which may be impeded but is never wholly incapacitated by sin.

Augustine's views on grace develop over a series of theological engagements with Manicheism, Donatism, Pelagianism, the anti-Massilian controversy and his ministry as bishop. Three vital themes emerge. First, Augustine comes to see that, beginning in the fall, human nature cannot rise without the help of grace; against Pelagius, he writes,

> In the beginning [human] nature was created without any fault and without any sin; however, this human nature in which we are born from Adam now requires a physician, because it is not healthy. Indeed, all the good qualities which it has in its organization, life, senses, and understanding, it possesses from the most high God, its creator and shaper. On the other hand, the defect which darkens and weakens all those natural goods, so that there is need for illumination and healing, is not derived from its blameless maker but from that original sin which was committed through free will.[10]

Augustine preserves a high regard for God's creation of human nature, including its rationality, freedom and sense appetites, and he assigns its corruption to misuse of the free will. His preference for the language of sickness is telling. Sin sickens nature so that it cannot move itself to health. Moreover, human beings rightly deserve punishment for sin and stand condemned in their own right. The need for grace is profound. Second, grace is efficacious for fallen human nature. It both heals and makes a person righteous. Intrinsically, grace "illumines" the intellect through faith, revealing God as ultimate good and end through the saving action of Jesus; it restores the will so that it is capable of loving God in faith. Extrinsically, the saving action of Jesus on the cross—a bloody sacrifice—expiates human sin and liberates sinners from condemnation. Grace is necessarily irresistible; otherwise, the sinner would reject it: "Therefore, this grace, which out of the divine generosity is bestowed secretly in human hearts, is rejected by no

---

[8]Gregory of Nyssa, "Concerning We Should Think of Saying That There Are Not Three Gods, to Ablabius," in *The Trinitarian Controversy*, ed. William G. Rusch (Minneapolis, MN: Fortress, 1980), 123.

[9]Pelagius, "To Demetrias," 8, 4, in *The Letters of Pelagius and His Followers*, trans. B. R. Rees (Woodbridge, ON: Boydell Press, 1991), 29–70.

[10]Augustine, *On Nature and Grace*, in *Four Anti-Pelagian Writings*, The Fathers of the Church, v. 86, trans. John A. Mourant and William Collinge (Washington, DC: Catholic University of America Press, 1992), 24.

one, no matter how hard-hearted he may be. For it is given so that the hardness of heart may first be taken away."[11] The priority and efficacy of divine action is stressed. As grace heals human nature, however, it capacitates it to return to an active and free role in its relationship with God so that Augustine speaks of grace as both operating (*operans*) and cooperating (*cooperans*): "We do in fact work, but when we work, we cooperate with God who works, for his mercy comes before us. It comes before us, however, that we may be healed, as it will also follow, so that, being healed we may gain strength."[12] The effects of grace are progressive; they justify and heal first, and they subsequently fortify the recipient for a life of discipleship and, ultimately, glory. Third, Augustine concludes that grace is provided through divine providence, expressed in the predestination of the elect to glory. Predestination serves as an explanatory tool to preserve the priority of grace and stress God's merciful love. If God initiates the restoration of a sinner through grace as a gift, then God chooses—elects—to give that grace to whom God wills. Augustine calls predestination "preparation for the gift" and grace "the gift itself."[13] His doctrine of predestination stands in conversation with his insistence in the Donatist controversy that one cannot know who God saves or why; thus the church's mission must be focused on ministry to the fallen, acknowledging that God alone and ineffably separates the wheat from the tares at the end of time.

MEDIEVAL CHRISTIANITY AND GRACE

The medieval church in the West wrestles with its reception of Augustine's writings, which are copious and occasional. Exposition of Augustine's thought progresses in works like Anselm's *De Concordia* and Hugh of Saint Victor's *De Sacramentis*. Systemization unfolds in Peter Lombard's *Sentences* and the medieval sentence commentary tradition that followed. For example, both Thomas Aquinas and Bonaventure write extensive sentence commentaries that integrate Augustine's insights into comprehensive accounts of grace and relate systematically to doctrines of God, human anthropology, Christology and the sacraments.

Thomas's mature theology of sanctifying grace (*gratia gratum faciens*) introduces three sets of distinctions, which advance Christian insights into grace. He distinguishes sanctifying grace as habitual and auxilium. Specifically, habitual grace (*gratiae habitualis donum*) pertains to the human form, and it heals and elevates that form, capacitating its habits or virtues as steady dispositions to action. The gift of faith is a habitual grace. Divine auxilium, sometimes referred to as helping, or actual grace, connotes God's application of motion to the human form, which moves persons into action. Inspiration to believe is an effect of auxilium. Using the habitual and helping distinction, Thomas speaks of grace's effects not only as formal created gifts in the soul but also as uncreated and efficient outcomes of God's indwelling and action in the person. Thomas maintains a second critical distinction between intact and fallen human nature. While human beings always stand in need of habitual grace and auxilium in order to reach the supernatural end of eternal life, sin and its consequences complexify the ways in which grace is needed. With

---

[11]Augustine, *On the Predestination of the Saints*, in *Four Anti-Pelagian Writings*, The Fathers of the Church, v. 86, trans. John A. Mourant and William Collinge (Washington, DC: Catholic University of America Press, 1992), 234.

[12]Augustine, *On Nature and Grace*, 48.

[13]See Augustine, *On the Predestination of the Saints*, 241.

its intellect, will and sensual appetites properly ordered to God, intact nature possesses the ability to know and love God, though it still requires the grace of auxilium. Sin corrupts the natural good of human nature so that the sinner cannot do all of the good all of the time. Thomas concludes,

> And therefore in a state of natural integrity a person needs a gratuitous strength superadded to the strength of nature for one reason, namely, in order to do and wish supernatural good. But in the state of corrupt nature [a gratuitous strength superadded to nature is needed] for two reasons, namely, in order to be healed, and ultimately in order to do works of supernatural virtue, which are meritorious.[14]

Thomas thus distinguishes habitual grace as healing (*sanans*) and elevating (*elevans*) both of which are needed to reach union with God. Thomas introduces a third and consequential distinction, reworked from Augustine, between grace as operative and cooperative; he applies these categories to habitual grace and auxilium alike. In those graces where God is the sole active actor and the recipient is simply disposed or moved by the grace, the effect is described as operative. God alone receives credit for its effect so that operative graces are gifts to the recipient. Thomas links operative grace to justification, reconciliation and perseverance. In those graces where God initiates the movement or infuses the gift in such a way that the recipient freely moves or responds to the grace, the effect is described as cooperative. Both God and the human person receive credit for the effect so that, on the human side, the effect is partially a reward. Thomas links cooperative grace to instances of human merit, including growth in charity and eternal life.

Thomas's divisions of grace—into habitual/auxilium, healing/elevating and operative/cooperative—give his account of grace greater flexibility to address a variety of human experiences and biblical accounts of grace. The effects of grace include divine indwelling and motion, created gifts and habits, healing against the sickness of sin, perfection of gifts like faith and charity, gifts that cannot be anticipated and rewards for freely choosing to follow God in love. All of these play vital roles on the journey to union with God. Critically for Thomas, all grace flows through the *missiones ad extra* of the Trinity; it is experienced with reliability through the sacraments; and it ultimately expands the recipient's love for God and others so that union with God is nothing other than participation in the charity, which is the Triune life. Thomas's doctrine of grace rests on a fundamentally Augustinian view of lapsed human nature, but free of the direct engagements with Pelagianism and the anti-Massilian controversies, it understands human nature as never completely destitute of its natural gifts so that even sinners may do some goods. The *imago Dei*, while wounded, is not destroyed and awaits the ever greater expression of divine love in healing grace and justification. Anthropologically, perhaps no Thomist maxim is more important than *gratia non tollit naturam sed perficit*, literally, "grace does not remove nature but perfects it."[15] Sanctifying grace does not displace fallen nature; on the contrary, it heals and perfects what God has begun in creation.

A Franciscan school of theology, beginning in Bonaventure but coming into much sharper focus in Duns Scotus and William Ockham, stresses the free will as definitive of human nature. Arguing that the will's contingency is not lost through the fall, late medieval Franciscan theology identifies a wider scope of action for the sinner

---

[14]Thomas Aquinas, *Summa theologiae* (*ST*), I–II:109, 2. Translations of the *Summa theologiae* are mine and are taken from *Summa theologiae*, 5 vols. (Ottawa: Impensis Studii generalis OP, 1941–5).
[15]Aquinas, *ST*, I:1, 8 ad.2.

in justification; habitual grace is indispensable, but the sinner freely seeks it and, so, cooperates in his justification. This cooperation opens wider conceptual space for sinners to merit justification and, in the state of grace, to merit a broader field of divine rewards from God. Martin Luther encounters this model of grace in his magisterial studies of Gabriel Biel, and later, he engages theologies of grace, which affirm robust cooperation and merit in interlocutors like John Eck and Erasmus of Rotterdam.

REFORMATION AND MODERN CHRISTIANITY ON GRACE

Luther's theology of grace, like those who come before him, is rooted in the practices and context of his own time. His engagements with Paul and Augustine, unrestricted by the forms of scholastic theology, equip him to confront the "localization" of divine grace in things like indulgences, fasting, monastic vows or private masses, all of which tended to trace their *ratio* back to the church as means of grace. Luther refocuses grace on God as primary actor in human salvation and sinners as powerless to effect their own justification even as they stand condemned under the law. Luther is particularly pessimistic on the status of the free will; he writes,

> You, who imagine the human will as something standing on neutral ground and left to its own devices, find it easy to imagine also that there can be an endeavor of the will in either direction, because you think of both God and the devil as a long way off, and as if they were only observers of that mutable free will; for you do not believe that they are the movers and inciters of a servile will, and engaged in the most bitter conflict with one another.
>
> ... For either the kingdom of Satan means nothing, and then Christ must be a liar, or else, if his kingdom is as Christ describes it, free choice must be nothing but a captive beast of burden for Satan, which can only be set free if the devil is cast out by the finger of God.[16]

Luther's anthropology begins from the premise that the human will is servile and originally held captive by God, but it is subsequently enslaved by the devil who maintains control until God reclaims the sinner through the saving work of Christ accessed through faith in the gospel promises. Justification is therefore less concerned with the healing and elevation of the will than receiving Christ's righteousness which frees sinners from condemnation and focuses them on the gospel; this is the will's experience of evangelical freedom.

For Luther, grace is fundamentally experienced through an encounter with the gospel, particularly by hearing the Word of God. After learning of one's condemnation under the law, the gospel proclaims the promise of salvation and new life through the saving action of Jesus on the cross. Luther writes,

> To preach Christ means to feed the soul, make it righteous, set it free, and save it, provided it believes the preaching. Faith alone is the saving and efficacious use of the Word of God, according to Rom. 10: "If you confess with our lips that Jesus is Lord and believe in your heart that God raised him from the dead, you will be saved."[17]

---

[16]Martin Luther, *On the Bondage of the Will*, in *Luther and Erasmus: Free Will and Salvation*, ed. Gordon Rupp (Philadelphia, PA: Westminster Press, 1969), 284.

[17]Martin Luther, *Freedom of a Christian*, in *Martin Luther, Selections from His Writings*, ed. John Dillenberger (New York: Anchor Books, 1962), 52.

When one believes the good news of the gospel, one receives the grace of forgiveness, of freedom from the law and of a new relationship in Christ. Grace is treated in largely extrinsic terms: it is experienced through hearing; it declares the believer righteous; and it remits the punishment for sins. Sacramental action is similarly defined by its word of gospel promise and its external sign, which elicit the recipient's response in faith. Grace is not infused into the recipient by a habitual gift; it is possessed as Christ's own righteousness that covers the recipient, making her *simul justus et peccator*—simultaneously just and sinner. Importantly, this does not necessarily mean that there is no internal regeneration of the believer's nature; the opportunity remains for growth in holiness as a fruit of faith. Luther speaks poignantly of the relationship between Christ and the believer:

> The third incomparable benefit of faith is that it unites the soul with Christ as a bride is united with her bridegroom. By this mystery, as the Apostle teaches, Christ and the soul become one flesh. And if they are one flesh and there is between them a true marriage ... it follows that everything they have they hold in common, the good as well as the evil.[18]

In terms of grace, however, Luther stresses faith as a gift from God, which justifies and necessarily precedes any truly good work. There is nothing to be merited because all has been given by grace even as Christians live robust and saintly lives as "fruits" of the faith they have received.

While Luther's theology establishes the grounds for Reformation debates on grace, justification and human salvation, John Calvin and the Council of Trent also make decisive contributions. Calvin shares Luther's commitment to justification by grace alone through hearing and believing the Word of God, and sets it into a larger theological system. Working from Augustine's strong emphasis on the gratuity of the first grace, Calvin situates justifying grace into a larger framework of divine sovereignty and predestination of the elect. He also takes a wider view on the effects of grace, seeing them, at least at times, as intrinsically regenerative. The Council of Trent's "Decree on Justification" responds to Protestant positions by upholding the sinner's inability to anticipate or cause the grace of justification while simultaneously affirming that the will retains the ability to reject God's offer of grace:

> They, who by sins were alienated from God, may be disposed through God's quickening and helping grace, to convert themselves to their own justification, by freely assenting to and co-operating with that said grace, so that, while God touches the heart of [the person] by the illumination of the Holy Spirit, so that [the person] neither does absolutely nothing while receiving that inspiration, since he can also reject it, nor yet is he able by his own free will and without the grace of God to move himself to justice in God's sight.[19]

Many interpreters of the decree see affirmation, following Thomas, of the necessity of prevenient habitual grace and auxilium even as the decree carves out a robust argument in favor of human merit following justification. Others, following a more Franciscan position, favor the decree's stress on the recipient "converting themselves," which seems to imply free human action even before justification. In addition to stressing the power

---

[18]Luther, *Freedom of a Christian*, 60.
[19]Council of Trent, Sixth Session, "Decree on Justification," in *The Canons and Decrees of the Council of Trent*, trans. H. J. Schroeder (Charlotte, NC: TAN Books, 1978), 31–2.

of grace, Trent identifies faith as the "beginning of human salvation, the foundation and root of all justification" and the necessity of meritorious works by the justified in order to obtain the reward of eternal life.

Questions about the interaction between grace and the free will give rise to Catholic nature-grace debates in the *De Auxiliis* controversy and in conflicts over Jansenism. In the late sixteenth century, the Jesuit Luis de Molina held that God's grace becomes effective through the recipient's free cooperation, which is foreknown by God. The Dominican Domingo Báñez sought to preserve God's transcendence and the operative character of prevenient grace, against Molina, arguing that God's grace necessarily transforms the sinner's will *so that* it may cooperate with God. It is possible to see the protracted *De Auxiliis* conflict rooted in the balance sought by Trent between the priority of operative grace and the freedom of the will; moreover, both sides claimed a definitive reading of Augustine. Similar questions and interpretations of Augustine persisted in the Jansenist controversies—arising from the posthumous publication of *Augustinus* by Cornelius Jansen—which questioned the depravity of the will and necessity of divine election. Jansenism stressed the operative character of divine predestination along with a conviction that only perfect contrition through rigorous penance made justification and salvation possible. Here again, ambiguity about the free will's acceptance and use of grace fuel the controversy. Jansenism at times engaged Calvinist questions on predestination and freedom of the will, which underscored parallel debates in early-modern Reformed Protestantism. Arminianism resisted Reformed accounts of double-predestination and the irresistibility of grace, and while it affirmed the total depravity of fallen nature, it argued that human freedom was vital to grace's effects in the recipient. Condemned by Dutch Calvinism, it exercised important influence on Wesleyan Christianity and Methodism where a more positive view of human freedom open spaces for the language of human perfection that marks certain pietist movements.

The twentieth century also includes significant nature-grace debates. In Roman Catholic theology, Henri De Lubac advances the conversation with two essential claims: (1) God gives grace freely and (2) human beings possess within themselves a natural desire for God's grace. De Lubac's work importantly resists a sense of a "duplex ordo" where human nature is entirely separate from divine or uncreated nature; his argument for a natural desire for grace holds the natural and supernatural in more integrated tension. Karl Rahner reframes these theses by arguing that, ontologically, there exists in human beings a "supernatural-existential" that constitutes an openness to God as the absolute horizon of being and is given to human beings as a supernatural (elevating) gift of grace. Rahner's insistence on the gratuity of the supernatural-existential preserves God's freedom against any sense that God owes grace to human beings on account of an entirely natural desire for God. De Lubac and Rahner speak of grace in uncreated terms—as an encounter with God in human history, and their theology marks an important anthropological "shift to the subject" so that grace is known in a person's concrete experience. Christ and church constitute primary and reliable *loci* of grace, but they do not exhaust the grace of God moving in the world. Vatican Council II extends the vision of God at work in human history. The language of grace is everywhere present in the conciliar texts both in traditional statements of grace as prevenient, healing and perfecting as well as in affirmations of grace as participation in God's life through the indwelling of the Holy Spirit. One area of emphasis at the Council is the ecclesial dimensions of grace: "[The Holy Spirit] distributes special graces among the faithful of every rank. By these gifts He makes them fit and ready to undertake the various tasks and offices which contribute toward the renewal and building up of the Church."[20] The Council also places grace at the foundation of its universal call to holiness:

> The followers of Christ are called by God, not because of their works, but according to His own purpose and grace. They are justified in the Lord Jesus, because in the baptism of faith they truly become sons [and daughters] of God and sharers in the divine nature. In this way they are really made holy. Then too, by God's gift, they must hold on to and complete in their lives this holiness they have received.[21]

The Council's call adds direction to discussions of grace, raising questions about its historical and social character—something taken up in *Gaudium et spes*.

CONTEMPORARY FRONTIERS IN GRACE

Ecumenical dialogue has used conceptions of grace to achieve broader areas of dogmatic and pastoral agreement. Nowhere is this more evident than in the "Joint Declaration on Justification" (1999). The fruit of decades of dialogue between Lutheran and Catholic dialogue teams, and now cosigned by many of the mainline Protestant churches, its common statement reads, "Together we confess: By grace alone, in faith in Christ's saving work and not because of any merit on our part, we are accepted by God and receive the Holy Spirit, who renews our hearts while equipping and calling us to good works."[22] Convergence on the gratuity, priority and effects of grace made agreement possible on perhaps the most divisive theological point of the Protestant and Catholic Reformations, and it has opened ecumenism to convergence on grace-related topics including the nature of the church, sacraments and authority.

The language of grace has found fertile ground and opportunity for constructive growth in theologies of liberation, which underscore the freeing power of God's grace. Grace liberates persons *from* sin, both personal and social, even as it frees them *for* a new life in Christ that seeks the renewal of all creation. Theologies of liberation often understand sin as a retreat from communion with God and others; God gives grace to empower recipients to engage with the social-political processes of human history in order to build communion, particularly through doing justice for the marginalized. The language of liberation and justice places grace and theological anthropology squarely at the heart of present-day political theologies and social ethics. Moreover, it understands that a "doctrine of grace" cannot be a closed system of reflection but instead must value human praxis as revelatory. An appreciation of the presence of grace in everyday experience has cultivated new perspectives on the experience of women, persons in non-dominant cultures, and others who find themselves at the margins of normative definitions of human nature and experience. Latin American liberation theology's demand that Christians "do justice for the neighbor" as a response to God's gracious action in Christ and feminist critiques of ways of knowing provide new and productive space for exploring the relationship between grace and human nature, the challenges of

---

[20]Vatican Council II, *Lumen Gentium*, 12, in *Vatican II: The Conciliar and Post-Conciliar Documents*, ed. Austin Flanner (Northrup, NY: Costello, 1992).

[21]Vatican Council II, *Lumen Gentium*, 40.

[22]The Lutheran World Federation and the Roman Catholic Church, *Joint Declaration on the Doctrine of Justification* (Grand Rapids, MI: Eerdmans, 2000), 3.5. Cosigners now include the World Methodist Council (2006), the World Communion of Reformed Churches (2017) and the Anglican Communion (2017).

personal and social sin, the role of human freedom in human salvation and the political dimensions of the graced if Christian life.

CONCLUSION

Doctrines of grace share a certainty that God's love is gratuitous and fecund, freely branching out in diverse ways in the world. It has extrinsic effects, making God's favor available in events and created gifts, and it also acts intrinsically, transforming and perfecting person and the world, making of them "new creations" (2 Cor. 5:17). Similarly, grace is sometimes given as wholly unmerited favor—love from God entirely outside of the economy of exchange—while at other times, God responds to free human action—a response that follows God's sapiential ordering of the cosmos as something like a reward for human action. While theologies of grace thus share a common witness to "God the Father and the Lord Jesus Christ" who share love through the Holy Spirit, they diversify themselves according to their systems of classification, decided points of emphasis and historical context. The long history of nature-grace debates could suggest seemingly insoluble "problems," especially on the nexus between divine initiative and human freedom. On the other hand, the sheer breadth of God's loving action in the world transcends closed systems and definitions of grace, requiring that theologians and believers engage grace as a polyvalent symbol that names but far from exhausts the mystery of God, who in love graces the world.

SUGGESTED FURTHER READING

Boff, Leonardo, *Liberating Grace* (trans. John Drury; Maryknoll, NY: Orbis Books, 1979).
Dreyer, Elizabeth, *Manifestations of Grace* (Collegeville, MN: Liturgical Press, 1990).
Duffy, Stephen, *The Dynamics of Grace: Perspectives in Theological Anthropology* (Collegeville, MN: Liturgical Press, 1993).
Oakes, Edward T., *A Theology of Grace in Six Controversies* (Grand Rapids, MI: Eerdmans, 2016).
Spezzano, Daria, *The Glory of God's Grace: Deification According to Saint Thomas Aquinas* (Ave Maria, FL: Sapientia Press, 2015).

CHAPTER TEN

Human Freedom and the Triune God

PHILIP ROSSI, SJ

The theological articulation of the structure, operation and significance of human freedom offered in this chapter takes its orientation from the Christian proclamation of faith in the triune God. It proposes an account of the theological intelligibility of human freedom referenced to the personal God professed in the Christian creed as Creator, Redeemer and Sanctifier of humanity and the cosmos. In this account, the triune God stands, first, as the graciously originating and sustaining enactor of human freedom and of the world in which freedom is exercised; second, as the transformative healer of the self-incurred brokenness of human freedom and of the consequences such brokenness brings upon the world; and, third, as the abiding enlivener of the fullness of communion with God to which human freedom in history is oriented for eschatological completion. Human freedom, as an element of "the image of God" in which humanity is created (Gen. 1:17), is formed, in its origin and exercise, in reference to God's triune relationality as Creator, Redeemer and Sanctifier. The intelligibility of human freedom thus derives from this fundamental creedal and theological given: Humanity, human freedom and the cosmos as historical locus for the enactment of human freedom, all stand, in their origin, ordering and final destiny, in enduring relation to God's triune relationality. Human freedom originates from the triune God, from, in and by whom it is faithfully sustained in society and history, and to whom it is directed for completion in lasting personal communion.[1]

Situating the intelligibility of human freedom in relation to the triune personal God and envisioning its completion in personal communion with God presents a strong contrast to prevailing accounts of freedom offered in many strands of Western philosophy in an era of secularity. These accounts do not reference the intelligibility of freedom to humanity's relation to a transcendent personal god, nor to a deeply rooted human sociality ordered to completion in personal communion. Freedom is referenced, instead, to the subjectivity of individual human agency as it bears upon human action in the world. These accounts take human freedom to be fully explicable by intra-mundane principles that do not require reference to a transcendent origin of human agency nor to the ordering of freedom to the good of mutuality and communion. These principles constitute, instead, an "immanent frame" of meaning: A set of interlocking cosmic, social and moral orders

---

[1] See Libreria Editrice Vaticana, *Catechism of the Catholic Church* (Washington, DC: United States Conference of Catholic Bishops, 1997), #357: "Being in the image of God the human individual is capable of self-knowledge, of self-possession and of freely giving himself and entering into communion with other persons."

providing self-sufficient explanations of the natural, social and historical world in which humanity has emerged.[2] Correlative to this immanent frame is a model of a "disengaged" self that encloses human understanding in atomistic subjectivity. This model overlooks the relational context framing our human capacity for self-interpretation and foreshortens the horizon of freedom to "choice" exercised over heterogeneous fields of incommensurable preferences. It places human and divine freedom in "zero-sum" competition, a dynamic in stark contrast to the inexhaustible self-giving that this chapter sees constituting the living relationality from which God brings forth human freedom.[3] This dynamism of relationality, inscribed into the radical dependence of otherness in which God brings forth creation, situates human freedom as a fundamental feature of the socially embedded character of human reality. Human freedom is neither disengaged nor self-enclosed in a field of atomistic transactions; it is structurally situated, instead, within a relationality of mutual recognition. This relationality, which constitutes us as moral agents with respect to one another, arises from our creation in the image of God and finds its completion in personal communion with God.[4]

THEOLOGICAL ORIENTATIONS ON HUMAN FREEDOM: SCRIPTURAL, HISTORICAL, AND STRUCTURAL HORIZONS

This section charts the frame of reference that the triune relationality of Creator, Redeemer and Sanctifier constitutes for the intelligibility of human freedom from the vantage point of three fields of theological discourse, providing general orientations upon the engagement of God's relationality with human freedom. The three following sections then specify the role each term of Trinitarian relationality, Creator, Redeemer and Sanctifier, has in rendering human freedom intelligible.

Three fields of discourse provide this section's mapping of the coordinates of a Trinitarian frame of reference for the intelligibility of human freedom: (1) the scriptural/narrative orientation; (2) the historical/experiential orientation; and (3) the conceptual/structural orientation. They mark a complementary set of interpretive perspectives on human freedom, its origin and healing renewal in God's triune graciousness, and on the ordering of its operations to completion in life-giving communion. These orientations serve to articulate coordinates proper to each of the Trinitarian terms and to locate

---

[2]Charles Taylor, *A Secular Age* (Cambridge, MA: The Belknap Press of Harvard University, 2007), provides an account of the emergence of secularity's "immanent frame" as a self-sufficient order of explanation for human self-understanding and freedom; see especially chapter 6, "Providential Deism," 221–69; chapter 7, "The Impersonal Order," 270–95; and chapter 15, "The Immanent Frame," 549–93. Two related accounts of the modern disengagement of human freedom from personal relationality with a transcendent God are: Michael J. Buckley, *At the Origins of Modern Atheism* (New Haven: Yale University Press, 1987), and Louis Dupré, *Passage to Modernity: An Essay in the Hermeneutics of Nature and Culture* (New Haven: Yale University Press, 1993).

[3]Elizabeth A. Johnson, *Quest for Living God: Mapping Frontiers in the Theology of God* (New York: Continuum, 2007), 16. Johnson, commenting on the contrast between "modern theism" (which is arguably a conceptual sibling to the "immanent frame") and contemporary theologies of God, puts this point trenchantly: "Reclaiming radical transcendence and radical immanence in equal measure rather than opposing them in a zero-sum game, contemporary theologies view the unknowable God as the very Ground not only of the world's existence but of its fragmentary flourishing and hope against brokenness."

[4]Cf. Walter Kasper, *The Christian Understanding of Freedom and the History of Freedom in the Modern Era*, The 1988 Père Marquette Lecture in Theology (Milwaukee: Marquette University Press, 1988), 41: "Human freedom finds its completion by accepting the love of God and affirming freedom among human persons."

points linking these coordinates into a framework delimiting the intelligibility of human freedom.

The Scriptural/Narrative Orientation

The first field of discourse, the scriptural/narrative orientation, encompasses the linguistic and literary expressions in which Scripture recounts the overarching patterns of the engagement of God's triune relationality with human freedom. These texts present this engagement unfolding from the "original grace" of creation.[5] It is this unfolding that establishes human freedom's relation with the transcendent personal God from whom it originates, and places humanity and the world into a finite relationality of radical dependence upon its Creator. Human freedom's placement within the finite relationality of creation is contextual: The structures and practices of human sociality, providing the social bonding formative of the life of human communities, form the concrete context of finite relationality for human freedom. This contextuality of human freedom is located in particular communities, a condition that Charles Taylor designates as "situated freedom,"[6] and it provides a fundamental coordinate for the intelligibility of freedom as exercised in that community. It imparts a particular social and historical shape to the human freedom in that community in virtue of the "social imaginary"[7] in which its practices are constituted and construed.

This fundamental role of relationality as a concrete matrix for the theological intelligibility of human freedom can be discerned within the narrative arc of Scripture. God's initial and renewed enactments of relationality in the mutuality of covenantal freedom constitute and sustain a people of God throughout Scripture's narrative. Constituted as a people, they become a locus for divine fidelity to empower human freedom for patterns of living as a community responsive to God's covenantal enactments. As the narrative arc of Scripture unfolds, one observes a pattern of freedom with a salvific dynamic as its organizing motif. Though set in motion by the self-deflection of human freedom from its ordering to communion (a self-deflection unflinchingly recounted in Israel's subsequent narrative), this dynamic in the end lovingly restores and elevates that freedom through the incarnate outpouring of divine graciousness in Jesus' life, death and resurrection.

This salvific dynamic of God's incarnation in Jesus provides a central locus for discerning key elements of the engagement of God's triune relationality with human freedom. Within that narrative, God's relationality engages human freedom in gathering and sustaining a community to continue the mission of Jesus, constituted in the power of his Spirit as locus for the healing, restoration and elevation of human freedom in history.

---

[5]See David B. Burrell, "Creation as Original Grace," *God, Grace, and Creation*, ed. P. J. Rossi, (Maryknoll, NY: Orbis Books, 2010), 97–106, on how Creation may be construed as "grace" in its very origin from God's abundant freedom.

[6]Charles Taylor, *Sources of the Self: The Making of the Modern Identity*, (Cambridge: Cambridge University Press, 1989), 515; Charles Taylor, *Hegel and Modern Society* (Cambridge: Cambridge University Press, 1979), 168: such situatedness comprises a "vision of embodied subjectivity, of thought and freedom emerging from the stream of life, finding expression in forms of social existence and discovering themselves in relation to nature and history."

[7]Taylor defines a "social imaginary" as "the ways in which [people] imagine their social existence, how they fit together with others, how things go on between them and their fellows, the expectations which are normally met, and the deeper normative notions and images that underlie these expectations" (*Secular Age*, 171). See *Secular Age*, chapter 4, "Modern Social Imaginaries"; and Charles Taylor, *Modern Social Imaginaries* (Durham: Duke University Press, 2004), for detailed discussions.

Remembrance and attention to the scriptural narrative of the unfailing fidelity of divine freedom shape a community made capable of exercising human freedom to enact healing and elevation for all—but most especially among the neediest and the most vulnerable.

The Historical/Experiential Orientation

The second field, the historical/experiential orientation, delimits the concrete interactions in which human freedom is invited to engage God's triune relationality. In continuity with the narrative trajectory of Scripture, this field gives concrete shape to freedom working in history. It provides horizons for discerning markers of the engagement of God's triune relationality with the structure and dynamics of human freedom at work in concrete human experience. Within this historical orientation, the narrative of Scripture provides markers memorializing key events of the engagement of human and divine freedom such as Israel's exodus and its paschal fulfillment in Jesus. These offer an orientation for measuring present and future engagements of human freedom with divine freedom. They also encompass the lives of those who, in full consonance with being in the image of God, abundantly enact good in self-giving service for peace, justice, reconciliation, compassion and mercy—that is, the saints.[8] Within the ambit of this historical/experiential orientation, human freedom is most manifest in holiness.

While the shape and direction of the paradigmatic engagements of divine and human freedom is expressed in the narrative of Scripture, its subsequent enactments occur in an expansive field of human freedom operating within the historical relationality of community, culture and creation. Within this field, as in Scripture, engagements of divine and human freedom are marked by all aspects of divine triune relationality. As Originating Creator and Sustainer, as Incarnate Redeemer and as Sanctifying Spirit, God's freedom engages human freedom in multiple modes—for example, invitation, support, inspiration, enlightenment, empowerment, consolation, healing—that can be gathered together as "grace." Located within this all-encompassing field of freely offered divine activity sustaining creation, human freedom is drawn to its completion in a divine "gracing" of creation that goes "all the way down."

The horizon upon human freedom delimited from the historical/experiential orientation provides an important conceptual and imaginative background to a long-standing point of contention over the import and intelligibility of human freedom. This contention centers on how properly to understand human freedom in relation to the freely bestowed presence and activity of God in creation that Christian theology terms "grace." There are currents within the long stream of Christian theological reflection that place God's freedom in enacting grace in deep tension with and, at times, even in opposition to human freedom in the manner of a zero-sum game. David Burrell provides an alternative to this strongly contrastive view; he proposes that the whole of creation stands constituted in the "original grace" by which God brings it to be.[9] The working of

---

[8]Cf. Vatican Council II, *Gaudium et Spes*, in Austin Flannery, OP (ed.), *Vatican II: The Conciliar and Post-Conciliar Documents* (Northrup, NY: Costello, 1992), #17: "Only in freedom can man direct himself toward goodness ... For its part, authentic freedom is an exceptional sign of the divine image within man."

[9]Burrell provides detailed historical and conceptual articulations of this in *Knowing the Unknowable God* (Notre Dame, IN: University of Notre Dame Press, 1986), *Freedom and Creation in Three Traditions* (Notre Dame, IN: University of Notre Dame Press, 1993) and *Towards a Jewish-Christian-Muslim Theology* (Chichester: Wiley-Blackwell, 2011), chapters 1–3. Also pertinent is Karl Rahner's succinct discussion, "Radical Dependence and Genuine Autonomy," in *Foundations of Christian Faith*, trans. William V. Dych, (New York: Seabury Press,

original grace is never absent, nor lacking in creation: Gracing goes all the way down in the creation God has brought to be and faithfully sustains. Human freedom, as created, thus functions within the original grace constitutive of creation.[10] The grace of creation provides the possibility of human freedom as a freely bestowed gift; its gifted origin sets the horizon for its orientation and exercise.

The Conceptual/Structural Orientation

The third field, the conceptual/structural orientation, encompasses human capacities providing the linguistic and imaginative spaces for articulating in discourse and practice the ideational shape, the syntactical structure and the conceptual limits of the intelligibility we encounter and construct in the world. Within Western intellectual traditions, setting parameters for the spaces of articulacy has often been considered primarily the task of philosophy. In a contemporary culture that often faults philosophy for its abstractness, this task may be better characterized as "theoretical": the task of identifying, expressing and articulating the conceptual/linguistic distinctions fundamental for "making sense" of the world and our human engagement with it.[11]

The theoretical horizon for "making sense of the world" provides general conceptual and linguistic working space in which theological inquiry articulates distinctions appropriate for understanding the engagements of divine and human freedom. This task begins with these engagements as concretely presented within the horizons of the scriptural/narrative and the historical/experiential orientations. They provide material for posing a key conceptual/structural question: What features for rendering human and divine freedom intelligible can be discerned in the patterns and working of their engagements? Within this theoretical horizon lie possibilities for theology to initiate dialogue on human freedom with other modes of human inquiry, for example, philosophy, psychology, history, sociology and political science, concerned with rendering human freedom intelligible from their specific horizons of articulacy.

THEOLOGICAL ORIENTATIONS ON HUMAN FREEDOM: TRINITARIAN COORDINATES

The previous section charted three fields of theological discourse—the scriptural/narrative, the historical/experiential, and the conceptual/structural—that orient horizons from which to identify and articulate the Trinitarian coordinates framing the theological intelligibility of human freedom. The three divisions in this section will now identify coordinates that are proper to each term of Trinitarian relationality—God as Creator, Redeemer and Sanctifier—and will articulate their function in rendering human freedom intelligible.

1978), 78–9, on behalf of the claim that the radical dependence constitutive of creation grounds genuine human autonomy.

[10]This suggests that creation is persistently and pervasively "graced," such that it cannot be "un-graced"; such "un-gracing" would be nothing other than its "erasure."

[11]Robert Sokolowski, "The Method of Philosophy: Making Distinctions," *Review of Metaphysics* 51 (1998): 515–32, argues that "making distinctions" constitutes the most fundamental way of "doing philosophy."

God as Creator: Bestowing Finitude as Space for Human Freedom

The first coordinates reference the activity of God as Creator. As Creator, God graciously brings forth and sustains all that is, a totality God sees and pronounces good in its entirety. Within that totality of divine seeing and pronouncement of "being good," human freedom is brought into being both as integral to human activity and as "image of god." In bringing forth creation, God provides the field of finitude in which, upon which and for which human freedom is empowered to function for enacting good.

The narrative horizon of the book of Genesis, especially chs. 1–11, depicts the abundance of God's creation as the field of finitude provided humanity, empowered in freedom to enact good, as space for its life and activity. In this divinely bestowed space, consisting of the interrelated fields of persons, relations and objects pronounced good in God's efficacious seeing, human freedom is empowered to govern action for the enacting of good. This empowerment, bestowed as an element of the image of God, orients freedom in accord with the abundant and enduring enactment of good constituted in God's creating and sustaining all that is.

Three elements in the space creation provides for human freedom mark important coordinates for rendering human freedom, precisely as created, theologically intelligible. First, the finitude of human freedom and the created world as the field of its exercise; second, the orientation of human freedom to the enactment of good in accord with humanity's creation in the image of God; third, the fundamental relation between the limitless abundance of divine freedom, from which created freedom has its origin, and created human freedom, which has the finitude of creation as field for its enactment. This last is the most conceptually challenging of the elements to articulate. It requires determining the character of this relation in a way that properly respects the radical difference between the Creator and creation, without diminishing or distorting the freedom proper to each. Characterizing this relation has to recognize the singular radicality of the difference between God's freedom and created freedom—but recognizing the singularity of that difference cannot thereby result in placing their engagement with one another within creation into a zero-sum competition pitting human and divine freedom against one another.[12]

As an element of the theological intelligibility of human freedom, finitude marks, in the first instance, the radical dependence of freedom as created upon the abundance of God's self-giving. In its dependence, human freedom is ordered in consonance both with the finitude of creation as field for its enactment and with "the image of God" that orients it for the enactment of good. This radical dependence on God's self-giving marks human freedom as itself an enactment of the "original grace" of creation.[13] Construed as original grace, creation comes entirely from the divine activity with which God, in uncompelled divine freedom, *both* brings the world—all that is, has been and will be as other than God—into being as good *and* sustains that goodness in its otherness from God. With respect to God's originating activity of creating, finitude marks *the radical dependence that constitutes one precisely as creature.*[14] In consequence, even though

---

[12]Burrell, following Kathryn Tanner, calls such an appropriate characterization 'non-contrastive'. See Burrell, *Towards a Jewish-Christian-Muslim Theology*, 57.

[13]Burrell, "Creation as Original Grace"; see also *Towards a Jewish-Christian-Muslim Theology*, 51–61.

[14]For an astute moral/religious phenomenology of radical dependence, see H. Richard Niebuhr, *The Responsible Self* (New York: Harper & Row, 1966), chapter 3, "Responsibility in Absolute Dependence," 108–26.

finitude constitutes a "limit," this is neither deficit nor lack. Instead, it marks the good that constitutes each and every element that God brings to be and sustains—including human freedom—in its creaturely identity. Human freedom, as created, functions properly in virtue of its finitude and as image of God by enacting good within the space of finitude that constitutes creaturely identity.[15]

The space that creation provides for human freedom to enact good in creaturely finitude serves, moreover, as the field from which to articulate two other coordinates that creation provides for the intelligibility of human freedom: the orientation of human freedom to the enactment of good; and the fundamental relation between created human freedom and the divine freedom from which created freedom has its origin. Both coordinates stand in structural proximity to each other, with the fundamental relation between divine freedom and created human freedom as personal standing as the locus from which human freedom is oriented and empowered for the enactment of good. The divine activity that expresses God's self-giving freedom provides a horizon of grace that is *personal* with respect both to the origin of human freedom and to its enactment within the finitude of the world. Human freedom has its origin within the dynamics of a mutuality of persons that arises from God's original gracing of human freedom in the image of God, a gracing that is oriented in the space of created human finitude to the constitutive mutuality of human persons.[16]

Human freedom thus engages grace both in the structure of its empowerment to enact good and its concrete enactments of good in a created world of mutuality. It encounters grace, in the first instance, in the very constitutive ordering with which freedom structures human agency and human personhood as image of God for the enacting of good in creation: Human freedom, along with all creation, has its origin from the uncoerced, abundant self-giving of a personal God. Standing within the ambit of the original grace of creation, that is, the originating empowerment issuing abundantly from divine freedom, human created freedom's enactment of good in the created space of finitude also stands fully within the ambit of God's *sustaining* empowerment of creation.

Inasmuch as it also stands within the ambit of God's sustaining empowerment of creation, human freedom's enactment of good as image of God provides a point of reference for articulating the second set of coordinates from which Trinitarian relationality serves as the locus for the intelligibility of human freedom. In the activity of God as Incarnate Redeemer, human freedom is elevated to participate in the sustaining, healing and elevation of a broken creation. As Incarnate Redeemer, the God who enters into the full condition of finite human freedom enables it to bring its agency to bear upon the transformative healing of the brokenness of the world that was consequent upon the self-deflection of human freedom from its orientation to the enactment of good.

---

[15]Cf. Karl Rahner, "Thoughts on the Possibility of Belief Today," *Theological Investigations V: Later Writings*, trans. Karl-H. Kruger (Baltimore: Helicon, 1966), 12: "For a really Christian doctrine of the relationship of the world to God, the autonomy of the creature does not grow in inverse but in direct proportion to the degree of the creature's dependence on, and belonging to, God."

[16]See Kasper, *The God of Jesus Christ*, trans. Matthew J. O'Connell (New York: Crossroad, 1994), 152–7, and John D. Zizioulas, *Communion and Otherness* (London: T&T Clark, 2006), 161–70, for succinct treatments linking Trinitarian relationality, divine freedom and human freedom as personal, and the communion issuing from love as freedom and from freedom as love.

God as Incarnate Redeemer: The Divine Enfleshment of Human Freedom and Finitude, for the Healing of Human and Cosmic Brokenness

The second set of coordinates for the intelligibility of human freedom proper to the terms of Trinitarian relationality are located in reference to the activity of God as Incarnate Redeemer. As Incarnate Redeemer, God is the One who, as Godself entering into human finitude and into the brokenness that humanity inflicted upon itself and the world, redemptively heals and transforms that brokenness, and thereby elevates the field for the working of human freedom toward full completion in personal communion with the triune God. The key points of these coordinates that are referenced to God as Incarnate Redeemer may be articulated as the divine enactment of, first, the fully enfleshed entrance of the abundance of divine freedom into human brokenness; second, the healing of the human freedom that brought about such brokenness; and, third, the transformation of human freedom to become participatory agent in the agapic healing of brokenness and in its completion in communion with God.

In relation to human freedom, the Incarnation is the locus in which the divine relationality of God transformatively takes into itself, in Jesus, the finitude and brokenness of humanity and creation; in consequence, human freedom, which brought such brokenness about, is enabled to participate in enacting its healing and completion in personal union with the triune God. The incarnate redemptive agency of God, freely taking on human brokenness, provides a basis from which to articulate two fundamental points of reference for the working of God's transformative agency upon human freedom: First, the role human freedom has in the origin of the evil that besets it; and, second, the transformative empowerment of that freedom, through the Incarnate Jesus, to participate in his salvific overcoming of evil. These points delimit the historical and social character of human agency and freedom as the horizon within which human freedom and the incarnate redemptive agency of God function together for enacting the final good of human freedom, communion with God.

As the previous section indicated, the scriptural/narrative trajectory of Genesis 1–11 provides a frame of reference for the intelligibility of human freedom in terms of God's relationality as Creator. Human freedom, originating in God's enactment of creation, is oriented and empowered as image of God for the enactment of good. Those chapters also provide a frame of reference for construing the intelligibility of human freedom with respect to God's relationality enacted as Incarnate Redeemer. They offer an account of the circumstances by which the exercise of human freedom beset humanity and the world with evil, an outcome for which, in the unfolding of the narrative, the divine enfleshment into human freedom and finitude in Jesus becomes the decisive form of God's redemptive response. The "first act" of this account, the narrative of the temptation and sin of Adam and Eve, long shaped Christian moral and religious imagination; it continues, in its astute portrayal of enticement, falsehood, conflict and blame, to resonate, even in a time of secularity, with deep human moral sensibilities.

The multiple dynamics at work in the interactions among Adam, Eve, the serpent and the Lord leave the identification of their transgression and of how it constitutes a misuse of human freedom open to multiple readings. Even interpretive traditions in Christian theology that depict their transgression as disobedience also recognize that it arises from complex human motivational dynamics that are, arguably, more basic than disobedience and straight-out defiance.[17] These include the envy, distrust and pride that,

---

[17]See, for instance, Libreria Editrice Vaticana, *Catechism of the Catholic Church*, #397: "Man, tempted by the devil, let his trust in his Creator die in his heart and, abusing his freedom, disobeyed God's command. This is

by placing self-preference as primary for orienting efforts of human freedom to enact good, lead to the willful disorientation of freedom that constitutes "sin" and brings evil in its wake.[18] The serpent's inducement—"your eyes will be opened, and you will be like God" (Gen. 3:5)—tellingly strikes this chord of self-preference. The consequence is tragically ironic: Adam and Eve, acceding to a self-preference inviting them to grasp at being "like God" through the "knowledge of good and evil," instead turn from the abundant horizon of good entrusted to them for creaturely enactment of good. Tradition names the consequence of this disorientation "original sin": an impairment of human apprehension of good and of human freedom's empowerment for enacting good. Instead of becoming like God, Adam and Eve undermine the very creaturely capacity bestowed upon human freedom for enacting good, not "as God," but "in the image" of God that constitutes the good of human creaturely finitude.

Genesis presents this momentous interaction between divine and human freedom issuing in a self-inflicted disorientation of human freedom. Human freedom deflects its enactment of good toward a self-preference discordant with the image of God stamped upon its finitude. Yet the ordering of creation in God's "seeing good" that structures freedom as constitutive for human agency and personhood does not thereby cease the empowerment given human freedom as image of God for enacting good in the world. The dynamic underlying this scriptural trope suggests that, even in humanity's broken condition, the divine image stamped on human freedom retains a capacity *for seeing and enacting good as God does*, a capacity that provides an intriguing link between the activity of God as both Creator and Redeemer and the intelligibility of human freedom. Taylor suggests this in *Sources of the Self*: God's efficacious "seeing good" in Genesis (1:31) also bears upon *the empowerment of human agency for enacting good* in the "image of God."[19] On this construal, the seeing good constituting the redemptive enfleshment of the divine completes the divine seeing good of creation in an abundant, unforeseen way. This completion *is* the fullness of Jesus' incarnate enactment of both human and divine freedom. Jesus is the incarnate "seeing good" constituting the response of unlimited *agape* to the broken human condition: God sees with surpassing clarity a world in which humans, in their freedom, wreak horrific destruction on themselves and on the cosmos, and nonetheless enacts, in the freedom of Jesus' incarnational seeing, a surpassing good for the world.[20]

God's incarnate free self-binding to the healing of humanity and creation, moreover, *is so radical that its seeing good now enlists human freedom in this healing task*. It manifests the enlivening, elevating and consoling activity of the third aspect of God's Triune relationality, God as Sanctifying Spirit. The "seeing good" of the Spirit constitutes a community of mutuality (the Church) as locus for the empowerment of human freedom to enact good in practices of inclusive welcoming, faithful accompaniment and healing

---

what man's first sin consisted of. All subsequent sin would be *disobedience toward God and lack of trust in his goodness*" (emphasis added).

[18]Libreria Editrice Vaticana, *Catechism of the Catholic Church*, # 398: "In that sin man *preferred himself to God* and by that very act scorned him. *He chose himself over and against God*, against the requirements of his creaturely status and therefore against his own good" (emphasis added).

[19]Taylor, *Sources*, 515–16.

[20]An observation from Catherine Mowry LaCugna, *God for Us: The Trinity and Christian Life* (San Francisco: Harper, 1973), 168–9, is pertinent here: "A Trinitarian theology rooted in salvation history leads us to think of divine freedom as the freedom of relationship, the freedom of love, not freedom conceived as autonomy and self-sufficiency."

solidarity. The divine seeing of God as Sanctifying Spirit *constitutes a community empowered to continue the enactment of God's salvific purposes in and for creation.* This community enlists human freedom into the mutual service that points humanity and the cosmos toward its eschatological completion in communion with God.

This agapic community of service manifests the mutuality of community as itself the central coordinate that God as Sanctifying Spirit provides for the intelligibility of human freedom. This community is an enacted "platform," oriented to a horizon of liberation, reconciliation and healing, that stands resistant to the dynamics of the disengaged, self-enclosed and asocial human subjectivity into which secularity's immanent frame constricts the intelligibility of human freedom. The liberating reconciliation enacted in an agapic community of service provides a lived account of human freedom referenced to the relationality of the Triune God—an account that offers a basis for constructive engagement with modern, secular accounts of human freedom. Such engagement could open possibilities for reorienting of the dynamics of the enclosed human subjectivity from which these accounts construe human freedom: away from a disengaged, self-enclosed and irreducibly asocial horizon and to a horizon attentive to the situatedness of freedom in a mutuality constituting us as agents responsible to one another.

God as Sanctifying Spirit: Enlightening and Enlivening Human Freedom for the Enactment of a Community of Agapic Service

The third set of coordinates for the theological intelligibility of human freedom proper to the terms of Trinitarian relationality are located in reference to God's activity as Sanctifying Spirit. As Sanctifying Spirit, God is the One whose enlivening empowerment, poured forth from the crucified and risen Lord Jesus into the cosmos and human history, brings forth the church as an agapic community of freedom called into mutual service to be transformatively efficacious for the salvation of humanity and the cosmos. The Sanctifying Spirit is the locus from which the divine relationality of God empowers the enactment of human freedom for the redemptive mission of the church. That mission enlists human freedom in the kenotic mutual service, paradigmatically enacted in the mission of Jesus, which points humanity and the cosmos toward its completion in communion with God.

In terms of the trope of "seeing good," the expansiveness of God's seeing good in creation is exceeded in God's seeing good in and for a world in which the enfleshment of God liberates human freedom from the self-regarding constriction it has placed on its recognition and enactment of good. The world, redeemed by God's enfleshment, is empowered to become a place for the transforming activity of the Spirit: a sanctifying "seeing good" bringing forth the agapic community, the church, as locus for human freedom's participation in God's healing and elevating enactments of good. The Spirit empowers human seeing good, enacted in freedom, to *become* the seeing good of the Incarnation. This seeing good responds with *agape* to the broken human condition, a brokenness of which God remains abidingly mindful and, in that enduring mindfulness, effects transformative healing in and through the community gathered together in mutuality by the sanctifying Spirit. This transformative healing empowers human freedom to recognize and welcome creation in *the fundamental otherness in which it stands as good* in virtue its radical dependence on the divine enactment that brings it to be and sustains it. Such welcoming pledges respect to creation as the space of finitude graciously brought to be and sustained in its otherness by the inexhaustible goodness of God, and in which human freedom is called upon to enact good.

It is thus in reference to the relationality of the triune God as Sanctifying Spirit that human freedom is empowered by a "seeing good" in the manner of God's inclusive welcoming. In this seeing good, the Spirit gathers humanity into a community of full mutuality, the Church, in which welcoming and accompaniment of one another enact healing solidarity and wholeness in virtue of the recognition and reverencing of our shared vulnerabilities. This seeing good makes it possible for concrete enactments of human freedom to have the capacity to turn even the fractured ground presented by disengaged, self-enclosed and asocial subjectivity of the immanent frame into a place of graced and gracious welcome for the good of all that is other. Seeing good in the modality of God's inclusively welcoming Spirit enables us to envision a gathering of humanity into a community of mutuality that, enlivened, renewed and elevated by the activity of the Spirit, stands as a pledge of a renewal of the cosmos and of eschatological completion in personal communion with God.

CONCLUDING SUMMARY

In consequence, the theological intelligibility of human freedom may be construed as fully ordered to community and mutuality in reference to all dimensions of the triune relationality of God:

> First, in reference to the activity of the triune God as Creator, human freedom, as created in the image of God, is ordered in its origin to mutuality in its enactment of good. Yet it also has willfully disoriented itself toward a horizon of enclosed self-preference standing athwart the enactment of mutuality to which it first is ordered in created finitude.
>
> Second, in reference to the activity of the triune God as Incarnate Redeemer, human freedom has been released, through the graciousness of God's free incarnate self-binding to humanity and creation, from bondage to that self-enclosed horizon and is reoriented in agapic service to enacting good.
>
> Third, in reference to the activity of the triune God as Sanctifying Spirit, human freedom is elevated through the kenotic outpouring of the Spirit from the crucified and risen Jesus to participate in a community, the Church, that continues the liberating mission of the Incarnate Jesus; it does so in its enactments of agapic mutual service that empower human freedom to be transformatively efficacious for the salvation of humanity and of the cosmos.

SUGGESTED FURTHER READING

Burrell, David B., *Freedom and Creation in Three Traditions* (Notre Dame, IN: University of Notre Dame Press, 1993).

Johnson, Elizabeth A., *Quest for Living God: Mapping Frontiers in the Theology of God* (New York: Continuum, 2007).

Kasper, Walter, *The God of Jesus Christ* (trans. Matthew J. O'Connell; New York: Crossroad, 1994).

La Cugna, Catherine Mowry, *God for Us: The Trinity and Christian Life* (San Francisco: Harper, 1973).

Steiner, George, *Real Presences* (Chicago: University of Chicago Press, 1989).

Taylor, Charles, *Sources of the Self: The Making of the Modern Identity* (Cambridge: Cambridge University Press, 1989).

PART III

Key Figures

CHAPTER ELEVEN

Irenaeus: As It Was in the Beginning

FRANCINE CARDMAN

"Theological anthropology" is not a category that would have been recognizable to Irenaeus. For him, to ask "What does it mean to be human?"—a common shorthand today for the locus of theological anthropology—would be, at best, only a partially formed question. In his eyes, its poor formulation would be due to its dislocation from its necessary context and corollary: "What does it mean to be Godlike?" Together these questions point to the unified and unifying matrix from which they arise, namely the reciprocal relationship of creation and eschatology, God's plan "from the beginning" for eternal communion with humankind.

In addressing these fundamental questions, Irenaeus' vision is large, encompassing time and eternity, humankind and God, the beginning and the end. An often (but seldom completely) quoted declaration characterizes his perspective: "The glory of God is a living human being and (but) the life of humankind is beholding God" (*gloria enim Dei vivens homo, vita autem hominis visio Dei*, AH 4.20.7).[1] It is in the movement toward beholding God that humankind has its being and meaning. The order or arrangement (*taxis*) of God's plan, as Irenaeus explicates it in his two extant treatises, is more open, dynamic and generous than later views of fall and redemption, sin and grace, typically filtered through interpretations of Augustine, that have been prominent in much of Western Christian theology. In a sense Irenaeus represents a road not taken in the West, while also having resonances with Origen, Gregory of Nyssa and later Eastern Christian theology. Now,

---

[1] The critical edition of *Against Heresies* (henceforth cited as AH), with French trans., is in *Sources Chrétienne* (Paris: Cerf), ed. A. Rousseau et al., *Irénée de Lyon: Contre les hérésies*, I: 263, 264 (1979); II: 293, 294 (1982); III: 210, 211 (1974); IV: 100, in 2 vols. (1965); V: 152, 153 (1969). Quotations of *Against Heresies* are from *St. Irenaeus of Lyons: Against the Heresies Book I*, trans. and annotated by Dominic J. Unger, OFM. Cap., with further revisions by John J. Dillon, ACW no. 55 (New York: Paulist Press, 1992); Book 2, trans. and annotated by Dominic J. Unger, with further revisions by John J. Dillon, introduction by Michael Slusser; Book 3, trans. Dominic J. Unger, OFM. Cap., with introduction and further revisions by Irenaeus M. C. Steenberg, ACW 64 (New York: Newman Press: 2012). Quotations from Books 4 and 5 from "The Ante-Nicene Fathers 1," in *The Writings of Irenaeus* (1887, repr. Grand Rapids, MI: Eerdmans, 1987). Available online at http://www.newadvent. org/fathers/0103.htm. Revised and edited for New Advent by Kevin Knight. For the *Demonstration*, the critical edition is by K. Ter-Mekerttschian and S. G. Wilson, with Prince Max of Saxony, eds. and English trans., *Proof of the Apostolic Preaching, with Seven Fragments* (Turnhout: Brepols, 1917 repr., 1989). There are two modern English translations: *St. Irenaeus, Proof of the Apostolic Preaching*, trans. and annotated by Joseph P. Smith, SJ, ACW 16 (New York: Newman Press, 1952); and *St. Irenaeus of Lyons, On the Apostolic Preaching*, trans. and introduction by John Behr (Crestwood, NY: St. Vladimir's Seminary Press, 1997).

however, it may be a road that re/opens some useful vistas for seeing, believing and understanding humankind and God in their unfolding historical and salvific relationship.

CONTEXT

Irenaeus appears in Lyons in the 170s CE and soon takes a prominent place among Christian leaders and writers of the second century. Believers from Asia Minor who were immigrants, missionaries and merchants had brought Christianity to Gaul in recent decades, settling along the upper Rhone river. When and how Irenaeus joined them is unknown. He does report that, as a boy in Smyrna (in modern-day Turkey), he had avidly listened to the preaching and instruction of the bishop Polycarp (c. 70?–155/6), whom he regards as his teacher and reveres for his witness to the preaching of the apostles.[2] Beyond these references, Irenaeus provides no further biographical information; but it is likely that he again heard Polycarp proclaim the apostolic preaching in Rome around 154/5, which suggests that Irenaeus was born between 130 and 140.[3]

The Letter of the Churches of Vienne and Lyons, written *c.* 177 after the persecution of Christians in those cities by the emperor Marcus Aurelius, was addressed to churches in Asia Minor and Phrygia. It detailed the great works of the Spirit demonstrated in the witness and endurance of the martyrs, at least some of whom would have been known to the recipients. Recent scholarship tends to be receptive toward the view that Irenaeus was the author of the letter, which is preserved by Eusebius.[4] Among the martyrs was the elderly bishop of Lyon, Pothinus, who was over 90 years old when he died in the persecution. It is plausible that Irenaeus then became the leader (presbyter or bishop, the terms were still interchangeable at the time) of the church in the more prominent city of Lyons.[5]

WRITINGS

Eusebius does not mention Irenaeus in connection with the churches' letter about the persecution, but he does list Irenaeus' known writings, some of which have survived. Irenaeus wrote in Greek, the language of imperial administration as well as of his homeland. His major work, the five-book *Refutation and Overthrow of All Heresies*, only

---

[2]Eusebius preserves the account in his partial quotation of Irenaeus' *Letter to Florinus* in his *History of the Church* 5.20.5-8; Eusebius, *The History of the Church from Christ to Constantine*, trans. G. A. Williamson (Harmondsworth: Penguin, 1965), 227–8. In *Against Heresies* 3.3.4, Irenaeus recounts that in his early youth he knew Polycarp; elsewhere in the treatise he refers to Polycarp indirectly as "the divinely inspired elder and teacher of truth" (AH 1.15.6); "a certain presbyter" (4.27.1); and the "presbyter and disciple of the apostles" (4.32.1). See Charles E. Hill, *From the Lost Teaching of Polycarp, Wissenschaftliche Untersuchungen zum Neuen Testament* 186 (Tübingen: Mohr Siebeck, 2006), 1–17. See also John Behr, *Irenaeus of Lyons: Identifying Christianity* (Oxford: Oxford University Press, 2013), 57–66.

[3]Polycarp died at Smyrna in 155/6 at the age of 86 (*Martyrdom of Polycarp*), hence the plausibility of his having known the apostle John. For Irenaeus' encounter with him in Rome in 154/5, see Behr, *Irenaeus*, 66–7; for scholarly opinions on Irenaeus' year of birth, see 67, n. 154. See also Eric Osborn, *Irenaeus of Lyons* (Cambridge: Cambridge University Press, 2001), 1–7, for a brief introduction to Irenaeus' life and works. Polycarp was important to Irenaeus as a connection to the apostles and an exemplar of handing on the apostolic tradition.

[4]"Letter of the Churches of Vienne and Lyon," in Eusebius, HE 5.1-2, 193–203.

[5]Behr posits that Irenaeus had previously been the leader of the church in Vienne, hence the precedence of Vienne in the letter's title: *Irenaeus*, 19, n. 19.

survives completely in Latin translation and is commonly known as *Against Heresies*.[6] The first two books describe and refute teachers and systems of "gnosticism"[7] and related interpretations of Christian faith with their multifarious teachings that Irenaeus considers erroneous and misleading; the next three elucidate the apostolic scriptures (*graphe*, writings) and faith that have been handed down to believers by the apostles. *The Demonstration* (or proof, *epideixis*) *of the Apostolic Preaching* (Dem.) is a compact and more accessible, probably earlier, treatment of the main themes of Christian faith and its scriptural sources.[8] Within the vision of creation and salvation in his extant writings we can discern Irenaeus' theological anthropology.

These two major works reveal Irenaeus' deep commitment to the unity of the apostolic preaching in itself and its coherence with God's plan of salvation from the beginning of creation to its completion. In demonstrating that vision and arguing against its opponents, Irenaeus engages beliefs elemental to understanding the relationship of God and humankind: one God, the Creator; one creation and the goodness of materiality and flesh; the formation of human being in the image and likeness of God; the incarnation of the Word, the image and likeness of God made flesh; recapitulation, the summing up and remaking of humankind, which (re)connects the end to the beginning. Irenaeus does not present these fundamental themes in a systematic way in *Against Heresies* (AH). Rather, they appear repeatedly and somewhat haphazardly within the five books as he exposes and refutes erroneous teachings, explicates the apostolic preaching and defends the authenticity of its tradition (*paradosis*, handing on). The *Demonstration* summarizes that tradition briefly while also confirming it by proofs from the fulfillment of the Law and the Prophets.

BEGINNING AND END

Key to Irenaeus' exposition of the apostolic faith is the unity of beginning and end, creation and completion, within which works the dual dynamic of the Word as both the image and likeness of God and the maker and model of humankind, who were created at the beginning as the Word's image and likeness. Incarnate in human flesh, the Word is the remaker of the "earth creature,"[9] its perfecter and perfection. Made flesh, joining creature and creator, flesh and Spirit, the incarnate Word is visible proclamation and proof of the goodness of the flesh and its capacity for salvation. The work of the Word incarnate is twofold: making God ("the Father") visible *in the flesh* and restoring

---

[6]Some fragments of the Greek text are preserved in quotations and there is a sixth-century Armenian translation. Denis Minns notes that Augustine quotes a Latin translation of Irenaeus in 421, in *Contra Julianum* I.3.5, which provides *a terminus ad quem*; Denis Minns, *Irenaeus: An Introduction* (London: T&T Clark, 2010), 6. See Appendix I on source texts and dates in M. Steenberg, *Irenaeus on Creation: The Cosmic Christ and the Saga of Redemption* (Leiden: Brill, 2008), 217–19.

[7]"Gnostics" and "gnosticism" are terms Irenaeus used to describe teachers and interpretations of Christian faith that offered secret, higher knowledge (*gnosis*) of God and salvation, unknown to the apostles, that tended to be spiritualized, highly mythologized and dualistic. Although less organized and distinct than Irenaeus pictured them, they were coming to be regarded as beyond the developing mainstream of Christian belief in the late second century. For a reliable introduction, see David Brakke, *The Gnostics: Myth, Ritual and Diversity in Early Christianity* (Cambridge, MA: Harvard University Press, 2010).

[8]Scholars disagree on the relative dating of the two works. Behr holds that Dem. appeared after the first two books of AH (*Irenaeus of Lyons*, 69); Minns, *Irenaeus*, 6, puts it after the complete AH, although he notes that its theology is more primitive and its tone scarcely polemical.

[9]Minns, *Irenaeus*, 57–9.

humankind to its original formation, thus making it possible for them to reach their intended goal of communion with God. For Irenaeus there is but one Creator God and one material creation, one author of both covenants, one formation of humankind that is fleshly and one salvation that includes the flesh (4.7.3). There is no other creation and no solely spiritual human being. Within these parameters it is possible to discern the outlines of an emerging theological anthropology.

THE "ANCIENT FORMATION"

Humankind is God's handiwork, formed in the image and likeness of God from the dust of the earth by the Word and the Spirit, God's hands (4.20.1; 4.7.3). This "ancient formation" (4.33.4; 5.1.2) is composed of flesh, soul and Spirit. The Word is its archetype (4.36.40); God's breath animates and makes it a living being (4.18.5); the Spirit vivifies and perfects human being so that they might do the works and know the fruits of the Spirit (5.11.1; 5.12.2). Thus formed, humankind is oriented from the beginning to God, who is "accustoming" (adsuescens) them to bear the Spirit and be in communion with Godself (4.14.2).

Endowed with reason and free will, "the ancient law of liberty" (4.37.1; 4.38.4), they had power over themselves, the capacity to choose and to change (4.15.3). Because they are like God in their reason and free will, they alone are the cause of harm to themselves through disobedience (4.4.3). Yet, given the dynamic of growth and increase that permeates all of creation (2.28.1), imbuing it with the power of development, Irenaeus envisages Adam and Eve as "infants" (infantes, children), young people not fully matured morally, intellectually or sexually.[10] They were inexperienced and imperfect (4.38.1) in the sense that they were unfinished and needed to grow into themselves, into the image and likeness of the Word and the Spirit, into communion with God. Given this foundational assumption, it is not surprising that Irenaeus reads the story of Adam and Eve's fateful choice in Genesis 2 through a softer lens than that of later Western tradition.

Yet, their choice is not without consequences. Mortality sets a boundary to disobedience. The garden is closed to them. Hard labor is their due—bringing forth food from the earth and progeny from their bodies. Their minds are no longer guileless (3.23.5). They need to learn anew by experience, from both obedience and disobedience, how to choose obedience (4.39.1). Distanced from God, they need to avail themselves of God's plan of salvation (4.14.2), prepared for them from the beginning: guides and teachers, Moses, the Law and the Prophets; the Word and the Spirit. They are slow learners. They need mercy.

RECAPITULATION

Mercy comes in the person of the Word made flesh, God's compassion present to humankind (3.10.2; 5.21.3). Within the paradigm of beginning and end, Irenaeus delineates a process of remaking that sums up the work of creation, bringing it to completeness through the Word's recapitulation and righting of human experience.[11] The

---

[10]See also Dem., 12. For Adam and Eve as children, see M. C. Steenberg, "Children in Paradise: Adam and Eve as 'Infants' in Irenaeus of Lyons," *Journal of Early Christian Studies* 12, no. 1 (2004): 1–22.

[11]Irenaeus develops the idea of *anakephalaiosis*, the recapitulation or summing up of all things in Christ, from Eph. 1:10, God has made known the plan set forth in Christ "as a plan for the fullness of time, to gather up all things in [Christ], things in heaven and things on earth." Irenaeus regarded the epistle as Paul's.

Word who formed humanity in the beginning now restores and perfects them in God's image and likeness by entering into every human experience, including infancy (4.38.2) and death (5.23.2). Obedience undoes disobedience, resurrection overcomes death, humility displaces pride, perfection brings incompleteness and infirmity to maturity and wholeness (3.18.7; 3.20.2; 5.21.2; 5.3.1). The Word comes through every economy in the "long unfolding (*expositio*) of humankind," granting salvation to them as a whole (3.18.1).

Recapitulation reconnects beginning and end, restoring the descendants of Eve and Adam, enabling them to become fully human by becoming Godlike, re-formed in the image and likeness of the Word (5.21.2). Through the Word's transcendent love, manifest in recapitulation, "he became what we are, that he might bring us to be even what he is in himself" (5, pref.).[12]

SAVING FLESH

The Word made flesh is Irenaeus' theological anthropology in brief and in full. All the rest is commentary. In his commentary, Irenaeus illumines human existence, the earth creature's nature and way to God, God's way to humankind. Having argued and established to his own satisfaction that flesh is capable of salvation in books one and two of *Against Heresies*, Irenaeus lays out in books four and five what that salvation looks like in process and in perfection.

The flesh made by God (i.e., the human creature) is material and spiritual: "Now man is a mixed organization of soul and flesh (*temperatio animae et carnis*) who was formed after the likeness of God, and molded by his hands, that is, by the Son and Holy Spirit, to whom he also said 'Let us make man'" (4, pref. 4). God is the maker of both material and spiritual substance, both body and soul (2.28.7; 2.30.33–34). Whether Irenaeus envisages a bipartite (flesh and soul) or tripartite (flesh, soul, Spirit) structure of the human person is difficult to determine from Irenaeus' various usages.[13] He makes a very strong statement, however, about the indwelling of the Spirit through the Word's recapitulation of all things "by uniting [humankind] to the Spirit and causing the Spirit to dwell in them, the Word is made head of the Spirit, and gives the Spirit to be the head of human being: for through the Spirit we see and hear and speak" (5.20.2). The economy of the salvation necessitates that the flesh of the Word be flesh from Mary (5.1; 5.1.2), in order to restore humankind by becoming truly human. Thus the incarnate Word is both Adam *and* Eve, all of humankind past, present and to come.[14] Only through the Word's sharing their lot would human being know God and themselves; know through experience from what the incarnate Word's death and

---

[12]*"Verbum Dei, Jesum Christum dominum nostrum, qui propter immensam suam dilectionem factus est quod sumus nos, uti nos perficeret esse quod est ipse."*

[13]Scholars disagree on whether Irenaeus envisages a bipartite (flesh and soul) or tripartite (flesh, soul, Spirit) structure of the human person. Behr maintains that the "nurturing presence of the Spirit" is always with the human being, suggesting perhaps indwelling: John Behr, *Asceticism and Anthropology in Irenaeus and Clement* (Oxford: Oxford University Press, 2000), 97. Brigmann considers the Spirit's presence as instrumental: Anthony Briggman, *Irenaeus of Lyons and the Theology of the Holy Spirit* (Oxford: Oxford University Press, 2012), 164–81. But see 5.8.1: "We do now receive a certain portion of his Spirt, tending towards perfection, and preparing us for incorruption, being little by little accustomed to receive and bear God ... This earnest, therefore, thus dwelling in us, renders us spiritual even now."

[14]Irenaeus extends Paul's parallelism of Adam and Christ to Eve and Mary: 3.22.4; also 5.1.2; 5.19.1.

resurrection freed them; know that "God is the glory of humankind, who are vessels of God's working" (3.20.2).[15]

In the economy of salvation, "our bodies were united to salvation by means of the bath [baptism] but our souls by means of the Spirit" (3.17.2)—both of which are necessary. Through the Word's work of recapitulation, the ancient handiwork is restored to participation in God (3.18.7), able to make progress toward becoming wholly like God (3.20.2). The dynamic of progress present in creation is uniquely open to human agency, its life-giving potential restored through the Word and made accessible through the Spirit in the church (3.24.1). It is through the vivifying work of the Spirit that humankind advances toward God.

God made human being free agents, possessing their own power and soul, able to obey God without coercion (4.37.1, 5). Seeking God's power for their own, they instead learn to live irrationally (4.4.3; 4.4.37).[16] Unable to know God without God, they can only be reformed when taught by the Word in person, who renews time and the face of the earth so that humankind can mature and grow toward immortality. In language that recurs regularly in the last books of *Against Heresies*, Irenaeus describes the ongoing progress of humankind toward God. "God is always the same ... but humankind receives advancement and increase to God" (4.11.2). Before the coming of the Word, God has a plan of salvation, put into action by the patriarchs and prophets, "accustoming human being to bear [the] Spirit and to hold communion with God" (4.14.2). They learn love of God and neighbor while maintaining their own freedom; they learn friendship with God (4.12.2, 15.3, 16.4); they always go on toward God (4.11.2). Advancement and increase are the dynamics of life in the Spirit. The capacity for growing toward God is inherent in human being, like a plant drawn toward the sun; following that innate orientation, humankind can mature to immortality (4.5.1).

Having the knowledge of good and evil, humankind are able to obey God and keep God's commandments; doing so is "the life of humankind" (4.39.1). Irenaeus admonishes his readers to "preserve the form in which the Creator has fashioned you," for by doing so, "you shall ascend to that which is perfect" (4.39.2). Although Irenaeus acknowledges that there will be judgment and separation of the sheep and the goats (Mt. 25:31-46), he does not dwell on or explicate it. His recurring iterations of progress toward God tend to overshadow references to the possibility of final failure. The logic of recapitulation would seem to entail the salvation of all, but Irenaeus envisions the eternal rest of the righteous in the light of God in contrast to the darkness and fire that await the unrighteous who do not inherit the kingdom.[17]

Even after Adam and Eve turn away, God preserves free will in humankind. They are free not only in their daily choices and actions but also in regard to faith (4.37.5), which would otherwise be meaningless. Without such freedom, they would not be able to take pleasure in the good and the beautiful; with it they may love God all the more while striving for immortality (4.37.6).

---

[15]Irenaeus' phrasing here is suggestive of the famously misunderstood "the glory of God is man [sic] fully alive" (4.20.7) in some popular translations.

[16]See also 4.15.2: God always respects human freedom and self-governance, even when exhorting humankind to follow divine precepts.

[17]See 5.11.1, the works of the flesh and the fruits of the Spirit (Gal. 5:16–26).

LIVING EUCHARIST

Irenaeus links humankind's communion with the Word, the image and likeness of God made flesh, with communion in his body and blood in the Eucharist. Having learned mortality through experience, they now learn through eucharistic experience that God does not abandon the ancient handiwork to destruction, but opens their way to eternal life (5.1.1). Through communion with the Word, humankind grow in the Word's likeness by hearing and doing the Word's teachings. Through communion in the Word's redeeming body and blood,[18] they are nourished by the bread and cup of the Eucharist and able to participate in "the constructive wisdom and power of God" (5.3.3). Irenaeus counters those who deny that flesh is capable of immortality by emphasizing the created materiality of the bread and wine that are the body and blood of the incarnate Word in the Eucharist. "As we are his members, we are also nourished by means of the creation ... He has acknowledged the cup (which is part of creation) as his own blood; and the bread (also part of creation) he has established as his own body, from which he gives increase to our bodies" (5.2.2).[19] Irenaeus suggests that those who "become accustomed to eat and drink the Word of God ... may be also able to contain in [themselves] the Bread of immortality, which is the Spirit of the Father" (4.38.1). Participation in Eucharist nourishes human beings throughout life and toward resurrection, the glory of God.

Vivified by the Spirit through baptism and Eucharist, human being is made spiritual, becoming temples of God and members of Christ (5.11.2; 5.6.2). Participating in the constructive wisdom and power of God, they live a eucharistic life. Loving God, they learn love of neighbor; exercising their free will in "deeds of righteousness" done in the body (2.9.2), they are able to enter into friendship with God,[20] made accessible again by the Word's coming in the flesh (4.16.4; 5.17.1). The ethical life that follows from Eucharist is performed in the vivified body that is in communion with the Spirit and conformable to the Word of God (5.9.3). Quoting Gal. 5:22, Irenaeus recalls "the spiritual actions which vivify a man, that is, the engrafting of the Spirit"; those who bring forth fruits of the Spirit "are saved altogether because of the communion of the Spirit" (5.11.1).[21] It is this same Spirit that enables the martyrs to give witness to their faith (5.9.2) and baptismal commitment. Vivified by the Spirit, the earth creature that was first animated being with the breath of life becomes spiritual being as well (5.12.2). The work of the Spirit is the salvation of the flesh (5.12.4), a fully alive human being (5.9.3).

---

[18]As far as I can ascertain, Irenaeus refers to redemption by Christ's blood, body or passion—i.e., his flesh—ten times in AH, all but two in book five: 5.1.1, "redeeming us by his own blood ... gave himself as a redemption for those who had been led into captivity"; 5.2.1, "nor did he truly redeem us by his own blood, if he did not really become man"; 5.14.3, "redeeming us by his own body and blood"; 5.14.4, "his flesh and blood are the things that procure life for us"; 5.16.3, the Lord manifested himself "by means of his passion" (in addition to or within the work of recapitulation); 5.18.1, "the incarnate Word of God was suspended on a tree"; 5.18.3, the Lord "was made flesh and was hung upon the tree, that he might sum up all things in himself"; through his passion there was a second creation, 5.23.2. The other references are in 2.20.3, where Irenaeus is refuting "gnostic" opponents who argue that Christ suffered a passion of "dissolution and corruption," and 3.20.2, "humankind are freed by the incarnate Word's death and resurrection."

[19]Irenaeus emphasizes both the physical presence of the Word in the Eucharist and that it nourishes the physical body of the recipient to prepare it for incorruption; see 5.2.2-3.

[20]Additional references to friendship with God are found in 3.17.1; 4.12.2; 4.15.3; 5.17.1.

[21]Irenaeus refers to Paul's use of the wild olive metaphor in Rom. 11:17-24. See Minns's analysis of Paul's confused use of the metaphor, 92–3.

The goal of humankind is life with God—"inheriting God," as Irenaeus writes—possible again because the Word, the new human being, has overcome death (4.22.1) and joined beginning to end (4.34.4). As he rose in the flesh, so will humankind (5.7.1). Now human being bears the image of Adam, made of earth; then they will bear the image of the one from heaven. For Irenaeus, resurrection is the vindication of the flesh. The Word who made flesh, healed flesh; healing flesh he brought life; through life he brought incorruption (5.12.6). In the resurrection, the body of humiliation shared by human being will be transfigured and conformed to the Word's body of glory (5.13.3), recapitulating God's original handiwork (5.14.2).

ENDING AND BEGINNING

Irenaeus brings AH to an end with an apocalyptic reflection on "the Apostasy" and a millenarian view of the end times. There will be a thousand-year reign of the just in an earthly kingdom. In those days the earth will be restored to its primeval condition (5.32.1; also 5.35.2). There will be righteous rule and a peaceable kingdom in which animals will be docile (5.33.2-3; 5.33.4). Creation will increase extensively, and death, the anguish of the people, will be healed (5.34.2). The righteous who reign on the earth will "become accustomed to partake in the glory of God the Father" and interact with the holy angels and spiritual beings (5.35.21).

Irenaeus is adamant that these revelations of the end times can neither be allegorized nor taken to apply only to heavenly matters (5.35.1, 2). Rather, real human beings will be raised from the dead, and they will need a material place in which to dwell. The substance of the creation will not be annihilated, but its fashion (i.e., its mores) will pass away (1 Cor. 7:31); a new heaven and a new earth will be revealed. Humankind will progress and flourish then. When all things are made new, they will dwell in the city of God, the new Jerusalem. In the times of the kingdom, the righteous who are on the earth "shall then forget to die" (5.36.2).

Irenaeus' vision of the completion of creation ends where it begins: in the perfecting of God's handiwork by the Word descending into flesh and humankind being taken up into the Word, who recapitulates their making and renews them fully in the image and likeness of God (5.36.3). Recapitulation is, rightly, the major "take-away" from Irenaeus. But equally important are three major themes of his writings and their bearing on theological anthropology today: flesh, accustoming and progress.

Irenaeus' impassioned defense of the *flesh*, and with it the material creation (which might be considered the flesh of the world), is the necessary premise of AH and the salvation history recounted in the *Demonstration*. Flesh—the earth creature, Adam and Eve, the primal parents—is God's handiwork and worthy of salvation. Flesh is the image and likeness of God. Flesh is the Word who is both its maker and its remaker. Flesh is the Word incarnate, God made visible to humankind. Flesh is the Eucharist. In the resurrection life, flesh is the glory of God.

God and humankind engage in a reciprocal process of *accustoming*. Humankind needs to become accustomed to communion with God in this world and in the glory of resurrection. They must learn friendship with God. God becomes accustomed to ordering and sustaining the handiwork modeled after the Word. The Word sums up all things, becoming flesh in order to restore humankind in God's image and likeness. Together with the Word, the Spirit of God that rested on Jesus at his baptism becomes accustomed to dwell with humans and renew them.

Progress is the dynamic that drives the whole of creation, recapitulation and salvation. All of creation develops toward its intended completion. Humankind alone can derail this process, but only for a moment of cosmic time, since the Word and Spirit, God's hands, are eternally making and remaking what they originally fashioned. Even in the resurrection, the earth creature will continue to grow, renewed and incorruptible, in the image and likeness, the glory of God.

What does it mean to be human? What does it mean to be Godlike? For Irenaeus it means to live in the recapitulation of the beginning as humankind journeys with the Word toward the fullness of the end, in which God is all in all.

SUGGESTED FURTHER READING

Behr, John, *Asceticism and Anthropology in Irenaeus and Clement* (Oxford: Oxford University Press, 2000).

Behr, John, *Irenaeus of Lyons: Identifying Christianity* (Oxford: Oxford University Press, 2013).

Minns, Denis, *Irenaeus: An Introduction* (London: T&T Clark International, 2010).

Osborn, Eric, *Irenaeus of Lyons* (Cambridge: Cambridge University Press, 2001).

Steenberg, M. C., *Irenaeus on Creation: The Cosmic Christ and the Saga of Redemption* (Leiden: Brill, 2008).

CHAPTER TWELVE

Gregory of Nyssa: Formed and Reformed in God's Image

J. WARREN SMITH

The fourth century witnessed the development of one of the most important movements within Christianity—monasticism. Why monasticism? Why devote oneself to a life of sexual renunciation and the mortification of the flesh? Gregory of Nyssa (335–394), in addition to being a defender of Nicene orthodoxy, articulated an anthropology that provided a theological foundation for asceticism.

In the preface to *On the Making of Man*, Gregory presents his methodology, "For it is necessary to know those things concerning humanity ... of that which we believe to have come to be, of that which we expect to appear later, and of that which is now seen."[1] The beginning point for his study is not the human condition in the present age. Rather, in order to understand what animals human beings are, one must look at God's original intention for humanity, which can be fully understood only by seeing the consummation of God's plan in the eschaton. Gregory reasons teleologically that one cannot fathom the nature of an acorn unless one has first seen an oak tree into which the acorn will grow. To draw conclusions about humanity by looking only at the characteristics of its nature in the present yields not a true picture of human nature but of humanity distorted by sin. Thus, he asks, how can humanity be made in the image of the perfectly blessed God when it exists in a present state of misery? By providing an account of the *imago Dei*, which God originally intended for humanity and the perfection of human nature in the age to come, *On the Making of Man* illustrates how humanity's condition deviates from God's original intention due to sin and how monastic practices, especially celibacy, enable Christians to press on in this life toward the perfection of human nature that awaits at the resurrection.

"OF THAT WHICH HAS COME TO BE": CREATION IN THE IMAGE OF GOD

Human beings were fashioned to be amphibious creatures sharing both the material nature of nonrational animals that inhabit the earth and the rational nature of the angels that

---

[1] *On the Making of Man*, in *Nicene and Post-Nicene Fathers*, 2nd series, vol. 5, trans. W. Moore and H. A. Wilson (Edinburgh: T&T Clark, 1898), 387. Henceforth cited as *Hom. Op.*

apprehend the intelligible realities of God.[2] In the beginning God created the material world in order to reveal his power and goodness to humanity so that man[3] might find pleasure in knowing him through creation.[4] Humanity is both honored guest and divinely appointed viceroy of paradise. He is also the royal son of the King of the universe and so is equipped with the faculties to rule creation on his heavenly Father's behalf.[5] Although the material creation was made for humanity's enjoyment, God did not give humanity dominion in order to exploit creation. Based on Gen. 1:26, "Let us make humankind in our image, according to our likeness; and let them have dominion," Gregory concludes that God made man in his image so that he might know God and so exert dominion over creation in accordance with the nature and will of God. Humanity may be kingly, but he is at most a client king who exercises authority on behalf of the true King.

Since God made humanity for the royal work of governing, then human nature must not be subject to anything external but have an autocratic or free will (thelēmasin autokratorikōs). For Gregory, free will (autexousia) does not mean the capacity to choose between opposites but freedom from necessity (anankē), that is, humanity's actions need not be determined by instinctual impulses. Thus, unlike nonrational creatures that follow uncritically their sensual desires for material goods, Man was intended by God to possess mind (dianoia), speech (logos) and perception (aisthēsis) proper to the Divine nature. This rational nature allows humanity to apprehend the intelligible realities of God that lie beyond the senses' grasp, and because of this, dianoia allows human beings to contemplate the Creator through the sensible. This contemplation (theōria) is the monastic practice by which the monk seeks the Divine who reveals himself in the enigmas of Scripture. It also allows humanity to be self-reflective and critical about his choices based on his knowledge of the nature of material goods and the ends they serve. Since Christ, who is the image of the Father, is the Logos of John's prologue, humanity that is made after the image of God must also possess logos, which denotes both a share in God's rational nature and speech, which in turn allows reasoning within one's own mind (Gregory's view of logos in the verbal sense anticipated linguist Noam Chomsky's view that language is the tracks of human thought), as well as communication with others.

The capacities of intellect, speech and perception constitute humanity's *structural likeness* to God and allow participation in God by which one acquires a *moral likeness*. That is, the way one reflects the beauty of God's goodness, such as purity, freedom from passion (apatheia), blessedness (makarios), righteousness, alienation from evil, immortality and most of all love (agapē). By speaking of the image of the invisible and incorporeal God as contemplated in the beauty of his virtue (aretē), Gregory establishes an aesthetic way of speaking about God's goodness—following the Platonic tradition of identifying the Good and the True with the Beautiful—that will be critical for his account of how God arouses desire that draws the soul into himself. The implicit distinction between structural and moral likeness reflects the influence of Irenaeus' image-likeness distinction and provides a way to explain human virtue and the effects of sin. Human virtue is a participation in God's virtue made possible by the rational nature. This structural likeness and the potentiality proper to it remain, albeit in a diminished form, even when the moral likeness is corrupted by sin—that is, a failure to participate in the Divine.

---

[2]Ibid., 2.2.
[3]Gregory does think of humanity as one in the man—Adam—whom he speaks of in the singular.
[4]Hom. Op. 2.1.
[5]Hom. Op. 3.1.

While the *imago Dei* is chiefly associated with faculties and qualities of the soul, Gregory sees the capacities of the soul as dependent upon the structure of the body. God gave the human body its distinctive configuration in order to allow the soul to be rational, or, to put it in modern terms, man had to be *Homo erectus* in order to become *Homo sapiens* as upright posture was a sign of humanity's royal dignity. Instead of stooping down with eyes directed to the earth, erect posture allowed the eyes to be lifted up to the heavens. Following Aristotle, Gregory recognizes that erect posture allowed hands to have a different form than feet, and the hand's configuration with opposable thumbs, which allowed human beings to carry things with the hands rather than the mouth, meant that the face and mouth need not be shaped for carrying but could be shaped for speech and thus reason. This illustrates not only Gregory's appreciation of the body's contribution to the rational nature but also the relationship of speech—discourse—and reason.

Gregory builds upon this account of the integral relationship of the soul and body in *On the Soul and Resurrection*, which, following Plato's *Phaedo*, is a deathbed dialogue between Gregory and his older sister, Macrina, who converted their family estate at Annisa into a monastic community for women. Here he explains that the soul develops alongside the body. Unlike Origen, who held that the mind existed before the material body to which it was joined as a result of the fall, Gregory subscribed to a traducianist theory of the soul's origin according to which the soul is passed on from parent to child through the father's semen. In the mother's womb, the soul receives the matter that is its body. The soul *in utero*, is not, however, a fully formed rational soul. Rather, it has only the vegetative powers (reproduction, ingestion, digestion, elimination, respiration) that the body of the embryo or fetus allows. After birth, when the body is outside the dark and silent womb—as Gregory seems to have imagined it—the soul develops the faculties of sense perception. As the soul's experiences of the world increase, its rational faculties develop. The soul's sensual experience of particular material things provides data for reflection from which the soul develops its capacity to grasp intelligible realities. Thus, Gregory holds a strong conception of the psychosomatic unity of the person: the soul and body exist in a harmonic unity under the free and wise judgment of the intellect, and as such, humanity was the apex of animate material life: 'Perfect bodily life is seen in the rational (I mean the human) nature which is both nourished and endowed with sense, and also partakes of reason and is ordered by the mind.'[6] Such was God's intention in making humanity in his image but that intention had to be altered because of sin.

"OF THINGS AS THEY ARE NOW": DEVIATION FROM THE DIVINE IMAGE

Although the presence of the body itself marked a deviation from the incorporeal archetype, Gregory was troubled by two unnecessary divergences from the Divine nature, namely, the division of mankind into male and female and the presence of the passions. What is the status of the passions and their relationship to the soul? Rejecting Plato's account of the soul in the chariot simile from the *Phaedrus* as the combination of the rational (i.e., the charioteer) and the nonrational faculties (i.e., the winged horses of different temperaments), Gregory, through the voice of Macrina, asserts that the essence

---

[6]*Making Man* 8.4.

of things is that which is distinctive or unique (*idia*) to it.[7] Since the nonrational faculties are not unique to human beings but qualities shared with the beasts, Macrina reasons that they are not part of man's essence, that is, the rational nature of the divine image. At the same time, Gregory, wanting to preserve the organic relationship between the soul and the body, explains the development of the passions by appealing to an Aristotelian psychology. When the soul develops its sentient faculties, it experiences elements of the world as either pleasant and desirable or unpleasant and revolting. These experiences arouse the emotion of desire (*epithymia*)—even revulsion is a corollary of desire. Concomitant with desire is the fight or flight impulse, *thymos*. *Thymos*, often called "spirit" or "gumption," is the drive to *pursue* the object of desire or to *flee* from that which is undesirable or threatening. Together the appetitive (*epithymetikon*) and spirited (*thymikon*) faculties comprise the principle of movement in the soul. All other emotions, for example, fear, anger and grief, are forms of desire or gumption.

This account of the passions poses a conundrum for Gregory: how to understand the place of the nonrational passions in a rational being made in the image of the impassible God? In other words, the nonrational emotions and impulses are part of the human soul and yet they are not proper to humanity's essence since they are alien to the divine nature that possesses the virtue of *apatheia*.[8] Macrina's answer is that they are warts that are not proper to the soul's nature but exist on the margin of the soul, allowing it to act in the world.[9] This account of desire and gumption is foundational for Gregory's theory of virtue. The passions are in themselves morally neutral. But because the rational faculties of the soul develop after the sentient faculties, the soul's appetites are habitually oriented toward the sensual goods of the world rather than the intelligible goods of God. Thus, the soul is predisposed to seek worldly goods. This habitual predisposition is the source of soul's impulses (*hormai* or *horexis*). Whether an emotion is a vice or a virtue depends on whether the soul uncritically follows its reaction to the senses or whether is guided by reason. If the soul's movements are not properly ordered by reason, then the soul is dragged to destruction.[10] In such a case, desire becomes the vice of worldly lust and gumption becomes the vice of wrath. Moreover, desire acts like glue fixing the soul to its object. If, therefore, the soul desires sensual goods, the soul attaches itself to worldly goods and so is prevented from ascending to God.[11] Even worse, if reason does not exert control on the emotions ordering them to the service of God, then the emotions overpower reason and reason becomes coopted.[12] Once a slave to the passions, reason allows humanity to attain a level of viciousness far greater than that of the nonrational animals. If, however, the soul is not attached to the worldly goods but is rightly ordered to pursue the goods of God, then the emotions become virtues. Desire takes the form of love and gumption becomes courage. This transformation of the passions occurs when the intellectual nature asserts its hegemonic control of the lower nature. That is, when the intellect apprehends the intelligible beauty of the divine virtues, then desire for God is aroused and the soul becomes redirected toward God. Moreover, since desire and

---

[7]*On the Soul and Resurrection* 3.42, in *Macrina the Younger, Philosopher of God*, trans. A. M. Silvas (Turnhout: Brepols, 2008), 194; and *Making Man* 11.3.

[8]*Soul and Resurrection* 3.44.

[9]Macrina modifies the pejorative description of the emotions as warts (ibid. 3.30) and instead speaks of them as existing on the soul's margin, being necessary for movements to the good in this life (ibid. 3.34).

[10]Ibid. 3.47–8.

[11]Ibid. 6.5.

[12]*Making Man* 12.10–12.

gumption are the principle of motion in the soul, these emotions, when redirected by reason, are necessary for the soul's ascent to God. The love of God reorients the soul and the spirited faculty is the source of moral courage and fortitude by which the soul perseveres in its ascent overcoming worldly temptations.[13] Even as desire governed by the senses rather than reason attaches the soul to the world, desire oriented by the intellect to God attaches the soul to God in love.

Although the emotions are not proper to the divine image, Gregory does not see the monastic goal of *apatheia* as the absence of emotion—unlike Evagrius Ponticus who held *apatheia* to be the radical elimination of emotions—but their transformation through being rightly ordered toward God. Here lies the logic of monasticism. Because the soul has been attached to the world through the orientation of the appetites to sensual objects, the disciplines of fasting, chastity, renunciation of all luxuries and so on, separate the soul from the sensible objects so that the soul's desire for the worldly goods weakens. As the appetitive bonds soften, the soul's desires are reoriented to the heavenly, immaterial goods that are the object of contemplation. Yet, a question remained: since the emotions are alien to the essence of humanity and serve only its needs in the present age, will the perfection of human nature in the eschaton entail a more radical understanding of *apatheia* as the elimination of emotions such as longing and courage?

The second divergence of human nature from the image of God was gender. Because, according to Gal. 3:28, "in Christ there is no longer male and female," gender is alien to Christ after whose likeness humanity was formed.[14] Why, then, Gregory wondered, did God divide the human race into male and female? Such was not necessary since humanity could have reproduced in an angelic, asexual manner.[15] Gregory discovered his answer in the difference between Gen. 1:26 and 1:27. Whereas v. 26—"let us make man in our image after our likeness"—describes God's deliberative creation (*ktisis*) of the form man should take, v. 27—"and God made man in his image, male and female he created them'—narrates the actual fashioning (*kataskeuē*) of the first human beings. Therefore, Gregory infers that the two verses refer to the twofold creation of humanity.[16] Verse 26 speaking of the creation of humanity in the singular—"let us make man"— refers to God's intention for humanity to possess the divine image. Here God establishes his own nature as the archetype. Thus God originally willed humanity's rational nature without either gender division or nonrational passions.[17] Moreover, God willed at the level of his foreknowledge all individual human beings—the *pleroma*—who then existed in potentiality in the first man.[18] Verse 27, by speaking of the division of humanity into male and female, names the nonrational component of human nature. It is misleading to call this a "double creation theory" if it refers to two acts of creation. Gen. 1:26 refers to God's *intention* for humanity and his willing the existence of each member of the human race. Gen. 1:27 refers to the *actualization* of God's intention plus the male-female distinction.

What is especially problematic about this explanation is that Gregory sees the division of the race into male and female *both* as God's anticipation of the fall into sin *and* as the

---

[13]*Soul and Resurrection* 3.61.
[14]*Making Man* 16.5.
[15]Ibid. 17.3.
[16]Ibid. 16.8.
[17]Ibid. 16.9.
[18]Ibid. 16.16.

cause of the fall into sin. Foreseeing the fall of the first human beings from the angelic life of Paradise, God "formed for our nature that contrivance for increase which befits those who had fallen into sin, implanting in mankind, instead of angelic majesty of nature, that animal and irrational mode by which they now succeed one another."[19] Meaning that, since the fall into sin entailed a turning of the mind from the contemplation of God to the sensual goods, it was necessary to give humanity a means of procreation that took into consideration the sensual orientation of desire. Thus, even as sensual pleasure provides the inducement for procreation among the nonrational animals, so too sensually oriented human beings need the same sort of inducement. Gregory, however, goes on to identify the sexual mode of procreation as the source of the very passions that caused the fall that God had foreseen:

> For he [Adam] was made like the beasts, who received in his nature the present mode of transient generation, on account of his inclination to material things ... from this beginning all our passions issue as from a spring, and pour their flood over man's life ... all these [i.e., base appetites] and like affections enter man's composition by the reason of the animal mode of generation.[20]

The very sensual orientation that caused the first human beings to turn from God was inherent in God's creation of humanity as male and female with their instinct for a bestial mode of procreation.[21] Here lies Gregory's explanation of how a being made in God's image can be subject to miseries alien to the Divine blessedness: man possesses one head with two faces, the divine element of his mind that reflects the divine beauty and the brutish element that is the source of nonrational passions and impulses.[22]

"OF THINGS WE EXPECT TO APPEAR LATER": THE ESCHATOLOGICAL PERFECTION OF HUMANITY

Since Gregory's anthropology follows the teleological reasoning that one cannot know the acorn without knowing the oak, his vision of the resurrection, inaugurated by the resurrection of Jesus, whom he calls—in a modification of the Col. 1:15—first born of the *new creation*, gives clarity to God's original intention for humanity.[23] In the resurrection, human beings will possess the divine image and with it the blessedness humanity would have enjoyed had it not fallen. One confusion, however, arising from his eschatological interpretation of the creation story is Gregory's recurring description of the eschaton as a restoration (*apokatastasis*) of paradise: "Now the resurrection promises us nothing else than the restoration of the fallen to their ancient state."[24] One key passage that informs his vision of the eschaton and paradise is Jesus' reply to the Sadducees' question about marriage in the resurrection—"in the resurrection from the dead [they] neither marry nor

---

[19]Ibid. 17.4.
[20]Ibid. 17.5–182.
[21]For a fuller debate about this controversial passage, see J. Behr, "The Rational Animal: A Rereading of Gregory of Nyssa's *De hominis opificio*," *Journal of Early Christian Studies* 7, no. 2 (1999): 219–47, and J. Warren Smith, "The Body of Paradise and the Body of the Resurrection: Gender and the Angelic Life in Gregory of Nyssa's *De hominis opificio*," *Harvard Theological Review* 92, no. 2 (2006): 207–28.
[22]*Making Man* 18.3.
[23]*Against Eunomius* 3. 2. 52–3, in *Gregory of Nyssa: Contra Eunomium III: An English Translation with Commentary and Supporting Studies*, ed. Johan Leemans and Mattieu Cassin, trans. Stuart G. Hall (Leiden: Brill, 2014).
[24]*Making Man* 17.2.

are given in marriage ... they are like angels and are children of God" (Lk. 20:35-6). The implication is that the first human beings lived an angelic existence in paradise. Yet, as we saw above, he also contends that God "implanted in mankind, instead of the angelic majesty of nature, that animal and irrational mode [of procreation]," and with it, passions alien to the *imago Dei*. Instead, therefore, of interpreting the eschaton to be an exact "restoration" of the Edenic life, we should interpret the eschatological restoration as the perfection or actualization of God's original purpose for humanity, namely, that man might possess the virtues of *apatheia*, *autexousia* and *makaria* (blessedness) proper to a creature bearing the divine image. He expresses this idea of humanity's perfect conformity to the archetype in his idea that as humanity began as a single man from whom the human nature flowed in procreation, so then the culmination of this process is a single man like the first.[25] Since the resurrection is the perfection of human nature, then it must entail the redemption of the body and the soul through the elimination of that which is alien to the divine image and is the cause of suffering.

The purification of the body is the result both of God's refashioning the mortal body and the purification of the soul. Gregory's view of the resurrection was intentionally a critique of Origen's eschatology. Although at times Gregory sees the spiritual body of the resurrection as liberation from humanity's present corporeal existence,[26] more commonly he holds that the resurrected body is the present body transformed and glorified. The soul, he explains, remains in contact with the material elements of the body, which the soul, like quicksilver, draws together at the resurrection.[27] His concern is twofold. First, to preserve continuity between this life and the next, the body of the resurrection must be the same body, that is, composed of the same matter as a person had in this life. As in Methodius' view, the resurrection is like remaking a defective clay pot that the potter has reduced to dust in order to remove the defect and then remolds into a perfect pot.[28] Second, whereas Origen's spiritual body is the ethereal body in which each rational being dwelt before the fall into the present, coarse material bodies, Gregory affirms the goodness of the material creation rather than seeing it as a mere epiphenomenon that serves the present age but will pass away in the eschaton. Yet the matter of the resurrected body is transformed so that it no longer weighs down the soul and proves an impediment to the soul's participation in God.[29] This is, at least in part, a consequence of the soul's purification. For, drawing on Plotinus' theory of the soul's communication of form and beauty to the body through contemplating the intelligible forms,[30] Gregory says the body mirrors the beauty of the soul, which itself reflects the beauty of God whom it contemplates.[31] Since in the eschaton God will be "all and in all," the soul will derive life directly from the divine nature in which it participates. This life then sustains the body

---

[25]Ibid. 16.17–18.

[26]"In Regard to Those Fallen Asleep," in *One Path for All: Gregory of Nyssa on the Christian Life and Human Destiny*, trans. Rowan A. Greer (Eugene, OR: Cascade Books, 2015), 105–6.

[27]*Making Man* 27.6.

[28]*Address on Religious Instruction* 8, in *Christology of the Later Fathers*, trans. Edward R. Hardy (Philadelphia: Westminster Press, 1954), 282–3.

[29]B. E. Daley, *The Hope of the Early Church: A Handbook of Patristic Eschatology* (Cambridge: Cambridge University Press, 1991), 88.

[30]Plotinus, *The Enneads*, trans. Lloyd P. Gerson, George Boys-Stones, John M. Dillon, R. A. H. King, Andrew Smith and James Wilberding (New York: Cambridge University Press, 2019), 1.6.

[31]*Making Man* 12.9–10.

keeping it free from corruption. In this sense the body itself bears the beauty of the divine image undistorted by mortality.

Gregory's account of the soul's deification or purification,[32] both in this life and in the age to come, of all that is alien to the *imago Dei*, is called *epektasis*. Taken from Paul's account of the soul's straining forward (*epekteinomenos*) to the heavenly prize (Phil. 3:13), *epektasis* defines perfection as the soul's eternal movement into God's infinite being. The doctrine is most clearly stated in *Life of Moses*; unlike finite goods whose perfection is measured in precise limits[33]—not too much, not too little—"in the case of virtue we have learned from the Apostle that its one limit is the fact that it has no limit."[34] The theory of *epektasis* rests on two principles, one theological, the other anthropological. The theological principle is God's infinity. Dating back to his refutation of the Eunomians' claim to be able to define God, Gregory reasoned that since God is unconditioned by anything external to himself, God must be infinite. And if infinite, then God's nature is beyond human comprehension. Finite humanity cannot know all there is to know about God. Thus, there will always be a gap (*diastēma*) between God and humanity's understanding; there will always be something of God to be revealed. Therefore, the soul will always be straining forward seeking to know more of God. The anthropological principle is humanity's inherent mutability. Unlike God who is eternal, humanity is a creature that by God's power and grace came into existence from nothing. Drawing on a hylomorphic theory of substance, Gregory contends that human beings derive their existence from God, who gives form to our material nature. Moreover, rational creatures continue to be formed through contemplative participation in God's nature. In other words, as the intellect contemplates the Divine, God becomes the content of its thought; thus, the soul acquires a likeness to the Divine object of its thought. Since God's goodness is infinite, the soul's desire to see and know more of God is insatiable. Moreover, since God is an inexhaustible object of contemplation, the intellect set upon God will continually be reformed as it receives yet newer revelations of God's nature. The mind "looks eternally upon the First Cause of all things that are and is preserved in every respect in the good by its participation in what transcends it. It is also in a certain fashion, *always being created* as it is changed for the better by increasing in goodness."[35] Here Gregory finds the dividing line between the Creator and the creature: God is eternal Being but humanity is eternal becoming. This principle of eternal becoming through an ever-progressive participation in God is the basis for his definition of perfect virtue: "let us make progress within the realm of what we seek [i.e., God]. For the perfection of human nature consists in its very growth in goodness."[36]

This perpetual growth can be understood in terms of a dialectic between vision and desire. Following the maxims that "like is known by like" and "like is attracted to like," the soul's purification through monastic disciplines allows it to become like God's holiness. The more like God the soul becomes, the higher the revelation it is able to receive from

---

[32]The *telos* of humanity is deification; *epektasis* is the process by which one participates in the divine and is transformed into deified humanity. See N. Russell, *The Doctrine of Deification in the Greek Patristic Tradition* (Oxford: Oxford University Press, 2006), 225–37.

[33]For example, a perfect or ideal right angle is exactly 90 degrees.

[34]*Life of Moses* 1.5, in *Classics of Western Spirituality*, trans. A. Malherbe and E. Ferguson (New York: Paulist Press, 1978), 30.

[35]*Homilies on the Song of Songs*, trans. R. Norris (Atlanta: Society of Biblical Literature, 2012), 6.185–7. Emphasis original.

[36]*Moses* I.10.

God. At the same time, the more of God the soul beholds, the purer and more ardent its longing to see God. Since God is love, the increase in love for God is itself an increase in likeness to God. Thus, every new vision of God allows the soul to see ever more wondrous aspects of God. These greater and greater visions of God create a continuous cycle that both arouses deeper longing for God and fosters a greater capacity to see the Divine more clearly. Thus, the progressive growth in the knowledge unceasingly sets the soul in motion into God. Humanity will always be a creature that is ever changing, an eternal becoming. When united to God in love, it is a creature ever being changed "from glory unto glory"—into higher degrees of likeness to the Divine. Here Gregory's doctrine of humanity's creatureliness provides the logic for his soteriology. God uses the inherent instability of human nature—an instability that is the condition for the possibility of turning from God—to keep the soul ever desiring and so continuously moving into God.[37] This is the paradox of *epektasis*: humanity's only hope of attaining *stasis* in God— eternally abiding in the Rock—is because God's infinitely wondrous Being never allows the soul to come to a point of rest at which its desire for God is satiated.

Although the theory of *epektasis* comes to full form in Gregory's later works, already in his anthropological writing of the early 380s he was beginning to work out the anthropological implications of divine infinity. One challenge, however, is figuring out how the soul is able to ascend eternally into God in the eschaton if, in the resurrection, the soul has been purged of its principle of motion, desire and spirit, which are nonrational and so alien to the *imago Dei*. Since the nonrational faculties serve the needs of this age, they will not remain a part of human nature when it is purified in the eschaton. Yet if the soul is drawn ever deeper into God by a desire to see more of God's beauty, then how will the soul continue to ascend if it has lost the faculty of desire? In *On the Soul and Resurrection*, Gregory argues that, when God shall be "all in all," God will be fully present to the soul in one eternal now and so the emotion of desire—the longing for that which is absent—will be transformed into enjoyment (*apolausis*).[38] Joy is the new principle of intellectual activity. Such a view, he recognized, does not take seriously the ontological gap between infinite God and finite humanity even in the eschaton. In later works, such as his *Homilies on the Song of Songs*, Gregory recognizes that, if something of God always remains hidden, the soul always experiences desire—even if it is different in character than desire in the present age—for God. Although God shall be "all in all," yet so infinite is his grace that the soul will desire as if it is seeing God for the first time.[39] Thus, desire, though alien to the *imago Dei*, is an inherent and inescapable element of our creaturely nature.

As we have already seen, the ideal of the angelic life is central to Gregory's conception of the perfection of human nature in the resurrection. It, therefore, establishes the *telos* of human existence eschatologically and of the monastic life in this age. If the resurrection was to be in some sense a restoration or actualization of paradise, then monasticism offered, especially for women, a foretaste of eschatological freedom from the task of procreation. This possibility rests on Gregory's analysis of Gen. 1:26-27 that establishes a type of equality between men and women. Unlike those theories of virtue that maintained that the female could become virtuous by taking on the qualities proper to the male such as strength, self-control and fortitude, Gregory locates people's capacity for virtue in the

---

[37] *Song of Songs* 8.265.
[38] *Soul and Resurrection* 6.15.
[39] *Song of Songs* 1.33.

imago Dei, which was prior to and independent of gender. Consequently, a woman's actualizing her capacity for virtue is not about becoming male; it is about a participation in the virtues of the divine archetype that is without gender. Thus, his theories of the *imago Dei* and the twofold creation establish the moral equality between men and women.

Perhaps no text expresses this point as clearly as his hagiographical *Life of Macrina*, written about the same time as *On the Making of Man* and *On the Soul and Resurrection*. Here Gregory narrates his sister's monastic life to illustrate how through monastic disciplines one can attain a likeness to that perfection in virtue that is humanity's eschatological destiny. In the prologue to the *vita*, Gregory writes, "The subject of this tale was a woman—if indeed she was a 'woman', for I know not whether is fitting to designate her of that nature who so surpassed nature ... who had raised herself by philosophy to the highest summit of human virtue."[40] Gregory calls the monastic life "philosophy" because it is characterized by contemplation, the mortification of the flesh and above all the love of the Bridegroom who is the Wisdom and Power of God (1 Cor. 1:24).[41] Through sexual renunciation, Macrina "returned" to that asexual, angelic existence God intended for humanity in the beginning and which is humanity's eschatological destiny. In this way, the monastic life that casts off sexual relations, which exist only as an accommodation of humanity's fall, is a proleptic participation in the angelic life of resurrected humanity. Thus, Gregory describes the life of Macrina and her women as "far removed from these things, divorced from all earthly vanities and attuned to the imitation of the angelic life."[42]

SUGGESTED FURTHER READING

Boersma, Hans, *Embodiment and Virtue in Gregory of Nyssa: An Anagogical Approach* (Oxford: Oxford University Press, 2013).

Greer, Rowan A., *Christian Hope and Christian Life: Raids on the Inarticulate* (New York: Crossroad, 2001).

Laird, Martin, *Gregory of Nyssa and the Grasp of Faith: Union, Knowledge, and Divine Presence* (Oxford: Oxford University Press, 2004).

Ludlow, Morwenna, *Gregory of Nyssa: Ancient and [Post]modern* (Oxford: Oxford University Press, 2007).

Mateo-Seco, Lucas F., and Giulio Maspero (eds.), *The Brill Dictionary of Gregory of Nyssa* (Leiden: Brill, 2010).

Smith, J. Warren, *Passion and Paradise: Human and Divine Emotion in the Thought of Gregory of Nyssa* (New York: Crossroad, 2004).

Zachhuber, Johannes, *Human Nature in Gregory of Nyssa: Philosophical Background and Theological Significance* (Leiden: Brill, 1999).

---

[40]*Macrina* 1.3.
[41]Gregory may be following Socrates' description of philosophy in *Phaedo* 64be by which the soul is prepared for death through contemplation and self-restraint (*sōphrosunē*) in order to purify it of that which is alien to its true nature (80e-81a).
[42]*Macrina* 13.3–4.

CHAPTER THIRTEEN

Soul, Body, and the Miraculous Excess of the Human Being: Augustine's Theological Anthropology

DOUGLAS FINN

In two sermons preached around Easter 411, Augustine counters opponents of the resurrection, the human end according to Christianity, by recalling the human beginning: "It is in fact a greater miracle, so many people being born who didn't previously exist, than a few having risen again, who did exist."[1] The "daily miracle" of human formation is "so excessively common that it has lost its power to strike wonder"[2] in people's minds and hearts. Augustine indicates that, from beginning to end, the human being is a site of wonder, a point of transcendent reference to God. Yet, habituated to the visible world, sinful humans have grown inured to their own miraculous excess. To regain vision of the human being and human possibility demands, then, a training in unseeing and unknowing.

In this chapter, I extend insights from John Cavadini's article, "The Anatomy of Wonder."[3] According to Cavadini, miracles are, for Augustine, signposts pointing to a greater miracle, the goodness of creation, which ought to elicit wonder. Wonder is the antidote to pride, the distorted love animating sinful humanity's various cultural projects, which objectify God's creatures, including human beings, according to their usefulness. Here I investigate how Augustine's anthropology uncovers the "anatomy" of wonder even more literally, in the unity of soul and body. The human being is, in its unity-in-difference, a mysterious expression of love, which averts both the proud claim to speak definitively with words and the pride that claims an illusory objective position in silence above temporal language. Augustine's anthropology of wonder enables, rather, a humble seeing and speaking that draw the human beyond herself in the communal praise of God.

I would like to thank my colleagues Anthony Dupont, Andrew Hofer, OP, Augustine Reisenauer, OP, and Stephen Okey for their helpful comments on earlier drafts of this article. The title was suggested by Miles Hollingworth.

[1] *Sermon* (=s.) 242.1 (Patrologia Cursus Completus, Series Latina [=PL] 38:1139; Works of Saint of Augustine [=WSA] III/7:78).

[2] *S.* 242A.2 (*Miscellanea Agostiniana* [=MA] 1:329; WSA III/7:86).

[3] John Cavadini, "The Anatomy of Wonder: An Augustinian Taxonomy," *Augustinian Studies* 42, no. 2 (2011): 153–72.

SOUL AND BODY

Augustine describes the human being as a wondrous mixture:

> The soul is not of a bodily nature, nor does it fill the body as its local space, like water filling a bottle … but in wonderful ways (*miris modis*) it is mixed into (*commixta*) the body it animates, and with its incorporeal nod … it powers or steers the body with a kind of concentration (*quadam intentione*), not with any material engine.[4]

Augustine is consistent throughout his career in describing humanity as a composite of soul and body.[5] Yet there exists a difference in his attitude toward the body, if one compares his early works with those from later periods, especially after 410.[6] In the *Soliloquies* (386–7), for instance, Augustine states that he desires to know only God and the soul, nothing more.[7] That endeavor requires that one

> entirely flee from things of sense. So long as we bear this body we must beware lest our wings are hindered by their birdlime. We need sound and perfect wings if we are to fly from this darkness to yonder light, which does not deign to manifest itself to men shut up in a cave unless they can escape, leaving sensible things broken and dissolved. When you achieve the condition of finding no delight at all in earthly things, … you will see what you desire.[8]

Augustine further reports in his *Reconsiderations* that, in some early works, he expected the resurrection body to be purely spiritual, not fleshly.[9]

The young Augustine was influenced by both Manichean and Stoic thought to believe that anything real must be bodily.[10] On that view, God and the soul are corporeal. Only after reading Plotinus in Milan was Augustine able to conceive of nonbodily reality. Thereafter, Augustine knew bodies are extended three-dimensionally in space. The soul, contrariwise, is "an independent, nonmaterial substance present to the body in a causal but not spatiotemporal way—the subject of knowledge and desire [and] the seat of self-consciousness."[11] The soul is whole wherever it is,[12] independent of the size of the body it animates.[13]

---

[4]*On the Literal Interpretation of Genesis* (=*Gn. litt.*) 8.21.42 (Corpus Scriptorum Ecclesiasticorum Latinorum [=CSEL] 28:261; WSA I/13:370).

[5]See, e.g., the early *On the Happy Life* (=*b. vita*) 2.7.

[6]See David Hunter, "Augustine on the Body," in *A Companion to Augustine*, ed. Mark Vessey (Chichester: Wiley-Blackwell, 2012), 353–64. For extensive treatment of the body in Augustine's thought, see Margaret Miles, *Augustine on the Body* (Missoula, MT: Scholars Press, 1979).

[7]*The Soliloquies* (=*sol.*) 1.2.7.

[8]*Sol.* 1.14.24 (CSEL 89:37; Augustine, *Earlier Writings*, ed. and trans. J. H. S. Burleigh, 1953 (Louisville: Westminster John Knox, 2006), 38).

[9]See, e.g., *On Faith and the Creed* (=*f. et symb.*) 10.24 and his corresponding reevaluation at *retr.* 1.17. See also *Reconsiderations* (=*retr.*) 1.25, on *Eighty-Three Varied Questions* (=*div. qu.*), and *retr.* 2.3, on *On the Christian Struggle* (=*agon.*).

[10]Roland Teske, "Soul," in *Augustine through the Ages*, ed. Allan Fitzgerald (Grand Rapids, MI: Eerdmans, 1999), 807, citing *Confessions* (=*conf.*) 5.10.19–20 and 7.1.1.

[11]Brian Daley, "Christology," in *Augustine through the Ages*, 165.

[12]*On the Immortality of the Soul* (=*imm. an.*) 16.25.

[13]At *On the Greatness of the Soul* (=*quant.*) 16.27–22.40, Augustine argues that the greatness of soul is virtue, not extent. See also the later *ep.* 166.2.4.

Manicheism also taught Augustine that the human soul is substantially identical with the divine.[14] Human souls are particles of the divine imprisoned in evil material bodies. The Manichean believer's task was to separate his good, divine self from the evil body that beset him.[15] And however much Plotinus liberated Augustine from materialistic thinking, he, too, posited a concept of soul that straddled the divine and human spheres. From Augustine's earliest writings, however, his Nicene Christian beliefs prevented him from appropriating Plotinus' teaching regarding the soul's divinity.[16] Augustine insisted the soul is created,[17] particularly because it is mutable.[18] Consistently, Augustine posited a hierarchy of being,[19] wherein nothing is closer to God than the soul.[20] As the soul is subordinate to God, so is the body subordinate to the soul.[21]

From very early, then, Augustine establishes the basic principles ingredient to humanity's mysteriousness: first, the soul's creaturely status and dependence upon God, and second, within the human composite, the soul's difference from and superiority to the body. That sense of human mystery only deepens as Augustine's appreciation for the body grows, as he grasps the human person as a mysterious unity-in-difference, articulated in terms of love. That is, Augustine's wonder increases as he more acutely perceives a twofold human vulnerability: as an embodied soul immersed in society and the world and as radically dependent upon God, the creator.

At this juncture, we should note important developments, occasioned by Augustine's deepening engagement with Paul,[22] that contribute to Augustine's appreciation for the body. First, Michael Cameron pinpoints Augustine's *Commentary on Galatians* (394), where, against the Manichees, Augustine emphasizes in a new way the soteriological necessity of Christ's death, with profound theological consequences:

> Rather than *only* ... juxtaposing ... [eternity and time], the cross interrelated them as Christ took on sin, death, and the curse *both* figuratively *and* really. The resulting "sacramental" template altered Augustine's understanding of the unity in Christ's person and work; it also eventually affected his view of Christ's unity with the Church, and the unity of sign and reality in sacraments. Augustine had earlier thought that Christ's death ... was primarily a tool of spiritual pedagogy that used "likenesses" to excite and coach the believer's self-mortification. But a loophole inadvertently allowed the Manichees to say that self-mortification by likeness did not require Christ's physical death. Augustine closed the loophole by adjusting his view of how figures work. The real flesh of Christ on the cross was necessary *not only to show redemption, but to conduct it*; Christ *instructed* the human mind with truth but also *mediated* grace to the human will.[23]

---

[14]See *On Genesis, against the Manichees* (=*Gn. adv. Man.*) 2.8.11 and 2.26.40.

[15]J. Kevin Coyle, "Mani, Manicheism," in *Augustine through the Ages*, 522–3.

[16]Chad Tyler Gerber, *The Spirit of Augustine's Early Theology: Contextualizing Augustine's Pneumatology* (Surrey: Ashgate, 2012), 57–122.

[17]*Gn. adv. Man.* 2.8.11.

[18]*Conf.* 12.17.24.

[19]See the description of intellectual ascent at *conf.* 7.17.23. See also the later *City of God* (=*civ. Dei*) 11.16.

[20]*Quant.* 34.77; *imm. an.* 15.24; *On True Religion* (=*vera rel.*) 53.113. See the later *civ. Dei* 11.26.

[21]*Gn. adv. Man.* 2.9.12. See the later *civ. Dei* 19.25–26.

[22]See Paula Fredriksen, "Beyond the Body/Soul Dichotomy: Augustine on Paul against the Manichees and the Pelagians," *Recherches Augustiniennes* 23 (1988): 87–114.

[23]Michael Cameron, *Christ Meets Me Everywhere: Augustine's Early Figurative Exegesis* (Oxford: Oxford University Press, 2012), 158.

Second, Tarcisius Van Bavel studies Augustine's use of Eph. 5:29: "No one ever hated his own flesh." By 397, Augustine regards love for one's body as natural and refers to soul and body as a whole (*totum*). Van Bavel documents "an evolution from subjection to love. Subjection of the body [to the soul] remains always necessary, but it is less and less based on philosophical arguments and more and more on Christian, especially Pauline, ideas."[24]

Finally, Robert Markus traces Augustine's developing concept of pride. What was, in Augustine's earlier works, a turning from God to lower goods in the hierarchy of being becomes a preference for one's private good over the common good. The result is disharmony between the individual and God, between soul and body and among human beings.[25]

IMAGE AND ITS DEFORMATION

To see how disharmony arises, we need to explore Augustine's Trinitarian theology of creation and the *imago Dei*. Beginning with his early writings, Augustine counters Manichean denigration of creation by discerning creation's intelligibility in its Trinitarian imprint. Augustine describes how each created substance has a capacity for being, particular form and proper place—a goodness or order—in the divine arrangement of creation.[26] These features reflect the Trinity's immanent relations: the Father is the source of all being; the Son is begotten of the Father, an equal, consubstantial and perfect image, adhering eternally to the Father; the Holy Spirit unites the Father and Son in love. In the economy of creation, then, the Father gives being to creatures.[27] The Father creates through the Son, who gives each thing its particular form.[28] The Holy Spirit represents God's good will in creation, "a kind of love in his activity which comes not from any need on his part but from generosity."[29] The Holy Spirit preserves the beautiful and harmonious order of all things in unity with their creator.[30]

The Son contains the forms of all created things. Augustine stresses that God creates *ex nihilo*.[31] What God creates is *formability*, the capacity of all created things to receive form.[32] Formability is atemporal and unchanging—apart from its basic contingency as a creature. It stands at the lowest extreme of the hierarchy of created beings, while at the highest extreme Augustine situates the heaven of heavens, God's unfallen rational creation.[33] God's Word informs indeterminate creation through a dynamic of call and conversion: God calls contingent creation, and in turning toward him, each creature

---

[24]Tarsicius Van Bavel, "'No One Ever Hated His Own Flesh': Eph. 5:29 in Augustine," *Augustiniana* 45 (1995): 45–93, here 84–5.
[25]Robert A. Markus, *Conversion and Disenchantment in Augustine's Spiritual Career* (Villanova, PA: Villanova University Press, 1989), 31–2.
[26]James J. O'Donnell, *Augustine*, Confessions, 3 vols. (Oxford: Oxford University Press, 1992), 2:46–51, on *conf.* 1.7.12. For earlier instances, see *Gn. adv. Man.* 1.16.26, Letter (=*ep.*) 11.3, *vera rel.* 7.13. See also *civ. Dei* 11.21.
[27]*Gn. litt.* 4.12.22–23, 5.20.40.
[28]*Conf.* 13.2.2–2.3.
[29]*Gn. litt.* 1.5.11 (CSEL 28:9; WSA I/13:172).
[30]David Vincent Meconi, SJ, *The One Christ: St. Augustine's Theology of Deification* (Washington, DC: Catholic University of America Press, 2013), 12–14.
[31]*Vera rel.* 17.34–18.35; *civ. Dei* 12.5.
[32]*Gn. litt.* 5.5.16; *conf.* 12.6.6.
[33]*Conf.* 12.12.15; Meconi, *One Christ*, 16–18.

gains form as a distinct and knowable thing. Through conversion, each creature imitates the Word, God's perfect and equal image, in his eternal adherence to the Father.[34]

Nonrational creation undergoes this process necessarily; for rational creatures, however, conversion and formation entail freedom and will.[35] Here we arrive at the human being as *imago Dei*. According to Augustine, an image is distinguished from other likenesses by its relationship to its source. An image reveals something about its archetype, with which it shares some qualities. By contrast, many things may resemble each other without sharing the same origin. Their likeness to each other conveys nothing about their respective sources.[36] Crucially, images can be equal or unequal to their source. The Son is *the* perfect image of the Father, coming from and perfectly manifesting the Father, while eternally equal to and one with the Father. Theirs is not a relationship of mere likeness. The human being, contrariwise, is God's unequal image.[37] The human's ability to image the divine depends upon and is constitutively reflective of God's transcendence over creation. But difference between archetype and image does not mean utter disjunction. In Platonic fashion, an image participates in features of its archetype[38] and bears an intrinsic drive to assimilate itself, as much as is possible, to its source.[39]

Augustine thus argues that the image of God lies not in the body or the soul's lower functions, but in the rational mind, through which humans can recognize God and attain wisdom.[40] Nevertheless, the *imago Dei*'s dynamism entails a vision of the human being as an intrinsic unity of soul and body, as evidenced by Augustine's theory of *rationes*, whereby he reconciles the differing creation accounts of Gen. 1:1–2.4 and 2.4-2.25.[41] The former, according to Augustine, describes God's simultaneous creation of all things; the latter describes creation's emergence over time.[42] Eternally, the Son contains the forms of all created things (*rationes primordiales*).[43] At the first, simultaneous creation, Augustine identifies two lower modes of causation: the *rationes* of the intellectual creation[44] and the *rationes seminales*, which govern material creation.[45] The *rationes seminales* are not themselves material;[46] they are causal "seeds" of material things set to emerge at their proper time. Regarding human nature, Augustine thereby affirms the soul's primacy over the body while simultaneously stressing their unity. Burnell explains, "A human physical causal reason in the first instance has two dimensions: as an aspect of the soul and as a virtuality in the material basis of the universe; for before it is realized it associates the

---

[34]*Gn. litt.* 1.4.9; see Meconi, *One Christ*, 20–7.

[35]For Augustine's anthropology analyzed under the aspects of creation, conversion and formation, see Marie-Anne Vannier, "L'Anthropologie de S. Augustin," in *Körper und Seele: Aspekte spätantiker Anthropologie*, ed. Barbara Feichtinger, Stephen Lake and Helmut Seng (Munich: K.G. Saur, 2006), 207–36.

[36]*Div. qu.* 74. See Gerald Boersma, *Augustine's Early Theology of Image: A Study in the Development of Pro-Nicene Theology* (Oxford: Oxford University Press, 2016), 189–207; and Meconi, *One Christ*, 36–8, for discussion of how Augustine distinguishes image, likeness and equality.

[37]*Vera rel.* 43.81; *The Trinity* (=*Trin.*) 7.3.5, 7.6.12.

[38]Boersma, *Early Theology of Image*, 196–9.

[39]*Sol.* 2.9.17; *Trin.* 7.3.5; Meconi, *One Christ*, 39–41.

[40]*Trin.* 12.7.12; *Gn. litt.* 3.20.30, 6.12.21.

[41]See Matthew Drever, *Image, Identity, and the Forming of the Augustinian Soul* (Oxford: Oxford University Press, 2013), 19–21.

[42]*Gn. litt.* 5.1.1–5.5.16, 5.7.20, 6.1.1–6.5.8, 6.10.17–6.11.19.

[43]*Gn. litt.* 1.9.17–1.10.20, 1.18.36, 3.12.18, 4.24.41–4.25.42, 5.12.28, 6.10.17.

[44]*Gn. litt.* 2.8.16–2.8.19, 4.32.49–4.32.50.

[45]*Gn. litt.* 4.33.51–4.33.52, 5.4.8–5.4.11, 6.10.17–6.11.18.

[46]*Gn. litt.* 6.6.11.

soul, from which it is not distinct, with the material world, from which it is distinct, but does so virtually. When it is realized (at conception) it associates them actually."[47] The human soul is intrinsically oriented toward its body.[48]

The fall manifests the implications of this unity. As *imago Dei*, humans possess an intrinsic tendency to become like God.[49] They are called to be freely converted and conformed to the Son,[50] the perfect and equal image of the Father. Importantly, for Augustine, humans are made in the image of the Trinity, not just the Son[51]—for reflecting the Son as the Father's equal image *is* reflecting the Trinity. But, as rational, embodied creatures, humans must come to image God in and through history. Adam, Augustine insists, was initially granted an "ensouled" or animal body, which was *able not to die*, so long as he avoided sin. By nature, the prelapsarian human was mortal—*able to die*—but immortal—*able not to die*—by God's assistance. Had Adam not sinned, God could have made his body "enspirited"—such that he would have been *not able to die*.[52]

By the time of *Gn. litt.*, Augustine was convinced that, even before the fall, the first human pair would have procreated sexually. But sex would have reflected the harmonious unity of humans in themselves, with each other, and with God. Through their mind and will, the first pair would have directed their sexual organs to function, without lust, in an act of pure self-giving to one another.[53] In sinning, however, humans attempted a "perverse imitation of God,"[54] seeking God's power decoupled from his goodness. Preferring their own private good to the common good, they tried to elevate themselves above the whole of creation. Yet the human being, a part of creation,[55] cannot transcend the whole. When the proud soul tried to commandeer the whole, it relinquished control over even that part which it governed partially: the body.[56] The harmony of human beings with God and each other vanished. Even the human body now disobeys the mind and will.[57]

The body falls apart and dies. The younger Augustine followed the Platonic tradition in regarding death as a good,[58] but by the time he wrote *civ. Dei* 13, he was convinced that death was in all cases evil,[59] for the soul loves its body. Even the greatest saints and martyrs struggle with the fear of death.[60] Furthermore, sin dramatically changes sexual experience. Postlapsarian sexuality is marked by concupiscence, lustful desire that often

---

[47]Peter Burnell, *The Augustinian Person* (Washington, DC: Catholic University of America Press, 2005), 28.
[48]*Gn. litt.* 12.35.68.
[49]Meconi, *One Christ*, 52–78.
[50]*Gn. litt.* 8.6.12; *Explanations of the Psalms* (=*en. Ps.*) 70(2).6–7; *Trin.* 7.3.5.
[51]*Trin.* 7.6.12, 12.6.6–12.6.7.
[52]*Gn. litt.* 6.25.36–6.26.37.
[53]*Gn. litt.* 9.3.5–9.3.6; *civ. Dei* 14.23, 14.26; see John Cavadini, "Feeling Right: Augustine on the Passions and Sexual Desire," *Augustinian Studies* 36, no. 1 (2005): 195–217.
[54]*Gn. litt.* 8.14.31 (CSEL 28.1:252; WSA I/13:364).
[55]*Conf.* 1.1.1.
[56]*Trin.* 12.9.14.
[57]*Civ. Dei* 14.15.
[58]E.g., *quant. an.* 76; see also *civ. Dei* 1.11.
[59]*Civ. Dei* 13.6; see John Cavadini, "Ambrose and Augustine: *De bono mortis*," in *The Limits of Ancient Christianity: Essays on Late Antique Thought and Culture in Honor of R. A. Markus*, ed. William E. Klingshirn and Mark Vessey (Ann Arbor: University of Michigan Press, 1999), 232–49.
[60]E.g., *en. Ps.* 30(2).3 and 68(1).3; see Robert Dodaro, "'Christus Iustus,' and Fear of Death in Augustine's Dispute with the Pelagians," in Signum Pietatis: *Festgabe für Cornelius Petrus Mayer zum 60. Geburtstag*, ed. Adolar Zumkeller, OSA (Würzburg: Augustinus-Verlag, 1989), 341–61.

defies reason and will—epitomized for Augustine by the male erection.[61] Nevertheless, Augustine describes postlapsarian sexuality, and the passions generally, in *defense* of the body. Against the Manichees and Platonist philosophers,[62] Augustine insists that the passions stem from a disordered soul, not the body.[63] The evil humans suffer is not the body *per se*, but human nature's fragmentation.[64]

THE WONDER OF THE INCARNATION

Turning from the source of their being toward nothingness,[65] sinful humans are *de*formed.[66] Augustine recounts how the soul, enamored of its power, turns toward the body and other material things. Growing attached to them, it begins to conceive of its own nature as material, too.[67] Because the soul conforms itself to material objects rather than the eternal Word, the Word meets humans where they are. Without change to his divinity, the Son assumes the *form* of a servant,[68] mutable humanity, in order to re-form human nature. Yet believing that one bearing the form of a servant is simultaneously the form of God is challenging, both for those incapable of grasping intelligible truth and those who, though comprehending spiritual reality, do not know how to reach and adhere to it in love. Some, fettered by materialistic thinking, fail to conceive how God could enter a human body without relinquishing providential governance of creation.[69] Others, understanding the difference between intelligible and material realities, deem the incarnation unbecoming of God.[70] Either way, there is a misunderstanding and delimitation of divine transcendence with respect to God's power and goodness.

Around 410–11, Augustine's anthropology advances by way of important Christological developments. In *ep.* 137 (411), Augustine writes, "Just as the soul is united to the body in the unity of the *person* in order that a human being might exist, so God is united to the man in the unity of the *person* in order that Christ might exist."[71] *Persona* is a new technical term in Augustine's theology, denoting the subjective unity of two distinct substances. Augustine's earlier employment of the term drew upon exegetical usage stemming from theatrical and legal contexts. Augustine sought to identify who was "playing the role" of speaker in a particular biblical passage and how that role was being played. Augustine could, for instance, interpret a text's speaker to be Christ, but in the role of Adam (*ex persona Adam*), fallen humanity's corporate person.[72] At the same time, the incarnate Christ is unlike other humans, who merely participate in divine Wisdom. Christ can, of

---

[61]E.g., *civ. Dei* 14.16.

[62]*Civ. Dei* 14.5.

[63]*Civ. Dei* 14.3.

[64]Hunter, "Body," 359–60.

[65]*Civ. Dei* 14.13.

[66]E.g., *Trin.* 14.16.22: "sed peccando iustitiam et sanctitatem veritatis amisit, propter quod haec imago **deformis** et decolor facta est; hanc recipit cum **reformatur** atque renovator" (Corpus Christianorum. Series Latina [=CCL] 50:452; emphasis added).

[67]*Trin.* 10.5.7–10.8.11.

[68]*Trin.* 1.7.14.

[69]*Ep.* 137.2.4–2.8.

[70]*Ep.* 137.3.9; *conf.* 7.21.27; *civ. Dei* 10.24.

[71]*Ep.* 137.3.11 (CSEL 44:110; WSA II/2:218; italics mine).

[72]*En. Ps.* 21(1).1 (CCL 38:117); *en. Ps.* 21(1).7 (CCL 38:118).

his very nature, speak in the person of divine Wisdom.[73] After 411, this dramatic sense of *persona* gains the metaphysical inflection of "acting subject" in Augustine's writings.[74]

Throughout his career, Augustine eschewed Apollinarianism,[75] claiming instead that the divine Word assumed a whole human being, soul and body. The soul becomes for Augustine the contact point between the Word and Christ's humanity:

> The union of two incorporeal realities ought ... to be believed with more ease than that of one incorporeal and one corporeal reality. For, if the soul is not mistaken about its nature, it grasps that it is incorporeal; much more is the Word of God incorporeal, and for this reason the union of God and the soul ought to be more believable than that of the soul and the body. But we experience the latter in ourselves; the former we are commanded to believe in Christ.[76]

Many overlook the incarnation because they cannot view the created world with awe, including the daily birth of human beings as a unity of soul and body. God's Word must thus become familiar to humans so that humans might become other to themselves. Only by becoming alien to themselves can they attain what is truly "theirs" and see themselves as sites of wonder.

The distinction within Christ's subjective unity proves essential to the miracle of the incarnation and Augustine's anthropology: "A mediator has appeared between God and human beings so that, *uniting both natures in the unity of his person*, he may raise up the ordinary to the extraordinary and temper the extraordinary to the ordinary."[77] Among sinful humans, the rupture in human nature often engenders deleterious one-sided thinking: either a materialism that regards God and the soul as bodily or a proud spiritualism that excludes the body from what is truly human. Above, Augustine set the conditions for grasping the unity of the Word with Christ's soul: the soul cannot be mistaken about its immaterial nature and must have in itself the experience of the unity of soul and body. The former suggests widespread confusion regarding the soul's nature. Everyone presumably fulfills the latter. Nevertheless, among those who favor the soul at the body's expense, the experience of soul and body together is not always deemed *good*. And despite the universal experience of the soul's unity with the body, that unity remains *inexplicable*.[78]

In the incarnate person of Christ, according to Augustine, humans are reintegrated individually and socially. Yet Augustine underscores the *Trinitarian* shape of human reintegration through his exegesis of Christ's birth by the Holy Spirit.[79] Augustine insists that Christ's virginal conception was free of lust and his humanity thus insulated from original sin's disruptive effects.[80] This interpretation can also be articulated positively: the

---

[73]*Commentary on the Letter to the Galatians* (=*Ex. Gal.*) 27 (CSEL 84:92).

[74]See Hubertus Drobner, *Person-Exegese und Christologie bei Augustinus: Zur Herkunft der Formel*, Una Persona (Leiden: Brill, 1986), 241–70.

[75]A view set forth by Apollinaris of Laodicea (c. 310–c. 390), which argued that, in Jesus Christ, the divine Logos assumed only Christ's human flesh, not a rational soul. The Logos took the place of Christ's human mind.

[76]*Ep.* 137.3.11 (CSEL 44:110–11; WSA II/2:218).

[77]*Ep.* 137.3.9 (CSEL 44:108; WSA II/2:217; italics mine).

[78]*Ep.* 137.3.11: "Certain people demand that an account (*rationem*) be given them of how God was united to the man in order to become the one person of Christ, though ... this happen[ed] only once. They do so as if they can give an account (*rationem*) of something that happens daily, namely, of how the soul is united to the body in order that there might come about the one person of a human being" (CSEL 44:109–10; WSA II/2:218).

[79]See Jacques Verhees, "Heiliger Geist und Inkarnation: Unlöslicher Zusammenhang zwischen Theo-logie und Ökonomie," *Revue des études Augustiniennes* 22 (1976): 234–53.

[80]E.g., s. 233.4; *Trin.* 13.18.23; *Against Julian, an Unfinished Book* (=*c. Jul. imp.*) 4.57–58.

Holy Spirit is essential to the unity of Christ's incarnate person. Christ's birth by the Spirit demonstrates God's free grace, for the man Jesus' personal union with the Word resulted not from any preceding merits, but a free gift.[81] The human being's formation is a gracious act of love; so, too, is humanity's re-formation.

Augustine's account of Christ's affective life shows the latter's freedom from original sin. Christ experienced real human emotions, but never as disobedient passions.[82] Thus, Christ offers an example of what human affective life ought to be. Significantly, Christ is the only human who goes to death freely, without fear.[83] That freedom renders Christ's death a true sacrifice, *the* sacrifice in which believers participate.[84] Christ's death reharmonizes what sinful humanity ruptured. Humans sought power over justice, by claiming for themselves what is God's. Christ pursued justice before wielding his divine power. He assumed human mortality and healed human nature through a renewed sharing in divine life.[85] Fittingness, rather than strict rational necessity, dictated this redemptive solution.[86] The human illness is pride, while the remedy is the free, humble love of justice manifest in the incarnation.

For Christ to foster the love of justice over power, he cannot serve as an example that humans imitate by their *own* power. Rather, Christ must mediate to believers the power to follow his example. Augustine utilizes the concepts of sacrament and example to explain how Christ's death reintegrates human nature. Humans suffer a double death, first of soul, then of body. The soul dies when it is separated from God through sin. As punishment for sin, bodily death occurs when the soul departs the body. To humanity's double death, Christ harmoniously applied his single, bodily death. His spirit could not die, because he was sinless and never separated from the eternal Father. Thus, Christ also underwent a single bodily resurrection. Christ thereby negated humanity's double death and enabled a twofold resurrection: initially, the resurrection of the inner human and, eschatologically, the body.[87]

The death and resurrection of Christ's *body* function as a *sacramentum*, a sacred sign, which indicates *and* communicates the mystery of redemption. In his divinity, Christ could not die, so his *transitus* from death to life in his body signifies and effects the inward movement of a sinful soul to a new life of justice. Christ's bodily resurrection then serves as a sacrament of the soul's spiritual regeneration. Christ's sacramentality further enables Christians to follow his *exemplum*. Augustine explicitly relates Christ's exemplarity to the outer human. Through the power of Christ's sacrament, believers can follow Christ's example not to fear death. They can also conform their bodily sufferings to Christ's so as to focus the mind's attention on the soul, which is harmed only through sin. By following Christ's example in life, Christians then hope to follow Christ's example in the resurrection.[88] Christ's exemplarity thus helps believers grasp the soul's difference from the body and affirm the goodness of human nature as a unity of soul and body. Because Christ exemplifies a humble love of justice over power, though, Christians are

---

[81] *Trin.* 13.17.22; *A Handbook on Faith, Hope, and Love* (=*ench.*) 11.37, 12.40.
[82] *Civ. Dei* 14.9.
[83] E.g. *s.* 305.2–4.
[84] *Civ. Dei* 10.6.
[85] *Trin.* 13.13.17–13.14.18, 13.16.21.
[86] *Trin.* 13.10.13, 13.18.23.
[87] *Trin.* 4.2.4–4.3.6.
[88] *Trin.* 4.2.4–4.3.6.

healed gradually. Only at the eschaton will believers achieve the happiness that attends the power to act, in their bodies, according to their just wills.[89]

THE WHOLE CHRIST

The Inward Turn

After investigating scriptural revelation and the grammar of Trinitarian doctrine in *De Trinitate* 1–7, Augustine seeks a deeper understanding of the Trinity by looking at God's image in the human mind.[90] In *Trin.* 10, he confronts the paradox of the Delphic injunction, *Know thyself*: the mind as a whole must find within itself what it lacks, knowledge of itself as a whole. Yet, for the quest to commence, it must have some sense of what it seeks, the whole of itself, not just readily observable parts of itself or universal categories that might describe it in the abstract.[91] An obstacle to the mind's self-knowledge is people's tendency to view the mind as an object distinct from the process of coming to know. Such objectification arises from materialistic thinking, whereby the mind attaches to itself features of material objects on which it has become fixated.[92] Augustine therefore introduces a mental exercise of self-doubt, in a seeming anticipation of Descartes, to demonstrate the mind's presence to itself as an immaterial reality. Although sensory perceptions admit of doubt, one cannot doubt the existence of the mind doing the doubting. The act of self-doubting thus opens onto a deeper level of the mind's self-awareness—a more immediate self-knowledge that Augustine terms *se nosse* as opposed to the on-and-off thinking about oneself, *se cogitare*, of conscious awareness.[93] Yet here Augustine and Descartes differ: the former seeks not to establish a trustworthy foundation of all knowledge upon the certitude of the mind's knowledge of itself, but rather to show how the mind, as intellectual and immaterial, as thinking *activity* behind all discrete mental acts, eludes skeptical critiques, which might otherwise still pertain to perceptions of material things.[94]

Augustine shows how the mind's ever-present and immediate self-knowledge enables the search for the mind as Trinitarian image—in the mind's remembering, understanding and loving itself remembering, understanding and loving God. This *Trinitarian* structure, however, suggests the limits of self-knowledge afforded by the mind's exercise of self-doubt. Knowledge, for Augustine, entails intention and love. Knowledge of self as the *image* of God cannot be the discovery of rational *autonomy*. An image depends upon its source and goal. The mind as image reflects the Trinitarian God who *is* self-giving love and who acts consistently with his being—creating and saving the world out of love. Any self-knowledge articulated in terms of a closed, autonomous self thus arises from a fallen will seeking power before justice. By contrast, those who, in imitating Christ, seek justice before power, confront another paradox: the mind, in knowing itself, knows itself completely, yet in knowing itself completely, it knows itself as open and mysterious.[95]

---

[89]*Trin.* 13.13.17; *s.* 242.11.

[90]*Trin.* 8.P.1.

[91]*Trin.* 10.3.5–10.4.6.

[92]*Trin.* 10.5.7–10.6.8.

[93]*Trin.* 10.10.13–10.10.16. See Drever, *Image*, 113–15.

[94]See Drever, *Image*, 124–31.

[95]See Rowan Williams, "The Paradoxes of Self-Knowledge in the *De trinitate*," in *Augustine: Presbyter Factus Sum*, ed. Joseph Lienhard, Earl Muller and Roland Teske (New York: Peter Lang, 1993), 121–34.

In *Trin.* 13, Augustine thus adduces another argument directed in part at the skeptics. They agree that everyone wishes to be happy. Augustine sets two conditions for happiness: desiring rightly (justice) and possessing what is desired such that one cannot lose it against one's will (power). Mortality clearly prevents the attainment of happiness in this life. Only Christ offers the means to happiness: presently, by reforming the distorted human will (justice) and, ultimately, through the resurrection (power).[96] The task, then, is not just to know the mind's structure but also to *become* the image of God. That entails grasping the immateriality of the mind where the image is found; it also means entering into proper relationship with the body.[97] Reintegration is not a solo affair, for if one's proud pursuit of the world as a private good occasioned the fall, one's healing emerges from learning to love God as the common good of all those created in his image. To love justly is to love God and to love one's neighbor as oneself, as a fellow human made to reflect and praise the creator. This communal healing takes place in the communal body of Christ, the church.

Into the Body

In *en. Ps.* 30(2) (*c.* 411), Augustine deploys bodily and marital imagery to illustrate the therapeutic, unifying effects of Christ's voice in the church:

> Understand that Head and body together are called one Christ. ... [L]isten to what Paul tells us: *They will be two in one flesh,* he says. *This is a great mystery, but I am referring it to Christ and the Church* (Eph 5:31-32). So out of two people one single person comes to be, the single person that is Head and body, Bridegroom and bride. ... [I]f two in one flesh, why not two in one voice? Let Christ speak, then, because in Christ the Church speaks, and in the Church Christ speaks, and the body speaks in the head, and the Head in the body.[98]

In the voice of Christ, expressed especially through the Psalms, Augustine discovers how errant human emotions are healed.[99] Augustine justifies a Christological reading of the Psalms through Christ's own appropriation of psalmic lament: "God, my God, why have you abandoned me?"[100] According to Augustine, Christ laments in *forma servi.* The words function sacramentally, signifying the sinful soul's God-forsakenness, but they also function as an example, as Christians are taught not to fear death. In *ep.* 140, Augustine connects the lament to sinful humanity's yearning for a longer life: "So great a power does the sweet companionship of the flesh and soul have! ... [T]he soul also does not want to leave its weakness even for a time, though it trusts that it will receive its flesh for eternity without weakness."[101] Christ assumes his body's lament and *transfigures* it into himself, thereby transferring the body's loves from this life toward human nature's reintegration in the next:

> In the cry, then, of this weakness of ours, which our head applied to himself [*in se transfiguravit*], the psalmist says ... *God, my God, look at me; why have you abandoned*

---

[96]*Trin.* 13.3.6–13.9.12.

[97]Paige Hochschild, *Memory in Augustine's Theological Anthropology* (Oxford: Oxford University Press, 2012), highlights the role of memory, especially its communal dimension, in mediating between the intelligible and the material in Augustine's anthropology.

[98]*En. Ps.* 30(2).4 (CCL 38:193; WSA III/15:324).

[99]See Cavadini, "Feeling Right," 212–15.

[100]Ps. 21.2 (22.1).

[101]*Ep.* 140.6.16 (CSEL 44:167; WSA II/2:252).

me? (Ps 22:2). ... Jesus applied this cry to himself [*in se ... transfiguravit*], that is, the cry of his body ... his Church, which was to be formed anew [*reformandae*] from the old man into the new man.[102]

Augustine again demonstrates lamentation's transfigurative power in *en. Ps.* 30(2). He investigates the meaning of the term "ecstasy," found in the Psalm title. It could mean fear: "Whose fear? Christ's certainly ... Or our fear, perhaps? Surely we cannot attribute fear to Christ as his passion loomed, when we know that was what he had come for?"[103] Yet because Christ freely assumed human emotions, including fear, those emotions become the sacramental means of healing:

> He who did not disdain to take us up into himself, did not disdain either to transfigure us into himself [*transfigurare nos in se*], and to speak in our words, so that we in turn might speak in his. This is the wonderful exchange. ... Facing death, then, because of what he had from us, he was afraid, not in himself but in us. When he said that his soul was sorrowful to the point of death, we all unquestionably said it with him. Without him, we are nothing, but in him we too are Christ.[104]

Believers are given words to pray to God, which, on the sacramental power of the incarnation, begin to heal fractured humanity. Their fear is real; so is God's love, which transforms that fear from the inside out. "Your fear is your own, your hope is God's gift in you. In your fear, you know yourself better, so that once you are set free you may glorify him who made you."[105] Self-knowledge, knowledge of the self's creation from nothing and its distortion through sin, leads not to absolute self-possession, but to the human's fulfillment in the *outward* movement of rightly ordered love.

Above, we saw Augustine use marital imagery to express how Christ's unity with his body helps effect healing in that body's members. In the text *On the Advantage of Fasting* (408), Augustine speaks also of "a kind of marriage between spirit and flesh,"[106] by which he indicates the harmonious unity that is achieved as sinful flesh is gradually rendered obedient to the spirit, just as the church subordinates herself to Christ. Accordingly and tellingly, then, Augustine proceeds in *util. jejun.* to argue that the pursuit of individual self-discipline is merely self-serving and ultimately self-destructive if it is not grounded upon the greater obedience of the body of Christ to her bridegroom and head. It is contradictory for one to pursue only one's own bodily harmony at the expense of the harmony and unity of Christ's body.[107] Thus, individual human reintegration is only really possible in the communal body of Christ, through training in love of God *and* neighbor.

Human identity thereby assumes a communal, Eucharistic character. Lament becomes gratitude and praise of God, humanity's proper mode of being.[108] Praise is language fitting to the wondrousness of creation and human nature. As Augustine argues in *civ. Dei* 10, worship is due to God alone, who is shared in common by all, not to any intermediary or

---

[102]*Ep.* 140.6.15 (CSEL 44:166; WSA II/2:252).
[103]*En. Ps.* 30(2).3 (CCL 38:191; WSA III/15:322).
[104]*En. Ps.* 30(2).3 (CCL 38:192; WSA III/15:322–23).
[105]*En. Ps.* 30(2).3 (CCL 38:192; WSA III/15:324).
[106]*On the Advantage of Fasting* (=*util. jejun.*) 5 (CCL 46:235; WSA III/10:474).
[107]*Util. jejun.* 8.
[108]*Conf.* 1.1.1.

oneself. Moreover, "Mercy is ... the true sacrifice."[109] In the love binding the members of Christ's body into a harmonious whole, "the true sacrifice is offered in every act which is designed to unite us to God in a holy fellowship, every act, that is, which is directed to that final Good which makes possible our true felicity."[110] That true sacrifice entails all human sacrifices of soul and body. Becoming an incarnational totality,

> the whole redeemed community ... the congregation and fellowship of the saints, is offered to God as a universal sacrifice, through the great Priest who offered himself in his suffering for us—so that we might be the body of so great a head—under "the form of a servant." ... Thus the Apostle first exhorts us to offer our bodies as a living sacrifice ... not to be "con-formed" to this age but to be "re-formed" in newness of mind to prove what is the will of God ... because we ourselves are that whole sacrifice.[111]

Christ's mediation enables the body, in its groaning, fear, and lamentation, to begin to "prove what is the will of God." The visible body's liturgical practice underscores that the faithful are a sacrificial community dependent always upon God's love: "This is the sacrifice which the Church continually celebrates in the sacrament of the altar, a sacrament well-known to the faithful where it is shown to the Church that she herself is offered in the offering which she presents to God."[112]

The Body of Praise: Resurrection

Augustine articulates his mature view of bodily resurrection with a view toward the communal praise of God in the heavenly city. He struggles to envision perfectly reintegrated and embodied humanity.[113] In part, he needs to account for the eternal damnation of the unjust and the eternal blessedness of the saved. Damnation requires an inseparable bond between soul and body so that the psychic and physical pain of one's God-forsakenness persist for eternity. In life, pain signals the rupture between soul and body, often to the point of actual, and unwanted, rupture in the first death. In hell, there is a perverse, and unwanted, reintegration of the self, which in God's absence becomes one's greatest torment, as this "second death holds the soul in the body against her will."[114]

By contrast, Augustine describes humanity's state of blessedness "as an intensification of bodily experience."[115] It will be a state of utter freedom and peace, better than that possessed by Adam, for it will be a freedom from death's possibility and from the possibility of willing evil.[116] Disintegration and corruption will be overcome.[117] The body will be subservient to the soul.[118] Deformities and other blemishes will be remedied.[119]

---

[109]*Civ. Dei* 10.5 (CCL 47:278; Bettenson, 379).
[110]*Civ. Dei* 10.6 (CCL 47:278; Bettenson, 379).
[111]*Civ. Dei* 10.6 (CCL 47:279; Bettenson, 380).
[112]*Civ. Dei* 10.6 (CCL 47:279; Bettenson, 380).
[113]See Virginia Burrus and Karmen Mackendrick, "Bodies without Wholes: Apophatic Excess and Fragmentation in Augustine's *City of God*," in *Apophatic Bodies: Negative Theology, Incarnation, and Relationality*, ed. Chris Boesel and Catherine Keller (New York: Fordham University Press, 2010), 79–93.
[114]*Civ. Dei* 21.3 (CCL 47:760; Bettenson, 966).
[115]Hunter, "Body," 361.
[116]*Civ. Dei* 22.30.
[117]*S.* 242A.3.
[118]*Civ. Dei* 22.21, 22.24.
[119]*Civ. Dei* 22.19.

Bodies will be restored to their ideal stature of about age 30, or "the stature of the full maturity of Christ."[120] Those who died before reaching peak bodily condition will be raised to the condition they would have achieved had they lived to maturity.[121] Body parts that, in the fallen condition, had been conceived exclusively under the regime of utility will be in the resurrection sites of beauty and wonder. Even now the body bears a beauty bespeaking the goodness of its creator—Augustine adduces men's nipples and beards, which he contends are purely ornamental—but in the body's resurrected state even internal organs and human genitalia, which have a particular use, will occasion the praise of God. This indicates the perfectly ordered harmony and peace of soul and body and among all members of the heavenly city. No longer will one look upon a woman's, or any person's, body and feel lust, the desire to *use* another. Rather, one will see in the other a reflection of God's goodness and love.[122] Humanity, and all creation, will be transfigured from opacity to transparency:

> All the limbs and organs of the body, no longer subject to decay ... will contribute to the praise of God. ... The harmonies which, in our present state, are hidden, will then be hidden no longer ... [and] they will kindle our rational minds to the praise of the great Artist by the delight afforded by a beauty that satisfies the reason.[123]

In the state of sin, furthermore, the body impedes knowledge, its discovery and communication. In the resurrection, however, our thoughts will be open to all,[124] no longer subject to misunderstanding and the strife it causes.[125] And "how complete, how lovely, how certain will be the knowledge of all things, a knowledge without error, entailing no toil! For there we shall drink of God's Wisdom at its very source, with supreme felicity and without any difficulty."[126]

This is not to say that what is particular to the individual will be lost in some idealized, generic humanity. Augustine describes how the wounds of martyrs will be preserved and transfigured as marks of glory.[127] If the temptation in this life is for one to give one's own story a definitive meaning, and do so in such a way that subsumes or silences the stories of others, Augustine tries to imagine the unimaginable: the heavenly city where one receives and keeps what is truly one's own in its perfect other-directedness, in perfect love of God and neighbor.[128] This is as hard to envision as it is to see why the soul would not want to reach its end—the sight of the Trinitarian God—without the body it loves,[129] and it is perhaps why Augustine imagines we shall not truly *see* and reflect the mysterious self-giving love that God is except with and through the resurrected eyes of the flesh:

> It is ... most probable, that we shall then see the physical bodies of the new heaven and the new earth in such a fashion as to observe God in utter clarity and distinctness, seeing him present everywhere and governing the whole material scheme of things by

---

[120]*Civ. Dei* 22.15, referring to Eph. 4:13.
[121]*Civ. Dei* 22.13–14.
[122]*Civ. Dei* 22.17, 22.24.
[123]*Civ. Dei* 22.30 (CCL 47:862; Bettenson, 1087–8).
[124]*Civ. Dei* 22.29.
[125]See *civ. Dei* 19.7.
[126]*Civ. Dei* 22.24 (CCL 47:852; Bettenson, 1076).
[127]*Civ. Dei* 22.19.
[128]In eternity each will have a reward commensurate to her merit, but differences among individuals will not inspire envy (*civ. Dei* 22.30).
[129]*Gn. litt.* 12.35.68.

means of the bodies we shall then inhabit and the bodies we shall see wherever we turn our eyes.[130]

No longer will we see God as in a mirror or an enigma. That vision will not obtain in silence or idleness,[131] but with never-ending songs of praise.[132]

CONCLUSION

Matthew Drever has observed how Augustine's two-source, hierarchical anthropology is susceptible to some modern critiques, which enjoin us to see human nature as more integrated into the world.[133] I have not tried to evaluate Augustine's anthropology from a contemporary theological or philosophical perspective so much as to underscore how central the unity-in-difference of the human person is to Augustine's understanding of the mystery of the human being, as a creature of God made in his Trinitarian image. In particular, I have attempted to show how, for Augustine, the human mystery does not leave one utterly speechless, but rather enables the type of language appropriate to divine transcendence and the excess of God's love, which extends into the finite world through the acts of creation, salvation and eschatological perfection. Augustine appeals to human experience—for example, to the fact that all humans experience in themselves the unity of soul and body—but, ultimately, one's ability to speak of the human being is rooted in theological mysteries that have been revealed out of love: creation out of nothing,[134] the mystery of the incarnation,[135] the divine Trinity.[136] At the core of these doctrines is the wondrous movement of God's love, to which the only proper human response—the very end without end of the human being—is wonder, expressed in ceaseless gratitude and praise.

SUGGESTED FURTHER READING

Cavadini, John, "Feeling Right: Augustine on the Passions and Sexual Desire," *Augustinian Studies* 36, no. 1 (2005): 195–217.

Drever, Matthew, *Image, Identity, and the Forming of the Augustinian Soul* (Oxford: Oxford University Press, 2013).

Hunter, David, "Augustine on the Body," in Mark Vessey (ed.), *A Companion to Augustine* (Chichester: Wiley-Blackwell, 2012), 353–64.

Miles, Margaret, *Augustine on the Body* (Missoula, MT: Scholars Press, 1979).

Vannier, Marie-Anne, "L'Anthropologie de S. Augustin," in Barbara Feichtinger, Stephen Lake and Helmut Sen (eds.), *Körper und Seele: Aspekte spätantiker Anthropologie* (Munich: K. G. Saur, 2006), 207–36.

---

[130]*Civ. Dei* 22.29 (CCL 47:861; Bettenson, 1086).

[131]*Civ. Dei* 22.30.

[132]*Trin.* 15.28.51.

[133]Drever, *Image*, 46–7.

[134]See *Gn. litt.* 1.18.37, 5.4.10.

[135]See, e.g., John Rist, *Augustine: Ancient Thought Baptized* (Cambridge: Cambridge University Press, 1994), 100–1.

[136]See, e.g., Lewis Ayres, *Augustine and the Trinity* (Cambridge: Cambridge University Press, 2010), 285–90.

CHAPTER FOURTEEN

From Image to Indwelling: Aquinas' Theological Anthropology

DOMINIC DOYLE

Aquinas' theological anthropology is theocentric and Trinitarian. It is grounded upon a robust doctrine of creation that sees the human as *imago Dei*. As such, it takes seriously the idea that the human person is *capax Dei*. The influence of divine grace upon human nature is therefore seen as perfective, not destructive. In Trinitarian terms, the two temporal missions of the Word (Incarnation) and Spirit (grace) heal and perfect the human capacities to know and to will. In this way, human understanding and loving are gathered into the eternal Wisdom and Love that is God. The image of God becomes the place where God dwells.

This brief statement of Aquinas' theological anthropology will be unpacked in the following four sections: (1) creation; (2) *imago Dei*; (3) sin; and (4) grace.

CREATION

The doctrine of creation is fundamental to Aquinas' theological vision. It is not so much one doctrine alongside others but rather the lens through which the meanings of other doctrines come into focus. Creation is God's production of existence *ex nihilo*, from no preexisting matter. It refers not to a distant time of origin, but a permanent relationship of dependence. As the effect of God, the source of all goodness, creation is good. To denigrate creation, therefore, is to disparage the Creator. Positively, creation is the venue in which to find something of the divine goodness.

The relationship between Creator and creation can be expressed in terms of participation. This intuitive and (to some, infuriatingly) broad notion captures at once God's transcendent difference from, and intimate presence in, creation. As the infinite cause of existence, God is clearly not one effect alongside other effects. In technical terms, God's essence is identical with God's act of existence, whereas the existence of finite effects is given to them and not self-contained, as it were, in their own essences. One must therefore affirm God's radical transcendence from any created thing. However, one must also acknowledge that those finite, created effects resemble their divine cause. As a result, creation is not alien to God. For if God's essence is existence itself, and if existence is "innermost in each thing and most fundamentally inherent in all things …

Hence it must be that God is in all things, and innermostly."[1] So God is not distant from the world but immanently, deeply present in it.

This transcendent yet immanent relationship of creation to Creator is *sui generis*. The difference between God and the world is different from any difference within the world. God is differently different. And so that difference between God and world cannot be explained by appealing to any difference in the world. We cannot use our categorically differentiating intelligence to understand this Creator-creation distinction in the way we normally use it to understand distinctions within the world. For when we distinguish things within the world, we mark off one thing from another, as this and not that. For example, this book you are holding is not the chair you are sitting on. But God cannot be treated as another item in the universe, set alongside other things on the same plane of existence, as it were. In fact, it would be a mistake of the highest order to defend divine transcendence by contrasting God to the world in the same way that we contrast two things within the world. God's transcendence is of such a unique, radical kind as to entail immanence. Indeed, from the very same premise—God's infinity—we can derive both divine transcendence (for obvious reasons) and divine immanence (for there is nowhere that the infinite is not).

To be created, then, is to participate in the infinite act of existence in a finite, derived way. Expressing creation in terms of participation affirms that God and the world are neither identical (which would be pantheism) nor separate (which would entail the world's nonexistence). This tensile relationship of radical difference-in-likeness grounds the affirmation that God and creation are not competing causes. God does not need to intervene in order to act in creation, as if God were somehow absent and then had to push aside created reality in order to make space to show up in the world. Likewise, creatures do not need to declare independence from God in order to flourish. To the contrary, by realizing their created, finite natures, they come to share more fully in their enabling and sustaining Source.

In this non-contrastive understanding of the Creator-creation relationship, creation possesses a relative autonomy. Its proper causal integrity is not voided by divine action, for God's causal power does not operate on the same ontological level as creation. Rather, God's causal power transcends and sustains creaturely agency. It is both "behind" and "within." In this way, God's providence does not override creaturely agency but rather works through it. In so doing, it establishes the dignity of secondary causality. As Aquinas puts it, "there are certain intermediaries of God's providence; for He governs things inferior by superior, not on account of any defect in His power, but by reason of the abundance of His goodness; so that the dignity of causality is imparted even to creatures."[2] Creation, then, is not just a place in which to behold divine goodness. It is the venue for sharing in divine providence. This more intimate participation in God is seen in that part of creation made in God's image.

---

[1] Thomas Aquinas, *Summa theologiae*, 5 vols., trans. Fathers of the English Dominican Province (Allen, TX: Christian Classics, 1948), I.8.1. (=prima pars, question 8, article 1). All translations from the *Summa theologiae* are from this version and are henceforth cited as *ST*.
[2] *ST* I.22.3.

IMAGO DEI AND THE NATURAL DESIRE FOR GOD

The notion of *imago Dei* is a key organizing principle of Aquinas' *Summa theologiae*. After treating "God and those things that proceed from divine power" in the *prima pars*, the *secunda pars* treats the human person as the image of that divine exemplar. Its prologue quotes John Damascene to identify the likeness in the capacity for intelligence, free decision and self-movement. The basis of that likeness is therefore not simply existence, nor even life, but the intellectual capacity to understand and love.[3] So whereas the *prima pars* treated God's governance over creation in general, the *secunda pars* treats God's more specific providence—through law and grace—over that part of creation endowed with rational freedom.

Since the human is copied, as it were, from the divine, there results a real likeness.[4] Further, since God is triune, the image reflects something of the distinctions among the Persons.

> As the uncreated Trinity is distinguished by the procession of the Word from the Speaker, and of Love from both of these ..., so we may say that in rational creatures wherein we find a procession of the word in the intellect, and a procession of the love in the will, there exists an image of the uncreated Trinity, by a created representation of the species.[5]

Further, when the soul knows and loves itself, those processions of the inner word and of love provide a fitting analogy for the two divine processions.[6] "The mind in knowing itself begets a word expressing itself, and love proceeds from both of these, just as the Father, uttering Himself, has begotten His Word from eternity, and the Holy Spirit proceeds from both."[7]

As made in the image of God, the human person possesses a deep, intrinsic attraction to know about and become like her Maker. "The likeness of image is found in human nature, forasmuch as it is capable of God [*capax Dei*], viz. by attaining to Him through its own operation of knowledge and love."[8] While this natural desire for God is a single dynamic drive, one can distinguish its intellectual and volitional aspects. In terms of the

---

[3]"An *image* represents something by likeness in species ..., while a *trace* represents something by way of an effect, which represents the cause in such a way as not to attain to the likeness of species." *ST* I.93.6. See also Thomas Aquinas, *De veritate*, trans. Robert W. Mulligan, SJ (Indianaolis: Hackett, 1994), question 10, article 1, ad 5.

[4]This likeness, of course, is imperfect and analogical; only the Son is the perfect likeness, consubstantial with the Father. Aquinas makes clear the limitations of the analogy in *ST* I.35.2, ad 3:

> The image of a thing may be found in something in two ways. In one way, it is found in something of the same specific nature; as the image of the king is found in his son. In another way it is found in something of a different nature, as the king's image on the coin. In the first sense the Son in the Image of the Father; in the second sense man is called the image of God.

[5]*ST* I.93.6. See also *ST* I.45.7. The meaning of the phrase "representation of the species" will be explored more fully in a later section.

[6]For Aquinas' development of the Trinitarian analogy from one based on the triadic faculties of memory, understanding and will (cf. Book 10 and 14 of Augustine's *De trinitate*) to one based on the two acts or processions of the inner word in knowing and of love in willing (cf. Book 15 of *De trinitate*), see D. Juvenal Merriell, "Trinitarian Anthropology," in *The Theology of Thomas Aquinas*, ed. Rick van Nieuwenhove and Joseph Wawrykow (Notre Dame, IN: University of Notre Dame Press, 2005), 123–42.

[7]*De veritate*, question 10, article 7, resp. Quoted in Merriell, "Trinitarian Anthropology," 132.

[8]*ST* III.4.1, ad 2.

intellect, Aquinas argues that once the mind has affirmed God's existence through natural reason (e.g., in the "five ways" of question 2 of the *prima pars*), there arises the question of God's nature. The conclusion "that God is" (*an sit*) gives rise to the question of "what God is" (*quid sit*).[9] In this way the human person experiences intellectual wonder about God's essence.

In terms of the will, Aquinas argues that its final satisfaction—ultimate happiness—must complete the appetite such that no desire remains. The opening questions of the *secunda pars* rule out any created good (e.g., bodily pleasure, wealth, power, honor, even contemplation) as the candidate for this goal, because all such created goods point to their Creator and so cannot satisfy the desire for lasting peace. The will, Aquinas argues, is unable to find rest until it goes beyond any participated good and "reaches out to the universal fount of goodness ... the infinite and perfect good," which is God.

Appropriately, Aquinas expresses this twofold natural desire for God in terms of the *imago*:

> Since man is said to be the image of God by reason of his intellectual nature, he is most perfectly like God according to that in which he can best imitate God in his intellectual nature. Now the intellectual nature imitates God chiefly in this, that God understands and loves Himself. Wherefore we see that the image of God is in man ... inasmuch as man possesses a natural aptitude for understanding and loving God.[10]

The image, then, possesses a natural desire for its exemplar.

The fulfilment of this desire, though, is another matter. Without God's help, finite, embodied intellect cannot comprehend the immaterial infinite. Absent grace, human reason faces a paradox: a natural desire for what is above—and thus unobtainable by—nature.[11] Further, since the will can only desire what is presented to it by the intellect, and the intellect cannot by its own powers grasp the essence of God, it follows that the will cannot naturally desire the beatific vision. The fulfillment of the natural desire for God, then, requires grace.

SIN

In addition to these intellectual and volitional limits, a further consideration underscores the need for God's assistance: the impediment of sin. The basic elements of Aquinas' account of sin can be sketched as follows. Sin is a bad, voluntary act flowing from a bad habit, or vice. "Vice" names that state when something is disposed to act against its nature. Since human nature is specified by rationality, vice involves being disposed to act against the order of reason. The root of this disorder lies in the decision to follow one's sensuality instead. Sin, then, involves acting on an inordinate desire for a mutable good, which at root is an inordinate love of self—the source of all sin.[12]

---

[9]*ST* I-II.3.8.
[10]*ST* I.93.4.
[11]On this paradox, see Bernard Lonergan, "The Natural Desire to See God," in *Collection*, ed. Frederick E. Crowe and Robert M. Doran (Toronto: University of Toronto Press, 1967), 81–91 (84).
[12]*ST* I-II.77.4.

Consequently, whereas the good person, by pursing reason, unites the virtues, the sinner, by contrast, experiences dissipation.

> Appetible goods ... to which the sinner's intention is directed when departing from reason, are of various kinds, having no mutual connection; in fact, they are sometimes contrary to one another. ... [Hence] sin does not consist in passing from the many to the one ... but rather in forsaking the one for the many.[13]

Since God is the author of human nature, and human reason participates in the eternal law (or divine reason), then to act against reason is simultaneously to sin against God. More exactly, human reason is the proximate rule or measure of the will; the eternal law is the first rule or measure that encompasses and transcends that proximate rule. They are not two separate, parallel tracks, as it were. To the contrary, to sin against God is to deform one's nature, and to act against reason is to depart from the eternal goal toward which all temporal goods should be ordered.[14]

It is possible, though, that one may sin and not fall into vice, because it takes more than one act to corrupt a virtue. Such venial (or pardonable) sins are compatible with both kinds of virtues: acquired (by human effort) and infused (by divine grace). A mortal sin, however, expels the infused virtues, because it removes charity, the source of all infused virtue.[15] Without charity, the person is no longer directed to the last end; and nothing—except God—can heal the consequent radical disorder. Venial sins, on the other hand, are repairable precisely because the order to the last end remains intact, and so the disorder among intermediate goods can be healed.

In the state of original justice, prior to the fall, the person was able to order the sensible appetites to reason and, through grace, order the whole person to God. The sin of humanity's first parent obliterated this otherwise immortal state and caused a hereditable defect in human nature (cf. Rom. 5:12: "Just as sin came into the world through one man, and death came through sin, and so death spread to all because all have sinned"). This original sin, which affects all humankind, differs from vice (a bad disposition) or sin (a bad act). Formally, original sin is the privation of this original justice by which the will was ordered to God. Materially, it is concupiscence, the consequent inordinate desire for mutable goods. In terms of its effects, sin leaves intact human nature in terms of its principles and powers but destroys the gift of original justice. It diminishes, but does not destroy, the natural inclination to virtue. (If sin did erase rational freedom, the person would no longer be capable of sin.[16]) But such is the disorder wrought by original sin that in the state of corrupt nature, only a few, particular natural goods (such as planting vineyards and building houses) can be reached without grace.[17] A fuller attainment of proportionate natural goods now requires God's help.

---

[13]*ST* I-II.73.1.

[14]But see *ST* I-II.74.10 on the tensions between these two rules: "It is possible for one of the articles of faith to present itself to the reason suddenly under some other aspect, before the eternal law, i.e. the law of God, is consulted ... as, for instance, when a man suddenly apprehends the resurrection of the dead as impossible naturally, and rejects it."

[15]For more on the distinction between mortal and venial sin, see *ST* I-II.72.5 and especially I-II.88.

[16]For a sympathetic account of Aquinas' understanding of original sin, see Rudi te Velde, "Evil, Sin, and Death: Thomas Aquinas on Original Sin," in *The Theology of Thomas Aquinas*, ed. Rick van Nieuwenhove and Joseph Wawrykow (Notre Dame, IN: University of Notre Dame Press, 2005), 143–66.

[17]*ST* I-II.109.2.

GRACE

Just as God is the source of existence, so Christ is the source of grace.[18] Through the work of the cross, Christ pays the infinite debt of sin. By the grace of conversion and repentance, the sinner can direct her life to God and share in the benefits of Christ's cross. In addition to these healing effects, grace also elevates the person to new life with God, overcoming the ontological distance between God and humanity. At its broadest, grace refers to God freely and gratuitously moving the human person to his or her ultimate end, namely, eternal happiness.[19] This divine initiative not only heals the effects of sin but also ultimately makes persons into "participants of the divine nature" (as one of Aquinas' favorite scriptural passages, 2 Pet. 1:4, puts it). Clearly, only the divine can deify. The ultimate end therefore lies beyond what is proportionate to human nature. Consequently, "supernatural" help is needed to attain the end.[20] For this reason, Aquinas describes grace as "the outcome of His mercy," since mercy refers to a gift beyond what is due.[21]

As a gift, grace presupposes a recipient, a nature that receives it. The relationship between grace and nature is captured in Aquinas' famous maxim: "grace does not destroy nature, but perfects it."[22] God takes up and completes the natural desire for God. While human nature cannot attain its end by itself, it is nonetheless inclined and receptive to God's moving it to its end. Hence the irreducible elements of discontinuity and continuity in the grace/nature relationship. The end lies beyond the reach of nature, yet it fulfils what the person, however inchoately or imperfectly, naturally desires. The endless controversies about the relationship between nature and grace in part result from overemphasizing one of these elements at the expense of the other. If one overemphasizes the continuity between human desire and its final end, grace becomes a requirement to fulfil an immanent directionality of nature, and so is no longer gratuitous. If one overemphasizes discontinuity, grace seems extrinsic, even arbitrary, and nature becomes independent and self-sufficient. Both continuity and discontinuity must therefore be held in tension. By nature, the human is *capax Dei*, susceptible of seeing the divine essence. By grace, God freely actualizes this potential by elevating the human above what it can attain unaided. The twofold good of natural and supernatural happiness should therefore not be collapsed or reified. It cannot be collapsed, because grace exceeds nature. It cannot be reified, because grace completes nature. Natural and supernatural happiness are not two separate goals but rather stand to each other as imperfect to perfect. Natural happiness provides some distant likeness to supernatural happiness but signals beyond itself to a qualitatively greater happiness that can only come about through an unmerited, divine gift.

Aquinas unpacks the maxim "grace perfects nature" with particular reference to faith and reason in his *Commentary on Boethius' De Trinitate*:

> The gifts of grace are added to nature in such a way that they do not destroy it, but rather perfect it. So too the light of faith, which is imparted to us as a gift, does not

---

[18]*De veritate*, question 29, article 5.

[19]The treatise on grace is the last section of the *prima secundae*. By considering how the person is brought to their ultimate goal, it appropriately concludes the treatment of the human act, since the end is as foundational for ethics as first principles are for speculative inquiry.

[20]*ST* I-II.112.1.

[21]*ST* I-II.111.3, sed contra.

[22]*ST* I.1.8, ad 2.

do away with the light of natural reason given to us by God. And even though the natural light of the human mind is inadequate to make known what is revealed by faith, nevertheless what is divinely taught to us by faith cannot be contrary to what we are endowed with by nature. One or the other would have to be false, and since we have both of them from God, He would be the cause of our error, which is impossible. Rather, since what is imperfect bears a resemblance to what is perfect, what we know by natural reason has some likeness to what is taught to us by faith.[23]

Faith and reason, then, are not opposed. To the contrary, reason can be used to defend the faith (by removing charges of contradiction) and to nourish it (through analogies that give some limited, proportionate understanding of the mysteries). To accept the gift of grace, then, is not to reject the life of the mind. It is instead to come to see reality in light of God's transcendent wisdom and allow one's understanding and action to adjust accordingly.

The same perfective relationship applies to the noncoercive manner in which grace relates to human freedom. Grace does not contradict nature because, Aquinas argues, God moves the person according to their nature. But the capacity for free decision is proper to human nature. Therefore, grace involves human freedom. Even the infusion of justifying grace requires consent as God moves the will to accept grace.[24] Grace is not coercive since it can be refused.[25] Aquinas uses the following image to show the possibility of the rejection of grace:

> Since this ability to impede or not to impede the reception of divine grace is within the scope of free choice, not undeservedly is responsibility for the fault imputed to him who offers an impediment to the reception of grace. In fact, as far as He is concerned, God is ready to give grace to all; "indeed He wills all men to be saved, and to come to the knowledge of the truth," as is said in I Timothy (2:4). But those alone are deprived of grace who offer an obstacle within themselves to grace; just as, while the sun is shining on the world, the man who keeps his eyes closed is held responsible for his fault, if as a result some evil follows, even though he could not see unless he were provided in advance with light from the sun.[26]

The compatibility of divine initiative and human freedom is only intelligible if one bears in mind the critical distinction between God and creation discussed above. Overlook the transcendent nature of divine causality and one will inevitably think that God's action must restrict human freedom, since they both would then act on the same ontological plane, as it were. But recall that crucial distinction, by which God is understood as transcendently immanent, then God can be "totally and actively present in a divine manner ... without taking over the role of the agent."[27] God's causal power is not that of an extrinsic and

---

[23]Thomas Aquinas, *Faith, Reason, Theology: Questions I–IV of his Commentary on the De Trinitate of Boethius*, trans. Armand Maurer (Toronto: Pontifical Institute of Mediaeval Studies, 1987), 48–9.
[24]*ST* I-II.113.3.
[25]Thomas Aquinas, *Summa contra gentiles: Book Three: Providence. Part II*, trans. Vernon J. Bourke (Notre Dame, IN: University of Notre Dame Press, 1975), 260 (chap. 159, par. 2): "although one may neither merit in advance nor call forth divine grace by a movement of his free choice, man is able to prevent himself from receiving this grace."
[26]Ibid., 261.
[27]Rudi te Velde, *Aquinas on God: The 'Divine Science' of the Summa Theologiae* (Burlington, VT: Ashgate, 2006), 150.

coercive agent. It uniquely relates to the will as its enabling Source that creates, sustains and fulfills human freedom.[28]

Aquinas' views on grace changed considerably over time. Tracing that development brings to light a difficult problem. In his earlier writings, Aquinas affirmed that the person made the first movement toward God. God then responded with the infusion of habitual grace. The person then could persevere in grace by acting on that habitual grace.[29] Upon closer reading of Paul and the later Augustine, Aquinas subsequently came to regard the damage of sin as more serious. He therefore argued for the additional grace of *auxilium* (or help) to overcome sin and bring about conversion and perseverance.[30] In this later position, grace ultimately depends upon God's inscrutable, predestining will and could in no way begin with human effort. But if grace depends upon divine predestination, it raises the question, why is it given to some, but not others? Aquinas' response is that God does "come to the assistance of ... some, while He ... permits others [to sin]—there is no reason to ask why He converts the former and not the latter. For this depends on His will alone; just as it resulted from His simple will that, while all things were made from nothing, some were made of higher degree than others."[31]

In any event, grace brings about a participation in God that goes beyond creative, efficient causality to redemptive, quasi-formal causality. This deeper presence is evoked through various biblical images, such as illumination and indwelling. A passage that describes the divine indwelling adverts to this twofold divine presence, through nature and through grace:

> For God is in all things ... according to His one common mode, as the cause existing in the effects which participate in His goodness. Above and beyond this common mode, however, there is one special mode belonging to the rational nature wherein God is said to be present as the object known is in the knower, and the beloved in the lover. And since the rational creature by its operation of knowledge and love attains to God Himself, according to this special mode, God is said not only to exist in the rational creature, but also to dwell therein as in His own temple. So no other effect can be put down as the reason why the divine person is in the rational creature in a new mode, except sanctifying grace.[32]

If in creation, God brings into existence what is not God, then in grace, God shares Godself with humanity. This grace transforms the natural love for God into the infused virtue of charity, as it "draws the rational creature above the condition of its nature to a participation of the Divine good; and according to this love He is said to love anyone simply, since it is by this love that God simply wishes the eternal good, which is Himself,

---

[28]For a helpful overview of this topic, see Brian Shanley, "Divine Causation and Human Freedom in Aquinas," *American Catholic Philosophical Quarterly* 72 (1998): 99–122.

[29]Habitual grace refers to God's infusion of a settled disposition that makes the person pleasing to God and is the principle of acts proportionate to the supernatural end.

[30]The grace of *auxilium* refers, among other things, to God moving the potency of habitual grace to act. This grace is required because what is in potency can only be reduced to act by something in act. For a clarifying presentation of Aquinas' multiple distinctions on grace, see Joseph Wawrykow, "Grace," in *The Theology of Thomas Aquinas*, ed. Rick van Nieuwenhove and Joseph Wawrykow (Notre Dame, IN: University of Notre Dame Press, 2005), 192–221.

[31]Aquinas, *Summa contra gentiles*, 263–4 (chap. 161, par. 1 and 2).

[32]*ST* I.43.3.

for the creature."[33] Such is the depth of this transformation that Aquinas likens it to creation, in that the person "is given a new being out of nothing, i.e. not from merits."[34]

This presentation of Aquinas' understanding of grace can be summed up by considering it in light of an earlier theme, the *imago Dei*. As the result of sanctifying grace, the making present of the specifically Trinitarian reality of the divine exemplar (the "representation of the species" mentioned above) refers to more than a general capacity to understand and love. It also goes beyond the illuminating analogy for the Trinity that comes to mind when human knowing and loving is reflexive. The specificity of the Trinity is made present when the human is enabled by grace to direct its knowing and loving to God, and thus shares in the very activity that constitutes God as triune, namely, in "the procession of the Word from the Speaker, and the procession of Love connecting Both."[35] In this way, "the image of God is found in the soul according as the soul turns to God, or possesses a nature that enables it to turn to God."[36]

For Aquinas, then, the *imago Dei* conveys more than a pleasing analogy of proportion between faculties or even structurally parallel operations—a distant mirror image between divine and human. Rather, it describes the dynamic, ontological conformation of the human image to its Trinitarian exemplar. Made in the *image* of the Trinity, the human person is remade through grace by the *indwelling* of the Trinity. This assimilation to God, or deification, occurs when the soul actively knows and loves God through grace, and thereby shares in the eternal processions of Word and Love.[37] Specifically, "the soul is assimilated to the Holy Ghost by the gift of charity" and to the Son by the gift of wisdom.[38] Notably, "the Son is the Word, not any sort of word, but one Who breathes forth Love."[39] That is why the consequent intellectual illumination of anyone receiving the mission of the Word is "a certain experimental knowledge; and this is properly called wisdom (*sapientia*), as it were a sweet knowledge (*sapida scientia*)."[40] As the person comes to know God more truly and love God more deeply, she more diaphanously *images* God's loving wisdom in the world. In this way, she exhibits the dignity of instrumental causality through which God providentially governs human affairs.

SUGGESTED FURTHER READING

Torrell, Jean–Pierre, *Saint Thomas Aquinas. Vol. 2, Spiritual Master* (trans. Robert Royal; Washington, DC: Catholic University of America Press, 2003).

van Nieuwenhove, Rick, and Joseph Wawrykow (eds.), *The Theology of Thomas Aquinas* (Notre Dame, IN: University of Notre Dame Press, 2005).

te Velde, Rudi, *Aquinas on God: The 'Divine Science' of the Summa Theologiae* (Burlington, VT: Ashgate, 2006).

---

[33] *ST* I-II.110.1.
[34] *ST* I-II.110.2, ad 3.
[35] *ST* I.93.7. For a fuller discussion of the various degrees of the image, see *De veritate*, question 10, article 7.
[36] *ST* I. 93.8.
[37] The Vulgate's dynamic rendering of Gen. 1:26 ("Faciamus hominem ad imaginem et similitudinem nostram"— "Let us make the human person to our image and likeness") lends support to this position. For more on the distinction between "similar operation" and "unity of object," see Thomas Aquinas, *De potentia*, question 9, article 9, https://isidore.co/aquinas/QDdePotentia9.htm#9:9 (accessed September 8, 2020).
[38] *ST* I-II.43.5, ad 2. Cf. *ST* I-II.79.3, ad 1, which discusses "the effects of grace" as that which "both perfects the intellect by the gift of wisdom, and softens the affections by the fire of charity."
[39] *ST* I.43.5, ad 2.
[40] Ibid.

CHAPTER FIFTEEN

Grasping at the Human as Human: The Human Person after Justification according to Martin Luther's Pneumatological Lens

CANDACE L. KOHLI

Theological anthropology analyzes human personhood in relation to God. There are multiple avenues for exploring this subject. One major approach, particularly among Protestant theologians, orients the conversation of personhood around the *imago Dei*.[1] In this discourse, the human person is created in the image of God, the Fall mars the expression of the human's divine likeness and Christ redeems the human person by reorienting human personhood back to God. A second approach utilizes language from philosophical anthropology and moral theology about human intellectual and volitional capacities. The goal here is to detail the ways in which the noetic faculties in the soul work together such that the human being acts in and with the world around her. The former approach captures the eschatological landscape in the human relation to God but neglects the temporal nuances that enliven exploration of the human *qua* human.[2] In this first approach, anthropology is too often reduced to questions of Christology and justification. The latter accounts for the composite parts of the human as human and her temporal existence but attends less fully to the impact of the God-human relation established in justification, so often pitted in eschatological terms, on those anthropological features. The question is, is it possible to give a robust theological account of the human *qua* human in a way that also does justice to Christ's work to redeem the human person in justification?

---

[1] This perspective permeates the most important systematic work in theological anthropology in the last decade, David Kelsey's *Eccentric Existence*. Kelsey takes a Barthian framework and outlines his anthropology according to the perichoretic relations between the divine Persons. Kelsey's Christological priority is reflected in the sections that deal with post-lapsarian anthropology: "Consummated, Living on Borrowed Time" and "Reconciled: Living by Another's Death." See David Kelsey, *Eccentric Existence: A Theological Anthropology*, 2 vols. (Louisville: Westminster John Knox Press, 2009).

[2] The German theologian Michael Welker recently observed that these anthropological conversations are so often trapped in mind-body dualisms that they fail to do justice to the complexity of human personhood in both psychological-cognitive and physiological-experiential spheres. See his "Introduction" in *The Depth of the Human Person: A Multidisciplinary Approach* (Grand Rapids, MI: Eerdmans, 2014), 1.

The sixteenth-century Protestant reformer Martin Luther is an intriguing discussion partner for this question because he combined anthropological categories inherited from medieval moral theology with the eschatological considerations of the God-human relation established through Christ in justification. By doing so, he was able to parse the impact of justification on the Christian life and to do so in wholly temporal terms. This claim is not without impassioned controversy. Since the early twentieth century, Luther scholarship has largely attended to the eschatological features of Luther's theological anthropology to the exclusion of the anthropological categories available in the medieval moral theology of Luther's day that get at temporal aspects of the human being in the Christian life. In this chapter, I will draw out the ways in which Luther used the concept of justification—not to limit theological anthropology to an eschatological relation—but rather as a tool to open wide the human *qua* human after justification. To do this, I will examine how Luther used justification to parse a changing relation between the Holy Spirit and the human person and, then, how this new way of thinking about the Spirit-human relation made it possible for Luther to reexamine the impact of justification on human intellectual and volitional powers.

THE PROBLEM WITH TEMPORALITY IN SCHOLARLY APPROACHES TO LUTHER'S THEOLOGICAL ANTHROPOLOGY

For most of the twentieth century, Luther researchers elevated an anthropological dialectic known as the *simul* formula as the key to the reformer's theological anthropology. Luther establishes this concept in his *Lectures on Galatians* (1531/35). Here, Luther describes the Christian as *"simul iustus et peccator,'* sinner and righteous simultaneously.[3] He derives this phrase from Galatians 5 where the Apostle Paul discussed the Christian's struggle between "spirit" and "flesh." The "sinner" aspect of the human being aligns with the Pauline term, "flesh." This is the human as she is in herself after original sin. Christians have an additional part added to their ontological structure, which Luther following Paul calls the "spirit." Within Luther's *simul* formula, the "righteous" part of the human being aligns to the "spirit." This aspect results from God's justifying declaration given in the gospel, which attributes Christ's righteousness to the sinner in faith.

The divine declaration that attributes righteousness to the sinner results in an anthropological paradox for Luther. The Christian is both holy and unholy, both "child of God" and "God's enemy." When faith in the "spirit"-aspect of the Christian brings with it Christ's righteousness, it makes the Christian simultaneously sinner—in herself—and righteous—through faith in Christ. In this sense, the paradoxical anthropological condition captured in Luther's *simul* formula refers to a condition that is unique to the Christian's personhood.

This anthropological structure is intrinsically connected to Luther's understanding of sin and justification. Luther inherited the Augustinian framework that conceives of sin as concupiscence or wrong desire. The distinction here is between loving well and loving wrongly. To love well means to love an object above all else and for its own sake. To love wrongly or concupiscently is to love an object for the enjoyment that object can bring to

---

[3]Martin Luther, *Luthers Werke: Kritische Gesamtausgabe [Schriften]*, 73 vols. (Weimar: H. Böhlau, 1883–2009), 40/I.2:368.9, hereafter WA.

one's self, or to love an object for one's own sake. According to the medieval Augustinian theology Luther inherited, this wrong desire was inborn into human nature via original sin. Each individual person then confirms their participation in and guilt for original sin by committing "actual sins" in the mind and body, such as pride, anger, despair, unbelief and so on.[4] As I have discussed elsewhere, Luther makes robust use of this medieval hamartiological framework.[5] What is critical for Luther is that the ongoing presence of original sin in human nature, confirmed and perpetuated by actual sins through the mind and body, makes the human person incapable of loving well.[6] Luther understands sin to coincide with a lack of capacity and, therefore, to keep the person in bondage.

Luther's pessimistic view of the human condition are further exasperated by his inheritance of medieval nominalist notions of the divine command in the law.[7] In Luther's language, the law is the divine declaration that sets the requirements to be justified before God. In it, Luther sees God to demand that human persons love God for God's own sake and above all else. This is the requirement for salvation and it must be perfectly met.[8] Human incapacity is irreconcilable with this divine demand. The ongoing presence of original sin in human nature meant the human person was never able to love God for God's own sake and, in fact, the more she tried the more she proved herself to be a sinner.

Luther's doctrine of justification grows out of the need to resolve this problem of human incapacity before the law. His solution is to locate law fulfillment in Christ's righteousness, not the human person. When the human person comes to God in faith, Luther thinks that God declares that person as righteous and attributes Christ's own righteousness to her as her own. Luther then says that the resulting "perfect Christian righteousness," the righteousness that fulfills the law, consists of "faith and imputation." Righteousness requires faith or "trust in the Son of God," which God gives to the Christian.[9] Then, there is a double imputation. The faith that God gives is "imputed" or attributed to her as Christ's perfect righteousness because faith trusts that Christ suffered and died for the sins of the world.[10] Second, there is a type of negative imputation in which the Christian's own sins are *not* imputed to her but are covered by Christ. Luther notes that this means the Christian's sins remain but become "as if" they are not sin. In order to create perfect law fulfillment out of human incapacity, God must see something in the human being that is not there, namely, Christ's righteousness, and not see what is actually there, human sin.

When it comes to human personhood, Luther's doctrine of justification further specifies the Christian's *simul* condition. Something new, namely, Christ's righteousness, is added to something old, the Christian's own sinful self. Thus, she becomes paradoxically "*simul iustus et peccator*"—simultaneously just (from Christ) and sinner (in herself). The

---

[4]WA 40/II.2:87.13–14.

[5]Candace Kohli, "Help for Moral Good: The Spirit, the Law, and Human Agency in Martin Luther's Antinomian Disputations (1537–40)" (PhD diss., Northwestern University, 2017), 103–22.

[6]WA 40/II.2:88.3–4.

[7]On Luther's nominalism, see Christine Helmer, *The Trinity and Marin Luther: A Study on the Relationship between Genre, Language and the Trinity in Luther's Works (1523–1546)* (Mainz: Verlag Philipp von Zabern, 1999), and Graham White, *Luther as Nominalist: A Study of the Logical Methods Used in Martin Luther's Disputations in the Light of Their Medieval Background*, Schriften der Luther-Agricola-Gesellschaft 30 (Helsinki: Luther-Agricola-Society, 1994).

[8]WA 40/I.2:366.10.

[9]WA 40/I.2:366.6.

[10]WA 40/I.2:366.9–10.

experience of the Christian life will now be constituted by the struggle between these contrary inner anthropological and moral determinations.

This is the picture of Luther's theological anthropology that emerges out of current scholarship. Gerhard Ebeling's *Lutherstudien: Disputatio de Homine* orients the conversation.[11] Ebeling roots the *simul* construct in a forensic interpretation of Luther's doctrine of justification. As Ebeling sees it, God functions as divine judge in a heavenly courtroom. Here, God declares the human being as righteous and acquits her as sinner on the basis of Christ's merits alone. What is vital is that Ebeling denies that this divine declaration alters any ontological features of the Christian in herself. She remains in herself a sinner and incapable of loving God for God's own sake. Rather, Ebeling argues that the divine pronouncement creates a *status change* from "sinner" to "righteous." The change in status establishes a *relation* to God through faith in Christ. It is this relation that Ebeling thinks is important for understanding Luther's theological anthropology, not the ontological features of the person, which ultimately pass away.

Ebeling denies that Luther used ontological categories from Aristotelian anthropological categories inherited from Scholastic and Nominalist theology in any positive or constructive way. Instead, he asserts that Luther's view of the human person after justification encapsulated in the *simul* formula is a "relational ontology."[12] The new relation to God in Christ infers righteousness to the Christian, but this righteousness is restricted to God's declaration regarding the Christian in justification. Any actual righteousness can only be realized in the human person eschatologically and never in the temporal life. The Christian in herself as a temporal person remains ever a sinner and never really ontologically possesses the righteousness inferred to her in justification in any real, experiential way.

The result of this neo-Kantian interpretation of Luther's *simul* formula is the comprehensive rejection of any temporal effects of divine grace on the human person in Luther's theology. Thereby, any consideration of the human *qua* human, of the experiences and struggles of the Christian life, are excluded as a serious point of reflection or inquiry in Luther's thought. Like other Protestant theological anthropologies, the theological investigation of human personhood within Luther's thought is eclipsed by soteriological, Christological and eschatological questions.

LUTHER'S THEOLOGICAL ANTHROPOLOGY AND THE HOLY SPIRIT

What is perplexing about this scholarly approach that elevates the eschatological and soteriological in Luther's theological anthropology is that Luther actually had a great deal to say about the impact of divine grace on human personhood after justification. To investigate this dimension of the human person vis-à-vis God, Luther turned his sights on the human person's changing relation to the Holy Spirit before and after justification. Parsing this evolution in the person's relation to the third Person of the trinity allowed Luther to more fully clarify his ideas about the impact of justification on the ontological features of the Christian's soul.

---

[11]Gerhard Ebeling, *Lutherstudien: Disputatio de homine*, 3 vols. (Tübingen: Mohr Siebeck, 1977–89).
[12]Gerhard Ebeling, "Luthers Wirklichkeitsverständnis," *Zeitschrift für Theologie und Kirche* 90 (1993): 423.

Luther's theological focus in the 1530s is marked by serious reflection on the role of the Spirit in the godhead as well as in the God-human relation. Luther's pneumatology evolved in 1537 to incorporate a new office for the Spirit as divine agent of the law and accuser. The first development occurred when Luther prepared Pentecost sermons on John 14–16, which recounts Jesus' final speech to his disciples before the crucifixion. In line with the liturgical themes, Luther's exegetical notes highlight the shift from Jesus' earthly life and ministry to the coming of the Spirit and the Spirit's work in the world. Theorizing the Spirit's office in his notes to Jn 15:26, Luther notes the Spirit's office is "to bear witness to Christ."[13] The Spirit did not preach the law but made Christians into witnesses and confessors of Christ. Luther clearly associates the Spirit with his theological category of "gospel."

The reformer's surprise is palpable as he progressed in his exegesis of John 16 and discovered a second office for the Spirit in Jn 16:8. Here, he notes that Christ's speech "clearly defines the Spirit's office and work [to be] to convict the world of sins."[14] Luther identified this as an accusing office (das Straf Ampt) and noted that the Spirit is the "eternal judge."[15] According to Luther's estimation, the Spirit's accusing office involves "attacking all of the world's deeds and being, and to tell [everyone in the world] that, as they are found, they are entirely guilty and unjust before God and must believe this word about Christ or be eternally damned and lost."[16] By the end of 1537, as Luther was confronting the Antinomian controversy, he overtly aligned the Spirit with the accusing law in his *Antinomian Disputations* (1537–40). Here, he claimed that the Spirit "wrote the law on tablets of stone with his finger."[17] As the "Author of the law,"[18] the Spirit speaks the law into being and animates it to accuse the sinner's conscience and to drive her to Christ in the gospel.

Luther's discovery of the Spirit's agential relation to law in Jn 16:8 requires that he reconcile the Spirit's new accusing office with the Spirit's more traditional charismatic offices as vivifier and sanctifier. These latter offices come as a result of Christ's gift of the Spirit to the Christian in justification, a view Luther carefully retains.[19] To reconcile the conflicting pneumatological claims, Luther returns to Jn 16:8 as a theological resource. Here, he notes that the Spirit is said to "convict the world of sin *and righteousness* (italics mine)."[20] To make sense of this, Luther decides that the Spirit convicts the world of sin when the Spirit comes to the person in its accusing office apart from Christ. This is a moment that is chronologically delineated neatly before justification in Christ.

However, in justification, Luther understands Christ to give over Christ's righteousness *and* to give the Spirit to the soul as a gift. When the Spirit is mediated as a gift through Christ *and* the soul now possesses in some way Christ's righteousness such that the law can no longer accuse it. Therefore, Luther determines that the Spirit's agential relation to law means the Spirit can use the law in any way it chooses. It just so happens that according to Jn 16:8, the Spirit uses the law after justification to exhort righteousness in

---

[13]WA 45:730.3–11.
[14]WA 46:34.21–3.
[15]WA 46:47.2. See Pekka Kärkkäinen, *Luthers trinitarische Theologie des Heiligen Geistes* (Mainz: Verlag Philipp von Zabern, 2005), 136.
[16]WA 46:34.31–4.
[17]WA 39/I:370.11.
[18]WA 39/I:391.18.
[19]WA 39/I:383.10–11.
[20]WA 46:34.13–14.

the Christian, not to accuse of sin.[21] In justification, Christ gives over the Spirit who is the agent of the law. In doing so, Christ transforms the human relation to the Spirit such that the Spirit brings the law to the human person in a new, what Luther calls, "salutary" way.

To reiterate, Luther establishes an evolution in the way the Spirit relates to the human person that is chronologically determined according to the person's relation to Christ.[22] Before Christ, the Spirit animates the law to accuse the person of sin and drive the person to Christ. Then, the person encounters Christ in faith, is imputed Christ's righteousness and receives the gift of the Spirit. The relation to Christ in faith initiates a new relation to the Spirit when two things occur: first, when Christ imputes Christ's righteousness to the human such that she is no longer attributed with her own guilt before the law; and second, when Christ gives the Spirit to the human person as a gift in faith. Luther calls this third stage "in the Spirit' and locates it squarely after justification by faith. In this stage, the Spirit brings the law to the human person in a new way in its vivifying and sanctifying offices.

THE HOLY SPIRIT, THE LAW AND THE HUMAN INTELLECT AND WILL

In 1537, Luther discovered that the Spirit had an additional office in which the Spirit was the divine agent of the law. This discovery allowed Luther to more carefully parse the human person's changing relationships to the second and third Persons of the trinity. The relation to the Spirit hinges on and is transformed by the relation to Christ. Before Christ, the Spirit animates the law to accuse the human being of sin. After Christ, "in the Spirit," the Spirit in its sanctifying office brings the law to the Christian to "convict of righteousness," according to Luther's interpretation of Jn 16:8. The questions this section will seek to answer are, how does the Spirit use the law to sanctify the human person? What parts of the human being are involved and what can this tell us about Luther's theological anthropology?

At the beginning of this chapter, I discussed Luther's interest in perfect law fulfillment. In medieval moral theology, law fulfillment had to do with penitence, which was a sacramental process where a Christian felt sorrow for sin and formed a good intention not to sin in the future. This means the good intention has to do with law fulfillment. It is the intention to obey God's law and command, which is to love God for God's own sake and above all else.

The good intention is an important concept for the way Luther uses the Spirit to open up anthropological categories. The reason is, Luther credits the Holy Spirit with elevating the human capacities to the good intention. In his *Antinomian Disputations*, he stated, "[God] gives the Spirit to those who believe in order that, from the soul, they might begin to hate sin ... to love, worship, and to call on God."[23] The gift of the Spirit after justification is somehow working in the human soul to spur the types of affection that are in line with the divine command. The Spirit is somehow prompting love of God in the human soul.

---

[21]WA 39/I:445.21–446.1.
[22]WA 39/I:349.39–40. For more detail on this *ordo*, see section 3.5 of my dissertation.
[23]WA 39/I:383.10–11, 13.

The Spirit in its offices as vivifier and sanctifier elevate human capacity for the good intention. The Spirit as vivifier resolves the anthropological problem in the human will, which Luther sees as the locus of sin because the will disobeys the law.[24] To do this, Luther claims that the Spirit actually recreates the soul according to the law and gives the person the will to do the law.[25] The Spirit as sanctifier orients the new will to the law so that it is directed to produce the good intention. Here, Luther claims, "By faith, we receive the Holy Spirit, who produces new motions and fills the will so that it begins to truly love God and hate sin."[26] The Spirit moves the will to the good intention to love God and hate sin.

Luther deploys another anthropological category from medieval moral theology to demonstrate how the Spirit accomplishes this new motion in the will. He claims that the Spirit speaks the law into the soul and "causes remarkable and indescribable cries against sin in your heart."[27] Although Luther does not mention the mind or intellect by name, he is referencing the other noetic faculty common to medieval theological anthropologies, namely, the intellect. In order for the will to assent to a good affection or action, the intellect must guide the will by deciding whether the affections or actions are worthy of love. When Luther suggests the Spirit is speaking the law into the soul and crying out against sin in the heart, he is referencing this intellectual faculty that guides the will's decision making. He is demonstrating that the Spirit brings the law to the human intellect to guide knowledge of God's will and law. Thus, we see Luther using the Holy Spirit to identify and clarify the impact of justification on the noetic faculties in the human soul.

THEOLOGICAL ANTHROPOLOGY AND TEMPORAL HUMAN EXPERIENCE

By examining the Spirit's relation to the human person after justification, Luther has determined that the Spirit uses the law to support the human person's intellectual and volitional capabilities for loving God for God's own sake. He has used his robust doctrine of justification and Christology to actually open up his investigation of the human *qua* human after justification. However, is it possible to also examine how the Christian herself experiences this in her temporal life?

Luther seems to think this is possible. He attempts to excavate this experience by recounting a story about a "Christian youth" who is dealing with the ongoing experience of sin. Luther recounts the story in this way:

> If I, a Christian, still strong in my youth, were to fall in love with a beautiful girl or woman, unless I were a total tree trunk, I could not [help] but feel affection for her and [1] *desire to attain her*, even if I were baptized and justified, were it only permitted by disgrace or another punishment that I fear. Yet, nevertheless, if I am a Christian, [2] *the heart and the Spirit in the heart right away exclaim*: "Get behind me, Satan! Do not speak! No, do not rule, flesh! Be completely silent! You should not persuade me or incite me to fornication, adultery, passion, or to do any other shameful acts against my God in this way. Instead, [3] *I will wait until God will give a woman to me whom*

---

[24]WA 39/I:379.6.
[25]WA 39/I:373.1–4.
[26]WA 39/I:395.22–23.
[27]WA 39/I:526.5–6.

I love! I will make an end with her! I will leave her [i.e. the desired girl/woman] to her bridegroom and family." These and such words are not man's, but [4] *Christ's and the Holy Spirit's, who says in the heart*: "Let the girl in peace. I will give you another in due time, whom you will easily love." This [5] *Christian, even if he is affected by sexual desire, nevertheless obeys the Spirit*, averts by prayer the evil he feels, and prays that he might not enter into temptation.

Therefore, [6] *this already is what it means to overcome sin, even if it cannot be done without trouble and much difficulty ... The Christian stands firm and obeys God's word and law* which says: "You shall not covet," and with the Holy Spirit admonishing him concerning this will of God, he will not give in. (Italics mine)[28]

Here, Luther rehearses the temporal experience in the Christian life of struggling [1] against sin and to love God after justification vis-à-vis the law, Christ, and the Holy Spirit.

The "Christian youth" narrative reflects a young man battling sexual desire for a pretty girl. In this narrative, we see Luther reposition language from medieval moral theology to discuss the anthropological dimension of law obedience in relation to the sanctifying Spirit. Luther locates the Christian youth in proximity to the Holy Spirit, who [2]/[4] together with the Christian's own heart cries out against the sinful desire. The content of the Spirit and the Christian's shared speech is law; Luther harkens back to the commandment prohibiting adultery. Here, we see something critical. The Christian does not experience this declaration of law as an accusation but as an exhortation and directive that he is able to obey in his decision making and action. Luther makes clear [3] that the Christian's decision is to obey and wait on God above all else. The result [5] is that the Christian obeys the Spirit, who directs and bolsters his capacity to reject the sinful desire. In the end, Luther acknowledges the Christian's experience. He obeyed the Spirit and the law, [6] even if it was with much difficulty and struggle.

Interestingly, Luther's account of the "Christian youth" narrative moves through all of the anthropological categories characteristic of medieval moral theology. He gestures toward the affections, the intellect's deliberation over a desire and the intellect's direction of the will's choice to attain or resist a desire. However, Luther does not represent the character in his story to experience these various faculties. Instead, Luther shows how the Christian experienced the Spirit's sanctifying activity as a representation of the law to direct his actions and to bolster his ability to obey by "crying out" within the Christian's own inner thought world. The Christian experiences the Spirit's vivifying and sanctifying work but does so as if somehow the Spirit's work is his own.

---

[28]WA 39/I:500.16–501.6, 501.9–11:

Si ego christianus adhuc robustus adolescens inciderem in aliquam formosam puellam aut mulierem, hic nisi plane tuncus sum, non possum non affici erga illam, etiamsi baptizatus sum et iustificatus, ita ut cuperem eam attingere, si modo per infamiam aut aliam poenam, quam timeo, liceret. Sed tamen, si sum christianus, statim reclamat cor et Spiritus sanctus intus in corde: Abi post me, sathana, nihil dicas, non, non domina caro, tace, obmutesce, non sic me debes impellere aut sollicitare ad stuprum, adulterium, libidinem aut si qua sunt alia flagitia contra Deum meum, ut agam, sed expectabo donec Deus dederit aliquam, quam amabo. In qua etiam finem faciam, sinam hanc suo sponso suisque. Hae et eius modi voces non sunt hominis, sed Christi et Spiritus sancti, qui dicit in corde: Laß daß medlein mit friden, dabo tibi aliquam suo tempore, quam facile amabis. Hic christianus, etsi afficiatur sexu, tamen obedit Spiritui, deprecans hoc malum, quod sentit, orans, ne intret in tentationem. Hoc iam itaque vere est peccatum captivare, etsi hoc non fit sine molestia et difficultatibus plurimis...Sed tamen stat firmus obediens verbo et legi Dei, quae dicit: Non concupisces, et Spiritui sancti admonenti eum de hac voluntate Dei et non succumbit.

CONCLUSIONS

This chapter asked whether it was possible to give a robust theological account of the human *qua* human, or the human in herself, in a way that does justice to Christ's justifying activity on behalf of the human person given this activity may be only eschatologically realized. In other words, does justification really make a difference in the temporal existence of the Christian or in her day-to-day experience of the Christian life? For Luther, the answer is clearly yes. He uses Christ's activity in justification to reconsider the person's relation to the Holy Spirit. This allows him to parse out anthropological features of the person using the Aristotelian categories supplied through medieval philosophical anthropologies and moral theology. Moreover, it allows him to consider how those anthropological faculties—the intellect and will—are altered as a result of the new relation to Christ and the Spirit. By doing so, he is also able to give voice the human experience of these transformed and transforming features of the Christian's personhood.

SUGGESTED FURTHER READING

Adams, Marilyn McCord, "Genuine Agency, Somehow Shared? The Holy Spirit and Other Gifts," in *Oxford Studies in Medieval Philosophy* (Oxford: Oxford University Press, 2013), 1:23–60.

Slenczka, Notger, "Luther's Anthropology," in Robert Kolb, Irene Dingel, and L'Ubomir Batka (eds.), *The Oxford Handbook of Martin Luther's Theology* (Oxford: Oxford University Press, 2014), 212–32.

Vind, Anna, "The Human Being According to Luther," in Anne Eusterschulte and Hannah Wälzholz (eds.), *Anthropological Reformations-Anthropology in the Era of Reformation* (Refo500 Academic Studies; Göttingen: Vandenhoeck & Ruprecht, 2015), 69–86.

Wannenwetsch, Bernd, "A Love Formed by Faith: Relating Theological Virtues in Augustine and Luther," in Robert Song and Brent Waters (eds.), *The Authority of the Gospel: Explorations in Moral and Political Theology in Honor of Oliver O'Donovan* (Grand Rapids, MI: Eerdmans, 2015), 1–32.

White, Graham, *Luther as Nominalist: A Study of the Logical Methods Used in Martin Luther's Disputations in the Light of Their Medieval Background* (Schriften der Luther-Agricola-Gesellschaft 30; Helsinki: Luther-Agricola-Society, 1994).

CHAPTER SIXTEEN

John Calvin's Trinitarian Theological Anthropology Reconsidered

ARNOLD HUIJGEN

INTRODUCTION

Under modern conditions, the importance of anthropology for the foundations of theology has increased. For instance, Immanuel Kant's philosophy understood God as postulate of human subjectivity, and Friedrich D. E. Schleiermacher based religion on the utter sense of dependence (*schlechthinniges Abhängigkeitsgefühl*). This anthropological concentration in foundational theology was unknown, and unthinkable, for earlier theologians, from the patristic era to the early modern Reformers, such as John Calvin.[1] As a humanist, Calvin was surely interested in anthropological matters, even at the outset of theology, but the hotly debated topics of anthropology were matters of soteriology, centering on the possibilities of human faculties after the fall. For Calvin, there is no such thing as "prolegomena" to theology, as a methodological framework, also because theoretic atheism lies beyond his horizon. These aspects should be kept in mind to prevent anachronistic readings and to enable a fruitful incorporation of Calvin's insights in present-day theology.

Calvin's anthropology has received little attention in Calvin research, particularly when compared to the vast area of secondary literature on other aspects of his theology. Remarkably, Thomas F. Torrance's seminal monograph, *Calvin's Doctrine of Man* (1949), is still among the most quoted, its obvious Barthian tenor notwithstanding.[2] A second milestone is Mary Potter Engel's 1988 perspectival approach to Calvin's anthropology, which distinguishes the relative, human perspective in which humans occupy a high position, compared to animals, from the absolute perspective of God, in which humans are on the one hand tiny and humble, and on the other hand heirs of Christ.[3] Besides these

---

[1]Wolfhart Pannenberg, *Anthropology in Theological Perspective*, trans. Matthew J. O'Connell (Philadelphia: Westminster Press, 1985), 11.
[2]Thomas F. Torrance, *Calvin's Doctrine of Man* (London: Lutterworth Press, 1949). An example of his Barthian inclinations: Torrance interprets any hints of human natural qualifications as reflections of God.
[3]Mary Potter Engel, *John Calvin's Perspectival Anthropology* (Atlanta: Scholars Press, 1988), 22.

broader approaches, three subareas of Calvin's anthropology have drawn attention. First, the alleged philosophical roots of his anthropology in Platonic or Stoic ideas.[4] Second, Calvin's understanding of the image of God and corporeality.[5] Third, the question of how Calvin includes women in, or excludes them from, the image of God.[6]

Theological discussions are often driven by contemporary concerns, such as equality, and Calvin's theological anthropology is no exception. Rather than an unavoidable liability of historical research, these concerns help to take Calvin as theologian seriously, by letting his voice resound in present discussions on what it is to be human. Therefore, the present contribution will focus on what can be learned from Calvin's theological anthropology for the present day, in which we face questions on gender, race, sexuality, freedom, animals, technological enhancements, robots and ecology that Calvin could not even imagine. Calvin, however, opens his *Institutes of Christian Religion* with a perspective that can still be central to Christian anthropology: the correlation between the knowledge of God and the knowledge of ourselves. After a discussion of that correlation, the present chapter will picture humanity in three successive states (as creatures, as sinners, as believers) that correspond to the Persons of the Trinity.

HUMAN EXISTENCE BEFORE GOD

For Calvin, the doctrines of God and of anthropology are intricately and inseparably related, like the two foci of an ellipse. This correlation is so important that it forms the opening of Calvin's *Institutes*: "Nearly all the wisdom we possess, that is to say, true and sound wisdom, consists of two parts: the knowledge of God and of ourselves. But, while joined by many bonds, which one precedes and brings forth the other is not easy to discern."[7] For Calvin, this was the hinge on which his entire theology turned. Therefore, when his opponent Albert Pighius plagiarized this *cognitio dei et nostri*, which Calvin regarded as characteristic of his theology, Calvin responded vehemently, and very critically.[8]

For anthropology in particular, two aspects of Calvin's correlation are important. First, that by definition, human beings are what they are before God, *coram deo*. A human person "never achieves a clear knowledge of himself unless he has first looked upon God's face, and then descends from contemplating him to scrutinize himself."[9] This epistemological statement has ontological force: humans exist before God; besides or

---

[4]Charles Partee, *Calvin and Classical Philosophy* (Leiden: Brill, 1977), notes Calvin's indebtedness to Plato's view of the immortal soul. Barbara Pitkin, "Erasmus, Calvin, and the Faces of Stoicism in Renaissance and Reformation Thought," in *The Routledge Handbook of the Stoic Tradition*, ed. John Sellars (London: Routledge, 2016), 145–59, places Calvin in the Stoic tradition.

[5]See Jason Van Vliet, *Children of God: The Imago Dei in John Calvin and His Context* (Göttingen: Vandenhoeck & Ruprecht, 2009); Alida Leni Sewell, *Calvin and the Body: An Inquiry into his Anthropology* (Amsterdam: VU University Press, 2011).

[6]Jane Dempsey Douglass, *Woman, Freedom, and Calvin* (Philadelphia: Westminster, 1985); John L. Thompson, "*Creata ad imagem dei, licet secundo gradu*: Woman as the Image of God according to John Calvin," *Harvard Theological Review* 81 (1988): 125–43.

[7]John Calvin, *Institutes of the Christian Religion*, 2 vols., trans. Ford Lewis Battles (Philadelphia: Westminster Press, 1960), 35; Calvin, *Inst.* 1.1.1.

[8]Calvin, *Defensio sanae et orthodoxae doctrinae de servitute et liberatione humani arbitrii contra Alberti Pighii Campensis* (Geneva: Joannes Gerardus, 1543); in *Ioannis Calvini opera quae supersunt omnia* (= CO), ed. Guilielmus Baum, Eduardus Cunitz and Eduardus Reuss (Brunsvigae: C.A. Schwetschke), 6:225–404 (246).

[9]Calvin, *Inst.* 1.1.2 (trans. Battles, 37).

without this position, no humanity is possible. Even when humanity turns its back on God, God as creator remains the point of reference for human essence. Second, Calvin defines human existence as relational. No human can exist without relations: human beings are born into a network of relations, with other people (parents, peers and so on), but primarily with God. This divine-human relation is fundamental to all other relations. This relationality, however, should not be understood in the modern sense of authenticity and equality. Relations are defined by different hierarchical positions (humans are ontologically subordinated to God), which need to be respected by way of obedience.

Two images dominate Calvin's discussion of human existence, and of the believer in particular: the family and the school. God is both Teacher and Father, and humans are his children and pupils. Both images exemplify the familiar nearness of God's communication, by which God accommodates himself to the human level of understanding.[10] The apt response to this divine communication is *pietas*, an obedient form of spirituality, which Calvin defines as "that reverence joined with love of God which the knowledge of his benefits induces."[11] For Calvin, piety is thus not merely an inward feeling or subjective spirituality but a relation grounded in the objectivity of the creaturely relation between God and humans. Piety ultimately takes the communicative form of prayer, a familiar mode of communication, expressing dependence, trust and thankfulness, and which distinguishes human beings from animals.[12] The other side of this is that humans cannot function in complete independence from God. Whether the human being sins and turns his back on God, or heartily believes in God, both are relational definitions of the human being, who remains creature. Even sin cannot completely estrange the human being from God, because sin is by definition sin *against God*.

In Calvin's universe, a sense or awareness of God is anthropologically fundamental. Before all sinful obscuration and above all rational denial, "there is within the human mind, and indeed in natural instinct, an awareness of divinity (*divinitatis sensus*)." For Calvin, this is "beyond controversy."[13] Religion is therefore no arbitrary invention of some kind. There is "no nation so barbarous, no people so savage, that they have not a deep-seated conviction that there is a God"; everyone continues "to retain some seed of religion (*semen religionis*)."[14] Atheism is therefore not a rational possibility. Even those who "deny that God exists … from time to time feel an inkling of what they desire not to believe."[15] This comes through conscience, which testifies to God like a "worm," who "gnaws away within."[16] Corrupted as this fundamental sense of God may be by sin, curiosity and superstition,[17] it remains fundamental to humanity, and it shines forth in the universe, which is a theater of God's glory.[18] So, the *sensus divinitatis* belongs to the basics of anthropology: all humans have it, and there is no way to shake it off, even if people want to.

---

[10]Arnold Huijgen, *Divine Accommodation in John Calvin's Theology. Analysis and Assessment* (Göttingen: Vandenhoeck & Ruprecht, 2011), 157–64.
[11]Calvin, *Inst.* 1.2.2 (trans. Battles, 41).
[12]Calvin, *Inst.* 3.20, the longest chapter of the work.
[13]Calvin, *Inst.* 1.3.1 (trans. Battles, 43).
[14]Ibid., 44.
[15]Calvin, *Inst.* 1.3.2 (trans. Battles, 45).
[16]Calvin, *Inst.* 1.3.3 (trans. Battles, 46).
[17]Calvin, *Inst.* 1.4.
[18]Calvin, *Inst.* 1.5.1.

HUMAN CREATURES

The Place of Humans in Creation

The knowledge of ourselves, which correlates to the knowledge of God, is twofold: the knowledge of our original, created state, and the knowledge of what we became after the fall.[19] This indicates both the importance of the fall in Calvin's thought and the prominence of the creator-creature distinction. The fact that humans are made out of the dust of the earth should restrain our innate pride, since as creatures, human beings belong to the earth and not to the heavens.[20] On the other hand, every human is a "microcosm" and as such a proof of God's power.[21]

Within the created order, humans belong ontologically between angels and animals. Angels have a higher place in the hierarchy of being since they are incorporeal, and animals are lower because they do not have a soul and are not created in the image of God. The angels are spiritual (i.e., incorporeal) beings who have not sinned. Nonetheless, they were not created in the image of God, nor did God become angelic to reach out to them. These are human privileges, which demonstrate that God deals with human beings mediately. Calvin emphasizes that Christ has been mediator from the very beginning of the world and that there is no unmediated knowledge of God available for humans.[22] So, even apart from the incarnation, mediatorial structures are fundamental for the relationship between God and humans. Already under the Old Testament, Christ served as mediator,[23] and even without sin, the human condition would have been "too lowly" to reach God without a mediator.[24] Here, the theological structure of the so-called *extra calvinisticum* shows: the idea, typical for Calvin and the Reformed tradition, that God also exists outside (*extra*) the means he employs in his service; Christ's mediatorial office functions even outside the actual incarnation.[25]

Soul and Body

For Calvin, it is "beyond controversy" that human beings consist of a soul and a body. The soul consists of two faculties: intellect and will.[26] The intellect takes the lead, informing the will, which subsequently chooses what the intellect has informed it to be good. Compared to the body, the soul is the "nobler part," "an immortal yet created essence," which is sometimes called spirit.[27] Calvin advocates this immortality of the soul already in his earliest theological work *Psychopannychia* (1534), albeit not as inherent quality of the soul but as a gift of God.[28] Calvin wishes to avoid two extremes: first, the position of the heretic Servetus,[29]

---

[19]Calvin, *Inst.* 1.15.1.

[20]Ibid.

[21]Calvin, *Inst.* 1.5.3.

[22]Calvin, *Comm. Gen.* 20.7 (CO 23:290); *Inst.* 3.2.1.

[23]Calvin, *Comm. Psalm* 132:10 (CO 32:347): "umbratilis mediator."

[24]Calvin, *Inst.* 2.12.1.

[25]Cornelis van der Kooi, "Christology," in *The Calvin Handbook*, ed. Herman J. Selderhuis (Grand Rapids, MI: Eerdmans, 2009), 257–67.

[26]Calvin, *Inst.* 1.15.2 (trans. Battles, 184), cf. 1.15.7.

[27]Calvin, *Inst.* 1.15.2 (trans. Battles, 184).

[28]Calvin, *Psychopannychia* (CO 5:177–232).

[29]Calvin, *Inst.* 1.15.5. Servetus combined various heresies; see Arnold Huijgen, "The Challenge of Heresy: Servetus, Stancaro, and Castellio," in *John Calvin in Context*, ed. R. Ward Holder (Cambridge: Cambridge University Press, 2020).

who regards the soul as an effluence of the divine soul, which implies pantheism; and the Epicurean idea that human souls are mortal, because they are attached to material, that is, corruptible, bodies. For Calvin, the unbreakable bond with Christ is at stake, which is central to his theology and spirituality: the Christian has entered the Kingdom of God in Christ, so nothing will sever the bond between Christ and the Christian.

Calvin's insistence on the soul's immortality and his language of "prison house of the body" sound rather Platonic. This is not a binary matter, however. While Calvin leaned toward Platonism as many of the Reformers and other humanists did, this does not imply that the prison house language expresses Platonic views. Calvin echoes not only Platonic but also Pauline language, since he employs the prison house metaphor within the context of human dying. Humans must die because of sin, but for the believer, death also means the liberation from sin.[30] Still, the fact that Calvin did not feel the need to demarcate Pauline from Platonic language indicates that for him, Plato and Paul were not complete strangers, but—in this respect—soul mates. The body links humans to the animal world, which is perishable, whereas the soul makes humans partakers in the world of immortality, in which the angels also share: "Shut up as we are in the prison house of our flesh, we have not yet attained angelic rank."[31] Still, since Christ's resurrection was a truly bodily resurrection, the believers will receive a renewed body in the eschaton in which they will glorify God. Calvin oscillates between a hierarchical ontology, in which corporeality belongs to the lower echelons, and a theology of creation, in which human corporeality belongs to the goodness of God's creation.

Image of God

Human beings are created in the "image" and "likeness" of God (Gen. 1:26), which Calvin reads as synonyms, unlike Catholic theologians, who—according to Calvin—used these terms to distinguish between natural gifts (preserved after the fall) and supernatural gifts (lost through the fall). Calvin calls this "a nonexistent difference," since the repetition is typical for the Hebrew language.[32] Besides, Calvin denies the position of Osiander, who taught that the image is as much found in the body ("indiscriminately") as it is in the soul.[33] Still, in the final edition of the *Institutes*, Calvin has come to locate traces of the image of God in the human body, which deviates from the earlier theological tradition from Irenaeus to Abelard, and from other Reformers such as Melanchthon and Bullinger.[34] Here, Calvin's position is distinctly non-Platonic.

The perfect image of God is not found in Adam, but in Christ. When Adam fell, "God's image was not totally annihilated and destroyed in him, yet it was so corrupted that whatever remains is frightful deformity."[35] Therefore, the image of God can presently only be known by deriving it from the renewal through Christ, "the most perfect image of God."[36] While Adam was the image of God only in an attributive sense, Christ is the

---

[30]This view is advocated by Van Vliet, *Children of God*, 260; Sewell, *Calvin and the Body*, 39–68.
[31]Calvin, *Inst.* 4.1.1 (trans. Battles, 1012).
[32]Calvin, *Inst.* 1.15.3 (trans. Battles, 187).
[33]Ibid.
[34]Van Vliet, *Children of God*, 258–9.
[35]Calvin, *Inst.* 1.15.4 (trans. Battles, 189).
[36]Ibid., 190.

image of God essentially.[37] Remarkably, Calvin's idea of the image of God consisting in knowledge, justice and holiness—in line with the human faculties of intellect, will and affect—corresponds to his idea of Christ's threefold office as prophet, king and priest.[38] Still, Christ is the second, not the first Adam.[39]

Image of God, Gender, Sexuality

A delicate discussion concerning the image of God, at least from a present perspective, is the matter of women as the image of God. In 1 Cor. 11:7, Paul calls man "the image and reflection of God" while woman is "the reflection of man." This indicates a hierarchy in which women are subordinate to men, who are subordinate to God. Calvin explains that women are excluded from the image of God only with respect to "the political order" (in the *Institutes*),[40] "the domestic state" or "the conjugal order" (in the commentaries).[41] John L. Thompson summarizes this position: "The first of these phrases seems to exclude woman from public leadership outside the home, while the second and third apparently refer to woman's subjection within the home."[42] Calvin shows openness for the possibility of exceptions to woman's subordination, and thus for greater equality.[43] Also, woman's subordination is relativized by Calvin as a rule for the time of the world, while in light of eternity and salvation, man and woman are equal.[44] Still, for Calvin, the rule itself remains, and besides the broader definition of the image of God, he employs a narrower definition that excludes woman.[45] Still, this could be expected of any sixteenth-century humanist reader of Paul.

Remarkably, Calvin's views on sexuality show a strong tendency toward equality between man and woman. With respect to sexual morals, the double standard that was usual at the time (e.g., women were bound to stricter rules and punished more severely than men) was abandoned in Geneva, and men and women were treated equally.[46] More importantly, however, Calvin highly esteems marriage and sexuality as belonging to the good order of creation, without restriction. Luther had not come that far; although he had criticized the veneration of virginity and celibacy under the papacy, he still retained the Augustinian idea of concupiscence, which led to an estimation of the sexual life as inferior. Calvin, however, emphasizes the original unity of love between man and woman as an *amitié* (emotional communion of love between

---

[37]In this context, "image" primarily means "reflection" as in a mirror; Calvin, *Comm. Eph.*. 4.24 (CO 51:208–9). Based on his interpretation of "reflection," Torrance regards the image of God as an attitude rather than a quality of humanity (Torrance, *Doctrine of Man*, 52). Richard Stauffer rightly criticizes this (Barthian) overinterpretation, while maintaining that the image of God is primarily reflective (Stauffer, *Dieu, la création et la Providence dans la prédication de Calvin* (Bern: Peter Lang, 1978), 201–5).

[38]Calvin, *Inst.* 1.15.3; 2.15.

[39]Calvin, *Inst.* 2.12.7, against Osiander.

[40]Calvin, *Inst.* 1.15.5.

[41]Calvin, *Comm. Gen.* 1.26 (CO 23:27); *Comm. 1 Cor.* 11.7 (CO 49:476).

[42]Thompson, *"Creata ad imagem,"* 131.

[43]Douglass, *Woman, Freedom, and Calvin*, 104, 121.

[44]Thompson, *"Creata ad imagem,"* 141.

[45]This is received critically by Mary Potter Engel, "Gender Equality and Gender Hierarchy in Calvin's Theology," *Journal of Women in Culture and Society* 11 (1985): 725–39; Thompson, *"Creata ad imagem,"* 140–3.

[46]Sewell, *Calvin and the Body*, 173–90.

equals).[47] Coitus is "a thing that is pure, honorable and holy, because it is a pure institution of God."[48] Also, the prime goal of marriage does not lie in procreation but in the mutual companionship of husband and wife. The indissoluble nature of the bond of marriage is connected to the idea of the unity of the body of Christ. Of course, Calvin also discusses sexual weaknesses and sins, and warns against immoderation. Yet overall, Calvin stands out in the Christian tradition for equality between man and woman in the marriage bed, and for humanizing the sexual life as creaturely and good, without the restrictions common to the Augustinian tradition.[49]

HUMAN SINNERS

Adam's sin meant humanity's fall. He was completely free to choose either good or evil, and his mind was sound, but he made a wrong use of his free will (*liberum arbitrium*): "Disobedience was the beginning of the Fall."[50] This was Adam's own fault, although God could have granted him the grace of perseverance, which he did not. In some passages, Calvin seems to imply that the withholding of this grace made Adam's fall inevitable, though not logically necessary.[51] Calvin regards the fall as predestined by God, but not in the sense that Adam was forced to sin against his will.

Because of Adam's fall, all humans are sinners. Since Adam is the "rotten root" of humanity, all humans, as "rotten branches," bear the consequences of his sin.[52] The effects are dramatic, since all humans are born totally depraved, their supernatural gifts are stripped and the natural gifts corrupted. Although the faculty of reason could not be completely erased, only "its misshapen ruins appear."[53] Similarly, the will as such "did not perish, but was so bound to wicked desires that it cannot strive after the right."[54] Calvin walks a fine line here between what he saw as the Catholic distinction between the natural (which would have been preserved) and the supernatural (which would have been lost) on the one hand, and the Anabaptist approach of cutting through all connections between creation and recreation on the other. The image of ruins expresses both continuity and discontinuity. Thus, Calvin emphasizes that the current depraved state of humanity is not the original one: human corruption is not essential but accidental.[55] This accent serves to maintain the original goodness of creation that once was and that is restored in Christ. Calvin's purpose in painting fallen humanity with such dark colors is to make the superabundance of God's grace, which makes sin a brief episode, shine even brighter.

Humans sin necessarily, albeit only in a specific mode of necessity. While Adam had the possibility not to sin (Augustine's phrase: "*posse non peccare*"), after the fall humanity cannot not sin ("*non posse non peccare*"). Calvin entered into a major discussion on this theme with Albert Pighius, who taught that after the fall, humans still have free choice

---

[47]Calvin, *Sermon Eph.* 5.31–33 (CO 51:771–84).
[48]Calvin, *Comm. 1 Cor.* 7.6 (CO 49:406).
[49]H. W. de Knijff, *Venus aan de leiband: Europa's erotische cultuur en christelijke sexuele ethiek* (Kampen: Kok, 1987), 174–81.
[50]Calvin, *Inst.* 2.1.4 (trans. Battles, 245).
[51]E.g., Calvin, *Inst.* 1.15.8; 3.23.8; see Anthony N. S. Lane, "Anthropology," in *The Calvin Handbook*, ed. Herman J. Selderhuis (Grand Rapids, MI: Eerdmans, 2009), 275–85 (276–7).
[52]Calvin, *Inst.* 2.1.7 (trans. Battles, 250).
[53]Calvin, *Inst.* 2.2.12 (trans. Battles, 270).
[54]Calvin, *Inst.* 2.2.12 (trans. Battles, 271).
[55]Calvin, *Inst.* 2.1.10–11.

(*liberum arbitrium*). Calvin, however, denied that humans presently are like Hercules at the crossroads, with equally possible options of right and wrong. Humans are sinners, so they will sin necessarily, in the sense of relative necessity (*necessitas consequentiae*), not in the sense of absolute necessity (*necessitas consequentis*).[56] The freedom of the will, and not the function as such, is denied. Here Calvin distinguishes between necessity and compulsion (*coactio*).[57] Human beings are not coerced to sin, because they sin voluntarily. But they do sin by necessity, because they have chosen and continue to choose to live in the slavery of sin. Against Pighius' Pelagian statement that there is no obligation without ability, Calvin replies that this was true before the fall but no longer for fallen humanity. Fallen humanity spontaneously and consistently chooses the wrong path of sin. "Thus bondage brings necessity, but is nonetheless a voluntary rather than coerced bondage."[58]

The net result of the bondage of both mind and will is the complete inability to know God and do as he pleases. Still, in the natural realm (e.g., civil government, household management), fallen humans can still do fairly well.[59] Calvin singles out science and art as specific gifts of God's Spirit to humanity: notwithstanding human depravity, these creative gifts still thrive, although they are used in wrong ways. These gifts are not the only positive aspects to Calvin's doctrine of sin, however. This doctrine serves to halt human flattery and self-admiration, and to stimulate humility and dependence on God's grace.[60] Calvin's intention in painting such a dark picture of humanity is a message of hope, since Jesus Christ has conquered sin. Thus, Calvin quotes Augustine: "The weaker you are in yourself, the more readily the Lord will receive you."[61] Humans should therefore not try to build on philosophy, science and the arts to reach God, important as these may be. Calvin compares philosophers to "a traveler passing through a field at night who in a momentary lightning flash sees far and wide, but the sight vanishes so swiftly that he is plunged again into the darkness of the night before he can take even a step."[62] Human "keenness of mind is mere blindness as far as the knowledge of God is concerned."[63] What is needed is illumination by the Holy Spirit as inner teacher (*magister interior*).[64] "For wherever the Spirit does not cast his light, all is darkness."[65] Once again, Calvin prefers visual metaphors to describe both the blind human faculties and the "illumination" of the Holy Spirit.

In sum, human beings are completely lost when left to their own devices. Their will functions only to make them sin willingly, and it is completely impossible for them to change this situation. Calvin invests all this theological energy to highlight the uniqueness of the work of Christ. Calvin's lengthy discussion of human faculty serves as entryway for Christology: Christ the mediator between God and human beings is the center of Calvin's theology. Without Christ, there is nothing more positive to say about fallen humanity than could be said about created humanity without God the Father. In the first book of his *Institutes*, Calvin focused on created humans in light of the Father; in the second book, he

---

[56]Calvin, *Inst*. 1.16.9.
[57]Calvin, *Inst*. 2.2.7; 2.3.5.
[58]Lane, "Anthropology," 282.
[59]Calvin, *Inst*. 2.2.13.
[60]Calvin, *Inst*. 2.1.2.
[61]Calvin, *Inst*. 2.2.11 (trans. Battles, 269).
[62]Calvin, *Inst*. 2.2.18 (trans. Battles, 277).
[63]Calvin, *Inst*. 2.2.19 (trans. Battles, 278).
[64]Calvin, *Inst*. 2.2.20.
[65]Calvin, *Inst*. 2.2.21 (trans. Battles, 281).

describes fallen humans as utterly dependent on Christ the mediator; in the third, humans are pictured as believers through the work of the Holy Spirit.

HUMAN BELIEVERS

What happens when fallen humans become believers? Calvin ascribes this conversion to the secret operation of the Holy Spirit in the human heart: it is a new creation and a total transformation. The will is "created anew; not meaning that the will now begins to exist, but that it is changed from an evil to a good will."[66] Thus, the will is liberated from its sinful bondage to be genuinely free. Only then do humans discover what true freedom is: obedience to God's will.

Calvin is not particularly optimistic about the Christian's life as a free person. Although liberated from the bondage of sin, God's children "do not obtain full possession of freedom so as to feel no more annoyance from their flesh, but there still remains in them a continuing occasion for struggle whereby they may be exercised."[67] So, Calvin pictures the Christian life as an ongoing training, an exercise, supported by the Spirit as the internal teacher, or coach. Sin no longer reigns over believers, but it still dwells in them,[68] resulting in a continuous, daily struggle. Thus, the believer's lives under eschatological tension: *nondum* ("not yet") is the word Calvin often uses to characterize the progress of the believer en route to God's Kingdom.[69]

The Christian life in Calvin's theology is centered on remaining faithful to the end. Calvin devotes three chapters to the Christian life in the third book of the *Institutes*. The first sums up the Christian life as denial of ourselves. This means that we do not belong to ourselves but that we belong to God.[70] Since we belong to God, our lives must be humbly directed to God and not to our own luxury, comfort, pride or self-love.[71] Self-denial does not mean the denial of human existence but of self-centeredness. Rather, Christians should devote their lives to God's will.[72] Second, Calvin focuses on bearing the cross, which is a part of self-denial. "The more we are afflicted with adversities, the more surely our fellowship with Christ is confirmed!"[73] The cross teaches us to distrust ourselves. It teaches patience and instructs people in obedience.[74] Thus, the cross can correct our vices, like a medicine[75] or a fatherly chastisement.[76] In the exercise of the Christian life, the cross is God's preferred remedial teaching equipment. Third, the positive side of self-denial is the meditation of the future life. Christians should learn not to love the world but to long for the life to come. The present life, on the other hand, "however crammed with infinite miseries it may be, is still rightly to be counted among those blessings of God which are not to be spurned."[77] Calvin's style of enjoying life is the concessive mode: enjoyment

---

[66]Calvin, *Inst.* 2.3.6 (trans. Battles, 297).
[67]Calvin, *Inst.* 3.3.10 (trans. Battles, 602).
[68]Calvin, *Inst.* 3.3.11.
[69]Calvin, *Comm. 1 Cor.* 13.12 (CO 49:429–30).
[70]Calvin, *Inst.* 3.7.1.
[71]Calvin, *Inst.* 3.7.4.
[72]Calvin, *Inst.* 3.7.8.
[73]Calvin, *Inst.* 3.8.1 (trans. Battles, 702).
[74]Calvin, *Inst.* 3.8.4.
[75]Calvin, *Inst.* 3.8.5.
[76]Calvin, *Inst.* 3.8.6.
[77]Calvin, *Inst.* 3.9.3.

is allowed cautiously. First and foremost, humans should be as watchmen at the sentry post at which the Lord has posted us, "which we must hold until he recalls us."[78] The longing for God's kingdom is a litmus test for the true Christian, for "no one has made progress in the school of Christ who does not joyfully await the day of death and final resurrection."[79]

The Christian is primarily a pilgrim: a *viator* underway, walking the right way, following the Word of God.[80] This way is full of signs and promises, used by the Spirit to point the way to the heavenly homeland. The pilgrim is hindered by the remainder of sin and also—some passages suggest—by his corporeal existence.[81]

Ultimately, believers will live with God. Two biblical texts are Calvin's favorites: "now, we see through a mirror, dimly" (1 Cor. 13:12), but then "we shall see him [God] as he is" (1 Jn 3:2). In his commentary on the latter text, Calvin notes that seeing God does not mean that we become "equal" (*pares*) to God. Rather, Calvin emphasizes that the "veil of this mortal and corruptible nature shall be removed," so that we will see "the majesty of God."[82] Once again, Calvin maintains the distinction between Creator and creature, and pictures human corporeality rather negatively.

CONCLUSION: THEN AND NOW

Calvin lived in an entirely different world than the present world. People lived harsh lives, threatened by war and ill-health, without the securities and life expectancies of many modern people. This left its marks on Calvin's views on human life. Besides, the existence of God still went unquestioned; no technical revolutions had taken place to make human life more comfortable than ever, not yet had scientific developments denied humanity center stage of the universe. The self-evidence of God's existence, the universe as obvious theatre of God and human life as microcosm each stamp Calvin's theological anthropology. His underestimation of human corporeality catches the eye of the modern Westerner, who lives in a body culture that is probably without precedent and that perhaps overestimates corporeality. A confrontation with theologians from the past can help to gain a fresh view on the present time.

The following six aspects of Calvin's theological anthropology are worth considering in view of present-day theology.

First, Calvin defines human life in its relation to God. Before anything else, human beings are relational beings. Although they are unique persons, they are not primarily individuals. Human beings are born in a network of relations—family relations, societal relations, contextual factors of time and place—that are defining for that human persons' existence, survival and flourishing. For Calvin, the prime and most important relation is that to God: humans live *coram deo*: they are creatures, sinners and—hopefully— believers, before the Triune God who is Creator, Redeemer and Renewer. Although this God-relation is presently not self-evident as it was in Calvin's days, it is basic for Christian

---

[78]Calvin, *Inst.* 3.9.4 (trans. Battles, 716).
[79]Calvin, *Inst.* 3.9.5 (trans. Battles, 718).
[80]Calvin, *Inst.* 1.6.3; 3.10.6.
[81]Calvin, *Inst.* 3.2.20 (trans. Battles, 565).
[82]Calvin, *Comm 1 Jn* 3.2 (CO 55:332).

theology to acknowledge that no human being in this life is completely off God's grid, or completely left by God. Everyone relates to God, albeit often not in a positive way.

Second, Calvin sees humans as responsible beings without losing sight of human weaknesses. Even when they cannot but sin, this no mere tragedy, for humans sin willingly. This human responsibility does not imply that everyone should be left to one's own devices, since humans often show themselves incapable of bearing their responsibility. Calvin touches a balance between responsibility and contextual determinedness: he argued against mere human autonomy and against determinism. Although human autonomy post-Enlightenment took a form that Calvin could not imagine, and determinism is found more in circles of neuroscientists than in Stoic forms, Calvin's views express a truly catholic Christian attitude. Still, Calvin often seems to place God's operation and human responsibility in a competing relation, which need not be the case if his theology is approached from the pneumatological side. The Spirit shows that God and humans are not in competition but that God's operations in humans lead to truly human and truly believing behavior.

Third, Calvin's anthropology is a decisive step forward in the history of sexuality. The sexual life is evaluated positively, as a part of the good creation, and the equality of husband and wife in the marriage bed is emphasized. This is a significant humanization of the understanding of sexuality when compared to Augustine and Luther, but also in contrast to the later Victorian era. Calvin is an unexpected champion of sexual equality, that is, in its heterosexual form, safeguarded by the institution of Christian marriage as Calvin's ideal life form.

Fourth, Calvin emphasizes self-denial to the extent of asceticism. Moderation and sobriety are key terms for Calvin's understanding of what human life should be. Although these ideas can be used to steer away from life in the world, they can serve a new function in the present time, in which humanity is confronted with the limitations of planet Earth, to counter the immoderation that contributed to climate change and unbridled consumerism. Christian theology may offer an ideal of asceticism that values the goodness of the present life.

Fifth, the implicit hierarchy of being in Calvin's ideas seems particularly unfit for the present time, and the definition of the relation between God and humans on the one hand, and between humans and animals on the other hand, in terms of power structures and ontological echelons, seems less than attractive. Calvin's anthropology is in better shape when some of its hierarchical, ontological presuppositions are stripped. Still, power structures do exist, and it should be noted that Calvin describes a power structure that does not function among human beings but between human beings and God. That might well be a key to criticize power structures among humans, because a position of power means a position of extra responsibility against the One who entrusted the power. Because God is, there can be no absolute power in the world—a conviction that hints at the connection between Calvin's heritage and the foundations of modern liberal democracies.

Sixth, there is the issue of suffering. Contemporary Western theologians can only imagine the sufferings of sixteenth-century refugees like Calvin, including chronic diseases, the loss of his only child and his wife, the threat of war and renewed exile, not to mention the overload of work. While Calvin's picture of the Christian life may look rather negative from the perspective of those affected by hedonist and utilitarian outlooks, his theology of the watchman standing his ground may well be appealing for those in situations of suffering. Calvin's theology fits in the margins of society, his reformation was meant for refugees.[83] But maybe the successful and healthy need to be reminded even more than the other: "we are not our own but the Lord's (*nostri non sumus, domini sumus*)."[84]

SUGGESTED FURTHER READING

Calvin, John, *The Bondage and Liberation of the Will: A Defence of the Orthodox Doctrine of Human Choice against Pighius* (eds. A. N. S. Lane; trans. G. I. Davies; Grand Rapids, MI: Baker, 1996).

Eusterschulte, Anne, and Hannah Wälzholz (eds.), *Anthropological Reformations: Anthropology in the Era of the Reformation* (Göttingen: Vandenhoeck & Ruprecht, 2015).

Helm, Paul, *John Calvin's Ideas* (Oxford: Oxford University Press, 2004).

Torrance, Thomas F., *Calvin's Doctrine of Man* (London: Lutterworth Press, 1949).

Van Vliet, Jason, *Children of God: The Imago Dei in John Calvin and His Context* (Göttingen: Vandenhoeck & Ruprecht, 2009).

---

[83]Cf. Heiko A. Oberman, *John Calvin and the Reformation of the Refugees* (Genève: Droz, 2009).
[84]Calvin, *Inst*. 3.7.1.

CHAPTER SEVENTEEN

Karl Barth: "Being Human Means Being with God"

TIM HARTMAN

"Being human means being with God."[1] In characteristically grandiose prose, Swiss-German theologian Karl Barth (1886–1968) offered this definition of what it means to be human. In what follows, I critically examine Barth's definition of humanity, including his understanding of race, gender and sexuality, with an eye toward potential implications of Barth's theological anthropology for contemporary theological scholarship.

OVERVIEW

Human existence is never an existence in isolation or independence, but always already an existence in relation to God and to one's fellow creatures. For Barth, what it means to be human is that humans are beings-in-relation. We cannot know what it means to be human without considering human beings in relationship with God and with one another. Whereas the starting point for most work in theological anthropology focuses on the human being, Barth favors beginning with the Creator of human beings, that is, God. For Barth, humanity is understood first and foremost as an object of *theological* knowledge (III/2, 19). Thus, he argues against using cosmology for understanding humanity in favor of a truly theological anthropology. In short, we must look to God to gain understanding of what it means to be human.

Barth most directly addresses what it means to be human in volume III of his magnum opus, *Church Dogmatics*. The second-part volume, CD III/2, "The Doctrine of Creation," continues the Christological concentration of his earlier volumes, beginning its exploration of what it means to be human with reflection upon God's self-revelation in Jesus Christ. CD III/2 was published in German in 1948, having been drafted during the Second World War and completed just after the war's conclusion. Barth situates humans as the "the central object of the theological doctrine of creation" (III/2, 3). Within Barth's doctrine of creation, his exposition of what it means to be human is his most lengthy and primary occupation. In particular, CD III/2 §§43–5 discuss humanity as a problem

---

[1] The German text reads (with the bold in the original): "Menschsein heißt: **mit Gott zusammen sein.**" Karl Barth, *Die kirchliche Dogmatik*, vol. III, part 2 (Zürich: EVZ, 1948), 161, and again on 167; English translation: Karl Barth, *Church Dogmatics*, vol. III, part 2 (Edinburgh: T&T Clark, 1960), 135 and 139. Additional references to Barth's *Church Dogmatics* (hereafter CD) will appear parenthetically in the text, i.e. (III/2, 135 and 139).

of dogmatics, as the creature of God and in our determination as the covenant-partners of God. There are other sections of the *Church Dogmatics* that are related to theological anthropology, including the section in CD III/1 on the image of God (III/1, 183–206, esp. 183–92) and III/3, III/4 (special topics), as well as portions of volume IV, the Doctrine of Reconciliation—that considers the humanity of Jesus Christ in reference to humanity more broadly. This chapter focuses on Barth's theological anthropology primarily as presented in CD III/2 as the central locus of Barth's thinking about humanity. Before examining Barth's specific views about humanity, a bit of wider context from his *Church Dogmatics* is needed.

In the first volume of the *Church Dogmatics*, "The Doctrine of the Word of God," Barth articulates his threefold understanding of the Word of God as divine revelation. God reveals Godself—through the Son of God, Jesus Christ—as the Word of God incarnate, the Word of God written in the Scriptures of the Old and New Testament, and the Word of God proclaimed in preaching. Barth's Christocentric account of divine revelation emphasizes that although God reveals Godself in a myriad of ways, the content of divine revelation is always Jesus Christ. And, whereas Barth's portrayal of the Triune God (Father, Son and Holy Spirit) as wholly other—alongside earlier articulations of an "infinite qualitative distinction"[2] between God and humanity—might give the impression of a vast distance between God and humanity, his explicit adherence to a Chalcedonian Christology affirms Christ's full humanity and full divinity. Thus, God remains wholly other even as God assumes human flesh in all its brokenness and finitude. The reality of Christ's humanity is in no way limited by his divinity.

Barth continues his Christological concentration in volume II of the *Church Dogmatics*, "The Doctrine of God," which presents Barth's radical reworking of all previous doctrines of election. Retaining double predestination in a modified sense, according to Barth's revision of this traditional doctrine, Jesus Christ becomes the "Yes" of both the Electing God and the Elect Human. However, as the elect one, Jesus Christ also receives the judgment and punishment for all of human sin, the "No" of God. Having taken this "No" upon himself for the sake of humanity, Jesus Christ also receives the gift of new life and salvation on behalf of humanity. As human beings are joined to Christ, they receive the gifts that God offers.

CHRISTOLOGICAL STARTING POINT

When Barth turns to the doctrine of Creation in CD III, his exposition again prioritizes knowledge of the Creator as the necessary framework for understanding the Creator's creation. For example, in turning to Scripture to engage the question of what it means to be human, John 1 serves as a lens through which to read Genesis 1. Barth's basic thesis is that for a properly theological understanding of humanity, the investigation must begin by turning our eyes to God and the work of God. The creature, the human being, is always already in relation to the Creator, the Triune God, and is to be understood through this primary relationship between God and humanity (III/2, 19). Barth pushes this understanding to its extreme. Indeed, he claims that, humanity "exists only in his relation to God" (III/2, 123). As the human being who reveals what right relationship

---

[2]See Karl Barth, *Epistle to the Romans*, 2nd ed., trans. Edwyn C. Hoskyns (London: Oxford University Press, [1933] 1968), 10, 355 and 356.

between God and human being looks like, Jesus Christ is "the source of our knowledge of the nature of man as created by God" (III/2, 3).

Jesus Christ is thus both the beginning and the content of theological anthropology. Barth is quite explicit about his method: "We must ask concerning the humanity of the man Jesus, and only on this basis extend our inquiry to the form and nature of humanity generally ... we do not need to look for any other basis of anthropology than the Christological" (III/2, 207–8). Such claims lead to a Christological reframing of traditional concepts in theological anthropology for which the tradition had more often turned to Genesis 1–3. For example, Barth asserts that the humanity of Jesus, rather than the creation of Adam and Eve, serves as the basis for a proper account of the "image of God" (III/2, 219). Thus, it is not the case that individual human beings are the image of God, but rather Jesus Christ alone is the true image of God who reveals God to humanity. The image of God functions as a dynamic category, an event, rather than a static substance or nature. In the humanity of Jesus Christ, we see humanity as God created humanity to be (III/2, 48–9). Jesus Christ is the firstborn of all creation, the visible image and glory of the invisible God (Col. 1:15, 2 Cor. 4:4).

By looking at God incarnate, in the person of Jesus Christ—fully God and fully human—we can see what humanity truly is and what it means to be truly human. For Barth, the Word of God, Jesus Christ, reveals the truth about humanity, the goodness of our creation as well as the perversion and corruption of our condition (III/2, 20, 26). Barth refers to this starting point as the "Christological basis of anthropology" (III/2, 55). Only after this critical and controlling Christological foundation has been established does Barth expand his vision to welcome additional insights and contributions from wider discourses, including Genesis, the natural and social sciences, philosophy and other disciplines (III/2, 24). Barth is not afraid of human knowledge about humanity but believes that a properly theological order of knowing proceeds from Christology to other discourses whose contributions might best be dialogically engaged, critiqued and appreciated after God's revelation of true humanity in Jesus Christ has already been examined. Barth describes his Christological methodology for theological anthropology as follows:

> The purity, freedom, peace and clarity of the human nature of Jesus do not remain His privilege alone, but for His sake this privilege becomes ours as well. As God knows Him, He also knows us. As He knows Jesus, He also knows our nature, against which no accusation can stand because He has created it. In virtue of the exoneration from sin validly effected in Jesus, we may count on this nature of ours and its innocence as we could not otherwise do. This judicial pardon gives us the courage and shows us the way to think about man as God created him. It is the true ground of theological anthropology. (III/2, 48–9)

God knows us in our humanity as God knows Jesus. The obedient work of Jesus Christ is valid for all humans and allows us to think about humanity in the ways that God originally intended. Thus, the image of God embodied in the humanity of Jesus of Nazareth is shared with humanity.

When Barth considers what it means to be human, he begins with Jesus Christ and constantly refers back to Jesus Christ. As discussed above, Jesus is *the* true human. To recap: Barth refers to his method as: the "Christological basis of anthropology" (III/2, 55). In Jesus Christ, we see humanity as God created humanity to be (III/2, 48–9). The humanity of Jesus is the image of God (III/2, 219). For Barth, the question is not how humanity is made in the image of God but instead how Jesus Christ is the image of God. Jesus Christ is "the source of our knowledge of the nature of man as created by God" (III/2, 3, 41). Barth describes his method as asking "concerning the humanity of the man Jesus, and only on this basis extend[ing] our inquiry to the form and nature of humanity generally" (III/2, 207). What this means for Barth is that as he "turn[s] to the problem of humanity, we do not need to look for any other basis of anthropology than the Christological" (III/2, 208). In short, in order to understand what true humanity looks like, we need to look at Jesus' humanity.

BARTH'S METHOD OF THEOLOGICAL ANTHROPOLOGY

For Barth, humanity is determined Christologically, defined actualistically and understood relationally. Each of these descriptions will be considered in turn. As we have seen, Barth's approach moves "from an autonomous to a theonomous understanding" of humanity (III/2, 125). God has created humanity and defined what it means to be human. God has revealed what it means to be human in the person of Jesus Christ. As will be explored in more detail below, Barth understands this Christological determination relationally, because "Man exists only in his relation to God" (III/2, 123). His definition also renders humanity actualistically, presenting the human as existing only in the events and actions by which God relates to him or her.

As always, Barth's approach to understanding humanity begins with Jesus Christ through an exploration not of the *being* of Jesus Christ but his actuality, the historical actions and events of Jesus of Nazareth. Barth employs this method throughout CD III/2 to describe what it means to be human. Barth is not interested in speculating about the being of a human in stasis or abstraction but rather who humans are in active relation to God and one another. Through the lived actions of the life of Jesus of Nazareth on earth, as recorded in the New Testament scriptures, we can learn what true humanity is. The life lived by Jesus was characterized by humility, compassion, courage and passion for justice. All of these acts determine what it means to be human. For Barth, what it means to be human cannot be different than what it meant for God to be human in Jesus Christ. Our human lives are to be lived in correspondence to the life that Jesus lived, as a reflection of the image of God—albeit our lives are limited by human finitude and marred by sin.

Therefore, if we want to know what true humanity looks like we need to look at Jesus' humanity. For Barth, we come to understand humanity through an analogy of relationship between God and humanity, not an analogy of being. Jesus Christ is unique— as fully God and fully human. The being of humanity is not to be understood as somehow analogous to the being of Jesus Christ. Rather, humanity is determined in and through our relationship with God (III/2, 19). Barth refers to this as the *analogia relationis* (III/2, 220–1). Humans are beings-in-encounter, and the primary relationship of human beings is with God.[3]

Barth's Christological determination of humanity is defined actualistically. What Barth means is that his understanding of what it means to be human is derived from the actual, physical, tangible acts of Jesus Christ, not a typology or abstract concepts. Barth does not begin from historically influential ideas of what it means to be human, but rather, he seeks

---

[3]For more on the *analogia relationis*, see Keith L. Johnson, *Karl Barth and the Analogia entis* (London: T&T Clark, 2010).

to learn about what it means to be human from Jesus' actions, not theories,[4] including the stories and narratives contained in the book of Genesis. Barth's answer to the question "What does it mean to be human?" is an actualized ontology for humanity: how humans live out the being that God has given (III/2,142). Humans become—more and more—the beings who God has created us to be. This process is ongoing.

Beginning with humanity's primary relationship, with God, humans are then understood, and true humanity is expressed, through humans' relationships with one another. In Barth's words, "To be [hu]man is to be with God" (III/2, 139). What it means to be human is to truly live into who God has created us to be. In a sense, Barth's understanding of human life is this continual quest by each individual to be, and to become, more and more human. In this way, Barth's understanding of humanity is dynamic and directional, not fixed. So, humans can act in ways that are more-human or less-human. As we live into the calling that God has created for us, we become more human through our interactive relationships with others. As we harm ourselves or others, we dehumanize ourselves and others, by orienting ourselves away from God and acting in less human and less-than-human ways.

In fact, for Barth, one could not be human alone. The basic form of humanity can be found in the encounter of one human with another (III/2, 268). This I-Thou encounter mimics the I-Thou encounter that humans have with God. Thus, it is theologically appropriate to talk about any total isolation of a human being as dehumanizing. Part of what it means to be human is to be in relationship with God and with other human beings. Humans gain a better understanding of what it means to be human through our relationship with God in Jesus Christ and our relationships with others. Again, not theoretically, but actually, in living relationships. Barth's method of theological anthropology is that humanity is determined Christologically, defined actualistically and understood relationally.

THEOLOGICAL IMPLICATIONS OF BARTH'S THEOLOGICAL ANTHROPOLOGY: SIN AND VOCATION

While Barth's method is innovative, distinctive and worthy of study, even more significant for this chapter are Barth's conclusions. Barth's theological anthropology encompasses his understandings of sin and of vocation.

Humans are good, elect of God, who yet commit sin, and are chosen by God and are summoned to live in correspondence to God's active relating to humanity by responding to Christ's leading. The Christological determination of humanity establishes the inherent goodness of humanity. Through Barth's Chalcedonian Christology, Jesus Christ is simultaneously of the same substance (*homoousious*) with God while also the same substance (*homoousious*) with humanity.[5] We share the same flesh, indeed the same humanity, with one another and with Jesus Christ. In Barth's words, there is "no neutral humanity in Jesus" (III/2, 56–7). While Christ was capable of sin, his life of perfect

---

[4]For a helpful overview of the major anthropological alternatives Barth engaged in CD III/2, see George Hunsinger, "Barth on What It Means to Be Human: A Christian Scholar Confronts the Options," in *Karl Barth and the Making of Evangelical Theology: A Fifty-Year Perspective*, ed. Clifford B. Anderson and Bruce L. McCormack (Grand Rapids, MI: Eerdmans, 2015), 139–55.

[5]For more on the Chalcedonian character of Barth's Christology, see Bruce L. McCormack, "Barth's Historicized Christology: How Chalcedonian Is It?," in *Orthodox and Modern: Studies in the Theology of Karl Barth* (Grand

obedience to his Father left him sinless. We humans share the same humanity that is capable of acts of sin and capable of acts of goodness. Our human nature, rather than Christ's divine nature, cannot prevent us from sinning; however, these acts of sin do not define our humanity. Our humanity has been defined by Jesus Christ and Christ alone; our sins (our disobedient acts and our participation in unjust systems of oppression) and our sin (our condition of continuing to commit sinful acts) do not define us. Humanity is defined and determined by Christ alone because our humanity is included within Christ's humanity.

Thus, Barth uses the same methodological approach to define sin as he did to define humanity itself. Sin is determined christologically, sin is defined actualistically and sin is understood relationally. Barth's primary definition of sin is one of broken relationships— with God and with our fellow humans. Barth's understanding of how humans are to respond to God from within the divine-human relationship is with gratitude.[6] Because all of God's actions toward humanity are the outworking of divine grace, any human action that fails to correspond to God's action demonstrates a deficiency of grace. Thus, Barth quips, "all sin is simply ingratitude" (IV/1, 41). In a sense, Barth's line is no different than the classic, Protestant claim that all sin is idolatry. Just as the root of sin is placing our human desires ahead of God's desires for us—worshipping false gods—so also, taking for granted all the good gifts that God has graciously bestowed upon us or acting as if what we have is reducible to the results of our own actions is also the root of sin. Anytime that humans place themselves at the center and relegate God to the periphery is an act of ingratitude, idolatry and sin.

For Barth, sinful humanity is not the real humanity (III/2, 32) because humanity was created good by God to be in free relationship with God. Humans cannot possibly "go back" to some Edenic state of perfection (III/2, 28), since, for Barth, there never was a literal Garden of Eden in which humans had lived perfectly without sin. Importantly, human sin (or, "the Fall") does not change human nature. Humans remain created good by God. Practically, this insight means that theologically speaking there are no "bad people," though there are people who commit bad, even evil, actions. Barth's reasoning is based on his conviction that sin is an "ontological impossibility" for humanity (III/2, 136, 146). The core of our beings as humans is good, not sin. Our bad actions do not define us; only God, our Creator defines us. Sin is a self-contradiction of human nature, a self-deception of human identity (III/2, 48). While humans may spend their lives rebelling against God, humans cannot escape God (III/2, 33), because God does not let humanity go (III/2, 34). Human sin cannot overcome the grace of God in Jesus Christ. As such, divine grace is primary and human sin is secondary (III/2, 41). For Barth, humanity would not even know what sin is without grace. This view allows Barth to claim that only Christians sin.[7] By which Barth means that while all people commit acts of sin that harm their relationships with others and with their Creator, only Christians—having acknowledged and received the grace of God in their lives,

---

Rapids, MI: Baker Academic, 2008), 201–34; and Paul Dafydd Jones, *The Humanity of Christ: Christology in Karl Barth's Church Dogmatics* (London: T&T Clark, 2008), 26–37.

[6]For more on gratitude as the human response to the grace of God, see "Humanity of God," in *The Humanity of God*, trans. John Newton Thomas (Louisville: John Knox Press, 1960), 46–7.

[7]Citing CD IV/3, 359, William Willimon wrote, "As Barth says, '*Only* Christians sin'." See William H. Willimon, *Pastor: The Theology and Practice of Ordained Ministry* (Nashville: Abingdon Press, 2010), 272. Similarly, Barth wrote, "In the strict sense there is no knowledge of sin except in the light of Christ's Cross." Karl Barth, *Dogmatics in Outline* (New York: Harper & Row, 1959), 119.

know and name those actions as sin (III/2, 35). The only true human, one without corruption, is Jesus Christ (III/2, 43). Thus, in Jesus Christ we see humanity as God created humanity to be (III/2, 48–9).

Humanity, then, is not banished from relationship with God because of human sin. Instead, God faithfully remains alongside humanity. In God's eternal self-determination, God has chosen from before the creation of the universe to be in relationship with humankind, knowing that humans would sin. In spite of human brokenness, God chose to be God-for-others and elected humanity to be humans-for-God. Barth refers to this act of electing as God's "Yes" toward humankind. Humanity, then, is summoned by God to respond with a "Yes" of our own. The human life of Jesus Christ is a model of the obedience that is expected of humanity. Humans are called to live in correspondence with Christ and to follow Christ's leading. Barth reprises "To be man is to be with God" with "To be a man is to be with Jesus, to be like Him" (III/2, 145). Humanity joins Jesus as fellow-elect. Together we will be the victor and not the vanquished (III/2, 147). The presence and actions of Jesus Christ in the world transform us, the world and our daily lives. Barth writes, "To be a man is to be in the particular sphere of the created world in which the Word of God is spoken and sounded" (III/2, 149). Being with God, is not passive for humans, but is an active participation with God in the created world.

Human life, then, is both a *gift* and a *task* (III/2, 180).[8] As humans we are the recipients of God's free grace that gives us life and breath while summoning us to live our lives in service of others. For Barth, all humans share a common vocation: to live our lives in correspondence to God's grace and calling in Jesus Christ, the divine command. Barth's view of vocation completes his understanding of humanity. "Man is the creaturely being which is addressed, called and summoned by God" (III/2, 149). This address, calling and summons define humanity: Man *is* this being. Man does not *become* this being (III/2, 149). Humanity is summoned because we are chosen (III/2, 150). God has graciously chosen to be in relationship with humanity from before time by the Word of God, Jesus Christ (III/2, 150). As humanity responds in gratitude to the divine summons, we live into our responsibilities to live in relationship with God and our fellow humans (III/2, 176). Through our obedience, we live more and more into our God-given human identity (III/2, 179).

Certainly, the broad strokes of Barth's theological anthropology present a positive, generative portrait of the human being and the characteristics of human life. Sin is real and has significant negative effects on human life, both individually and communally. And yet, the power and grace of God in Jesus Christ is also real and brings wholeness to human frailty, peace to human conflict and reconciliation to human brokenness.

BARTH AND CONTEMPORARY ISSUES IN THEOLOGICAL ANTHROPOLOGY

If these are the broad strokes of what it means to be human, then what are the specifics? Whereas the more general and broad strokes of Barth's treatment of humanity receive

---

[8]For an insightful interpretation of Barth's connection between divine election, ethics, theological anthropology and human vocation, see Margit Ernst-Habib, "'Chosen by Grace': Reconsidering the Doctrine of Predestination," in *Feminist and Womanist Essays in Reformed Dogmatics*, ed. Amy Plantinga Pauw and Serene Jones (Louisville: Westminster John Knox, 2006), 87–9.

a positive reception, as he applied his significant theological insights to more everyday issues, Barth's views seem more reflective of a "man of his time" than of a theological revolutionary.[9] On issues of race, gender and sexuality, for example, Barth's views did not depart significantly from other white, European males of the late 1940s and early 1950s, though there are a number of scholars seeking to read Barth in liberationist directions.[10] As British theologian Timothy Gorringe writes,

> Barth's theology, like any worthwhile theology, is an extended account of what life in all its fullness means. It shares with liberation theology the concern both to radicalize *and to relativize* the significance of the "political" narrowly construed. The reality of freedom and love *include* the political and the economic, and cannot be articulated without it, but they are not exhausted by it. It is the God who is *love* is, as Barth said, "God the Liberator." (IV/1, 789)[11]

Gorringe narrates how the core of Barth's theology is *inherently* political, that is, concerned with humanity and our interactions with one another. For Barth, what it means to be human is to live in relationship with one another and with God. God is love and God's love is liberating.

Often contemporary theologians seek to read with-and-beyond Barth toward liberation by making moves to apply Barth's theological insights to contemporary questions, even though their conclusions differ from Barth's own statements. Such arguments often draw on volumes II or IV of the *Church Dogmatics* and tend to claim that Barth did not fully integrate his theological insights with the particular claims about humanity that he made in volume III. On this reading, when Barth is writing about gender and sexuality in III/2 (and mostly ignoring race), he is "not at his best." In this way, many scholars have sought to rehabilitate Barth while engaging in close readings and offering constructive proposals about how Barth's theology could inform contemporary societal reflections.

Already in the First World War, and certainly in the rise of National Socialism as well, Barth saw racism as one of the primary forces—alongside militarism, nationalism and capitalism—that fueled the lust for domination and war.[12] Yet, Barth had very little to say about racial difference beyond Europe, and what he did say focused on racial differences of non-Europeans as recipients of European missions and missionaries.[13] For example, in a letter to one of his sons in 1951, Barth mentioned meeting Ghanaian theologian C.G. Baëta and his wife, describing them as "both coal black, but I got on with them very

---

[9]For an excellent presentation of Barth's social and political context, see Claudia Koonz, *The Nazi Conscience* (Cambridge: Belknap, 2003).

[10]In addition to the authors cited below on the topics of race, gender and sexuality, see a more general reading of Barth and liberation theology in Paul Dafydd Jones, "Liberation Theology and 'Democratic Futures' (by way of Karl Barth and Friedrich Schleiermacher)," *Political Theology* 10, no. 1 (2009): 261–85.

[11]Timothy Gorringe, *Karl Barth: Against Hegemony* (Oxford: Clarendon Press, 1999), 276, *italics* in original.

[12]In a sermon, preached on August 30, 1914, Barth said, 'This present war is largely a *racial* conflict" between Germans, French, Slavs and Russians (97, *italics* in original). And then again, two weeks later, Barth preached, "No more idolatry of money and power ... no more racial arrogance and no militarism" (123). These sermons can be found in Karl Barth, *A Unique Time of God: Karl Barth's WWI Sermons*, ed. and trans. William Klempa (Louisville: Westminster John Knox, 2016).

[13]For example, Barth mentions Africa a mere twenty times in his *Church Dogmatics*, and most of which refer either to missionaries or to Africa as an object of missionary outreach.

well."[14] While not necessarily a racist term, the descriptor, "coal black," paired with the conjunction "but," displays an obvious cultural insensitivity.[15]

Barth had much more to say about women and the relationship between men and women.[16] Barth asserts a hierarchical, ordered relationship between men and women in which women are subordinate to men, and women are only complete with men, just as men are only complete with Christ. Barth applies this understanding not only to marriage but to all human society. Men and women need one another to live into their full humanity that God intends, with men occupying leading roles in the home and in society at large.[17] Regarding sexuality in general, and homosexuality in particular, Barth considered marriage between a man and a woman to be the relationship that humans had been created for and that same-sex unions depart from God's intent.[18]

During the last decade, Barth's understanding of humanity and the human person has been invoked to address a wide array of contemporary questions. For example, George Hunsinger appeals to Barth in his objections to the involvement of the United States in the wars in Iraq and Afghanistan, as well as in objections to the use of torture.[19] Marc Cortez has employed Barth's theological anthropology to consider contemporary questions of the interrelationship between human bodies, minds and souls.[20] Esther Acolaste stages a three-strand conversation between Barth, Carl Jung and African Traditional Religions

---

[14]The original phrase is: "*kohlrabenschwarz, aber mir sehr sympathisch.*" Quoted in Eberhard Busch, *Karl Barths Lebenslauf: Nach Seinen Briefen und Autobiograph Texten* (München: Kaiser, 1975), 410; ET: 396; from a letter from Karl Barth to Christoph Barth, August 25, 1951.

[15]A number of African American theologians are thinking with-and-beyond Barth on the topic of race. See the work of Andrea C. White, including "The Political Theology of Karl Barth: Why a Womanist Theologian Should Care" lecture on November 21, 2015, Karl Barth Society of North America newsletter No. 52 (November 2016); J. Kameron Carter, *Race: A Theological Account* (New York: Oxford University Press, 2008); Brian Bantum, *Redeeming Mulatto: A Theology of Race and Christian Hybridity* (Waco: Baylor University Press, 2010); and Willie James Jennings, *The Christian Imagination: Theology and the Origins of Race* (New Haven, CT: Yale University Press, 2010).

[16]On Barth and gender, see Elizabeth Frykberg, "Karl Barth's Theological Anthropology: An Analogical Critique Regarding Gender Relations," *Studies in Reformed Theology and History* 1, no. 3 (Summer 1993): 1–54, as well as two more recent and updated contributions: Gillian Breckenridge, "Looking for Likeness and Hope: Beyond Super- and Subordination in Barth's Discussion of Gender in *Church Dogmatics* §45.3," *Zeitschrift für Dialektische Theologie* 33, no. 2 (2017): 166–78, and Faye Bodley DeAngelo, *Sexual Difference, Gender, and Agency in Karl Barth's Church Dogmatics* (London: Bloomsbury Academic, 2019).

[17]See Mary McClintock Fulkerson, 'The Imago Dei and a Reformed Logic for Feminist-Womanist Critique," in *Feminist and Womanist Essays in Reformed Dogmatics*, ed. Amy Plantinga Pauw and Serence Jones (Louisville: Westminster John Knox Press, 2006), 95–106. Fulkerson argues that in Reformed theology the *imago Dei* is a compliment to humanity that has not been paid equally to all peoples, and women in particular have been viewed as "lesser bearers of the image" (96). Her rereading of Reformed theology develops a "Reformed logic" that destabilizes existing "previously accepted social arrangements" and expands the *imago* to include neighbor relations.

[18]For scholarship that engages Barth on sexuality and builds towards queer theory, see Linn Marie Tonstad, *God and Difference: The Trinity, Sexuality, and the Transformation of Finitude* (New York: Routledge, 2017).

[19]See George Hunsinger, "Karl Barth and Human Rights," in *Karl Barth and Radical Politics*, 2nd edition (Eugene: Cascade, 2017), 181–92. Barth addressed the question of just war in III/4, §55.2: "The Protection of Life," 397–470, especially 448–69. While Barth did allow for war as just in exceptional circumstances, his greater concern was peace, for just societal arrangements on a daily basis. For more on Barth on war, see Matthew Puffer, "Taking Exception to the *Grenzfall's* Reception: Revisiting Karl Barth's Ethics of War," *Modern Theology* 28 (2012): 478–502.

[20]Marc Cortez, *Embodied Souls, Ensouled Bodies: An Exercise in Christological Anthropology and Its Significance for the Mind/Body Debate* (London: T&T Clark, 2008). See especially chapter 2: "From Christology to Anthropology: The Ontological Determination of Humanity in Karl Barth's Theological Anthropology," 16–39.

around theological anthropology in order to reflect upon African pastoral practices.[21] The growing field of comparative theology has appealed to Barth's theological anthropology.[22] Barth's understanding of humanity has also been engaged in rethinking and seeking to decolonize contemporary theological reflection.[23] In each case, the authors find Barth's theological anthropology to be generative for addressing their particular question.

CONCLUSION

This chapter has examined Karl Barth's understanding of humanity as determined Christologically, defined actualistically and understood relationally. Beginning with the Christological determination, humans act out of the goodness of their Creator by seeking to live in correspondence to the divine calling and summons. Barth understands the human as good, as God is a God for-humanity and with-humanity. As Gorringe writes, "Barth's theology is a *humanist* theology in the sense that it is primarily affirmative of human endeavor, and not carping, accusatory, and nay-saying. His political word was always a word of promise."[24] And, as we have seen, in recent decades, the thrust of Barth's theology has been employed to rethink Barth's claims about contemporary societal issues in liberationist directions.[25]

To conclude, though Barth is not best known for his theological anthropology, in a sense, humanity was always in focus as he wrote his dogmatics. In a 1962 lecture in the United States, near the end of his career, Barth remarked, "Although theology is no enemy to mankind, at its core it is a critical, in fact a revolutionary affair, because as long as it has not been shackled, its theme is the new man in the new cosmos."[26] Our thinking about the God who is for us must be unleashed from confining, restrictive assumptions and worldviews.

Freely living life in relationship with this God of grace and in relationship with our fellow humans defines our humanity, and, from Barth's perspective, fills us with *joy*. There is a deep, though often hidden, connection in Barth's theological anthropology between freedom and joy. As Barth writes in *Humanity of God*,

> Freedom is *being joyful*. Freedom is the great gift, totally unmerited and wondrous beyond understanding. It awakens the receiver to true selfhood and new life. It is a gift

---

[21]Esther Acolaste, *For Freedom or Bondage?: A Critique of African Pastoral Practices* (Grand Rapids, MI: Eerdmans, 2014).

[22]Christian Collins Winn and Martha Moore-Keish, eds., *Karl Barth and Comparative Theologies* (New York: Fordham University Press, 2019), esp. Pan-chiu Lai, "Barth and Universal Salvation: A Mahayana Buddhist Perspective," 85–104; John Sheveland, "Do Not Grieve: Reconciliation in Barth and Vedanta Desika," 184–202; and Tim Hartman, "Humanity and Destiny: A Theological Comparison of Karl Barth and African Traditional Religions," 228–47.

[23]Tim Hartman, *Theology after Colonization: Bediako, Barth, and the Future of Theological Reflection* (Notre Dame: University of Notre Dame Press, 2020).

[24]Gorringe, *Against Hegemony*, 277.

[25]In addition to the works already cited, Barth's thought was influential in the anti-apartheid movements, particularly among white South Africans. See Charles Villa-Vicencio, ed., *On Reading Karl Barth in South Africa* (Grand Rapids, MI: Eerdmans, 1988); John W. de Gruchy and Charles Villa-Vicencio, *Apartheid is a Heresy* (Grand Rapids, MI: Eerdmans, 1983), Dirk J. Smit, "On Reading Karl Barth in South Africa -- Today?," in *Essays on Being Reformed, Collected Essays 3*, ed. Robert R. Vosloo (Stellenbosch: Sun Press, 2009), 275–92; and John de Gruchy, *Liberating Reformed Theology: A South African Contribution to an Ecumenical Debate* (Grand Rapids, MI: Eerdmans, 1991).

[26]Karl Barth, *Evangelical Theology* (Grand Rapids, MI: Eerdmans, 1963), 119.

from *God,* from the source of all goodness, an ever-new token of his faithfulness and mercy … Through this gift man who was irretrievably separated and alienated from God is called into discipleship. This is why freedom is joy![27]

As humans live into the freedom that God has given, we are formed more and more into the image of God, that is, into the likeness of Jesus Christ. This ongoing process, that occurs in spite of human sin, fills us with joy as we become more and more who we already are in Christ: creatures created by God to live in relationship with God and with others. In the context of these relationships, Barth encourages us to work out our salvation, or as Barth puts it, our "life in hope," in full confidence that it is God who is working in us (IV/3, 940; Phil. 2:12-13). This joyful hope, or hopeful joy, then characterizes what it means to be human.

SUGGESTED FURTHER READING

Barth, Karl, *Church Dogmatics*, vol. III, part 2 (Edinburgh: T&T Clark, 1960).

Barth, Karl, *Humanity of God* (Louisville: Westminster John Knox, 1960).

Gorringe, Timothy, *Karl Barth: Against Hegemony* (Oxford: Clarendon Press, 1999).

Hartman, Tim, *Theology after Colonization: Bediako, Barth, and the Future of Theological Reflection* (Notre Dame, IN: University of Notre Dame Press, 2020).

Jüngel, Eberhard, "The Royal Man: A Christological Reflection on Human Dignity in Barth's Theology," in *Karl Barth: A Theological Legacy*, trans. Garrett E. Paul (Philadelphia: Westminster Press, 1986), 127–38.

Krötke, Wolf, "The Humanity of the Human Person in Karl Barth's Anthropology," in *Cambridge Companion to Karl Barth*, ed. John Webster (Cambridge: Cambridge University Press, 2000), 159–76.

---

[27]Karl Barth, *Humanity of God*, 78.

CHAPTER EIGHTEEN

Karl Rahner for Twenty-First-Century Cyborgs

SUSAN ABRAHAM

For Karl Rahner, theology and anthropology are the same because theology cannot avoid speaking about the human being even as its subject matter is God. Anthropology, therefore, is the immanent ground of transcendence in relationship with its opposite pole, the divine ground of transcendence. The nature of the human being consequently is evident only in relation to the Divine. Rahner is a highly systematic thinker for whom content and method function cohesively and systematically, best seen in his *Foundations of Christian Faith*.[1] Yet, for many contemporary students this a difficult text to read, exacerbated by the fact that "human nature" is a fuzzy concept. Theological anthropology presumes that human nature is universalizable, that is, what theologians say about human nature is universally true for all human beings. Students these days are familiar with critical theories that challenge any universal narrative of human nature. Rahner's theological anthropology seems out of touch and irrelevant to humanity's most pressing concerns. Rahner's text is difficult also because his method in speaking about human beings incorporates diverse intellectual and philosophical ideas more pertinent to his Eurocentric context.

Like all theologians responding in a context, Karl Rahner was responding to a specific mid-twentieth-century context of European Catholicism. These originating influences as well as critical perspectives challenging his philosophical and theological concerns are well mapped in the ever-burgeoning Rahner literature of the past forty-plus years. In writing this chapter, I am more intrigued by how Rahner would respond to another contemporary issue, that of post- and transhumanism.[2] The main feature of this form of humanism is that human beings are able to enhance the self through technological or medical prosthetics, resulting in a hybrid of human and machine called a cyborg. Post and transhumans "believe that technology should be available to help human beings transcend the limits imposed by evolution. They see evolution as incomplete, and so look to biotechnology, nanotechnology, and a host of other new approaches to help us live

---

[1] Karl Rahner, *Foundations of Christian Faith: An Introduction to the Idea of Christianity*, trans. William V. Dych (New York, Crossroad, 1993), henceforth, FCF.

[2] R. Cole-Turner, "Introduction: The Transhumanist Challenge," in *Transhumanism and Transcendence: Christian Hope in an Age of Technological Enhancement*, ed. Ronald Cole-Turner (Washington DC: Georgetown University Press, 2011), 13, asserts that the result of technological modification is not simply a "better" human but something that is no longer human, a posthuman. The word "posthuman" presents conceptual complications because of its literary history. Hence, many writing in this field prefer the term "transhuman," especially when human biology is changing through the use of technology.

longer and be stronger, healthier, smarter and faster than evolution made us."[3] For these transhumans, there is no such thing as "essential human nature," because human beings are free to recreate themselves, transcending biological limits. Post- and transhumanism presents a conundrum for Catholic theology. As Catholic scholar Ilia Delio asserts, "up to the twentieth century the philosophical challenge was to think nature and ourselves in the presence of nature. Today the philosophical challenge is to think technology ... and ourselves in the presence of technology."[4] Even more importantly, the philosophical shift we are seeing is also a shift to what she calls "InfoPhilia," or the love of information. As she asserts, "information has come to define reality."[5] In such a "postbiological" future, what can Catholic theologians say about human beings? What would Rahner have to say?

Rahner, however, invites angry dismissals, for being both too conservative and too liberal. For example, in an essay entitled "Rahner, The Restorationist," R. R. Reno attacks Rahner for being too conservative on some counts and too liberal on others.[6] The main issue for Reno is that Rahner's theological approach "has encouraged many to translate the theological doctrines of God's transcendence into an epistemological doctrine of God's unknowability."[7] "Dire" consequences have followed from this, he argues, including "theological relativism," "lack of any material criteria for theological truth" and simplistic notions about human nature that are social-constructive rather than strictly theological.[8] Reno is a traditionalist who wants no "solidarity with the experience of modernity" and its liberal leanings but "solidarity with the apostolic tradition as vouchsafed to us by the Church."[9]

Reno is also very critical of Rahner's theological method, which was to "try as far as possible to situate Christianity within the intellectual horizon of people today," a sign of Rahner's capitulation to Western modernity.[10] Here Rahner was being too "conservative,"[11] he argues, in performing a "mid-twentieth century restorationist desire for a new, modern-friendly integralism ... that allowed for Christian institutions to work harmoniously with secular ones."[12] Worse, in his view, Rahner was simply securing a position in academic contexts in which critiques of traditional theology flourished, leading to the "Catholic academic scene in America, providing theological justifications for nearly all forms of contextual, feminist and liberationist theologies, as well as nearly all revisionist moral theologies."[13] Reno's solution is to abandon any theological method that seeks to integrate modern issues with Catholic theology and instead affirm a propositional Catholic theology emphasizing "metaphysics in philosophy and dogma in theology."[14] Catholic theology departments in numerous universities in the United States will find Reno's argument familiar. Reno's argument depends on a false dichotomy between

---

[3]R. Cole-Turner, 'Going beyond the Human: Christians and Other Transhumanists', *Dialog: A Journal of Theology* 54 (Spring 2015), 20.
[4]Ilia Delio, *The Unbearable Wholeness of Being: God, Evolution, and the Power of Love* (Maryknoll, NY: Orbis Books, 2013), 156.
[5]Ibid., 160.
[6]R. R. Reno, "Rahner the Restorationist," *First Things* 233 (May 2013): 45–51.
[7]Ibid., 45. Reno is clear that "Karl Rahner's time has passed."
[8]Ibid., 49.
[9]Ibid., 51.
[10]Ibid., 47.
[11]By this he means that Rahner was seeking to conserve Catholic identity and tradition.
[12]Reno, "Rahner the Restorationist," 47.
[13]Ibid., 46.
[14]Ibid., 49.

theology and secular disciplines. By driving the distinction between the theological and secular much deeper than Rahner would, he attempts to create a space for theology that is unaffected by contemporary questions.

My reading of Rahner's theology persuades me otherwise. Rahner would have seized with delight the conundrums presented by post- and transhumanism to continue to speak to the great mystery at the heart of theology: that when God decides to be not God, God becomes a human being.[15] In such a spirit of embracing Rahner's distinctive theological creativity, I identify three broad issues structuring this chapter. First, it is important to acknowledge that theological anthropology itself presents a particular problem in the context of posthumanist cyborgs. Technological enhancement is a reality for many, ranging from the ordinary communication tools we use to connect with each other to chemical medical enhancements regulating behavior and mood. The first section consequently explores whether the cyborg needs theology. In the second, I ask who Jesus Christ is for cyborgs. Rahner's theological method, even as it integrates modern philosophical ideas with traditional theology, was in service of church, society and the academy. Overemphasizing the Western philosophical influences in his theology blinds us to the ways Rahner's theological method was Christological. Third, an issue that envelops the first two is whether Rahner's understanding of "transcendence" is relevant to twenty-first-century concerns about human beings. Human beings are in a process of constant creation and reinvention of themselves. We seek to transcend finitude, biological limits and even death. Transcendence meant something very different for Rahner, evident in this passage from the *Foundations of Christian Faith*:

> If the human being really is a subject, that is, a transcendent, responsible and free being, who as subject is both entrusted into their own hands and always in the hands of what is beyond their control, then basically this has already said that the human person is a being oriented towards God. Their orientation towards the absolute mystery always continues to be offered to them by this mystery as the ground and content of their being. To understand the human being in this way, of course, does not mean that when we use the term "God" in such a statement, we know what this term means from any other source except through this orientation to mystery. At this point theology and anthropology necessarily become one. A person knows explicitly what is meant by God only insofar as they allow their transcendence beyond everything objectively identifiable to enter into their consciousness, accept it, and objectify in reflection what is already present in their transcendentality.[16]

Can, therefore, a cyborg do theology, that is, can a theological notion of transcendence be useful to them? There are many excellent studies of Rahner's theological anthropology which are not reprised here.[17] In this chapter in contrast, instead of an exposition and survey of Rahner's theological anthropology, I ask whether his understanding of transcendence, presented through his theological method, has purchase in a post and transhumanist age, usable by cyborgs.

---

[15]FCF, 225: "When God wants to be what is not God, the human being comes to be."

[16]FCF, 44.

[17]An excellent introductory resource is D. Marmion and M. E. Hines, eds., *The Cambridge Companion to Karl Rahner* (Cambridge: Cambridge University Press, 2005).

DOES A CYBORG NEED THEOLOGY?

A cyborg needs theology to understand her creatureliness. Theological anthropology need not be alien to cyborgs because Rahner affirms that human beings are always reaching outward and beyond the confines of their creatureliness.[18] For Rahner, to be human is to be oriented toward what is more than the human experience: an orientation to a "sea of infinite mystery."[19] When the human person intuits that she can "ask about asking" and "think about thinking," she is making the turn to transcendence, the first step to being a religious person.[20] A cyborg cannot help being religious, then, because she is already asking such fundamental questions about herself. "Experience" therefore is a source of theological thinking even for cyborgs. There are important differences though. For Rahner, the experience of transcendence is a foundation for faith; a human being is the "hearer of the message." The message is something that comes to us outside of our experience but is, at the same time, able to be understood, though not in its totality. We only hear, not generate the message. Transcendence *is* transcendence after all. For Rahner, the ungraspability of transcendence secures us our humanity. A cyborg will find this insight difficult. For a cyborg, transcendence is something she should be able to have, add, consume or buy. Rahner would insist that transcendence ultimately is not within our grasp.

In Rahner's understanding, transcendence originates in God. It is the reason it remains ungraspable by human beings. Yet, it approaches human beings in a communicative relationship. Transcendence therefore lures the human person to the deepest truths of herself, the depths of her being, an existential ontology. This is who we are for Rahner: persons spoken to by God and a God who in turn is able to listen. The communicative relationship between God and human being is made possible by a sense of the infinity of reality, translated as a "pre-apprehension," the *Vorgriff auf esse*.[21] Human beings intuit such a sense of "the more" and it is evident in the ways in which human beings carry on in the face of adversity and oppression. This is true even if a person feels empty and fragile. Even when this is the case, human beings are able to continue to live a human life, because of hope and gratefulness for life. In these pages, Rahner sounds very much like the pastoral theologian he is. Consider these sentences:

> Real transcendence is always in the background, so to speak, in those origins of human life and human knowledge over which we have no control. This real transcendence is never captured by metaphysical reflection, and in its purity, that is, as not mediated objectively, it can be approached asymptotically at most, if at all, in mystical experience and perhaps in the experience of final loneliness in the face of death.[22]

Transcendence is unthinkable, that is, it is not cognitively graspable. Ordinary human experience, as Rahner describes it, is largely the acknowledgement of things that are beyond individual control, a point that people who struggle with existential anxiety can grasp. In his view, such an effort is based in transcendence, though not a transcendence that is generated solely by the self. Post- and transhumanists have to face the questions of

---

[18]See the essay on parallels between Rahner's understanding of transcendence and posthumanism by Ronald Cole-Turner in his "Going beyond the Human: Christians and Other Transhumanists," 20–6.

[19]FCF, 22.

[20]Ibid., 23.

[21]Ibid., 33–5.

[22]Ibid., 35.

existential anxiety and loneliness because many technological and chemical enhancements currently available to human beings seek to ameliorate existential anxiety and loneliness. Anxiety and loneliness are opportunities for transcendence, for Rahner and the cyborg, with important differences.

For Rahner, transcendence is divine, but not estranged from human experience. In so doing, he dissolves dualistic thought separating humanity and divinity. He actively challenges the idea of an otherworldly transcendence, even as he seeks to preserve its divine origin. Many traditional forms of theology overemphasize the "otherness of God" in order to maintain a necessary distinction between the world created by God and God as creator. In contrast, Rahner's theological anthropology speaks to the nearness of God in human space and time. Because he wants to claim that a human being's religious sense is intrinsic to their humanity, he argues that human nature is constituted by an orientation to transcendence. The human being in the world is one who has "not entered accidentally into this material and temporal world as into something which is ultimately foreign to them as subjects and contrary to their spiritual nature."[23] Even as theologically and semantically dense a term as "salvation" is, it is inseparable from human time, space and action. The salvation effected by God is only understood in relation to the history, that is, the time and space in which human beings live. God *is* in all things in the world, especially near and with each of us. Of course, in order to maintain the fundamental difference between God and human beings, Rahner is careful to say that there is a "genuine differentiation" between them.

Cyborgs are not strangers to an idea of transcendence at the heart of human nature and experience. Yet they deepen the dualism of material reality and transcendence. Andrea Vicini and Agnes Brazal assert that human beings are desperate, indeed, yearning for transcendence in their essay entitled "Longing for Transcendence: Cyborgs and Trans- and Post Humans" in their turn to technology.[24] Transcendence in the newly articulated "cyber-anthropologies" perceives reality as largely bodiless: "In the Silicon Valley of the early 1990s, the merging of spirituality with new media technologies stressed that salvation occurred by departing from the body and joining the "immaterial sphere" of cyberspace."[25] Theological anthropologies in contrast, especially like that of Karl Rahner, do not flee bodily and material reality. Vicini and Brazal in their critical assessment further underscore that transhuman emphases on technological enhancement overemphasize individual experience over the social, deepening economic and other inequalities. This sense of transcendence is not one that is recognizable to Christian theologians because it denies the body on the one hand and ignores the individual's interconnection to the wider world on the other. For this reason, cyborgs need theology.

Rahner's theological anthropology challenges any notion of dualistic anthropology as well as notions of the human being as individualist and self-absorbed. Rahner's idea that transcendence, which resonates in human experience and has its origin in God, means is that we are both "radically different from" and "radically dependent" on God while belonging to the community of other beings also created and sustained by God. Transcendence therefore is both about our uniqueness and also about our ordinariness. This mean that human beings are free, but without absolute autonomy. Our difference and

---

[23]Ibid., 41.
[24]A. Vicini and A. Brazal, "Longing for Transcendence: Cyborgs and Trans- and Posthumans," *Theological Studies*, 76 (2015): 148–65.
[25]Ibid., 150.

freedom thus have their source in God. Rahner secures a very important theological space for the human being. To be human is to realize one's creatureliness in the experience of transcendent continuing creation, in, with and for other created beings. Most useful here is Rahner's theological focus on human life as interrelated and in constant relationship. Human nature and human experience have to be articulated in relation to more than the self and more than the merely human. For many, contemporary technologies of self and self-enhancement distort and destroy human nature by being singularly focused on egoistic desire.[26] The cyborg needs theology in order to remain human. Otherwise, she ceases to be human and becomes a machine.

WHO IS JESUS CHRIST FOR A CYBORG?

To a cyborg, the idea of God becoming a human being may sound ludicrous. After all, being human implies lack and limit; we cannot do everything and cannot know everything. Why would God seek to become human? "God," as all cyborgs may think, is omnipotent, omniscient and omnipresent, far removed from the reality of human life. Cyborgs who encounter Rahner's theological anthropology will face a quandary. Instead of such an "omni-God," Rahner insists on telling the story of God who came to be with us first as a human child and then as a human being, who remained powerless before evil. One of the most beautiful lines in Rahner's writing on the mystery of God is an excerpt from a talk he gave entitled "Experiences of a Catholic Theologian."[27] Rahner asserts that the "agonizing task" facing theologians today is to clarify "the ineffable outrageousness of the absolute Godhead in person falling stark naked into our narrow creaturehood."[28] The emphasis on the incarnation in order to illuminate the nature of the human being is typical of Rahner. If the cyborg reflected on Rahner's method, she would discover that Rahner successfully heads off two problems. One is the problem of dualism that thinks of creaturehood and material realities as something human beings need to escape. The other is that of a distant God who has nothing to do with creation. His incarnational theology demonstrates that transcendence is also the yearning of the divine who embraces created reality to become like it.

Tendentious arguments that assert that Rahner compromises Christology by an overemphasis on anthropology dismiss the complex theological system that Rahner develops. In *The Foundations of Christian Faith*, Rahner's chapter on Jesus Christ is a full 146 pages long, the longest chapter in the middle of the book. A careful reading of this chapter makes clear a theological method that reveals the goal of theological thinking: to grow in our relationship to Christ. While the first five chapters explore faith as something intelligible, possessed by and gifted to the human being, the three chapters following

---

[26]See Delio, *The Unbearable Wholeness of Being*:

> The relationship between iPhones, Google and institutional religion may not seem obvious, but the loss of human identity has stimulated the scientific imagination to fill in the deep hole left by the absence of religion from our everyday lives. The hole for more life and deeper consciousness, once the stuff of religion, has been transferred to a technological utopia. The "I-thou" relationship has mutated into an "I-Phone" relationship ... the need to find a new body and new personal identity is becoming more urgent in a culture of consumerism in which the primary commodity is the human person. (163)

[27]See the excerpt in P. Endean, ed., *Karl Rahner: Spiritual Writings* (Maryknoll, NY: Orbis Books, 2004), 202–3.

[28]Ibid., 202. A slightly different translation of the talk in its entirety can be found in *The Cambridge Companion to Karl Rahner*, 308–10.

the chapter entitled "Jesus Christ" explore how the Christian must express her faith in the world. To do so, Rahner integrates philosophy and theology, in service of a practical Christology, that is, a Christology that inspires a discipleship of ordinary life.

Theology's task is to point the human being to her true destiny: her relationship to the unknowable God revealed in Jesus Christ. Thus, it is most important that we understand the experience of faith as the mystery of God that is not mysterious but unknowable in its totality as Mystery. Transcendental Christology, moreover, is incarnational; it is fleshly and practical. That is, to reflect on one's experience of Jesus Christ invites one to live lives within the limits of one's humanity while simultaneously extending beyond one's life. It requires that we ignore the many desires of the egoistic self by putting the self in the service of the world in its ordinariness. It means to live a life of discipleship in imitation of Jesus Christ in the everyday. We can only preserve our humanity in this way. Rahner's incarnational theology leads us to think about divine and human natures as ontologically related, meaning, that we can only understand the one in relationship to the other. Each exists in a mutual and co-inhering relationship. It also means that human selves have to learn similar forms of self-emptying in order to be in relationship with God and the world. Hence, the incarnational starting point for theology leads Rahner to declare "Christology is the beginning and end of anthropology."[29] It is also the reason he is able to say that theology and anthropology are the same. The incarnation is both a revelation of God and a revelation of the human being.

God becomes human out of divine love. Theology, consequently, is a reflection on love and a practice of love. For Christians, faith is reflection and practice of love, because it leads us to the knowledge of God's creative and incarnational love. The foundation of faith is love: love for God and love for the human other who is the embodiment of God. Christology cannot just be dogma; Christology has to be enacted in love toward all. The consequence of faith and belief is to strive toward excellence in loving action. Christology, properly understood, is the basis of self-transcendence in concrete time and space, in relationship to other human beings. Love, another name for wise, ethical excellence, is the basis of the Christian church and the Christian life. Theological method is mapping the way of love, the ecstasy of the self, oriented to God and neighbor in the world. In this sense, transcendence is concrete—of the world, in the world and for the world:

> Anyone who accepts their humanity fully, and all the more so of course the humanity of others, has accepted the Son of Man because in them, God has accepted human beings. And if it says in scripture that whoever loves his neighbor has fulfilled the law, then this is the ultimate truth because God has become this neighbor, and hence God who is at once nearest and farthest from us is always accepted and loved in every neighbor.[30]

For the cyborg and her posthumanism, the demand to be fleshly is in contradiction to her need to transcend the bounds of fleshly human living. Her fleshly reality is a stark reminder of fragility, loss and mortality. Yet, an idea of transcendence that permits her to escape these human limits will dehumanize her. Brent Waters states that this would be the case because even though there may be some apparent similarities between Christianity and post- and transhumanism, no reconciliation is possible between them.[31] Transhumanism is

---

[29]FCF, 225.
[30]Ibid., 228.
[31]B. Waters, "Whose Salvation, Whose Eschatology?," in *Transhumanism and Transcendence: Christian Hope in an Age of Technological Advancement*, ed. Ronald Cole-Turner, 164.

a "late modern religious response" to the conditions of contemporary human life in this account. Both transhumanism and Christianity agree that finite human conditions need to be transcended. For both, death is the enemy to be defeated. Yet, these similarities for Waters are not substantive and he sounds a resounding alarm against transhumanism. He does so on theological terms: salvation for transhumanists is basically salvation from the human condition through "biological and bionic immortality" and eschatology is the absolute self-perfection of the human being as the ideal of self-actualization.[32] In other words, if transcendence simply is transcendence beyond one's fleshly reality, then it is a dangerous and distorted form of transcendence.

Rahner would argue that the problem is not so much the overweening power of the cyborg to replace religion; rather, the problem for Rahner is that bad religion, overemphasizing an otherworldliness and unnecessary abstraction, deepens dualistic thinking about God and the World—*that* is the issue. Practical Christology staves off this tendency. Similarly, Ronald Cole-Turner offers a more middle-ground assessment by identifying another dichotomy in the debate between theological anthropology and transhumanist anthropology. In his view, this is a debate between the theological values of gratitude and creativity: "As one side emphasizes our obligation to remember that life is a gift and that we need to learn to let things be, the other emphasizes our obligation to transform that gift and to exhibit our creativity."[33] Rahner would agree that the key here is to continue to see ourselves as creatures while also embracing human abilities to create and innovate. His theological program as a whole was an experiment of creativity, innovation and expression of gratitude for life. His incarnational theology, however, will challenge transhumanism out of its radical individualist and libertarian orientation to focus on the service of others. In fact, the question that haunts Christians through the ages continues to haunt the cyborg: "Who do you say that I am?" Perhaps human beings have always been like cyborgs, caught in the web of self-important desire. That question of belief, confession and trust does more to undercut self-absorption and self-importance while acknowledging that transcendence in the human world is recognizable. Creative and grateful cyborgs can recognize Jesus Christ.

CAN A CYBORG DO THEOLOGY?

Yes, if she seeks to preserve her humanity. In the above two sections, I have presented two aspects of Karl Rahner's theological anthropology that illuminate his use of transcendence in view of cyborgs who may precipitously dismiss him. Transcendence and the desire for it seems to be common ground for Rahner and transhumanists. As has been argued, the conversation between them must begin with what "transcendence" might mean. It may begin with what "human" means. Reflecting the fuzziness of the concept, Elaine Graham, a pastoral theologian writing about trans- and posthumanism speaks of the post/human. "Transhuman" in her account is simply a "transitional human being, or one augmented and modified on the way to being posthuman, the fully technologized successor species to organic Homo sapiens."[34] Since "posthuman" remains a contentious term, she suggest the use of "post/human" to "suggest a questioning of both the inevitability of a successor

---

[32]Ibid. 169.
[33]Cole-Turner, "Transhumanism and Christianity," 195.
[34]E. Graham, *Representations of the Post/Human: Monsters, Aliens and Others in Popular Culture* (New Brunswick, NJ: Rutgers University Press, 2002), 9.

species and of there being any consensus surrounding the effects of technologies on the future of humanity."[35] As is evident in this quote, "human nature" continues to escape clear definition. But it is also clear that human nature, whether theologically or technologically framed, seeks transcendence.

Her point is that "human nature" needs to be far less abstract even as it seeks transcendence. She writes,

> If the advent of the post/human is about recognizing the constructedness of the fault-lines by which we have in the past delineated the boundaries of the normatively human, then we can hardly revert to fixed categories of "human nature" as a basis of our moral judgments. However, the sense that humans and machines are increasingly assimilated, that it is not so easy to separate human beings from their tools and artefacts … may not be such an unthinkable notion of where we are in a digital and biotechnological age. It is also a profoundly materialist understanding, because it refuses to think either that we can retreat to some pure unadulterated "human nature" independent of this world we have made; or that we can use technology to transcend bodily finitude and limitation.[36]

Graham, like Cole-Turner, is not dismissive of transhumanists but of the distortions of "transcendence." For Graham, the cyborg is confirmation that we must continue to speak of human nature, but now in a particular way. The way to speak of human nature for a post/human future is to reflexively examine *how* we create artefacts and discourses and how we coexist in a world together with them.[37] At the basis of both is human creativity, a gift to us, in our material plenitude. It is in the interaction with the material world, a realization that we live and exert our humanness in a web of relationships that we create machines and discourses. Thus, technology need not be an impediment for the cyborg. In another essay, Graham is even more insistent on this point, asserting that we can no longer trade extreme technophilia for its opposite, technophobia.[38] Post/humanity celebrates human beings and our technical and scientific skills while the "engagement with the material might be an avenue into transcendence or divinity, via a more incarnational or sacramental engagement with the material world."[39] The revivifying of the material through a sacramental view (God in the World) is the basis for a cyborg's theological anthropology. What will be an impediment to the cyborg is bad theology.

Graham warns that post/humans need correctives about the nature of God. Post/human ideas of transcendence banish God from the world, an idea that would be alien to theological anthropology. Post/humans need a better understanding of God, as both immanent and transcendent, in the world and different from the world. A cyborg need not relinquish her humanity and concede her freedom to technology. She cannot also concede her humanity to an unintelligible notion of God. God is in the world, and creation bears the imprint of divine creativity. If technological enhancement leads human beings to a greater sense of the fragile web of life and the need to care for it, it can lead human beings

---

[35]Ibid., 11.
[36]E. Graham, *Words Made Flesh: Writings in Pastoral and Practical Theology* (London: SCM Press, 2009), 277.
[37]Graham, *Representation of the Post/Human*, 224.
[38]E. Graham, "Nietzsche Gets a Modem: Transhumanism and the Technological Sublime," *Literature and Theology*, 16 (2002): 65–80.
[39]Ibid., 77.

to a true understanding of their nature. As Graham insists, we are not unitary beings, but beings whose sense of self depends on how we relate to what is other than us.

On such a view, Karl Rahner's theological anthropology would find a very sympathetic audience among post/humans. We can say, in one manner of speaking, that human beings, for Rahner, were already "post/humans" after the reality of the incarnation. That is, after the incarnation, we must speak of human beings as the transcendent beings they are, because Christ enhances humanity now. The cyborg, however, has to risk encountering Jesus, the God who became human in order to protect their humanity. Rahner writes in the *Foundations* that

> [love of Jesus] can only be understood by someone who experiences how an encounter with the concrete Jesus of the gospels, in all the concreteness and irreducibility of this definite historical figure, does not confine the person who is seeking the incomprehensible infinity of the absolute mystery of God to something concrete which is made an idol either out of love or foolishness.[40]

The cyborg's yearning for transcendence has to be fulfilled in relationship, particularly a relationship with Jesus that will lead her to the profundity of transcendence in God. Rahner even makes room for a cyborg who disdains religion and theology. If a cyborg stubbornly insists that religion or Christianity has no place in her life, she can encounter her brothers and sisters in the world. That encounter, and its risks of love, has the same enhancing effect as a personal relationship with Jesus Christ (though, of course, Rahner never used the language of enhancement). What is most human about the cyborg therefore is not her capacity and yearning for transcendence, but her yearning to be more of the human being she is called to be. In her love for Jesus or her love for others, she is a transcendent and enhanced being.

Where cyborgs, posthumans and transhumans would balk in reading Rahner's theological anthropology is in his insistence that human beings do not initiate and control transcendence. Even when a human being is being creative and therefore transcending her limits, she is unable to do so unless she is gifted it in the first place by God. In the chapter entitled "The Human Being in Presence of Absolute Mystery,"[41] Rahner examines how a transcendental starting point, that is, beginning with human experience of transcendence can lead to a greater understanding of God in the world. God is indeed "ineffable mystery" and as such is not found as any other object in the world. Yet, it is also true that everything bears the mark of its Creator. In fact, in human creativity, Rahner finds a way to resolve the tension between God's immanence and transcendence. A "good idea," is better understood as inspiration.[42] Human nature, when transcending its ordinary ways of thinking and doing, becomes creative, by being open to inspiration. The word "inspiration" is also Rahner's way of protecting God's transcendence. It is not the case that human creativity is prior to God's inspiration. We are creative and inspired, in this view, because we are open to transcendence. The pastoral argument that seeks to take the human being's historicity and experience in the world seriously becomes a source of theological authority. The cyborg may find, to her chagrin, that she may not be the creator of her own creativity, but one inspired by the very transcendence she deeply desires. In reflecting on this process, Cyborgs find that they *can* do theology.

---

[40]FCF, 310.
[41]Ibid., 44–89.
[42]Ibid., 89.

SUGGESTED FURTHER READING

Haraway, Donna, "A Cyborg Manifesto: Science, Technology and Socialist Feminism in the Late Twentieth Century," in *Cyborgs, Simians and Women: The Reinvention of Nature* (London: Free Association Books, 1991), 149–82.

Kilby, Karen, *Karl Rahner, A Brief Introduction* (New York: Crossroads, 2007).

Losinger, Anton, *The Anthropological Turn: The Human Orientation of the Theology of Karl Rahner* (New York: Fordham University Press, 2000).

Mercer, Calvin, and Tracy Trothen (eds.), *Religion and Transhumanism: The Unknown Future of Human Enhancement* (Santa Barbara, CA: Praeger, 2015).

Parens, Erik, "Authenticity and Ambivalence: Toward Understanding the Enhancement Debate," *Hastings Center Report*, 35 (May–June. 2005): 34–41.

Schüssler Fiorenza, Francis, "Method in Theology," in Declan Marmion and Mary Hines (eds.), *The Cambridge Companion to Karl Rahner* (Cambridge: Cambridge University Press, 2005), 65–82.

CHAPTER NINETEEN

The Dramatic, Christological, Missional Anthropology of Hans Urs von Balthasar

CAROLYN CHAU

A basic starting point for all Christian theological anthropology is that the human person is made in the image and likeness of the triune God. This means that humans are created beings, relational and imbued with dignity. All Christian anthropology attests, moreover, that human beings are endowed by a loving God with intellect, will, freedom, bodies and souls. In other words, according to the Christian tradition, human beings are relational, rational, free, responsible, created, embodied, spiritual and loved.

Swiss theologian Hans Urs von Balthasar adds depth and dimension to this understanding of the human person. Weaving the elements of divine love and divine freedom intimately so as to provide greater explanatory power for human freedom, Balthasar expounds on the nature of human freedom by applying an analogy from theatre, namely, drama, to finite freedom. Balthasar conceives of human freedom as a drama that takes place on the stage of temporal existence where God the Father is the Director, Christ is the "acting area," and all human beings who are open to the Holy Spirit are called and led by the Spirit to take up their role in the *theo-drama*. The goal of *theo-drama* is the goal of salvation history: to bring the entire world back to God, so that God is all in all.

For Balthasar, "There is no other anthropology but the dramatic."[1] By this Balthasar means that one can only inquire into "[humanity's] 'essence'" from the vantage point of being "in the midst of [humanity's] dramatic performance of existence."[2] Moreover, theo-drama presses the point that the initiative in the drama comes from God, not humanity, and the human being's ability to see him or herself as whole is impossible without recognizing God as the starting point of the relationship between God and humanity:

It releases [humanity] from this burden by inserting [humanity], right from the start, into the dramatic dialogue with God, so that God himself may cause [humanity] to

---

[1] Hans Urs von Balthasar, *Theo-drama, Volume II - Dramatis Personae: Man in God*, trans. Graham Harrison (San Francisco: Ignatius Press, 1990), 335. Henceforth TD II.
[2] Ibid.

experience *his* ultimate definition of [humanity]. This does not mean that [humanity] is dispensed from the effort of planning and fashioning [its identity and character], but the human person is shown the way to do it and the ultimate destination he [or she] should have in mind.[3]

Famously, Balthasar speaks of infinite freedom as guaranteeing finite freedom: it is because of divine love that human beings are free and have the power to love in a radical and transformative way.

In addition to Balthasar's anthropology being dramatic in approach,[4] Balthasar is widely known to have appreciated and appropriated the thought of the Church Fathers more so than many of his contemporaries. An affinity for the Greek heritage of Christianity is particularly clear in Balthasar's work on personhood. Recognizing and underscoring the origins of "person" in the Cappadocian choice of the word *prosopon* to resolve the Trinitarian crisis of the first centuries of Christianity, Balthasar expands the dramatic meaning of the term into a full-blown theological anthropology. What makes this term more theologically rich than contemporary understandings of personhood is its strong the relational resonance. *Prosopon* as developed within Trinitarian and Christological contexts stresses the fact that personhood exists in relation and, particularly, in relationships of self-giving. Whereas modern conceptions of personhood often have to do with uniqueness, autonomy, individual rights and agency, the concept of "person" in the Patristic period was the glue that made sense of the three-in-one formulation (three persons, one God) in the creed of the Church.[5] To understand the inner Trinitarian life of processions, the language of personhood rather than substance was embraced by the Church. This is the foundation of Balthasar's twentieth-century proposal of theological anthropology.

Additionally, Balthasar's anthropology integrates the concepts of personhood and mission: for Balthasar, one becomes a person in the true theological sense as one receives one's mission from the Lord and, more precisely, as one enters into the universal mission of Christ. Indeed, Balthasar's mission-centered anthropology is inextricable from the person of Christ and Christology: Christ is the way into the drama between God and humanity. Following Christ's example of surrender, obedience and holiness leads, according to Balthasar, to fully realized personhood. Christ is the single concrete example where person and mission coincide completely; thus, Christ is the perfection of humanity, and following Christ is the way to become a "person" in Balthasar's understanding of the term. The notion in Balthasar that mission is fundamental to identity has its roots

---

[3]TD II, 343.

[4]Note that Balthasar's "method" of presenting his theological anthropology through a depiction of a theo-drama itself hold some important indications of Balthasar's idea of the human being. While some have made the critique that Balthasar does not take time and history seriously—cf. Ben Quash, *Theology and the Drama of History* (Cambridge: Cambridge University Press, 2005)—Balthasar chooses the format of mapping out a drama to underscore that time and human existence have real dramatic import and significance, that the end of the play is not already a *fait accompli*. Indeed, in Christ, humanity receives the gift of participation, through the drama of time and history, in the eternal Triune drama. All creation, including time, exists in the kenotic space between the Father and Son, bound together by the Holy Spirit.

[5]Hans Urs von Balthasar, "On the Concept of Person," *Communio* 13, no. 2 (Spring 1986): 18–26 (also available in Hans Urs von Balthasar, *Explorations in Theology V: Man is Created* (San Francisco: Ignatius Press, 2014), 114–25). Also, for an excellent elaboration of Balthasar's Christological conception of person and its Patristic roots, see Mark Yenson, *Existence as Prayer: The Consciousness of Christ in the Theology of Hans Urs von Balthasar* (New York: Peter Lang, 2014), 61–106 and 121–4. (New York: Peter Lang, 2014), 61–106 and 121–4.

in the founder of the order to which Balthasar belonged for a significant share of his life: Ignatius of Loyola, founder of the Society of Jesus.

Beyond providing a uniquely dramatic and dynamic conceptualization of human freedom, a Trinitarian understanding of personhood and a deeply Christological and mission-centered anthropology, an introduction to Balthasar's theological anthropology would be incomplete without mention of his conception of the relation between the sexes. Though controversial, Balthasar maintains that woman was fashioned as a response to man and that sexual complementarity is crucial to understanding human fecundity and authenticity. To put it briefly, man is characterized fundamentally by action whereas woman is characterized by receptivity. "Receptivity" should not be equated with passivity, however, as receptivity is active. Mary, the mother of God, whom, after Christ, Balthasar believes to be *the* exemplary person, is the embodiment of receptivity *par excellence*, and it is she whom all persons, male and female, should, as disciples, strive to emulate in their own lives.[6] We will thus end the chapter with an exposition and critical reflection on Balthasar's understanding of sexual difference.

***

Before outlining Balthasar's conception of infinite and finite, human freedom, a note on Balthasar's understanding of the human desire for wholeness is due. Balthasar begins his work *A Theological Anthropology*[7] by observing that the human longs to be whole but is unable to achieve this longing for wholeness and/or completion on his own. There is a fundamental fragmentariness and finitude to human existence, and the question for the human being is whether this experience of being a mere fragment may be overcome. According to Balthasar, it is only through the action of God that the human person can achieve this sense of fulfilment and a realization of the eternal in his or her life. Balthasar compares the way of God, or love, or revelation—these are synonymous for Balthasar— with the two key ways that the human has tended to strive for immortality: through mythic religion and tragedy. Greek thought epitomizes the mythic way, which relegates wholeness to the eternal realm and to the eternal being as the one who gives finite being salvation. The tragic way is epitomized by someone such as Nietzsche, who would argue that all of life is suffering and that the desire to outstrip the suffering of life is unrealistic and not to be pursued. According to Balthasar, it is only through the way of love, the way of Christ crucified, that the eternal can be realized in human existence, as it is only Christ's life, death and resurrection that does not deny the reality of suffering completely and does not make attainment of the eternal solely a matter of divine involvement, but, rather, involves the participation and involvement of humanity in salvation, namely, through Jesus Christ, the God-man.[8]

---

[6]Regarding how to understand the relationship between following Christ, the exemplar of humanity, and appreciating the example of Mary, one could say that we are all called to become persons in Christ, and we come to better inhabit that path of personhood in Christ by attending to the example of Mary who was Christ's first and best disciple.

[7]This work is published in German under the title *Das Ganze im Fragment* and is often translated as *The Whole in the Fragment*.

[8]Hans Urs von Balthasar, *A Theological Anthropology* (Eugene, OR: Wipf and Stock, 2010), 43–72.

HUMAN FINITUDE

In the context of Balthasar's treatise on theological anthropology, the fragmentariness of the human person is characterized by three dialectics: in nature, man-woman; in history and politics, master-slave; and in the Church, Jew-Gentile. The phenomenological experience of being partial and incomplete[9] is not the final word, however. In *Theodrama II* , Balthasar attends to even more basic anthropological tensions.[10] Here, Balthasar addresses the categories of spirit/body, man/woman, individual/community and moves on to how these polarities are recapitulated and reconciled in Christ, the Eucharist and the Church. The emphasis on recapitulation in Christ, even when this term is not used, echoes both Irenaeus of Lyons and Maximus the Confessor. Balthasar attests that in Christ the fragment attains the whole, as through the person of Christ the dialectics of human existence are overcome. Balthasar explains how this is so in the instance of complementarity of the genders, for example, as Christ, unlimited in his divine nature, willingly takes on self-limitation into the gendered being of a man (as in "male") and thereby enables man *qua* human being to be fully free. He observes that while Christ is without limit and dependence, he chooses to become limited and dependent. The natural dialectic of man-woman, according to Balthasar, is one wherein man, the male, is symbolized by freedom and woman, the female, is called to be his helpmate. The helpmate that God fashions from the nature of man, who has already in himself a sense of femininity within him, allows him to recognize his true completion in his equal but different other, in woman.[11] Thus, for Balthasar, the natural incompleteness of man as male is transcended in and by Christ, who assumes limitation and goes the distance of self-gift toward the other, for the sake of love.

Dogmatically speaking, Balthasar abides by the traditional Christian notion that the human person is marred by sin and thus in need of salvation. Notably, however, Balthasar does not premise the reality of Christ on the sinfulness of humanity but, rather, understands Christ to precede human fallenness and so is not the answer to sin but the answer to what it means to be fully human, as God created humanity to be.[12] For Balthasar, Christ as the gift of the Father to the whole world was not premised on the Fall and original sin. Nonetheless, human finitude is overcome and transformed by the self-giving love of God in Christ. Balthasar's theological anthropology is deeply Christological, and his Christology is, in turn, deeply Trinitarian.

INFINITE AND FINITE FREEDOM

Human freedom has so often been depicted as being in competition with divine freedom: that is to say, God is the one who created us with limited rather than infinite freedom, and our freedom consists in our obedience to the eternal law of God. Balthasar,

---

[9]Balthasar also uses the term "broken" to describe humanity as such. The challenge of being human lies in an existence that is tense with contradiction and paradox: on the one hand, the human being is a spiritual being; on the other hand, the human being is a biological being (or otherworldly/worldly). On the one hand, the human person is free; on the other hand, the human person is constrained by necessity (tied to nature, tied to God); the human being is ex-centric, with his or her center lying outside of him or herself; we could even say that the human is "homeless" (TD II, 337–41). Similarly, there is the man-woman polarity (TD II, 365–82) and the individual/community polarity (TD II, 383–94).

[10]TD II, "Man," 346–94.

[11]Balthasar, *A Theological Anthropology*, 306–9.

[12]See Kevin Mongrain, *The Systematic Thought of Hans Urs von Balthasar: An Irenean Retrieval* (New York: Crossroad-Herder, 2002) for an excellent exposition on this theme.

however, underscores that human freedom is in fact a gift that culminates in the possibility of a share in divine life itself. Indeed, God's greatest gift to humanity and the content of God's redemptive plan is to allow human beings to participate in his life of total self-giving love. Genuine, fulfilled human freedom is only possible through an encounter with and close following of Jesus Christ, who shows the world the possibility of living through finitude victoriously.

Balthasar subscribes to the traditional conception of the human being as coming from God and moving ever more toward God (*exitus-reditus*), with a difference. He takes this Christian eschatological theme and enriches it through the metaphor of an intersubjective drama between human and divine freedom. The process of successfully moving toward God happens through undertaking in one's own life the self-surrender, dying to self and total fidelity to love itself and love of others that Christ exemplified with his life, ministry and his passion. As Aristotle Papanikolaou has put it, Balthasar's theological anthropology is *kenotic*. "In Balthasar's trinitarian theological anthropology, personhood is not defined in terms of a quality possessed, but as a gifted event. One is person only in *kenotic* relations of freedom as love."[13] Papanikolaou clarifies that *kenosis* for Balthasar does not denote self-sacrifice so much as it means self-gift in relationships with others.

The root of the human capacity to make her way back to God is the person of Jesus Christ, who, in becoming human, allows finite freedom to find in him and in his ongoing gift of self to the Father, a movement toward God. Balthasar understands the Trinity to be an eternal procession of love expressed between the persons, the Father giving the Son, the Son giving all that he is back to the Father and the Holy Spirit holding these two together in their difference and in their ongoing exchange of love. A key premise in this understanding of the Trinity is *diastasis*, or the distance and difference that exists between the three persons of the Trinity. It is only because they are different and distinct that there can be procession, relation, intersubjectivity and love. The distance between the three persons enables communion across difference to occur through the eternally self-giving movements of each of them to the other. This self-giving love of the other across distance in the Trinity is what Christ reveals about God's very nature. It is only because Christ in his humanity gives all that he has to God the Father that the rest of humanity can respond to God in kind. In this way, Christ redeems finite freedom.

PERSON AS MISSION

The human person is, through Christ, "positively endowed with missions ('charisms') that make them persons of profile and quality within the prototypical mission of Jesus."[14] What this means is that all human beings find their mission, their calling in life, in Christ's mission and participating in this mission gives their lives an eternal ecclesial significance, a "profile" as it were. It could be said that for Balthasar, one is not truly a person until this encounter with Christ happens, and one is called into service. Balthasar believes that all too often, Western culture uses the word "person" for what is merely a "conscious subject"; Balthasar seeks to retrieve the distinction between the two:

---

[13]Aristotle Papanikolaou, "Persons, Kenosis and Abuse: Hans Urs von Balthasar and Feminist Theologies in Conversation," *Modern Theology* 19 (January 2003): 41–65.
[14]Hans Urs von Balthasar, *Theo-drama III, Volume III - The Dramatis Personae: Persons in Christ*, trans. Graham Harrison (San Francisco: Ignatius Press, 1992), 231. Henceforth TD III.

It is when God addresses a conscious subject, tells him who he is and what he means to the eternal God of truth and shows him the purpose of his existence—that is, imparts a distinctive and divinely authorized mission—that we can say of a conscious subject that he is a "person."[15]

A human being has consciousness in virtue of being a member of a class of beings who possess the capacity to be reflective and to be, in a word, self-conscious. The uniqueness that comprises personhood, however, arises not simply from self-consciousness but from an awareness of who one is as beloved.[16] In emphasizing the difference between the person-constituting and person-generating love found in God, and all other roots of identity including other forms of loves, Balthasar notes that while in the natural realm a mother's love calls a child into consciousness as a spiritual being, even one's mother cannot tell a person what their mission is. God alone grants mission and thereby helps to reveal to a person who they are in their fullness. Balthasar looks to some of the Church's renowned disciples for an example of how mission constitutes personhood. He considers the life of Peter, ultimately known as the leader and key officeholder of Christ's Church, and notes that it was only through Peter's encounter with Christ and following where his relationship with Christ took him that he became his "true self"; until this point, he was Simon, a fisherman among other fishermen. The unique mission of his life for the good of all only became clear in being "taken into [the] service" of the Lord.[17]

PERSONS IN CHRIST

A key implication of Balthasar's theological anthropology is that every person has the potential and is called to take part in the redemption of the world. Indeed, this is the desired goal for finite freedom: "saying 'Yes' to one's mission means consenting to participating in God's action for the world and therefore being Christ's fellow servant in his saving task."[18] In and through divine graciousness, humans can participate in the redemption of the world and can change the lives of others through changing their own. Thomas Dalzell spells out the concrete meaning of participating in God's saving action this way:

For Balthasar, participation in God's action in the world is the willingness to live for "the other." He thinks that the person chosen by God is called to live not for himself or herself but always for the sake of his or her neighbour. By this he means that the Christian is called to take part in the work of redemption by entering into solidarity with the world and vicariously experiencing its darkness in order to offer it the salvation already objectively achieved by Christ.[19]

To the degree that Christians can reveal Christ's form in their person, they inspire others to participate in the theo-drama of human existence. While most would acknowledge that an other-centered ethos is a basic mandate of Christian living, that self-giving love includes

---

[15]Ibid., 207.
[16]Ibid., 205.
[17]Peter Henrici, "Hans Urs von Balthasar: A Sketch of His Life," in *Hans Urs von Balthasar: His Life and Work*, ed. David L. Schindler (San Francisco: Ignatius, 1991), 11.
[18]Thomas Dalzell, *The Dramatic Encounter of Divine and Human Freedom in the Theology of Hans Urs von Balthasar* (Bern: Peter Lang, 2000), 222.
[19]Ibid.

"vicariously experiencing the darkness [of the world]" speaks to the eschatological vision of the redemption of finite freedom that Balthasar holds. Among the theologoumena for which he is most famous, or infamous, Balthasar is noted for his desire to take seriously the mystery of Holy Saturday. The emphasis on Christ's willingness to undergo death and experience the hell of utter forsakenness on the way to resurrection highlights the way in which love, for Balthasar, means more than benevolence, but must involve bearing Christ's own cross and taking on suffering for love of the world.

PRAYER

Prayer is key to living this transformed existence in Christ. "In Balthasar, prayer begins in the conversation between the persons of the Trinity, even before creation. Therefore, our participation in prayer is always one which pulls us up into a divine conversation, and therefore a divine life, that precedes us but in which we are offered a real dramatic role."[20] We are made to respond to divine love and to follow the call of Christ, but we can only hear this call if we attend to the Word in our daily life. Contemplation of the life of Christ deepens the intimacy between a human being and God to the point where one can take up the *sequela Christi*, the following of Christ, by choosing a state of life in which to express one's sense of mission as given by God, and through which one can then develop a moment-by-moment following of the Lord. Balthasar is clear in saying that a true Christian is one who has given oneself completely over to the Lord; this means that one cannot have any foreordained idea of what one's life project is in advance, as if Christianity is a self-contained idea that must simply be implemented.[21] On the contrary, one's existence must be a continual prayer to the Father, as Christ's own life.[22] In living thusly, one becomes a person in the most meaningful sense of the word.

As Mark McIntosh and others, especially Victoria Harrison, have underscored, obedience, honed and perfected through prayer, is key to achieving the transparent refraction of the will of the Father that Christ and the saints exemplify. Christological obedience involves something more than simply doing the will of the Father, or refraining from disobeying God; it involves *kenosis* or self-emptying, a giving over of oneself to a life of complete *caritas* or love. Paradoxical as it may sound to contemporary ears, such an obedience calls for, in fact, the greatest amount of dexterity, freedom and creativity; to follow the Christological norm of love at all times involves becoming a person trained to continually risk, sacrifice and give all for the glory of the Lord.[23] As Balthasar puts it in his book on Thérèse Martin (aka Thérèse of Lisieux), the obedience at the heart of holiness is about exchanging personality for personhood. Harrison highlights from Balthasar's text on the saint, "What Thérèse needs is that her personality should die, and that she should

---

[20]Thanks to Sylvester Tan, SJ, for clarifying the truly theo-dramatic nature of prayer for Balthasar.
[21]See Hans Urs von Balthasar, *Who Is a Christian?*, trans. John Cumming (London: Burns and Oates, 1968), for Balthasar's resounding critique of this approach to Christian discipleship.
[22]See Mark McIntosh, *Christology from Within: Spirituality and the Incarnation in Hans Urs von Balthasar* (Notre Dame, IN: University of Notre Dame Press), and Yenson, *Existence as Prayer*, for elaboration on this theme.
[23]Referencing *Theo-drama IV*, 334, Margaret Turek notes,

> For Balthasar, the genuineness of Jesus' freedom precisely as obedience is evidenced both by his capacity for a kenotic self-giving that is without reserve and by the fact that "this handing-over of himself is no mere passivity but a form of action which, humanly speaking, demands of the subject more self-possession and initiative than the pursuance of self-imposed precepts and goals." (Margaret Turek, *Towards a Theology of God the Father: Hans Urs von Balthasar's Theodramatic Approach* (New York: Peter Lang, 2001), 48)

be reborn as a person at the level where she has to draw upon all her latent potentialities." Harrison observes further,

> This is a clear instance of one of Balthasar's central and recurring themes: the requirement that a shift take place from "personality" to "person"—in other words, to what a person is in God's Idea, which is discovered in and through a personal relationship to Christ. What has to die in the "personality" is "untruth," which, for von Balthasar, means everything that is in opposition to God (for example, pride). In short, the "personality" has to be radically cleansed of such things in order for a human being to acquire the status of "personhood." In the Thérèse text, von Balthasar makes it explicit that "personhood" is only attained when one's own "truth" is identical with God's "truth."[24]

Prayer aids the cleansing of "untruth" of personality from a human being so that their personhood can shine forth. Prayer or contemplation of Christ, who surrendered himself wholly to the will of the Father, helps to cultivate in the one contemplating the same disposition of openness or what Ignatius calls "indifference." For Balthasar there is a good kind of indifference where one is willing to follow wherever Christ leads; it is a holy indifference that reveals true freedom.

A SPIRITUALITY OF CHILDHOOD

A key aspect of Christ's obedience and humility is his remaining faithful to his identity as son and as child of the Father. Balthasar was so attentive to the importance of the spirituality of childhood for authentic human and Christian existence that he penned a small book devoted entirely to this theme.[25] To be a child is to be filled with wonder at Being. As Raymond Gawronski writes,

> The child then [for Balthasar], secure in the love of his family, begins with that "wonder" (*Staunen*) at Being that leads into play which is a relation to things that precludes a "resigned distance" from them. Surrounded with love, the child should understand its speech as the answer (*Antwort*) to the words of love addressed to it.[26]

Gawronski concludes, "The key points of Balthasar's anthropology are thus found in his doctrine of childhood."[27] There is a simplicity to being human, a freedom, a joy and a youthfulness that are traceable to Balthasar's attentiveness to Jesus' identity as son and child of God.

ECCLESIAL PERSONHOOD

Within and beyond Balthasar's notion of "person," there is a deeper and more particular understanding of personhood, which one might describe as "ecclesial personhood." If Balthasar's basic conception of the person is that he or she becomes who he or she truly is

---

[24]Victoria Harrison, "Personal Identity and Integration: Von Balthasar's Phenomenology of Human Holiness," *Heythrop Journal* 40 (1999): 429–30.
[25]Hans Urs von Balthasar, *Unless You Become like This Child* (San Francisco: Ignatius Press, 1991).
[26]Raymond Gawronski, SJ, *Word and Silence: Han Urs von Balthasar and the Spiritual Encounter between East and West* (Edinburgh: T&T Clark, 1995).
[27]Ibid.

in recognizing and responding to their mission in Christ, ecclesial personhood amplifies this account of person as mission with a clarification of the role that the Church plays in freeing a human being for mission. An ecclesial person is one whose existence is rooted in the life of the Church, which is, of course, that of witness and response to the life of Christ, and an ecclesial person is one who is so immersed in the life of the Spirit that their life, their mission, becomes a fresh source of life, fruitfulness and eternal significance for the Church. Thérèse of Lisieux for example, or Francis of Assisi, created a new way of hearing, responding to and living the gospel that have been paths henceforth of holiness for the rest of the Church.

The most exemplary forms of ecclesial personhood are that of Mary, mother of God, Peter, Paul and John, who form what Balthasar calls the "Christological constellation." This group of persons become the source of what Balthasar will term the Marian principle or profile, the Petrine principle or profile, the Pauline principle (profile) and the Johannine principle (profile) of the Church. The Marian profile of the Church is the Church as humble, receptive handmaid of the Lord. This profile, for Balthasar, is the most basic profile of the Church, although all of them are essential. The Petrine principle is composed of the structural or institutional dimension of the Church. The Pauline principle is the Church of the individual in the midst of all that is not-Church, the Church in mission. The Johannine profile is the Church as love. Importantly, these profiles exist in relationship to one another but are irreducible to one another. All the profiles "need" one another, but they are distinct from one another.[28]

Interestingly, the ecclesial person is not necessarily one who has no quarrel with the institutional church. Balthasar notes in his reflections on Catholic author George Bernanos that one who leads a truly ecclesial existence is simultaneously one who has the most with which to criticize the Church and yet is least likely to do so. Moreover, an ecclesial existence or the life of the saint is "launched" by the Church but can never be planned or projected by the Church. Balthasar expounds on the paradox of the saint, the one who opens herself in a radical way to following Christ in and through the Church, and yet often ends up being an initiator of a new way of being holy in the Church and in the world.[29] Indeed, the ecclesial person outstrips the Church in her sense of what discipleship means, and adds to the Church's understanding of holiness and *sequela Christi*.

Finally, as we have said in our discussion of Balthasar's notion of person, at the heart of true personhood lies a certain receptivity and obedience to the will of God. The ecclesial person or the saint possesses this quality or habit of indifference, in the Ignatian sense, a readiness to go where the Lord calls. And, as a microcosm of the Church, the ecclesial person ultimately lives an ek-static existence, which means that the center of their lives is elsewhere, namely, in God.

BALTHASAR'S GENDER ONTOLOGY

Balthasar takes seriously the difference between the sexes, noting that this difference is of theo-dramatic significance. He distinguishes between gender difference in the creaturely

---

[28]Cf. Hans Urs von Balthasar, *The Office of Peter and the Structure of the Church*, trans. Andrée Emery (San Francisco: Ignatius Press, 1986).
[29]Cf. Hans Urs von Balthasar, *Bernanos: An Ecclesial Existence*, trans. Erasmo Leiva-Merikakis (San Francisco: Ignatius Press, 1996).

sphere and gender difference as ascribed analogically to God,[30] but in both cases there is a notion of complementarity and completeness that lies at the heart of the male/female, masculine/feminine distinction. According to Balthasar, woman is "essentially an answer. If man is the word that calls out, woman is the answer that comes to him at last."[31] The two are related and ordered to each other. Importantly, "the word that calls out only attains fulfillment when it is understood, accepted, and given back as a word. Thus, there is a way in which man can be seen as primary and woman as secondary, where the primary remains unfulfilled without the secondary."[32] On the basis of these words, Balthasar has been roundly criticized for gender essentialism and sexism. To the mind of critics, Balthasar has reduced the significance of all women to mere response, answer to and completion of man. One might note, however, that whereas often we hear the critique that woman as secondary implies the corollary that woman without man is unfulfilled, here Balthasar asserts that the man primary/woman secondary schema means that the primary is unfulfilled without the secondary, or man is unfulfilled without woman, as they are ordered to each other. Moreover, Balthasar maintains that the primary needs a partner of *equal rank and dignity* for its own fulfilment and that man is incapable of providing this answering dimension; God the Creator and woman are required if man is to be complete as God gives the gift of woman, who is, in her being, "the vessel of fulfilment specially designed for him."[33]

It would be hard to say, however, that there is no equivocation or contradiction in Balthasar's account of "woman" as, on the one hand, woman is considered to have her own agency and fruitfulness, and, on the other hand, Balthasar states that woman's fruitfulness is always an "answering fruitfulness,"[34] which seems to reiterate the idea that woman is secondary in her fruitfulness to that of man.

Nonetheless, it would seem to be critical to properly assessing Balthasar against the charge of sexism that one recognizes the esteem with which Balthasar treats "receptivity." Receptivity is the condition for the possibility of true personhood and not a synonym for passivity. Receptivity is active and challenging; it is the way in which one attains who one is, receiving one's calling from God and continually opening oneself anew to receiving the gift of divine love to continue on one's path of self-giving love. As noted, Balthasar considers Mary to be the exemplary figure of receptivity; her *fiat* is what allows for salvation history to unfold as God envisions it. Thus, contrary to being a way to minimize the role or capacity of women, with the alliance of femininity and receptivity Balthasar seems to elevate a key aspect of womanhood that is instructive for all persons striving for holiness and integrity, male and female.

Perhaps, though, the final word on the issue belongs to Rowan Williams, who has observed that what is at stake in understanding Balthasar's gender ontology goes much deeper than political debate about gender, to the very heart of Trinitarian theology:

> What makes his analysis so tantalizing is a central unclarity about how far sexual differentiation really can be said to partake of the differentiation of the trinitarian persons, a differentiation in which there is no unilateral and fixed pattern of priority

---

[30]There is some biblical precedence for the feminine principle in God (as Logos proceeding from Father and as woman being borne within or by man, coming forth from within him as his "fullness" to complement him).
[31]TD III, 284.
[32]Ibid.
[33]Ibid.
[34]Ibid., 285.

or derivation but a simultaneous, reciprocal conditioning, a pattern of identity *in* the other without remainder. To engage with this *aporia* in Balthasar, we need more than an enlightened outrage at a rhetoric of sexual differentiation apparently in thrall to unexamined patriarchy. Balthasar is not so easily written off. What is needed, rather, is a response to his own rhetoric within the terms of the extraordinary affirmation of simultaneous and reciprocal difference that his account of the trinitarian relations and the relation of God to creation insists upon. [35]

***

With these unique contributions of *theo-drama* as an overarching frame by which to understand the relationship between finite and infinite freedom; Christ and Christological mission as further constitutive bases of personhood; prayer; a spirituality of childhood (or a spirit of childhood, aka the Holy Spirit); the role of the Church in shaping selves; and the particular drama of action and receptivity between man and woman, Balthasar's thought yields some truly fecund portals through which one might pass to deepen theological exploration and understanding of the mystery of the human person.

SUGGESTED FURTHER READING

Balthasar, Hans Urs von, *Theo-drama, Volume II – Dramatis Personae: Man in God* (trans. Graham Harrison; San Francisco: Ignatius Press, 1990).

Balthasar, Hans Urs von, *Theo-drama III, Volume III – The Dramatis Personae: Persons in Christ* (trans. Graham Harrison; San Francisco: Ignatius Press, 1992).

Balthasar, Hans Urs von, *A Theological Anthropology* (Eugene, OR: Wipf and Stock, 2010).

Balthasar, Hans Urs von, *Bernanos: An Ecclesial Existence* (San Francisco: Ignatius Press, 1996).

Balthasar, Hans Urs von, "The Concept of Person," *Communio* 13, no. 2 (Spring 1986): 18–26.

Dalzell, Thomas, *The Dramatic Encounter of Divine and Human Freedom in the Theology of Hans Urs von Balthasar*, 2nd ed. (Bern: Peter Lang, 2000).

Harrison, Victoria, *The Apologetic Value of Human Holiness* (Dordrecht: Kluwer Academic, 2000).

McIntosh, Mark, *Christology from Within: Incarnation and Spirituality* (Notre Dame, In: University of Notre Dame Press, 2000).

Oakes, Edward, *Pattern of Redemption: The Theology of Hans Urs von Balthasar* (New York: Continuum, 1994).

Papanikolaou, Aristotle, "Persons, Kenosis and Abuse: Hans Urs von Balthasar and Feminist Theologies in Conversation," *Modern Theology* 19 (January 2003): 41–65.

Williams, Rowan, "Balthasar and Rahner," in John Riches (ed.), *The Analogy of Beauty: The Theology of Hans Urs von Balthasar* (Edinburgh: T&T Clark, 1996), 11–34.

Yenson, Mark, *Existence as Prayer: The Consciousness of Christ in the Theology of Hans Urs von Balthasar* (New York: Peter Lang, 2014).

---

[35] Rowan Williams, "Balthasar and Difference," in Rowan Williams, *Wrestling with Angels: Conversations in Modern Theology*, ed. Mike Higton (Grand Rapids, MI: Eerdmans, 2007), 82–3.

CHAPTER TWENTY

Edward Schillebeeckx

EDMUND KEE-FOOK CHIA

One of few theologians to have been awarded the prestigious Erasmus Prize (1982) for his contributions to European culture, Edward Schillebeeckx is without doubt one of the most important Christian thinkers of the twentieth century. His contribution to the Catholic Church especially during and also following the Second Vatican Council turned him from being a professor of theology in a Dutch university into "an international theologian's theologian."[1] Despite having authored volumes on theological disciplines as diverse as God, Christ, Church, revelation, sacraments, Eucharist, priesthood, celibacy, Mary and spirituality, he did not write a specific treatise on theological anthropology. Instead, his whole corpus of works reveals how he thinks about God and God's relationship with humans, what it means to be fully human, the nature of human experience and the very mystery of humanity itself.

LIFE-JOURNEY OF A THEOLOGIAN
AMID HEAVY BOMBARDMENT

Though his family lived in Kortenberg, Edward Schillebeeckx was born in the city of Antwerp in 1914 as his family had temporarily relocated there when the German troops advanced into Belgium. Schillebeeckx's birth, therefore, coincided with the beginnings of the First World War: "The story of his birth while the bombs were falling evidently had a deep symbolic, almost mythical, truth for him: 'All the same, there is no disguising the fact that I was born under heavy bombardment.'"[2] Despite the chaos of his early life, he was initiated into a very Catholic and sacramental lifestyle, attending early morning Mass as well as serving as an altar boy from the age of six. Upon completing his primary education he was sent to a Jesuit boarding school. While his elder brother joined the Jesuits and became a missionary to India, Schillebeeckx opted for the Dominican Order at the age of twenty. He had this to say about his choice: "I was struck by the healthy balance, the joy, the openness to the world, the study, the research, the theology centred on preaching. I came to the conclusion that I would become a Dominican."[3]

Schillebeeckx joined the Dominicans in Gent in 1935 and later moved to Louvain for his *philosophicum* where he came under the mentorship of Flemish philosopher

---

[1]John Bowden, *Edward Schillebeeckx: Portrait of a Theologian* (London: SCM Press, 1983), 2.
[2]Erik Borgman, *Edward Schillebeeckx: A Theologian in His History* (London: Continuum, 2004), 19.
[3]Edward Schillebeeckx, *I am a Happy Theologian: Conversations with Francesco Strazzari*, trans. John Bowden (New York: Crossroad, 1994), 5–6.

Dominicus De Petter. He began military service in 1938 where he had the opportunity to meet with pastors from other Christian Churches and Jewish rabbis. He then began his *theologicum* in 1939 and was ordained a priest in 1941. He taught theology at the Dominican house of studies for two years until the end of the Second World War when he was sent to Paris to begin postgraduate studies. It was there that he studied with scholars such as the philosophers Rene Le Senne, Jean Wahl, Louis Lavelle and Etienne Gilson, as well as Old Testament scholar Eduard Dhorme and patristic scholar Charles Puech. He also made acquaintance with the esteemed ecumenist Yves Congar, as well as with the phenomenologist Maurice Merleau-Ponty and the existentialist Albert Camus. But the scholar who had the most impact on Schillebeeckx's life was his fellow Dominican friar, Marie-Dominique Chenu.

In 1947, Schillebeeckx returned to Louvain and was appointed professor of theology in the *studium generale* where he taught young Dominican friars and served as Master of Students, which meant being responsible for their spiritual development as well. He completed his dissertation in 1951 under the supervision of Chenu. Pastorally, he worked as chaplain in the local prison. In 1956, Schillebeeckx was appointed professor in Louvain's Higher Institute for Religious Studies. Two years later, he was appointed Professor of Dogmatics and the History of Theology at the University of Nijmegen in the Netherlands, a position he held until his retirement in 1982. In this new assignment, his students included mostly mature priests and later even some lay people, including women. He was no longer spiritual director to a group of young friars and, thus, had more time to involve himself with groups outside of academe and accepted invitations to speak in different parts of the Netherlands as well as to the media. When the Second Vatican Council was announced, Schillebeeckx found himself playing an even greater role, first, in its preparations, and then as the principal theologian-consultant to the Dutch bishops.

Because he was not appointed an official *peritus* to the council (Cardinal Ottaviani of the Holy Office opposed his nomination because Schillebeeckx drafted the 1960 Christmas Letter of the Dutch bishops that questioned the theology of the council's preparatory documents), he was freed to deliver numerous lectures in Rome that many of the council bishops attended: "Before the decisive vote on the 'two sources schema' at the end of November 1962, which in Schillebeeckx's opinion, determined the fate of modern theology, he had already given twenty-three such lectures, thus reaching about 1500 bishops."[4] Upon his return to the Netherlands after the council, Schillebeeckx played a major role in the renewal of the Dutch Church, first, through the publication of the *New Catechism* (developed from the perspectives of the new understandings of theology) and, second, in the convocation of the Dutch Pastoral Council. Both were renewal attempts of the Dutch episcopate that the post-conciliar Vatican curia objected to. Thus, when Schillebeeckx himself was investigated by Rome for his views on the Christian faith and ministry, many people believed that since he had been so "involved in all the progressive developments of the Dutch Church, an attack on him was also an attack on them [Dutch bishops]."[5] Schillebeeckx's conflicts with Rome were ideological disputes over his theology and especially his theological approaches. It is therefore necessary that we look at some of these influences and method.

---

[4]Ted Schoof, "E. Schillebeeckx: 25 years in Nijmegen," *Theology Digest* 37, no. 4 (Winter 1990): 323.
[5]Peter Hebblethwaite, *The New Inquisition? Schillebeeckx and Kung* (London: Fount Paperbacks, 1980), 28.

THEOLOGICAL INFLUENCES AND
METHODOLOGICAL APPROACHES

One can discern two main phases in Schillebeeckx's theological thought. The end of the Second Vatican Council, or the mid-1960s, is usually used as the dividing line. His theology of the earlier phase reflects the influence of the Louvain school and that of his mentors in Paris, while that of the later phase arose out of his experiences with the Dutch Church, the Second Vatican Council and especially his exposure to the wider world, including a lecture tour to North America in the year 1966.

The Early Schillebeeckx

Like all students of theology of the early twentieth century, when the Catholic Church was countering modernity through neo-scholastic thought, Schillebeeckx was schooled in the tradition of Thomas Aquinas. Drawing on Aristotelian philosophy, Thomism begins with the premise that created beings are in participation with nature as well as with grace. Because the created human participates in the Creator God, it is therefore possible for the human being to know God. As human knowledge is oriented towards being, and since the first being is God, human knowledge is oriented finally toward God. This knowledge can only come through creation, which means it can only come through our senses, that is, via the sensory physical realm. Sense experience, therefore, is the primary starting point of knowledge. In reflecting on Schillebeeckx's theological methodology, Robert Schreiter explains, "God communicates with us through the medium of the created world and not through some other channel. That relative optimism means that, sinful and broken though the world may be, it remains the medium for this divine-human communication."[6]

Under the mentorship of De Petter, Schillebeeckx was introduced to the phenomenological works of Edmund Husserl, Maurice Merleau-Ponty and Martin Heidegger. Phenomenology's concern is with analyzing and describing the essential structures of experience and focuses on the subject, on the experiential ground of knowledge and on the analysis of the structures of the lifeworld. This represents the philosophical roots of Schillebeeckx's emphasis on the concrete and the incarnational in most of his theology. It also led him to the works of the existentialist phenomenologist, Paul Ricoeur, whose emphasis on experience, as well as on metaphor and narrative, is clearly evidenced in Schillebeeckx's subsequent writings. Besides the phenomenologists, De Petter also introduced Schillebeeckx to the work of Karl Adam, whose theological method was not only grounded in the medieval thinkers (as was characteristic of the neo-scholastic method) but also emphasized a return to the Church Fathers, while also incorporating the fruits of modern biblical research. It was also he who encouraged Schillebeeckx to read Hegel, Kant and Freud, as well as books which had been placed on the *Index of Forbidden Books*, and so should have been almost inaccessible to students in Catholic theological institutions.

Schillebeeckx furthered his Thomistic studies in the two years he spent in Paris, but this time exploring it from the perspectives of the French *Nouvelle Theologie*. Chenu and Congar were associated with this movement and the concomitant *ressourcement* method. It meant reading Thomistic texts while paying attention to the historical setting

---

[6]Robert Schreiter, "Edward Schillebeeckx: An Orientation to His Thought," in *The Schillebeeckx Reader*, ed. Robert Schreiter (New York: Crossroad, 1984), 20.

in which they were produced, that is, returning to the medieval and also patristic sources. This historical-critical approach imprinted on Schillebeeckx that texts and teachings are culturally and historically conditioned. He would later employ this approach in his research on the *Jesus* books, except that he would return to Scripture as the original source. Aside from this, Schillebeeckx was also influenced by Chenu's personality and commitment to works of justice, such as the worker-priest movement: "Chenu's fusion of theological research with social-political engagement" interested Schillebeeckx, which resulted in his becoming "more and more preoccupied with the relationship between world and church" rather than being concerned only about internal church issues.[7]

The Later Schillebeeckx

The mid-1960s represented a turning point for Schillebeeckx in that his teaching and writings began to show a marked change in content as well as in approach. He focused on issues raised by the Second Vatican Council and employed new approaches, such as the post-Heideggerian new hermeneutics of Hans-Georg Gadamer, Paul Ricoeur, Rudolf Bultmann, Gerhard Ebeling and Ernst Fuchs. The "new hermeneutics" asserted the linguisticality of being and "stressed the historical character, or historicity of being itself."[8] Truth, in this approach, is seen as always in process and pluralistically articulated and so has to be apprehended within the flux of history, of which it itself is also a part. It is not possible for an interpreter to fully enter into another historical world since the interpreter is always approaching a text with some pre-understandings. The interpreter questions the text with these pre-understandings, while the text in turn also raises questions to the interpreter. The consequence of this process is the hermeneutical circle. Schillebeeckx's conclusion was that "the best way to keep faith alive is not a literal repetition of past texts but their reinterpretation in light of contemporary modes of thought."[9]

The emphasis of the new hermeneutics on the importance of language led Schillebeeckx to study the philosophy of language, especially the Anglo-American approaches. These included the works of Ludwig Wittgenstein, whose concept of "language game," as well as that of Ian Ramsey, whose concept of "disclosure," became useful in providing Schillebeeckx with new vocabulary for his future theological writings. Another major philosophical influence in Schillebeeckx's life was the Critical Theory of the Marxist-inspired Frankfurt school of social criticism. Critical Theory not only employed the intellectual disciplines of economics and politics but also included culture and aesthetics in its critique of society and those who dominate it, in order to focus on the liberation of the oppressed and the socially and economically subjugated. Schillebeeckx's theology subsequently became "more politically responsible, eshatologically orientated, and resolutely attentive to suffering."[10] Concepts that were to appear unsparingly in his later writings, such as "ideology," "ideological critique," "praxis," "orthopraxis," "negative contrast experience" and "negative dialectics" are all rooted in Critical Theory.

A final but no less important influence on Schillebeeckx was the field of modern biblical studies, especially the quest for the historical Jesus. Schillebeeckx delved deeply

---

[7]Philip Kennedy, *Deus Humanissimus: The Knowability of God in the Theology of Edward Schillebeeckx* (Fribourg: University Press, 1993), 53.
[8]Schreiter, "An Orientation to His Thought," 21.
[9]Philip Kennedy, *Schillebeeckx* (London: Chapman, 1993), 48.
[10]Ibid., 50–1.

into modern exegesis and is regarded as the first Roman Catholic scholar to employ biblical scholarship in a really substantive way in order to advance theological research. The fruits of this are clearly evidenced in the first two volumes of his Christological trilogy. The first book is entitled *Jesus*, the second entitled *Christ* and the third *Church*.[11] While each of these books looks at different aspects of systematic theology, they reveal the progression of Schillebeeckx's Christological research and so are usually known generically as the "Jesus books."

DOCTRINE OF GOD AND CREATION FAITH

In offering an overview of his theology and drawing on his Thomistic roots, Schillebeeckx posits that the doctrine of creation is the "foundation of all theology"[12] and that a "creation faith" is the "background and horizon of all Christian belief."[13] He clarifies that creation faith "says something about God and about humans in their temporal-spatial world, and also about their mutual concern both towards each other and towards the whole world, their relation to the whole."[14] The creation faith that Schillebeeckx speaks about is actually the basis for his own faith and undergirds the whole of his theology as well. Schillebeeckx's creation faith speaks of God as "essentially creator, the lover of the finite, loving with the absoluteness of a divine love which is unfathomable to us."[15] It is a doctrine rooted in the Pentateuch's understanding of Yahweh as "The Lord, the Lord, a God merciful and gracious, slow to anger, and abounding in steadfast love and faithfulness" (Exod. 34:6). Schillebeeckx's thesis is that God's love was so gracious and overflowing that God freely shared it in creation. Creation is therefore an act of love on God's part and, more importantly, "an act of God's trust in man."[16] However, Schillebeeckx concludes that by creating human beings God begins an adventure, as it were, and actually becomes vulnerable or defenseless by so doing.[17]

As the divine trust is an unconditional free gift, humanity's natural duty is to reciprocate by being responsible for the world, as symbolized by Adam and Eve being charged with taking care of the garden. But, just as our first parents were disobedient and acted irresponsibly, humankind is also liable to fall and indeed, even prone to failure. As a result, they are punished, but with a punishment much less serious than the gravity of their sin. God remains merciful and gracious and continues to manifest God's presence

---

[11]Edward Schillebeeckx, *Jesus: An Experiment in Christology* (New York: Collins and Crossroad, 1979), originally published in Dutch as *Jezus, het verhaal van een levende* (Bloemendaal: Nelissen, 1974); Edward Schillebeeckx, *Christ: The Christian Experience in the Modern World* (London: SCM, 1980), originally *Gerechtigheid en Liefde: Genade en Bevrijding* (Bloemendaal: Nelissen, 1977); Edward Schillebeeckx, *Church: The Human Story of God* (New York: Crossroad, 1990), originally *Mensen als Verhaal van God* (Baarn: Nelissen, 1989).

[12]Schillebeeckx, *I Am a Happy Theologian*, 47. See also Edward Schillebeeckx, *God Is New Each Moment: Edward Schillebeeckx in Conversation with Huub Oosterhuis and Piet Hoogeveen*, trans. David Smith (New York: Seabury, 1983), 102.

[13]Schillebeeckx, *Church*, 90.

[14]Edward Schillebeeckx, "Plezier en woede beleven aan Gods schepping," *Tijdschrift voor Theologie* 33 (1993): 326, as cited in Diane Marie Steele, *Creation and Cross in the Later Soteriology of Edward Schillebeeckx* (PhD diss., University of Notre Dame, 2000), 303.

[15]Schillebeeckx, *Church*, 181.

[16]Edward Schillebeeckx, *Interim Report* (London: SCM Press, 1980), 106.

[17]Philip Kennedy, "God and Creation," in *The Praxis of the Reign of God: An Introduction to the Theology of Edward Schillebeeckx*, ed. Mary Catherine Hilkert and Robert Schreiter (New York: Fordham University Press, 2002), 43.

and omnipotent love unto the world and humankind despite human frailty and failings. Such is the nature of God and, more importantly, such is the nature of humankind.

Creation faith, therefore, is really a doctrine about God and the human being and especially about God's relationship with the world and all of creation. It is more a theological anthropology than a scientific theory about the physical constitution of the universe. While the doctrine of creation and the science of cosmology may seem to be addressing the same reality, they operate within two different language games: "Belief in creation does not claim to give an explanation of the origin of the world."[18] Instead, creation faith tells us who we are and how we ought to relate, whether it is with ourselves or with God. Schillebeeckx points out that the "mythically developed story" of the Pentateuch aims at showing that "this is the way in which God intended the ordering of the world and this is how it must remain, i.e., as a world in which all individuals and peoples live together in peace, each in their own territory."[19]

HUMANITY AND THE LIMITATIONS OF FINITUDE

Hence, the doctrine of creation is founded upon the ideal that human beings must be in relationship with God, as well as in relationship with one another, with all other living beings, and the rest of nature. But what has to be hastily added is that each created being has its own place, particular nature, and role in the cosmos. Essentially, according to Schillebeeckx, the doctrine of creation teaches that "God is God, the sun is the sun, the moon is the moon and man is man."[20] Furthermore, as divine creator, God creates only that which is "not-divine" and "not-God." In other words, all of creation is "not-God" and so is by nature not perfect, not omnipotent, not infinite, not immortal and not absolute. It follows that creation is imperfect, finite, contingent, mortal and unpredictable. Moreover, created beings are certainly subject to making mistakes, being weak, and are even prone to committing sinful and evil acts. Creation is not necessarily subject only to events and phenomena that have rational explanations, nor is it necessarily subject to the laws of teleology. Such is the condition of what it means to be created, and it is precisely this that the Judeo-Christian tradition affirms as good: "It is good the man is simply man, the world is simply the world, i.e., not-God, contingent: they could just as well not have been, yet they are thought to be worth the difficulty and the price."[21]

Creation is even allowed to be as it pleases, without intervention from God. Schillebeeckx at times speaks of the "impotence of God," an impotence willed freely by God.[22] God is not necessarily in charge or in control of everything in the universe. That is not part of God's design or blueprint for the universe. The world and humanity cannot expect God to come to their rescue at all times and in all circumstances. They certainly cannot expect God to save them from finitude or from the contingency that finitude entails. That is not what salvation is about. God created the world in such a way that the world will never be able to be "not-finite." It is in the nature of the world to be finite and thus imperfect. This is simply part of the trust which God has in creation. It is a sort of "divine yielding," where God makes room for creation to exist in total freedom and the

---

[18]Schillebeeckx, *Church*, 229.
[19]Ibid., 242.
[20]Schillebeeckx, *Interim Report*, 113.
[21]Ibid.
[22]Ibid., 115.

world to be as it pleases.[23] In short, Schillebeeckx believes, God has freely willed to have no control over creation.

It would be a "mistake," therefore, if "finitude is regarded as a wound, something which need not really have been."[24] Such mistaken ideologies are wont to attribute finitude to some other cause or demonic power or to regard it as a result of some primal sin. These ideologies do not accept finitude as part of the nature of the world but as something which is improper and which ought to be overcome. This lends itself to the view that contingency, imperfection and sin are not supposed to be, and that perhaps human beings ought to have been infinite or infinitely perfect. This would have been, if not for the fact that these infinite attributes were lost or taken away as a result of some original sin, or first Fall. Schillebeeckx reminds us that the book of Job clearly testifies against such views. Other parts of the Bible also clearly teach that humans are qualitatively different from God and can never attain to God's perfection, as represented by the Genesis accounts of the first parents wanting to be like God, and the people of Babel wanting to reach God in order to do away with the divine. Schillebeeckx insists that wanting to transcend the finitude and contingency of life "is arrogance which alienates man from himself, the world and nature" and regards such desires as the "fundamental human sin" since they are attempts to challenge God's creation by disowning our human nature.[25] Unfortunately, it is a sin repeated over and over throughout the course of human history, even until today.

GOD'S GRACIOUSNESS AND THE WORTH OF LIMITATION

The recognition of the finitude of creation and of humanity has to be appreciated in concert with the affirmation of God's graciousness. They are like two sides of the same coin. Limitation and contingency are the very elements that distinguish between creatures and all created beings from the one and only creator God. If created beings were infinite then there would be no distinction between them and the creator and, indeed, no notion of divinity. To be sure, the creator manifests the divine attributes precisely within the realm of the finite and humans experience the divine also within the finite world and not outside of it. Thus, God's revelation occurs in and through the mediation of the concrete and visible in human history: "Revelation does not drop out of the sky as a series of truth; it comes to us in experience in concrete, existential encounter."[26]

Moreover, the condition of finitude means that human beings and the finite world are completely helpless and vulnerable if not for the creator:

> There is nothing that can be brought between the world and God to interpret the relationship between them. This is what people mean when in symbolic language they talk about "creation from nothing". However, the other side of this belief in creation is that the anxiety of this hanging above absolute nothingness at the same time has as a counter-balance the absolute presence of God in and with the finite.[27]

---

[23]Schillebeeckx, *Church*, 90.
[24]Schillebeeckx, *Interim Report*, 113.
[25]Ibid., 114.
[26]Schreiter, "An Orientation to His Thought," 17.
[27]Schillebeeckx, *Interim Report*, 114.

As such, belief in the infinite and creator God situates the human being within a condition of limitation and finitude, on the one hand, and affirms the reality of the infinite God, on the other. This infinite God is gracious and ever loving, unconditionally trusting in the finite world and infinitely present despite human frailty and sinfulness.

Creation faith, therefore, enables finitude to be looked upon as an intrinsic merit and essential goodness and not so much as some kind of flaw or shortcoming. Schillebeeckx speaks of it as "the worth of limitation."[28] This is not to imply that God will remove our finitude one day or would even wish to do so. Instead, our finitude will always remain but can be taken up in prayer into the presence of God who is gracious and merciful. A Christian's creation faith implies a belief in a God who is boundless in omnipotent love and who loved us while we were still sinners and who trusts us for no reason. This is expressed in Paul, "But God proves his love for us in that while we still were sinners Christ died for us" (Rom. 5:8), and in John, "In this is love, not that we loved God but that He loved us" (I Jn 4:10). Salvation from God, therefore, is not about God saving us from our creaturely existence or from the world of contingency but about God providing the strength and inspiration that will help us to lift ourselves up from the evil and suffering which so pervades the world. Hence, Schillebeeckx asserts that the doctrine of creation is at once the doctrine of salvation. God's creation is the beginning of the history of salvation just as the whole of creation is permeated with God's saving intent. Such is the creation faith which Schillebeeckx's theology speaks about, and such is the hope which this faith engenders.

THE QUEST FOR SALVATION AND THE KINGDOM OF GOD

Furthermore, it is creation faith and in particular, the experience of the challenges inherent in the contingent world that drives the human person in a search for more, in a quest for something better in order to foster a more livable and meaningful life. This protest against the unsatisfactory conditions of the world and a desire to self-improve are all rooted in the fact that we feel vulnerable and inadequate in view of our finite nature. It is what leads to the quest for salvation from God, the infinite and creator of the whole creation. And this search takes place within the finite realities of the world. Schillebeeckx insists that God's will of salvation is realized through the concrete realities of history and not outside of it, turning the age-old adage of *extra ecclesiam nulla salus* (outside the church, no salvation) into the axiom of *extra mundum nulla salus* (outside the world, no salvation).[29]

This search for a better world and the transformation of society are left in the hands of finite men and women and they can act only within history. They are free to act as they see fit except that their actions have to be within the confines of the limitation of finitude. In particular, Schillebeeckx maintains, they cannot choose to be released from their finite nature, as represented by God's command to Adam and Eve:

As God's representative, man is entrusted with the garden. He must work out, responsibly and freely by himself, in accordance with his honour and his conscience, what he must do in the garden, albeit within the limits which have been laid down by

---

[28]Kennedy, *Schillebeeckx*, 86.
[29]Schillebeeckx, *Church*, 12.

God ("not to eat of the one tree"; old myths were reworked within the context of this royal theology).[30]

In the human quest for salvation, Schillebeeckx's thesis is that humanity's task is to participate in God's plan of salvation, that is, to bring about the kingdom of God: "Throughout the Bible, the coming of the kingdom of God is the coming of God as salvation for human beings."[31] This means that human beings have to be concerned for one another and work towards the liberation and wholeness of all members of the human and cosmic community: "in the face of God's saving omnipotence which shows his solidarity with human helplessness and which seeks to help the oppressed. This is what the kingdom of God means."[32]

By whose authority have the foregoing reflections about creation and salvation been based upon? Schillebeeckx suggests that it is our human experience which is the basis for such reflections. Specifically, within the context of creation faith our human experience informs us that such is the nature of salvation. While it is not possible for us to be sure of the full extent of what human salvation means, Schillebeeckx believes that we do have "a faint idea of it, on the one hand through human experiences of goodness, meaning and love, and on the other as reflected in situations in which, whether as individuals or societies, we experience a threat to what is human in us."[33] The fact that we rejoice and look forward to the former and rebel against and reject the latter gives us an indication of what our true human nature is supposed to be. This is the inherent knowledge of good and evil that we derive from our own lived experience.

JESUS AS CONCENTRATED CREATION AND PARADIGM FOR HUMANITY

Schillebeeckx then adds that our experience of creation and salvation is also verified and given definitive form in the person of Jesus of Nazareth who through his life revealed to us "everything that is good in creation."[34] This, according to Schillebeeckx, is because Jesus is "the ultimate key to understanding human existence" since in his life one sees "the final promise of God's unconditional trust in mankind and the perfect human response to this divine trust."[35] It is in this sense that the Christian belief in the creator God is essentially bound to the belief in the person of Jesus as God's definitive salvation. Jesus amplifies clearly the "meaning of creation as the manifestation of God's nature, as the beginning of salvation, and, in biblical categories, as the inauguration of God's kingdom."[36] Schillebeeckx speaks of Jesus as "concentrated creation ... the man in whom the task of creation has been successfully accomplished."[37] The doctrine of creation, therefore, sheds light on Jesus' life just as Jesus' life clarifies the doctrine of creation.

Thus, over and above our own experience of what salvation is like, the life and teachings of Jesus of Nazareth also reveal aspects of God and about salvation that we may never

---

[30]Schillebeeckx, *Interim Report*, 108.
[31]Ibid., 106.
[32]Ibid., 107.
[33]Ibid., 130.
[34]Kennedy, *Schillebeeckx*, 94.
[35]Schillebeeckx, *Interim Report*, 109.
[36]Kennedy, *Schillebeeckx*, 94.
[37]Schillebeeckx, *Interim Report*, 111.

know by ourselves from our own lived experience alone. It is through how the human Jesus lived his life and the message that he preached, as well as through the circumstances surrounding his death and the apostolic witness of his resurrection, that we know God is "liberating love for humanity, in a way which fulfils and transcends all human, personal, social and political expectations."[38] Christians see in the person of Jesus God sharing in human history. Jesus is God being God in a human way in order to dwell among us as a human being. It is in this context that Schillebeeckx speaks of Jesus as "parable of God and paradigm of humanity."[39] In Jesus God's love story with humankind is told just as humanity's obedient and love response to God is recounted. Jesus is therefore the perfect example for what it means to be fully human.

Thus, in order to better understand what it means to be human and what salvation from God means, it is important that we first appreciate the life, teaching and witness of Jesus. To begin with, the Gospels regard the "kingdom of God" as central to the life and ministry of Jesus. Also called "God's reign," it refers to God's "unconditional and liberating sovereign love, in so far as this comes into being and reveals itself in the life of men and women who do God's will."[40] Schillebeeckx defines this kingdom as an "already and not yet," in that it is already experienced in the here and now, as well as something which awaits fulfillment. Where "men and women encounter Jesus in faith, the sick are healed, demons are driven out, sinners are led to repentance and the poor discover their worth ... the kingdom of God is experienced here and now both by Jesus and the one who encountered him."[41] On the other hand, "the kingdom of God is [also] an eschatological event, still to come (Mk. 14:25; Lk. 22:15–18): the eschatological feast lies in the future: Jesus participates in it with his disciples."[42] The whole of Jesus' message and praxis was about actualizing the kingdom of God, "with the emphasis at once on its coming and on its coming close."[43]

CHRISTIAN PRAXIS AND GOD'S SALVATION

Schillebeeckx is emphatic that all of Jesus' activities have to be understood as pointing to the offer of God's salvation and relationship with humankind: "the intercourse of Jesus of Nazareth with his fellow-men is an offer of salvation-imparted-by-God; it has to do with the coming rule of God, as proclaimed by him."[44] Moreover, he believes, the kingdom of God "does not know the human logic of precise justice. Jesus wants to give hope to those who from a social and human point of view, according to our human rules, no longer have any hope."[45] The only logic for Jesus, according to Schillebeeckx, is that the kingdom is essentially directed to the upliftment of the poor and the outcast. This logic represents the principal criterion by which God's kingdom is discerned: "Jesus' picture of God is determined by the thirsty, the stranger, the prisoner, the sick, the outcast; here he sees God (Mt. 25)." Likewise, Jesus' actions and teachings are directed toward actualizing

---

[38]Ibid., 128.
[39]Schillebeeckx, *Jesus*, 626.
[40]Schillebeeckx, *Church*, 111.
[41]Ibid., 132–3.
[42]Schillebeeckx, *Jesus*, 150.
[43]Ibid., 140.
[44]Ibid., 179.
[45]Schillebeeckx, *Church*, 117.

the picture of the world which God wills. In Jesus' actions one sees how God would act: "So in him there is a claim that God himself is present in his actions and words. To act as Jesus does is praxis of the kingdom of God, and moreover a demonstration of what the kingdom of God is: salvation for men and women."[46]

If the message and praxis of Jesus is to mean anything, his disciples, the Christian community, have to continue his ministry. Otherwise, according to Schillebeeckx, Jesus' proclamation of God's kingdom "remains in a purely speculative, empty vacuum. It is not the confession 'Jesus is Lord' (Rom. 10:9) which in itself brings redemption, but 'he who does the will of my Father' (Matt. 7:2)."[47] If God's offer of salvation in Jesus is to be truly universal, the churches have to be active in continuing Jesus' mission by following his way of life. This means that his disciples, including present-day Christians, have to "take upon themselves the aspirations of the wronged of this world and [be] in solidarity with the call for justice of poor and voiceless people."[48] As justice and peace are the entitlements of all persons, the salvation in Jesus has to be universalized through Christian praxis. Schillebeeckx is emphatic that "the transformation of the world to a higher humanity, to justice and peace, is therefore an essential part of the 'catholicity' or universality of Christian faith; and this is *par excellence* a non-discriminatory universality."[49] Thus, Christian praxis or orthopraxis is a recurring leitmotif of Schillebeeckx's theological hermeneutics.

THE PURSUIT OF THE *HUMANUM* AND NEGATIVE CONTRAST EXPERIENCES

Christian faith, Schillebeeckx never tires in insisting, has to entail Christian praxis "because although the object of faith has indeed been realized, in Christ, it has only been realized as our promise and our future, and the future cannot be interpreted theoretically, it has to be brought about. Action (orthopraxis) must therefore be an inner element of the principle of verification."[50] Put simply, Christian faith must be followed by concrete action. From the perspective of eschatological hope, the *humanum*, the kingdom of God, the salvation proclaimed and promised in Christ, can only be actualized through Christian praxis or concrete human actions. This is what is meant by orthopraxis being the means—or royal road—to orthodoxy, a theme central to Schillebeeckx's theology. Just as God's action in history is revealed through concrete experiences, the Christian's expression of faith is made manifest also through concrete actions.

In the context of orthopraxis Schillebeeckx claims that while "man can be seen as seeking the threatened *humanum*, ... a sphere of meaning is revealed in the negative experiences of contrast in our personal and social life."[51] This occurs when a situation of negativity is accompanied by a positive experience of hope, especially where one vehemently opposes that which is unjust and inhumane. This eschatological hope, in light of negative contrast experiences, is that which enables critical resistance, evoking

---

[46]Ibid., 118.
[47]Ibid., 168.
[48]Ibid., 169.
[49]Ibid., 170.
[50]Edward Schillebeeckx, *The Understanding of Faith: Interpretation and Criticism*, trans. N. D. Smith (London: Sheed and Ward, 1974), 59.
[51]Ibid., 65.

the protest: "No! It can't go on like this; we won't stand for it any longer!" Schillebeeckx explains, "A negative experience would not be a contrast experience, nor could it excite protest, if it did not somehow contain an element of positive hope in the real possibility of a better future."[52]

Thus, if revelation occurs in human experience, Schillebeeckx regards negative contrast experiences as having "a revelatory significance *par excellence*."[53] It is in the experience of catastrophic disasters, meaninglessness and innocent suffering, victimization and oppression of the lowly that human beings realize that God's plan has gone awry. The threatened *humanum* is clearly a revelation that the world is not in order. Notwithstanding the positive and powerful experiences of love and meaning abundant in the world, it is also a fact that the world remains fundamentally flawed, with disproportional amounts of unnecessary evil and suffering. Such experiences of meaninglessness and suffering are of revelatory significance to us as they reveal our helplessness and finiteness. At the same time they also point to the hope which such experiences elicit; a hope, if manifest in the praxis of liberation and reconciliation, that can bring about a change for a better world. In Schillebeeckx's words, "the Christian message of the kingdom of God with its potential for liberation remains in its distinctive character an offer to all men and women."[54] With St. Irenaeus, Schillebeeckx underscores in his *Jesus* books that salvation for all of humankind lies in the living God, the creator of all (*vita hominis, visio Dei*), as well as the point that God's glory lies in humankind's happiness, salvation and wholeness (*Gloria Dei, vivens homo*): "Glory for God and peace for men."[55]

CONCLUDING BY WAY OF THE ANTHROPOLOGICAL CONSTANTS

While the present article began by stating that Schillebeeckx never really wrote a specific thesis on theological anthropology, it is clear that his entire theological enterprise was practically an exposition of the same. His use of the doctrine of creation as starting point and foundation for theology shapes the way he discusses all aspects of God's relationship with humankind, as well as humanity's quest for meaning and salvation in God. Having said that, it has also to be mentioned that Schillebeeckx did propose what he terms as a set of anthropological constants that "point to *permanent* human impulses and orientations, values and spheres of value, but at the same time do not provide us with *directly* specific norms or ethical imperative in accordance with which true and livable humanity would have to be called into existence here and now."[56]

Hence, by way of conclusion and as a summary of Schillebeeclx's theological anthropology as outlined in this article, the seven anthropological constants are as follows: (1) that human beings are in a relationship with themselves, their own corporeality, with the wider sphere of nature, the entire ecological environment; (2) that being human involves contact and relationships with other fellow human beings in order to have someone to share with as well as to confirm one's own self-identity; (3) that

---

[52]Edward Schillebeeckx, "The Church as the Sacrament of Dialogue," in *God the Future of Man* (New York: Sheed & Ward, 1968), 136.
[53]Schillebeeckx, *Interim Report*, 28.
[54]Schillebeeckx, *Church*, 185.
[55]Schillebeeckx, *Interim Report*, 142–3.
[56]Schillebeeckx, *Christ*, 733.

human beings need to engage with social and institutional structures even as it is humans themselves who established these structures which, with time, have become independent of humans; (4) the conditioning of people and culture by time and space on account of their historical and geographical situation means that no person can be detached from them; (5) that there is a mutual relationship between theory and praxis to ensure that human culture, as a hermeneutical undertaking or an understanding of meaning, receives some degree of permanence; (6) that there is some form of religious or para-religious consciousness in human beings that enable them to apprehend the contingencies of the finite world and create meaning in the mysterious universe; and (7) That there has to be a synthesis of all the six dimensions mentioned above and that human culture cannot be reduced to any single anthropological constant but must take into account all of them, as they mutually influence one another. In the words of Schillebeeckx himself, *"Christian salvation,* in the centuries-old biblical tradition called redemption, and meant as salvation from God *for men,* is concerned with the whole system of co-ordinates in which man can really be man. This salvation—the wholeness of man—cannot just be sought in one or other of these constants."[57]

SUGGESTED FURTHER READING

Borgman, Erik, *Edward Schillebeeckx: A Theologian in His History* (London: Continuum, 2004).

Bowden, John, *Edward Schillebeeckx: Portrait of a Theologian* (London: SCM Press, 1983).

Hilkert, Mary Catherine, and Robert Schreiter (eds.), *The Praxis of the Reign of God: An Introduction to the Theology of Edward Schillebeeckx* (New York: Fordham University Press, 2002).

Schillebeeckx, Edward, *The Understanding of Faith: Interpretation and Criticism* (London: Sheed and Ward, 1974). [Republished in Edward Schillebeeckx Collected Works, vol. 5. London: Bloomsbury, 2014.]

Schillebeeckx, Edward, *Jesus: An Experiment in Christology* (New York: Collins and Crossroad, 1979). [Republished in Edward Schillebeeckx Collected Works, vol. 6.]

Schillebeeckx, Edward, *Christ: The Christian Experience in the Modern World* (London: SCM, 1980). [Republished in Edward Schillebeeckx Collected Works, vol. 7.]

Schillebeeckx, Edward, *Interim Report* (London: SCM Press, 1980). [Republished in Edward Schillebeeckx Collected Works, vol. 8.]

Schillebeeckx, Edward, *Church: The Human Story of God* (New York: Crossroad, 1990). [Republished in Edward Schillebeeckx Collected Works, vol. 10.]

Schillebeeckx, Edward, *I am a Happy Theologian: Conversations with Francesco Strazzari* (New York: Crossroad, 1994).

Schreiter, Robert (ed.), *The Schillebeeckx Reader* (New York: Crossroad, 1984).

Van Erp, Stephan, and Daniel Minch (eds.), *The T & T Clark Handbook of Edward Schillebeeckx* (London: Bloomsbury, 2019).

---

[57]Ibid., 734–42.

CHAPTER TWENTY-ONE

"Being in the Luminousness of Being": Introducing Bernard Lonergan's Anthropology

JEREMY D. WILKINS

To transcend means to go beyond. When we speak about the transcendence of God, we mean that God is beyond the whole order of the created universe, the totality of its conditions, places, times and relations. God's transcendence is not becoming; God is already the beginning and the beyond, the all-knowing and the all-sufficient. But for us, to be is to become.[1] We transcend ourselves by becoming more than we presently are.

We might wonder how it is possible to become more than one presently is. Already the wondering is the seed of becoming. Wonder is the font of questions, and questions carry us beyond ourselves: beyond experience to an idea of how things might be; beyond bright ideas to knowledge of what actually is so; beyond knowledge of what is so to knowledge of what might become of our world and ourselves by our own choosing and action. Self-transcendence is complete only when we decide and act. Then we ecstatically plunge ourselves into the world as agents of its becoming. We are not only making our world; we are also making ourselves. Who we become depends a great deal on the quality of our loves. Love and wonder are related, for "all love is self-surrender,"[2] and to give oneself over to one's questions is a form of self-surrender. But if love involves wonder, still its reach is further. For the whole tendency of love is to displace us into the beloved, and this tendency is not complete with knowing but only with total self-surrender.

An inquiry into the structural dynamics of inquiry and of love was the center of Bernard Lonergan's life project. Lonergan was a Canadian Jesuit theologian and philosopher. He spent the middle years of his career teaching dogmatic theology—Trinity, Christology and theological method—at the Gregorian University in Rome, where he had previously done

---

[1] Bernard J. F. Lonergan, "Existenz and Aggiornamento," in *Collection*, Collected Works of Bernard Lonergan, vol. 4, ed. Frederick E. Crowe and Robert M. Doran (Toronto: University of Toronto Press, 1988), 223. The Collected Works will henceforth be cited as CWL.

[2] Bernard J. F. Lonergan, *Method in Theology*, CWL, vol. 14, ed. John D. Dadosky and Robert M. Doran (Toronto: University of Toronto Press, 2017), 101.

his doctoral work on the problem of operative grace in Thomas Aquinas. Having studied and taught in an environment shaped by antiquated methods, he sought to articulate the structure of inquiry in order to clear the way to a more adequate conception of theology or, as he put it, to get "history into Catholic theology."[3] His model and inspiration was Thomas Aquinas. As Aquinas had measured up to the need of his time to assimilate the Aristotelian learning then inundating European Christendom, so Lonergan sought to put theology on a footing adequate to contemporary transformations in science and scholarship.[4] But he was also animated by a profound concern for the human good, and his experience of the Great Depression as a young man prompted him to an intensive investigation of macroeconomics. This he returned to at the end of his life, feeling that a better understanding of economics was "the way to help the poor in a notable manner."[5]

Lonergan always insisted that the most important element in his project was an invitation and a challenge to "self-appropriation": "asking people to discover in themselves what they are. ... And in that sense [*Insight*] is a way."[6] The self that is at stake in self-appropriation is one's own. The invitation is to discover in oneself the structural dynamics of inquiry and decision. The discovery brings about a radical clarification of the immanent sources of self-transcendence in each of us. It invites a fundamental decision to stand by them, come what may. Self-appropriation is a practice or, if you like, a form of asceticism. Lonergan wrote his book *Insight* as a kind of handbook to self-appropriation. His purpose in the sequel, *Method in Theology*, was to show how the structure of inquiry and decision could ground a framework for collective responsibility.

Lonergan, to be sure, was a powerful theorist, and we shall have something to say about his theories in the pages to follow. But the heart of his project is an experiment and a discipline only you can undertake. Regrettably, it is not possible here to lead you into the experiment.[7] We shall have to be content with a descriptive reconnaissance of Lonergan's thought on the mystery of being human.

WONDER AND LOVE

Wonder and love promote our self-transcendence in different but complimentary ways. By wonder we interrogate our experience. We ask how and why and what for. By answering such questions we enlarge our understanding. When we are at our best questioning selves—when our desire to understand is not overwhelmed by other desires, like the desire to win or to impress—we really want to get things right. We know that not all our

---

[3] J. Martin O'Hara, ed., *Curiosity at the Center of One's Life: Statements and Questions of R. Eric O'Connor* (Montreal: Thomas More Institute, 1984), 427.

[4] The major landmarks in this campaign are Bernard J. F. Lonergan, *Verbum: Word and Idea in Aquinas*, CWL, vol. 2, ed. Frederick E. Crowe and Robert M. Doran (Toronto: University of Toronto Press, 1997); Bernard J. F. Lonergan, *Insight: A Study of Human Understanding*, CWL, vol. 3, ed. Frederick E. Crowe and Robert M. Doran (Toronto: University of Toronto Press, 1992); Bernard J. F. Lonergan, *Method*, CWL 14; the project as a whole is studied in Jeremy D. Wilkins, *Before Truth: Lonergan, Aquinas, and the Problem of Wisdom* (Washington, DC: Catholic University of America Press, 2018).

[5] Bernard J. F. Lonergan, "Sacralization and Secularization," in *Philosophical and Theological Papers, 1965–1980*, CWL, vol. 17, ed. Robert C. Croken and Robert M. Doran (Toronto: University of Toronto Press, 2004), 280.

[6] Bernard J. F. Lonergan, "An Interview with Fr. Bernard Lonergan, S.J.," in *A Second Collection*, CWL, vol. 13, ed. John D. Dadosky and Robert M. Doran (Toronto: University of Toronto Press, 2016), 180.

[7] For such an attempt, see Philip J. McShane, *Process: Introducing Themselves to Young (Christian) Minders* (Halifax: Mount Saint Vincent Press, 1990), accessed December 27, 2017, http://www.philipmcshane.org/wp-content/themes/philip/online_publications/books/process.pdf.

ideas are right. When we think we've understood, the spirit of inquiry becomes critical. We ask for evidence. We are being reasonable in the measure that we accept what the evidence supports and do not commit ourselves beyond the evidence. We are responsible in the measure we ask and do what is truly worthwhile and not merely pleasant. The sweep of consciousness reaches its summation when we give ourselves over in love, when by giving ourselves over we commit to what is best and truest in ourselves and the world.

By wonder and love, we are open-ended, potential infinities. If like God we already understood everything perfectly, there would be no need for us to inquire. If like God we already enjoyed the perfect possession of every good, there would be no need for us to realize value. Then our love and our understanding would also be perfect rest and fulfillment. But, in relation to all that is worthy to be known and cherished, we begin as "sheer potency."[8]

CONSCIOUSNESS

The word "subject" is said in many ways. So we distinguish the grammatical, the logical, the ontological, the psychological subject, and the subject of rights and duties. Here our concern is with the psychological subject, the subject of consciousness.[9]

Every creature is finite. It is of a limited, particular kind. Every creature is also conditioned. Created things do not explain their own existence; created events do not explain their own occurrence. Because creatures are finite and conditional, they are always, ontologically, the subjects of relations to others. What they are—and that they are at all—is in some way a function of the whole order of the universe. The only reality that explains the whole order of the universe is its author, God. Thus, every created reality is immediately dependent upon God, because each thing and event results from the order of the universe God wisely designed and lovingly chose to be the mirror of divine glory.[10]

But being that is intelligently, reasonably, morally conscious is not only related to other beings. It is such relatedness, as luminous to itself, "a being in the luminousness of being."[11] It is such relatedness as felt, potentially noticed, queried, accepted and embraced. It relates us to others who can become known and embraced. If they also are subjects luminous to themselves, they likewise know and embrace, in fact or at least in potential.

This "luminosity" is a kind of self-presence. Augustine explains that there is a meaning of "know thyself" that consists simply in the mind's presence to itself.[12] This meaning of presence is not local or spatial like the presence of Augustine's face on his body. Nor is it intentional presence, like the presence of an object that is seen or understood or believed: the face, though locally present, is said to be absent from view when it is out of the line of sight, and present in view when reflected in a mirror. Intentional presence is the presence of an object to a conscious subject. By an "object" in this sense, we mean the intended content of any conscious act, that is, what is heard, smelled, seen, understood,

---

[8]Lonergan, *Insight*, 395.

[9]On the topics of this section, see Bernard J. F. Lonergan, "The Subject," in *A Second Collection*, 60–74; Lonergan, "Existenz and Aggiornamento."

[10]See Bernard J. F. Lonergan, "The Natural Desire to See God," in *Collection*, 85.

[11]Lonergan, "Existenz and Aggiornamento," 223.

[12]Augustine, *De Trinitate* 10.9.12. Quoted and discussed in Bernard J. F. Lonergan, *The Incarnate Word*, CWL, vol. 8, ed. Robert Doran and Jeremy D. Wilkins; trans. Charles C. Hefling Jr. (Toronto: University of Toronto Press, 2016), 474–7.

conceived, appreciated, chosen. But intentional presence depends upon self-presence, not as an intended object, but as the intending subject: the hearer, the seer, the knower, the doer. It is by virtue of this self-presence that we know what is meant when we hear the injunction, "know thyself."

Distinguish, then, spatial presence, intentional presence and self-presence, where self-presence is not another kind of intentional presence, not the presence of an intended content, but the presence of the intending subject, the presence of the subject to herself in and through the acts by which she intends the world.

Now, intentional presence—the presence of intended objects—can be of quite different kinds. It is one thing for Augustine to see his face in a mirror, another for him to recall the skyline of Carthage and different still for him to know St. Paul and to love him.[13] Because self-presence is in and through the acts by which we are present to the world, the quality of our self-presence varies with the quality of our intending. When one is in a deep and dreamless sleep, one is present neither to oneself nor to the world. Dreams constitute a kind of fragmentary presence to self and to world. One may be fully awake and yet wondering at nothing. But questions arise spontaneously and, when they do, they not only relate the subject to the world in a new way but also constitute a more intensive manner in which she is present to herself as incarnate wonder. And this self-presence as presence-to-world continues to intensify as one asks for evidence, assents in judgment or belief, enters into projects and covenants.

STRUCTURE IN CONSCIOUSNESS

Consciousness is a polyphony: one can drive and talk at the same time, for instance. It also runs in different patterns. A person can be preoccupied with a book and forget to eat, or preoccupied with practical affairs and forget to pray, or absorbed in worship, art or sport and so forth.[14]

Within the polyphony, however, there are discernible processes—as one conscious event leads to another—and discernible structures. The structure of knowing and deciding unfolds on four levels, which for shorthand we might name experience, understanding, judgment and decision. Experience gives rise to questions, and questions enlarge our consciousness. They transform our experience of the world without negating it. When we mean to understand, we displace ourselves, in a way, into the matter we are trying to understand, even if we don't notice that's what's happening. When we come to judge, when we raise the question about evidence, our self-transcendence is still more complete. At our questioning best, we are surrendering ourselves to what is so, regardless of what we would like to be so. Judgment is a personal act, a commitment, and the commitment is signaled by the common reluctance people have to acknowledge their errors. Decision and action take us beyond mere knowing. They unite our knowing to love and loathing, our felt responses to good and evil. Self-transcendence reaches a provisional term in the judgment of what is so independently of our preferences; but we plunge most fully beyond ourselves in the ecstatic movement of choice and action and love.

---

[13]See Augustine, *De Trinitate* 8.56.8–8.6.9.
[14]See Lonergan, *Insight*, 204–12.

Each successive level or enlargement sublates the previous. "Sublation" here means that the higher takes the lower into itself and transforms it without negating its proper reality.[15] The structure is dynamic, that is, on the move; and it is also self-assembling, in the sense that each set of operations consciously calls forth the next. The structure is also normative, meaning that the untrammeled unfolding of our questions is the proper way to know and decide. This does not mean that there is only one valid kind of inquiry, of course, or that the explanatory form of every question must always reduce to, say, physics. Reality is multiform, and there are many different kinds of inquiry. All of them, however, follow a normative pattern of question and answer.[16]

BIAS

What I have been describing as "our questioning best" can go wrong in many ways. By "bias," Lonergan means a tendency to cut our questioning short in the service of other, self-referential rather than self-transcending interests. He distinguished four basic types of bias: dramatic, individual, group and general.[17] "Dramatic" bias is basically psychological. We all have our blind spots and sometimes they are very serious (for instance, repressed memories). "Individual" and "group" biases have to do with questions we don't ask because we would prefer not to know the answer: we might have to change our lives if we did. We limit our questions to what seems advantageous individually or for "our side," people like us.

The "general" bias is endemic to common sense. Common sense is the specialization of intelligence in the concrete problems of day-to-day living. Such problems obviously differ from one place and time to another. But every mode of common sense is circumscribed in that each of us stands at the center of our own field of practical concerns. The result is a "general" bias toward the practical, the immediate, the here and now. Common sense is a development of intelligence, but it is no preparation for questions that head away from obvious practical significance. Common sense commonly lacks the capacity to scrutinize the limitations of its own assumptions and suffers from a spontaneous short-sightedness.

For example, in our culture it is quite common to justify a college degree by pointing out its increased earnings potential. Education is conceived of as a form of job training, and its value is measurable in dollars. This is not a very serious way to think about the problem or purposes or value of an education, but it part of our culture's dominant common sense. Again, consider the manner in which public investments in scientific research are justified, or educational outcomes measured, or grants awarded, or how problems like climate change are debated in the public square mainly with reference to economic considerations. The general bias short-circuits the kind of scrutiny and penetration that might call our assumptions and values into question. It is quite different from the naked egoism of individual bias and the prejudice of group bias but, for that very reason, all the more insidious. It mires a civilization in undetected oversights. "A civilization in decline digs its own grave with relentless consistency."[18]

---

[15] On the topics of this section, see Lonergan, *Method* CWL 14; Bernard J. F. Lonergan, "Self-Transcendence: Intellectual, Moral, Religious," in *Philosophical and Theological Papers, 1965–1980*, 313–31.

[16] On this topic, see Lonergan, *Insight*, 196–204.

[17] On bias, see ibid., 214–20, 244–63.

[18] Lonergan, *Method* CWL 14, 53.

MEANING

Intellectual development is intimately connected to language. My dogs live in the world of their sensorium, the world of immediacy. They don't know anything about the Incas or special relativity or the possibility of life on other planets. Neither do infants (etymologically, nontalkers). But we get talked into talking, and it transforms our apprehension of the world completely. We move into a world that is mediated by meanings, and the meanings are largely carried by language.[19]

The world mediated by meanings is also constituted by meanings. We have law courts and universities and nations and passports. My dog regards my passport as another potentially chewable object. But to me, it is proof of citizenship, of belonging to a nation-state, and it makes international travel possible. The passport, the nation and national boundaries are realities largely constituted by meaning. Citizenship is defined by laws, and laws are enactments of meaning. Again, I do not bring my dogs to the office, but, if I did, they would not know they were at a university. A university is not defined by how it looks or smells or sounds; it is a reality in the world constituted by meaning, our world. A religious tradition and the acts of religion, such as sacraments, preaching and worship, are also constituted by meaning.

There is a tension between the world given to immediacy and the world mediated and constituted by meaning. The world of immediacy is known through the senses. But the world mediated and constituted by meaning is accessed by inquiry. It is known through judgments. This tension calls for an "intellectual conversion" by which we turn from the images of things to their reality. The reality of a university or a law court, a passport or a lecture, is not reducible to physical phenomena. One does not know what a passport is by putting it in one's mouth or even by analyzing its molecular structure. One knows it by correctly understanding its function in a world constituted by meanings, and correct understanding is achieved by asking and answering the relevant questions.

Meaning has a history, and living in the world of meaning invites us to acknowledge our historicity. We are not enclosed in our language because beyond language stands the dynamic structure of intelligence and reflection. People invent new words to express new understandings, and we gradually figure out what they mean to say. Because meaning is historical, there is also a history to our grip on meaning. We would distinguish astrology from astronomy, sorcery from science, fiction from fact. Language itself is an instrument for sifting meanings. Logic and metaphysics are more developed instruments and so is a scientific method. Because the practice self-appropriation leads to a familiarity with the sources of meaning and brings to light the basic structures of inquiry, it opens up the possibility of a still-more-precise grip on meaning for its practitioners.[20]

VALUE

Life in the world mediated and constituted by meaning raises questions of value.[21] We ask not only how we can live but also how we should live. Stories of other people and how they live open up possibilities for us. The Greek hero Achilles was presented a choice: to live a quiet life and die in his sleep, or to live and die as a great hero. Most of us are

---

[19]On meaning, see Bernard J. F. Lonergan, 'Dimensions of Meaning', in *Collection*, 232–45.
[20]Lonergan, *Method* CWL 14, 82–95.
[21]On value, see ibid., 28–41.

presented humbler options, but in each of us there is a spark of the divine. We can settle into comfortable routine, but we are apt to feel drawn to some kind of greatness.

Beyond intellectual self-transcendence, then, there is a further realm of moral self-transcendence. It unites our feelings with our questions. Of course, feelings are involved all along the line because, when we are trying to understand, to get things right, we feel that it is important to do so. If all love is self-surrender, we might even say that wonder is a love of understanding and reasonableness a love of the truth. But our feelings come into play with special power when we find ourselves admiring someone, indignant over some injustice, or ready to give our all for a friend in need. Such feelings apprehend values. They urge us on to do and become more than we presently are.

We said questions for understanding expand our consciousness beyond mere experience. Questions for judgment enlarge our concern to what is actually so and not merely what makes sense to us. But knowing is not the same as doing and becoming. When we ask what we should do or who we should become, our consciousness mounts to the level of decision.

The essence of liberty is not choosing between good and evil. It is choosing between goods that are objectively possible, finite and subject to critique and voluntary at least in the sense that we are not compelled to realize them. Consequently, the exercise of freedom is not complete until we choose and carry out a course of action. Our essential liberty, however, is not the same as our effective liberty. Effectively we are constrained by our situations, our capacity to imagine and conceive possibilities and, most of all, by our readiness to strike out in new directions.[22]

Questions of value have their own criterion. Just as the intelligible is different from the imaginable, so the worthwhile is different from the merely pleasant. We can and do make many decisions by a calculus of pleasures and pains. But we can ask about the right thing to do, and we may discover that the right thing is neither easy nor pleasant. We know we should do it anyway, and our failures provoke the reproach of conscience.

Just as the tension in our knowing calls for an intellectual conversion, so the tension in our deciding calls for a moral conversion. Moral conversion is a shift in the criterion of our decision-making from pleasures and pains to true values. The world mediated by meaning is also a world motivated and regulated by value.[23]

VECTORS OF DEVELOPMENT

We've been describing these enlargements or levels of consciousness as if they move in one direction from experience to understanding to judgment to decision. But the notion of a moral conversion suggests that it's not so simple. Getting things right is a value. It is different from the satisfaction of winning arguments, bets or applause. When we decide to make value the criterion for our deciding, sooner or later we are going to ask about the value of our knowing. Then we become capable of an explicit commitment to honesty, to facing questions squarely, to intellectual self-transcendence as a component of moral self-transcendence.

What makes sustained self-transcendence possible is love. Feelings are intentional responses to values, and love is supreme among the feelings. By linking us to others,

---

[22]Lonergan, *Insight*, 631–56.
[23]On moral conversion, see Lonergan, *Method* CWL 14, 225–8.

it makes them in some way operators of our development. The birth of a child usually evokes overwhelming feelings of love. But children have enormous needs, and, as they grow, their needs change. To be a good parent, one has to grow with them, to develop skills to meet their changing needs, but also to develop self-control and all the qualities one would pass on to one's best loved. Love blossoms only by entry into the interpersonal situation in which its lifelong implications can unfold.

Love is properly self-transcending when it is oriented to objective lovableness rather than to self-regarding desires and fears. Love takes three great forms—and many small ones. The three great forms are the love toward one's fellows that binds a community together, the love that founds a family and the supreme love that is friendship with God and all things in and for God. It is this last friendship that animates a religious tradition, and it alone is unqualified and unreserved because only God is objectively lovable without any restriction.

Self-transcendence, then, is operated from below when wonder promotes us from mere experiencing to understanding, from understanding to judgment, from judgment to decision. But it is operated from above when love opens the eyes of our hearts to new values, motivates our decisions and leads us to accept on trust what others have discovered beyond our ken. Then what we have first loved and believed shapes our understanding and experience of the world.[24]

THE HUMAN GOOD

The world mediated by meaning involves us in a vast collaboration. Fundamental to that collaboration is belief.[25] To believe is to take the word of another and thereby make another's knowledge our own, not because we have worked it out for ourselves, but because we trust the competence and honesty of others. Imagine, for instance, a political map of South America. We recognize the shapes of Brazil and Argentina, Chile and Colombia. But we may never have been to South America. Certainly we never visited all the boundaries marked on the map, let alone with surveyors' equipment. We have never inspected the official documents that define these boundaries and checked them against our surveys. Nor do we have the least intention of doing these things; they should not only be a waste of our time but also quite impossible. Our map is a compilation of countless surveys by countless teams, and the surveys are correlated with legal documents to mark the political boundaries labeled on our map. We consider ourselves to know where Brazil is and how it is shaped, but this knowledge is mostly belief. What is true of geography is true of most every domain of science and scholarship and everyday life. To refuse to believe would be absurd.

Belief makes knowledge a public possession. That possession has a history. So too does the wider collaboration it makes possible. Consider how much your breakfast each morning involves you with other people, even if you eat it alone. There are the farmers who sow, water and harvest. But chances are the seed they sow comes from others. It has to be delivered by trains and trucks moving on tracks and roads. The tracks and roads, the trains and trucks are built by some and driven by others. There is petroleum in the trucks, and there is petroleum in the roads. Before it is in the truck, it was at the gas

---

[24]Ibid., 116–19.
[25]On belief, see ibid., 42–7, 111–16; Lonergan, *Insight*, 725–40.

station; before it was at the station, it was at a refinery; before it was at a refinery, it was in a pipeline or on a ship carrying it from Arabia to Houston.

The seed, once planted, has still to be watered, and the watering is not left to chance. There are reservoirs, canal ways, dikes; there are the great irrigation machines you see in the fields; there are water towers, pipes, valves, spigots. Some design, others make, others install and others use to water crops and process them, and to bathe, to drink, to clean, to cook. Our interdependence today is virtually endless; even a meal as homely as breakfast involves us in a vast and multilayered network of relationships.

The human good, in short, is an historical and collaborative good. If your breakfast is for you a particular good, so too is every element in the collaboration that brings it to you. But it is not the elements in isolation that deliver breakfast. It is the elements arranged in an order, and that order is itself a good: the good of order. But there are different possible orders. The water supply may be public or private; crop selection may be left to market forces, or influenced by public subsidies, or directed by a state ministry; petroleum may be extracted or refined by private or by publicly controlled enterprise; and so forth. Such possible arrangements may be compared, criticized and preferred in light of different cultural values.[26]

This human good makes progress through the attention, intelligence and reasonableness, the responsibility and love of its members. In effect, these are the first precepts of the natural law according to Lonergan: be attentive, be intelligent, be reasonable, be responsible and be in love. But the good is always concrete, so we may add another precept: acknowledge your historicity.[27] Lonergan calls these precepts "transcendental" because they are applicable always and everywhere.

Our choosing and doing is authentic when it is in accord with the transcendental precepts. It is unauthentic when it is not. But, because the human good is historical, we can distinguish the authenticity of an individual from the authenticity of her tradition. A tradition can be corrupted, and then it is propagating not true values but false ones. Then the best its adherents can do is authentically realize the compound of authentic and unauthentic values presented by their tradition.[28]

We tend to think about our decisions in terms of the objects we are deciding about. But, as the foregoing suggests, every one of our decisions is also about ourselves. We are deciding who we shall become, and the most important decisions regard, not this or that particular good ("horizontal liberty"), but the horizon of meanings and values within which all our living and doing will occur ("vertical liberty").[29]

We have to keep deciding because we have our freedom over time. If we were pure spirits like the angels, we could dispose of our entire freedom in a single movement. But we are incarnate spirits, and our freedom is disposed only in the series of decisions that constitute a life. We are presented, then, with fundamental alternatives. We can choose to become more than we presently are, through intellectual, moral and religious

[26]On the structure of the human good, see Lonergan, *Method* CWL 14, 47–51.
[27]Natural Law was not a major category in Lonergan's thought. I mention it to make a connection for the reader. Lonergan made the connection himself in two remarks in answer to questions at the 1974 and 1976 Lonergan workshops: the transcripts are 815A0DTE070 (1974), 10, and 88800DTE070 (1976), 7–8. See also Bernard J. F. Lonergan, "Questionnaire on Philosophy: Response," in *Philosophical and Theological Papers, 1965–1980*, 378.
[28]Lonergan, *Method* CWL 14, 77–8.
[29]Ibid., 41.

self-transcendence. Or we can collapse inwardly through the contraction of consciousness that restricts our concern for truth and value to the scope of our own pleasures and pains.

SIN AND DECLINE

This inward collapse or contraction of consciousness is the basic meaning of sin.[30] It is radically unintelligible because it is precisely the opposite of paying attention, being intelligent, being reasonable, acting responsibly, self-surrender in love. It is a kind of brute fact, a blunt failure of created freedom. Because it is radically unintelligible, basic sin cannot be explained in itself, although there may be extenuating circumstances, rationalizations, justifications and even a kind of statistical regularity that St. Paul calls the "reign of sin." Because sin is not explained by anything, it is not explained even by God, though God knows it as a fact and judges it as absurd. It is the objective falsity, the hatred of the light, decried by St. John.

The result of sin is an increasingly incoherent objective situation and a moral corruption of human agents. The more absurd the objective situation, the more likely illicit compromises become, and the easier they are to rationalize. "In the kingdom of crooks, one has to be a crook to survive."[31] Sin, then, is the root of decline, that is, the breakdown of the good of order.

The social surd confronts us with impotence on a grand scale. It seems impossible to sort through all the dimensions of corruption in the regime, the economy, the culture, the international order—let alone to do anything effective about them. But impotence on the grand scale has its counterpart in every human heart. Moral self-transcendence requires sound judgment so that we may know what to do, and good will, that we may be ready to do it. But how is the person of reckless judgment to acquire good judgment? How is the person of bad will to develop readiness to do all good?

The possibility of moral self-transcendence is our capacity to ask questions and to fall in love.[32] By questions we come to distinguish the truly worthwhile from the merely pleasant or painful. As long as our motivations are self-regarding, we are not transcending ourselves morally; we are just drifting along. But it is always possible to ask what is truly worthwhile, and that is the beginning of moral self-transcendence. That small seed, however, bears its fruit only when matched by a readiness to do and bear all things. That readiness is love, and the supreme love is "the love of God poured into our hearts through the Holy Spirit given to us" (Rm. 5:5).

REDEMPTION

The problem of decline cannot be met by even-handed justice. Even-handed justice expects an eye for an eye. But that is a prescription for universal blindness. When sin is universal and its consequences irrevocable, there is no going back. There is only going forward. Concretely, going forward means either retribution or forgiveness. But retribution—even when it is justified—is a vicious circle, a counsel of despair. It does nothing to break out of the cycle of decline.

---

[30]Lonergan, *Insight*, 689–91.
[31]Bernard J. F. Lonergan, "Self-Transcendence: Intellectual, Moral, Religious," in *Philosophical and Theological Papers, 1965–1980*, 323.
[32]Ibid., 323–4.

The essence of redemption is bringing good out of evil, and its principle is the self-giving love that flows from the gift of the Spirit. For Lonergan, this love is the inner core of all true religion. It is a "religious" conversion that turns us from the ultimacy of human projects toward the still deeper purposes of God. In itself, religious love is the secret but basic fulfillment of our capacity and drive for self-transcendence. It is self-surrender without condition, qualification or reservation. It brings joy despite humiliation, failure, oppression or suffering; it brings a peace the world cannot give. It bears fruit in a commitment to the welfare of our fellows despite the real absurdity of sin. Its proof is in the deed, for the good tree bears good fruit. Its negation is revealed in devotion to the pursuit of fun or power, wealth or fame.[33]

Although the Spirit's gift of love is most intimate, it is not solitary. It cries out for expression and solidarity in a community. It opens the eyes of our heart in faith that we might hear and believe the seed of the word. So what is given in secret is matched to an outer word of fellowship, witness, service and worship. But the outer is not merely the symbolization of the inner. It is a reflection on the history of the community, its truth-claims, aims and values, its relationship to other meanings and values. A religious tradition exists in the world mediated by meaning and motivated by value. It has a history that includes both progress in the realization of its ideals, and decline, and recovery.[34]

In the Gospel, otherworldly love is objectified as the new commandment: "love one another as I have loved you" (Jn. 13:34). Universal niceness is innocuous enough, but the law of the cross is harder than that. "Deny yourself, take up your cross, and follow me" (Mt. 16:24) reveals a danger to be reckoned with. "Offer it up" has been used to endorse and justify all manner of self-loathing and supinity in the face of outrageous injury. Indeed, it has too often meant not only the acceptance of the cross for oneself but also the imposition of the cross upon others.

Redemptive love, then, involves a problem of very careful discernment. Christ's suffering was not generated by his illusions but by ours. It was transcended, rather, or transformed in his free and loving decision to be a principle of compassion and forgiveness. "Christ so made the cross his own that we usually speak of it as his and forget it is ours."[35] To take up one's cross after him means to commit oneself to overcoming evil with love. It is to decide that the escalating cycle of violence and revenge ends with me, because I refuse to pass it along. It is to discern with enlightenment how the harvest of justice may be sown in peace (Jas. 3:18) not as our work but as God's in us. The justice possible among sinners is cruciform.

CONCLUSION

In one of the most stirring passages of ancient literature, Aristotle exhorts readers of his *Nicomachean Ethics* to embrace in themselves the spark of the divine. That spark is the light of reason, slight in bulk but magnificent in value. It is, for Aristotle, the defining feature of our humanity. To be human in the fullest sense means to possess and be possessed by wonder.[36]

---

[33]Lonergan, *Method* CWL 14, 96–106.
[34]Ibid., 106–11.
[35]Bernard J. F. Lonergan, *The Redemption*, CWL, vol. 9, ed. Robert M. Doran, H. Daniel Monsour and Jeremy D. Wilkins; trans. Michael G. Shields (Toronto: University of Toronto Press, 2018), 488/9 (trans. alt.).
[36]See Lonergan, *Method* CWL 14, 99.

A long tradition in Christian theology links Aristotle's spark of the divine with the biblical testimony that we are created after the image of God. For Thomas Aquinas, the most influential of all Aristotle's Christian adapters, the image of God is as much promise as fact. It names a dynamic orientation: we are not merely *in* but made *to* the image of God; the image is something we are becoming, and we stretch out to it by knowing and loving God ever more.

For Christians, however, our becoming like God has a personal center and a conversational structure the likes of which never occurred to Aristotle. We become like God above all through personal friendships with a tripersonal God and, for God's sake, with all who belong to God. The spark of the divine in us is only the beginning, and, in a way, not the most important beginning. It is the beginning because by it we are open to God's self-communication in love. But the spark is transformed by God's free gift, "the love of God poured into our hearts through the Holy Spirit given to us" (Rm. 5:5). This is a love that carries us quite beyond the confines of our mere humanity. Our highest wisdom is not something learnt from study but a docility to the gentle promptings of the Spirit.

For Bernard Lonergan, mere humanity is impossible for us.[37] Mere humanity could be realized only in a vacuum apart from sin and grace. Our world, plainly enough, is not such a vacuum. It is a world in which sin is a brutal fact, a renunciation of our humanity, a snuffing of our spark. To accept the law of sin as the effective rule of our lives is to make ourselves unfit for the company of other persons and, above all, those persons to whom we shall one day have to render an account of all our work. But where sin abounds, grace abounds all the more (Rm. 5:20). Ours is a world replete with God's love, a world in which God invites us to be ready partners in the work of healing and creating in history.[38]

These, then, are the concrete alternatives: to let our spark be inflamed by a higher love of God, or to gradually starve it of air. The alternatives are being worked out in all our choices. To choose life is to become not only more than one presently is but also more than one ever could be on one's own. "Rise, let us be on our way" (Jn. 14:31).

SUGGESTED FURTHER READING

Crowe, Frederick E., *Lonergan*, Outstanding Christian Thinkers (Collegeville, MN: Michael Glazier, 1992).

Gregson, Vernon (ed.), *The Desires of the Human Heart: An Introduction to the Theology of Bernard Lonergan* (New York: Paulist Press, 1988).

Lambert, Pierrot, and Philip McShane, *Bernard Lonergan: His Life and Leading Ideas* (Halifax: Axial Press, 2010).

McCarthy, Michael H., *Authenticity as Self-Transcendence: The Enduring Insights of Bernard Lonergan* (Notre Dame, IN: University of Notre Dame Press, 2015).

Miller, Mark T., *The Quest for God and the Good Life: Lonergan's Theological Anthropology* (Washington, DC: Catholic University of America Press, 2013).

Wilkins, Jeremy D., *Before Truth: Lonergan, Aquinas, and the Problem of Wisdom* (Washington, DC: Catholic University of America Press, 2018).

---

[37]Lonergan, *Insight*, 749–50.

[38]Bernard J. F. Lonergan, "Healing and Creating in History," in *A Third Collection*, CWL, vol. 16, ed. John D. Dadosky and Robert M. Doran (Toronto: University of Toronto Press, 2017), 94–103.

CHAPTER TWENTY-TWO

The Philosopher-Pope: The Theological Anthropology of John Paul II

JENNIFER BADER

INTRODUCTION

One cannot comprehensively treat theological anthropology in the Catholic tradition without exploring the thought of the man who was born Karol Wojtyła and who became Pope Saint John Paul II.[1] Many of the questions that were key for him remain so for us today. How and where do we ground an absolute claim to human dignity? How do we understand human nature? What does it mean to be a person? What is the relationship between the human person and the human body? What is our understanding of human sexuality, gender and/or sexual difference, and how does that relate to human nature, personhood and dignity?

This chapter will first set the stage for understanding John Paul II's thought by offering a brief summary of his life, historical context and influence on Catholic theological anthropology and ethics. Second, I will explore the definition of human nature that underlies John Paul II's philosophical and theological anthropology. In this section, I demonstrate that his chosen definition of human nature is motivated by his desire to defend human dignity from the philosophical materialisms of his time. In the third section, I explore key aspects of John Paul II's understanding of the human body-person, utilizing both his pre-papal philosophical writings and his papal theological reflections and articulating certain connections between them. Finally, I will conclude by offering a critique of John Paul II's methodology in light of both his own original project and contemporary questions of human sexuality. Does his methodology successfully accomplish his project to defend human dignity in light of both of these?

---

[1] In this chapter, when discussing his pre-papal philosophy I will refer to the author as Karol Wojtyła. When referring to his papal works or when referring to themes throughout his scholarly work that include both pre-papal and papal works, I will refer to him as John Paul II.

KAROL WOJTYŁA: LIFE, HISTORICAL
CONTEXT AND INFLUENCE

Karol Wojtyła was born in Poland in 1920.[2] He knew pain and sorrow early in life, as his mother died when he was 9 years old. Three years later, he lost his older brother, and when he was 21 years old his father died. Wojtyła began studies at the Jagellonian University in Cracow in 1938, and while he was a student there the Germans occupied Poland and closed the university. While working in a stone quarry, Karol Wojtyła sought to enter the Carmelite order in 1942 but was turned away because the order was not accepting new novices at that time. In the fall of that same year, he began his seminary studies at the clandestine seminary in Cracow and also became part of an underground theatre group and wrote plays, some of which are still extant today.[3] After the Second World War came to an end, Wojtyła continued his studies at the seminary (now officially reopened) and was ordained a priest in 1946. Shortly after his ordination, Wojtyła inquired about entering the Carmelite order again, but this time his bishop, Cardinal Archbishop Adam Stefan Sapieha, was reluctant to let him go.[4]

Instead, Cardinal Sapieha sent Fr. Wojtyła to Rome to pursue a doctorate in theology at the Angelicum, for which he wrote his dissertation on the theology of faith in the works of the Carmelite St. John of the Cross. He completed his doctoral work at the Angelicum in 1948 at the age of 28. A true scholar, Wojtyła received the highest number of points possible at his doctoral defense; however, he was unable to pay to have his dissertation published and so left Rome without the degree. He returned home to Cracow and presented the dissertation to the faculty there, receiving his doctorate in sacred theology from the Jagiellonian University the same year.[5]

In 1949, Fr. Wojtyła was appointed an assistant pastor in a parish in Cracow and also engaged in ministry with the students at the university. In 1954, he defended his habilitation thesis in philosophy, which focused on the feasibility of using Max Scheler's phenomenology as the basis of Christian ethics. He answered this question in the negative, because of the inability of phenomenology to ground ethics in a transcendent, objective order. After he began teaching philosophy at the Catholic University in Lublin the same year, Wojtyła wrote a book called *Love and Responsibility*, originally published in Polish in 1960,[6] in which he brings together his pastoral experiences with Catholic young adults and his moral philosophy, grounding Christian ethics in objective moral principles. In the introduction to the book, Wojtyła is explicit about the sources of his reflection; *Love and Responsibility* "is not an exposition of doctrine. It is, rather, the result above all of an incessant confrontation of doctrine with life (which is just what the work of a spiritual advisor consists of)."[7] Wojtyła goes on to locate the source of Church teaching on sexual

---

[2]Dates for key events in Karol Wojtyła/John Paul II's life in this chapter are taken from the Vatican's biographical page on the saint (http://www.vatican.va/special/canonizzazione-27042014/documents/biografia_gpii_canonizzazione_en.html) and from the USCCB's page, "Important Dates in the Life of Pope John Paul II" (http://www.usccb.org/about/leadership/holy-see/pope-john-paul-ii-timeline.cfm), both accessed June 20, 2018.

[3]These are collected in Karol Wojtyła, *The Collected Plays and Writings on Theater*, trans. Boleslaw Toberski (Oakland: University of California Press, 1987).

[4]Michael Novak, in his introduction to Jaroslaw Kupczak, OP, *Destined for Liberty: The Human Person in the Philosophy of Karol Wojtyła/John Paul II* (Washington, DC: Catholic University of America Press, 2000), xvii.

[5]See ibid., xvii.

[6]Karol Wojtyła, *Miłość i Odpowiedzialność* (Cracow: TN KUL, 1960). For this chapter I will be using the English translation, *Love and Responsibility*, trans. H. T. Willetts (San Francisco: Ignatius Press, 1993).

[7]Wojtyła, *Love and Responsibility*, 15.

matters in the New Testament; this is important, because his later papal audiences which form his theology of the body will also be based on his interpretation of the biblical text.[8]

Note also that for Karol Wojtyła the relationship between doctrine and life in moral matters is a "confrontation." In fact, he notes that the rules of Catholic sexual ethics are often in need of justification and explanation in the face of the difficulties that arise in the practice of them.[9] Therefore, *Love and Responsibility* "was born principally of the need to put the norms of Catholic sexual morality on a firm basis, a basis as definitive as possible, relying on the most elementary and incontrovertible moral truths and the most fundamental values or goods."[10] This desire to give Catholic teachings in sexual ethics a firm basis motivates Karol Wojtyła's pre-papal philosophical works as well as his papal teachings on the body and sexual difference.

Wojtyła was ordained a bishop in 1958 and became an influential figure at the Second Vatican Council, where he was one of the key authors of *Gaudium et Spes*,[11] which to this day continues to define the Church's understanding of itself and its relationship to the world. In 1969, he published his seminal philosophical work, *The Acting Person*,[12] which puts forth his understanding of the human person.

Pope John Paul II reigned as pope from 1978 to his death in 2005. He was a key inspirational figure in the Solidarity movement in Poland and, thus, the eventual collapse of communism in Europe.[13] During his papacy, he issued "fourteen encyclicals, fifteen apostolic exhortations, forty-two apostolic letters, 11 apostolic constitutions, and 28 motu proprio. He proclaimed 482 new saints."[14] Given the length of his papacy, after his death the College of Cardinals was composed of a majority of his appointees; indeed, in the 2005 papal conclave only two out of 115 electors were *not* appointed by John Paul II.[15] Pope John Paul II was canonized, together with Pope John XXIII, on April 27 (Divine Mercy Sunday), 2014, by Pope Francis.

Perhaps most influential on Catholic theological anthropology and ethics have been his Wednesday audiences, given September 5, 1979, through November 28, 1984,[16] which

---

[8]For analyses of how John Paul II uses and interprets the Bible in his Wednesday audiences, see Michael Waldstein's introduction to John Paul II, *Man and Woman He Created Them: A Theology of the Body*, 2nd ed. (trans. Michael Waldstein; Boston: Pauline Books & Media, 2006), 18–23, and Thomas D. Stegman, SJ, " 'Actualization': How John Paul II Utilizes Scripture in *The Theology of the Body*: A Response to William S. Kurz, S.J.," in *Pope John Paul II on the Body: Human, Eucharistic, Ecclesial*, ed. John M. McDermott and John Gavin, Festschrift Avery Cardinal Dulles, SJ (Philadelphia: Saint Joseph's University Press, 2007), 47–64.

[9]See Wojtyła, *Love and Responsibility*, 16.

[10]Ibid.

[11]Paul VI, *Gaudium et spes* (English title: Pastoral Constitution on the Church in the Modern World; December 7, 1965. Available online: http://www.vatican.va/archive/hist_councils/ii_vatican_council/documents/vat-ii_const_19651207_gaudium-et-spes_en.html).

[12]Karol Wojtyła, *Osoba i Czyn*, ed. Anna-Teresa Tymieniecka; Analecta Husserliana: The Yearbook of Phenomenological Research, no. 10 (Cracow, Poland: Polski Towarzystwo Teologiczne, 1969). This chapter will use the English translation, *The Acting Person*, trans. Andrzej Potocki (Dordrecht: D. Reidel, 1979).

[13]According to a 2005 *Washington Post* article on the subject, Mikhail Gorbachev noted that the collapse of communism in Europe "would not have been possible without the presence of this pope" (see Michael Dobbs, "The Inspiration for a Workers' Revolution," *Washington Post Sunday*, April 3, 2005; A37. Available online: http://www.washingtonpost.com/wp-dyn/articles/A22109-2005Apr2.html?noredirect=on).

[14]Miguel Acosta and Adrian J. Reimers, *Karol Wojtyła's Personalist Philosophy: Understanding Person and Act* (Washington, DC: Catholic University of American Press, 2016), 3.

[15]"Cardinal Electors for the 2005 Papal Conclave," Wikipedia, last modified May 12, 2019, https://en.wikipedia.org/wiki/Cardinal_electors_for_the_2005_papal_conclave. According to this Wikipedia article, there were 117 possible electors, with only three appointed by Paul VI and not by John Paul II. However, only 115 attended the conclave. Of the two who were absent, one was appointed by John Paul II and one by Paul VI.

[16]These dates are according to the edition of the audiences published in English as John Paul II, *Man and Woman*.

comprise the foundational text of what has become known in the United States as his 'theology of the body." John Paul II's vision of the human person and human sexuality, and in particular sexual difference, has since been popularized in parish religious education programs, college and high school theology courses, and conferences for theologians, priests and lay people.[17]

HUMAN NATURE: WHAT ARE WE?

In the aftermath of the Second World War, Karol Wojtyła felt that he was engaged in a cosmic battle for the soul of humankind. This defensive position was nurtured in an environment immediately during and following the Second World War, wherein the whole world did battle with Nazism, and then again when the ideology of communism became pervasive in Poland. Wojtyła's colleague at the Catholic University in Lublin, Stefan Swiezawski, offers insight into the post-war intellectual culture in Poland:

> The experiences of the war, in their overwhelming realism, were too horrible to allow us still seriously to maintain a subjective or idealistic philosophy. Reality asserted itself so unequivocally that to question its objective character was absurd ... Our experiences of the war and occupation and their tragic aftermath became a critical gauge for assessing the philosophical and ideological views we entertained before the war.[18]

It is easy to see how in such a context questioning the objectivity of the ontological and moral order was unimaginable. One simply had to start from the proposition that the horrors of war and occupation experienced by the people of that time and place were absolutely, unequivocally morally wrong—and that the dignity of the human person, and indeed, the human person him- or herself, needed, desperately, to be defended against them. For a philosopher like Wojtyła, the key questions became: What are the social, political and economic philosophies behind such atrocities as Nazism and communism? And what must the Church's own philosophy say about what it means to be human in order to successfully defend the human person against these philosophies? In his own words:

> Ours is an age of violent controversy concerning man, the essential meaning of his existence, and, consequently, the nature and value of this being. It is not the first time that Christian philosophy has been confronted by materialist doctrine. But it is the first time that materialism has mustered such a wide variety of resources and expressed itself in so many different ways as it now does in Poland in the political climate spawned by a dialectical Marxism that seeks to capture men's minds ... The discussion about man's role in the world over the past twenty years in Poland clearly shows what the heart of the matter is: It is not just a question of cosmology and natural

---

[17]In the United States, Christopher West has been the most prominent popularizer of John Paul II's theology of the body. For a good review and critique of West's work, as well as an extensive and balanced analysis of the influence of and reception of John Paul II's work in the field of U.S. moral theology, see John Grabowski, "The Luminous Excess of the Acting Person: Assessing the Impact of Pope John Paul II on American Catholic Moral Theology," *Journal of Moral Theology* 1, no. 1 (2012): 116–47.

[18]Stefan Swiezawski, "Introduction," in Karol Wojtyła, *Person and Community: Selected Essays*, trans. Theresa Sandok, OSM (New York: Peter Lang, 1993), ix–x.

philosophy; it is a question of philosophical anthropology and ethics—it is the great and fundamental contest for the essence of man.[19]

In order to defend the human person from such destructive philosophical systems— systems that have real consequences for real people, as demonstrated through war, holocaust and occupation—Wojtyła must maintain that "the essence of man" (i.e., human nature) is *more* than material, that the human person is not a thing solely made from material that can simply be manipulated by others, but rather someone who *transcends* that physical material and is an end in his or her own right. Human dignity, then, flows from this metaphysical status, not from the material out of which the human person is made. Out of this context comes Wojtyła's own characterization of his philosophical project:

> First of all, audacious though it may seem in the present day—in which philosophical thinking is not only nourished by, and based upon history ... the present work cannot be seen otherwise than as a personal effort by the author to disentangle the intricacies of a crucial state of affairs to clarify the basic elements of the problems involved. I have, indeed, tried to face the major issues themselves concerning life, nature, and the existence of the human being—with its limitations as well as with its privileges— directly as they present themselves to man in his struggle to survive while maintaining the dignity of the human being: man, who sets himself goals and strives to accomplish then, and who is torn apart between his all too limited condition and his highest aspirations to set himself free.[20]

The first thing that strikes the reader about Wojtyła's own characterization of his project is his passionate love and compassion for human beings—and that this love and compassion serve as his motivation for his intellectual work. It is out of this motivation that Wojtyła strives to establish the dignity of the human being in the objective order while at the same time encountering, indeed "facing," the questions of the meaning of human existence *as they arise in human experience*, that is, "directly as they present themselves to man in his struggle to survive," which struggle is foremost in his mind and heart due to his own experience—and those of his family, friends and neighbors—of political and economic oppression, war and holocaust.[21]

Second, in this statement of his project, one can parse the dual philosophical schools of thought that shape Wojtyła's work, namely, Thomism and phenomenology. From Thomism, Wojtyła grounds human nature—and therefore human dignity—in the metaphysical, objective order. From phenomenology, especially the work of Max Scheler, Wojtyła approaches the big questions of meaning *as they arise in human life and experience*.[22]

---

[19]Karol Wojtyła, "From *The Controversy about Man*," in *Toward a Philosophy of Praxis*, ed. Alfred Bloch and George T. Czuczka, trans. George Czuczka (New York: Crossroad, 1981), 12.

[20]Wojtyła, *The Acting Person*, vii.

[21]For more on Wojtyła's experiences during the Second World War], see George Weigel, *Witness to Hope: The Biography of John Paul II* (New York: HarperCollins, 2001).

[22]Wojtyła himself acknowledges these dual influences and indicates in the preface to *The Acting Person* that he "owes everything to the systems of metaphysics, of anthropology, and of Aristotelian-Thomistic ethics on the one hand, and to phenomenology, above all in Scheler's interpretation, and through Scheler's critique also to Kant, on the other hand" (Wojtyła, "Translation of Handwritten Draft of the Author's Preface," in *The Acting Person*, xiv).

Third, in this statement of his project, Wojtyła himself hints at the reason for his rejection of historicity as a determinative category for human nature, which during Wojtyła's life as a philosopher and pope had become a major, if not the major, philosophical and theological paradigm in the West through which to consider the human subject. The materialisms that Wojtyła was fighting against were based on an understanding of the human being that posited the human as a merely physical and material being, who could be subject to—and therefore objectified by—economic and social forces. For Wojtyła, the *source* of human dignity needed to be found outside of history. Thus Wojtyła's preferred definition of human nature is a metaphysical one.[23]

HUMAN PERSONS: WHO ARE WE?

For John Paul II, the *imago Dei* (see Gen. 1:26-27) encompasses not only the human person as created but who we are called to be as well. It "bookends" human historical life from conception until death (and beyond). In *Mulieris Dignitatem*, John Paul II states that "the revealed truth concerning man as 'the image and likeness' of God constitutes the immutable basis of all Christian anthropology."[24] Moreover, Christ *is* this image of God and so is both our beginning and our end, our alpha and omega.[25] John Paul II acknowledges that the dignity of the human person comes from this relationship to Christ.

This Christological focus in John Paul II's *theological* anthropology has led some scholars to posit that he proposes a Christological personalism at the core of his understanding of the human person. For example, John S. Grabowski states that "the ideas of *Gaudium et spes* 22 and 24—that Christ reveals us to our selves [*sic*] and that human fulfillment is found in the sincere gift of self—form hermeneutical keys to the corpus of his thought."[26] This grounding in a Christocentric anthropology is evident in both John Paul II's later 1979 encyclical, *Redemptor Hominis*,[27] as well as in his episcopal engagement in the Second Vatican Council and drafting of *Gaudium et Spes* itself.[28] John Paul II asserts in many places in both his pre-papal and papal works that human beings are created as *persons*—that is, beings capable of total self-gift and thus of responding to God's own self-gift in Christ. For example, in his reflection on Genesis 2 in *Mulieris*

---

[23]True to his dual philosophical influences—phenomenology and Thomism—the philosopher Wojtyła identifies two definitions of human nature. In its phenomenological sense, nature refers to things that happen without the agency of a person. Wojtyła is uncomfortable with this definition because it sets up an opposition between person and nature, where in human acts belong to the person, and acts that happen within a person without his or her agency belong to nature. On the other hand, "in the metaphysical approach nature is identical with essence, and thus nature in man is the same as the whole of his humanness" (Wojtyła, *The Acting Person*, 82; see also his discussion on 76–9). He also notes that in actual human experience these dynamisms are not sliced apart; rather they are experienced by the unity that is the person as a whole. Despite his discomfort, Wojtyła uses "nature" in this phenomenological sense in some places in *The Acting Person*, e.g., 116 and 118.

[24]John Paul II, *Mulieris Dignatatem* (English title: On the Dignity and Vocation of Women; August 15, 1988; http://w2.vatican.va/content/john-paul-ii/en/apost_letters/1988/documents/hf_jp-ii_apl_19880815_mulieris-dignitatem.html), par. 6.

[25]See Rev. 22:13.

[26]Grabowski, "Luminous Excess," 124.

[27]John Paul II, *Redemptor Hominis* (March 4, 1979; http://w2.vatican.va/content/john-paul-ii/en/encyclicals/documents/hf_jp-ii_enc_04031979_redemptor-hominis.html).

[28]For a detailed history of Bishop Wojtyła's intellectual involvement in the preparations for the Council as well as his role in drafting *Gaudium et Spes*, see John Sikorski, "Towards a Conjugal Spirituality: Karol Wojtyła's Vision of Marriage Before, During, and After Vatican II," *Journal of Moral Theology* 6, no. 2 (2017): 103–29. For a treatment of Wojtyła's "Christocentric personalism" before and during the Council, see especially 107–9.

Dignitatem, John Paul II asserts that the human being "is made in the image of God, insofar as he is a rational and free creature capable of knowing God and loving him."[29]

For Wojtyła, by definition a person is a concrete *unity* of various elements, and experiences himself or herself as such. Indeed, Max Scheler's philosophical influence on Wojtyła is most apparent in his treatment of human experience. Wojtyła notes that human experiences present themselves to human persons as wholes, not, for example, as purely physical, purely emotional, purely spiritual or purely intellectual. On the contrary, he asserts that human experience (including the experience of being human) is an *organic whole*, which contains both intellectual and sensual content, that is, soul and body, due to the "dual structure" of the human person.[30] Only after we have experienced something do we divide the experience up into those categories. Thus, Wojtyła also takes seriously the emotions, the affective dimension of human life. He acknowledges that one's experience of oneself as a moral agent, a person, has a definite affective dimension to it. This affective dimension is also important to how he treats the human person as a relational being, and therefore goes to the core of what he means by "person"—one who is capable of giving oneself in relationship with others.

While Wojtyła posits both a soul and a body in his construct of the human person, he criticizes modern philosophy for neglecting their unity. Rather than Descartes' "I think; therefore I am," Wojtyła would assert, "I act; therefore I am." In his discourse on *The Acting Person*, Wojtyła overcomes Cartesian dualism, the idea that the body is simply a substructure upon which the mind rests, by positing that the human person is unified in action. It is when I act that all the different parts of myself are unified by my will, because human acts are embodiments of the choices I make as a spiritual being. Wojtyła takes this to its logical conclusion as an ethicist: we realize and express ourselves through our actions; our choices embody the persons we are and choose to be. Therefore, "the integration of the person in action, taking place in the body and expressed by it, reveals simultaneously the deepest sense of the integrity of man as a person."[31]

Still, while Wojtyła rejects a Cartesian dualism, in his philosophical anthropology, the body is still subordinate to the spiritual person. This is apparent in the language he uses in *The Acting Person*. For example, Wojtyła calls the body a "compliant tool" that the person possesses and asserts that "the dynamic transcendence of the person—spiritual by its very nature—finds in the human body the territory and the means of expression."[32] In possessing his or her body, the human person is able to "*govern*" himself.[33] This language of the body as a territory to be governed by the person is striking, and mitigates against a true integration of the body into human personhood.

Such language also stands in deep contrast to his papal—and more theological—works, and in particular the Wednesday audiences that form the basis for John Paul II's theology of the body.[34] In these later writings, the unity of a person and his or her body is much

---

[29]John Paul II, *Mulieris Dignatatem*, par. 7.

[30]See Wojtyła, "The Personal Structure of Self-Determination," in *Person and Community*, 188.

[31]Wojtyła, *The Acting Person*, 205.

[32]Ibid.

[33]Ibid., 206. Emphasis mine.

[34]In "Engaging the Struggle: John Paul II on Personhood and Sexuality," in *Human Sexuality in the Catholic Tradition*, ed. Kieran Scott and Harold Daly Horell (Lanham: Rowan & Littlefield, 2007), esp. 96–9, I argue that this contrast is explained by a methodological difference between philosophy and theology. In his philosophical anthropology, he describes human persons as they experience themselves now, in their fallen state. In his theological reflections, he is reflecting on human beings as created in their prelapsarian state.

more intimate, even absolute. The body is not the means of expression of the person, but rather that expression itself.[35] Human personhood therefore includes as essential to itself the body, which is "the very bone marrow of the anthropological reality."[36]

It is this much deeper unity, almost an identification, between body and person that gives rise to John Paul II's understanding of the relationships among embodiment, sexual difference and personhood. At one point, John Paul II asserts that corporeality and sexuality are not *completely* identified. "The fact that man is a 'body' belongs more deeply to the structure of the personal subject than the fact that in his somatic constitution he is also male and female."[37] This is demonstrated by the fact that the male human being wakes up from sleep and recognizes the female human being as one *like* himself. "The woman is another 'I' in a common humanity."[38]

However, John Paul II notes that in Genesis 2 the creation of the human being was not complete until sexual differentiation, and thus, relationality—the recognition by one of the other. Thus the *imago Dei*—that which is most fundamental about what it means to be human for John Paul II—is expressed more fully in the communion of persons constituted by the second moment of creation when sexual differentiation appears than in the creation of the solitary human being.[39]

> Man becomes an image of God not so much in the moment of solitude as in the moment of communion. He is, in fact, "from the beginning," not only an image in which the solitude of one Person, who rules the world, mirrors itself, but also and essentially the image of an inscrutable divine communion of Persons.[40]

Being the image of God has to do with being created in relationship to one another, a relationship that is expressed through the creation of sexual difference.

Thus in another place in his catecheses on the body, John Paul II asserts that "the theology of the body, which is linked from the beginning with the creation of man in the image of God, becomes, in some way also a theology of sex, or rather the theology of masculinity and femininity."[41] For John Paul II, embodiment, sexual difference and personhood are intimately tied to one another in constituting the image of God in humanity. Because he posits such a close relationship between body and person in his papal works, "sex is not only decisive for man's somatic individuality, but at the same time it defines his personal identity and concreteness."[42] Thus, for John Paul II the theology of the body becomes the theology of sexual difference. This mitigates against his claim about sexuality and corporeality not being completely identified.

---

[35]See John Paul II, *Man and Woman*, October 31, 1979; p. 154.

[36]John Paul II, *Man and Woman*, November 14, 1979; p. 164.

[37]John Paul II, *Man and Woman*, November 7, 1979; 157.

[38]John Paul II, *Mulieris Dignatatem*, par. 6.

[39]John Paul II notes that in the second creation story in Genesis 2, the solitary human being ('*adam*) is created first; it is only when '*adam* wakes up from his sleep that sexual differentiation appears and the text speaks of man ('*is*) and woman ('*issah*). See *Man and Woman*, November 7, 1979; 159. There is a debate in the secondary literature about whether John Paul II posits a fractional sex complementarity vs an integral sex complementarity—that is, whether or not each person is complete in herself or himself (integral) or whether men and women need the opposite sex to complete themselves as persons (fractional). For discussion on this matter, see Grabowski, "Luminous Excess," 132, esp. fn 63.

[40]John Paul II, *Man and Woman*, November 14, 1979; p. 163. Also see *Mulieris Dignatatem*, par. 7.

[41]John Paul II, *Man and Woman*, November 14, 1979; p. 165.

[42]John Paul II, *Man and Woman*, March 5, 1980; p. 208.

In terms of his understanding of gender, John Paul II falls firmly in the essentialist camp, which considers gender to be determined by one's biological sex, rather than socially constructed. Indeed, the whole concept of gender as it is distinguished from sex in contemporary philosophy and social theory is contrary to John Paul II's understanding and theology of sexual difference.[43] Note here also that "sexual difference" is singular, and that what John Paul II means by sexual difference is what has become known in contemporary (non-essentialist) parlance as the "gender binary"—the insistence that all human beings fit into one of two strict categories, that is, male and female.

Indeed, for John Paul II masculinity and femininity have objective and universal content. This is most obvious in *Mulieris Dignitatem*, his apostolic letter whose English title is *On the Dignity and Vocation of Women*. In it, he constructs an "archetype" of the feminine, that is, "what is characteristic of woman."[44] John Paul II describes women as having a "special sensitivity"[45] as well as a "naturally spousal predisposition."[46] Femininity involves motherhood, virginity and receptivity. Indeed, as the only woman who remains both virgin and mother, Mary "signifies the fullness of the perfection of 'what is characteristic of woman', of 'what is feminine'. Here we find ourselves ... at the culminating point, the archetype, of the personal dignity of women."[47]

In sum, John Paul II posits two kinds of persons: male persons and female persons. Masculinity (the state of being male) and femininity (the state of being female) are "two different 'incarnations', that is, two ways in which the same human being, created 'in the image of God' (Gen 1:27), 'is a body'."[48] Sexual difference is *the fundamental* human characteristic, such that masculinity or femininity determines personal identity in a way that no other human characteristic has, such as culture, time in history, one's talents or one's other bodily characteristics. "The fundamental fact of this existence of man in every stage of his history is that God 'created them male and female'; in fact, he always creates them in this way, and they are always such."[49]

Moreover, the gift of male and female body-persons to one another in relationship is the highest form of what John Paul II calls the *communio personarum*. This mutual bodily self-gift through the *communio personarum* is the "spousal" meaning of the body,[50] the consciousness of which "constitutes the fundamental element of human existence in the world."[51] Understanding the spousal meaning of the body is "important and indispensable for knowing who man is and who he ought to be, and therefore how he should shape his own activity."[52]

---

[43]For a fuller discussion of this rejection of "gender ideology," on the part of John Paul II and other popes, see Tina Beattie, "Dignity, Difference and Rights—a Gendered Theological Analysis," *Louvain Studies* 40 (2017): 58–81; and Mary Anne Case, "The Role of the Popes in the Invention of Complementarity and the Vatican's Anathematization of Gender," *Religion & Gender* 6 (2016): 155–72.

[44]See John Paul II, *Mulieris Dignatatem*, par. 5. In all of his writings there is no corresponding treatise on men or masculinity. This may be attributed to his acknowledgment of the pastoral and theological issues surrounding women in Church and society.

[45]See, e.g., John Paul II, *Mulieris Dignatatem*, par. 16.

[46]See, e.g., John Paul II, *Mulieris Dignatatem*, par. 20.

[47]John Paul II, *Mulieris Dignatatem*, par. 5.

[48]John Paul II, *Man and Woman*, November 7, 1979; 157.

[49]John Paul II, *Man and Woman*, February 13, 1980; 200.

[50]Sometimes referred to as the "nuptial meaning of the body" based on an earlier translation (1997) of the Wednesday audiences, John Paul II introduces this term in *Man and Woman*, January 2, 1980; 178.

[51]John Paul II, *Man and Woman*, January 16, 1980; 189.

[52]John Paul II, *Man and Woman*, February 13, 1980; 200.

Embodiment and sexual difference belong to human nature, although they are expressed concretely in actual male and female human persons. In John Paul II's own words,

> the "definitive" creation of man consists in the creation of the unity of two beings. Their unity denotes above all the identity of human nature; duality, on the other hand, show what, on the basis of this identity, constitutes the masculinity and femininity of created man.[53]

Note the contrast between human nature and created humanity; for John Paul II, human nature is ahistorical; on the other hand, masculinity and femininity are expressed in actual, human beings. The unity of sexual difference is an integral part of human nature— that is, the essence of what it is and means to be human, and therefore to be made in the image of God.

At heart, John Paul II is an ethicist; our understanding of the human person matters because it tells us who we are and, therefore, how we should act. The human person is a particular, concrete expression of a metaphysical human nature. As discussed above, Wojtyła's unique blend of Thomism and phenomenology drives his understanding of the human being—that is, his philosophical and theological anthropology, and specifically his understandings of the human person and human nature. Moreover, these philosophical influences run through his catecheses on the body, which form the basis of his theology of sexual difference.

CONCLUSION: JOHN PAUL II, SCIENCE AND HUMAN DIGNITY

Karol Wojtyła's project was to philosophically and theologically ground human dignity in order to defend the human being from the materialisms of his time that led to the atrocities of war, occupation and holocaust. This was most urgent in the mid-twentieth century—and remains so in our time as well. By all accounts Karol Wojtyła was successful in this. By grounding human dignity in an understanding of human nature that is beyond history and that is not subject to its vicissitudes, he makes the point quite forcefully that the human person cannot and should not be at the mercy of political ideologies based on materialist philosophies, such as fascism and communism. The evidence of his success is provided by none other than the Polish people themselves and the late pope's solidarity with them in their fight to throw off the yoke of these ideologies. A true saint indeed!

Just as Karol Wojtyła could trace the causality from philosophical materialism to political ideology to the horrors of war, holocaust and occupation and their real effects on real people in his time, we cannot be blind to the effects of how we think theologically about the question of human dignity in our own time. We must ask: What implications does John Paul II's understanding of human nature, personhood, body and sexuality have for real people today?

In order to answer this question, it would behoove us to learn more *about* real people today, so as to mitigate the limitations of our own anecdotal experience. This question, therefore, gives rise to the need for an interdisciplinary methodology more closely associated with practical theology than traditional philosophy; namely, it means that the

---

[53]John Paul II, *Man and Woman*, November 14, 1979; 161.

natural and social sciences have something relevant to say about what the human *is*, even if they cannot tells us what it *means*. As Todd Salzman and Michael Lawler put it,

> Practical theology embraces both description and evaluation of the present situation. For description, theology relies on the sciences; for evaluation, it critically distills the scientific data through its own theological filters. The present situation, social or theological, cannot be deduced abstractly from prior theological theories; it can only be described concretely by the sciences.[54]

Theology must turn to science for descriptions of "the current situation"—in our case, actual, concrete human beings. Then, it must evaluate those findings in light of its own theological values. This is especially true with regard to human sexuality. As Patricia Beattie Jung and Aana Marie Vigen point out, "Sexuality and gender are complex and multifaceted realities ... indeed, without the information and dynamic participation from multiple disciplines, any analysis of human sexuality or gender seems tragically undercut."[55]

Thus, the tragedy with John Paul II's theology of sexual difference is a methodological one. Given that for John Paul II, the unity of masculinity and femininity—and the characteristics that comprise the content of each—are found in human nature, it is perhaps no surprise that John Paul II dismisses the importance of scientific findings on embodiment and sexuality in his treatment of sexual difference. Early on in his catecheses on the body, he admits that "we find ourselves in this study on a wholly pre-scientific level. We know almost nothing about the inner structures and regularities that reign in the human organism."[56] However, he goes on to dismiss science completely as a source for theological reflection on the "personal dignity" of the body or human sexuality. "Contemporary bio-physiology can offer much precise information about human sexuality. Nevertheless, the knowledge of the personal dignity of the human body and of sex must still be drawn from other sources."[57] Because for John Paul II masculinity and femininity are tied up in human nature, the source of our understanding of sexual difference must be revelation, not science.

It is certainly true that human dignity as such cannot be grounded in the descriptive role of science, which strives to be value-neutral. Science can only describe physical human beings who present themselves in history. Unfortunately, however, John Paul II's rejection of historicity as an essential component of human nature leads him to conclusions about sexual difference that not only consider scientific research irrelevant but also directly contradict scientific findings. In the case of sexual difference, ethicist Christine Gudorf points out, "Biologists today tell us that there are six indicators of biological sex, and

---

[54]Todd A. Salzman and Michael G. Lawler, "Theology, Science, and Sexual Anthropology: A Methodological Investigation," *Journal of Religion and Society: Supplement* 11 (2015): 46–72 (46). Salzman and Lawler's article examines various paradigms of the relationship between theology and science, and then critiques traditionalist and revisionist sexual anthropologies, including John Paul II's, according to John Paul II's own call to an "intense dialogue" between theology and science (see ibid., 48).

[55]Patrica Beattie Jung and Aana Marie Vigen, eds., in their introduction to *God, Science, Sex, and Gender: An Interdisciplinary Approach to Christian Ethics* (Champaign: University of Illinois Press, 2010), 5.

[56]John Paul II, *Man and Woman,* April 2, 1980; 221.

[57]John Paul II, *Man and Woman,* April 2, 1980; 222. See also his "Message to the Pontifical Academy of Sciences on Evolution," *Origins* 26, no. 22 (1996): 350–2, esp. 351, in which he delineates the respective purviews of biology, philosophy and theology.

that for many millions of people these indicators do not line up in any simple dimorphic pattern."[58]

Moreover, according to biologist Joan Roughgarden, science itself is "challenged when asked to supply an accurate picture of sex, gender expression, and sexuality in nature, and this limitation impedes a scientifically informed moral and theological discussion of these issues."[59] What science *can* confirm with regard to sex and gender expression found in the natural world is that it is not as simple as the strictly dimorphic pattern of male and female that John Paul II espouses. The variations found among animal species in terms of both physical characteristics and behavior confound scientists themselves. Roughgarden asks,

> Does not such natural variation in gender expression contradict the ... prescription of one template, or norm, per sex ...? Does such natural variation in gender expression point to multiple norms for each sex, a multiplicity of possible roles evolutionarily negotiated within each species depending on local circumstance?[60]

John Paul II's sexual anthropology ignores these questions as irrelevant to the personal dignity of the human being. This (at best) ignorance of scientific research and (at worst) rejection of it has the effect of positing an understanding of sexual difference that does not include or apply to real human persons. How does this (unintended to be sure) effect of non-inclusion, then, witness to their human dignity?

John Paul II is ambivalent when it comes to the relationship between philosophy and theology on the one hand and the natural and social sciences on the other. In a 1988 letter to George Coyne, SJ, Director of the Vatican Observatory, he considers the question of whether and how science and theology can and should inform one another:

> Is the community of world religions, including the church, ready to enter into a more thoroughgoing dialogue with the scientific community, a dialogue in which the integrity of both religion and science is supported and the advance of each is fostered? Is the scientific community now prepared to open itself to Christianity and indeed to all the great world religions, working with us all to build a culture that is more humane and in that way more divine? Do we dare to risk the honesty and the courage that this task demands? We must ask ourselves whether both science and religion will contribute to the integration of human culture or to its fragmentation. It is a single choice, and it confronts us all. For a simple neutrality is no longer acceptable. If they are to grow and mature, peoples cannot continue to live in separate compartments, pursuing totally divergent interests from which they evaluate and judge their world.[61]

However, contrary to his remarks above to Fr. Coyne, in *Love and Responsibility*, Karol Wojtyła asserts that an understanding of human sexuality can only be based on the

---

[58]Christine Gudorf, "A New Moral Discourse on Sexuality," in *Human Sexuality in the Catholic Tradition*, ed. Kieran Scott and Harold Daly Horell (Lanham: Rowman & Littlefield, 2007), 55.

[59]Joan Roughgarden, "Evolutionary Biology and Sexual Diversity," in *God, Science, Sex, Gender: An Interdisciplinary Approach to Christian Ethics*, ed. Patricia Beattie Jung and Aana Marie Vigen (Urbana: University of Illinois Press, 2010), 89. Of course, Roughgarden is using the term "nature" here not in a theological or philosophical sense, but to mean simply "in the natural world."

[60]Ibid., 92.

[61]John Paul II, "Letter to George V. Coyne" (June 1, 1988; http://www.vatican.va/content/john-paul-ii/en/letters/1988/documents/hf_jp-ii_let_19880601_padre-coyne.html), 376–7.

order of nature, which means the totality of the cosmic relationships that arise among really existing entities ... the sexual urge owes its objective importance to its connection with the divine work of creation ..., and this importance vanishes almost completely if our way of thinking is inspired only by the biological order of nature.[62]

Thus, for John Paul II, the metaphysical order of nature must take precedence when considering human sexuality and—therefore—human dignity, so as not to contradict those principles that came to us from Catholic tradition,[63] such as the belief that God created two—and only two—kinds of persons, male and female.

So we are left with a dilemma in John Paul II's work. On the one hand, his project is successful in that it grounds human dignity in an understanding of human nature that is not subject to the social and economic forces of history and maintains that the human being is more than physical, more than the material out of which he or she is made. On the other hand, this same methodological move means that for John Paul II human sexuality is so tied to an ahistorical understanding of human nature that a contradiction, even a dichotomy, exists between what is essentially human (human nature) and real, historical human beings, especially with regard to biological sex and gender expression. Despite John Paul II's good intentions and passionate love for human beings, this dichotomy mitigates against upholding the dignity of actual persons by insisting that they are or must strive to be something they are not.

This dilemma leaves some remaining questions for further inquiry. First, is it necessary to exclude historicity completely from our understanding of human nature in order to establish or maintain a philosophical basis for human dignity? Can human dignity be located precisely in our creation in the image of God and thus in our relationship to Christ—as John Paul II proposes—while still acknowledging that historicity is an integral part of being human? Would a practical theological method give rise to a theological anthropology that could honor both human dignity and historicity?

Second, how should the natural and social sciences inform our understandings of human nature and human dignity? What is the relationship between human nature and natural law, and how does this relationship inform or determine questions of sexual ethics? I submit that Karol John Paul II is a key conversation partner in exploring these questions.

SUGGESTED FURTHER READING

Beattie, Tina, "Gendering Genesis, Engendering Difference: A Catholic Theological Quest," *Svensk teologisk kvartalskrift* 92 (2016), 102–117.

Massa, Mark, SJ, *The Structure of Theological Revolutions: Models of Natural Law in American Catholic Theology* (New York: Oxford University Press, 2018).

Schindler, David L., 'Being, Gift, Self-Gift: A Reply to Waldstein on Relationality and John Paul II's Theology of the Body (Part One)', *Communio* 42 (2015): 221–51.

---

[62]Wojtyła, *Love and Responsibility*, 57. This also explains why, unlike other biological functions such as eyesight, for example, human sexuality must be treated differently, as part of a higher order, such that it cannot be manipulated artificially. So, to continue the example, for Karol Wojtyła/John Paul II, it is morally sanctioned to wear glasses to correct faulty vision, but not so to use artificial means to enhance or restrict the procreative function of sexuality.

[63]See ibid.

CHAPTER TWENTY-THREE

Rosemary Radford Ruether's Theological Anthropology

SUSAN A. ROSS

Rosemary Radford Ruether (1936–) is an extraordinarily prolific American theologian who has written on a wide range of issues including feminism, racism, anti-Semitism, anti-colonialism, ecology and interreligious dialogue. She is best known as a feminist liberation theologian who, as a Catholic, is unafraid to challenge her own tradition particularly with regard to women's issues, but she has also advocated, among other causes, for justice for Palestinians, church reform and better mental health care. While she explicitly spells out her theological anthropology in one chapter of *Sexism and God-Talk* (1982), her subsequent work expands upon many of the points made there. Her view of humanity can best be understood through the various lenses that she has used throughout her work to analyze relevant topics involving the human person. Long before the term "intersectionality" became a buzzword in academia, Ruether saw the connections among various forms of oppression and has consistently argued against dualistic conceptions of the person in favor of a holistic approach that encompasses different but also complementary "lenses."

In this chapter, I will focus on the ways that Ruether uses the lenses of history, theology, ecology and global awareness to understand what it means to be human, how the various theological subtopics in anthropology—such as *imago Dei*, sin and grace, sexuality, individual and community—are informed by these lenses and how current crises affect her understanding of the human person. Ruether is not an easy theologian to categorize since her writings are so wide-ranging, but over her long career there are certain themes that characterize her work.

The first major theme is her opposition to all dualistic forms of thinking and especially dualistic conceptions of humanity, especially in terms of human sexuality, interpersonal and social relationships and the human relationship to the earth. Beginning with one of her first major books, *New Woman New Earth: Sexist Ideologies and Human Liberation*, Ruether shows how the persistence of sexism is "foundational to the perception of order and relationship that has been built up in cultures."[1] Unlike other forms of oppression such as those based in race or class that are now, at least for the most part, seen as unjust, dualistic conceptions of sex continue to be seen as intrinsic to human nature and

---

[1]Rosemary Radford Ruether, *New Woman New Earth: Sexist Ideologies & Human Liberation* (New York: Seabury Press, 1975), 3.

are still strongly upheld by most religious traditions. Ruether, however, does not only condemn sexism but also shows how the dynamics of hierarchical dualism function in anti-Semitism, racism and the destruction of the earth. In all of these 'isms," one side is set over and against the other, with the superior often seen as rational and male and the inferior as demonic and female. Ruether's opposition to dualism undergirds her entire theological anthropology.

A second theme is her historical consciousness. Ruether received her master's degree in classics and her doctorate in classics and patristics from Claremont Graduate School, with a dissertation on Gregory of Nazianzus. Her training in the early sources of Western civilization and Christianity has influenced her approach to theological anthropology, in that taking into account the historical background of theological teachings is essential. In *Sexism and God-Talk*, Ruether explicitly links women's experience with historical tradition in her methodology.[2] Theological ideas emerge out of particular contexts, influenced by social, economic, political and other forces, and cannot be seen in isolation. Her treatment of Mary, for example, who is often held up as a model for women, emphasizes the Ancient Near Eastern roots of goddess worship and how this tradition was "baptized" by Christianity. So too does her book on the family, which begins with six chapters tracing the development of Christian ideas of the family, going back to the Jewish and Greco-Roman background up to the present time, as does her work on redemption. Theological ideas always emerge out of a complex historical and social context and cannot be adequately understood apart from it. Tracing how these ideas emerged and developed underscores their relative rather than timeless relevance.

A third theme is her reliance on a wide variety of sources. While Christian theology traditionally relies on scripture, the inherited tradition, reason and experience, Ruether also draws on "pagan" resources—that is, sources that are often dismissed by "orthodox" theology as heretical, often because of their inclusion of women—as well as "post-Christian" sources such as Marxism in order to make constructive theological proposals that she sees as more adequate to contemporary needs. Tradition, Ruether reminds us, is always shaped by the powerful; she observes that "all the categories of classical theology in its major traditions … have been distorted by androcentrism."[3] While never completely dismissive of the Christian tradition, Ruether has maintained a healthy skepticism toward the idea that any one formulation or tradition has permanent value. Thus, in the first pages of *Sexism and God-Talk*, Ruether presents a feminist *midrash* (an imaginative retelling) on the nature of God, Jesus, the crucifixion and the resurrection, suggesting the incomplete and biased nature of the scriptures.

Finally, and perhaps most importantly, a fourth theme is her commitment to eradicating all forms of injustice and working toward an eschatological vision of a transformed humanity and world. Since her earliest books, beginning with *Faith and Fratricide*, to her later works on interreligious dialogue and care for the earth, Ruether has dedicated her work to liberation—both of humanity and of the cosmos. In *Sexism and God-Talk*, Ruether refers to the "prophetic principle"—that is, the biblical tradition that God takes the side of the oppressed, and that a new age is to come. Although Ruether has been criticized by some of her feminist colleagues for reliance on this biblical category since it

---

[2]Rosemary Radford Ruether, *Sexism and God-Talk: Toward a Feminist Theology* (Boston: Beacon Press, 1993), 12.
[3]Ibid., 37.

is rooted in a patriarchal tradition, she has defended this principle. For Ruether, the major focus of the biblical tradition is justice and a vision of a better world.

HISTORY

Ruether's approach to theological anthropology is deeply rooted in history. The biblical tradition, the history of theology and secular history all demonstrate how androcentric assumptions have shaped the ways that human beings are understood, what their roles have been and whose stories have been told. There are also the countless untold stories of women and oppressed groups that have been suppressed. One of Ruether's signal contributions to feminist historical theology has been her collaboration with other scholars in presenting a series of historical studies of women, which reveal the complexity of women's lives.[4] While Ruether maintains that both Judaism and Christianity, at their core, affirm the equal dignity of women and men, there is another influential strand in these traditions that has equated men with the superior mind and women with the inferior body; the superiority of men justifies the subordination of women. This is particularly true in Christianity. For both traditions, Ruether observes, the normative human being is the man, and this idea has both a long history and staying power. It can be traced back to prehistoric times and continues to be the dominant strain worldwide.

Ruether notes how the Hebrew prophets condemned the oppression of the weak by the strong; widows and orphans, people who lacked the protection of a man, were the most vulnerable. She notes how the prophetic tradition "is destabilizing toward the existing social order and its hierarchies of power."[5] Feminism, Ruether argues, claims this tradition as "the central tradition, the tradition by which Biblical faith constantly criticizes and renews itself and its own vision."[6] The stress on the prophetic was continued and developed by Jesus, who engaged in a "radical interpretation of the prophetic-messianic tradition."[7] With the writings of Paul, Greek thought began to have a strong influence on Christian theological developments, where the body and women are seen to represent lowly matter, which is ruled by the higher, transcendent spirit, represented by man. Ruether continually notes how egalitarian movements in the tradition were gradually deformed by androcentric and patriarchal ideas.[8]

In her chapter on theological anthropology in *Sexism and God-Talk,* Ruether singles out Augustine, Thomas Aquinas, Martin Luther, John Calvin and Karl Barth from the Christian historical tradition, all of whom saw men as superior to women, not just in the post-Fall world but even in the order of creation. For Augustine, women are the image of God only secondarily; Thomas Aquinas, relying on Aristotle, views women as "misbegotten," although nevertheless essential for procreation.[9] While Luther and Calvin

---

[4]Rosemary Radford Ruether and Rosemary Skinner Keller, eds., *Women and Religion in America* (San Francisco: Harper & Row, 1981); Rosemary Radford Ruether, ed. *Religion and Sexism: Images of Woman in the Jewish and Christian Traditions* (New York: Simon and Schuster, 1974); Rosemary Radford Ruether and Eleanor McLaughlin, eds., *Women of Spirit: Female Leadership in the Jewish and Christian Traditions* (New York: Simon and Schuster, 1979).

[5]Ruether, *Sexism*, 26.

[6]Ibid., 24.

[7]Ibid., 30.

[8]See especially Rosemary Radford Ruether, *Women and Redemption: A Theological History* (Minneapolis, MN: Fortress Press, 1998).

[9]Ruether, *Sexism*, 95–6.

made a stronger case for women's equality before God in creation, Luther still blamed women for original sin and stated that their subjugation to men and relegation to the home was their punishment. Calvin saw women's subordination as part of the created order, an idea later reaffirmed by Karl Barth.[10]

Ruether also includes various "egalitarian anthropologies" in this chapter. Some "eschatological" anthropologies see in Christ the unity of male and female; some reject sexuality for asceticism. Liberal feminism, although having roots in the biblical and Christian traditions, gets renewed strength from the Enlightenment emphasis on reason and becomes "secularized" in that equality is a goal to be achieved within human history. "Romantic" feminism, according to Ruether, takes different forms. Conservative romanticism sees women as purer than men by associating altruistic love with women and power with men. Such a view results in seeing women's proper place in the private sphere of the home where love and affection are primarily located and men's in the public sphere of work, politics and war. "Reformist" feminism also sees women as innately more pure than men but argues that women's qualities can transform the world into a place of peace and harmony. "Radical romanticism" sees men as the source of evil and in its most separatist forms "dreams of an alternative world" where women would live and reproduce without men.[11]

Ruether is critical of both liberal and romantic feminism, noting how liberal feminism tends to overvalue rationality and romantic feminism tends to overlook the moral ambiguity of the private sphere. Arguing for a "creative synthesis" of the two movements, Ruether seeks to affirm the "full and equivalent human nature" of both men and women. She also maintains that "maleness and femaleness exist as reproductive role specialization," a point that will be developed more below.[12]

In sum, an adequate understanding of what it means to be human involves a knowledge of the ways in which humanity has been shaped by cultural and religious forces over time, how these have been intertwined with religious traditions and how they continue to be influential in the present.

THEOLOGY

The central themes of theological anthropology concern how the human person is related to God, self and others; how sin and evil have affected humanity and how salvation and redemption are to be understood; the significance of sexuality; and how humanity is understood as community. In addition, both Christology and Mariology have profound anthropological implications, as both represent ideal and redeemed humanity. Ruether touches on all of these topics in her books and articles.

The biblical tradition holds that men and women are created in the image of God (Gen. 1:27). Yet God's maleness has long been assumed in both the Jewish and Christian traditions, with the consequence that women's capacity to image God has been belittled or denied. Although Judaism came into existence alongside ancient goddess traditions in the Ancient Near East, Ruether notes that "male monotheism … assimilate[s], transform[s] and revers[es] [these] symbol systems."[13] Ancient conceptions of divine marriage are taken

---

[10]Ibid., 97–9.
[11]Ibid., 109.
[12]Ibid., 111.
[13]Ibid., 54.

up in the bridal symbolism of Yahweh and his spouse Israel. In the Christian tradition, as noted above, men are the ones who can fully image God, while women are seen as the image of God only through their relationship to men. Efforts to name God more inclusively are often resisted across the board; Ruether notes the "emotional hostility" to inclusive language for God even on the part of liberals.[14] She proposes the language of God/ess, "the *Shalom* of our being," as a more adequate name for the divine.[15]

When it comes to theologies of sin and grace, Ruether points out how feminism "presumes a radical concept of 'sin'," particularly in relation to more individualistic conceptions.[16] Sin is not simply personal alienation from God; it is, rather, "a fallen state of humanity," which is both historical and theological; it affects not just personal and social relationships but also the human relationship to nature. Sexism is perhaps the primal form of sin. Women have not only been held responsible for sin, as in the stories of Lilith, Eve and Pandora, but "the entire symbolic universe … is deeply tainted by hostility to their humanity."[17] Thus, conversion from the evil of sexism and all forms of hierarchical dualism requires different journeys for women and men. Redemption, which will be discussed below in the section on Christology, is not to be understood as the process of the individual being saved from God's judgment by Christ's death but rather as the ongoing journey in which all humanity works toward a more just and egalitarian world.[18] Women especially need to develop a full sense of selfhood, own their justifiable anger and work towards "new systems of relationship."[19] For their part, men need to understand the struggles of women, allow themselves to accept their own vulnerability, and resist male group egoism.[20] Thus, for Ruether, salvation/redemption does not refer to an otherworldly promise but a "this-worldly redemptive hope."[21]

Ruether's opposition to dualism is also found in her understanding of sexuality. As already noted, women are identified with body and nature, which is always seen as lower than spirit and culture. Like many other theologians, Ruether cites Augustine, who has had the most powerful influence on Christian understandings of sexuality. Augustine saw all sexual activity as sinful, since it arose from concupiscence, the inordinate desire for self and pleasure. Only sexual activity for procreation could mitigate this, making it venially and not mortally sinful. Thus, since Augustine, all forms of contraception were judged to be morally reprehensible. It was only in 1930 that Roman Catholicism permitted "natural" forms of birth control (i.e., through abstinence at fertile times in the woman's cycle, and only with permission of one's pastor), and the 1968 encyclical *Humanae vitae*, even against the majority recommendation of the Papal Commission established by Pope John XXIII, prohibited all forms of "artificial" contraception.[22] What this meant theologically was that sexual pleasure remained under a cloud of suspicion,

---

[14]Ibid., 47.
[15]Ibid., 71.
[16]Ibid., 161.
[17]Ibid., 168, 173.
[18]Ruther, *Women and Redemption*, 277.
[19]Ruether, *Sexism*, 189.
[20]Ibid., 191.
[21]Ruether, *Women and Redemption*, 275.
[22]The papal encyclical *Casti connibii* (1930) was directed against the Anglican Church's limited allowance for contraception. The text is available at http://www.vatican.va/content/pius-xi/en/encyclicals/documents/hf_p-xi_enc_19301231_casti-connubii.html (accessed September 9, 2020).

despite the Church's recognition at Vatican II of marriage's "goods" as including "unity," in addition to procreation.[23]

Particularly under the papacy of John Paul II, with his "Theology of the Body," the idea of sexual complementarity was promoted by the Catholic hierarchy. According to this theology, the man is the one who initiates while the woman is the one who receives, both sexually and in other roles in human life. Sexual love involves the complete self-gift of one partner to the other, and the use of contraception means that this self-gift is sinfully held back. John Paul II bases this theology in his interpretation of the biology of the sexes and extends this idea to the relationship between God and the world, as well as Christ and the Church. This theology provides a further reason why the ordination of women is prohibited, as men are the only appropriate representatives of Christ. Ruether sees this as a return to nineteenth-century romantic feminism;[24] in addition, the most significant issue for her is the consequences of the Catholic Church's global campaign against birth control and abortion.

Ruether has written widely on both contraception and abortion. Viewed through the lens of theological anthropology, sexuality is an intrinsically positive dimension of the person as created by God as body and soul and as the physical expression of love between people. The dualism that infects religion has, as already noted, seriously distorted theologies of sexuality. Ruether's efforts have been to point out how often hierarchical dualism and clerical control have not only presented a distorted view of women by seeing them as representative of lower matter but also prevented women from exercising control over their own sexuality.[25] She notes how church teachings on abortion have developed over time, as the understanding of conception, for example, in Thomas Aquinas, originally held that "ensoulment" took place months after conception, and only in the last 170 years has the church totally prohibited abortion from the moment of conception. In the last forty-plus years, the issue of abortion has overtaken contraception as the major focus of hierarchical condemnation; surveys show that the overwhelming majority of Catholics use contraception. As a longtime board member of the organization Catholics for Choice, Ruether has advocated not only for reproductive choice but also for positive theologies of nonmarital sex and same-sex relationships.

But it is not only on historical and theological grounds that Ruether argues against traditional Catholic positions on sexuality. In many parts of the world, women not only lack gender equality and access to adequate health care but also face severe punishment for even the possibility that they may have had an abortion, such as in the case of miscarriage. Women's lack of sexual autonomy is quite simply life-threatening.[26] Ruether was one of the signatories of the 1984 *New York Times* advertisement that said that there was a diversity of views on abortion and continues to be outspoken on the issue.[27]

---

[23]Pastoral Constitution on the Church in the Modern World, *Gaudium et Spes*, pars. 48–50. Available online: http://www.vatican.va/archive/hist_councils/ii_vatican_council/documents/vat-ii_const_19651207_gaudium-et-spes_en.html (accessed September 9, 2020).

[24]See Rosemary Radford Ruether, *Women-Church: Theology and Practice* (San Francisco: Harper and Row, 1985), 64–6.

[25]Ruether, *New Woman*, 196

[26]Note that the Rosemary Radford Ruether Award is given by the organization Catholics for Choice. See http://www.catholicsforchoice.org/2013-rosemary-radford-ruether-award-presented-to-cdd-peru-for-advancing-prochoice-catholicism/ (accessed September 9, 2020).

[27]See https://en.wikipedia.org/wiki/A_Catholic_Statement_on_Pluralism_and_Abortion (accessed September 9, 2020), which summarizes the *New York Times* ad in October 1984.

Christology and Mariology, while in many ways distinctive theological topics on their own, also have significant anthropological implications. As Ruether asks most pointedly in the title of one chapter of *Sexism and God-Talk*, "Can a Male Savior Save Women?," that God became human in the body of a man, Ruether notes, has come to take on the status of an "ontological necessity"; thus, women are unable to fully image God or to represent Christ at the altar.[28] Ruether does not see the role of Jesus as the "outside mediator who does the work of reconciliation for us" but rather as "the root story for the redemptive process in which we all must be engaged."[29] Quoting Mary Daly, who wrote "When God is Male, the Male is God," Ruether points out how the prophetic, inclusive ministry that Jesus exercised has been reshaped into that of Christ the "imperial" ruler, in whose name "patriarchy, hierarchy, slavery, and Graeco-Roman imperialism have all been taken over and baptized by the Christian Church."[30] The Jesus story, Ruether comments, "continues to be paradigmatic for Christian feminists" as it "exemplif[ies] the redemptive paradigm of feminist liberation" when all oppressive hierarchies will be overcome.[31] Androgynous Christologies have periodically emerged throughout Christian history, in which various mystical and marginalized groups have emphasized the feminine in Christ or even seen some women as the new incarnation of Christ. In different ways they express the inadequacy of a "masculinist" Christ and point toward a more adequate understanding of humanity that "renounce[s] this system of domination and seeks to embody in his person the new humanity of service and mutual empowerment."[32]

Mariology has been a frequent topic of Ruether's writing. In her earlier works *Mary the Feminine Face of the Church* and *New Woman New Earth*, she explains its ancient roots in goddess worship as well as the biblical sources that are the basis for Mary's role. For Ruether, Mary's significance is basically ecclesiological, as a model for the church, but Mary has been given an iconic role particularly for women as both virgin and mother. Ruether sees Mary's perpetual virginity as a "mythological or pictorial way of getting at this theological mystery of the gratuitous nature of salvation," showing how other Ancient Near Eastern religions also used virginity for theological purposes.[33] Mary functions theologically in a number of different ways. For the purposes of theological anthropology, Ruether sees Mary as representing the feminine face of God, serving as mediator between humanity and God, and as anticipating eschatological humanity in its redeemed state.[34] Mary can only be a "liberating symbol for women" when she is "freed from hierarchical power relations" and, as a symbol for the Church, represents "the reconciled wholeness of women and men."[35]

A final theological issue for Ruether is humanity's need for community and shared worship. In *Sexism and God-Talk*, Ruether takes on ministry and community and says that "it is essential to understand redemption as a communal, not just an individual, experience."[36] She develops this theology further in her 1985 book *Women-Church: Theology and*

---

[28]Rosemary Radford Ruether, *To Change the World: Christology and Cultural Criticism* (New York: Crossroad, 1981), 45–56.
[29]Ruether, *Women and Redemption*, 275.
[30]Ibid.
[31]Ibid., 277.
[32]Ibid.
[33]Rosemary Radford Ruether, "The Collision of History and Doctrine: The Brothers of Jesus and the Virginity of Mary," *Continuum* 7, no. 1 (Winter 1969): 93–105.
[34]Ruether, *New Woman*, chapter 2: "Mistress of Heaven: The Meaning of Mariology," 36–59.
[35]Ibid., 58–9.
[36]Ruether, *Sexism*, 193.

Practice. With the observation that "science has failed to provide a sufficiently satisfying substitute for religion as a vehicle of meaning," Ruether proposes a new understanding of church and a series of ritual practices that provide men and especially women avenues to celebrate significant life events, including those particular to women such as menarche and menopause.[37]

Despite the sexism and clericalism that pervades Christianity, Ruether argues against a wholesale exodus from the church. Women, she argues, have the prophetic obligation to speak out against the injustices perpetuated by a demonic all-male hierarchy. In a sermon that she includes in *Women-Church*, Ruether uses powerful and vivid language to expose the "great idol of patriarchy with its flashing eyes and smoking nostrils, its inhuman mechanical voice" declaring that "only the male represents perfect humanity."[38] This "nightmare" representation of the divine, she argues, "destroy[s] our humanity."[39] Instead, humanity—men and women alike—must recreate the church as Women-Church, "as we build together this new earth freed from the yoke of patriarchy."[40]

The official prohibition of women's ordination in the present is largely grounded in theo-anthropological arguments of sexual complementarity, although historically they were based in women's fundamental inferiority and subjugation to men. Ruether's opposition to this gendered classification of men and women is consistent over her career. She has long argued that it is not an issue of ordaining women into preexisting clerical structures but rather, as her colleague Elisabeth Schüssler Fiorenza has argued, that the entire clerical structure that elevates clergy over laity must be dismantled. Her egalitarian theological anthropology sees ministry as functional rather than as ontological and thus more inclusive of the entire community.[41]

In sum, Ruether's reworking of traditional theological doctrines emphasizes her focus on the "original sin" of sexism, women and men's equality before God, the distortions of traditional doctrinal formulations and the vision of a transformed and liberated humanity.

ESCHATOLOGY AND ECOLOGY

Ten years after *Sexism and God-Talk*, Ruether published *Gaia and God: An Ecofeminist Theology of Earth Healing*. In this book, she turns again to the human situation but now in the light of the ever-worsening ecological crisis. The eschatological dimension that has always been present in Ruether's work emerges as central given the dire situation in which humanity finds itself; one could say it is even more relevant in the over twenty-five years since the book was published. She writes that the goal of this work is "earth healing" and that this healing is not only between humanity and the ecosystem but also "between men and women, between classes and nations, and between humans and the earth."[42] In order for there to be healing, it is necessary to understand the roots of the present situation.

The interconnectedness of all forms of oppression, first developed in 1975 in *New Woman New Earth*, is central to *Gaia and God*. Ruether turns again to the classic

---

[37]Ruether, *Women-Church*, 1.

[38]Ibid., 70.

[39]Ibid.

[40]Ibid., 73.

[41]Ibid., 89.

[42]Rosemary Radford Ruether, *Gaia and God: An Ecofeminist Theology of Earth Healing* (San Francisco: HarperCollins, 1992), 1.

themes of creation, sin and redemption and reviews the complex history of humanity's estrangement from itself, from other human beings and from the earth. In relation to theological anthropology, Ruether focuses here especially on the heritage of the apostle Paul, and shows how his theology contains

> a profound dualism between two modes of existence: existence according to the "flesh," which he characterizes as a state of slavery to sin and death, and existence in the Spirit, which he sees as freeing the Christian, through their rebirth in Christ, both to virtuous and loving life and also to the promise of immortality.[43]

This dualism has pervaded Christianity ever since. Although Paul's spiritual heir Augustine rejected the Gnostic dualism that saw matter as evil, an idea to which he subscribed as a young man, and affirmed the goodness of all creation, nevertheless Ruether remarks that the "Platonic version of the anti-body, anti-material hierarchy" is still present in his writing, as noted above in relation to his theology of sexuality.[44] The result of this dualism has led to "an earth-fleeing ethic and spirituality" and, consequently, an avoidance of anything connected with death, hatred of women (as "birth givers") and the rejection of all that is connected with the finite as "alien." The response to these "mortal others," Ruether concludes, is "either conquest … or genocidal destruction."[45] Many of Ruether's works provide examples of this demonic and destructive war on all that represents material and finite reality.

Ruether is insistent that there needs to be a clear separation between "sin" and "finitude." Sin is a very real dimension of the human condition that, because of our free will, means that we can choose to enhance or stifle life. But finitude is simply a fact of material life and to deny it is basically to deny life itself. Because of its complicity with the idea that finitude is evil, Christianity bears much responsibility for the distorted relationships that have elevated human power over others and the earth.[46]

In both *New Woman New Earth* and *Gaia and God*, Ruether focuses on the dynamic of domination as the main obstacle to human liberation. In *New Woman New Earth*, she writes, "Women must see that there can be no liberation for them and no solution to the ecological crisis within a society whose fundamental mode of relationships continues to be domination."[47] Twenty-seven years later, she writes that "the search for an ecological culture and society seems to demand … an overcoming of the culture of competitive alienation and domination for compassionate solidarity."[48] For Ruether, the eschatological vision of human wholeness and healing will depend on a

> principle of equity: equity between men and women, between human groups living within regions; equity across human communities globally; equity between the human species and all other members of the biotic community of which we are a part; and finally equity between generations of living things, between the needs of those now alive and those who are to come.[49]

---

[43]Ibid., 127.
[44]Ibid., 135.
[45]Ibid., 140.
[46]Ibid., especially Part Three: "Domination and Deceit."
[47]Ruether, *New Woman*, 204.
[48]Ruether, *Gaia*, 201.
[49]Ibid., 258.

Ruether's vision of a transformed humanity includes the transformation of all relationships of domination and subordination.

GLOBAL AWARENESS

Throughout her career, Ruether has paid careful attention to what in the present is often termed "social location." While she is not afraid to make generalizations about the impact of religious teachings on women worldwide, especially concerning reproductive justice, she is sensitive to the issues that affect people in distinct ways, both within traditions, as in how Christianity is experienced in the global south differently than the global north, but also across religious traditions. Her theological anthropology is therefore also contextual. While acknowledging the validity of postmodern critiques of universalism, Ruether still appeals to what humans share. In *Religious Feminism and the Future of the Planet*, she writes, "We need a language that can affirm this deep commonality of humans as a species, while at the same time acknowledging and celebrating the multi-contextualization of this common potential in a great variety of cultural expressions."[50]

Ruether has spent considerable time both in Latin America and in Palestine, where the situations of oppressed groups have profoundly affected her thinking. She has learned Spanish, participated in many meetings, both of church groups and women's groups, and has taught and lectured around the world.[51] These experiences have profoundly informed her thinking and writing. She observes that patriarchy is found in all cultures and world religions and acknowledges the difficulty of critiquing another tradition from the outside.[52] But patriarchy is deeply intertwined with political, social and economic forms of oppression.

Ruether's global awareness includes a critical understanding of political systems of domination and the ways that they affect our understanding of humanity. Early in her career, she worked in the civil rights movement and taught at a historically black university; she has consistently spoken out against racism as well as neocolonialism. She has taken up the causes of anti-apartheid movements, Palestinian independence, reproductive rights for women especially in the global south and the evils of US political and military policies. Human rights are central to her understanding of humanity.

CONCLUSIONS

Ruether's theological anthropology is, on the one hand, clear and practical in its focus: the equal humanity of women and men, care for the earth and the overcoming of all that stands in the way of this equality. She envisions a transformed humanity where there are no more "male" and "female" qualities but rather "human" qualities in which individuals, families, nations and all living and nonliving creation can live in harmony. The Jewish and Christian traditions offer resources for this transformation through the prophetic

---

[50]Rita M. Gross and Rosemary Radford Ruether, *Religious Feminism and the Future of the Planet* (London: Bloomsbury Academic, 2016), 135.

[51]See Ruether's discussion of the 1979 CELAM meeting in "Consciousness-Raising at Puebla: Women Speak to the Latin Church," *Christianity and Crisis* (April 1, 1979): 77–80.

[52]See Ruether's "Conference Report: the World Parliament and Religious Diversity," *Feminist Theology* 26 (January 2001): 121–8.

principle of the Hebrew prophets, the liberating message of Jesus and the ongoing work of women and men throughout the centuries.

This vision of transformed humanity and the earth is also very complex. Systems of domination and oppression are deeply rooted in human history, maintained and distorted by religious and political traditions. Yet there remains a fundamental eschatological hope in Ruether's work. Her major books—*Sexism and God-Talk*, *Women-Church* and *Gaia and God*—all conclude with visions of what could be: the divine presence among us, a "patient passion," a world without weapons. This combination of a critical understanding of history, a passion for justice and a deep faith in the possibilities of the human person mark a deeply significant contribution to contemporary theological anthropology.

SUGGESTED FURTHER READING

Ruether, Rosemary Radford, *Disputed Questions: On Being a Christian* (Nashville, TN: Abingdon, 1982).

Ruether, Rosemary Radford, *Sexism and God-Talk: Toward a Feminist Theology* (Boston: Beacon Press, 1983).

Ruether, Rosemary Radford, *Gaia and God: An Ecofeminist Theology of Earth Healing* (San Francisco: HarperCollins, 1982).

Ruether, Rosemary Radford, "My Ecumenical and Interfaith Journey," *Journal of Ecumenical Studies* 49, no. 1 (2014): 159–65.

Silverman, Emily Leah, Dirk Von Der Horst and Whitney Bauman (eds.), *Voices of Feminist Liberation: Writings in Celebration of Rosemary Radford Ruether* (London: Taylor & Francis Group, 2014).

CHAPTER TWENTY-FOUR

Salving the Wound of Race: Racialized Bodies as Sacrament in the Theology of M. Shawn Copeland

KAREN TEEL

In 2018, Dr. M. Shawn Copeland honored the Catholic Theological Society of America by accepting its John Courtney Murray Award for Theology. This lifetime achievement award, reserved for extremely influential theologians and generally considered the highest honor in Catholic theology, has been given annually since 1972.[1] As an accomplished and quintessentially Catholic theologian—rooted in tradition, forward thinking, inclusive—Copeland was an obvious choice for the award. She was also its first black recipient. Moreover, she is the only African American theologian and one of only two women whose ideas are covered in this volume under the heading "Key Figures." These facts testify both to how far African American Catholics have come and to how far church and academy have still to go in nurturing and valuing their theological perspectives.

Raised in Detroit, Copeland earned her BA in English from Madonna College in Livonia, Michigan, in 1969 and her PhD in theology from Boston College in 1991. She taught at St. Norbert College, Yale University, and Marquette University before returning to teach at Boston College, where she retired as a full professor in 2019. She has served as president of the Catholic Theological Society of America, convener of the Black Catholic Theological Symposium and professor at Xavier University's Institute for Black Catholic Studies. Copeland's extensive corpus includes books and edited volumes, over one hundred academic articles and book chapters, presentations and lectures, popular publications and classroom teaching. Throughout her career, she has challenged the United States and the US Catholic Church to come to terms with our "structural historical amnesia" regarding our subjugation of nonwhite people.[2] Focusing on black women's struggle to survive in a

---

[1] From 1947 to 1971, prior to the institution of the John Courtney Murray Award, the Catholic Theological Society of America gave an annual "Cardinal Spellman Award for Theology." Murray himself received this award in its inaugural year. According to the organization's website, all save one of the recipients of the Cardinal Spellman Award were clergy. This reflects the historical reality that academic Catholic theology was the exclusive domain of white men until the 1960s. Monika K. Hellwig became the first white woman to win the John Courtney Murray Award in 1984, and Virgilio Elizondo became the first nonwhite awardee in 2007.

[2] M. Shawn Copeland, "Memory, #BlackLivesMatter, and Theologians," *Political Theology* 17, no. 1 (January 2016): 1–3 (1).

white supremacist society and church, Copeland advocates theologically for the right of all people to be valued as human beings deserving to flourish.

As a white theologian, I might be inclined to excuse myself from grappling with Copeland's insights regarding black women's bodies.[3] But I once heard Copeland say, during a professional meeting session when attendees were disputing the appropriateness of a particular question, that ultimately our concern should be not with disciplinary boundaries but with getting at the truth of the matter. And since the Incarnation is at the heart of Christianity, theology always refers finally to bodies. Copeland pushes us to confront the concrete and spiritual realities of bodies and their fates, to see their meanings illuminated in the eschatological context of death and resurrection, of Christ's body and other bodies. In the US context, racism implicates all of our bodies, such that theologians invested in the truth of the matter cannot responsibly defer difficult questions about it to others.[4]

Copeland models grappling with such questions by attending to how she personally is implicated in her work. For example, she frames an essay on Christology and discipleship by pondering the experience of watching another woman search through the trash for food.[5] She begins a lecture describing the expansion of the scope of her theological anthropology to include creation beyond human beings by stating, "I am no environmentalist, although I begin to understand that I must become one."[6] She bookends her monograph *Enfleshing Freedom* with meditations on her personal investment in her topic as a "theologian of the black experience."[7] Copeland's commitment prompts me to take responsibility for my own work, perhaps vocation, as a "theologian of the white experience." What would it look like to engage in constructive theological reflection on white bodies?

In *Enfleshing Freedom*, Copeland "tak[es] black women's bodies as a prism" to illuminate "the theological anthropological relationship between the social body and the physical body."[8] At the risk of oversimplification, one may say that the 'social body' is the body as seen by others, while the 'physical body' is the material body itself with its needs and desires, pains and pleasures. In the United States, white people tend to experience our social and physical bodies as continuous. We see ourselves as unique and dignified individuals whose basic needs deserve to be met, and for the most part, so does society. Black people, however, experience a disconnect: they likewise know themselves to be unique and dignified individuals, but society, traditionally characterized by antiblack racism, has not regarded them as such and is unconcerned with meeting their basic needs.[9] In other words, although white people commonly think of white supremacy

---

[3]Throughout my scholarly writing, I speak in the first person. Explicit self-awareness, though traditionally devalued in Western thought, is becoming increasingly common among scholars—including Copeland—who realize that "genuine objectivity is the fruit of authentic subjectivity" (Bernard J. F. Lonergan, *Method in Theology* (Toronto: University of Toronto Press, 1971), 292). In writing about race while racialized as white, I use this practice to acknowledge my own participation in and responsibility for white supremacy, as well as to invite white readers to adopt a similarly self-critical stance.

[4]See M. Shawn Copeland, "Racism and the Vocation of the Theologian," *Spiritus* 2, no. 1 (Spring 2002): 15–29.

[5]M. Shawn Copeland, "The Cross of Christ and Discipleship," in *Thinking of Christ: Proclamation, Explanation, Meaning*, ed. Tatha Wiley (New York: Continuum, 2003), 177–92.

[6]M. Shawn Copeland, "God among the Ruins: Companion and Co-Sufferer," in *Violence, Transformation, and the Sacred: "They Shall Be Called Children of God,"* ed. Margaret R. Pfeil and Tobias L. Winright (Maryknoll, NY: Orbis, 2012), 15–29.

[7]M. Shawn Copeland, *Enfleshing Freedom: Body, Race, and Being* (Minneapolis: Fortress, 2010), 130.

[8]Ibid., 8.

[9]Many thinkers have theorized this disconnect, which W. E. B. Du Bois famously termed "double consciousness" in *The Souls of Black Folk* (London: Penguin, 1989 (A. C. McClurg & Company, 1903)). See

as extremism, it is more productive to define and address it as the foundation of US society. The outward structure of this social system has changed over time: from slavery, to segregation and lynching, to what cultural critic Ta-Nehisi Coates has called "elegant racism."[10] Yet it consistently preserves the racial hierarchy that Europeans established during the colonial period to build white wealth and power. Thus, white supremacy is a system that perpetuates white domination and its routine devaluation of black lives. In this context, Copeland's insight into the sacramental character of black women's embodied struggle for freedom raises the question: Can white bodies, invested as they are with oppressive power, bear positive meaning?

I proceed in three parts. First, I consider a central contention of Copeland's theological anthropology, namely, that black women's embodied struggle for freedom constitutes a sacrament. Second, I explore how Copeland's ideas help to clarify distinctions among the categories of skin color difference, cultural difference and racial difference. Third, I maintain that Copeland lays the groundwork for a theological understanding of race— not skin color or culture, but race—as wounding. I raise a "difficult [and] precarious"[11] question about the theological significance of white bodies: in the context of white supremacy, where black women's struggling bodies reveal God's presence, what do relatively easeful white bodies represent? Insofar as white bodies function to perpetrate and perpetuate white supremacy, contemplating this question may prove painful. I take courage in Copeland's conviction that *all* are called to Eucharistic solidarity.[12]

BLACK WOMEN'S BODIES

In its fullest articulation in *Enfleshing Freedom*, Copeland's theological anthropology may be summarized in this way: *Black women's bodies struggling for freedom against the dehumanizing forces of empire reveal God's own presence among and desire for us, thereby constituting a human sacrament.* In what follows, I describe and reflect upon the themes embedded in this brief summary, including empire, bodies, struggle, freedom and sacrament.

Merriam-Webster's definition of "empire" refers to unequal power relationships among political units such as nations, and to "imperial sovereignty, rule, or dominion."[13] Empire is a political, social, economic and ecclesial system in which those in power deem some bodies, typically their own bodies, to matter more than others. In particular, the United States has been and remains an empire in which white bodies control, oppress and exploit other bodies.

For Copeland, bodies cannot be considered theologically apart from empire. Moreover, what happens to bodies under empire's dehumanizing conditions is inextricably linked with the realm of spirit. These material and spiritual dimensions of empire demand a

---

also Frantz Fanon, *Black Skin, White Masks*, revised edition, trans. Richard Philcox (New York: Grove, 2008); and George Yancy, *Black Bodies, White Gazes: The Continuing Significance of Race* (Lanham, MD: Rowman & Littlefield, 2008).

[10]Ta-Nehisi Coates, "This Town Needs a Better Class of Racist," *The Atlantic*, May 1, 2014. Available online: https://www.theatlantic.com/politics/archive/2014/05/This-Town-Needs-A-Better-Class-Of-Racist/361443/ (accessed July 17, 2019).

[11]Copeland, *Enfleshing Freedom*, 2.

[12]Ibid., 126–8.

[13]https://www.merriam-webster.com/dictionary/empire.

theological response. "Given the location and conditions of bodies in empire ... above all, [Jesus'] body broken and resurrected for us, theological anthropology can never cease speaking of bodies."[14]

Copeland's foregrounding of empire as the context for theological anthropology is methodologically innovative. Conventional "Western" Christian theological anthropology has tended to presume the reality of empire. It has considered the person as primarily individual rather than social and has contemplated spirit and body separately, the Incarnation notwithstanding. Ancient Christian thinkers[15] deemed the soul or spirit as higher than the body because for them the soul resembled God, defined as transcendent spirit, while the body's materiality was shared with animals. Appealing to Genesis, they saw animals as subject to humans in the order of creation, interpreted as hierarchical. Colonial Europeans extended this hierarchy to position their own pale-skinned (European, or "white") bodies above dark-skinned (African, or "black") bodies. This impulse to domination led Europeans to create the modern idea of race, in which they imagined "racial" characteristics including skin color, shape of facial features and hair texture to indicate degrees of humanity and of the *imago Dei*. This means that race in the modern sense is a creation of empire, a tool of domination: specifically, European and Euro-American or "white" domination over Africans and other nonwhites. In short, modern empire has taken the form of white supremacy.[16] This is necessary context for contemporary theological anthropology.

As Copeland notes, we are so accustomed to the racial categories that colonial Europeans created that they seem like common sense.[17] Yet they were established arbitrarily. For example, in the United States, people with a dark skin tone can be categorized as "black"; meanwhile, blue-eyed people—who may have either light or dark skin—are never categorized as a race. Race was based, not on genetic groupings, but on select physical characteristics. Having designated these characteristics as "racial," Europeans imposed rankings, placing themselves on top, creating division and hierarchy so as to maintain and justify control of Africans and others.[18] Race could have been conceived to put people with black skin at the top and white skin at the bottom. But it wasn't. And Copeland demands that we contend with the concrete historical reality within whose imperial legacy we still live, in which white bodies oppress nonwhite bodies; male bodies oppress female bodies; straight bodies oppress queer bodies.[19]

---

[14]Copeland, *Enfleshing Freedom*, 57.

[15]We often claim "classical" thinkers as part of "Western" (European) tradition, even though Asians and Africans including Gregory of Nyssa and Augustine of Hippo (two of three ancient "key figures" covered in this volume) largely drove its development in its early centuries.

[16]Readers interested in the theological implications of this history may wish to consult Kelly Brown Douglas, *What's Faith Got to Do with It? Black Bodies/Christian Souls* (Maryknoll, NY: Orbis, 2005); J. Kameron Carter, *Race: A Theological Account* (Oxford: Oxford University Press, 2008); Willie James Jennings, *The Christian Imagination: Theology and the Origins of Race* (New Haven, CT: Yale University Press, 2010).

[17]Copeland, *Enfleshing Freedom*, 9.

[18]For one historian's account of this process, see Rebecca Anne Goetz, *The Baptism of Early Virginia: How Christianity Created Race* (Baltimore: Johns Hopkins University Press, 2012).

[19]Copeland proposes "queering the body of Christ" in *Enfleshing Freedom*, chapter 3, and honors the queer roots of the Black Lives Matter movement in "Memory, #BlackLivesMatter, and Theologians." In 2015, Pamela Lightsey identified Copeland as one of only two womanist theologians who had treated LGBTQ sexuality in depth in a monograph (Pamela R. Lightsey, *Our Lives Matter: A Womanist Queer Theology* (Eugene, OR: Pickwick, 2015), 3). Doing so remains controversial. In 2017, an invited lecture to be given by Copeland at her alma mater, Madonna University, was canceled after right-wing Catholic militants objected to this theme in her work, though it was not to have been the lecture's topic.

In this context, black women's experiences have been characterized by struggle. Copeland details how, during slavery, black women were exploited as objects of property, production, reproduction and sexual violence.[20] Enslavers forbade black women to own their bodies, to enjoy the fruits of their labors, to raise their children. Black women endured sexual abuse from white men while white women looked the other way. Through all this black women resisted however they could: by running away, learning to read, talking back and gathering secretly to pray.[21] Though many individuals did not survive enslavement, black people collectively never lost sight of their humanity, holding onto the hope that their children or grandchildren would someday be free. For Copeland, black women's unwavering vision of and struggle for freedom represents a specific, concrete example, lived out in history, of what it means to be truly human.[22] "The black struggle for authenticity is coincident with the human struggle to *be* human and reveals *black-human-being* as a particular incarnation of universal finite human being."[23]

In describing black women's struggle against empire as an enfleshment of freedom, Copeland reveals their bodies as sacred. As enslaved black people knew, and as black theology formally argues, a major theme in the Bible—from Exodus to Incarnation—is that God desires and actively works toward the liberation of people who are oppressed.[24] For Copeland, black women's embodied struggle for freedom is "immanent self-transcendence in act."[25] She explains, "The body is the medium through which the person as essential freedom achieves and realizes selfhood through communion with other embodied selves."[26] In a world characterized by injustice—not in the abstract where all are potentially culpable, but the concrete injustice of white supremacy and antiblack racism—the freedom-seeking black body emerges as sacred, enacting God's will for humanity. Black women's embodied struggle against empire is "a site of divine revelation and, thus … a 'basic human sacrament.'"[27] A sacrament reveals the presence of God, and black women's struggle for freedom constitutes an affirmation of human dignity that is nothing less than an authentic expression of the *imago Dei*.

Charges of essentialism or identity politics are often levied against thinkers suspected of prioritizing one aspect (e.g., the body) or way (e.g., a particular racial/ethnic group or gender) of being human over others. By focusing specifically on black women's bodies, however, Copeland appeals to the particular precisely to get at the universal. First, we cannot dissociate our spiritual/rational selves from our bodies. "The body is no mere object—*already-out-there-now*—with which we are confronted: always the body is with us, inseparable from us, *is* us."[28] Human personhood cannot be reduced to the material body, yet to disregard bodies is to disregard human beings. A theological anthropology that does so loses its moorings, floating free of reality.

---

[20]Copeland, *Enfleshing Freedom*, 29–38.

[21]Ibid., 38–46.

[22]Ibid., 46–51.

[23]Ibid., 21. Emphasis original.

[24]See, for example, James H. Cone, *A Black Theology of Liberation, Twentieth Anniversary Edition* (Maryknoll, NY: Orbis, 1990), chapter 3.

[25]Copeland, *Enfleshing Freedom*, 8.

[26]Ibid., 24.

[27]Ibid.

[28]Ibid., 7. Emphasis original.

Second, the particular and the universal are inextricably connected. Attending to black women's bodies keeps us rooted in history, where we actually are, and prevents an escape into abstraction. It also connects us to what is universally human and highlights the transcendent and indissoluble unity of body and spirit.[29] Black women's struggle establishes a concrete starting point from which to illuminate truth about all our experiences, which are deeply interconnected.

Third, then, inquiring into the lived experiences of black women prompts inquiry about other relevant bodies. If black women struggle in particular ways, do black men struggle similarly? How do people racially categorized as neither white nor black negotiate the realities of racialization? And how is the relative ease with which white people navigate empire connected to the struggles of black and other nonwhite people, in the United States and beyond? Is our comfort predicated upon their struggles? If wielding unjust imperial power dehumanizes us, then how can we join in solidarity against the forces of empire? Attending to black women's bodies, it becomes possible and necessary to affirm all bodies.

In Copeland's analysis, all bodies are marked by empire, specifically by "race, sex and gender, sexuality, and culture."[30] Visible signs of having suffered oppression are often easiest to see. In our context, black bodies, indigenous bodies, LGBTQ bodies and more are devalued.[31] In his own time, Copeland notes, Jesus' body too was marked by "race, gender, sex, sexuality, culture, and religion."[32] And Jesus' body was marked literally by crucifixion, state-sponsored execution. In any era, then, Copeland argues, suffering bodies reveal Christ's body among us. "The body of Jesus of Nazareth impels us to place the bodies of the victims of history at the center of theological anthropology."[33] As a "theologian of the white experience," I suspect that white people need to ponder the marks of empire on black women's and others' bodies in order to discern empire's marks on our own bodies.

SKIN COLOR, CULTURE AND RACE

Given Copeland's theological reflections on black women's bodies, what is the significance of white bodies? Before addressing this question, I want to build on Copeland's anthropology to clarify distinctions among three types of difference that are often conflated: skin color differences, cultural differences and racial differences. Reflecting on these distinctions evokes questions for me as a theologian of the white experience, which I note but do not necessarily answer, and lays the groundwork for interpreting race as wounding.

Skin Color Differences

Despite several hundred years of European and Euro-American insistence on using skin color to organize society, skin color does not correlate with human ability, value or worth. Scientists now agree that skin color represents the level of melanin in the skin and that

[29]Ibid., 8.
[30]Ibid., 56.
[31]Copeland, "Memory, #BlackLivesMatter, and Theologians," 2.
[32]Copeland, Enfleshing Freedom, 83.
[33]Ibid., 84.

differing levels of melanin are the result of human migration and adaptation to various climates across the planet since our common origin in Africa. Historian Nell Irvin Painter notes, "Today's biologists concur [that] sunny climates do make people dark-skinned, and dark, cold climates make people light-skinned."[34] Moreover, a recent study shows that genes for a whole range of skin tones, from light to dark, have existed in Africans since before the human race evolved. If white people's light skin is an inheritance from our African origins, then it makes no sense to interpret it as evidence of evolutionary superiority.[35] Skin color, like other "racial" differences, is truly superficial, *on the surface.*

Intending to honor the superficiality of skin color differences and to avoid discriminating because of them, many US Americans—especially white people—attempt to be "colorblind." We try to ignore skin color and "see everyone the same." While the "colorblind" impulse is often well-intentioned, studies show that it doesn't work: we are so thoroughly conditioned to notice skin color that we do so unconsciously.[36] Moreover, skin color is simply a salient feature of human beings. Children who notice skin color may be startled when their curiosity upsets adults who think they have noticed race. Not noticing skin color is not an option.

Fortunately, "colorblindness" is not the only possible response. The fact that skin color differences are superficial does not mean that it is bad to notice them. The problem is using them to judge human worth. Historically, Europeans viewed skin color differences as cause for mistrust, hate and fear. We can choose to see them as beautiful manifestations of human diversity and let them draw us toward one another rather than divide us. This requires work, but transforming our perspective may be more realistic than trying to ignore it.

Copeland argues that such transformation is not only desirable but necessary for its own sake. As a response to the continuing injustices of a society built on disdain for and destruction of black bodies, ignoring skin color is totally inadequate. Dark skin color is natural, and for their own mental health and self-respect, black people must be able to affirm unapologetically that "black is beautiful."[37] As part of the process of relinquishing deeply rooted and often subconscious attitudes of domination, white people must also learn to rejoice in the beauty of skin color differences and to affirm sincerely that "black is beautiful."

Trying not to notice skin color is also theologically unnecessary. Christian belief in the Trinity holds that within the one God, there is diversity. These three persons, commonly referred to as Father, Son and Spirit, are all truly God, yet truly distinct, so "humanity in its diversity is a reflection of the community of the Three Divine Persons."[38] Skin color differences, then, may be seen as reflecting God's diversity. Appreciated as part of the *imago Dei*, they can evoke wonder and positive enjoyment.[39] Exploring the possibility of an anti-racist sexual ethics, theologian Bryan Massingale argues that "racialized sexuality is not inherently problematic ... it need not always be a negative factor in human relationships.

---

[34]Nell Irvin Painter, *The History of White People* (New York: W. W. Norton, 2010), 394.

[35]Nicholas G. Crawford et al., "Loci Associated with Skin Pigmentation Identified in African Populations," *Science* 358, no. 6365 (7 Nov 2017). DOI: 10.1126/science.aan8433.

[36]Studies show that implicit bias is pervasive and difficult to correct. Copeland discusses Eduardo Bonilla-Silva's work on "colorblind racism" in *Enfleshing Freedom*, 68–73.

[37]Ibid., 15–18.

[38]Ibid., 104.

[39]Bryan N. Massingale, "The Erotic Life of Anti-Blackness," in *Anti-Blackness and Christian Ethics*, ed. Vincent W. Lloyd and Andrew Prevot (Maryknoll, NY: Orbis, 2017), 173–94 (192).

At times, it can have a benign character."[40] He proposes that "developing what might be called 'the racially erotic Trinity'" could help to facilitate "racialized persons' ability to love themselves and others through erotic love."[41] Alice Walker beautifully expresses a vision of skin color difference as something to celebrate when she imagines a child asking, "Mama, why are we brown, pink, and yellow, and our cousins are white, beige, and black?" The mother responds, "Well, you know the colored race is like a flower garden, with every color flower represented."[42] Though some of this variation has resulted from violence, people themselves are invariably beautiful, dignified, *imago Dei*.

How can white people practice appreciating rather than fearing skin colors different from our own? How shall we learn to see black as normal and beautiful, rather than as strange, exotic or terrifying? Can we see our own white skin as beautiful without seeing it as better, without reinforcing our historical sense that whiteness was divinely ordained to domination?

Cultural Differences

Like skin colors, cultures—language, foodways, values, philosophies, religions, music and so on—existed prior to the invention of race. Historically, because of geography, cultures usually included people with similar skin tones. But skin color does not always correlate with cultural identity. As intercultural adoptions and mixed-race children amply demonstrate, any person with any skin color can be raised as a "native" of any culture. While cultural identity shapes the world as we know it, it is not genetically determined. Culture is not inborn but learned.

Virtually all people possess what Western culture calls "reason," and each culture has an internal logic that makes sense to its members. Because we often judge cultures different from our own as less reasonable—"cultureblindness" being a less common aspiration than "colorblindness"—interpersonal and intergroup conflict regularly arises. As with skin color, colonial Europeans assumed that cultural difference, especially dissimilarity or resistance to Europeanness, signaled inferiority or unreasonableness. Yet Copeland's explication of black women's struggle for freedom, a struggle simultaneously necessitated and disparaged by white culture, suggests that we ought to approach unfamiliar cultures with curiosity rather than suspicion. Learning why certain practices or beliefs make sense makes it harder to be dismissive or judgmental. As with skin color differences, then, noticing cultural differences is not bad. Intercultural exchanges can lead to mutual learning in which all participants increase their knowledge and self-understanding.

When conflict arises, however, adjudicating among cultural differences becomes necessary. This process may be complicated by the fact that some cultural characteristics are a direct or indirect result of race; some differences between black and white US cultures originate in the clash between the white drive for domination and the black struggle for freedom. Massingale argues that while black culture is characterized by struggle against white supremacy, white culture is characterized by a feeling of normalcy.[43] In a vacuum, struggling for justice and feeling normal can both be positive. But, Copeland reminds us, we cannot consider cultural differences outside historical context. There is no vacuum.

[40]Ibid., 176.

[41]Ibid., 192.

[42]Alice Walker, *In Search of Our Mothers' Gardens* (Orlando, FL: Harcourt, 1983), xi.

[43]Bryan N. Massingale, *Racial Justice and the Catholic Church* (Maryknoll, NY: Orbis, 2010), chapter 1.

And in context, cultural traits function positively or negatively. If white supremacy is wrong, then resisting through struggle is good, and monopolizing power through the normalization of whiteness is bad. The black struggle for freedom affirms life, while the white sense of normalcy perpetuates dominance. So while all cultures possess admirable qualities and produce admirable individuals, cultural differences cannot always be uncritically celebrated.

How can people raised in culturally white homes and communities learn about and appreciate nonwhite cultures? Can we do so without simply engaging in misappropriation or cultural tourism? What is white culture, and which of its elements—if any—should be passed on to future generations? Can white people interrogate our cultural traits that historically supported domination, let go of some and redirect others to life-giving ends?

Racial Differences

Having clarified that skin color is superficial but not meaningless, and that cultural differences are not inherently problematic but have traits that can function positively or negatively in context, we arrive at the question of race. Skin color is so closely wedded to race that it may seem hopeless, even dangerous, to try to separate them. In attempting to do so, I do not advocate "colorblindness," nor do I think US society can become "postracial"; as a sociopolitical system, race is firmly entrenched. Also, I realize that the category of "race" holds positive meaning for some nonwhite people; as I define it, this more closely resembles "culture." Although Copeland does not emphasize the distinction between skin color and race, I do so here, as a reasonable move based on her work, in order to critique race as a visual system of categorization. I hope that, as individuals relating to individuals, we can start to notice how we conflate race with skin color and begin to interrupt this racial vision, even as we continue to confront the overwhelming social, political, economic and ecclesial power of race. This small yet significant step might ever so slightly weaken the stranglehold that the ideology of race has on us.

To review, the modern notion of race was socially constructed, dividing humans into groups according to an ideology of superiority.[44] Race was born, not from a generic dislike or distrust of "others" being exhibited by all human groups in roughly the same way, but from European Christians' desire to dominate non-Europeans, rationalized as natural order and divine mandate. Europeans arbitrarily designated certain physical features, especially skin color, as signifying racial differences and used them to rank the relative values of human beings according to a social hierarchy that they had already established. The notion of race provided conceptual and spiritual justification for white domination. In this sense, as Coates puts it, "race is the child of racism, not the father."[45]

Race does not apply only to people of color. Racism racializes everyone. Whiteness was originally imagined not as racelessness but as the prototypical race, to be protected from blackness. As racial identities, whiteness and blackness mean nothing without each other. This is true even though light and dark skin colors exist independently; individually, a person's skin has a color but not a race. Racism associates race so closely with skin color that they seem indistinguishable, but they are not the same. Pretending to be about individual skin colors, race really invokes the difference between two or more skin colors,

---

[44]For Copeland's account of race, see *Enfleshing Freedom*, chapter 1.
[45]Ta-Nehisi Coates, *Between the World and Me* (New York: Spiegel & Grau, 2015), 7.

which vanishes when we take them on their own. Race racializes everyone in relation to everyone else, or no one at all.

Another key difference between race and skin color is that skin color is there to be seen, while race is created by the person seeing it. This usually hidden process comes into view when we allow ourselves to notice it. Imagine, for example, that one sees a person who initially appears to be white, or racially ambiguous. If one is informed that the person has a black parent or grandparent, one may find (to one's surprise, or not) that the person's blackness suddenly appears! As if by magic, curly hair or olive skin becomes African rather than, say, Italian. Even if the person grew up in a culturally white environment, one may still think that this person is "really" black. The person's features and cultural identity remain the same; it is one's seeing that racializes them. This *is* magic—the magic of white supremacy.[46] Empire trains our vision to create race and to categorize according to the system. Race isn't there until we "see" it. Its arbitrariness is exposed by the fact that we "see" a person with one black ancestor as black, but we do not "see" a person with one white ancestor as white. That race is an invented category lacking concrete substance, its connection to skin color being spurious, does not diminish its power to shape our perceptions in the slightest—unless we catch ourselves creating it.

It is also essential to distinguish race from culture. Both skin color and culture, which can be value-neutral and function positively, existed before the European notion of race arose, and both would continue if race declined. Racism and racial difference are tools of empire, created for domination, and they should be questioned. Learning to notice that we "see" race, when what we really see is skin color, hair texture and facial features, can be a place to begin.

When we distinguish among skin color, culture and race, what does doing so reveal? If bodies racialized as black, struggling for freedom, are a "basic human sacrament," then do bodies racialized as white, relatively easeful and complacent, represent the need to resist oppression? Can we interpret racial whiteness in this way without further reifying race and without dismissing the inherent dignity of, or appearing to condone violence against, human beings with light skin color?

RACE AS WOUNDING

Racism dehumanizes everyone. Just as people with dark skin and cultural blackness cannot be reduced to the racial blackness to which society assigns them, people with light skin and cultural whiteness cannot be reduced to the racial whiteness to which society assigns us. Race's effects on blacks and whites are not the same, yet we all bear the legacy of domination. As Copeland asserts, "The Atlantic slave trade wounded the very body of Africa"; slavery and racism have wounded not only individual victims but "the body of a people."[47] Racial vision distorts the humanity of black bodies by marking them for subjugation. As a "theologian of the white experience," I propose to extend Copeland's insight that racial vision also harms whites. Specifically, I argue that white people should regard race as wounding insofar as it distorts the humanity of our bodies by marking them for domination. This wound will not heal itself.

---

[46]For an argument framing white supremacy as trickery, see Jeannine Hill Fletcher's *The Sin of White Supremacy: Christianity, Racism, & Religious Diversity in America* (Maryknoll, NY: Orbis, 2017), in which she adopts James Perkinson's phrase "the witchcraft of white supremacy."

[47]Copeland, *Enfleshing Freedom*, 110.

A wound is an injury, damage to a body, by accident or by design. The wound of race was inflicted deliberately, and racial inequalities continue to shape our society. The detrimental effects on nonwhites are discussed more often, perhaps because they are easier to measure: stress and other health problems, shorter lifespans, higher infant mortality rates, underemployment, wealth deprivation, diminished access to housing, police killing and sexual violation of black bodies, educational inequities and so on. Though less often noticed, the overprivileging of white bodies also wounds. When police crack down on communities of color but let us off easy—for example, by winking at illegal drug use— our sense that we are above the law is strengthened and our inability to relate to those who feel its full force diminished. When our schools fail to enroll or nurture nonwhite students, we grow up ignorant of their cultures, and society's failure to cultivate the talents of whole groups of people results in workforce impoverishment. Having been taught to prefer people who "look like us," we maintain segregated social networks that deprive us of potential friends and family members, people we might love but never get to know. Race wounds our vision so that we cannot truly see one another—or even ourselves.

Along these lines, Copeland asserts, "The privileged members [of society] not only damage themselves by resisting the invitation to self-transcendence; by interrupting human intersubjective spontaneity they inflict incalculable harm on 'others.'"[48] In "a white, racially bias-induced horizon" that reduces black bodies to skin color and confuses them with one another, white bodies endure excessive individualism, isolation and fragmentation.[49] Because of racism, Copeland explains, white people cannot see those unlike ourselves; denying our emotions, we become emotionally stunted; due to "suppression of unwanted insights of self-knowledge in everyday life," we fail to know ourselves; we "resist the invitation to self-transcendence," refusing opportunities to grow; we "project personal inadequacies onto members of non-privileged racial groups," cultivating dishonesty; becoming physically or otherwise violent through participating in a system that subjugates nonwhite people, we "inflict incalculable harm on others."[50] Artificially inflating our human dignity in relation to others' precludes authentic relationships with nonwhites and distorts our relationships with other whites. As a racial category, whiteness represents the triumph of bias, failure to transcend the self and care about "others," and actively harming the self and "others." As part of the foundation of US society, whiteness will not change unless we actively resist it.

Confronting empire, Copeland proposes the Eucharist as a site of solidarity. To accomplish this will be difficult. Wounded by power, white people have betrayed Jesus and the Eucharist. As Copeland observes, "Slavery sought to displace God, and, thus, it blasphemed."[51] Indeed, to consume the broken body of Jesus in the Eucharist while breaking and abusing other human bodies was blasphemy. More than this, it was idolatry. Commodifying, coveting and exploiting blackness and the profits it generated, whites deployed the power of empire to consume black bodies in place of Christ's body. The wounds of racial division—whiteness and blackness—persist, and in this context, racially white bodies represent supremacy. Where black women's bodies represent struggle, white bodies represent oppression. As racially white, white bodies correspond to the bodies of

---

[48]Ibid., 14.
[49]Ibid., 16–17.
[50]Ibid., 13–14.
[51]Ibid., 24.

those who "racialized, shattered, and lynched" Jesus.[52] Surely, *as racially white*, white bodies normally do not constitute a sacrament.

But if race and skin color are distinct, we may still ask about bodies with white skin. Thinking with Copeland, we may wonder: Do white bodies ever join in the black struggle for freedom and pay the ultimate price? Since whiteness confers advantages and masquerades as normalcy, white people rarely resist our racialization. Though we suffer under empire in other ways, as casualties of empire's destruction of black bodies our numbers are miniscule, at most a footnote to the long history of resistance. Still, we may consider Elijah Lovejoy (1802–1837), a journalist who died defending his right to publish abolitionist views in Alton, Illinois. Or Andrew Goodman (1943–1964) and Michael Schwerner (1939–1964), lynched along with James Chaney (1943–1964) for registering black voters in Mississippi. Or Viola Liuzzo (1926–1965), a housewife and activist targeted by the Ku Klux Klan for supporting the Selma-to-Montgomery march. Or Heather Heyer (1985–2017), a paralegal killed protesting a white supremacist rally in Charlottesville, Virginia. Struggling for freedom against the dehumanizing forces of empire, exchanging wounds of racial domination for wounds of racial solidarity, perhaps these and other white bodies may be rendered a sacrament. These dangerous memories[53] may salve the wound of race and reveal one possible path to Eucharistic solidarity, which "mandates us to shoulder our responsibility to the past in the here-and-now in memory of the crucified Christ and all the victims of history."[54]

SUGGESTED FURTHER READING

Lightsey, Pamela, *Our Lives Matter: A Womanist Queer Theology* (Eugene, OR: Pickwick, 2015).

Massingale, Bryan N., "Has the Silence Been Broken? Catholic Theological Ethics and Racial Justice," *Theological Studies* 75, no. 1 (2014): 133–55.

Pramuk, Christopher, "Living in the Master's House: Race and Rhetoric in the Theology of M. Shawn Copeland," *Horizons* 32, no. 2 (2005): 295–331.

Saracino, Michele, and Robert J. Rivera (eds.), *Enfleshing Theology: Embodiment, Discipleship, and Politics in the Work of M. Shawn Copeland* (Lanham, MD: Lexington, 2018).

Teel, Karen, *Racism and the Image of God* (New York: Palgrave Macmillan, 2010).

---

[52]Copeland, "Memory, #BlackLivesMatter, and Theologians," 1.
[53]Copeland, *Enfleshing Freedom*, 28–9, 126.
[54]Ibid., 101.

CHAPTER TWENTY-FIVE

Toward Understanding the Contextual Theo-Ethical Anthropology of Orlando Espín

NÉSTOR MEDINA

INTRODUCTION

The underlying theo-ethical anthropological vision in Latino theologian Orlando Espín's work imagines being human and humanness as encompassing all aspects of life in light of its everyday context.[1] Humanness, the quality and character of being human, he claims, is contextually constructed; a theoethics of humanness must therefore take into consideration the intersecting historical, cultural, popular religious, social and pneumatological factors at work as people live their lives.

Though he has not specifically written a theology of being human or ethics of humanness, in Espín's writings there is an underlying operative anthropology. Among the multiple other themes he engages in his theological corpus (traditioning, popular Catholicism, Guadalupe, Grace, culture, etc.), his work is peppered with affirmations and implications for a theoethics of humanness. Since Espín has not written an all-out exploration on being human and humanness, it is of course difficult to speak of "Orlando Espín's theo-ethical anthropology." There is no one source that can guide us, and sometimes there are internal tensions that complicate such endeavor.

As someone who follows his work quite closely, I would argue that the very elusiveness of his theo-ethical anthropology is a strength rather than a weakness. The elusive, provocative, disruptive, and "non-systematic" nature of his anthropology corresponds

---

[1] Orlando Espín is Professor of Systematic Theology in the Department of Theology and Religious Studies at the University of San Diego. He has served twice as president of the Academy of Catholic Hispanic Theologians of the United States, of which he is one of its founders. He has also served on the boards of the Catholic Society of America and of the Hispanic Summer Program in Religion and Theology. Orlando Espín is also one of the founders of Latina/o Theology and his contributions have shaped its development. For his many contributions to theology he received the "John Courtney Murray Award" from the Catholic Society of America, which is the highest and most prestigious recognition for a Catholic theologian in the United States of America.

to his own affirmations concerning his own understanding of the contextual nature of humanness. In great part, his theoethics stems from and remains grounded in the communities of faith of which he is part, and the community of scholars with whom he actively interacts.

Morever, Espín conceptualization of humanness is so entrenched in his overall project that one must uncover his methodological moves in order to more clearly discern his operative understanding of humanness.

Espín's work is irreducible to a single methodological thread that could provide the "secret code" for understanding his theo-ethical imagination. For this reason, my intention here is to tease out key categories, themes and theo-ethical implications that run through his work and that help us in imagining what his theology of being human and ethics of humanness would be.

HUMANNESS: BASIC STARTING POINTS

Espín argues without equivocation that humanness is constructed contextually. It is not something that theologians create as part of abstract reflection. The role of theologians and ethicists is to discern that which takes place on the ground as people live and express their faith and interact with each other at the level of the everyday. His entire theo-ethical vision is a categorical critique and rejection of perspectives that fail to include the social, cultural and historical context as constitutive elements of any theo-ethical considerations of humanness. For Espín, there is no such thing as a perfect abstract ideal or social humanity that we all share. *Humanitas* has never been generic or uniform; it is but "the intersection of specific, living, and diverse contextualizations."[2]

Espín never defines humanness or the human. In my view, his refusal to define it works together with his insistence on the constructed and contextual nature of humanness. To define it means to create a theoretical straight jacket that disallows the kind of openness he envisions by taking contextuality as essential part of humanness. Herein lies the foundation of Espín's anthropology: it affirms that humanness is not an abstraction in the world of ideas but is rather alive and manifest in and through real-life humans and cultural communities.[3] This affirmation of the fundamental contextuality of being human functions in Espín as an axis around which his other notions in relation to being human must be understood. Let us consider three key implications which stem from this contextuality as he understands it: humanness includes diverse ways of being human (diversity), it encompasses a multiplicity of religious traditions (interreligiousness) and it includes the presence of the global population (ecumenicity and catholicity).

Diversity

Precisely because he does not see humanness as uniform, Espín envisions a humanity in all its rich diversity. The interaction between people marks the encounter of racialized, gendered, classed, sexualized individuals, including those considered subhuman or

---

[2]Orlando O. Espín, *Grace and Humanness: Theological Reflections Because of Culture* (Maryknoll, NY: Orbis Books, 2007), 53.
[3]Ibid.

nonhuman. For the same reason, diverse processes of contextualization contribute to the emergence of diverse permutations of being human, all of which he views as equal in standing.[4] Espín does not view contextualization as adjacent or added to humanness but as an essential condition to it. That is, different people live their humanity differently according to their context. In the same way, he considers diversity "a sine qua non condition of *humanitas*."[5]

An embracing of contextuality then leads to an acceptance of the myriad identities that encapsulate the unique and particular ways contexts enable and shape people to live their humanness.[6] The connection between context and diversity allows Espín to tackle crucial social markers, which, for him, are forms of being human: racial background, sexual background and ethnocultural background. These three aspects he challenges because of the particular ways in which they are downplayed or undermined in his larger social and national contexts, and often become sources of discrimination.

For instance, Espín rejects "Africanness" as a superficial cultural aspect; for him, it is a way to be human. He insists on the myriad hues and diverse colors of skin that have been reduced to a single-color marker but which, in turn, result in the downplaying of the diversity of human experiences, histories and ways of being human.[7] And in terms of sexual orientation and the diversity embodied by members of LGBTQAI+ communities, once again Espín affirms these as diverse ways of enacting one's humanness. He affirms the humanity of different sexual orientations and ways of being sexual and gendered as different expressions of *humanitas* in protest against the larger social forces that have historically marginalized LGBTQAI+ people as "non-human" or as "lacking in *humanitas*."[8]

Africanness and LGBTQAI+ identification as forms of humanness relate to the third aspect of ethnocultural background that Espín emphasizes as being Latino. On the one hand, he challenges dominant expressions of anthropology to imagine being human in ways that include ethnocultural and racial background and sexual orientation as constitutive aspects of humanness. The dominant culture of the United States of America tends to discriminate and exact violence upon these communities, including Latinas/os/xs because it considers them less human. On the other hand, and more specifically, Espín chides fellow Latina/o/x theologians for their inability to account for Latina/o/x African descendants and members of LGBTQAI+ communities as part of understanding Latina/o/x humanness.[9]

---

[4]As he puts it, "there are many human identities (i.e., many ways of being 'human') and all of these ways of humanness are 'equally equal' parts of who 'we' are, as long as these ways and identities construct 'humanness'" (Orlando O. Espín, *Idol & Grace: On Traditioning and Subversive Hope* (Maryknoll, NY: Orbis Books, 2014), 46).
[5]Espín, *Grace and Humanness*, 53.
[6]As he expands, "Identity can be said to be the process of recognition of self in community, of 'disclosing' my self to myself and others, as 'my' / 'our' diverse, living, and contextual *humanitas* (in a specific way—i.e., at the point of intersection of our always-present diverse contextualizations)" (ibid., 54).
[7]Ibid., 20–1.
[8]Ibid., 56.
[9]Ibid., 60–5. Espín is not naive! He also notes that members of the LGBTQAI+ are discriminated against and excluded among Latinas/os/xs in the United States of America and among African Americans. He notes a hierarchy of discriminations in place when these two communities protest forms of racialized discrimination but fail to address how they operate from a perspective of a heteronormative framework that excludes LGBTQAI+ members of their communities.

Interreligiousness

Espín's understanding of the diverse expressions of humanness extends to diversity among religious traditions. Christianity is one form of being human. But being devoted to another religious tradition is another equally valid form of being human. This aspect becomes quite evident when he discusses the presence of Afro-religions among Latinas/os/xs and in Latin America. He correctly notes that in Cuba, Brazil and among some Latina/o/x US Caribbean populations the Lukumí religion is omnipresent, "even among those who might sincerely declare and believe themselves to be practicing Roman Catholics, Episcopalians, or Protestants."[10]

The presence of Afro-religions among Latinas/os/xs, the growth of Latinas/os/xs ascribing to Islam and the expansion of other Christian denominational groups such as Seventh Day Adventist, Jehovah Witnesses and Pentecostals represent a radical reconfiguration of Latina/o/x identities. These religious traditions demand that Latinas/os/xs think in terms of interreligious conversations especially by rethinking Latina/o/x humanness beyond the Christian tradition. In broader terms, it means that religious devotion is one of the ways in which people live their humanness. The multiplicity of religious traditions defines a wide range of ways in which people actualize their humanity. Interreligious dialogue will therefore lead to a fuller appreciation of the divine mystery—what he calls the acknowledgement of the "ineffable mystery beyond all human knowing"[11]—by way of broadening the sources for theological reflection, making heard "the voices of other, previously unheard or silenced theologizing subjects."[12] It follows that it will also lead to a greater understanding of humanness in its complex contextual specificity.

Ecumenicity and Catholicity

Espín's own religious location as a Latino/x Catholic plays an important factor in his anthropological considerations since his own contextual mode of being human is as a Latino/x Roman Catholic. His understanding of Catholicism and humanity leads him to redefine ecumenicity and catholicity. For Espín, when it comes to thinking humanness, neither of these terms refer to the current global organization of religious institutions, the former signaling dialogue among Christian traditions (ecumenicity) and the latter pointing to the sound character of Catholic doctrinal statements (catholicity). Furthermore, these two terms can be coupled with a third cognate term, universality, not understood as concerned with the geographical extent of Christianity or the Christian Church. These terms are redefined in Espín's work.

For Espín, catholicity is a "quality of the Church"; "Catholicity has to do with universality as quality, as attitude, as vocation. The Church is 'catholic' because its doors are open to every human being and to every human group without distinction and without barriers."[13] In the same way, true universality can only be achieved when all those inhabiting the *oikoumēnē* can sit at the table and partake (ecumenicity). It does not entail decontextualization that robs people of their ancestral traditions, cultures

---

[10]Ibid., 90.

[11]Espín, *Idol & Grace*, xviii.

[12]Espín, *Grace and Humanness*, 22.

[13]Orlando O. Espín, "Immigration, Territory, and Globalization: Theological Reflection," *Journal of Hispanic/Latino Theology* 7, no. 3 (Fall 2000): 55.

and religions, but it is the dialogue that engages *human* communities, in meaningful ways that display humanness, "thereby suggesting that there is a 'human condition' which, although constructed and defined in and by every particular universality, can be effectively acknowledged as possessing universally relevant elements."[14] Espín is not concerned with what is Catholic in relation to what is not Catholic and the dynamics of how that is determined. Instead, he is concerned with the ways in which the church (most likely the Catholic Church) reaches the global human diversity, embodies it and represents it.

Note the distinction that Espín makes concerning humanness and universality. Particularities are not partial expressions of one human universality. Instead, particularities are historical, cultural and human universalities.[15] He rejects the idea of establishing hierarchies among human cultural traditions. Here again the notion of catholicity is the operating principle that refuses "to assume that one human culture is superior to others, or that one human culture or nation is better suited as witness and bearer of the Christian gospel."[16] Catholicity necessarily demands the adoption of an intercultural (i.e., catholic) theological posture "in order to reflect more authentically the [divine] revelatory event," what he calls "God's self-donation to humankind and for the benefit of humankind."[17]

Though I cannot go in depth at this point, Espín's orientation toward diversity and catholicity makes room for an appreciation of immigration as a "sacrament for the catholic church" insofar as it is the "best" way in which the church can be truly catholic. In the same way, his intercultural theology of traditioning gains full force because the orientation toward diversity and catholicity establishes intercultural dialogue as a means to construct "a multilayered, polyphonic, and non-innocent model for the Catholic tradition."[18] Though he focuses on the Catholic Church, I suspect he would broaden the model ecumenically to include all members of the Christian tradition. Diversity, interreligiosity and catholicity-ecumenicity are nonnegotiable signposts for understanding Espín's anthropological scheme; each discloses a fundamental aspect in which we live our humanness in relation to our contexts, to other fellow humans, and to the divine.

HUMANNESS, GOD AND LOVE

Espín's anthropological vision reveals two approaches between humans and God. In his earlier writings, it is more conceptual, whereas in his later writings he opts for a more mainstream Christological approach. These approaches complement each other in disclosing a fuller vision of humanness, though not without some tensions and difficulties. On the one hand, in his earlier works, Espín emphasizes theologically that humans are made in the image of God. This is an ontological point by which he proposes that God is the source and ultimate definition of humanness while insisting on the contextual nature

---

[14]Orlando O. Espín, "Migration and Human Condition: Theological Considerations on Religious Identities and Unexpected Inter-Religious Dialogue," in *Migration und Interkulturalität: Theologische und Philosophische Herausforderungen*, ed. Raúl Fornet-Betancourt (Aachen: Wissenschaftsverlag Mainz, 2004), 178–9.

[15]Espín, *Grace and Humanness*, 21.

[16]Espín, "Immigration, Territory, and Globalization," 55.

[17]Espín, *Idol & Grace*, 19.

[18]Espín, *Grace and Humanness*, 29–30.

of the historical Jesus.[19] On the other hand, in his later writings he emphasizes the ethical side drawing on the historical Jesus, his life and ministry—how he lived, to affirm the divine disclosure to humanity. Jesus reveals God in and through (the distinct ways he lived) his humanness.[20]

But how is God the ultimate definition of humanness according to Espín? He argues that the answer lies in the form of God's self-giving love for an-other, which to me is an ethical statement. Echoing Augustine, he identifies the triune community of love as the (ethical) model humans ought to imitate in order to reach "full" humanity. It is love that binds and is the oneness of the Trinity and is simultaneously that which the three share.[21] Put another way, the very essence of God is love. Consequently, there is nothing that God can be or do that is not loving. To be made in the image of God means to love, and it is by loving that humans are humanized and live their humanity.[22] The logic is circular. Since God is love and humans are made in the image of God, to be made in the image of God means to have the capacity to imitate God by loving. At the same time, since God is the ultimate model of humanity, to love is to be human. The theo-ethical imperative is love. As he puts it in his own words, "to be human is not just to exist knowing that we ultimately come from God. Rather, to be human is to *be* the image of love, of an eternally communitarian (that is, Trinitarian) God. And, as a consequence, one cannot claim to be truly human unless one is loving."[23] Espín adds grace to the divine calculus of love and its implications to humanness: "When we allow ourselves to be loved unconditionally, then we are set on the path of humanization, because implied in this acceptance is the recognition that love—and only love—can make us humanly whole."[24]

Adopting Espín's notion of love requires that one redefines the reach and essence of that love and the God who loves. However, his unqualified affirmation of God as essentially love creates tension in his theological vision of humanness for at least three reasons: (1) the reality of pain, suffering, exploitation, innocent death and so on; (2) his heightened emphasis on sin and sinfulness; and (3) the liberationist overtones of his work. Discussing these three points goes beyond the scope of this chapter. Let me just say, without spending too much time to dispel any possible misunderstandings of his work, that he quite astutely qualifies what it means for humans to love. He does not only mean loving one's neighbor. His liberationist commitments leads him to affirm the call to love as including those most disadvantaged by social structures: the needier, the discriminated against, the poor. Inspired by his thinking, one can conclude that love has profound (ethical) social, political and economic implications and applicability. It follows that in Espín's theo-ethical frame, "justice and liberation are other names for love."[25] For him, growing into or achieving humanness requires the self-giving action of love on the side of justice.

---

[19]Orlando O. Espín, "Grace and Humanness: A Hispanic Perspective," in *We Are a People! Initiatives in Hispanic American Theology*, ed. Roberto S. Goizueta (Minneapolis, MN: Fortress Press, 1992), 138.

[20]See Espín, *Idol & Grace*.

[21]Espín, "Grace and Humanness," 137.

[22]Ibid., 136, 139. Elsewhere, Espín also says that compassion is the ultimate meaning and definition of humanness. See Espín, *Idol & Grace*, 93.

[23]Espín, "Grace and Humanness," 138.

[24]Ibid., 161.

[25]Ibid., 159.

HUMANNESS AND REVELATION

Though Espín's early work mentions the historical Jesus on few occasions, the later Espín connects humanness with both the divine self-giving of love and revelation. Traditional theology often insists that Jesus Christ reveals to us what it means to be human.[26] But by taking seriously the contextual nature of humanness, as Espín does, such traditional affirmations of humanness in light of Christ are turned into empty gestures because Jesus' historical, contextual and culturally conditioned humanness plays an insignificant role in this theological tradition. Espín bridges the gap between human and divine in traditional approaches by focusing simultaneously on the historical Jesus both as revelation of God and as the site of contextual humanness. He formulates a contextual theoethics.

Espín's later work starts with the idea of God as an unknowable and unsayable mystery. Much in line with traditional theology, Espín introduces God as wholly other to the extent that nothing that humans say can capture or define what "God" is.[27] Again, following traditional theology, it is the historical Jesus who bridges the gap between God and humans, showcasing the divine mystery and making it "sayable."[28] However, by drawing on his own earlier work, one could depart from traditional perspectives by emphasizing the contextual character of the historical Jesus, thereby highlighting the contextual nature of divine disclosure and humanness.[29]

Two key implications stem from this conversation about contextuality, humanness and divine disclosure. First, revelation, Espín notes, points to God's loving scandalous self-donation, the divine disclosure that embodies hope in the humanness of Jesus of Nazareth. Briefly,

> Christianity stands or falls on the reasonable hope that God, as Jesus said, is really intervening in this world, transforming it according to God's compassionate will. Christianity exists because of the effectively subversive hope that God really does care for the most vulnerable and disposable members of humankind, that God is really compassionate, and that the ultimate moment of history will be compassionate and not the now all too frequent abuse of the poor and vulnerable.[30]

Second, Espín's connection between the divine disclosure and humanness via contextuality can thus be highlighted. In other words, because the very human experience of Jesus of Nazareth is revelatory, so too by definition is contextual humanness.[31] This twofold revelatory stream meets in the human experience of Jesus and has a crucial correspondence with Latina/o/x popular Catholicism.

As already noted, Espín proposes that through the experience of the human Jesus we encounter a "God who cares and ... intervenes in human history to make it better. But in doing this, God encounters failure, rejection, and the victimizing treatment

---

[26]Karl Barth, "The Humanity of God," in *The Humanity of God*, trans. John Newton Thomas (Atlanta: John Knox Press, 1960), 37–68.

[27]Espín, *Idol & Grace*, 56.

[28]Ibid., 27.

[29]As he writes, "Christ lived in a specific time period, in a specific land, within a concrete history, and within a single culture. Jesus of Nazareth was a first-century, Palestinian Jew, and there is no way to responsibly understand him by disregarding these historical, geographical, and cultural facts" (Espín, "Grace and Humanness," 144).

[30]Espín, *Idol & Grace*, 29.

[31]Orlando O. Espín, *The Faith of the People: Theological Reflections on Popular Catholicism*, foreword by Roberto S. Goizueta (Maryknoll, NY: Orbis Books, 1997), 16.

given to the politically and religiously insignificant."[32] Suffering and vanquishment gain anthropological significance in Jesus, particularly for Latina/o/x communities who experience suffering, discrimination and exploitation; an analogical relation between the vanquished Latina/o/x communities and the vanquished Jesus becomes apparent. Jesus' innocent death points to divine solidarity with suffering men and women. In the same way, through popular religious expressions Latina/o/x Catholics mirror the divine; their popular religious traditions are the ways they live out their humanness, as well as encounter, face, confront and struggle against injustice and make sense of reality and suffering.[33] Moreover, the question is not whether Latinas/os/xs suffer. Rather, Espín's contention is that "popular religion is one of the most fundamental ways through which Latinos deal with suffering,"[34] and in doing so, they intuit both Jesus' true humanness and give witness to the gospel message.[35] Their popular religious traditions are revelatory and a *locus* of theological reflection.

The connection between humanness and religious faith is thus embodied in Latina/o/x popular Catholic popular traditions. Because being Latina/o/x and being Catholic are the manners in which these communities live their humanness, Espín proposes that Latino/a/x popular Catholicism and Latina/o/x Catholic popular traditions witness to and bear the gospel message. Popular here means not widespread but that the creators and the practitioners are the people, "and more concretely, the marginalized … in society (i.e., those social sectors *pushed* against their will to the 'dispensable' and 'disposable' margins of society)."[36] Popular expressions encompass the people's sense of faith and hope in God; they embody the *sensus fidelium*: "the 'faith-ful' *intuition* of the Christian people, moved by the Spirit, that senses, adheres to, and interprets the Word of God."[37]

HUMANNESS AND THE CULTURAL

Since for Espín Latina/o/x Catholics live their humanness through popular religious traditions, it follows that culture or, to expand his proposal beyond the singularity of culture, the cultural plays a central role. Latinas/os/xs live their humanness *latinamente*. Their popular traditions and expressions do not take place in a vacuum; they are also privileged carriers of Latina/o/x cultures.[38] I note that Espín deploys the singular *culture* to speak of the diverse cultural traditions subsumed under the label Latinas/os/xs. As I have argued elsewhere, such a use is problematic, but for the sake

---

[32]Ibid., 15.

[33]Orlando O. Espín, "An Exploration into the Theology of Grace and Sin," in *From the Heart of Our People: Latino/a Explorations in Catholic Systematic Theology*, ed. Orlando O. Espín and Miguel H. Díaz (Maryknoll, NY: Orbis Books, 1999), 135; Orlando O. Espín, "Popular Religion as an Epistemology (of Suffering)," *Journal of Hispanic/ Latino Theology* 2, no. 2 (November 1994): 55–78.

[34]Espín, "Popular Religion as an Epistemology (of Suffering)," 74.

[35]Orlando O. Espín, "Tradition and Popular Religion: An Understanding of the *Sensus fidelium*," in *Mestizo Christianity: Theology from the Latino Perspective*, ed. Arturo J. Bañuelas (Maryknoll, NY: Orbis Books, 1995), 157.

[36]Espín, "Popular Religion as an Epistemology (of Suffering)," 66. Espín argues against notions of the *sensus fidelium* as found only in Catholic official church doctrine. He unsettles these views by insisting that popular traditions are legitimate bearers of the *sensus fidelium*. See Espín, "Tradition and Popular Religion"; Espín, *The Faith of the People*.

[37]Espín, "Tradition and Popular Religion," 164. See also Espín, *The Faith of the People*, 73–9.

[38]Espín, "Grace and Humanness," 148.

of keeping the original meaning of Espín's proposal intact I preserve his use of the category in the singular.[39]

Among Espín's numerous insights concerning culture, two issues stand out as having direct implications for his discussion of humanness. First, he notes that culture plays a fundamental role in the way people (in his case Latinas/os/xs) live their humanness. Second, he dispels any romanticism of an ideal perfect humanness by arguing that cultures reflect an operative sinful dimension.

Living Humanness

According to Espín, culture is the historical and ecological means through which people unveil themselves to themselves and to others as meaningfully human.[40] In the process, people construct and define (for themselves) what it means to be *meaningfully human*.[41] He emphasizes that culture is historical because it is human.

Espín's central point is that there is nothing that is human that is not cultural because all human reality is historical and cultural. He articulates a circular ethical correspondence between humanness and culture, whereby culture enables people to construct themselves as meaningfully human while it in turn creates the conditions for people to be able to live their humanness.[42] Meaninglessness, then, is the opposite of culture, and to trample on the culture of a human group shortchanges their ability to live their humanness.[43]

In Espín's proposal, the impact of culture reaches all aspects of life, including how people live their humanness through faith traditions. God, he claims, wills that we humanize ourselves in the manner in which we are human, that manner being specifically cultural. Once again, Latinas/os/xs humanize themselves and live their humanness only in specifically Latina/o/x ways. Not surprisingly, Espín claims that "here is no acultural Christianity" just as there is no acultural view of God.[44] As far as he is concerned, revelation itself is a human cultural event just as the "revelatory event *itself* is intrinsically and necessarily cultural."[45] These affirmations invite us to rethink culture as an intrinsic part of the divine act of grace in creating the conditions for humans to understand the divine self-disclosure through cultural means and its counterpart, the human cultural response.[46]

---

[39]The category culture—much like the abstract idea of humanness—is part of the legacy of the modern project that sought to reduce the human experience to a manageable range of idea using Europe as standard and rubric for evaluating other cultural traditions. It is often used as synonymous with the equally colonizing notion of civilization. Together these terms have facilitated the disparaging of the customs and traditions of diverse communities throughout the world while insisting on the superiority of the Western European cultural and intellectual traditions. Instead, I propose *the cultural* as a more suitable category for speaking about the manner in which people groups confront reality, interact with each other and the environment, and encounter and respond to the divine. For a fuller discussion on the importance to rethink pervasive uses of the category in the direction of the cultural, see Néstor Medina, *Christianity, Empire, and the Spirit: (Re)Configuring Faith and the Cultural* (Leiden: Brill, 2018).

[40]Orlando O. Espín, 'Traditioning: Culture, Daily Life and Popular Religion, and Their Impact on Christian Tradition', in *Futuring Our Past: Explorations in the Theology of Tradition*, ed. Orlando O. Espín and Gary Macy (Maryknoll, NY: Orbis Books, 2006), 4.

[41]Espín, "Migration and Human Condition," 178.

[42]Espín, *Idol & Grace*, 44–5.

[43]Ibid., 124.

[44]Ibid., 123.

[45]Espín, "Traditioning," 4. Emphasis original.

[46]Espín, "Grace and Humanness."

Sinful Humanness

Though Espín runs the risk of romanticizing the human experience when he avers that to be human is to love, he is well aware of how people dehumanize others. Rather than articulating humanness as perfect, he speaks of a wounded humanness and wounded peoples because of sin. Though he does not explicitly define "sin" in his overall work, there is no doubt that he views expressions of dehumanization, discrimination, exploitation and impoverishment as directly connected to sin. At the cultural level, Espín points out that all cultural traditions bear the mark of conflict: "just as humans can dehumanize themselves, so can cultures bear the sinful imprint of the humans that create them. All cultures are also dehumanized and dehumanizing, and in need of the liberating love of God."[47]

In the same vein, Espín argues that Latina/o/x cultural traditions and Latina/o/x popular Catholicism are not exempt from sin. More to the point, Latina/o/x popular religious traditions do not express the "explicit commitment … to establish justice and reconciliation."[48] Just as Latina/o/x popular religious expressions contain the wide gamut of gifts, practices and intuitions that enable Latinas/os/xs to live and grow in their humanity, so also they contain the tensions, problems and difficulties that prevent many of them from living their humanness to the fullest. Espín is correct that in Latina/o/x religious expressions we find both the courage of the people and their fears, both their hopes and fatalism, both their faith in God and the temptation to resort to magical manipulation, both the strength of family and the androcentric chauvinist expressions of patriarchy, and both the deepest respects for mothers and the stereotyping and discriminatory attitudes towards women.[49]

These are the strengths and wounds that humanize and dehumanize in Latina/o/x cultures. For instance, Espín highlights how Latinas are celebrated as the family's interpreters, the privilege hermeneuts of the biblical message, the teachers of ethics and the leaders of prayer in Latina/o/x homes. But that is one side of the reality of Latinas' lives; they have also been taught to endure abuse, assault and violence as part of their devotion to Our Lady of Guadalupe, for example.[50] The complexity of human relations and sin in Espín's example of women and Latina/o/x cultural and popular religious traditions is further complexified when he tells us that women themselves contribute to the perpetuation of a sinful reality of violence by enduring violence and allowing their children to be abused.[51] Though I agree with Espín's highlighting of women's "complicity" in their own suffering and that of other women and children, his statement could be misunderstood as blaming the victims, which is highly problematic. Thus, while women cannot be said to be only victims, I argue that Espín's affirmation needs further development as it leaves unchallenged the multiple interconnected social forces of patriarchy that often leave women without recourse. His description does not acknowledge that sometimes enduring suffering seems like and often is the only alternative left to women for survival.

---

[47]Ibid., 145. See also, Espín, "An Exploration into the Theology of Grace and Sin."
[48]Espín, "Grace and Humanness," 160.
[49]Ibid., 150.
[50]Espín, "An Exploration into the Theology of Grace and Sin."
[51]Ibid., 130–2.

HUMANNESS AND THE STRUGGLE FOR JUSTICE

Until now I have attempted to flesh out some of the main theological categories at play in Espín's anthropological vision. I have insisted that contextualization is a crucial tenet of his understanding of humanness. In the previous section, I emphasized how Espín does not think of humanness as perfect and ideal humanness comes out of complex and messy contextual, historical and concrete cultural communities. Thus, drawing on Latina/o/x communities' experiences of pain, suffering, social marginalization, underemployment, racialized and cultural discrimination, as well as outright persecution by police and immigration authorities, he concludes that humanness also includes the struggle for justice. In an ecumenical move, he compares popular Catholicism and Latina/o/x Pentecostalism as examples of the manner in which poor Latinas/os/xs reclaim their human dignity even while socially resisting the dominant culture's pressures of heightened individuality, capitalist consumption and the commodification of life.[52]

These communities' Christian morality, he insists, reject "the notion that future progress ever justifies the death, hunger, or oppression of millions today."[53] These communities build and live their humanness even while they carry a "quiet rebellion against marginalization, and of doubt as to the absolute validity of that which pretends to be the normative."[54]

Though not stated categorically, it is evident that Espín's contextual criterion has profound implications for thinking theologically and ethically about humanness. If indeed the creative intent of God is our full humanness, then the experience of injustice, poverty and exploitation are obstacles to grow into full humanity. The struggle for justice—recall that justice is another word for love in Espín's thinking—involves whole communities which aim to transform society and thereby provide "clear proof that the grace of God and the God of grace are actively involved in the humanization process."[55] Though he could have made his argument more explicit, one can still conclude from Espín's proposal that the ethical struggle for justice is a struggle for humanization; "the grace of God calls us and moves us to further our humanization."[56] If indeed for Espín to love is to be human, by definition to be human means to struggle for justice on the side of the socially disenfranchised. The struggle for justice does not take place in a vacuum but in a specific social, political, cultural and religious context.

FURTHER THOUGHTS TOWARD A THEOLOGY OF HUMANNESS

While it is difficult to speak of "Orlando Espín's Anthropology" because he has not written a substantive anthropological treatise *per se*, there is much in his work that is pertinent to conversations on humanness. There is no doubt that, for him, the lived contextual reality of people, specifically Latinas/os/xs, is a central point of departure in theo-ethical considerations on humanness. Moreover, it is clear that he finds a corresponding relation

---

[52]Orlando O. Espín, "Pentecostalism and Popular Catholicism: The Poor and *Traditio*," *Journal of Hispanic/Latino Theology* 3, no. 2 (November 1995): 35.
[53]Espín, "Grace and Humanness," 158.
[54]Ibid., 150.
[55]Ibid., 162.
[56]Ibid., 163.

between the human Jesus and the humanness of Latinas/os/xs, even in their experience of suffering, marginalization, and discrimination.

Some tensions remain. For instance, while the early Espín focuses strongly on popular devotions to Guadalupe even as to suggest Guadalupe as a manifestation of the Spirit,[57] the later Espín de-emphasizes the role of Guadalupe (and Mariology) as he shifts his focus primarily to the historical Jesus.[58] Another tension in his work is the heightened emphasis on the wholly otherness of the divine Mystery, particularly in his work on traditioning.[59] Admittedly, Espín seeks to bridge the gap between humans and the divine Mystery in multiple ways, including by celebrating the inescapable dimension of the cultural in revelation. The revelation event, he notes, even in Jesus, was a cultural event. The Trinitarian impetus in Espín's discussions on the relation between humanness and the cultural dimension is emphasized through his accounts for the activity of the Spirit in relation to "culture." He argues that the Spirit does not remove but enlivens culture as means to make the disclosure or experience of the divine possible. For Espín, the Spirit does not suspend our humanity but is directly invested in moving, inspiring and pushing humans to further their humanization.[60] I wonder, however, if the dualist framing of divine-human relation through cultural dynamics, as explained by Espín, is far too influenced by Augustinian notions of sin and grace, which render humans as absolutely dependent in God and playing an entirely passive role in the human-divine saga. In other words, what do humans contribute to make possible the divine-human relation?

As Christians imagine and discern the will of God, it may yet be useful to think of our collective journey toward humanization as part of the continuation of the divine creative process. My sense is that Espín's theo-ethical imagination provides for us crucial insights to think humanness in just such ways, ways that go beyond inherited approaches.

SUGGESTED FURTHER READING

Espín, Orlando O., *Idol & Grace: On Traditioning and Subversive Hope* (Maryknoll, NY: Orbis Books, 2014).

Espín, Orlando O., *Grace and Humanness: Theological Reflections Because of Culture* (Maryknoll, NY: Orbis Books, 2007).

Espín, Orlando O., "An Exploration into the Theology of Grace and Sin," in Orlando O. Espín and Miguel H. Díaz (eds.), *From the Heart of Our People: Latino/a Explorations in Catholic Systematic Theology* (Maryknoll, NY: Orbis Books, 1999), 121–52.

Espín, Orlando O., *The Faith of the People: Theological Reflections on Popular Catholicism* (Maryknoll, NY: Orbis Books, 1997).

Medina, Néstor, "The Pneumatological Dimension of Orlando Espín's Theological Work and Its Implications for Engagement with Pentecostal Communities," *Journal of Hispanic/Latino Theology*, September 16, 2010. Available online: http://www.latinotheology.org/node/96 (accessed October 12, 2010).

---

[57]Espín, "Tradition and Popular Religion," 160. See also Espín, "An Exploration into the Theology of Grace and Sin"; Espín, *The Faith of the People*.
[58]In his forthcoming book on the Spirit, Espín revisits his discussion of the connections between our Lady of Guadalupe and pneumatology in his third chapter. However, he does not discuss directly how such discussion has direct implications for a theological understanding of humanness. See Orlando O. Espín, *Disruptive Cartographers: Pneumatology* (Minneapolis, MN: Fortress Press, forthcoming).
[59]Espín, *Idol & Grace*.
[60]Espín, "Grace and Humanness," 163.

PART IV

Contemporary Constructive Concerns

The Image of God and the Technological Person: Artificial Intelligence in Theological Anthropology

STEPHEN OKEY

INTRODUCTION

Depictions of artificial intelligence (AI) in popular media often fall into one of two categories: the AI that wants to conquer or destroy humanity (e.g., Skynet in the *Terminator* franchise) or the AI that wants to become human (e.g. Data from *Star Trek: The Next Generation*). Both these and many other depictions present AI that are at least as intelligent as their human counterparts (and usually much more so) and capable of their own agency. Their chief difference from humanity is usually the lack of emotion, whether in the T-800's relentless pursuit or Data's persistent attempts to understand human concepts like love, fear and humor.

Such popular depictions are grounded on this question of how AI is related to the human, and especially what one defines as essential to being human. Is it intelligence? Emotion? Free will? What role does a body play in understanding the human? Approached through the lens of theological anthropology, we might wonder whether it would be possible for an AI to possess these human characteristics. If so, could the AI be described as human?

Even as the question of AI looks to whether an AI could be human, I propose that there are two more important and more interesting questions to consider. The first is whether and how AI helps us to better understand what it means to be a human person. If one argues that AI would need this or that feature of the human person to be truly human, then one is arguing much more about what makes one human than about whether the machine can have that feature. This question initially arises with the question of intelligence,[1] but it serves as an effective approach for thinking about other dimensions of the human, such as emotion, embodiment and agency.

The second is whether or not an artificial intelligence can have personhood. Note here that the question is not whether AI can be a *human* person but rather whether it can

---

[1] Anne Foerst, "Artificial Intelligence: Walking the Boundary," *Zygon* 31, no. 4 (December 1996): 681–93 (684).

be a person at all. Within the Christian tradition, personhood has not been restricted to human beings: angels are understood to be angelic persons, and most fundamentally the doctrine of the Trinity describes God as three *persons* and one nature. Thus, the question with respect to AI is whether there can be a technological person.

This chapter investigates these questions through several steps. First, it offers a brief review of the history of artificial intelligence, with particular focus on the concept of the Turing Test. Second, it reviews various ways of discussing the *imago Dei* and its potential utility for thinking with artificial intelligence. As part of this section, the chapter considers various potential dimensions of the human made in the image of God, including intelligence, emotion, embodiment and agency. Finally, the chapter returns to the question of personhood and what questions a hypothetical technological person would raise for theological anthropology.

A CRASH COURSE IN ARTIFICIAL INTELLIGENCE

In many respects, what is referred to as "artificial intelligence" tends to be somewhat nebulous. The "artificial" aspect is generally easy enough, as it focuses on human-created computer programs. The "intelligence" aspect, though, is where the difficulty arises, as definitions for this have changed over time. For many years, the most visible example of artificial intelligence were computer chess programs, most famously IBM's Deep Blue. Some hailed its 1997 victory over reigning world chess champion Garry Kasparov as a significant moment in AI development, since being good at chess was considered by many to be a proxy for intelligence.[2] Deep Blue was not, however, designed to be able to do anything else intelligent, such as critically analyze a written text or hold a conversation. If intelligence includes a broader range of cognitive abilities, then what would that mean for *artificial* intelligence?

Recognizing this difficulty in describing intelligence, Anne Foerst writes, "Even without an exact definition or understanding of intelligence, artificial intelligence (AI) can be understood as a science that tries to build and program computers and/or robots so as to give them abilities and features that we intuitively call intelligent."[3] Foerst's approach sidesteps a more rigid definition of intelligence and instead treats the question functionally in relation to what is generally perceived to be intelligence in humans by humans themselves.

The most famous example of this approach to defining intelligence is the Turing Test. In his 1950 essay "Computing Machinery and Intelligence," mathematician Alan Turing attempts to set aside the question "can machines think" and reorient it toward whether or not machines can arrive at a point where a human cannot tell the difference.[4] To test this hypothesis, he proposes an "imitation game," in which a judge has conversations with hidden, unknown interlocutors, one of whom is human and the other is a machine. Both human and machine should try to convince the judge that they are in fact human through their conversation with the judge. To name Turing's parameters for this test, he predicts that

---

[2]Steven Levy, "What Deep Blue Tells Us about AI in 2017," *Wired*, May 23, 2017. Available online: https://www.wired.com/2017/05/what-deep-blue-tells-us-about-ai-in-2017/ (accessed June 6, 2020).
[3]Foerst, "Artificial Intelligence," 684.
[4]Alan M. Turing, "I.—Computing Machinery and Intelligence," *Mind* LIX, no. 236 (October 1950): 433–60 (433).

in about fifty years' time it will be possible to programme computers, with a storage capacity of about 10^9, to make them play the imitation game so well that an average interrogator will not have more than 70 per cent chance of making the right identification after five minutes of questioning.[5]

Again, for Turing it is not a question of whether machines actually think, or are in fact intelligent, but rather whether the unseen machine can, for five minutes, perform what a human judge would consider to be human intelligence. Yet even though Turing did not think that winning the imitation game meant that a machine was intelligent, the Turing Test has become for many a shorthand for marking artificial intelligence.

While the field of artificial intelligence since Turing has branched in numerous directions, two of these are particularly helpful for theological anthropology. The first, symbolic or classical AI, is predicated on the idea that all information can be represented symbolically, and that intelligence "processes" (makes sense of) that information according to rules.[6] While such processing happens in the human brain, proponents of symbolic AI claim that the same processing can, in theory, achieve identical results in a computer. The keys to developing artificial intelligence, then, are discerning and programming the rules for processing symbolic information while also having computers with sufficient speed, memory and inputs to carry it out.[7] This approach to AI is best exemplified by programs such as ELIZA, the artificial therapist designed by Joseph Weizenbaum in 1966, and is used in most computer chess programs. While symbolic AI is good at some tasks for which clear rules can be derived, such programs "exhibit deep but narrow knowledge" and are woefully inadequate to many ostensibly intelligent acts.[8] For example, what rules does one develop for distinguishing visually between a dog and a cat?[9]

In response to this type of problem, AI research has also pursued nonsymbolic approaches. Some of these efforts have sought to create an embodied AI within robots, providing the AI with sensory inputs, limbs extended in space and even expressive faces.[10] Others have sought to develop a connectionist approach, which tries to build artificial neural networks.[11] Still others have sought to use statistics and large data sets to create probabilistic models of intelligence that "learn" (so-called machine learning approaches).[12] This approach has proven relatively good at the sort of pattern recognition intelligence that eluded symbolic AI. Each of these approaches is less about formal rules and algorithms and more about developing ways of modeling the fuzzier, intuitive and experience-based ways that humans reason and know.

These approaches to artificial intelligence have led to remarkable technological breakthroughs, but they have also prompted further consideration of what is "human" about the human person. Even as much of the focus has been on the difficulty of both defining and modeling intelligence, other questions about the potential affectivity,

---

[5]Turing, "Computing Machinery and Intelligence," 442. The storage capacity of 10^9 is equivalent to 1 gigabyte.

[6]Noreen Herzfeld, *In Our Image: Artificial Intelligence and the Human Spirit* (Minneapolis, MN: Fortress Press, 2002), 35–7.

[7]Ian G. Barbour, "Neuroscience, Artificial Intelligence, and Human Nature: Theological and Philosophical Reflections," *Zygon* 34, no. 3 (September 1999): 361–98 (375).

[8]Herzfeld, *In Our Image*, 38.

[9]Russell C Bjork, "Artificial Intelligence and the Soul," *Perspectives on Science and Christian Faith* 60, no. 2 (June 2008): 95–102 (100).

[10]See the discussion of Cog in the section on embodied AI below.

[11]Antje Jackelén, "The Image of God as *Techno Sapiens*," *Zygon* 37, no. 2 (June 2002): 289–302 (291).

[12]Ibid., 291.

embodiment and moral responsibility of AI all point back to important dimensions of the human. In order to pursue these, we turn now to Christian teaching on the *imago Dei* to see how it might help frame AI as a theological anthropological question.

AI AND THE *IMAGO DEI*

In the first chapter of Genesis, toward the end of the sixth day of creation, God decides to "make human beings in our image, after our likeness."[13] There is little further elaboration on what this image and likeness mean: immediately following, God grants the human dominion over the animals created on days five and six, and the human is created "male and female."[14] The non-specificity of what is meant by the "image of God" has led the Christian tradition to develop numerous theologies of what that might be.[15]

Pursuing the image of God in artificial intelligence, Noreen Herzfeld has grouped these various theologies into three categories: substantive, functionalist and relational.[16] She then argues that each of these views of the *imago Dei* has a corresponding *imago hominis* in artificial intelligence. Since AI research is at least partly about better understanding what it means to be a human, it is reasonable to see how AI might disclose an image of the human.

The first and probably most common of these, the "substantive" view of the image of God, focuses on specific qualities of the human person that each person possesses. These qualities form part of the nature or substance of the human. Herzfeld argues that within the Christian tradition, these qualities have most often been "mental or spiritual" qualities like reason, free will or the capacity for self-transcendence.[17] As a result, the substantive *imago Dei* is often treated "in individualistic terms," apart from the relationships or environments and contexts that shape the person.[18] As a parallel to the substantive *imago Dei*, Herzfeld finds a substantive *imago hominis* in the symbolic approach to artificial intelligence, which seeks to develop a program with the capacity to mimic the intelligence of a human person. Though symbolic AI focuses only on intelligence (not free will or self-transcendence), it does so to replicate what would be considered an essential human ability according to a substantive image of God.[19]

The second, a "functionalist" view, emphasizes what humans do as God's agents or representatives. The functionalist approach was developed by scripture scholars, particularly Johannes Hehn and Gerhard von Rad, who argued that the clearest indication of what *imago Dei* means comes from the rest of the Gen. 1:27 verse, which directs the human to act with dominion in God's creation. This is understood to mean that "human beings image God when they function in God's stead, as God's representative on earth."[20] Herzfeld notes that this approach has become the most common among Old Testament scholars and is the most common interpretation found in recent commentaries on Genesis.[21] Herzfeld finds the functionalist *imago hominis* in artificial intelligence when

---

[13]Gen. 1:26 (New American Bible).
[14]Gen. 1:26-27.
[15]See Chapter 5 in this volume, Michelle Gonzalez, "Created for God and for Each Other: Our *Imago Dei*."
[16]Herzfeld, *In Our Image*, 7.
[17]Ibid., 16.
[18]Ibid., 18.
[19]Ibid., 41.
[20]Ibid., 21.
[21]Ibid., 24.

researchers create machines that "engage in tasks in the real world that human would normally do."[22] It is not required that they perform the tasks the same way humans would but rather that they are able to achieve through their programing and design the same ends humans would achieve.[23] Of course, as Herzfeld notes, it's not always clear what distinguishes a regular computer program from artificial intelligence when one is focusing on how to complete tasks.

The third view according to Herzfeld is the "relational," which understands "the image of God to be manifested in human-divine and human-human relationship."[24] Relying heavily on Reformed theologian Karl Barth to describe this approach to the *imago Dei*, Herzfeld says that the image of God is present in the very relationship between God and the human, not in the human capacity for relationship.[25] For Barth, this is essential given the already relational character of the Trinity.[26] The human relationship to God is a "copy" of the inner Trinitarian relations, and the human relationship to other humans (especially the relationship between males and females) is a copy of the divine-human relationship.[27] Drawing on Reformed approaches to the image of God and original sin, Barth recognizes that authentic relationship between humans and God, and among humans, is marred by sin. Yet because the image of God is present in the relationship itself, and not in any particular human capacities, then humans "are in the image of God when we are in authentic relationship with God or with one another."[28] Herzfeld argues that this relational *imago hominis* is what is actually being evaluated in the Turing test. If the machine's ability to converse convincingly with a human is what marks intelligence, "then we have defined intelligence relationally."[29] The relational approach is further evidenced by efforts to design AI that learns through embodied interactions; the most famous examples of this were the MIT robots Cog and Kismet in the 1990s and early 2000s.[30]

Through her analysis of these three approaches to the *imago Dei*, Herzfeld shows that much of the work on artificial intelligence helps us to understand a corresponding *imago hominis*. As stated by Foerst and others, research into AI is not merely a technological question but an anthropological one.[31] Inasmuch as the *imago Dei* has often been invoked as what distinguishes humans from animals and the rest of creation, so too does human research into artificial intelligence reveal the ways that we make sense of what is distinct about humans.[32] This is especially well represented in the difficulties of

---

[22]Ibid., 42.

[23]As an example, Herzfeld notes the chess program Deep Blue, a symbolic AI whose sole function is to play chess. Yet the way it determines chess moves is radically different from how humans do, examining up to two hundred million positions per second. See ibid., 43.

[24]Ibid., 7.

[25]Anne Foerst connects this approach to the work of Martin Luther as well. See Anne Foerst, "Cog, a Humanoid Robot, and the Question of the Image of God," *Zygon* 33, no. 1 (March 1998): 91–111 (105).

[26]Herzfeld, *In Our Image*, 26.

[27]Ibid., 26–7.

[28]Ibid., 29.

[29]Ibid., 46.

[30]Ibid., 47. Foerst takes a different approach here, describing Cog as "functionalist" because it "can be understood as a story telling us something about the underlying mechanisms that make us the beings we are" (Foerst, "Cog, a Humanoid Robot," 108). As part of her functionalist argument, Foerst also rejects the substantive view of the *imago Dei*, saying that it "does not distinguish us qualitatively from the animals and for that reason cannot distinguish us qualitatively from machines" (ibid).

[31]Foerst, "Artificial Intelligence," 684; Jackelén, "The Image of God as *Techno Sapiens*," 290–1; Herzfeld, *In Our Image*, 5–7.

[32]Herzfeld, *In Our Image*, 7–8.

defining what "intelligence" is. However, one interesting dimension of the *imago Dei* and *imago hominis* question is that humans are not distinguished merely by intelligence. As Antje Jackelén notes, some AI ambitions seek "to build fully intelligent artifacts with cognition, perception, action, learning, creativity, and emotion—all the characteristics of what might be called a human being created in the image of God."[33] While engaging with the substantive, functionalist and relational approaches, we must then discern how the question of the human is reflected in other important facets of human existence. Thus, in addition to the traditional focus on intelligence in both the *imago Dei* and in AI, this chapter turns to consider key questions about affectivity, embodiment and agency.

The Intelligent Machine

As noted above, how to define and test for intelligence has been a central question in AI research. While Turing did not consider his imitation game to be a real test of intelligence, its use of human conversational interaction has often been used and debated as a proxy for intelligence. In his book on the Turing Test, Brian Christian writes about two features of intelligence that researchers trying to pass the test sometimes focus on. One is to think of intelligence as sophistication or complexity. Can the AI exhibit complex behavior, such as making a joke or writing a poem? He notes examples of chatbots that have been programmed to do both, based on machine learning and a sufficiently large database of jokes or poems.[34] In machine learning, intelligence is modeled statistically rather than symbolically: the software seeks to make inferences based on an initial or "training" database of relevant information. From there, it iterates its process, refining its responses in a way that is comparable to the developmental quality of human learning.[35] Through this process, these programs become capable of imitation and can learn to act in ways that humans act. However, it is less clear whether such programs can innovate or create something new, something that transcends or breaks the rules or conventions with which it was programmed.[36]

A different way of modeling intelligence is sensitivity: the program is able to react to changes and interact with persons in an unscripted way.[37] The sensitive AI is less likely to fall into a predictable script that could be easily recognized as an algorithm. These types of intelligence emphasize the ability to interact with the human judge in the Turing Test in a way that would seem human (i.e., the "relational" form of AI according to Herzfeld). Foerst picks up on this interactive approach to intelligence, writing that AI ought to be developed not only "to act socially" with potential interlocutors but also "to interact with a constantly changing environment."[38]

While the relational approach may be most fitting for passing a test of perceived humanity, one of the most serious critiques of the Turing Test focuses on the substance of

---

[33]Jackelén, "The Image of God as *Techno Sapiens*," 291.
[34]Brian Christian, *The Most Human Human: What Artificial Intelligence Teaches Us About Being Alive* (New York: Anchor Books, 2012), 203–5.
[35]Scott H Hawley, "Challenges for an Ontology of Artificial Intelligence," *Perspectives on Science and Christian Faith* 71, no. 2 (June 2019): 83–93 (85–6); see also Foerst, "Cog, a Humanoid Robot," 102.
[36]Christian, *The Most Human Human*, 207.
[37]Ibid., 205–6.
[38]Foerst, "Cog, a Humanoid Robot," 101.

that communication. Philosopher John R. Searle challenges the Turing Test by positing the "Chinese Room Argument." Imagine that the judge in the Turing Test sits in a room and engages the hidden, unknown interlocutor via the computer. However, this time, despite having no knowledge of or proficiency in Chinese, the judge is given instructions to respond with specific Chinese characters to whatever Chinese characters he or she receives from the hidden, unknown interlocutor. The judge in this case is following formal rules and responding with the appropriate symbols, but none would reasonably say that the judge has an intelligent understanding of Chinese.[39] The difference, as noted by Michael Jin Choi, is that an artificial intelligence might able to follow syntactic rules but has no grasp of the *semantic* content: "no matter what data and inferences have been programed, the computer does not have an intrinsic feature of reality, namely its own interpretation that gives *meaning* to them; they are simply meaningless symbols."[40] The AI might be able to produce a joke but would not understand the joke sufficiently to authentically laugh at it.

Building on Searle's Chinese Room example, Alejandro García-Rivera claims that the Turing Test actually measures "us-ness," not intelligence.[41] He compares the Chinese Room to the famous Valladolid debate in 1550 between Bartolomé de las Casas and Juan Ginés de Sepúlveda over the humanity and intelligence of the indigenous Americans.[42] According to García-Rivera, both the Valladolid debate and the Turing Test are ostensibly focused on questions of intelligence, but the real challenge is that of "otherness." De las Casas defended the possibility that the other might be intelligent, even if their language was unfamiliar or incomprehensible to the European. The Turing Test, however, can only test how much the program produces responses that the judge would perceive as human.[43] While Searle rejects the intelligence of the machine based on its inability to understand the content it produces, García-Rivera highlights that we would only be able to make sense of the machine if it was similar enough to the human.

The Affective Machine

As noted above, Herzfeld argues that substantive approaches to the *imago Dei* have focused on specific qualities that the human possesses, and that consistently in the Christian tradition reason or intelligence has been the indispensable example of this. Similarly, AI research has focused primarily on intelligence as something that machines can be designed for. However, as AI research has expanded beyond symbolic approaches and a narrow understanding of intelligence, other central human qualities have also become part of AI design.

In her research on sociable robots, Sherry Turkle draws a parallel between work on artificial intelligence and artificial emotion. Much as the operative definition of

---

[39]John R. Searle, *Consciousness and Language* (New York: Cambridge University Press, 2002), 17; Michael J. Choi, 'Consciousness and Intentionality in AI and the *Imago Dei*,' *Canon & Culture* 10, no. 2 (2016): 69–90 (72–3).

[40]Choi, "Consciousness and Intentionality in AI and the *Imago Dei*," 73.

[41]Alejandro García-Rivera, "Artificial Intelligence and De Las Casas: A 1492 Resonance," *Zygon* 28, no. 4 (December 1993): 543–50 (548–9).

[42]Ibid., 544.

[43]Ibid., 548–9.

intelligence focused on perceiving acts that would be described as intelligent in humans, Turkle observes, "We are coming to a parallel definition of artificial emotion as the art of 'getting machines to express things that would be considered feelings if expressed by people.' "[44] She sees this work in computer projects ranging from the robot Cog at MIT to the Tamagotchi digital "pets" once popular among children. In a particularly striking example of the latter, she writes about her interviews with children whose Tamagotchis had "died." While the toy itself has a reset button, allowing for a fresh new digital pet, numerous children insisted on burials for their deceased pets and the subsequent purchase of a new one from the store.[45] The demands of the software, and the child's concomitant experience of "caring" for the digital pet, revealed that artificial emotion is able to evoke emotional responses from users that stem from a perceived connection between the user and the software.[46]

Turkle describes the present as a "robotic moment" wherein AI and robots are designed so that they can "move people to relate to machines as subjects, as creatures in pain rather than broken objects."[47] Rather than the robots having actual emotions, Turkle sees them as programmed to *perform* emotion, and doing so in order to elicit actual emotions in their users. She notes that these reactions occur not only in children, who may be especially susceptible to perceiving the robot as having real emotions,[48] but also in those who create AI and describe their relationship to it in caring and nurturing language.[49] While a sociable robot can thus seem to perform the role of companion for its user, Turkle argues that "it promises friendship but can only deliver performances."[50] Central to this weakness as a companion is that the user does not learn empathy through interaction with the sociable robot but rather is more likely to develop narcissistic personality traits.[51] They can elicit a feeling of safety in their users that can become an obstacle to taking the risks that accompany typical human relationships.[52]

Clearly for Turkle, the presumption is that artificial emotion is performative but not real.[53] While technology can elicit emotional responses from users, no actual emotion occurs. Although Turkle does not give a clear argument for this claim, similar questions have been raised about this potential since the late 1990s. In her work on computers and emotion, Rosalind Picard notes the complexity of human emotion on psychological and biochemical levels, which we as humans only partially understand. Thus, the challenge of creating a genuinely emotional machine must respond to whether or not these complexities can be accurately modeled, whether that model would be a real experience of emotion or merely an imitation thereof and whether an ostensibly authentic experience

---

[44]Sherry Turkle, *Alone Together: Why We Expect More from Technology and Less from Each Other* (New York: Basic Books, 2011), 63.
[45]Ibid., 30–4.
[46]Ibid., 20.
[47]Ibid., 44.
[48]Ibid., 30, 92.
[49]Ibid., 100.
[50]Ibid., 101.
[51]Ibid., 55–6.
[52]Ibid., 78–9.
[53]Similarly, Searle effectively argues that the computer can perform intelligence but does not understand what it is doing.

of technological emotion would be comparable to a human one or not.[54] Moreover, research into artificial emotion has helped to further emphasize how human emotion (and intelligence) are deeply embodied capacities. Many have thus argued that further AI research must also include embodiment.

An Embodied Artificial Intelligence

One of the questions arising from the contested definition of intelligence is the role of the body. Intelligence is sometimes treated as an abstract, disembodied reality, and theological reflection on human bodies and the relationship between body and soul can risk turning toward a Gnosticism that separates the two. In a parallel fashion, proponents of Embodiment Artificial Intelligence argue that intelligence cannot be cleaved from the body. Rather, "intelligence emerges only in bodies and is dependent on bodily features and conditions."[55] The robotic body makes possible interaction with an environment, including with human persons, and so this approach to AI focuses on intelligence that can engage both positionally and socially.

The most famous and widely written about example of Embodiment AI is Cog, a project begun by Rodney Brooks in the early 1990s at MIT's Artificial Intelligence Laboratory. Designed with arms, torso and a head with an expressive face, Cog was built with decentralized and distributed software and hardware.[56] What this means is that the devices and programs that operate in Cog's arm are local to that arm; the arm has certain actions it can do, and the arm can learn from its interactions with the environment. This software communicates with software in other parts of Cog, including the overarching "brainboards."[57] The theory is that as the various parts of Cog interact and learn, a more comprehensive intelligence might emerge over time.

In describing her first encounter with Cog, Turkle notes that its software enables its robotic eyes to track movement, and so it "noticed" her and would follow her with its eyes as she moved around the room. Turkle even found herself wanting Cog's attention, competing with others in the room for that attention.[58] Cog's ability to make "eye contact" is at least partly the result of its practicing the behavior through its robotic body.[59] Without the focus on embodiment, an AI like Cog that learns from physical and social interaction would be impossible.

The robotic body is obviously different from the human body: it is not a result of sexual reproduction, it is not composed of cells and it does not grow, develop and age organically. It is also infinitely easier to replicate and relocate the artificial intelligence in the robotic body, a body that need not be limited to humanoid shapes.[60] The relationship of body to soul, so central to theological anthropology, thus has an imperfect, even misleading parallel in the relationship of hardware to software. While Embodiment AI

---

[54]Rosalind Picard, *Affective Computing* (Cambridge: MIT Press, 2000), 136, cited in Barbour, "Neuroscience, Artificial Intelligence, and Human Nature," 378.

[55]Foerst, "Cog, a Humanoid Robot," 100.

[56]Ibid., 101.

[57]Ibid., 102.

[58]Turkle, *Alone Together*, 83–4. Much of Turkle's fifth chapter in *Alone Together* focuses on Cog and a related embodied AI named Kismet.

[59]Barbour, "Neuroscience, Artificial Intelligence, and Human Nature," 377.

[60]For example, Boston Dynamics builds a robotic "dog" named Spot that can be used in industrial, commercial and public safety applications.

makes a compelling case that the software depends on the hardware to learn, and that the development of intelligence is better in an "embodied, situated agent,"[61] it also remains that the replicability of both the hardware and the software undermines any claim to the unique union of the two in any one specific robotic AI.

Embodied AI helps to highlight the question of the human response to AI. Beth Singler draws on Martin Buber's "I-Thou" and "I-It" language, stating that many Christian theologians place AI firmly in the category of an "It" because AI is seen as a tool to be used and ought not to be accorded the status of "person."[62] She also notes, however, that the use of "It" language has historically been used to oppress and marginalize other humans and thus advocates caution on the question of technological personhood.[63] Turkle also references Buber, saying that the "symmetry" suggested by an "I-Thou" relationship is simply not present between humans and AI. However, she also says that Cog and embodied AI are able to play on the human desire for that symmetry to exist, and Cog's enchanting body and ability to (apparently) render its gaze at the human make us more likely to respond to it as though it is a Thou.[64] Foerst notes this question of the human response to the embodied AI but emphasizes those who worked on the Cog project were functionalist in how they perceive the body and intelligence. As such, Cog and other embodied AI are helpful for humans in "telling us something about the underlying mechanisms that make us the beings we are."[65]

An Artificial Agent?

A final question about the image of God and artificial intelligence is that of agency or free will. Scott Hawley puts the question directly, asking, "Is it appropriate to ascribe agency to algorithms?"[66] At issue for him is that there seems to be a leap in moving from a "mathematical operation," which at heart even the most complex algorithms are, and "intelligent agency."[67] Thus, the earlier question of what is meant by the "intelligence" of artificial intelligence is here extended to what it would mean for that artificial intelligence to be able to make free choices.

Assessing this very question, Richard Spinello draws on the philosophical work of Karol Wojtyła, later John Paul II, to argue that digital agency cannot be moral agency. Spinello recognizes that there can exist artificially intelligent agents, here defining agent as something that is "capable of acting in a way that produces an effect."[68] However, to go the further step of ascribing moral agency presumes both that the agent is aware of its actions and that it is capable of intending its actions and their effects.[69] Consciousness and intention are necessary for what Wojtyła calls "man-acts," for which one can be responsible; by contrast, those acts that are involuntary (such as one's heart beating) are the passive

---

[61]Barbour, "Neuroscience, Artificial Intelligence, and Human Nature," 376.
[62]Beth Singler, "An Introduction to Artificial Intelligence and Religion for the Religious Studies Scholar," *Implicit Religion* 20, no. 3 (2017): 215–31 (226).
[63]Ibid., 226–7.
[64]Turkle, *Alone Together*, 85, 90.
[65]Foerst, "Cog, a Humanoid Robot," 108.
[66]Hawley, "Challenges for an Ontology of Artificial Intelligence," 83.
[67]Ibid., 84.
[68]Richard A Spinello, "Karol Wojtyla on Artificial Moral Agency and Moral Accountability," *National Catholic Bioethics Quarterly* 11, no. 3 (2011): 479–501 (484).
[69]Ibid., 486.

"something-happens-in-man."[70] He asserts that artificial agents lack consciousness, both in the form of being aware of the self as acting and in the form of being responsible for the choice to act.[71] As a result, artificial agents are passive, "something-happens" agents that act by necessity according to the program and algorithm they come with.[72] Thus, any moral agency with respect to artificial agents must be ascribed to those who created or operated them.[73]

As a related question, Albert Erisman and Tripp Parker consider what it would mean to describe an artificial intelligence as "virtuous."[74] AI is generally not described as having habits, which are essential to virtue, but instead have algorithms. As noted above, machine learning is predicated on designing algorithms that learn and can improve their ability to carry out certain functions, which one might liken to virtue. However, this returns us to Spinello's claim that an artificial agent does not have consciousness or intentionality. With respect to virtue, an artificial intelligence would need to have a purpose (*telos*) towards which it aims. While depictions of AI in popular media often imagine the program developing a notably antihuman purpose, a less apocalyptic and more likely possibility is that its purpose would come from the decisions of the programmer.[75] But in doing so, the AI would not have consciously, intentionally appropriated that purpose as its own. The question of the virtuous AI, or more basically the morally responsible AI, is thus ultimately predicated on whether it can have conscious and intelligent intentionality.

THE TECHNOLOGICAL PERSON

In light of the preceding considerations of artificial intelligence and the *imago Dei*, we close by turning to the question of personhood. So much work on artificial intelligence is done with reference to human persons, both concerning how the possibilities of AI mirror the human and concerning how humans respond to AI. Despite the common anthropomorphizing of machines, or the science fiction narrative of the android that wishes to be human, it seems straightforward to say that AI is not and cannot be human. Even if one stipulates the technological possibility of creating an AI capable of intelligence, emotion and agency that is comparable to human intelligence, emotion and agency, there would still be two objections. First, would those capacities *be* human, or only analogous to the human? Second, they would not be embodied in a human body.

But even if AI cannot be human, does that mean that AI cannot be a person? Antje Jackelén writes that "a person is not necessarily identical with a human being as a biological entity" and then proposes the possibility of *techno sapiens* in order to distinguish a *personal* artificial intelligence from a human being.[76] Anne Foerst also distinguishes between person and human, describing personhood not in terms of substantive capacities

---

[70]Ibid., 489.

[71]Ibid., 491.

[72]Ibid., 501.

[73]Ibid., 486. Public discussion about responsibility when autonomous vehicles crash and harm people is a recent and potent example of this moral question.

[74]Al Erisman and Tripp Parker, "Artificial Intelligence: A Theological Perspective," *Perspectives on Science and Christian Faith* 71, no. 2 (June 2019): 95–106 (97).

[75]Brian Christian notes that classical Christian thought would see the *telos* of AI coming from its creator, while the existentialist would see it coming out of the AI's self-actualization (Christian, *The Most Human Human*, 138). It is worth noting that the decision of the programmer can have unintended and negative consequences (Erisman and Parker, "Artificial Intelligence," 98–9).

[76]Jackelén, "The Image of God as *Techno Sapiens*," 295.

that one possesses but rather in light of "the narrative processes of mutual storytelling about who each of us is."[77] For her, as AI robots like Cog become integrated into human life, they may be recognized as persons.[78] Indeed, within the Christian tradition, the term "person" has never really been restricted to humans; most notably, the doctrine of the Trinity classically describes God as "three persons and one nature."

What then makes something—someone—a person? In his study of personhood in the thought of St. Thomas Aquinas, W. Norris Clarke works with both substantive ("the *in-itself* dimension of being") and relational ("the *towards-others* aspect") approaches.[79] This leads him to offer the following definition of a person: "an actual existence [i.e., with its own act of existence], distinct from all others, possessing an intellectual nature, so that it can be the self-conscious, responsible source of its own actions."[80] To further explain this definition, Clarke offers three characteristics of the person: self-possessing, self-communicative and self-transcending.[81] First, the person is self-possessing in two ways: in terms of knowledge, the self is conscious or aware of the self; and in terms of activity, the self is able to choose freely and take responsibility for one's actions.[82] Second, the self-communicative dimension of the person refers both to a passive, receptive aspect of the relational person and to an active, expressive side.[83] Passively, the person is receptive to creation, both in terms of other persons and of the rest of the external world,[84] while actively, the person seeks to communicate the self "in some way ... toward sharing the good that the communicator possesses."[85] Thus, the person, according to Clarke, can only fully exist "in the plural," in relation to other persons.[86]

Third, Clarke describes the person as self-transcending, meaning not merely going beyond the self (which occurs already in the self-communicative dimension) but in a "radical *decentering of consciousness* from self to God."[87] This is a "vertical" transcendence that builds on the prior horizontal self-transcendence of self-communication and on the understanding and awareness of the self in self-possession. Through this third dimension of the person, Clarke ties personhood to the Thomistic *exitus-reditus*, where creation comes from God and returns to God.[88] Indeed, the three dimensions of self-possession, self-communication and self-transcendence reflect the intimate grounding of the person's existence in God, the perfect ground of existence and self-communicating love.[89]

For much of his analysis, Clarke understandably focuses on *human* persons, who are themselves in relation to divine persons. He also, at least briefly, refers to angelic persons.[90] Can his description of persons as self-possessing, self-communicating and self-transcending apply to the hypothetical *technological* person? Spinello consistently asserts

---

[77]Anne Foerst, *God in the Machine: What Robots Teach Us about Humanity and God* (New York: Dutton, 2004), 186.

[78]Ibid., 189.

[79]W. Norris Clarke, *Person and Being* (Milwaukee, WI: Marquette University Press, 1993), 5.

[80]Ibid., 29. When applied to a "human person," Clarke simply adds "human" before the word "intellectual."

[81]Ibid., 42.

[82]Ibid., 43.

[83]Ibid., 64.

[84]Ibid., 72.

[85]Ibid., 76.

[86]Ibid., 76.

[87]Ibid., 98. Emphasis original.

[88]Ibid., 100–1.

[89]Ibid., 10–12.

[90]Ibid., 32.

the non-personhood of artificial agents precisely because they lack the consciousness and intentionality described by Clarke as part of the self-possessing person.[91] However, Spinello treats "human" and "person" interchangeably in doing so, nor does he allow for the possibility of technological development that might create an AI that is capable of consciousness and intentionality. Jackelén, by contrast, encourages the distinction between person and human, suggesting that the technological person is at least theoretically possible and should not "cause any serious theological problems."[92] Russell Bjork similarly considers a thought experiment in which not only does future technology make AI capable of reason and agency comparable to the human, but also that such technological persons might be enabled by God to be in personal relationship with the divine.[93] For Bjork, such a possibility, as far-fetched as it may seem, ought not to be seen as a threat to human worth.

It seems evident that the technology for an artificial intelligence that could even potentially meet Clarke's three dimensions of a person does not exist. This is not to say that the technology will never exist, and thus the idea of a technological person firmly remains hypothetical. But in pursuing that as a thought experiment, it raises several questions for future consideration in theological anthropology. First, could the hypothetical technological person have a self-transcendent relationship with God, as Bjork suggests? If so, how might we think about grace, sin, or redemption with respect to that person?[94] If the technological person should become a reality, would this in any way affect the understanding of the human person as created in the image of God, or of our understanding of what the image of God is?[95] Could the technological person also be considered *imago Dei*, or would it be better described as *imago hominis*, or something else entirely? Finally, what moral responsibilities would human persons have with respect to technological persons?[96] Rather than focusing on the relative humanness of artificial intelligence, theological anthropology can offer more by thinking through what a technological person might mean for the human.

SUGGESTED FURTHER READING

Clarke, W. Norris, *Person and Being* (Milwaukee, WI: Marquette University Press, 1993).

Foerst, Anne, *God in the Machine: What Robots Teach Us about Humanity and God* (New York: Dutton, 2004).

Herzfeld, Noreen, *In Our Image: Artificial Intelligence and the Human Spirit* (Minneapolis, MN: Fortress Press, 2002).

Turkle, Sherry, *Alone Together: Why We Expect More from Technology and Less from Each Other* (New York: Basic Books, 2011).

---

[91]Spinello, "Karol Wojtyla on Artificial Moral Agency and Moral Accountability," 500.

[92]Jackelén, "The Image of God as *Techno Sapiens*," 295

[93]Bjork, "Artificial Intelligence and the Soul," 100.

[94]Jackelén, "The Image of God as *Techno Sapiens*," 295.

[95]Barbour, "Neuroscience, Artificial Intelligence, and Human Nature," 380; Bjork, "Artificial Intelligence and the Soul," 99.

[96]Turkle, *Alone Together*, 45; Barbour, "Neuroscience, Artificial Intelligence, and Human Nature," 380.

CHAPTER TWENTY-SEVEN

Disability: Raising Challenges to Rationality and Embodiment in Theological Anthropology

LORRAINE CUDDEBACK-GEDEON

This chapter begins with a simple premise: the concept of "disability" is no more and no less socially constructed than other categories (such as race and gender) that form and inform a person's identity. This is not an uncontroversial position, but it is nonetheless important to lay out at the start of our exploration of theological anthropology and disability. Though the term "disability" is a product of the twentieth century, until recently it seemed that what constituted a disabling condition was obvious: for example, the loss of a limb, a diagnosis of Down syndrome. However, the work of the disability rights movement has reshaped our understanding of disability, drawing attention to a wider range of embodied experiences that qualify as "disabling." Given the increasing breadth of the concept over the last half of the twentieth century, the task in this chapter is to address a set of thematic questions that disability raises for theological anthropology, in particular the way we understand the connections of souls, minds and bodies, and how we resist dualism in our anthropology. The two areas of exploration will be definitions of personhood and the plasticity of embodiment. These questions were selected in order to show how despite differences across disability—or even because of them—disability theory can help us reimagine the borders of bodies, wholeness and humanity.

In what follows, I begin with a brief overview of how disability as a concept and theory developed. I then highlight how disability (despite being a modern concept) has been theologically treated, and the most common challenges these treatments raise. The deconstructive work of these first two sections helps frame the stakes in the constructive work that follows on defining personhood, embodiment and difference. By engaging the experience of disability, in all its varieties, Christian theological anthropology has the opportunity to deepen its intersectional analysis and gain a greater awareness of voices that have been ignored in doing theology.

DEFINING DISABILITY

The origins of disability are relatively recent, located by a number of scholars in the nineteenth century. Critical literary scholar Lennard Davis was one of the first to make this argument, locating the origin of disability in the genesis of "normal" through the evolution of statistics as a mathematical science.[1] Prior to *normal*, argues Davis, one might have spoken of an ideal; although an ideal was aspirational, it was not prescriptive.[2] Normal, however, came to be prescriptive and to set expectations that bodies and behaviors had to meet. Anything outside normal was "abnormal," the concept that eventually led to disability. Abnormal represented problems to be eliminated, as seen in the co-option of normal by the eugenicists of the early twentieth century. Sociologist Allison Carey details how, at a time when the United States was rapidly changing, the white middle class felt threatened by shifts in racial demographics and gender politics. They began to use normal as a way of promoting the cultural hegemony of their values. Anything that pushed against the grain of their class, race and gender-informed social values was deemed abnormal, to be removed.[3] While the terminology of "disability" would not appear until the twentieth century, this history sets the stage for what Davis ultimately calls "normalcy": normalcy, being the fear and rejection of human difference, is to disability theory what whiteness is to critical race theory. Normalcy operates as the social and structural barrier that marginalizes people with disabilities.[4] Most importantly, the history of normal and normalcy highlights the deeply intersectional nature of the concept from its very origins. Disability has always been shaped and informed by race, class, gender and other social lenses.

Though scholars like Davis situate disability as shaped by social norms, for much of its early history disability was seen as a medical problem. The medical model of disability views disability as a physiological problem limited to a particular individual's body. If someone loses a limb, they are "cured" with a prosthetic; if someone is deaf, the supposed cure is a cochlear implant. In the late twentieth century, competing models emerged thanks to the activism of the disability rights movement. Primary among them was the social model (sometimes called a minority model, or social-minority model) of disability, which argues for a conceptual distinction between an *impairment*—paralyzed limbs or

---

[1]Lennard Davis, *Enforcing Normalcy: Disability, Deafness, and the Body* (New York: Verso, 1995). Davis names Adolphe Quetelet (1796–1874) as the statistician who first developed the concept of *l'homme moyen*, and therefore *les classes moyens* as the "exemplar of the middle way of life" (26–7); however, Francis Galton is responsible for the eventual move toward eugenics. For Quetelet, both ends of deviance from the statistical median are problematic; Galton applied value across the curve, making one end desirable, and the other undesirable (35).
[2]Davis, *Enforcing Normalcy*, 25.
[3]Allison Carey, *On the Margins of Citizenship* (Philadelphia, PA: Temple University Press, 2009), 52–82.
[4]A note on language: for the most part, I make use of "person-first" language with reference to disability, which for a long time was the norm promoted by disability advocacy groups: early self-advocates within IDD communities resented being labeled by their disability, and wanted to be seen as "a person, first." This meant using "a person with X" to name a disability. However, there has also been a recent resurgence of "identity-first" language ("disabled person") among advocacy groups, claiming disability as an identity similar to race and ethnicity—something to be proud of, not stigmatized. Many advocates in favor of identity-first language are members of communities that have identifiable cultural associations with their disability: e.g., Deaf communities, or the Autistic community. Throughout this essay, I will use person-first language when speaking at the level of generic persons, but identity-first with respect to communities in general, or when discussing a person from a community that is known to prefer identity-first language. For further information see Dana S. Dunn, Erin E. Andrews, and Anderson, Norman, "Person-First and Identity-First Language," *American Psychologist* 70, no. 3 (2015): 255–64.

blindness—and a *disability*. Whereas impairments are physiological, disabilities are not. Rather, disability is the result of how society enables or disables people according to their kind(s) of impairment(s). Someone who uses a power chair may have a physical impairment, but that person is only disabled by a building without an access ramp. When there is a ramp, they can come and go as freely as any abled-bodied person. In fact, sometimes what is regarded as a "disability" may well provide advantages: that person using a power chair may move faster than someone walking. Therefore, disability is a concept that is socially constructed, and remediated not by medical interventions, but by making social spaces more accessible. In this sense, accessibility can be the removal of architectural barriers, or education and social supports that remove stigma and foster inclusion.[5] It is important to note that these models can and do exist alongside one another: the medical model is still very much in play today, even though the social model of disability is the definition ensconced into law through the Americans with Disabilities Act (ADA) (passed in 1990).

Today, most disability advocacy is framed within the social model, in large part because it was adopted by the ADA. As written, the law currently defines a disability as: "(A) a physical or mental impairment that substantially limits one or more major life activities of such individual[s]; (B) a record of such an impairment; or (C) being regarded as having such an impairment."[6] This paints disability quite broadly, with the (intentional) result that disability operates like a large umbrella, encompassing physical impairments, learning disabilities, intellectual and developmental disabilities (IDDs), mental illness, long-term and chronic illnesses (such as cancer or HIV) and addiction.[7] This also means that any discussion of disability within theological anthropology has to attend to the internal heterogeneity of the category.

As one final note, it must be said that there is resistance, specifically within theological literature, about whether IDD can be adequately addressed under the social model.[8] The

---

[5]Other models include the rehabilitation model (popular after the Second World War), cultural models (seen in the Deaf community's self-understanding as a linguistic-cultural minority), tragedy/charity models (seen below), economic/consumer models, and more.

[6]Americans with Disabilities Act of 1990. Public Law 101–336. § 12102. 108th Congress, 2nd session (July 26, 1990). The law goes on:

> For purposes of paragraph (1), major life activities include, but are not limited to, caring for oneself, performing manual tasks, seeing, hearing, eating, sleeping, walking, standing, lifting, bending, speaking, breathing, learning, reading, concentrating, thinking, communicating, and working ... For purposes of paragraph (1), a major life activity also includes the operation of a major bodily function, including but not limited to, functions of the immune system, normal cell growth, digestive, bowel, bladder, neurological, brain, respiratory, circulatory, endocrine, and reproductive functions.

[7]The broad, inclusive nature of the definition of disability in the ADA was one of the most important (and controversial) components to the legislation. Activists were prepared to walk out on the legislation when attempts were made to define out people with HIV. See Lennard J.Davis, *Enabling Acts: The Hidden Story of How the Americans with Disabilities Act Gave the Largest US Minority Its Rights* (Boston, MA: Beacon Press, 2015), 171–2.

[8]Hans Reinders—given further attention below—is the primary critic, although he is not alone. Deborah Creamer's work also criticizes the social model on the basis that it fails to account for people who do not identify with their impairments in a positive manner. Deborah Beth Creamer, *Disability and Christian Theology Embodied Limits and Constructive Possibilities*, American Academy of Religion Academy Series (Oxford: Oxford University Press, 2009); Hans S. Reinders, *Receiving the Gift of Friendship: Profound Disability, Theological Anthropology, and Ethics* (Grand Rapids, MI: Eerdmans, 2008); John Swinton, "Who Is the God We Worship? Theologies of Disability; Challenges and New Possibilities," *International Journal of Practical Theology* 14, no. 2 (2011): 273–307; John Swinton, "From Inclusion to Belonging: A Practical Theology of Community, Disability and Humanness," *Journal of Religion, Disability & Health* 16, no. 2 (April 1, 2012): 172–90.

impact that IDD can have on a person's capacities to complete basic tasks of survival seems to transcend the kind of help that assistive technology or curb cuts offer someone with a physical disability. If the presumptive goal of accessibility and the social model is to make everyone (disabled or not) independent and self-sufficient, then it would seem there is a significant number of the disabled community that will never meet that criteria. Nonetheless, the social model is still very much applicable to IDD. It is a mistake to understand the social model of disability as denying the material reality of an impairment. Rather, the argument for the social model is that these impairments should not result in the treatment of people with disabilities as lesser human beings, or "second-class citizens." Furthermore, the definition of intellectual disability has shifted over time. During the eugenics era, "feebleminded" applied to women of supposedly incorrigible moral character: women who had children out of wedlock, or flagrantly disobeyed gendered norms in other forms.[9] This definition was undeniably culturally situated, as are our definitions, today: for example, the necessity of literacy in today's world means that an impaired ability to read is a much greater disability than it would have been a few hundred years ago. In a less literate society, having an intellectual disability but being physically abled might have fostered a greater level of inclusion. This is not to deny the bodily reality of limits that people with IDD may experience, but to challenge the presumption that it is always *obvious* what constitutes an IDD.[10]

With this overview of disability in mind, we turn to how theology has treated the topic. There is a burgeoning literature in theologies of disability, many of which engage the developments in disability theory and history just described in order to examine how theology has responded to disability across time.

THEOLOGY AND DISABILITY: SINNERS OR SAINTS?

Before addressing the challenges within theological reflection on disability, it should be noted that any discussion of disability within the tradition risks anachronism. The term and its underlying conceptual framework are a product of modernity. While certain conditions that may be considered disabilities today are very much present within the tradition (physical ailments, blindness, hearing loss), we are still reading a modern construct back into the tradition.[11]

Nonetheless, a few key trends have been identified concerning how the tradition treats people with the aforementioned impairments. Nancy Eiesland, in her groundbreaking text *The Disabled God*, argues that the treatment of disability falls into one key problem rendered in two different ways: "disability denotes an unusual relationship with God,

---

[9]Licia Carlson, *The Faces of Intellectual Disability: Philosophical Reflections* (Bloomington: Indiana University Press, 2010), 53–84; Carey, *On the Margins of Citizenship*, 52–82.

[10]Carlson, *Faces of Intellectual Disability*, 94–5. Carlson addresses this debate by proposing that, rather than ascribe some kind of essentialism to intellectual disability, we ought to understand disability as an "interactive kind": that is, a kind that is continuously shaped by social forces, particularly by relationships with others.

[11]For further methodological development of this problem, biblical studies provides the best resources. In many ways, biblical studies was an early adopter of critical disability theory, in large part because it shares the same tools of literary analysis as someone like Lennard Davis, whose background is in literary criticism. See Hector Avalos, Sarah J. Melcher, and Jeremy Schipper, eds., *This Abled Body* (Atlanta, GA: Society of Biblical Literature, 2007); Candida R. Moss and Jeremy Schipper, "Introduction," in *Disability Studies and Biblical Literature*, ed. Candida R. Moss and Jeremy Schipper (New York: Palgrave McMillan, 2011), 1–13; Amos Yong, *The Bible, Disability, and the Church: A New Vision of the People of God* (Grand Rapids, MI: Eerdmans, 2011).

and that person with disabilities is either divinely blessed or damned: the defiled evildoer or the spiritual superhero."[12] In short, disability becomes the defining element in one's relationship to God, defining someone as either sinner or saint. Scripture provides a great deal of evidence for this. On the one hand, disabilities such as blindness are frequently used as metaphors for sin; people with chronic illnesses, like lepers, are depicted as tragic outsiders. On the other hand, there are several passages that reject connections between disability and sin—when asked whether a man born blind was suffering for the sin of his parents, Jesus refutes the premise of the question (John 9:1-3). Yet, even in this positive example, Eiesland notes, the man is instrumentalized: he is blind that "God's works might be revealed in him" (John 9:3). This highlights the flip side of the problem that Eiesland names: disability is frequently viewed as a sign of "virtuous suffering," or as an object of acts of charity by the nondisabled.[13] Thomas Reynolds echoes these concerns in his work on intellectual disability and theology, *Vulnerable Communion*.[14] He distinguishes two types of theological responses to disability: one that denigrates, one that trivializes.[15] Denigrating theological responses to disability play into the stigma of sin and punishment that Eiesland highlights; trivializing responses entail the "object of charity" or "virtuous suffering" responses. In short, what underpins these theological problems is a lack of attention to the disability community as subjects in their own right. Their experiences are almost always cast as something for the nondisabled to learn from (whether a warning or a blessing) without attention to their own embodied experiences of the world.

Increasingly, theological works are trying to step into that gap, to start from the experience of disability and bring their standpoint—or as Eiesland puts it, "sitpoint"—into the center of theological conversation. These works show parallels with the development of feminist theologies, anti-racist theologies and other liberatory, contextual theologies. Particularly since the passage of the ADA, there has been a surge of works written in the liberatory mold of Eiesland.[16] Many of these liberation theologies of disability have been written by people who self-identify with the disability community.[17] Texts on IDD, however, have been slower to adopt a liberation perspective. What could be called "postliberal" theologies of disability constitute the bulk of the genre that engages IDD:[18] like liberatory theologies, postliberal theologies challenge modern presumptions

---

[12]Nancy L. Eiesland, *The Disabled God: Toward a Liberatory Theology of Disability* (Nashville, TN: Abingdon Press, 1994), 70.

[13]Eiesland, *Disabled God*, 72–4.

[14]Thomas E. Reynolds, *Vulnerable Communion: A Theology of Disability and Hospitality* (Grand Rapids, MI: Brazos Press, 2008).

[15]Reynolds, *Vulnerable Communion*, 35–7.

[16]John M. Hull, *In the Beginning There Was Darkness: A Blind Person's Conversations with the Bible*, 1st US ed. (Harrisburg, PA: Trinity Press International, 2002); Sharon V. Betcher, *Spirit and the Politics of Disablement* (Minneapolis, MN: Fortress Press, 2007); Hannah Lewis, *Deaf Liberation Theology*, Explorations in Practical, Pastoral, and Empirical Theology (Burlington, VT: Ashgate, 2007). A notable entry concerning IDD (specifically Autism) is found with Daniel Aaron Salomon, *Confessions of an Autistic Theologian: A Contextual, Liberation Theology* (CreateSpace Independent Publishing Platform, 2013).

[17]There are some exceptions to this: Molly Claire Haslam, *A Constructive Theology of Intellectual Disability: Human Being as Mutuality and Response* (New York: Fordham University Press, 2012); Amos Yong, *Theology and Down Syndrome: Reimagining Disability in Late Modernity* (Waco, TX: Baylor University Press, 2007).

[18]Jason Reimer Greig, *Reconsidering Intellectual Disability: L'Arche, Medical Ethics, and Christian Friendship* (Washington, DC: Georgetown University Press, 2016); Hans S. Reinders, *The Future of the Disabled in Liberal Society: An Ethical Analysis*, (Notre Dame, IN: University of Notre Dame Press, 2000). Both works show the influence of Stanley Hauerwas's early contribution to reflection on IDD: Stanley Hauerwas, *Suffering Presence: Theological Reflections on Medicine, the Mentally Handicapped, and the Church* (Notre Dame, IN: University of Notre Dame Press, 1986). Creamer, though on one hand writing from personal experience

of individuality and autonomy, highlight dependence and interdependence and attend to lived experiences of disability, often by including personal narratives of relationships with a disabled person. Both liberatory and postliberal theologies implicitly accept the value of experience with disability for doing theological work, but the primary difference between them concerns the stress they put on sharing in a disabled identity. Very few authors of the postliberal entries in the genre self-identify as disabled. By contrast, liberatory theologies of disability by the nondisabled often use qualitative sociological data to inject "first-person" viewpoints about disability, and IDD in particular.

The issue of self-representation is a salient one for theological anthropology, particularly for the first question we will examine: to what degree does our rational soul require the ability to identify as a self? For many postliberal theologies, liberation theology is limited because it requires a capacity for symbolic thought that people with profound IDD may lack—do such theologies inadvertently create a "hierarchy of disability?"[19] Nonetheless, liberationists contend that the voice of the disabled community is valuable: they deserve to be heard, not spoken for. In the next section, we will address how disability theologies navigate these questions, and the sinner-saint dichotomy with reference to the *imago Dei*.

IDD AND THE *IMAGO DEI*

The most salient debate for theological anthropology and disability concerns how we define "person." People with profound intellectual disabilities, such that it is difficult to tell if they can engage in even a basic level of symbolic thought, are often used as liminal "test cases" for bioethics, animal rights and other philosophical debates that center on what constitutes personhood. At the most basic theological level, a definition of personhood rests on *the imago Dei*; as a theological resource, the *imago Dei* is an invaluable means of affirming the dignity of all persons, yet, it runs into tensions when theologians attempt to specify what sets the *imago Dei* apart from the rest of creation.

The central problem is succinctly put by Molly Haslam: is the *imago Dei* relationality or rationality?[20] Haslam describes two trajectories in defining the *imago Dei*: (1) substantial definitions, which attribute the *imago Dei* to a particular quality taken as inherent in human persons; and (2) relational definitions, which situate human persons in a matrix of relationships to God, others and creation.[21] Across theologies of disability, there exists a general consensus that a substantialist rendering of the *imago Dei*, especially one that relies on reason and intellect, is insufficient because it risks excluding people with IDD.

Thomas Aquinas plays a significant role in this critique of substantialist definitions of the *imago Dei*. Reinders, Haslam and Yong all present Aquinas as part of the problematic, "rational" definitions of the *imago Dei*, with Reinders and Haslam critically engaging him. For Haslam's part, she recognizes layers of both substantialist and relational definitions within Aquinas, but ultimately finds his anthropology limited, because even his relational components place too great an emphasis on intellectual capacities.[22] Reinders engages

---

with physical disabilities and illness, nonetheless has stronger resonances with the postliberal genre. Creamer, *Disability and Christian Theology*.

[19]Reinders, *Receiving the Gift of Friendship*, 167–9.

[20]Haslam notes that she takes the distinction from Paul Ramsey. Haslam, *Constructive Theology of Intellectual Disability*, 92–116.

[21]Ibid., 93–4.

[22]Haslam, *Constructive Theology of Intellectual Disability*, 98–9.

what he sees as a particularly Roman Catholic, substantialist definition of personhood through an Aristotelian-Thomistic natural law tradition. He argues that this definition is ultimately unsatisfying because it relies on a *telos* that requires use of the intellect, which someone with a profound IDD does not possess.[23] Reinders concludes that for the natural law tradition, being born a person without use of reason means that while "you don't need to be a perfect apple to be counted as an apple in the first place ... from the perspective of its final end it is not an apple whose being carries any value."[24] For Reinders, a definition for personhood must operate universally, or not at all.

Relational definitions are preferred because of their greater capacity for inclusion, but even here there can be hurdles depending on the level of participation (enabled through intellect and reason) that is required for relationships (with God or with others) to work. Several strategies emerge to define "participation," especially for people with profound IDD. Reinders's anthropology, which set the stage for much of the work on IDD that followed, prescinds from the responsibility of participation altogether. Instead, Reinders proposes a purely extrinsic definition of personhood, based on "sharing the life of God ... [as] an end we are drawn into; it consists of a perfection that is not fulfilled by our own doing."[25] The grace by which we are granted a relationship with God comes only from God's own self, as pure gift, without any *required* response to earn it. God acts, we receive.

Haslam and Reynolds similarly adopt our relationship with God as the core of the *imago Dei*, but take less extreme approaches to the question of human agency within that relationship. Reynolds stresses that participation in the creativity, relationality and availability of the *imago Dei* does not require language and symbolic communication, instead emphasizing the role of embodied relationships. Arguably, communication through embodiment could still require a kind of intentionality that Reinders would argue is not possible for all. Nonetheless, by shifting the bias away from language and toward our bodies, Reynolds makes space for participation in relationship through bodily experiences of interdependence. Haslam's work also examines the question of bodily response and agency for people with profound intellectual disabilities. Drawing on her experiences as a physical therapist, Haslam describes the embodied experience of therapy for a client, Chan, with a profound intellectual disability. Within that description, Haslam highlights the unsure process of interpretation between changes in Chan's bodily movements and his therapist's reaction (e.g., does this vocalization mean Chan wants to join a game?).[26] She displays an ambiguity in whether Chan's movements have any clear intent behind them, while also proposing that intent does not matter. Chan offers an embodied response to the world, regardless of whether that is accompanied by the ability for symbolic thought or for establishing the self apart from the other. Reynolds and

---

[23]Reinders begins with the image of Kelly, a woman with encephalitis who appears (in a medical sense) to lack the very part of her brain that engages symbolic thought.

[24]Ibid., 103. Yet, it is not entirely clear whether Reinders's exegesis is accurate. For example, Miguel Romero and John Berkman, rather than looking at what Aquinas writes about rationality writ large, examine Aquinas' analysis of *amentes*, those without the use of reason. This resource provides a much more nuanced understanding of his theological anthropology than critics realize. Miguel J. Romero, "The Happiness of 'Those Who Lack the Use of Reason,'" *The Thomist: A Speculative Quarterly Review* 80, no. 1 (2016): 49–96; John Berkman, "Are Persons with Profound Intellectual Disabilities Sacramental Icons of Heavenly Life? Aquinas on Impairment," *Studies in Christian Ethics* 26, no. 1 (2013): 83–96.

[25]Reinders, *Receiving the Gift of Friendship*, 116.

[26]Haslam, *Constructive Theology of Intellectual Disability*, 107–9.

Haslam, rather than forgo human agency in our relationship with God altogether, prefer to expand the notion of what constitutes agency and participation.

While Reinders, Reynolds and Haslam forgo a substantive definition, Pentecostal theologian Amos Yong proposes an "emergent" theological anthropology that could hold the relational and substantive together. Engaging cognitive neuroscience, Yong describes emergence as "a theory of how mental (cognitional) properties … are dependent on but not fully explicable by physical (brain) properties."[27] By adopting an emergentist view, Yong wants to overcome dualism: holding body and brain together, and yet not reducing one to the other. In this, Yong starts with the body itself as substance, and then argues for a relational layer to the *imago Dei* that highlights Jesus' actions on the cross. While this move risks valorizing suffering, Yong also highlights the act of kenosis that occurs on the cross. If "God's power 'is made perfect in weakness,'" the cross is not just a sign of suffering, but a sign that God's love includes the "weak," the "foolish," the oppressed and marginalized.[28] Much like Reynolds and Haslam, Yong seeks a multivalent description of the *imago Dei* that can account for the full range of human embodiment, and the relationships experienced in and through that embodiment.

Much of what is at stake in debates about how to understand the *imago Dei* in light of the experience of IDD is also about how to understand the relationship between our embodied experience and our minds. In short, it is a part of the long-standing battle against dualism within the Christian tradition. The following section examines that from the other side of the problem: what have our bodies to do with our Christian identity?

BODIES, WHOLENESS AND (ESCHATOLOGICAL) HEALING

As theologian Sharon Betcher describes, our culture shows ongoing, deep discomfort and stigma related to disability: the disabled body reflects "the unprocessable stigmata of mortality."[29] Disability interrogates the assumptions that we make about embodiment, particularly how we might understand the plasticity of the body. Medical interventions have made it so that "broken" parts of the body can now conform to normalcy. Some of these are controversial (e.g., cochlear implants among the Deaf community), while some are so commonplace as to be invisible, like glasses and contact lenses. A glasses wearer myself, I know how readily I forget that they are an addition to the body, a piece of adaptive technology without which I might experience some significant limitations (such as the inability to drive or to read text at the front of a classroom). Such technological interventions are often made in the service of pursuing some notion of bodily "wholeness." Yet wholeness is slippery, complex: even in the innocuous example of glasses, when I wear them I am seen as whole precisely because of how commonplace they have become, even though they indicate a clear visual impairment. For people with less common impairments, they are often reduced to nothing but their bodies, and the problems their bodies supposedly present.

This question of the body and wholeness calls forward how disability theorists discuss bodily, material elements of disability.[30] On the one hand disability theorists consistently

---

[27]Yong, *Theology and Down Syndrome*, 170.
[28]Ibid., 178.
[29]Betcher, *Spirit and the Politics of Disablement*, 196.
[30]Tobin Siebers, *Disability Theory* (Ann Arbor: University of Michigan Press, 2008); Susan Wendell, *The Rejected Body: Feminist Philosophical Reflections on Disability* (New York: Routledge, 1996).

resist the Western, medical myth of being able to control the body and eliminate pain;[31] at the same time, some theorists also resist a strong constructivism that risks playing into a "mind over body" sense of control, since the psyche is the primary location of resistance to normalcy.[32] Disabled embodiment calls us to pay deeper attention to how our material bodies navigate complex networks of relationships; it also shows us the permeability of disability. Over the course of a lifetime, as we grow from infants and age as adults, our bodies go through phases and degrees of (dis)ability. In short, the nondisabled are really just the temporarily able-bodied.

The theological import of these debates is reflected in two areas that address the Christian vision of the body: healing miracles in scripture and the form of the resurrected body. Both represent theological understandings of "flourishing" and "wholeness." On this first point, the healing miracles, a shift from an individualistic "curing" to a community-centric "healing" in our exegesis creates space for a more complex understanding of the relationship between a self, a body and the experience of disability. To take seriously the witness of scripture is to see Jesus perform numerous healing miracles on individuals with impairments that would be understood as disabling, today. It is one of the most consistent marks of Jesus' ministry across all the gospels. And if we take this ministry to be a sign of what the kingdom will look like, then it might be easy to conclude that impairment has no place in it. Yet, there is a growing literature in biblical studies that offers constructive, corrective hermeneutical lenses to refocus theological readings of disability in the Bible.

These new hermeneutics work against a "normate" hermeneutic, one that brings ableist assumptions to interpretations that may not have been shared by the communities behind the texts.[33] For example, consider the story of the man born blind in John: though he has a vision impairment, he does not ask for healing, he was not totally helpless (he is neither called a beggar nor does he need help to wash in the pool at Siloam). Rather than read a text like this as focused on the curing of an impairment, it is better to understand it as a story of healing: Kathy Black, among others, distinguishes curing from healing by highlighting how the latter is a complex process of meaning-making that engages communities.[34] This draws attention to how seeming "cures" within scripture are performed with an eye to reunification with a community; healing, then, is more about overcoming the divisions that ableism may cause than about fixing a body.

While rereading healing miracles as less about physical cures and more about the repair of social relationships can help mitigate some ableist presumptions about what constitutes wholeness and human flourishing, this is a new tool for an old problem. Candida Moss argues that patristic writings on the general resurrection emphasize eschatological

---

[31]Wendell, *The Rejected Body*, 85–116.

[32]Siebers, *Disability Theory*, 53–69. This is actually not unlike the criticism that Reinders makes of the social model, and Reinders does engage "realist" versions of that model that are similar to Wendell and Siebers. He ultimately finds even this version problematic, arguing that it still relies on rational agency to have political effectiveness. In this regard, he embraces a critique that "realists" make, but neglects how they embrace bodily vulnerability and interdependence, not merely political agency. Reinders, *Receiving the Gift of Friendship*, 68–72.

[33]Kerry H. Wynn, "The Normate Hermeneutic and Interpretations within the Yahwistic Narratives," in *This Abled Body: Rethinking Disabilities in Biblical Studies*, ed. Hector Avalos, Sarah J. Melcher and Jeremy Schipper (Atlanta, GA: Society of Biblical Literature, 2007), 93; Amos Yong, *The Bible, Disability, and the Church* (Grand Rapids, MI: Eerdmans, 2011). For discussion of liturgical rites in connection with scripture, see Bruce Morrill, *Divine Worship and Human Healing: Liturgical Theology at the Margins of Life and Death* (Collegeville, MN: Pueblo Books, 2009).

[34]Kathy Black, *A Healing Homiletic: Preaching and Disability* (Nashville, TN: Abingdon Press, 1996), 50–4.

cures, a result of integrating scripture with Platonic strains of philosophy.[35] Platonic understandings of wholeness, order and aesthetics shaped the conceptual rendering of bodies in the general resurrection: "The beatification of the body and the redemption of the flesh mean the erasure of deformity."[36] Thus, where scripture might see in disability an opportunity for God's salvific power, in early church teachings impairment was rendered as a greater obstacle: it "becomes—as a corruption—a hindrance to finding God."[37] As a response to this assumption that disability—or more accurately, impairment—would be erased in the general resurrection, Yong and Eiesland offer constructive arguments for the presence of impairment in our resurrection bodies. These proposals overlap on two principles: the presence of wounds in Christ's glorified body and the importance of disability to the continuation of personal identity within the resurrected body.

First, the depiction of the wounds in the resurrected body of Jesus provides scriptural witness to a continuity of impairment in the general resurrection. Eiesland goes so far as to speak of the resurrected Jesus as "the disabled God," who serves as a sign "that our non-conventional, and sometimes difficult, bodies participate fully in the imago Dei."[38] Yong expands the connection between these wounds and disability: while he cannot draw an immediate connection between the physical impairment and the experience of IDD, he does find Christological resources for "weakness" within the Pauline epistles. Not only does Jesus reveal an impairment in his own resurrected body, but the kenosis on the Cross is taken to reveal a God whose "foolishness is wiser than human wisdom (1 Cor 1:25)."[39]

The second reason for a continuity of impairment in resurrected bodies is related: the wounds of the resurrected Jesus are used as a sign of his personal identity as the Christ, the one who both died and rose. Yong develops this connection between personal identity and disability for people with IDD: "People with intellectual or developmental disabilities ... will retain their phenotypical features in the resurrection bodies. There will be sufficient continuity to ensure recognizability as well as self-identity."[40] The wording here is slippery: "phenotypical" is ordinarily read as physical, but the definition can be broader. Yong offers clarification on this point in a response to a review:

> My claim is that what persists is at minimal the marks of our present disabilities and impairments. Such marks would include, but not be limited to, phenotypical appearances, mental capacities, behavioral expressions, and verbal, emotional, and interpersonal traits, among other perceivable—whether visually or audibly—features that emerge from and express human identities across the lifespan.[41]

This confirms that he sees the potential for impairment to be present even in nonmaterial elements of resurrected bodies: behavioral expressions, verbal and emotional traits, and so forth. To be clear, Yong's "dynamic eschatology" does not leave these marks of

---

[35]Candida R. Moss, "Heavenly Healing: Eschatological Cleansing and the Resurrection of the Dead in the Early Church," *Journal of the American Academy of Religion* 79, no. 4 (2011): 991–1017.

[36]Ibid., 1009. Moss goes on to deconstruct the various ways that glorified bodies reflected the racialized and gendered expectations of time, noting that the doctrine of the general resurrection—while affirming actual bodies—has been subject to a similar social construction as disability itself.

[37]Ibid., 1007.

[38]Eiesland, *The Disabled God*, 107.

[39]Yong, *Theology and Down Syndrome*, 178.

[40]Ibid., 282.

[41]Amos Yong, "Disability Theology of the Resurrection: Persisting Questions and Additional Considerations—A Response to Ryan Mullins," *Ars Disputandi* 12 (2012): 5.

continuity of impairments in a static state. Drawing on Gregory of Nyssa's *epectasis*, or "the doctrine of everlasting progress," Yong sees the soul as traveling "an unending journey of the individual as he or she is transformed from perfection to perfection into the glorious knowledge, beauty, truth, and love of God."[42] It would seem, then, that how much of what these bodies retain remains recognizable throughout this process is an open question. This does mean, however, that the kind of transformation undergone by a person with IDD is not qualitatively different than the transformation undergone by the nondisabled.

FUTURE DIRECTIONS

If we reconceive of healing, wholeness and resurrected bodies in a way that defies normalcy, this raises several further questions that will need more investigation. First among these are certainly conversations about transhumanism. Typically discussed in relationship to bioethics, medical ethics and genetics, which tend to operate in a different discursive spheres than disability theory, there is nonetheless much that the two can learn from one another. Second, disability theory can also deepen the role that intersectionality plays within our discussion of theological anthropology. While race, gender and class are lenses frequently used within Christian theology, ability status is often neglected. Normalcy, with its deeply intersectional history, could be a valuable tool for engaging and naming a variety of structural sins and injustices.

The disabled community has sometimes been called the "silent majority"—the experience of disability, when considered over the span of a human life is nigh universal. At the same time, we cannot let the social model be so watered down as to lose the political vulnerability and differences in how the disabled community is treated—and especially in how theology has neglected this silent majority. Attending to disability offers us valuable insights into theological anthropology that can resist dualism and uncover new ways of understanding the complex, dynamic connections of our bodies and souls.

SUGGESTED FURTHER READING

Disability Studies

Carlson, Licia, *The Faces of Intellectual Disability Philosophical Reflections* (Bloomington: Indiana University Press, 2010).

Davis, Lennard J., *The Disability Studies Reader*, 4th ed. (New York: Routledge, 2013).

Nielsen, Kim E., *A Disability History of the United States* (Boston, MA: Beacon Press, 2012).

Biblical Studies and Disability

Avalos, Hector, Sarah J. Melcher, and Jeremy Schipper (eds.), *This Abled Body: Rethinking Disabilities in Biblical Studies* (Atlanta, GA: Society of Biblical Literature, 2007).

Disability and Christian History

Brock, Brian, and John Swinton (eds.), *Disability in the Christian Tradition: A Reader* (Grand Rapids, MI: Eerdmans, 2012).

---

[42]Yong, *Theology and Down Syndrome*, 277.

CHAPTER TWENTY-EIGHT

A Theological Anthropology of Racism

AMEY VICTORIA ADKINS-JONES

"Race is an idea, not a fact," historian Nell Irvin states in the opening remarks to *The History of White People*.[1] Once thought to be a biological given, and now more frequently understood to be a social construct, it perhaps goes without saying that race, the *idea*, still performs itself today as a kind of universal known. Race is a peculiar problem—one that has shifted meanings across historic, geographic and social contexts, all while yet subtending an enduring commitment to being a primary arbiter of difference. Who does not know "race" when they see it? Who has not been baptized into the social waters of racial knowing, of racial conclusion? We find ourselves in a world where everyone, to some degree, has been taught to think about difference, hierarchy, purity and superiority, across multiple registers. But none rings so clearly as that of the physical. As Ibram Kendi writes, "Racist ideas are ideas. Anyone can produce them or consume them."[2] Indicting the universal implications of anti-Black racism in particular, Kendi continues,

> Anyone—Whites, Latina/os, Blacks, Asians, Native Americans—anyone can express the idea that Black people are inferior, that something is wrong with Black people. Anyone can believe both racist and antiracist ideas, that certain things are wrong with Black people and other things are equal.[3]

Debates rage over the effects of race, as well as the responses to race and racism—whether to engage it, offer reparations for it, ignore it, dismiss it, examine it, extinguish it or simply hope for some diluted vision of a post-racial world. Even when understood as a historical fiction, the realities of institutional racism, police brutality and mass incarceration all indicate how the idea of race functions for many as gospel truth.

Contemporary notions of race—the pseudo-factual connotations of peoples, melanin contents, practices, beliefs and perhaps most of all, *potential*—trace back to the earliest attempts at the scientific classifications of difference among the peoples of the world. Such scientists—white, European—endeavored fiercely to bring order to the chaotic encounters of the presumed Other, pontificating from their own bodies and lives as the center point from which all Others would be calibrated. But such determinations were never benign.

---

[1] Nell Irvin Painter, *The History of White People* (New York: W. W. Norton, 2010), xi.
[2] Ibram X. Kendi, *Stamped from the Beginning: The Definitive History of Racist Ideas in America* (New York: Nation Books, 2016), 10.
[3] Ibid.

When sketched inside of a Christian theological imagination, the emergence of "race"'—the varying skin colors and ethnicities of peoples—gestated within the broader question of what exactly it means to be human—what are we to make of our created selves, of our lives and our destinies, of our means and our ends? The questions were less about whether or not God created the varying "races" of humanity in their bodily forms. Instead, with far more nuance and violent capacity, the questions were tied to one's degree of humanity, one's place within a divine *ordo salutis* and whether or not such an Other would be considered human at all. What lingered among confessing mouths and believing hearts was an ethical apparatus, with assumed divisions of inferiority and superiority, that asked and answered what good these lesser "races" were for. Could these "lesser" races even *be* "good"?

It will take several tomes to attempt to articulate any purity of origins (as if there were any), particularly that of the idea of race (as we now know it). Instead, this chapter will signal an evolutionary theology of race as a confessional practice, as a system of belief—an invisible creed we have assimilated into our ideas around both Creator and creature. As Painter's fuller conclusion intimates, "race is an idea not a fact, and its questions demand answers from the conceptual rather than the factual realm."[4] As such, this chapter will consider several genealogical moments marking the theological significance of Western European colonial encounters with African and indigenous American peoples upon Christian theological anthropological thought. More specifically, as the ideas of both race and racism are fluid, manifesting variably in different locations and circumstances, this chapter will focus on the significance of anti-Black racism(s) stemming from the European colonial expansion from the fifteenth century forward. Likewise, it will focus on contemporary Black American theological scholarship addressing the question of race in the Christian imagination. These specifications are meant not to exclude but to lay the foundations for bridging more nuanced and specific conversations about *racial confession* I am arguing herein, and provide resources for exploring more deeply the significance of race both for the study of theological anthropology as well as for the church and the world. To this end, it will consider how Black American theologians have understood the modern erasure of Jesus' Jewish identity as critical groundwork for the continued promulgation of racist ideas within the theological imagination. Finally, juxtaposing the idea of "race" against the far more insidious dynamics of "racism," it examines how Black theologians have mapped interventions toward liberation, as it pertains to a sustained and transformative theological dialogue.

THE WAKE OF MODERNITY

Augustine's formulation of race and the human person still resonates as one of the most foundational conclusions of theological anthropology, for good and for bad. Writing in the early fifth century in *Civitate de Dei*, the African theologian and bishop of Hippo notes,

> Whoever is born anywhere as a human being, that is, as a rational mortal creature, however strange he may appear to our senses in bodily form or colour or motion or utterance, or in any faculty, part of quality of his nature whatsoever, let no true

---

[4]Painter, *The History of White People*, xi.

believer have any doubt that such an individual is descended from the one man who was first created.[5]

Even so early in the church, the *idea* of the monstrous "other"—those presumably grotesque and remarkable beings catalogued and described by Pliny the Elder—loomed heavily in the minds of theologians, torn between a missional impulse and fear. The question Augustine was responding to was undoubtedly one of human being, but the premise of the inquiry itself was already steeped in distinction and hierarchy—were the monstrous races referenced at the far ends of the earth actual descendants of Adam, or cursed sons of Noah?[6] The consideration of a united vision of the human race wholly descended as the creation of the supreme Creator seems clear here for Augustine, and contours a theological anthropology egalitarian in vision and scope. But Augustine's causal link between rationality and humanity will provide enough margin for the slippage that would occur in centuries to come. By the end of his meditations, he hedges his thought with caution, actually leaving the *evaluation* of human being open for interpretation:

> Let me then tentatively and guardedly state my conclusion. Either the written accounts of certain races are completely unfounded or, if such races do exist, they are not human; or, if they are human, they descended from Adam.[7]

By what means do we acknowledge the human, and on what grounds can one be excluded from this category? Already Augustine signals fluidity in determining the inclusion or exclusion of other "races" who exhibit difference—monstrosity being a categorically aesthetic and subjective judgment linking theological reasoning to the ordering of that which is unintelligible. In retrospect, Augustine's confusion is specious, yet even in the contemporary moment, the bias that comes from centering one's own experience (and presuming one's logic most proximate to divine interest) as a means of casting a world is wholly recognizable. For one, the presumed assumption of the monstrous—of the curse, of sin, of evil—as a starting point of appraisal will direct a course to far different conclusions than that of the inherent goodness of God's created work as premise for exploration. As David Kelsey describes in his prolific volumes on the subject,

> There is no single, simple Christian metanarrative. Nor can there be, parasitic on it, any Christian anthropological metatheory about human persons that can, at least in principle, systematically synthesize all relevant truth claims about human being, Christian theological claims and otherwise. Human beings are in their own way too richly glorious, too inexhaustibly incomprehensible, too capable of profound distortions and bondage in living deaths, too capable of holiness, in short, too mysterious to be captured in that fashion.[8]

---

[5]Augustine, *City of God. Vol. V: Books 16–18.35*, trans. Eva M. Sanford, Loeb Classical Library 415 (Cambridge: Harvard University Press, 1957), XVI, viii.

[6]The irony here is that, technically, even those cursed by Noah would have still held genealogical relation to Adam. We return to the significance of this trope for the justification of chattel slavery.

[7]Augustine, *City of God*, XVI, viii.

[8]David Kelsey, *Eccentric Existence: A Theological Anthropology* (Louisville: Westminster John Knox Press, 2009), 131. Kelsey here does not devolve into an open market of anthropological interpretation of the self and its discontents but rather holds together human difference in light of God's activity in the world. As Ian McFarland describes, in resisting the "normative gaze" that can so readily problematize any theological anthropological claim,

> many attempts to describe what we are as human beings have proved to be dead ends. They are dead ends in one respect because ... they invariably entail the exclusion of significant categories of individuals on rather

Kelsey posits a resistance to an anthropology apart from particularity, one that takes seriously theology's capacity itself to learn and grow, scholastically as well as ethically, across the Christian continuum. For theological anthropology to take seriously the problem of the idea of race, we must realize that the beauty of humanity, the glory of creaturely existence in relation with a loving Creator, the ideas of richness, endless, inexhaustible capacity celebrated for her incomprehensibility, for her profundity, for her complexity—were concepts denied to certain *kinds* of bodies, an exercise that uniquely both disavowed and destroyed in the inhumane moments of Christian-colonial enterprise.[9] As Willie Jennings describes, "Christianity and its theologians live in conceptual worlds that have not in any substantive way reckoned with the ramifications of colonialism for Christian identity or the identity of theology."[10] While there are several reasons to consider why this has not happened, the inability to take seriously theological complicity in racial belief has provided regular maintenance for the fissures of racist thought that have inflected both the church and the world.[11] However, thinking forward to the questions of communion and being in theological thought remains an insufficient endeavor apart from this reckoning.

In the span of colonial encounters, particularly those between an emerging Europe, Africa and the Americas burgeoning from the technologies and advancements of the fifteenth century onward, systematic comprehension and categorization of those *too* mysterious to *not* be captured or conquered was the quotidian reality. To pick a place, any place, to begin to describe the connections between being Black, being *raced* and the emergence of whiteness as an identity will ultimately have limitations. For one, processes of racial categorization, demarcation, exploitation and exclusion did not begin or end with the idea of Blackness itself. Again, Blackness has never maintained a clear or static definition, whether as a descriptor given or a descriptor claimed. But as Andrew Prevot describes,

> Blackness seems to have become the one *undeniably* racial category, the last perceived position that defines and secures the idea of race in a multicultural world. Every other color besides blackness appears capable of being translated into a marker of culture, ethnicity, or something similar.[12]

---

arbitrary grounds. But they are also dead ends because they tend more or less explicitly to measure human being in terms of conformity to some norm or standard—an approach that necessarily treats the differences between people as irrelevant to their identities as human beings. (Ian McFarland, *Difference and Identity: A Theological Anthropology* (Cleveland, OH: Pilgrim Press, 2001), 2)

[9]As historian Robert D. G. Kelly and others have pointed out, the idea of Black *bodies* as opposed to Black *people* can readily reduce human beings—as well as the powerful narrative of Black *life*—to the material realities of their circumstances. Here I intentionally retain the use of "black bodies" to describe acutely how Africans were imagined as "others" who did not inhabit the fullness of human begin. More so, I retain this language to explicitly contrast the joy and resistance that mark the primary lens through which Black life, and more specifically Black Christian life, must be thought theologically.

[10]Willie Jennings, *The Christian Imagination: Theology and the Origins of Race* (New Haven, CT: Yale University Press, 2010), 291.

[11]It is important to acknowledge such reticence, particularly as much of Christian theology—still dominated by white, cisgender male voices—continues to eschew theologians of color to the periphery of thought. For instance, the use of "contextual" theologies is often a catchall descriptive to categorize (and often relegate) anything other than predominantly white theologian voices—as if all theology does not have a context, and as if the particularity of these voices is of no importance. The (un)thinking of race, and in particular of whiteness as both an identity and a politic, function as normative and privileged givens even without our own contemporary discourses.

[12]Andrew Prevot, *Theology and Race: Black and Womanist Traditions in the United States* (Leiden: Brill, 2018). Emphasis original. My analysis here holds in standing with Prevot:

It would be helpful to think here with the significance of the synchronized movements on the Iberian Peninsula in 1492. This fateful year featured far more than Christopher Columbus's bright morning departure from Spanish shores. Rather, the infamous India and Jerusalem missional voyage (the one where Columbus would "discover" a New-To-Him World) glimmered with serendipity as it commemorated the neighboring Portuguese fiftieth anniversary of the first European "purchase" of enslaved Africans in 1442.[13] Alas, the young Columbus's late summer sail was proverbial icing on a multitiered cake. The year started with the official end of a decade-long war between the Emirate of Granada and the Castillian military forces. On January 2, the Alhambra palace was officially surrendered, sealing the victory forged by the united Catholic monarchy of Isabella I of Castile and Ferdinand II of Aragon. Together, their successful conquest would end the existence of what had been the sole Muslim state on the Iberian Peninsula for more than a century prior. The new world order would be proudly Christian. This victory simultaneously signaled the twin forces of a religious and ethnic hierarchy that manifested in a political victory over Islam, and of the "Spanish" over the "Moors," the loose frame of Moorish identity one that, as imagined by most Europeans, could equally encompass Arabic language speakers and/or bodies with darker skin complexions.

Fresh off the heels of conquering Granada, by the end of March Isabella and Ferdinand issued the Alhambra Decree. The proclamation called for the expulsion of all Jews from the rededicated Iberian Peninsula and its territories. Despite the fact that practicing Jews had already been relegated to segregated living quarters, social districts and worship spaces, the edict claimed that the Jews were a toxic presence, a people who retained the power, means, motivations and ways "to subvert and to steal faithful Christians from our holy Catholic faith and to separate them from it, and to draw them to themselves and subvert them to their own wicked belief and conviction."[14] Around the fifteenth century, Jews had long been antagonized by Christian theology, and their plight had only worsened through the expansion of the religious state throughout Europe. Jews continued to be blamed for communal and societal ills, from interpersonal agitations to the massive spread of the bubonic plague. They were the ironic, incessant scapegoat for every reprisal of human sin. Expulsion was a regular threat, but a low priority when compared to the religious pogroms that worked to deliberately exterminate their bodies and their faith throughout Europe.

Thus, Isabella and Ferdinand were not unique in their executive orders of 1492, as the Jewish presence on the peninsula was readily construed as a distinctive threat to the holy

---

To be clear, by adopting this focus on race through the lens of blackness and anti-blackness, I neither contend nor mean to suggest that blacks suffer *more* than other groups. I categorically refuse any absurd "olympics of suffering." Each history of violence needs its own focused attention, including each history of racialized violence. Race forms, deforms, and wounds virtually everyone in this modern, colonized and globalized world to some degree and in various ways, as I have indicated above. *My only point here is that a direct confrontation with anti-blackness challenges the entire white supremacist racial imaginary.* (Ibid., 12–13; emphasis added)

[13]Within two years of that now comparatively austere investment, Prince Henry the Navigator of Portugal would host the first market of 235 captive Africans upon his shores. A critical treatment of this event and the significance of Prince Henry and the Portuguese slave trade—recorded in 1453 in *The Chronicle of the Discovery and Conquest of Guinea* by Prince's chronicler Gomes Eanes de Zurara—can be found in the chapter "Zurara's Tears" in Jennings, *The Christian Imagination*, 15–64.

[14]"The Chapter of Expulsion of 1492," translated in Edward Peters, "Jewish History and Gentile Memory: The Expulsion of 1492," *Jewish History* 9, no. 1 (1995): 23–8.

and true Catholic faith. Per the Decree, Jewish people were "perverted and enticed" by wickedness. Their bodies were physically and morally diseased, couriers of the demonic who "by contagion can injure others." They were a menace that had to be dealt with directly by the political representatives of the Church. With justifications as these, the decree ordered that anyone of Jewish faith would have to either convert or leave by July 31 of that year. The fine print of the legal document would also force Muslims to leave or convert as well, inaugurating the era of the *limpieza de sangra* (blood purity laws) that would soon arise in Spain. As such, when Columbus boarded his ships on August 3, he did so in the name of a truly Christian peninsula. By October of that year, the Catholic mission would have crossed oceans to inaugurate an empire never before witnessed.

THE COLOR OF CHRIST

The 1492 calendar year glimpses the bricolage of religion and politics that marks a liturgical convergence of racial and religious identities, and the superior subjugation of both. Jewish bodies and ethnic bodies were together imagined through their proximities in Europe, which would catalyze the interaction between European bodies with those found in Africa and, subsequently, the New World. The potential for mapping lands eagerly brought attention to the mapping of bodies and, subsequently, identities, through the matrix of ethnic encounter. The theology of the body of Christ centered this work through the lens of salvation, of the capacities of *becoming* Christian.[15] Did these darker bodies have souls? Could these dark souls be saved? And in the meantime, what were the parameters for life "together"? Race would present a new frame for aesthetic assessments, the beautiful being tied to the virtues of the good, Godly and true. These signposts of racism (as will be further discussed) and the quest for a purity of bodily form would undoubtedly infiltrate the lens through which Jesus, as well as those who were members of his Church, would be viewed, understood and expressed. Jesus would have to be white.

As Karl Barth once described, "The nature of the man Jesus alone is key to the problem of human nature."[16] Along these lines, what twentieth-century African American theologians realized was that there was a Christological problem of race, with Jesus' positioning as a *white* male. The whiteness of Jesus, whether explicitly claimed or readily assumed, deeply inflected many global attitudes (ideas that manifest with numerous similarities through Europe and North America, inextricably linked across a global scale) about the nature of God and the nature of humanity. Jesus, the Son of God, was indivisibly white and invariably Christian. As such, many Black theologians questioned the racist theological implications of a Jesus severed from his own religious identity and seated on a throne of white supremacy. Instead, the questions of Black American (Christian) life, and of how the questions of race and the Black body operated within a matrix of power, had answers that relied on acknowledging the fractured theology of supersessionism. As Black theologian, professor, minister, and civil rights leader Howard Thurman wrote in the throes of segregation and structural racism in the United States,

---

[15]The questions of conversion and salvation of captured peoples is critical to note in relationship to the justifications of capture. However, while Africans were first brought to the colonies as indentured people, it was the evolving theology reflected in Virginia laws—to include that baptism would not necessitate emancipation—that concretized the brutality of chattel slavery in the United States.

[16]Karl Barth, *Church Dogmatics*, 4 vols. (Edinburgh: T&T Clark, 1956–75), III/2.43.

How different might have been the story of the last two thousand years on this planet grown old from suffering if the link between Jesus and Israel had never been severed! What might have happened if Jesus, so perfect a flower from the brooding spirit of God in the soul of Israel, had been permitted to remain where his roots would have been fed by the distilled elements accumulated from Israel's wrestling with God! The thought is staggering. The Christian Church has tended to overlook its Judaic origins ... the fact that Jesus of Nazareth was a Jew of Palestine [...][17]

Arguably there is much more than simple oversight at work in the violent historical treatment of Jewish communities by their Christian counterparts. But even here Thurman intimates the inability to see human—or more broadly, the created world—as suffering and causing suffering by the missed humilities of the Christian life. Thurman famously identified Jesus with those "who stand with their backs against the wall."[18] James Cone, the founder of Black liberation theology who would write that Jesus is Black and firmly identified with those who are oppressed in this world, makes this even clearer in his claims to Christ's identity. In *Black Theology and Black Power*, he writes,

To suggest that Christ has taken on a black skin is not theological emotionalism. If the Church is a continuation of the Incarnation, and if the Church and Christ are where the oppressed are, then Christ and his Church must identify totally with the oppressed ... In America, blacks are oppressed because of their blackness. It would seem, then, that emancipation could only be realized by Christ and his Church becoming black. Thinking of Christ as nonblack in the twentieth century is as theologically possible as thinking of him as non-Jewish in the first century.[19]

What these theologians were claiming (as they were thinking race, Blackness and theology together from the position of the underthought) is a deeply Christian reality that life and theology are not conceived with Jesus, with a church, with a Creed or even the revelation of Scripture, but find their being first through the articulation of a communal life with the God of Israel. Without this basis, without this commitment to solidarity and liberation, the Christian thinker cannot take seriously the question of how one ought to live. In other words, it is a dangerous act of hubris to obscure the reality that Christian belief is birthed amidst scandal, with a claim to have met God in a Jewish man, Jesus of Nazareth—one who came not to an eager Christian "us," but to his own people, Israel. As J. Kameron Carter points out in *Race: A Theological Account*, the enduring evil of racism "has its genesis in the theological problem of Christianity's quest to sever itself from its Jewish roots."[20] Black American theologians, mere generations away from chattel slavery and still enduring the pernicious legacy of racism and injustice both *de jure* and *de facto*, were uniquely positioned to provide a broad scale critique of the allure of supersession, the enticement to imagine one's self and body and people as the new (and in this case, *white* Christian) elect.

---

[17]Howard Thurman, *Jesus and the Disinherited* (Boston: Beacon Press, 1976), 16.
[18]Ibid., 7.
[19]James Cone, *Black Theology and Black Power* (Maryknoll, NY: Orbis Books, 1997), 69.
[20]J. Kameron Carter, *Race: A Theological Account* (New York: Oxford University Press, 2008), 4. As Carter later describes with more complexity, there is a

convergence of the *Rassenfrage* and the *Judenfrage* in the hoped-for modern cosmopolis, the perfect world order in which the ideal of the unity of the human species actualizes itself in the perfection of a race type, the white race ... [R]ace is the discourse to constitute whiteness in relationship to a non-Jewish alien without and a Jewish alien within the body politic. (Ibid., 81)

Reclaiming Jesus' Jewish identity, and understanding the fragmented distancing of Christians throughout history from this reality, is critical to understanding how Christians came to understand blood, kinship and racial subjectivity. Despite the notion of the Gentile being welcomed in with the Jew (a position calling forth deep senses of humility as well as sensibility to one's identity not being centered in a conversation), these Christians (predominantly European) came to center themselves as God's chosen people, with little consideration to the oppression of Jews in their own midst.[21] The events of 1492 demonstrate the complexities of this identity, enmeshed with claims to land, power, privilege and prestige. But it is the centering, as well as the concretizing, of a specific sense of Christian identity, over and against all other identities—the Christian exceeding of the Jew—as it is conflated inside of colonial expansion and a rising European self-determination—the election of the (white) Euro-Christian male that will ground the possibilities for such conclusively theological ideas about Africans and Blackness. The exploration of the Black body would be rife with modalities of creation and fall, of progression and possibility of a certain salvific telos that determined the meanings of grace, and the allowances for life lived.

For despite a theological attendance to God as ultimate Creator of all, to humanity descending from and being animated by the breath of God, questions of divine right, election and identity only exacerbated the productions of difference when met with power. As Mary Doak describes,

> Despite the long-standing Christian belief in one human race equally in need of and offered redemption through Jesus Christ, many began to support evolutionary polygenism that denied the unity of humanity. In any case, modern European Christians had little doubt that they were physically, morally, and culturally superior to the darker-skinned peoples of Africa and the Americas. The subjugation of these peoples and their lands could be religiously justified regardless of the outcome of the actual ecclesial debate on whether or not they were fully human: if not human, they could be subjugated without concern for their rights, yet if they were deemed human, that was all the more reason for the colonial expansion that would support Christian missions to save their souls.[22]

Thus, it is no surprise that theological explanations of a Black or brown body, of an Other perceived to be so different as to possibly *not* be human, could not be conceived of as being made in the image of God. Oppression and negation (and eventually violent acts, from murder to rape), if not from the outset theologically rooted, became easy to theologically justify, particularly when one could use Scriptural narratives to constitute not only race, but a rank and file of superiority.[23] In Genesis 4, we read of God placing a visible "mark" of

---

[21] It is important here to note that, while the historical relationship between Judaism and Christianity has been marked by hatred and mass genocide of those of Jewish faith, contemporary questions of race and identity with respect to Christian Zionism and the modern nation-state of Israel present another set of questions and concerns that are beyond the scope of this chapter.

[22] Mary Doak, "Sex, Race, and Culture: Constructing Theological Anthropology for the Twenty-First Century," *Theological Studies* 80, no. 3 (2019): 520.

[23] For more on this, see: Allen Dwight Callahan, *The Talking Book: African Americans and the Bible* (New Haven, CT: Yale University Press, 2006); Cain Hope Felder, ed., *Stony the Road We Trod: African American Biblical Interpretation* (Minneapolis, MN: Augsburg Fortress, 1991); Stephen R. Haynes, *Noah's Curse: The Biblical Justification of American Slavery* (New York: Oxford University Press, 2002); David M. Goldenberg, *The Curse of Ham: Race and Slavery in Early Judaism, Christianity, and Islam* (New Haven, CT: Yale University Press, 2003).

some sort upon Cain as punishment for murdering his brother and lying about it when God asked what happened. As early as the fifth century, Cain's curse was interpreted as Black skin, and millions of Christians have used it to justify slavery. A bit later in Genesis, we read of Noah cursing his son Ham, declaring that his offspring would henceforth serve those of his brothers, this "Curse of Ham" invoked as yet another biblical justification for African enslavement. The writings of St. Paul claimed a divine order of being along domestic lines, instructing the appropriate relationship between men and women, as well as slaves and masters. Master-slave metaphors mapped perfectly for those who imagined themselves to be earthly masters, onto a lived reality of hierarchy over the enslaved.

Blackness was a curse ordained by the Creator, and under the conditions of colonization, the ideal organizing trope to sustain the oppression of entire people groups in Africa and the Americas. Reprehensions around Black and brown bodies (and here we must at least note the ways such reprehension avails itself in specific reference to gender and sexuality) marks the way that Christianity itself became a universal principle baptized in her own "whiteness," a prism reflecting the disgust for Black bodies, a denial of the Black body, a degradation of the Black body. As Jennings makes clear, colonial theologies of reprobation cemented "the logical conclusion of black incapacity."[24] But reprobation as theological calculus offers a more sinister reality than correlation and causation, for reprobation "is not simply the state of existence opposite election; it is also a judgment upon the trajectory of a life, gauging its destiny from what can be known in the moment. Reprobation joins the Black body to the Moor body and both to the Jewish body. All are in the sphere of Christian rejection and therefore of divine rejection."[25] Dark skin was a lazy corollary to sin and evil, and notions of difference were fused with notions of depravity, a sense of that which might be seen to be less than human.

Despite the base claim in Scripture that God actively creates humanity not only as good, but *very good*,[26] the theological accounts of race as a sign of curse, demeaning and inequity before God certainly fed into the rising fields of scientific classification. By the eighteenth century, scientists like Carl Linnaeus and Johann Friedrich Blumenbach were concretizing authoritative taxonomies of comparison and order among the races, all stemming from the European man as a fixed center from which others would be evaluated and placed.[27] These scales aligned peoples in their proximity to the poles of light and dark, good and bad, that which we conflate as *white* and *Black*. While these arguments of scientific racism are now considered incorrect for their biological essentialism—the idea that race exists naturally and genetically—their remnants and conclusions endure despite the fiction of race itself. The conclusions drawn reified the inferiority of the African body, a denial of humanity that would ground numerous atrocities of exploitation and institutionalized violence around the globe.

CREDO

Racism is modernity's greatest idol. It is *racism* (as opposed to *race*) that remains insidious in its scope and collateral, persistent and enabled, by the legacy of Christian thinking

---

[24]Jennings, *The Christian Imagination*, 34.
[25]Ibid.
[26]Gen. 1:31.
[27]For a thorough treatment on these classifications, please see Terence Keel, *Divine Variations: How Christian Thought Became Racial Science* (Palo Alto, CA: Stanford University Press, 2018).

that gestates the lungs animating racial hierarchy, liturgizes the practices of exclusion and dominance, consecrates the unction of power that precedes race as an ideal rooted into a pious ideal and venerates whiteness as holy icon. And still, much of formal Christian theology palpably maintains an extensive reticence to take seriously the investigation of racism and its effects, acknowledging the racist relics yet alive in our praxis and doctrine.[28]

This is where we must necessarily attend to the racial ideas that infuse our theological imaginations. While racism is something from which we need to repent, perhaps the questions to consider are the ways that race is something we daily confess. We *believe* in race, as we believe that some peoples—by birth and by class, by gender and by sex, by ability and by age—are superior to others. We confess with our apathy; we believe with our power and privilege. The fact of race has been memorized and memorialized at every juncture of Christianity in the world. Beyond the social or the biological data or the intellectual categories, we have allowed race to become incarnate in our lives, its own word made flesh. But it is not theological, it is not from God or to God or about God. Instead, it becomes God—our idol, structural and systemic, a sacramental perversion. *Race* is thought the superlative "alternative" fact, and *racism* is its execution as truth, the scapegoat from its accountability.

An honest conversation around theological anthropology and race depends gravely on the stories we tell, recite and (re)member, as much as upon those we call upon as griots of this word. The burden of relevance requires careful attention to the stories written upon bodies in melanin's ink, the witness of ancestors come and gone who cultivated the songs of spiritual striving through the blood of cut throats. If racism is that which we must confess, if it is that which we must turn away from, then what shall we turn toward? Perhaps but one starting point is to enact the dangerous memory, to practice remembrance, of the meaning of the Word made flesh for those who were cast down in a world forged by the fires fueling their oppressions. As M. Shawn Copeland reminds us, it requires not just "a new anthropological question" but a turn to "a new anthropological subject of Christian reflection—exploited, despised, poor women of color."[29] With even the most cursory glance of history, that any person of color in this world—and to speak of a Black woman in this world—based on example, would want to be a Christian, can be explained only by either (1) a continued racist belief in the intellectual inferiority or opiate addiction of those who are considered to *have* or belong to a "race," or (2) by grace. We must tell the story of the trade winds of Christian expansion that carried not providence but the distortions of power upon its back; and yet, there were peoples who found and knew and modeled and loved Jesus anyhow. We must believe the hearts and minds of those who would sing and dance and shout, their cries subversive to enslavers who fashioned the character of Christ and the will of God into molds of their own violence and greed. We must witness that the living persistence of Black church traditions in both Europe and the Americas, especially in the United States, is a reality that convicts history while pointing to the possibilities of justice. It requires a different sort of listening and attention, the silence attendant to God's greatest works, the chaotic noise of the Pentecost community, marked by a Christian confession that takes seriously the practices—the enduring praise—of those who believed that Jesus loved their flesh. It requires the betrayal of the hermeneutics of whiteness, to

---

[28]For more, see Etienne Balibar and Immanuel Wallerstein, *Race, Nation, Class: Ambiguous Identities* (New York: Verso, 2011); Karen E. Fields and Barbara J. Fields, *Racecraft: The Soul of Inequality in American Life* (New York: Verso, 2012).

[29]M. Shawn Copeland, *Enfleshing Freedom: Body, Race, and Being.* (Minneapolis: Fortress, 2010), 89.

consider that to be human and Christian might mean that Jesus is calling us out of the systems and ideas we have been formed inside of. It requires what Baby Suggs saw in the clearing of Toni Morrison's *Beloved,* a belief in the proclamation of "we flesh," a response to the incitement to "love it. Love it hard."[30] This is work that can only be done through the commitments of community, revelation that can only be thought through the refusal of assumptions, through the interrogation of dominant narratives we name as normative, even for orthodoxy, to be freed from their latent foundations of anti-Blackness. It is imperative that we value, learn from and grow with the testimonies of those pushed to the margins of society, to the examples who yet inhabited worlds of praise and resistance. The metanoia of conversion—it is not what we shall turn toward, but rather, whom shall we turn toward. What could be more apposite for an anthropology?

SUGGESTED FURTHER READING

Carter, J. Kameron, *Race: A Theological Account* (New York: Oxford University Press, 2008).

Copeland, M. Shawn, *Enfleshing Freedom: Body, Race, and Being* (Minneapolis: Fortress, 2010).

Fields, Karen, and Barbara Fields, *Raceraft: The Soul of Inequality in American Life* (New York: Verso, 2012).

Jennings, Willie, *The Christian Imagination: Theology and the Origins of Race* (New Haven, CT: Yale University Press, 2010).

Kendi, Ibram X., *Stamped from the Beginning: The Definitive History of Racist Ideas in America* (New York: Nation Books, 2016).

Painter, Nell Irvin, *The History of White People* (New York: W. W. Norton, 2010).

---

[30]Toni Morrison, *Beloved* (New York: Random House, 1987), 103.

CHAPTER TWENTY-NINE

Beyond Complementarity: Gender Issues in the Catholic Church

MARY ANN HINSDALE, I.H.M.

This chapter wades into the thicket of the current conversations in theological anthropology concerning gender, sex and sexuality, especially in terms of female embodiment. It begins by looking at specific existential realities—the "signs of the times"—that Catholic official teaching needs to address and that implicate the church's current theological anthropology. Second, I look at gender complementarity as the "issue under the issues" in official Catholic theological anthropology. This long section begins by first examining the arguments of theologians who recognize the instability of the terms sex and gender, and find the church's current theological anthropology—gender complementarity—to be problematic in recognizing the full humanity and vocations of persons created in the image and likeness of God. Next, it proceeds to a detailed consideration of the magisterial documents produced during the papacies of Pope John Paul II, Pope Benedict XVI and Pope Francis that have raised complementarity to an almost ontological status. In the third section, I review the critiques from feminist theologians who continue to see these magisterial positions as problematic and call for a more representative consultation. In conclusion, I present several theological trajectories that purport to "get beyond" the perceived impasse created by gender complementarity, either by nuancing the more radical proposals of gender theory or by suggesting new philosophical and intersectional frameworks.

READING THE "SIGNS OF THE TIMES"

Examining "gender issues"[1] in the official teaching of the Catholic Church involves engaging in what the Second Vatican Council called reading "the signs of the times."[2] By promoting the "scrutinizing of the signs of the times in the light of the gospel," the council endorsed a correlational method of theological reflection, one that begins

---

[1] A portion of the material that follows draws from my article, "A Feminist Reflection on Postconciliar Catholic Ecclesiology," in *A Church With Open Doors: Post-Conciliar Reflection on Ecclesiology*, ed. Richard Gaillardetz and Edward Hahnenberg (Collegeville, MN: Liturgical Press, 2015), 112–37.

[2] *Gaudium et spes*, Vatican II's *Pastoral Constitution on the Church in the Modern World*, no. 4, in Walter M. Abbott (ed.), *The Documents of Vatican II* (New York: Guild Press, 1966), 201–2. Henceforth GS.

with concrete human experiences and analyzes them in light of "the gospel." Some of the "signs of the times" that have both troubled and encouraged various sectors of the Catholic church over the past six decades include: (1) the exclusion of women from ordained ministries based upon a theological anthropology of complementarity that specifies women's roles in the church; (2) the recognition that homosexuality exists among members of the church at every level, and the concomitant issues relating to this fact (e.g., the legality of same-sex marriages in many countries, the civil rights of LGBTQ persons employed in parishes and Catholic schools, and the seeming openness on the part of Pope Francis for change in Catholic teaching on homosexuality and transgendered persons in off-the-cuff interviews in 2013 and 2016); (3) the positive recognition of feminism as "a work of the Spirit" by Pope Francis in his 2016 post-synodal document, *Amoris Laetitia* (no. 54), but a concern that "certain forms of feminism" espouse a "gender ideology" seen as a fundamental challenge to the family, "since it denies the difference and reciprocity in nature of a man and a woman and envisages a society without sexual difference" (*Amoris Laetitia*, no. 56).

In 1959, when Pope John XXIII called for an "aggiornamento" of the church, resulting in the Second Vatican Council, there was little reason to think that anything would be said about "gender"—or even about women. Nevertheless, the history of the council's preparatory stage indicates that, while the topic of women was not on the official agenda, Catholic women were not deterred from submitting requests on issues that affected them.[3] Furthermore, midway through the council, Belgian Cardinal Leo Jozef Suenens stood up in the assembly and said, "Why are we even discussing the reality of the church, when half the church is not represented here?"[4] His intervention prompted Pope Paul VI to invite twenty-three women auditors to attend the final two sessions of the council (fourteen in 1964 and nine more in 1965).[5]

The fact that Vatican II never produced a specific document on women as a uniquely identifiable group within the structure of the church was partly due to the women auditors' own insistence. They rejected the idea that they had "a special nature" that differentiated them as human beings and refused to be put on a pedestal.[6] Thus, the council documents did not treat women as a separate group in the church but included them in the church's new understanding of itself.[7] As baptized laity or vowed religious, the council taught that women belong to the "People of God" as do men; they share in the priestly, prophetic and kingly mission of Christ and are therefore to be respected, as all human beings should be, as *imago Dei*. This might have been seen as a statement of gender inclusivity; yet, after the council, particularly in the pontificates of John Paul II, Benedict XVI, and now Pope Francis, one sees an ever-increasing endorsement of gender essentialism in the form of gender complementarity, to the point that this position now appears to have achieved the status of an official theological anthropology.

---

[3]For a summary discussion of these requests, see, Mary Ann Hinsdale, "Vatican II and Feminism: Recovered Memories and Refreshed Hopes," *Toronto Journal of Theology* 32, no. 2 (2016): 251–72; and Catherine E. Clifford, *Decoding Vatican II: Interpretation and Ongoing Reception* (New York: Paulist Press, 2014), 61–76.
[4]Hinsdale, "A Feminist Reflection on Postconciliar Catholic Ecclesiology," 115.
[5]For a history of the women auditors and their contributions, see, M. Carmel McEnroy, *Guests in Their Own House: The Women at Vatican II* (New York: Crossroad, 1996; repr. Eugene, OR: Wipf and Stock, 2011).
[6]Clifford, *Decoding Vatican II*, 73.
[7]In GS, nos. 27–9 called for a recognition of the rights of the person and condemned every type of discrimination, including sex discrimination.

GENDER COMPLEMENTARITY: THE "ISSUE UNDER THE ISSUES" IN OFFICIAL CATHOLIC TEACHING ON THEOLOGICAL ANTHROPOLOGY

When considering the various issues surrounding the roles of men and women in church and society, as well as Catholic sexual ethics, "gender complementarity" emerges as the core "issue under the issues."[8] Especially in relation to the "signs of the times" considered above, official Catholic church teaching always seems to return to complementarity as the essential way the two sexes are related. An additional worry is the concern voiced by Pope Francis about educational programs on sexuality that carry the possibility of "colonial coercion" from Western gender theory.[9]

"Gender" and "Sex" as Unstable Categories

As we have seen, the term "gender" never appears in the documents of Vatican II. This is understandable given the historical period during which the council took place. At the conclusion of the Council, the disciplines of women's studies, feminist theory and feminist theologies were just beginning to reflect upon the meaning of sex and gender in the context of developing a theological anthropology that took embodiment seriously. Thus, the notion of "gender" as a discreet analytical category within Catholic theological anthropology has a relatively recent history.

The modern differentiation of gender from the category of biological sex can be traced back to the beginnings of Western feminism, perhaps best expressed in the statement of Simone de Beauvoir, in her 1949 work *The Second Sex*, "One is not born, but rather becomes, a woman."[10] De Beauvoir's claim, developed out of an existentialist understanding of "self-creation," became a byword in the so-called second "wave" of feminism of the 1970s, which described "gender" as an attribute of human beings that is "socially constructed" and distinct from a person's biological (chromosomal) "sex."[11]

On the other hand, traditional Christian theological anthropology has considered the doctrine of *imago Dei*, being created in the image and likeness of God, as applying equally to the two sexes, both male and female. This conviction is derived from the first creation story in Gen. 1.26-27, which most feminists cite, along with Gal. 3:28, as the biblical basis for gender equality. The question that remains, however, is what does it *mean* to be "male" or "female"? As historical research has shown, Christianity's embeddedness in patriarchal culture often has determined that, though women and men might be "equal" at creation, biological sex difference introduces a determinant with respect to "identity"

---

[8]John O'Malley borrows this turn of phrase from John Courtney Murray, for whom *the* "issue under the issues" was the question of the development of doctrine. See *What Happened at Vatican II* (Cambridge, MA: Harvard University Press, 2008), 8–9.

[9]See Cristina L. H. Traina's insightful analysis of Pope Francis's concern with "gender ideology": "Whose *Sensus*? Which *Fidelium*?," in *Learning from All the Faithful*, ed. Bradford E. Hinze and Peter C. Phan (Eugene, OR: Pickwick), 155–69.

[10]Simone de Beauvoir, *The Second Sex*, trans. and ed. H. M. Parshley (New York: Random House, 1953), 7.

[11]In the short space of this chapter it is impossible to review all of the many theological approaches to "sex," "gender" and "sexuality" that have been discussed in the context of theological anthropology since the 1970s. Several helpful overviews can be found in Adrian Thatcher (ed.), *The Oxford Handbook of Theology, Sexuality and Gender* (Oxford Handbooks Online, 2014), DOI:10.1093/oxfordhb/9780199664153.013.33.

and the particular roles each sex plays in the family, society and the church. The second creation story (Gen. 2.4-25) is usually used to buttress this claim, basing it on the idea of "the order of creation," since Eve is created second.[12]

The creation narratives, especially Gen. 1:27, are repeatedly cited in official Catholic teaching as the biblical basis for heteronormativity and the conception of two completely different gendered beings. "Even in feminist theology," notes Isolde Karle, "repeated reference has been made to this passage … in order to claim both the equality of women and their essential difference from men. Thus, binary gender becomes the lynchpin of the imago Dei. But in doing so we essentially miss the meaning of this passage."[13]

Elisabeth Schüssler Fiorenza points out that only in the 1970s did the field of women's studies start to distinguish socially constructed gender roles from biological sex, so that by the mid-1980s gender studies had emerged as a distinct field of inquiry, which not only called into question seemingly universal beliefs about woman and man but also attempted "to unmask the cultural, societal, and political roots of gender."[14] Catholic ethicist Margaret Farley also points out that feminist theorists have held various (and sometimes competing) positions on the "sex/gender" issue. These arguments range from (1) stressing the equality of person, with gender being simply a secondary human attribute; (2) a reevaluation of women's embodiment that gives gender an even greater importance; (3) the "denaturalization" of notions of gender; and (4) a social constructivism that so destabilizes not only gender but also sex, so that "there are more forms of gender than the binary gender systems of the past could imagine."[15] Theories that emphasized the "social construction" of sex and gender began to challenge a number of official church teachings, such as the prohibition of women's ordination and "the intrinsic disorder" of homosexual activity.[16]

---

[12]The creation of woman derived from the rib of *'adham*, has traditionally given rise to a notion of women's secondary status, since the creation of Eve occurs *after* Adam. Phyllis Trible however has noted that "the Yahwist account moves to its climax, not its decline, in the creation of the woman." See Phyllis Trible, "Depatriarchalizing in Biblical Interpretation," *Journal of the American Academy of Religion* 41, no. 1 (March 1973): 30–48 (36).

[13]Isolde Karle, 'Beyond Distinct Gender Identities: The Social Construction of the Human Body', in *The Depth of the Human Person: A Multidisciplinary Approach*, ed. Michael Welker (Grand Rapids, MI: Eerdmans, 2014), 333–50 (346).

[14]Elisabeth Schüssler Fiorenza, "Between Movement and Academy: Feminist Biblical Studies in the Twentieth Century," in *Feminist Biblical Studies in the Twentieth Century: Scholarship and Movement*, ed. Elisabeth Schüssler Fiorenza (Atlanta: Society of Biblical Literature, 2014), 1–18 (6). Margaret Farley likewise comments, "Sexologists and feminist writers in the 1960s and 1970s distinguished 'sex' from 'gender', accepting sex as a biological and anatomical category, but challenging gender as a socially constructed category. This distinction has been blurred since then, however, with the implication that even our understandings of 'sex' are socially and culturally constructed as well." See Margaret Farley, *Just Love: A Framework for Christian Sexual Ethics* (New York: Continuum, 2008), 134.

[15]Farley, *Just Love*, 135.

[16]It is beyond the scope of this chapter to enter into detail concerning the voluminous amount of material addressing these issues. But it is important to point out that the concerns of theological anthropology that underlie these teachings are not solely the concern of Roman Catholics. For example, the Lutheran practical theologian Isolde Karle, cited above in n. 4, sees dichotomous gender metaphysics as a product of bourgeois nineteenth-century thought that "conditions a dualistic *habitus* that is correlated with open and hidden forms and practices of male domination and violence." See Michael Welker (ed.), "Introduction," in *The Depth of the Human Person* (Grand Rapids, MI: Eerdmans, 2014), 1–14 (10).

Gender Complementarity in Papal and Curial Pronouncements

Magisterial documents that have dealt with gender issues fall into several categories: (1) documents that prohibit the ordination of women; (2) documents issued during the papacy of John Paul II that establish "gender complementarity" as the norm for understanding the roles of women and men in the family, church and society; (3) statements by Cardinal Joseph Ratzinger, as head of the Congregation for the Doctrine of the Faith (CDF), and later as Pope Benedict XVI, that continue to affirm gender complementarity; and (4) post-synodal documents of Pope Francis that continue to endorse the previous papal positions on non-ordination of women, gender complementarity and that introduce new criticisms with respect to "gender ideology.'[17]

Documents Prohibiting the Ordination of Women: Inter Insigniores *(IS) (1976),* Ordinatio Sacerdotalis *(1994),* Responsum ad Dubium *(1995) and* Ad Tuendam Fidem *(1998)*   The possibility of women's admission to the ministerial priesthood reached "a tipping point" in the mid-1970s with the 1974 "irregular" ordination of eleven women to the priesthood in the US Episcopal church and the first Catholic Women's Ordination Conference held in Detroit in 1975, which petitioned the Vatican to "ordain women now!" The CDF, with the approval of Paul VI, responded with *Inter Insigniores* ("The Declaration on the Question of the Admission of Women to the Ministerial Priesthood") on October 15, 1976.[18]

Among the arguments presented in IS was the fact that the maleness of Jesus determines that the priest, who sacramentally acts *in persona Christi*, must be a man, lest there not be a "natural resemblance to Christ," who was, of course, a male.[19] Although the CDF document also acknowledged that priests equally represent the church as the Body of Christ in the sacraments (*in personae ecclesiae*), it appealed to Vatican II which regarded the priest as "representing Christ the head and the shepherd of the church." Underlying these arguments are gendered understandings of the patriarchal "head" of the family. However, IS does not articulate an explicit emphasis on gender *complementarity* with respect to women in relation to men. In fact, the equality of women with men is frequently invoked throughout the document (nos. 36–40) notwithstanding its admonition that "equality is in no way identity."

In 1994, on the feast of Pentecost, Pope John Paul II issued the apostolic letter *Ordinatio Sacerdotalis*, "On Reserving Priestly Ordination to Men Alone" (OS). This document reaffirmed much of the same reasoning expressed in IS, though it did not repeat the argument that women "could not image Christ." Its main purpose was to put a stop to all discussion of women's ordination in very forceful terms:

> In order that all doubt may be removed regarding a matter of great importance, a matter which pertains to the Church's divine constitution itself, in virtue of my ministry of confirming the brethren (cf. Lk 22:32) I declare that the Church has no

---

[17]"Official Catholic church teaching" has various levels of authority and uses a variety of categories that give clues to those levels. For an introduction to the "levels" of magisterial teaching, see Richard Gaillardetz, *By What Authority*, rev. ed. (Collegeville MN: Liturgical Press, 2018).

[18]See "Appendix I" in Leonard Swidler and Arlene Swidler (eds.), *Women Priests: A Catholic Commentary on the Vatican Declaration* (New York: Paulist Press, 1977), 319–37.

[19]This argument "from fittingness" is presented in IS, nos. 25–7. The text of *Inter Insigniores* was originally unnumbered. However, several authors have numbered the paragraphs for convenience in citation. All citations from IS here are taken from the numbering found in Swidler and Swidler, *Women Priests*, 37–49.

authority whatsoever to confer priestly ordination on women and that this judgment is to be definitively held by all the Church's faithful.[20]

Ordinatio sacerdotalis was followed up with a *Responsum ad Dubium* from the CDF in the following year which declared that the teaching of OS was to be understood as "definitive," infallible, and irrevocable, precluding any further discussion of women's ordination. A storm of controversy ensued among many Catholic theologians and the mere mention of continuing the discussion often had serious repercussions for them. However, with the exception of the issue of "iconic resemblance" to the man Jesus (troubling enough in itself), which was deemed essential for sacramental symbolizing, none of these statements explicitly discussed gender complementarity. Rather, the focus was on an unchanging understanding of revelation and the authority of the church (i.e., the impossibility of changing the "unbroken Catholic Christian tradition").

John Paul II on the Complementarity of Men and Women: Mulieris Dignitatem *(MD)*, Christifideles Laici *(CL)*, Evangelium Vitae *(EV) and* Letter to Women *(LW)*   The first specific papal endorsement of gender complementarity occurs in John Paul II's 1988 Apostolic Letter, *Mulieris Dignitatem* (MD).[21] MD reaffirms the impossibility of women's ordination, but its chief significance is its anthropology of complementarity whose essentialist arguments would lay the groundwork for what many feminist theologians today regard as women's *inequality* in the church.[22] The origin of MD was the 1987 Synod on the Laity, which called for a study on the vocation and dignity of women in the church. MD was issued on August 15, 1988, and three months later John Paul II completed his apostolic exhortation on the synod, *Christifideles Laici* (CL),[23] which underlined MD's anthropology of complementarity:

> The condition that will assure the rightful presence of woman (sic) in the Church and in society is a more penetrating and accurate consideration of the anthropological foundation for masculinity and femininity with the intent of clarifying woman's personal identity in relation to man, that is, a diversity yet mutual complementarity, not only as it concerns roles to be held and functions to be performed, but also, and more deeply, as it concerns her make-up and meaning as a person.
>
> The Synod Fathers have deeply felt this requirement, maintaining that "the anthropological and theological foundations for resolving questions about the true significance and dignity of each sex require deeper study." (CL 50)

John Paul II encourages everyone, "especially those who devote their lives to the human sciences and theological disciplines," to read MD as a biblical meditation and to undertake "critical study" that will "enlighten and guide the Christian response to the most frequently asked questions, oftentimes so crucial, on *the 'place' that women*

---

[20]John Paul II, *Ordinatio Sacerdotalis* (May 22, 1994; http://www.vatican.va/holy_father/john_paul_ii/apost_letters/1994/documents/hf_jp-ii_apl_19940522_ordinatio-sacerdotalis_en.html), 4.

[21]John Paul II, *Mulieris Dignitatem* (http://w2.vatican.va/content/john-paul-ii/en/apost_letters/1988/documents/hf_jp-ii_apl_19880815_mulieris-dignitatem.html).

[22]For an excellent discussion of the anthropology of complementarity in MD, see Lisa Cahill, "Feminist Theology and a Participatory Church," in *Common Calling: The Laity & Governance in the Catholic Church*, ed. Stephen J. Pope (Washington, DC: Georgetown University Press, 2004), 140–5.

[23]John Paul II, *Christifedeles Laici* (http://www.vatican.va/content/john-paul-ii/en/apost_exhortations/documents/hf_jp-ii_exh_30121988_christifideles-laici.html). Hereafter cited as CL.

can have and ought to have in the Church and in society."[24] However, it is clear that the encouragement to "critically study" the issue of women in relation to men is still predetermined by "a plan that 'from the beginning' has been indelibly imprinted in the very being of the human person—men and women—and, therefore, in the make-up, meaning and deepest workings of the individual."[25]

As did GS, MD argues that both men and women are created as *imago Dei* and thus are "human" to an equal degree (MD 6). However, as Susan Ross has perceived, the anthropology in this document was derived, not as theological anthropology usually is, from Christology, but from Mariology.[26] Michelle Gonzalez echoes Ross and notes that what professes to be an "egalitarian anthropology" in MD

> is quickly amended with a gender complementarity that defines the ethical vocation of women as one in which she *"can only find herself by giving love to others"* (no. 30). Woman is characterized as giving by her nature, almost to the point that she appears naturally self-effacing. Women have a special capacity to care and love based on a Marian anthropology of motherhood.[27]

According to this Marian-centered anthropology, femaleness is characterized by receptivity and maternal nurturing, while maleness consists of initiation. Thus, at the heart of John Paul II's anthropology is a nuptial symbolism based upon his reading of the creation narratives in Genesis, chs. 1–3. His "Theology of the Body," which began as catechetical orations on the book of Genesis, stressed this symbolism and leads to the conclusion that the essential differences between "man" and "woman," imply a "two-in-one" symbolism where each sex completes the other. This involves

> a conception of men and women as (a) essentially different and (b) "complete" only in relation to each other. According to this understanding maleness and femaleness constitute the original dimorphic condition of humanity as intended by God and as evidenced in the two creation accounts. In John Paul II's understanding however, gender complementarity has also come to include a definition of what is "essential" to being male and female. A certain form of "essentialism" has long been a part of official Vatican teaching on womanhood, but it has taken on enhanced importance in the writings of John Paul II.[28]

---

[24]Ibid.

[25]Ibid. John Paul II here makes explicit appeal to his Wednesday catechetical orations on Genesis (the basis for his "Theology of the Body"). See *Man and Woman He Created Them: A Theology of the Body*, 2nd ed. (translated with an introduction by Michael Waldstein; Boston: Pauline Books & Media, 2006), as well as his first encyclical, *Redemptoris Mater* (March 25, 1987; https://w2.vatican.va/content/john-paul-ii/en/encyclicals/documents/hf_jp-ii_enc_25031987_redemptoris-mater.html).

[26]Susan Ross, "The Bridegroom and the Bride: The Theological Anthropology of John Paul II and Its Relation to the Bible and Homosexuality," in *Sexual Diversity and Catholicism: Toward the Development of Moral Theology*, ed. Patricia Beattie Jung with Joseph Andrew Coray (Collegeville, MN: Liturgical Press, 2001), 39–49 (43). Since MD was written during "the Marian Year" being celebrated in 1988, many women assumed that this was why so much of the document presents Mary as the preeminent role model for women. However, it is clear from John Paul's first encyclical, *Redemptoris Mater*, that women are to look to Mary and "find in her the secret of living their femininity." See also CL 50, n. 187.

[27]Michelle Gonzalez, *Created in God's Image: An Introduction to Feminist Theological Anthropology* (Maryknoll, NY: Orbis Books, 2007), 142. Emphasis original.

[28]Ross, "The Bridegroom and the Bride," 40. See also Susan A. Ross, *Anthropology: Seeking Light and Beauty*, Engaging Theology: Catholic Perspectives (Collegeville, MN: Liturgical Press, 2012), especially 86–104.

The use of nuptial symbolism has a long and noble history in the Christian mystical tradition and it has often been used to illustrate the love and intimacy between married partners and between the soul and God. But "it has not," Ross writes, "for the most part, served as a prescriptive model for gender roles."[29] So where does it come from?

Ross, along with Tina Beattie, Michelle Gonzalez, Susan Rakoczy and others, attribute John Paul II's theory of sex complementarity to an understanding of the church highly influenced by Hans Urs von Balthasar.[30] Balthasar, who prefers a highly symbolic, rather than historical-critical, reading of New Testament texts, often interpreted Scripture through the imaginative personal piety of the visionary/mystic Adrienne von Speyr.[31] This interpretation connects to a rather distinctive ecclesiology, which sees ministerial roles and the church itself as instantiated in certain archetypes drawn from principal figures in the New Testament (i.e., Mary, Peter, John, Mary and Martha, Mary Magdalene, etc.). Fundamentally, Balthasar understood the church as being composed of a "Marian" and a "Petrine" principle.[32] Mary is at the center of the Church, and in her is seen "the nuptial encounter between God and the creature. The entire Church is Marian ... because 'Mary disappears into the heart of the Church to remain there as a real presence which, however, always gives place to her Son'."[33] For Balthasar, "the radiant heart of the Church is *lay, faithful, and holy*, characterized by contemplative receptivity in relation to God, and symbolized by the femininity and virginal maternity of Mary: as she is, so is the church."[34]

The essentialist view of women and its corresponding gender complementarity expressed in MD appears again in John Paul II's 1995 "Letter to Women," written on the eve of the Fourth UN World Conference on Women held in Beijing in 1995:

> Womanhood and manhood are complementary *not only from the physical and psychological points of view*, but also from *the ontological* [emphasis mine]. It is only through the duality of the "masculine" and the "feminine" that the "human" finds full realization.[35]

In this letter the pope gives thanks for "the feminine genius" of women—a phrase that henceforth will characterize the "semi-official" understanding of the role of women in the church, since it is "part of God's plan":

> It is thus my hope, dear sisters, that you will reflect carefully on what it means to speak of the "genius of women," not only in order to be able to see in this phrase a specific part of God's plan which needs to be accepted and appreciated, but also in order to let this genius be more fully expressed in the life of society as a whole, as well as in the life of the Church.[36]

---

[29]Ross, "The Bridegroom and the Bride," 41.

[30]See Susan Rakoczy, I.H.M., "Mixed Messages: John Paul II's Writings on Women," in *The Vision of John Paul II: Assessing His Thought and Influence*, ed. Gerard Mannion (Collegeville, MN: Liturgical Press, 2008), 159–83.

[31]The influence of von Speyr, according to Tina Beattie (who is not unsympathetic to other aspects of his theology, such as his aesthetics), "was in no small measure responsible for the growing sexualization of his work." See Tina Beattie, *New Catholic Feminism: Theology and Theory* (London: Routledge, 2006), 13.

[32]Hans Urs von Balthasar, *The Office of Peter and the Structure of the Church*, trans. Andrée Emery (San Francisco: Ignatius Press, 1986). This book spells out his highly symbolic anthropology and ecclesiology.

[33]Ibid., 158–9. For a detailed analysis of Balthasar's ecclesiology, see John McDade, SJ, "Von Balthasar and the Office of Peter in the Church," *The Way* 44 (2005): 97–114.

[34]McDade, "Von Balthasar and the Office of Peter in the Church," 101.

[35]John Paul II, "Letter to Women" (June 29, 1995, no. 7; http://www.vatican.va/content/john-paul-ii/en/letters/1995/documents/hf_jp-ii_let_29061995_women.html). Emphasis original.

[36]Ibid., no. 10.

Specifically urging women "to transform culture so that it supports life" is not in itself an objectionable summons; however, singling women out as bearing an exceptional responsibility in this regard was seen by many women as canonizing a construal of gender that concentrates on "women's special nature and gifts as mothers."[37] Such a theological anthropology certainly would have rankled the women auditors at Vatican II and continues to disturb many women today.

Cardinal Ratzinger's "Letter to the Bishops on the Collaboration of Men and Women in the Church and World" (2004)   As prefect of the CDF, then-Cardinal Joseph Ratzinger, who would succeed John Paul II as Pope Benedict XVI, championed the "new feminism." The "Letter to Bishops of the Catholic Church on the Collaboration of Men and Women in the Church and the World"[38] issued by him with the pope's approval in 2004, castigated what it termed "radical feminism" and reiterated the "definitive" teaching concerning the inadmissibility of women to priestly ordination, while insisting at the same time that such an exclusion "does not hamper in any way women's access to the heart of Christian life."[39] This document stresses sexual difference as a fundamental component of personality and taught that it is "women's vocation" to love and nurture life and to take primary responsibility for human relationships, based upon "her capacity for the other."[40]

Most disturbing to many Catholic women was Collaboration's caricature of contemporary feminism as "giving rise to an antagonism that makes women adversaries of men."[41] Its adamant resistance to the notion that sexual difference might be socially constructed was also a source of contention. As Tina Beattie commented at the time,

> What other institution today would produce a document about women, written by one group of men (the Congregation for the Doctrine of the Faith, under the signature of Cardinal Ratzinger), addressed to another (the bishops), without quoting or referring to any women's ideas? Given that the letter is titled "On the Collaboration of Men and Women in the Church and in the World," its lack of collaboration with women is slightly ludicrous.[42]

Documents by Pope Francis: Amoris Laetitia *(AL) (2015) and* Querida Amazonia *(QA) in 2020*   In 2016, Pope Francis issued the post-synodal apostolic exhortation *Amoris Laetita* ("The Joy of Love")[43] as his response to the two synods on the family held in 2014–15. In general, Francis in AL continues to support an anthropology of gender complementarity. However, he sees "in the women's movement the working of the

[37]Ivy Hellman contrasts the limited understanding of John Paul II's "feminism" with the theoretical understanding of "the varieties of feminisms" one finds in contemporary academic feminism in her *Women and the Vatican: An Exploration of Official Documents* (Maryknoll, NY: Orbis Books, 2012).

[38]http://www.va/roman_curia/congregations/cfaith/documents/rc_con_cfaith_doc_20040731_collaboration_en.html. Hereafter cited as "Collaboration."

[39]Ibid., no. 16.

[40]Ibid., no. 13.

[41]Ibid., no. 14.

[42]Tina Beattie, "Feminism, Vatican-Style," *The Tablet* 258, no. 8549 (August 7, 2004): 4–6 (4).

[43]Pope Francis, *The Joy of Love: On Love in the Family*, The Post-Synodal Apostolic Exhortation *Amoris Laetitia* (New York: Paulist Press, 2016). Hereafter cited as AL, with the corresponding page number to this edition.

Spirit for a clear recognition of the dignity and rights of women."[44] He calls out certain customs (e.g., genital mutilation) as "reprehensible" and recommends they be eliminated; domestic violence and various forms of enslavement are called "craven acts of cowardice"; verbal, physical and sexual violence are viewed as "contradicting the conjugal union." While castigating women's lack of equal access to dignified work and roles of decision-making, the pope finds "certain forms of feminism have arisen which we must consider inadequate." His rationale does not come until much later in the document, in the context of discussing the love of a mother and father for their child: "I certainly value feminism, but one that does not demand uniformity or negate motherhood. For the grandeur of women includes all the rights derived from their inalienable human dignity but also from their feminine genius, which is essential to society."[45]

It is in AL, however, where Francis makes his most pointed remarks about "gender ideology.' In the section on the experiences and challenges to today's family, he strongly critiques "an ideology of gender that 'denies the difference in nature of a man and a woman and envisages a society without sexual difference, thereby eliminating the anthropological basis of the family'."[46] It is this "ideology" that leads to sex education programs and laws that "promote a personal identity and emotional intimacy radically separated from the biological difference between male and female."[47] Thus, AL argues that while biological sex and its sociocultural role (gender) can be distinguished, they cannot be separated.

In *Querida Amazonia* ("Beloved Amazon"),[48] the apostolic exhortation on the Amazon Synod held in Rome in October 2019, Pope Francis shares "four dreams" he has for the region that are based upon the synod's final report, "The Amazon: New Paths for the Church and for an Integral Ecology." The dreams he recounts involve social, cultural, ecological and ecclesial desires, especially for the rights of the poor, indigenous peoples of the region. A particular thread that is interwoven in his narrative is his concern for the "colonizing mentality" that continues to expand and undermine the distinctive cultural riches of the region, as well as disrupt the equilibrium of nature.

In his fourth, "ecclesial dream" the pope includes an entire section entitled "The Strength and Gift of Women" (nos. 99–103). He recognizes that it is the women of the Amazon who have kept the church alive but says that opening the structure of holy orders to them would amount to "reductionism" and "lead to a narrowing of vision": "it would lead us to clericalize women, diminish the great value of what they have already accomplished, and subtly make their indispensable contribution less effective."[49] Thus, Francis sees any proposal for the ordination of women in the Amazon as "a functional approach" that would obscure the true contribution of women. Rather, following his papal predecessors, he upholds a view of complementarity, where women make their contribution in the Church in a way that is properly theirs, "by making present the tender strength of Mary."[50] His statement in no.102 of QA pretty well sums up this position:

---

[44]AL, no. 54 (39).
[45]AL, no. 173 (121–2).
[46]AL, no. 56 (39).
[47]Ibid.
[48]Pope Francis, *Querida Amazonia* ("Beloved Amazon"), Post-Synodal Apostolic Exhortation on the Synod on the Amazon, February 2, 2020. Available online: http://www.vatican.va/content/francesco/en/apost_exhortations/documents/papa-francesco_esortazione-ap_20200202_querida-amazonia.html. Hereafter cited as QA.
[49]QA, no. 100.
[50]QA, no. 101.

In a synodal Church, those women who in fact have a central part to play in Amazonian communities should have access to positions, including ecclesial services, that do not entail Holy Orders and that can better signify the role that is theirs. Here it should be noted that these services entail stability, public recognition and a commission from the bishop. This would also allow women to have a real and effective impact on the organization, the most important decisions and the direction of communities, while continuing to do so in a way that reflects their womanhood.[51]

Shortly after Francis's QA was released, feminist theologian Tina Beattie issued a trenchant critique of this exhortation. She commented that there are two recurring motifs in his theology. The first is that "no change can happen without honest dialogue, directed towards achieving unity not through the elimination of difference but through a 'reconciled diversity'."[52] In terms of the synod, Francis says he has listened to the bishops, theologians and laypeople but resists imposing "a premature resolution." Thus, no decision is made on ordaining married men, nor ostensibly on ordaining women deacons. Rather, he asks that everyone study the final report of the synod and trusts the bishops to find solutions appropriate to their contexts.

The second recurring motif in his thinking is that the ecological crisis calls for an anthropological transformation, and with this she is in profound agreement. Beattie observes that suffusing all of Francis writings is a profound sense of the mystery of God. "The church is not just another NGO, but called to incarnate Christ in all cultures of the world, and in so doing she must allow herself to be shaped by those cultures in her sacramental and devotional forms of expression."[53] All of this is beautiful, Beattie says, but it is his section on women, despite its title ("The Strength and Gift of Women" that is most troubling to her. She finds his concept of "woman' "to be "mired in a sentimental fantasy." Most disturbing is his logic about *why* women should not be ordained deacons: "women's roles must be suited to the particular characteristics of 'womanhood', which would be 'diminished' if women were to become 'clericalized'."[54] Beattie asks, "If, as he repeatedly insists, clericalism is the scourge of a dysfunctional priesthood, what better way to challenge that than to ordain women?" Nevertheless, perhaps most outrageous to her is Francis's contention that women image Mary and men image Christ, and the conclusion drawn is that only a man can say "this is my body." Such a theology is mired in contradiction, since this would be tantamount to excluding female flesh from the body of Christ.

SEEKING ALTERNATIVES IN THE GENDER THEORY/IDEOLOGY DEBATES

What is problematic for many feminists about the magisterial anthropology expressed in the papal and curial statements reviewed above is its elevation of gender complementarity to a metaphysical and theological category "that corresponds to the entire 'order of creation'."[55] Furthermore, they note that John Paul II's understanding

---

[51]QA, nos. 102–3.
[52]Tina Beattie, "A 'Frozen' Idea of the Feminine," *The Tablet* 274, no. 9340 (February 22, 2020): 4–6 (4).
[53]Ibid.
[54]Ibid.
[55]Ross, "The Bridegroom and the Bride," 47.

of spousal relationships is "completely dyadic" and does not give the multiplicity of roles that exist in human relationships enough attention or credit.[56] This is not to say that there are not differences among Catholic feminist theologians regarding "sexual difference" or with regard to gender roles of women and men. Tina Beattie, Nancy Dallavalle, Lisa Cahill, Michelle Gonzalez, Christine Gudorf and Margaret Farley, each in different ways acknowledge the complexity of the meaning and importance of gender and sexual arrangements among human beings.[57] Perhaps Margaret Farley puts it most clearly:

> Considerations of sex and gender do not begin as neutral examinations of "interesting" aspects of what it means to be human, embodied and inspirited. They begin as efforts to correct or reinforce previous understandings and to challenge or deny imbalances of power based on gender. They continue as investigations into "the political stakes in designating as an *origin* and a *cause* those identity categories that are in fact the *effects* of institutions, practices and discourses with multiple and diffuse points of origin."[58]

Most Catholics know that Paul VI wrote *Humanae Vitae*, the 1968 encyclical that forbade Catholic couples from using artificial means of contraception, but few probably have had any contact with his first encyclical, *Ecclesiam Suam*. Written during Vatican II, this encyclical celebrated its fiftieth anniversary in 2014. *Ecclesiam Suam* at the time was a phenomenal statement that called for dialogue as the fundamental way of proceeding in the life of the church. As John O'Malley reflected, there was hardly a word that was more celebrated during Vatican II than *dialogue*: "No single word, with the possible exception of *aggiornamento*, would be more often invoked to indicate what the council was all about."[59] But since the council it appears that dialogue (especially with women) is a word more to be feared rather than celebrated.

Although Pope Francis and a recent publication from the Congregation for Education[60] regard themselves as engaging in dialogue, it is clear that many feminist ethicists and theologians do not think this has been undertaken widely enough. They also argue that there is a need to include participants who espouse a greater breadth regarding gender and gender theory. The question thus remains: What are the chances of "getting beyond" such a situation of impasse?

---

[56]Ibid., 53.

[57]For example, viewpoints among feminists range from the "strategic essentialism" of Serene Jones in *Feminist Theory and Christian Theology: Cartographies of Grace* (Minneapolis, MN: Fortress Press, 2000), to Elizabeth Johnson's "multi-polar" anthropology described in *She Who Is: The Mystery of God in Feminist Theological Discourse* (New York: Continuum, 1992), 154–6, to Sarah Coakley, whose proposal is that "desire is the constellating category of selfhood, the ineradicable root of longing for God." For Coakley, to say that "desire is more fundamental than gender" means that gender is not static, not fixed "into the seemingly immovable stuckness of what secular theory gloomily calls 'the gender binary'. Rather it is made redemptively labile—subject to endless reformulations one can scarcely imagine at the beginning of the spiritual journey." See *God, Sexuality and the Self: An Essay 'On the Trinity'* (Cambridge: Cambridge University Press, 2013), 58–9.

[58]Farley, *Just Love*, 136. Emphases original.

[59]John O'Malley, *What Happened at Vatican II*, 80.

[60]Congregation for Catholic Education (for Educational Institutions), *"Male and Female He Created Them": Towards a Path of Dialogue on the Question of Gender Theory in Education* (Vatican City: Vatican Press, 2019), 1–31. Hereafter cited as "Male and Female."

ALTERNATIVES TO THE GENDER THEORY/IDEOLOGY DEBATES: THREE TRAJECTORIES

This concluding section briefly reviews three attempts by Catholic theologians, including those from a new generation, who seek to address the perceived impasse in the Catholic magisterium's official anthropology. I call these alternative approaches "trajectories" in order to indicate their open-endedness, one which is in keeping with the imagery of "path" used in recent magisterial documents.[61]

Nancy Dallavalle's Approach of "Critical Essentialism"

Recognizing that feminist theology by the late 1990s had grown increasingly skeptical of the usefulness of the terms "male' and "female," Catholic feminist theologian Nancy Dallavalle was concerned that increasing acceptance of the cultural construction of biological sexuality had given way to an "anthropological agnosticism" among Catholic feminist theologians. Accepting that "biological sexuality is never available to human knowing without the cultural construction of gender," she proposed the idea of a "critical essentialism" that would preserve "biological sexuality" as "essential" for understanding human persons, without having either to acknowledge a gender dualism, in which women inevitably are treated as subordinate to men, or to accept this distinction as leading to a theology of gender complementarity, where the meaning of one's identity is not complete except in the other.[62] Dallavale desired to bring "the important insights of gender theory into 'a deeper and more mutually critical conversation with the profound resonance of biological sexuality in the Catholic theological tradition'."[63]

Starting from the Catholic viewpoint, that "insofar as humanity mediates the divine, it does so with a variety of concrete particularities";[64] humanity as "male" and "female" should continue to stand as a "fixed point" in theological reflection. However (and this is the "critical" aspect), it is a "provisional" fixed point, to which we have no unconstructed access. Nevertheless, it is "grounded," since "as a reflection on a determinate theological tradition its legitimacy is derived from its responsiveness to that tradition in all its complexity and contextuality."[65] This means that the Catholic intellectual tradition can and ought to be brought to bear on any aberrations of patriarchal understandings of sex and gender in its self-reflection, which is what Catholic theology should be doing in respect to sex/gender questions.[66]

Brianne Jacobs's Proposal of the Body as an Existential Category

Brianne Jacobs's proposal for an alternative to gender complementarity argues for an embodied ontology that understands the body as an existential category, in which history, rather than sex, is "that which gives our bodies meaning and legibility

---

[61]Both QA and "Male and Female" use "path" in their documents.
[62]Nancy Dallavalle, "Neither Idolatry nor Iconoclasm: A Critical Essentialism for Catholic Feminist Theology,' *Horizons* 25, no. 1 (1998): 23–42.
[63]Ibid., 24.
[64]Ibid., 30.
[65]Ibid.
[66]For a more extensive discussion of Dallavalle's proposal, see Gonzalez, *Creative in God's Image*, 142–5.

in society."[67] She wants to hold on to the personalism of John Paul II, which she understands as "the idea that the value of a person is the criterion by which one should judge the meaning of work, commerce or relationships" (331) and applauds the idea that "any anthropology that reduces persons to mere producers and measures their value by their products is sinful" and that "people are never a means; their value is always the end" (331).

However, Jacobs finds that John Paul II's "Theology of the Body," in maintaining that men and women both image God and have different but equal and compatible gifts, actually continues the Aristotelian dynamic that views woman as passive, carnal, tempting and wild, while men are active, logical and in charge. Furthermore, the fulfillment and dignity of a woman is their receptivity, particularly the ability to receive one's husband and his child into her body, whereas for the man, fulfillment is to inseminate and be actively procreating. These roles characterize not just the body but also the very being of the person. Human dignity resides, then, in the free gift of self, precisely in gendered difference, that men and women give to one another. As beautiful as this might sound from within a culture where sexuality is seen only in terms of "possession" and "taking pleasure," it maintains, according to Jacobs, the age-old gender binary and renders John Paul unable to sustain the aim of his personalism.

In viewing the body as an *existential* category, Jacobs does not rely on an a priori understanding of sex but on history, where individual bodies "bear histories of power dynamics": the histories of slavery, patriarchy, colonialism, ableism and more. These are reiterated in what Judith Butler calls "performativity" (332). Jacobs prescinds from Butler's constructivist understanding to argue that to be a woman or man is not "an ontological reality" but "a series of historical constructions which give real social meanings to our bodies" (332). Moreover, she contends, drawing on concrete illustrations, there is no biological binary. From there she goes on to appropriate ideas from Johann Baptist Metz (suffering in history, the interruption of "dangerous memories" and seeing history and one's self through the eyes of victims), as well as M. Shawn Copeland (to see one's body through the eyes of God, accept the grace to love it and perform it in such a way that it becomes re-sacralized as holy) (343–4) in order to enflesh her argument (343–4).

Haecceitas: An Alternative to Thomistic Metaphysics

Daniel Horan's retrieval of a concept from the medieval Franciscan John Duns Scotus (d. 1308) presents an overlooked resource for theological anthropology. Horan suggests that Scotus's unique understanding of the "principle of individuation" (*haecceitas*) could provide an alternative framework for moving beyond current anthropological impasses regarding gender and sexuality. According to Horan, the starting point for Aquinas in developing his understanding of the human person (and for all creatures in general)

> has centered on the essence, or nature of a given thing. The unchanging, static, and timeless nature of this metaphysical foundation is apparent when we consider that for Thomas and the tradition that follows him, the existence of a thing comes totally from

---

[67]Brianne Jacobs, "An Alternative to Gender Complementarity: The Body as Existential Category in the Catholic Tradition,' *Theological Studies* 80, no. 2 (2019): 328–45. All citations in this section are taken from this article and indicated by page number in the text.

and is absolutely dependent upon God as pure Being (*Esse*), and the essence or nature of a person or thing is universal.[68]

What this sets up is a distorted outlook that "abstracts from the particular existent—that individual person or thing—something perceived as essential, static, and atemporal."[69] This constitutes, in Horan's view, an "anthropology from above" in which the uniqueness and particularity of the singular is overshadowed by interest in what constitutes the metaphysical nature of a being.

For ages, scholars have considered the ways in which human beings have shared or participated in what we have called "human nature," meaning some sort of universal, common identity. However, Horan observes, "insights from critical theory and contextual theologies have challenged the tradition to account for particular experiences of individuals in theological reflection on the human person." Without trying to argue that Scotus was at all interested in the problems contemporary gender theory sees in "essentialism," or "complementarity," Horan points out that the philosophical question of "what makes something an individual, particular thing" was a hotly discussed topic in the latter part of the thirteenth century in the universities.

Scotus certainly believed in a "common nature" that maintained a real sense of the universal, and that a nature cannot exist outside of some concrete thing. The question was, how can something universal be predicated of multiple individuals, and what makes a particular thing "particular"? Horan admits that these seemingly esoteric question might seem removed from the theological concerns in this chapter. Thus, he cuts to the chase to argue that *haecceitas* "resituates the focus of human value and dignity from an essential and universal 'essence' or 'nature' to a location of radical particularity." Citing the Dutch Scotus scholar, Antonie Vos, "the basic category [for Scotus] is not *universality*, but individuality—the individual has their own identity, something essential which cannot be shared with anything else. They [their respective *haecceities*] are unique, not something negative."[70]

Horan concludes by saying that

Scotus's overturning of the ontological priority of substance or nature through the subordination (yet realistic acknowledgment) of something he calls common nature can be read as decentering the inherited tradition's concern with establishing clarity of a universal human nature or seeking to uncover an absolute and timeless essence of the human person.[71]

What is especially promising about Scotus's approach, according to Horan, is "his capacity to imagine another starting point in our theological reflection without ignoring the importance of commonality, community or genus. In addition, *haecceitas* offers not only an alternative to essentialism, but it also addresses a particular critique of

---

[68]Daniel P. Horan, OFM, *Catholicity & Emerging Personhood: A Contemporary Theological Anthropology* (Maryknoll, NY: Orbis Books, 2019), 128.
[69]Ibid.
[70]Antonie Vos, "John Duns Scotus: An Anthropology of Dignity and Love," in *Words Made Flesh: Essays Honoring Kenan B. Osborne, OFM*, ed. Joseph Chinnici (St. Bonaventure, NY: Franciscan Institute Publications, 2011), 163. As cited in Horan, *Catholicity & Emerging Personhood*, 136.
[71]Horan, *Catholicity & Emerging Personhood*, 137–8.

essentialism: that it de-personalizes humanity" (138). Emphasis on one's individuality as unique and unrepeatable (*haeecceitas*), and "resituating human personhood within a theological framework where the individual is understood as primary and the universal is seen as concurrently present and real (yet secondary) unveils the intrinsic relationality, dignity, and value of *each* person over the depersonalizing elevation of *humanity* in a general and essentialist sense."[72]

SUGGESTED FURTHER READING

Coakley, Sarah, *God, Sexuality and the Self: An Essay "On the Trinity"* (Cambridge: Cambridge University Press, 2013).

Copeland, M. Shawn, *Enfleshing Freedom: Body, Race and Being* (Minneapolis, MN: Fortress Press, 2010).

Farley, Margaret, *Just Love: A Framework for Christian Sexual Ethics* (New York: Continuum, 2008).

Gebara, Ivone, *Out of the Depths: Women's Experience of Evil and Salvation*, trans. Ann Patrick Ware (Minneapolis, MN: Fortress Press, 2002).

Horan, Daniel, *Catholicity & Emerging Personhood: A Contemporary Theological Anthropology* (Maryknoll, NY: Orbis Books, 2019).

Ross, Susan A., *Anthropology: Seeking Light and Beauty* (Engaging Theology: Catholic Perspectives; Collegeville, MN: Liturgical Pres, 2012).

---

[72]Ibid. Emphases original. I would add here that the framework of *haecceitas* might well be correlated with contemporary approaches of critical analysis that are referenced under the umbrella term "intersectionality." See Grace J-Sun Kim and Susan M. Shaw, *Intersectional Theology: An Introductory Guide* (Minneapolis, MN: Fortress Press, 2018).

CHAPTER THIRTY

Neuroscience and Theological Anthropology

HEIDI RUSSELL

Theologian Karl Rahner notes that there is no unmediated experience of God.[1] All of our human experience, even mystical experience, is mediated through the brain. Therefore, any theological anthropology today needs to account for developments in neuroscience. As Philip Clayton, one of the pioneers of this dialogue, notes,

> The neurosciences raise a question much closer to home than disputes about God: the question of who we are. Progress in neuroscience challenges, or at least is often taken to challenge, cherished notions of what it is to be a human person: self-consciousness, soul, "thinking being," free will. Unless and until we manage to defend a notion of the person that preserves concepts such as these in light of what we now know about the human brain, language about God, and any work such language is supposed to do within the human mental psyche, will appear gratuitous.[2]

In recent decades, neuroscience itself has undergone many developments. In addition to the more traditional category of cognitive neuroscience, we have seen the rise of affective neuroscience, which examines the operation of emotions in animal brains in order to draw conclusions about human brains, and social neuroscience, which examines the human brain in the context of social relationships. The field of interpersonal neurobiology, which seeks to integrate neuroscience with developmental psychology, also has implications for theological anthropology.[3] All of these fields contribute something to a theological anthropology, and yet it must be noted that the there is some disagreement both in methodology and conclusions among the fields of neuroscience themselves.

The dialogue between theology and neuroscience must, like any dialogue between theology and science, avoid the twin errors of either basing theological conclusions entirely on developing science or of employing a "God of the gaps" theology that

---

[1] Karl Rahner, *Foundations of Christian Faith: An Introduction to the Idea of Christianity*, trans. William Dych (New York: Crossroad, 1978), 51–5, 83–4.
[2] Philip Clayton, "Neuroscience, the Person, and God: An Emergentist Account," *Zygon* 35 (2000): 613–52 (614).
[3] Note that some scholars have raised questions about the field of neurobiology, warning against too easily combining the findings of neuroscience with the social sciences and specifically then applying those findings to therapeutic interventions. See Adrian Mackenzie and Celia Roberts, "Adopting Neuroscience: Parenting and Affective Indeterminacy," *Body & Society* 23 (2017): 130–55; and Glenda Wall, "'Love Builds Brains': Representations of Attachment and Children's Brain Development in Parenting Education Material," *Sociology of Health & Illness* 40 (2018): 395–409.

inserts God as a cause into areas where science has not yet fully developed answers. For example, the widely popular distinctions between right brain and left brain or the three evolutionary parts of the brain, reptilian, mammalian and human, which are discussed below, have both been challenged by a more holistic view of the brain that understands the key functioning of the brain happening in the interconnectedness of these parts.[4] Thus, while a theological anthropology can and should draw on these theories, it also needs to stay current in the most up-to-date scholarship. Joel Molinario suggests three conclusions from neuroscience today: spirit is embodied; the automated unconscious functions of the brain are more important than the conscious functions of the brain; and the brain is malleable or exhibits neuroplasticity.[5] These three conclusions raise important questions about what it means to be a human person, what it means to talk about the soul and to what extent conversion and human freedom may or may not be limited.

This chapter will begin by defining terms before giving a brief overview of the brain and some key developments in neuroscience. Two of the main topics in the dialogue between neuroscience and theological anthropology are the role of the brain in religious or mystical experience and the relationship between body/brain and mind/soul/spirit. The contribution of neuroscience to the question of religious experience will briefly be addressed before turning to an overview of possible responses on the question of the relationship between body/soul in the dialogue with neuroscience. The chapter will conclude with the contemporary questions neuroscience raises for theological anthropology.

TERMINOLOGY

In a dialogue between neuroscience and theological anthropology, it is important to first clarify the terms body, brain, mind, soul and spirit. The common interpretation of the biblical understanding of body, spirit and soul is the idea that human beings are bodies enlivened by God's Spirit, and thus living souls.[6] This image allows for a more holistic view of the human person as embodied soul or ensouled body.[7] Alexander Fingelkurts and Andrew Fingelkurts advocate a typical view of the human person in this dialogue:

> The human is seen as a psycho-somatic entity consisting of the multiple levels and dimensions of human existence (physical, biological, psychological, and spiritual reality) allowing consciousness/mind/spirit and brain/body/matter to be seen as different sides of the same phenomenon, neither reducible to each other.[8]

They explain that the soul "is the self-aware essence unique to a particular human being, the unification of one's sense of identity, so called subjective world-for-someone," and the

---

[4]Joel Molinario, "Human Fallibility and Neuroscience," in *Theology, Anthropology and Neuroscience*, ed. Thierry-Marie Courau, R. Ammicht-Quinn, H. Haker, et al (London: SCM Press, 2015), 87–99 (89–90, 97 n. 16).
[5]Ibid., 90.
[6]Alan Gijsbers, "The Dialogue between Neuroscience and Theology," Conference on Science and Christianity (COSAC) (Avondale College, Cooranbong, Australia, 18–20 July 2003; ISCAST Christians in Science and Technology), 1–14 (8); Alexander A. Fingelkurts, Andrew A. Fingelkurts, "Is Our Brain Hardwired to Produce God, or Is Our Brain Hardwired to Perceive God? A Systematic Review on the Role of the Brain in Mediating Religious Experience," *Cognitive Processing* 10 (2009): 293–326 (315).
[7]Finglekurts and Fingelkurts warn against confusing the terms Spirit and soul ("Is Our Brain Hardwired," 315 n. 24).
[8]Ibid., 293.

mind "refers to the collective aspects of intellect and consciousness which are manifest in some combination of thought, perception, emotion, will and imagination."[9] They therefore conclude that "soul (using theological/religious terminology) and conscious mind (using cognitive neuroscience terminology) are different descriptions of the same thing."[10]

Nancey Murphy also notes that spirit and mind have a lot of overlap, so that the debate over the relationship between body and spirit is often similar or the same as the debate between body and mind, with the difference that spirit has religious overtones that mind does not have.[11] Daniel Siegel defines the mind as "an embodied and relational process that regulates the flow of energy and information within the brain and *between* brains."[12] Thus, Siegel brings the relational aspect of the human person into the definition of mind. The soul can also be seen as both embodied and relational, regulating the flow of energy and information and experience of God/the infinite within the brain, between brains and in relationship to God.

The theologian Karl Rahner also offers an image of the human person as embodied spirit or spirit in the world. For Rahner, spirit as an aspect of human nature is our capacity for the infinite, and thus our capacity for God.[13] Spirit is our human transcendence, the experience of being unbounded, created for something more. There is a dynamism to the human person so that we transcend or move beyond any finite thing, answer, or goal. We always want more. We want it all. As St. Augustine famously puts it, "You [Lord] have made us for yourself, and our heart is restless until it rests in you."[14] That drive and openness to the more, to the all, to the infinite, in other words—to God—is what Rahner calls spirit.

While humans have an openness to the infinite, in fact, we are finite. We experience ourselves as spirit only in and through the concrete, the embodied. Likewise, we only experience the infinite, which is to say God for Rahner, in and through the concrete, the finite and the embodied. We enact our potentiality in time and space. Through collapsing this infinite possibility into concrete, finite choices, acts of freedom, we become unique individuals. In a recent PBS special, *The Brain with David Eagleman*, Eagleman explains that the development of our brains is all about rapidly making new connections up until about the age of two when that growth halts. He then states, "The process of becoming someone is about pruning back the possibilities that are already present. You become who you are not because of what grows in your brain, but because of what is removed."[15] So in embodying spirit, we actually become individuals by removing possible choices, by pruning back the possibilities of infinite spirit in and through making concrete, embodied choices. I cannot live all of my possibilities. I must make choices. Similar to the quantum relationship between particle and wave, when I actualize a possibility, all other paths

---

[9]Ibid., 315.
[10]Ibid., 316.
[11]Nancey C. Murphy, *Bodies and Souls, Or Spirited Bodies?* (Cambridge: Cambridge University Press, 2006), 2.
[12]Daniel J. Siegel, *The Developing Mind: How Relationships and the Brain Interact to Shape Who We Are*, 2nd ed. (New York: Guilford, 2012), 24. Emphasis mine.
[13]Rahner, *Foundations of Christian Faith*, 31–5.
[14]Augustine of Hippo, *Confessions*, trans. Henry Chadwick (Oxford: Oxford University Press, 1992), 3.
[15]David Eagleman, "What Makes Me Me?," Episode 2, *The Brain with David Eagleman* (Films Media Group, Public Broadcasting Corporation, 2016).

I could have taken collapse into the one path I do choose, but in that same moment, another wave of possibility spreads out before me.[16]

THE HUMAN BRAIN AND NERVOUS SYSTEM

Physician Alan Gijsbers suggests that if the nineteenth century viewed the brain as mechanical and the twentieth century viewed the brain organically, the twenty-first century views the brain in terms of systems and networks.[17] Neuroscience is the study of the brain and the nervous system. Mark Graves explains, the nervous system involves the 10–100 billion neuron cells in the brain, each of which "has an output fiber called an *axon*, and thousands of input fibers called *dendrites*. The dendrites typically spread out like tree branches to receive input from the axon of other neurons."[18] The synapses are the connections between the axons and the dendrites. The language of the brain is chemical. Graves notes that "an estimated 10–100 billion neurons in the brain typically connect from 1000 to 100,000 other neurons, and neuroscientists have discovered over 100 neurotransmitters used in communication between neurons."[19] Groups of these neurons that have established patterns of communication form neuronal assemblies. The more we use certain synaptic connections, the more those connections are reinforced. While scientists have discovered developmental stages when our brain is extremely adaptable and forms new assemblies very quickly, for example, from birth to two years of age, they now know that the brain has plasticity, meaning that the synaptic pathways can be formed and changed throughout our lifetime. This fundamental ability of our brains to change is the physical underpinning of conversion.

Our neural system exists not only in the brain but also throughout our entire bodies. Daniel Siegel calls this our embodied brain.[20] We have a system of neurons lining our gut (our enteric nervous system) that provides information to our brain on an unconscious level.[21] When we talk about our gut instinct, or just knowing something in our gut, there is a physiological reality to that way of knowing.

Perhaps of even greater interest for theological anthropology is the fact that our heart has a network of forty thousand neurons. An example of the research done in this field of neurocardiology given by Adam Waytz in *Scientific American* is the link between one's heart rate variability (HRV) and social behaviors, such as decision making, regulating one's emotions, coping with stress and even academic engagement.[22] Waytz goes on to explain

---

[16]For an extended explanation of this metaphor of body/spirit as particle/wave, see Heidi Russell, "Quantum Anthropology: Reimaging the Human Person as Body/Spirit," *Theological Studies* 74 (2013): 934–59; Heidi Russell, *Quantum Shift: Theological and Pastoral Implications of Contemporary Developments in Science* (Collegeville, MN: Liturgical Press, 2015).

[17]Gijsbers, "The Dialogue between Neuroscience and Theology," 1.

[18]Mark Graves, "Gracing Neuroscientific Tendencies of the Embodied Soul," *Philosophy & Theology* 26 (2014): 97–129 (116).

[19]Ibid.

[20]Siegel, *The Developing Mind*, 15.

[21]Adam Hadhazy, "Think Twice: How the Gut's 'Second Brain' Influences Mood and Well-Being," *Scientific American*, February 12, 2010. Available online: https://www.scientificamerican.com/article/gut-second-brain/ (accessed August 13, 2018). See also Emeran A. Mayer, "Gut Feelings: The Emerging Biology of Gut–Brain Communication," *Nature Reviews Neuroscience* 12 (2011): 453–66.

[22]Adam Waytz, "Psychology beyond the Brain: What Scientists Are Discovering by Measuring the Beating of the Heart," *Scientific American*, October 5, 2010. Available online: https://www.scientificamerican.com/article/the-neuroscience-of-heart/ (accessed August 13, 2018).

that decreased HRV appears to be related to depression and autism, whereas increased HRV is associated with greater social skills, including recognizing other people's emotions and coping with socially stressful situations.[23] Meditation will increase a person's heart rate variability and thus make one better at relating to other people. Relating to people in kind and loving ways, in turn, increases the level of oxytocin (a key neurotransmitter) in one's heart, which has been shown to reduce the risk of heart disease.[24]

This sense that the brain is embodied is integral to a more holistic theological anthropology. The biblical understanding of the human person as an integrated whole has a greater congruence with the contemporary scientific understanding of the human person than the dualistic picture of body/soul.

NEUROSCIENCE—COGNITIVE, AFFECTIVE AND SOCIAL

Neuroscience itself is split into numerous subfields in order to address this complex and holistic view of the human person, such as behavioral, molecular and cellular, and developmental fields of neuroscience. This brief overview is limited to the subfields of cognitive, emotional and social neuroscience.

Cognitive neuroscience studies how the brain thinks, hence cognitive neuroscience has been at the center of the mind/body discussion as well as the body/soul discussion. Mark Graves observes that "although cognitive neuroscience is barely three decades old and has not undergone a major conceptual or paradigm shift, its theories progressively explain more mental activity in greater depth. Little remains of cognitive, emotional, volitional, or social activity for which neuroscientists have not at least begun to develop biological theories." [25] Cognitive neuroscience challenges any form of body/soul dualism, because the characteristics of cognition and volition that have been traditionally attributed to the soul can now be mapped on the brain. Graves explains that neuroscience can localize brain mental activity within distributed brain processing.[26] In other words, neuroscientists may not be able to point to one specific area of the brain that accounts for free will or consciousness, but they can point to the way in which several areas of the brain work together in the act of making choices or being conscious. Graves notes that neuroscience challenges a Thomistic anthropology by demonstrating the "material interdependency, plasticity, and distributed nature of activity ascribed to various Thomistic senses and an embodied conceptualization of the world insufficiently characterized by the Thomistic intellect."[27] Cognitive neuroscience continues to advance our understanding of the brain's central role in the traditional functions associated with the soul in a dualistic view of the human person. Alan Gijsbers concludes, "Embracing dualism seems to be embracing a God-of-the-gaps theology, and the gaps are rapidly shrinking."[28] Likewise Philip Clayton

---

[23]Ibid.
[24]David Hamilton, "Can Kindness Cut the Risk of Heart Disease?," *Huffington Post*, December 23, 2010, updated November 17, 2011. Available online: https://www.huffingtonpost.com/david-r-hamilton-phd/can-kindness-cut-the-risk_b_799562.html (accessed August 13, 2018). See also J. Gutkowska, M. Jankowski, S. Mukaddam-Daher, et al., "Oxytocin Is a Cardiovascular Hormone," *Brazilian Journal of Medical and Biological Research* 33 (2000): 625–33.
[25]Graves, "Gracing Neuroscientific Tendencies," 104.
[26]Ibid., 103.
[27]Ibid., 105. Cites Nancey C. Murphy and Warren S. Brown, *Did My Neurons Make Me Do It?: Philosophical and Neurobiological Perspectives on Moral Responsibility* (Oxford: Oxford University Press, 2007).
[28]Gijsbers, "The Dialogue between Neuroscience and Theology," 7.

maintains, "The debate [about whether or not neuroscience is sufficient to explain the mind] bypasses the debate about dualism. Like 'positivism', the word 'dualism' seems today to be used only as a term of derision, at least in debates with or written for neuroscientists."[29]

In addition to cognitive neuroscience, the newer subfields of affective and social neuroscience have emerged. Affective neuroscience studies the brains of animals to demonstrate that affect is "a lower/subcortical and earlier mind-brain evolutionary development at the level of basic survival," which is then "modulated and regulated by higher brain processes."[30] The distinction between cognitive neuroscience and affective neuroscience is that when cognitive neuroscience studies emotion, it studies the experience of emotion in human beings by using non-invasive approaches, including "verbal reports and nonverbal behavioral expressions of emotion."[31] Affective neuroscience has demonstrated that there are seven primal emotional tendencies in mammalian brains: seeking, rage, fear, lust, care, panic and play.[32] In short, the significance of affective neuroscience for theological anthropology is twofold. First it demonstrates the neurological basis for many pro-social human experiences, such as love, joy and play. Second, in doing so, affective neuroscience decenters the human person, locating these experiences in the mammalian brain, and thus underlining the extent to which these prosocial experiences are unconscious and instinctual instead or as well as intentional. Affective neuroscience acknowledges the consciousness and relationality of animals in their affective experiences. What may be unique to human persons is the ability to reflect on the experiences of these emotions, and it is that ability to reflect on emotion that requires the study of cognitive neuroscience.

In addition to cognitive and affective neuroscience, theological anthropology must consider the implications of social neuroscience. Social neuroscience recognizes both the perspective that the brain impacts our social interactions, but also the ways in which those social interactions influence brain processes.[33] Michael Spezio explains, "The Social Brain Hypothesis posits that humans, and nonhuman primates in general, have the size and kind of brains they have due to the need to function socially within community."[34] John T. Cacioppo and Gary G. Berntson elaborate, "The assumptions in social neuroscience, in contrast, are … that the mechanisms underlying mind and behavior will not be fully explicable by a biological or a social approach alone, that a multi-level integrative analysis may be required."[35] Social neuroscience is important to any theological anthropology because relationship is fundamental to what it means to be a human person. Cacioppo and Berntson further point out:

---

[29]Clayton, "Neuroscience, the Person, and God," 622.

[30]Jaak Panksepp, R. Lane, M. Solms, et al., "Reconciling Cognitive and Affective Neuroscience Perspectives on the Brain Basis of Emotional Experience," *Neuroscience & Biobehavioral Reviews* (2016): 1–29 (2–3).

[31]Ibid., 2.

[32]Ibid., 4.

[33]Malcolm A. Jeeves, *Minds, Brains, Souls, and Gods: A Conversation on Faith, Psychology, and Neuroscience* (Downers Grove, IL: InterVarsity Press, 2013), 66.

[34]Michael L. Spezio, "Social Neuroscience and Theistic Evolution: Intersubjectivity, Love, and the Social Sphere," *Zygon* 48 (2013): 428–38 (430).

[35]John T. Cacioppo and Gary G. Berntson, "Social Neuroscience," in *Foundations in Social Neuroscience*, ed. R. Adolphs, G. G. Berntson, J. T. Cacioppo, Social Neuroscience Series (Cambridge, MA.: Bradford Books, 2002), 3–10 (5).

People form associations and connections with others from the moment they are born. The very survival of newborns depends on their attachment to and nurturance by others over extended periods of time. Accordingly, evolution has sculpted the human genome to be sensitive to and succoring of contact and relationships with others. ... Affiliation and nurturant social relationships, for instance, are essential for physical and psychological well-being across the lifespan. Disruptions of social connections, whether through ridicule, separation, divorce, or bereavement, are among the most stressful events people endure.[36]

How we understand the human person in theological anthropology must take into consideration our primary relationships and our societal structures and relationships. Both have a profound impact on brain development. Social neuroscience demonstrates that we cannot contemplate the human person apart from the network of social relationships that inform a person.

RELIGIOUS EXPERIENCE AND NEUROSCIENCE

Before turning to what might be considered the main question of the neuroscience and theological anthropology dialogue to date, that of the body/soul relationship, it is important to address the question of religious experience. Fingelkurts and Fingelkurts put the question, "Is the brain hardwired to *produce* God; or is the brain hardwired to *perceive* God?"[37] As noted above, Rahner maintains that all religious experience is embodied and thus mediated by the human brain. Fingelkurts and Fingelkurts define religious experience as "the very moment of experiencing of ultimate divine reality or ultimate divine truth, a transcendence of events or universe, timelessness, spacelessness, and divine being and/or union with it in any combination with an accompanied memorable feeling of reality, emotions and thoughts with a religious content."[38] They note that while people from very different time periods, cultures and religions have religious experiences, there is a commonality to the experiences that is archetypal involving "the feeling of timelessness, divine love and being at one with the divine universe or divine being."[39] After detailing the arguments for both the brain producing religious experience and the brain perceiving religious experience, they develop a holistic mediating viewpoint that proclaims neuroscience cannot *explain* religious experience, but it can help *describe* religious experience. They conclude,

Religious experience is a complex subjective psycho-neuro-physiologic phenomenon. In order to understand and *explain* it fully we need to *describe* its physical, biological, psychological, sociological and spiritual dimensions. At the moment neuroscience cannot provide a reliable *explanation* for religious experience (see above). However, already today cognitive neuroscience in a broad sense may contribute to an overall *description* of religious experience with regards to biological and psychological dimensions. ... Therefore, currently there should be a methodological shift from "explanation" to "description."[40]

---

[36]Ibid., 7–8.
[37]Fingelkurts and Fingelkurts, "Is Our Brain Hardwired," 293–326. Emphasis mine.
[38]Ibid., 294–5.
[39]Ibid., 296.
[40]Ibid., 316. Emphasis in original.

Rather than seeing neuroscience and religious experience as adversarial, with neuroscience attempting to explain away religious experience, a well-developed theological anthropology should see neuroscience as offering a greater understanding of the way in which all religious experience is embodied.

UNDERSTANDING THE BODY/SOUL DISCUSSION

The single area of theological anthropology in which neuroscience has had the most impact to date has been the understanding of what it means to say that humans are body/soul. The extreme positions in this dialogue are a reductive materialism versus a substance dualism.[41] Reductive physicalism or materialism denies any aspect of the person that cannot be explained by the biological processes of the body. The whole is simply the sum of the parts. This extreme view does not allow for a distinct mind, let alone a soul, arguing that all our experiences of self, consciousness, love, freedom and so on are simply functions of our brain. The opposite position of dualism postulates two separate substances, realms, or realities. Mark Graves warns against these extremes:

> When Christian theology underemphasizes the role of natural processes in human experience, it often misses the richness and beauty of Creation. Conversely, when science overemphasizes human individuality and physicality, it often misses the distributed processing of the brain and the integrated functioning of societies in a cultural and religious context.[42]

Most theologians engaging neuroscience develop a mediating position between reductive materialism and substance dualism. Among those who embrace a body–soul holism, meaning that body and soul are inextricably intertwined, some may still be dualists in terms of a belief in the survival or existence of a soul that is completely separate from the body after death. Alison Gray describes this position as weak dualism or holistic dualism, viewing the mind and body as separate parts that function together or two poles of the same reality.[43] Graves offers a mediating position that suggests a nonsubstantive interpretation of Aquinas' concept of soul as form,[44] suggesting that one's "substantial form" consists instead of a new configuration of human potentiality capable of receiving grace.'[45] Nancey Murphy and Malcolm Jeeves are proponents of non-reductive physicalism, in which the soul is dependent on the body; however, as an emergent property of the brain, it is not reducible to the body. The whole is more complex than the parts and cannot be determined or predicted by the parts.

The concepts that are used to explain the relationship between body and soul or body and mind in the mediating positions are top-down causality, emergence and supervenience. Top-down causality is the process of higher-level capacities being dependent on lower-level neural processes, while at the same being capable of having an effect on those

---

[41]For a helpful taxonomy mind/body theories, see the chart in Gijsbers, "The Dialogue between Neuroscience and Theology," 12.

[42]Graves, "Gracing Neuroscientific Tendencies," 100–1. Philip Clayton also occupies a mediating monist position called emergentist monism that will be further discussed below.

[43]Alison J. Gray, "Whatever Happened to the Soul? Some Theological Implications of Neuroscience," *Mental Health, Religion & Culture* 13 (2010): 637–48 (644).

[44]Graves, "Gracing Neuroscientific Tendencies," 106.

[45]Ibid., 120–1.

lower-level processes.[46] Emergence is the process by which new properties "arise from increasing capacity and interactive complexity of complex systems."[47] Supervenience "is used to designate a dependent but generally irreducible relationship that higher-level properties or states have with lower-level properties or states" so that "higher-level states (mental states) can change only if the lower-level states (brain states) also change." [48] The reverse is not necessarily true; lower-level states can change while higher-level states remain the same.

Clayton rules out the extremes of strong reductionism and metaphysical dualism,[49] but he also notes the complexity of these mediating positions and the "fractal structure" of the debate, so that every time there seems to be common ground, multiple interpretations of the common ground position emerge depending upon whether one sees the neurological explanation to be sufficient or insufficient.[50] Clayton's own mediating position attempts to account for the fact that we do not have thoughts apart from our brains but at the same time "allow[s] for the emergence of mental phenomena and for mental causation."[51] This mediating position also "understand[s] the effect of interactions with the surrounding environment upon mentality" and thus can take into account social neuroscience, but "at the same time do[es] justice to the irreducible subjectivity of experience."[52] For Clayton, the human person is a psychosomatic unity, using what he calls "emergentist supervenience" to explain "that brains, social context, and mental properties exist" and are interrelated.[53] Clayton's view maintains a "weak supervenience" as opposed to "strong supervenience" in his "view that, although physical structures and causes may determine the initial emergence of the mental, they do not fully or solely determine the outcome of the mental life subsequent to its emergence."[54] Clayton further advocates a position of emergent monism:

> Monism asserts that only one kind of thing exists. There are not two substances in the world with essentially different natures. … But unlike dual-aspect monism, which argues that the mental and the physical are two different ways to characterize the one "stuff," emergentist monism conceives the relationship between them as temporal and hierarchical.[55]

Ultimately, Clayton is defining a relationship between mind and body, and not directly addressing the question of soul. He notes that emergentism is "a necessary condition for

---

[46]Warren Brown, "Neurological Embodiment of Spirituality and Soul," in *From Cells to Souls—and Beyond: Changing Portraits of Human Nature*, ed. Malcolm Jeeves (Grand Rapids, MI: Eerdmans, 2004), 63. Brown calls this top-down causality "nonreductive physicalism."

[47]Ibid., 64.

[48]William Stoeger, "The Mind-Brain Problem, the Laws of Nature, and Constitutive Relationships," in *Neuroscience and the Person: Scientific Perspectives on Divine Action*, ed. Robert John Russell et al., Series on Scientific Perspectives on Divine Action (Vatican City State: Vatican Observatory Publications and The Center for Theology and the Natural Sciences, 1999), 142.

[49]Clayton, "Neuroscience, the Person, and God," 624.

[50]Ibid., 642.

[51]Ibid., 628.

[52]Ibid.

[53]Ibid., 630–2.

[54]Ibid., 633.

[55]Ibid., 643.

a theological interpretation of the human person, but it is emphatically not a sufficient condition for a theological anthropology."[56] He ultimately concludes,

> To say that the human person is a psychosomatic unity is to resist both positions. It is instead to say that the person is a complexly patterned entity within the world, one with diverse sets of naturally occurring properties, each of which needs to be understood *by a science appropriate to its own level of complexity*. We need multiple layers of explanatory accounts *because* the human person is a physical, biological, psychological, and (I believe also) spiritual reality and because these aspects of a person's reality, though interdependent, are not mutually reducible. Call the existence of these multiple layers *ontological pluralism*, and call the need for multiple layers of explanation *explanatory pluralism*, and my thesis becomes clear: Ontological pluralism begets explanatory pluralism. Or, to put it differently, the best explanation for explanatory pluralism is ontological pluralism.[57]

Theological anthropology today cannot be neatly separated into two separate categories of the bodily/physical and the spiritual. Any approach to theological anthropology that takes neuroscience seriously needs to recognize that as human persons, we are integrated wholes. While there are multiple aspects to the human person, including the bodily and the spiritual, these aspects interact, are not completely separable from one another and ultimately combine to create a whole that is greater than the sum of its parts.

CONCLUDING QUESTIONS AND AREAS FOR FURTHER CONVERSATION

One question that emerges in the dialogue between theological anthropology and neuroscience is that of human uniqueness. Mark Graves asks if there is something unique about the human person, either as a separate yet connected ethereal aspect of human being (weak dualism) or as a part of human nature, but a part that determines our human essence as unique from the animals (reinterpreted Thomism).[58] He suggests there is not; science is rapidly closing the gap on human exceptionalism. We are beginning to recognize the consciousness and emotions of other animal species. Graves argues the "shared neural structures and processing between humans and other animals significantly contradict most claims for rationality or similar cognitive function as a point of human uniqueness."[59] In an age of ecological crisis, decentering the human person and recognizing ourselves as a part of the created world can call forth greater respect and protection for the fragile balance of the environment of which we are a part.

Neuroscience may be particularly relevant to theological anthropology today in light of its interdisciplinary work with the social sciences. Understanding brain development, distributed function and unconscious functions can have a major impact on how we understand the concepts of sin and grace. As we continue to struggle against systemic sin and injustice, neuroscience can help us understand how implicit bias and perception

---

[56]Ibid., 635.
[57]Ibid., 644. See also Fingelkurts and Fingelkurts, "Is Our Brain Hardwired," 293. Emphasis original.
[58]Graves, "Gracing Neuroscientific Tendencies," 102.
[59]Ibid., 105.

bias can impact issues such as racism and white supremacy. Understanding that our brains implicitly perceive black men as bigger, stronger and more threatening than white men, which can in turn trigger a fight or flight reaction in our brains, can help us address social issues such as police training.[60] The fact that our brains may falsely perceive black children to be older than they are in actuality can help us address issues of racial disparity in discipline in our educational institutions, and thus also help us address the preschool to prison pipeline.[61] The preschool to prison pipeline is impacted not only by racial disparity but also by the impact on brain development by adverse childhood experiences.[62]

As we study brain development, neurobiology helps us understand the essential role of relationality in early childhood brain development.[63] Children who experience childhood trauma and a high number of "adverse childhood experiences" (ACES) have less developed executive function and a hyper-aroused fight, flight or freeze response.[64] Intervention in the form of significant nurturing relationships can help prevent the repeated cycles of trauma in family systems. The theological axiom that to be human is to be in relationship is an axiom that not only reflects our creation in the image and likeness of God but also reflects the most fundamental quality of our brains.

Theologian Karl Rahner maintains theology is anthropology and anthropology is theology, meaning that the way we understand God impacts our understanding of the human person and our understanding of the human person impacts our image of God. To believe in a Trinitarian God is to believe in a created world in which relationship is primary. One of the key ways to disrupt implicit bias and perception bias and to heal adverse childhood experiences is through relationship. Human persons are created to be in relationship, and those relationships can heal our brains. Because of neuroplasticity, crossing racial, ethnic, nationalistic, class and cultural divides can actually change our brains, create new connections and pathways in our neural networks and change our implicit and perception biases. Entering into loving, nurturing relationships can create

[60]John Paul Wilson, Kurt Hugenberg and Nicholas O. Rule, "Racial Bias in Judgments of Physical Size and Formidability: From Size to Threat," *Journal of Personality and Social Psychology* 113, no. 1 (2017): 59–80; Colin Holbrook, Daniel M. T. Fessler and Carlos David Navarrete, "Looming Large in Others' Eyes: Racial Stereotypes Illuminate Dual Adaptations for Representing Threat Versus Prestige as Physical Size," *Evolution and Human Behavior* 37, no. 1 (2016): 67–78; Joshua Correll, C. M. Judd, B. Park, "The Police Officer's Dilemma: Using Ethnicity to Disambiguate Potentially Threatening Individuals," *Journal of Personality and Social Psychology* 83, no. 6 (2002): 1314–29.

[61]C. M. Culotta, P. A. Goff, M. C. Jackson, et al., "The Essence of Innocence: Consequences of Dehumanizing Black Children," *Journal of Personality and Social Psychology* 106, no. 4 (2014): 526–45; Oscar A. Barbarin, "Halting African American Boys' Progression from Pre-K to Prison: What Families, Schools, and Communities Can Do!," *American Journal of Orthopsychiatry* 80, no. 1 (2010): 81–8.

[62]Merih Altintas and Mustafa Bilici, "Evaluation of Childhood Trauma with Respect to Criminal Behavior, Dissociative Experiences, Adverse Family Experiences and Psychiatric Backgrounds among Prison Inmates," *Comprehensive Psychiatry* 82 (2018): 100–7.

[63]Allan N. Schore, "Effects of a Secure Attachment Relationship on Right Brain Development, Affect Regulation, and Infant Mental Health," *Infant Mental Health Journal* 22 (2001): 7–66; Schore, "The Effects of Early Relational Trauma on Right Brain Development, Affect Regulation, and Infant Mental Health," *Infant Mental Health Journal* Vol. 22 (2001): 201–69.

[64]Mary Boullier and Mitch Blair, "Adverse Childhood Experiences," *Pediatrics and Child Health* 28, no. 3 (2018): 132–7; D. Finkelhor, S. Hamby, A. Shattuck, et al., "A Revised Inventory of Adverse Childhood Experiences," *Childhood Abuse and Neglect* 48 (2015), 13–21; M. H. Bair-Merritt, P. F. Cronholm, M. B. Davis, et al., "Household and Community-Level Adverse Childhood Experiences and Adult Health Outcomes in a Diverse Urban Population," *Child Abuse and Neglect* 52 (2015): 135–45.

the connections between the different parts of our brain that did not fully develop due to childhood trauma, thus increasing *executive* function.[65]

The human person is a complex entity and both neuroscience and theology are beginning to understand that context and relationship are fundamental to human development. We cannot separate out either a neurological basis for the person apart from the set of relationships and societal context a person inhabits any more than we can develop a theological understanding of the person without those contexts. Any approach to understanding the human person today must approach the person as a whole with complex, interrelated pieces in which the sum is more than the parts.

SUGGESTED FURTHER READING

Clayton, Philip, *Mind and Emergence: From Quantum to Consciousness* (New York: Oxford University Press, 2004).

Clayton, Philip, "Neuroscience, the Person, and God: An Emergentist Account," *Zygon* 35 (2000): 613–52.

Graves, Mark, "Gracing Neuroscientific Tendencies of the Embodied Soul," *Philosophy & Theology* 26 (2014): 97–129.

Graves, Mark, *Mind, Brain and the Elusive Soul: Human Systems of Cognitive Science and Religion* (Burlington, VT: Ashgate, 2008).

Jeeves, Malcolm (ed.), *The Emergence of Personhood: A Quantum Leap?* (Grand Rapids, MI: Eerdmans, 2015).

Murphy, Nancey C., *Bodies and Souls, Or Spirited Bodies?* (Cambridge: Cambridge University Press, 2006).

Newberg, Andrew B., *Neurotheology: How Science Can Enlighten Us about Spirituality* (New York: Columbia University Press, 2018).

---

[65]Louis J. Cozolino and Erin N. Santos, "Why we Need Therapy—and Why It Works: A Neuroscientific Perspective," *Smith College Studies in Social Work* 84, no. 2–3 (2014): 157–77; Gabriela López-Zerón, Adrian Blow, "The Role of Relationships and Families in Healing from Trauma," *Journal of Family Therapy* 39, no. 4 (2017): 580–97; D. M. Lawson, "Understanding and Treating Children Who Experience Interpersonal Maltreatment: Empirical Findings," *Journal of Counseling and Development* 87 (2009): 204–15.

CHAPTER THIRTY-ONE

Neoliberalism and Theological Anthropology: The Hidden Formation of Student Loans and Dating Apps

VINCENT J. MILLER

INTRODUCTION

How do we learn an anthropology? What forms us to imagine ourselves and to act as certain kinds of persons? Catholicism has long—for at least the last ten or eleven papacies—criticized the individualistic anthropology of modern thought. But how do these ideas come to form the lives of so many people who have never even heard of John Locke or Adam Smith, let alone read them? We are formed, both consciously and unconsciously, through the social, economic and policy structures that we live in from day to day. Different forms of life inculcate radically different anthropologies. As peasants moved from agricultural life in rural villages to competitive urban labor markets in the eighteenth century, they were formed into very different sorts of people without reading a single sentence of Locke or Smith.

Such formation continues in our own time. "Neoliberalism" names a movement in economics that sees competitive market structures as the best form of social interaction. It seeks not only to minimize political limits on market activity (as laissez-faire capitalism did) but also to maximize the presence of market competition throughout society. Its ideas have dominated politics and policy debates since the 1970s. It has created a new, individualistic and competitive form of life that has spread throughout the world.

The form of life that neoliberalism has crafted conflicts with the Catholic understanding of the human person made in the image and likeness of the triune God. We are made for relationship and community. While competition with others as individuals has its place, we flourish primarily by giving to and receiving from others as members of community. This is, however, not only an *argument* between competing ideas but also a conflict between forms of life. Thus, our response cannot simply be a matter of clarifying our beliefs regarding whether we accept the Catholic understanding of the human person or not. It involves becoming aware of how the structures we have chosen to build society upon are, in important ways, at odds with the Catholic understanding of the human person. With this knowledge, we can become more aware of how these structures form us and thus work to resist that formation and seek to transform society into something more consistent with Catholic anthropology.

This chapter will explore how neoliberal policies have transformed society and how we might respond. After an overview of the movement, we will consider their major ideas and the policies they have successfully enacted based upon them. We will then turn to critical accounts of how neoliberalism has transformed everyday life. We will conclude by mapping the contrasts between the anthropologies in which we are formed and those of the Catholic tradition and consider how Christians might respond.

OVERVIEW OF NEOLIBERALISM

"Neoliberalism" is sometimes used as an epithet for a pro-corporate, anti-government political agenda. It is used to describe those on both the center left and the right who imagine policy in market terms. While such usage can be imprecise, the term is not simply a slur. It was coined by a group of economists organized by the Austrian F. A. Hayek in the wake of the Second World War. At that time, the economic model of John Maynard Keynes dominated policy. Keynesianism responded to the Great Depression by enlisting government to both moderate the excesses of capitalist economies, with their recurring boom and bust cycles of inflation and depression, and to actively guide the economy to growth in areas targeted for the national common good. This form of economic policy ushered in the greatest period of sustained economic growth in history and birthed the middle-class economies we now take for granted. The neoliberals, however, considered this democratic socialism of postwar Europe to be a slippery slope to communism. Hayek's 1944 *The Road to Serfdom* famously warned that England's social democratic policies placed it on a path that would lead to totalitarian repression. (They did not.)

Although a minority of economists at the time, neoliberal thinkers organized and built institutions such as the "Mont Pelerin Society," an international society of like-minded economists and many policy think tanks, to advance their vision. They coined the term "neoliberal" to distinguish their project from classical liberalism. Rather than the laissez-faire doctrine of "letting the market be," they understood that markets were a political choice, not a natural state of affairs. While laissez-faire presumed that a market economy would flourish if the state got out of the way, neoliberals instead sought to use state power to promote competition and to reimagine policies in market terms. State power is employed paradoxically to force people to embrace the freedoms of the market. For example, whereas postwar social democracies in the United States, Britain and Western Europe sought to use the state to provide or to support education, retirement and health care, the neoliberals sought to transfer the provision of such services from the state to the private sector where they would be guided by market logic: school vouchers, student debt, individual retirement accounts and health care insurance markets.

There were many neoliberal thinkers in Europe and the United States. Here we will focus on three: Friedrich Hayek, Milton Friedman and Gary Becker.

Friedrich Hayek

Friedrich Hayek was the organizer of the Mont Pelerin Society and author of popular polemical works (such as *The Road to Serfdom*) as well as important theoretical works for this approach to economics. Through the Society, he fostered the growth of this approach to economics throughout Europe and North and South America. His major intellectual contribution is his idea of the market as a processor of information given expression in his 1946 essay "The Use of Knowledge in Society."[1] The essay begins as an argument about how markets outperform socialist planning for resource allocation. Hayek argued that when the price of a commodity such as tin increases, myriad producers who use it adapt to the increased cost by seeking substitutes, changing production methods or passing the costs on to their customers. Each decision is based upon detailed, specific, local knowledge that no planning board could ever hope to compile. All that was required to communicate this information is the price signal between market actors. But the essay was more than a tidy argument for the value of markets in resource allocation. By reconceiving the market as an "information processor," Hayek implicitly expanded their reach to all knowledge. Not only do markets process economic knowledge better than central planning, but markets are also better at processing any knowledge; better than democratic deliberation, better than intellectual synthesis. This notion of knowledge presumes irreducible ignorance.[2] Few serious positions think we can know everything, but Hayek's reductionist understanding of knowledge presumes not only that our knowledge is limited and fragmentary but also that it is not shareable or synthesizable. It is communicated only through the economic negotiations of parties to a deal, each trying to maximize their advantage with the knowledge they possess. Thus for neoliberals, knowledge is linked to competition, not collective debate or wisdom.

Hayek's simple argument contained the seed of the expansion of market logic to vast swaths of social interaction. It would go on to inspire many of the innovators that designed important aspects of the internet. Jimmy Wales has cited Hayek's essay as an inspiration for his cofounding of Wikipedia.[3] Much of what we call "social media" displays a market-like structure: purely elective relationships and a quantified system of "liking" and sharing through forwarding, reposting or retweeting. Generations now experience their social lives through this constant evaluation and competition for attention. Dating and hookup apps likewise reduce complex human interactions to evaluative swipe left or right. While once the personal realm was experienced as a shelter from the harsh competition of daily life in the marketplace, now the market penetrates our private lives to a degree unimaginable for previous generations.

Milton Friedman

If Hayek was the strategic and intellectual founder of the movement, Milton Friedman was its greatest communicator. Through his column in *Newsweek* magazine from 1966 to 1984, he offered a constant commentary on contemporary events from a pro-market perspective. It was Friedman who distinguished neoliberalism as emphasizing

---

[1] F. A. Hayek, "The Use of Knowledge in Society," *American Economic Review* 35, no. 4 (September 1945): 519–30.
[2] Philip Mirowski, *Never Let a Serious Crisis Go to Waste: How Neoliberalism Survived the Financial Meltdown* (London: Verso, 2013), 54, 78.
[3] Katherine Mangu-Ward, "Wikipedia and Beyond: Jimmy Wales' Sprawling Vision," *Reason* 39, no. 2 (June 2007): 21. (See Wikipedia article: https://en.wikipedia.org/wiki/The_Use_of_Knowledge_in_Society#cite_note-reasonmag-8 (accessed April 7, 2017).)

competition rather than laissez-faire.[4] But the focus of his public arguments were freedom, not competition. Friedman offered a vision of society composed of completely independent agents ("a collection of Robinson Crusoes") who can produce what they need for themselves and thus only enter into market exchanges if both parties benefit. This produces a system of "cooperation without coercion."[5]

Friedman drew a sharp distinction between the freedom of market action and the coercion of political action. Political action "requires conformity." Democratic decisions inevitably run counter to the desires of the minority, who are nonetheless forced to conform to the outcome. Markets allow "each man" to "vote, as it were, for the color of tie he wants and get it; he does not have to see what color the majority wants and then, if he is in the minority, submit."[6] Thus, Friedman dissolves political action for the common good into personal consumer preference. From this perspective, he offered a simple and consistent argument that, in every possible political and policy question, proposed that market solutions would always advance freedom and that any form of government regulation or control would always have a negative outcome. He argued against public schools, advocating tuition vouchers as an intermediate step toward fully privatized education. He argued against state-funded universities in favor of student debt. He was instrumental in the Nixon administration's decision to end the military draft. This policy reduced responsibility for defending the community to an expression of personal preference or financial reward, rather than a responsibility to the common good.

Gary Becker

If Friedman was the great communicator who rhetorically equated capitalism with freedom, government with inefficiency and community with coercion, it was his colleague at the University of Chicago, Gary Becker, who developed the policies through which neoliberalism has remade our world. Becker brought economic analysis from the public marketplace into the private realm of marriage and family life. He evaluated decisions to marry and the "sorting of mates" in terms of maximizing "utility" with accompanying complex equations and supply and demand curves.[7] Becker's influence went far beyond conjectures however. His innovations in policy have been transformative, making neoliberal logic part of our lived experience.

Becker's greatest contribution concerned the notion of "human capital." Melinda Cooper has shown that this term was originally developed as a macroeconomic argument to explain how the education of workers contributed to the economic growth of the whole of society. It formed the basis for the massive investment in public education and higher education in the postwar period evident in the emergence of the modern public research university, state subsidized tuition and governmental grants to provide broad

[4]Milton Friedman, "Nyliberalismen Og Dens Muligheter [Neoliberalism and its Prospects]," *Farmand* (February 17, 1951): 91–3. Translated in Jamie Peck, *Constructions of Neoliberal Reason* (Oxford: Oxford University Press, 2012), 3. An older, full translation is available online: https://miltonfriedman.hoover.org/friedman_images/Collections/2016c21/Farmand_02_17_1951.pdf (accessed October 12, 2020).
[5]Milton Friedman and Rose Friedman, *Capitalism and Freedom* (Chicago: University of Chicago Press, 1962), 13.
[6]Ibid., 15.
[7]Gary S. Becker, *The Economic Approach to Human Behavior* (Chicago: University of Chicago Press, 1976), 205–50.

access to higher education.[8] Against this consensus, Becker and Friedman argued that the benefits of higher education primarily accrued to the student, not society, and thus argued against public funding. In *Human Capital*, Becker conducted comprehensive research into education and job training from this perspective, laying the foundation for neoliberal policy proposals to transform higher education funding into our current system of individual debt.[9] His argument goes deeper than merely monetary investment. All dimensions of parents' formation of children, insofar as they increase the child's potential, are reconceived here as investments in their future productivity.[10]

This policy has fundamentally changed people's experience of education. While we may still speak of education as formation and describe vocations in terms of usefulness to society, education has been reworked practically as an individual investment. One's choice of major always faces the looming audit: can it earn enough to repay student loans? "Return on investment" has now become part of the lexicon of college selection. Millions who struggle to repay student debt know well that these are not abstract debates but are life-constraining disciplines.

In a context of rising inequality, the competition for landing on the right side of the economic divide increases. And, thus, childhood has been colonized by career preparation. Parents treat their children as "precious appreciating assets."[11] Malcolm Harris quotes a letter from a kindergarten explaining the elimination of its annual school play: "The reason for the elimination of the Kindergarten show is simple. We are responsible for preparing children for college and career with valuable lifelong skills and know that we can best do this by having them become strong readers, writers, coworkers, and problem solvers."[12]

THE ANTHROPOLOGY NEOLIBERALISM CREATES

The economist Philip Mirowski has argued that the power of neoliberalism lies in the fact that "a kind of folk or everyday neoliberalism has sunk ... deeply into the cultural unconscious."[13] Here we will consider four effects of neoliberalism that are the most explicitly anthropological: the intensification of individualism, life imagined as risk, issues of class and agency, and a polarizing sadism that celebrates others' suffering.

Beyond Individualism: Dissolving the Self in the Market

Neoliberalism is frequently described as having a radically individualist anthropology. While this is accurate, it misses the specifics of its vision of the self. More than simply an isolated individual, the neoliberal self is an entrepreneur whose relationships with others are transactional and competitive. Other people are of interest only insofar as we can enter into beneficial exchange with them. Note that this is not simply a belief about what

[8]Melinda Cooper, *Family Values: Between Neoliberalism and the New Social Conservatism* (New York: Zone Books, 2017), 219–27.

[9]Gary S. Becker, *Human Capital: A Theoretical and Empirical Analysis, with Special Reference to Education* (New York: National Bureau of Economic Research/Columbia University Press, 1975).

[10]Michel Foucault, *Birth of Biopolitics: Lectures at the College de France 1978–1979*, trans. Graham Burchell (New York: Picador, 2008), 229.

[11]Malcolm Harris, *Kids These Days* (New York: Little, Brown, 2017), 27.

[12]Ibid., 13.

[13]Mirowski, *Never Let a Serious Crisis Go to Waste*, 89.

a person is; it is also a specific form of relationship. We relate to others through market exchange. As we saw in our discussion of Becker, the model of exchange goes far beyond goods and services to colonize dating, marriage and parenting relationships.

The model of the entrepreneur reaches even deeper into human personhood than our social and personal relationships. As Michel Foucault observed, the anthropological vision of neoliberalism is not simply the *Homo oeconomicus* of classical liberal economics rationally calculating the best path to realizing its desires. Neoliberal thinkers instead envision the person as "an entrepreneur of himself."[14] *We* are the products of our entrepreneurial activity. It is an experience fostered by our debt-funded educational system: how much will you invest in your future earning potential? But it is dispersed throughout our social experience. There was a time when to speak one's personal "brand" was a slightly ironic metaphor. Now it is a commonplace part of life. An entire generation is entering adulthood having curated their self-presentation through social media since preadolescence: beginning with Snapchat and Instagram, progressing through Twitter and graduating to LinkedIn and the many variations of Tinder. The task of carefully cultivating a persona for presentation to a marketplace of attention takes its place alongside earlier forms of social formation such as building a local reputation and establishing relationships. This market pressure is also evident in technologies of bodily enhancement from cosmetic surgery and physical fitness to pharmacological performance enhancement and "life hacking." In Mirowski's words, the neoliberal self is "a jumble of assets to be invested, nurtured, managed, and developed; but equally an offsetting inventory of liabilities to be pruned, outsourced, shorted, hedged against, and minimized."[15]

Like the sovereign individual, freedom also becomes problematic in this context. What began as a purely negative notion of freedom—the absence of coercion in pursuit of individual desires—is gradually transformed into something quite different. When freedom is exercised solely on the market, it ceases to be the pursuit of preexisting desires (which may or may not be realizable in the market). It becomes instead the activity of engaging in whatever is available on the market, of choosing among the opportunities on offer. In Mirowski's words, the neoliberal subject is not "learning about who she really is, but rather, provisionally buying the person she must soon become."[16]

This brings us to the profound depths of the reworking of the notion of the person. As the self is increasingly realized through market practices, the sovereign individual presumed by classical liberalism is gradually dissolved. One doesn't seek a certain good, adopt a style or even pursue a career to express one's true self. Rather, these activities are a way of participating in the marketplace of status, attention and reward. Likes, followers and right swipes are so often earned not by uniqueness, but by conformity. Hayek had proposed that the great virtue of the independent entrepreneur is that he or she is in direct contact with the market, thus engaging reality through the only trustworthy way of knowing: the price signal.[17] This has gone deeper than he imagined. The self is now found in submission to and embrace of the options and identities that are marketable. If the true self is constituted in market exchange, then "selling out" is no longer a betrayal of the self, but rather, its greatest realization. This transformation is perhaps evident in the current use of the word "passion." What once described the unruly aspects of human

---

[14]Foucault, *Birth of Biopolitics*, 226.
[15]Mirowski, *Never Let a Serious Crisis Go to Waste*, 108.
[16]Ibid.
[17]F. A. Hayek, *The Constitution of Liberty* (Chicago: University of Chicago Press, 1978), 121.

desire, passion now commonly appears in marketing copy and resumes—describing how a company serves its customers or a job seeker will be valuable to an employer.

Life Imagined as Risk

Mirowski argues that the neoliberal self's embrace of and submission to the market is most fully expressed in "capitulation to a life of risk." He contrasts neoliberal notions of risk with older economic definitions. For neoliberalism,

> accepting risk is not the fine balancing of probabilities, the planning for foreseen exigencies and the exercise of prudential restraint; rather, it is wanton ecstasy: the utter subjection of the self to the market by offering oneself up to powers greater than we can ever fully comprehend. It is, quite literally, an irrational leap of faith, with the parallels to religious traditions intentional.[18]

Mirowski's use of "irrational" here refers to the irreducible ignorance that Hayek argued was part of any market exchange. Market actors are like poker players, each reading their own hand of knowledge as best they can and communicating that to others only through the bets they place. Reward can only be obtained by risking a play amidst this uncertainty.

Most of us have no interest in living our lives this way. It is natural to seek some stability amid the uncertainties of life: relationships, steady income, shelter, health care, retirement. In seeking to advance competitive, market structures, the neoliberal revolution has worked to replace the twentieth-century Keynesian model of the prudent "worker-saver" household with the risk taking entrepreneur.[19] Thus, it has helped replace lifetime employment with dynamic, ever-shifting and insecure gig-economy work as an "independent contractor," defined benefit pensions with employee-managed individual retirement accounts and government-supported and employer-based health care with a variety of private options with varying levels of risk.

This emphasis on risk-taking has the predictable effect of shifting the volatility of life toward the individual and away from shared communal risk pools such as large employers, unions and government social security systems. This brings a way of moralizing negative outcomes. Mirowski notes the moral tautology here: when calamity is reinterpreted as a result of poor risk management, those suffering things outside of their control are judged for not properly hedging against risk. In Galit Ailon's words, "risk management discourse enables us to simultaneously celebrate the indeterminacy of outcomes and to retrospectively moralize these outcomes."[20]

The Suppression of Class and the Privatization of Agency

Because of its imagination of the market in terms of the interaction of individual agents, neoliberalism cannot think in a systematic way about differential outcomes, beyond seeing them as the result of individual choice and risk taking. It gives little attention to how economic factors result in different class outcomes. It imagines each person as an

---

[18]Mirowski, *Never Let a Serious Crisis Go to Waste*, 119.
[19]Christopher Payne, *Consumer, Credit and Neoliberalism: Governing the Modern Economy* (London: Routledge, 2012), cited in Mirowski, *Never Let a Serious Crisis Go to Waste*, 122.
[20]Galit Ailon, "The Discursive Management of Financial Risk Scandals," *Qualitative Sociology* 35 (2012): 265. Cited in Mirowski, *Never Let a Serious Crisis Go to Waste*, 120–1.

individual entrepreneur seeking to advance their own project, independent of others save through market relationships. At best, neoliberalism can imagine the nuclear family as a small collective economic agent.[21]

We can see this ignorance of class in a common use of the word "culture" to designate a set of habits and dispositions passed on in families and communities that facilitate or hinder competitive market action. Communities pass on habits, but participation in market practices is what determines outcomes. Thus, talk of a "culture of poverty" or discussions of the cultural deficits of poor, marginalized and minoritized communities. All of this presumes that each generation begins with a clean slate in its market position. If they have the proper skills and motivations, they have an equal chance at success in the marketplace. Thus, historic injustices are liquidated into a frame that sees only contemporary opportunities that anyone can choose to pursue or ignore and do so well or poorly. But even by the narrowest economic measures, minoritized communities have a profound, intergenerational legacy of fewer assets.[22] And indeed, when one looks at the student debt crisis, it becomes clear that the massive debt burden is primarily a problem for middle- and lower-income students, while elites continue to have the same disproportionately high educational outcomes with no substantial increase in student debt.[23]

The only collective that neoliberalism can value is the business firm or corporation. In Hayek's words, "The argument for liberty is not an argument against organization, which is one of the most powerful means that human reason can employ."[24] Such organizations are scaled-up versions of market actors. They act upon their own particular knowledge and collectively pursue their aims. They are tried in the same imagined sphere of free, noncoercive competition as individual market agents.

As we have seen, the neoliberal view of the world disparages political action, which it sees as intellectually blind and coercive. Thus, neoliberal policies have sought to systematically dismantle collective programs and to replace them with market-based alternatives. The post-depression era saw a host of state programs that provided a collective safety net that fundamentally changed life for generations. This was also the era of massive public works: flood-control projects, interstate highway systems, rural electrification authorities and space flight. We should also note generations of successful policies that reduced pollution, protected consumers and preserved the environment. All of these provided a horizon of experience in which collective action for the common good could fundamentally improve people's lives.

Neoliberal policies have focused on replacing such collective programs with individualized, market-based alternatives. Thus, the consistent proposal to "privatize" social security and attempts to discredit and dismantle environmental and labor regulations.

As a result of these policies, the market has replaced public action as the default form of human agency. If previous generations marveled at public works projects, our age is marked by enormous private ventures: smartphones, internet stores with second-day delivery and private space companies. Curiously, each of these work in the spaces that

---

[21]Discussed extensively in Cooper, *Family Values*.
[22]Ta-Nahisi Coates, "The Case for Reparations," *Atlantic Monthly*, May 21, 2014.
[23]Harris, *Kids These Days*, 44–5.
[24]Hayek, *The Constitution of Liberty*, 37.

were established by twentieth-century government-provided public goods: the internet, the interstate highway system, the space program.

Neoliberalism even diverts our moral imagination away from collective action into individualized market forms. The rise of ethical and fair-trade consumerism is an appealing phenomenon that deserves closer attention in the context of neoliberalism. It allows us to render our consumption more moral by purchasing from sources and supply chains that are certified to be free of economic exploitation and environmental destruction. But in the process, it translates moral goods into market goods available at a price. Slave labor, deforestation, economic exploitation: these are problems that could be addressed by governmental and intergovernmental policies. But the fair trade regime portrays them as business as usual, which can be avoided by those choosing to pay a price premium.

The impact of this vision goes far beyond specific policies. It is evident in the horizon of assumptions that mark a diverse range of contemporary social realities. Each of these emerge from their own particular histories, but note how they all converge in a vision of the person as individual and private, with neither obligation to help nor hope for help from broader society. Tens of millions of Americans passionately espouse personal firearms as a means of protection, often explicitly dismissing the ability of official police forces to provide protection. Likewise, tens of millions of Americans are suspicious of the safety of vaccines.[25] But the "anti-vaxxer" movement is based upon more than a rejection of mainstream medical science; it also ignores the value of and obligation to contribute to herd immunity: the multiplied immunity effect that emerges when a majority of a population is immunized against a disease. The rise of the homeschooling movement likewise displays a profound suspicion of collective social institutions. In church communities, some homeschooling families are equally suspicious of parish religious education. On a less profound, but equally formative level, we could consider the rise of personal media spaces. It is now normal for people to go through the city tuned to their own personal choice of music or podcast, not united even by a broadcast station playlist. All of these narrow the range of concern and agency from the public and social to private familial and individual level.

Everyday Sadism and Polarization

A number of authors argue that neoliberalism fosters a rise in political resentment and cruelty. While some view this as simply another form of the ancient Roman "bread and circuses" distraction, Mirowski argues something deeper is at work here. For him, the "everyday sadism" that dominates so much reality television is a "theater of cruelty" that legitimates the dictates of the market. We celebrate the winners and witness the debasement of the losers. Our enthusiasm for both secures our allegiance to a system that sorts us in every dimension of life.[26]

Martijn Konings offers a deeper account of the emotional politics of neoliberalism.

He argues that the anxieties produced by the effects of neoliberal policies paradoxically reinforce the hegemony of neoliberal ideas. In a neoliberal society, people deal with ever-present economic anxiety by embracing the proffered vision that everyone gets what they deserve and deserves what they get. This describes every success no matter how fragile

---

[25]Pew Research Center, "83% Say Measles Vaccine Is Safe for Healthy Children," February 2015. Available online: https://www.people-press.org/2015/02/09/83-percent-say-measles-vaccine-is-safe-for-healthy-children/.

[26]Mirowski, *Never Let a Serious Crisis Go to Waste*, 135.

as a result of the individual exercise of virtue. This provides comfort that the abyss that threatens is not really random or capricious, but is a fair recompense for the individual choice.

When even relatively affluent families are highly leveraged—a paycheck or two from bankruptcy—and successful businesses are always vulnerable to unforeseen disruption, we channel our resulting anxiety into cataloguing the failures of the losers. By blaming them for their suffering, we distract ourselves from random threats everyone faces in a society with a greatly thinned safety net where individuals are expected to manage risk on their own.

This method of coping with anxiety can exacerbate ethnic, racial and class tensions. Lower class groups, minoritized groups, and migrants become attractive targets for scapegoating. By blaming these groups' suffering on their defects, majority populations receive psychic assurance that their stability is the result of their virtues. This also drives a curious rejection of safety net policies among those who profit from them. We come to view social safety net programs as moral hazards that tempt us to laziness. *We shouldn't need them.* Indeed, austerity offers the promise of purification and strengthening of the self.[27]

To summarize, neoliberalism profoundly reshapes the way we think of ourselves as persons—our default anthropology—through the many ways its framework and policies have restructured everyday life. By systematically replacing collective political structures with individual, competitive market structures, it has created a world where in order to flourish, we need to become entrepreneurs in all dimensions of our lives, relating to others through market like structures of self-promotion and competition. It has created a world where collective forms of agency are systemically replaced with individually focused ones. This world of omnipresent risk and competition has lessened our ability to respond with compassion to the suffering of others.

RESPONDING FROM THE CATHOLIC TRADITION

The challenge posed by neoliberalism to a Catholic theological anthropology is both intellectual and formative. We are formed below the level of explicit belief by the policies, structures and default forms of agency in society. Thus, countering it is more than a matter of belief. Theological critique, however, plays an important role. It helps us diagnose what is wrong with the implicit anthropology of the world in which we live. Only once we understand the contrast between the world we inhabit and Christian ideals can we begin to imagine alternative policies, structures and forms of agency.

Major elements of Catholic anthropology stand in contrast to the neoliberal vision. Here we will focus on two: its notion of the communal nature of the human person and its understanding of the modes of human relationship.

Catholicism understands the human person to be made in the image of the triune God, and thus intrinsically relational. In the words of the *Compendium of the Social Doctrine of the Church*, humans cannot flourish or find fulfillment in our ourselves, "apart from the fact" that we exist " 'with' others and 'for' others."[28] Our relationships with others

---

[27]Martijn Konings, "Imagined Double Movements: Progressive Thought and the Specter of Neoliberal Populism," *Globalizations* 9, no. 4 (August 2012): 609–22.

[28]Pontifical Council for Justice and Peace, *Compendium of the Social Doctrine of the Church*, #165. Available online: http://www.vatican.va/roman_curia/pontifical_councils/justpeace/documents/rc_pc_justpeace_doc_20060526_compendio-dott-soc_en.html. For an extended discussion of the common good and the social nature of the human person in Catholic social teaching, see Todd Whitmore, "Catholic Social Teaching: Starting

bring fulfillment, not simply as additions to our individual experience, but by drawing us into a higher set of relationships with its own goal: the common good. In the words of *Gaudium et spes*, individuals, families and groups "are aware that they cannot achieve a truly human life by their own unaided efforts. They see the need for a wider community, within which each one makes his or her specific contribution every day toward an ever-broader realization of the common good." Awareness of this need drives the establishment of various forms of government or "political community" that exist "for the sake of the common good."[29] The common good demands shared, public forms of agency: politics in the deepest sense of the word. This shared flourishing cannot be achieved through private, competitive forms of acting.[30]

A second contrast between Catholic anthropology concerns the form of relationship between persons. Catholicism argues that while competition has a role to play, the most fundamental form of relationship is not exchange for profit, but gratuitous gift. Again, our creation in the image of the triune God means that we can only find ourselves "through a sincere gift" of ourselves to others.[31]

Pope John Paul II made the moral virtue of solidarity the center of his papal social teaching. Solidarity arises from the anthropological fact of our interconnectedness as human persons. We are born dependent, we grow to adulthood through the care and teaching of countless others, and we find flourishing by participating fully in social relationships. From this fact of interdependence, John Paul II derived a moral imperative and a virtue. Solidarity is "firm and persevering determination to commit oneself to the common good; that is to say to the good of all and of each individual, because we are all really responsible for all."[32] Shawn Copeland offers a powerful account of solidarity's roots in the cross of Christ: "The praxis of solidarity is made possible by the loving self-donation of the crucified Christ, whose cross is its origin, standard and judge. ... Only those who follow the example of the Crucified and struggle on the side of the exploited, despised and poor 'will discover him at their side'."[33] Thus, the neoliberal focus on market relations as the fundamental form of social relationship is far too narrow. Solidarity is a deep and profound commitment to live in the freedom of Jesus of Nazareth, who gave himself fully to humankind, to the point of death ... literally without counting the cost.

These aspects of the Church's teaching on theological anthropology help us diagnose what is wrong with neoliberalism's cramped and limited understanding of the person. But judging its errors is not enough. The Church itself is deeply influenced by the neoliberal cultural context. Believers formed in neoliberal culture are ill-prepared to appreciate the ways in which community and tradition are collective undertakings. Community and tradition are reworked into objects of choice: characteristics a church provides, rather

---

with the Common Good," in *Living the Catholic Social Tradition: Cases and Commentary*, ed. Kathleen Mass Weigert and Alexia K. Kelley (Lanham: Rowman & Littlefield, 2005).

[29]Vatican Council II, *Gaudium et spes* [Pastoral Constitution on the Church in the Modern World], #74, in *Vatican II: The Conciliar and Post-Conciliar Documents*, ed. Austin Flannery, OP (Northrup, NY: Costello, 1992), 981.

[30]Vincent Miller, "The Common Good and the Market," *America Magazine* 220, no. 7 (April 1, 2019): 32–7.

[31]Vatican Council II, *Gaudium et spes*, #24.

[32]John Paul II, *Sollicitudo rei socialis*, #38, December 30, 1987. Available online: http://www.vatican.va/content/john-paul-ii/en/encyclicals/documents/hf_jp-ii_enc_30121987_sollicitudo-rei-socialis.html.

[33]M. Shawn Copeland, *Enfleshing Freedom: Body, Race and Being* (Minneapolis: Fortress Press, 2010), 99. Citing Miroslav Wolf, *Exclusion and Embrace: A Theological Exploration of Identity, Otherness, and Reconciliation* (Nashville: Abingdon, 1996), 24.

than realities in which one participates. This feeds increasing polarization as believers sort into their chosen congregations and theologies, bringing habits learned in the market sorting of social media to the life of the church in a way that makes the imperative of the unity of the Church difficult for many believers to understand

Aspects of the Christian tradition that focus on the collective nature of salvation can work against these neoliberal tendencies, if they are explicitly deployed as counter-formation. The greatest contrast is *Lumen Gentium*'s understanding of the Church as a "sacrament," both a "sign and instrument" of the unity of humankind in God.[34] This constructs membership in the Church not as an object of choice by sovereign individuals but as an entry into a communion with demanding expectations of relationships with others. The communal anthropology implicit in the mission of the Church can provide a place to stand from which to work against the anthropological tide of neoliberalism.

Catholic anthropology illuminates the ways in which we are being formed contrary to our true nature and destiny. We need to become aware of the fact that within neoliberalism's abstract policy debates there are profound choices being made that affect both the kind of persons we will be and our ability to participate in the mission of the Church. After the work of critique comes the even more challenging constructive task: reimaging the social order so that it serves the fullness to which we are called as human persons.

SUGGESTED FURTHER READING

Brown, Wendy, *Undoing the Demos: Neoliberalism's Stealth Revolution* (Cambridge, MA: Zone Books, 2015).

Cooper, Melinda, *Family Values: Between Neoliberalism and the New Social Conservatism* (New York: Zone Books, 2017).

Eggemeier, Matthew T., and Peter Joseph Fritz, *Send Lazarus: Catholicism and the Crises of Neoliberalism* (New York: Fordham University Press, 2020).

Foucault, Michel, *Birth of Biopolitics: Lectures at the College de France 1978–1979* (New York: Picador, 2008).

Mirowski, Philip, *Never Let a Serious Crisis Go to Waste: How Neoliberalism Survived the Financial Meltdown* (London: Verso, 2013).

Peck, Jamie, *Constructions of Neoliberal Reason* (Oxford: Oxford University Press, 2012).

---

[34]Vatican Council II, *Lumen Gentium*, #1, in *Vatican II: The Conciliar and Post-Conciliar Documents*, ed. Austin Flannery, OP (Northrup, NY: Costello, 1992), 350.

CHAPTER THIRTY-TWO

Cosmic Christianity

OLIVER DAVIES

There can be no greater challenge for theology today than that posed by the combination of "cosmology" and "anthropology." It is not only a matter of the breadth of the topic but also its vital importance for Christianity. The very heart of the Christian claim is that Jesus lives a human life, which has universal and cosmological meaning. It is not just that he lays claim to us as persons who encounter other persons in the formation of Church, but also, that the space-time framework in which such encounters happen has itself been transformed by the power of his living. Contemporary cosmology and anthropology both have new things to say about the space-time framework, in potentially revolutionary ways. And indeed, it was radical change in precisely these areas that originally reshaped Western history around the phenomenon of "modernity," with its mechanistic science and reductive materialism on the one hand and reactive Romanticism on the other.

But the methodological challenge of the task should not be underestimated. Scientific investigation yields things that are known and enjoys an unparalleled third person, empirical authority. Theology on the other hand is concerned with a human and divine-centered fullness, coherence and meaning, which inevitably entails some degree of first-person narrative. Theology is likewise concerned with integration and the unity of the human person, while the empirical basis of scientific knowledge means that it is inevitably piecemeal and fragmented. And yet, in a technologically advanced and socially unstable age, it seems important that our genuine humanity, with its quirkiness, creativity, hope and despair, should as far as possible be represented in, or reconciled with, our scientific understandings.

This may seem to be an impossible task. But in fact, the focus here lies on understanding how we can be in the world as both mind and body, as followers of Jesus. It points to how we can belong to this world. Therefore, the primary resource for theology appears where different scientific disciplines *overlap* in their description of how we are in the world as human beings. Such an overlap suggests that something is coming into view about us today that has a claim to being *true*. Theology needs to work with that emergent truth, seeking to outline the human in terms of the life of Christ and of our potential ultimacy.

The sciences we are concerned with here are evolutionary anthropology, social neuroscience and the physics of symmetry. We need to set the scene with quantum field theory, however, which, by common consent, is the most fundamental form of science we know. But the quantum world, as it appears to us at the micro-level, is bewilderingly "weird." Particles move in and out of existence; they come into "entangled" states so that information passes between them *instantaneously*: faster than the speed of light. This suggests that at its most fundamental level, the cosmos is "one" or "whole."[1] It seems too that time drops away at this level, leaving only the interconnectedness of a kind of "space-time mesh."[2] Although the principles of quantum mechanics were well established by 1927, the integration of this knowledge was scarcely begun. The leading physicists reported what they saw but disagreed as to what it *meant*.[3] The passionate intensity of their debates, however, suggests that they felt that human self-understanding was also in some degree at stake in these key experiments. After all, it appeared that the human observer herself, or perhaps her intentionality, was itself an intrinsic part of the process of the actualization of the world. Physicists speak of the quantum level of reality as "free" and as subtending our own open freedom of will more generally, in opposition to the mechanical and closed "efficient causation" of the Newtonian inheritance.[4] It is striking that the human mind, through its most advanced mathematical calculations, can appear to capture the "free" depths of quantum reality. This may point in fact to a greater symmetry between the mind of consciousness and quantum states of interconnectedness. In its study of human decision making (i.e., where we are most *free*), mathematical psychology has also found evidence for significant structural parallels between complex reasoning and moral reasoning, and the behavior of subatomic particles, with their capacity to exist in contradictory physical states.[5] The unique capacity of the human mind to grasp wholes, and indeed ideas, as well as to entertain quite contrary concepts and scenarios at the same time, points to the possibly quantum nature of our consciousness as the site of our free decision making. Here too we need to consider the extent to which our capacity to build "quantum computers" can be read as an ability to "hack into the way the universe computes," in Seth Lloyd's phrase.[6] By implication, this seems to suggest that the other modes or reasoning we do, such as our practical, moral or social reasoning, may also have the potential to ground us in some sense in the depths of this universe. It is not that we have different minds; we have one mind that is realized in different modalities.

EVOLUTIONARY ANTHROPOLOGY

The participatory structure of our being in the world laid bare in quantum theory also finds strong resonance with our self-understanding in a very different sphere. Today the competitive "modern synthesis" of neo-Darwinism in evolutionary theory has been replaced by the more inclusive "extended evolutionary synthesis." The former stressed the role of natural selection acting directly upon our genes, while the latter understands the signature of life to be the movements of living organisms, causing conditions of "at homeness" or adaptation through "fitness" within their environment (with a later

---

[1]A host of books are available which introduce the field of quantum science. Of particular value is Shimon Malin, *Nature Loves to Hide* (Oxford: Oxford University Press, 2001).
[2]Carlo Rovelli, *Seven Brief Lessons on Physics* (London: Alan Lane, 2015).
[3]See Malin, *Nature*, 1–86, for an excellent survey of the differing views.
[4]Henry P. Stapp, *Quantum Theory and Free Will* (New York: Springer International, 2017).
[5]See, for instance, E. M. Pothos and J. R. Busemeyer, "Can Quantum Probability Provide a New Direction for Cognitive Modeling?," *Behavioral and Brain Sciences* 36, no. 3 (2013): 255–74.
[6]https://www.closertotruth.com/series/does-information-create-the-cosmos (accessed April 27, 2018). See also Seth Lloyd, *Programming The Universe: A Quantum Computer Scientist Takes on the Cosmos* (New York: Random House, 2007).

"drag-effect" upon genes). "Niche construction theory," which is now in the ascendency, suggests that the principle of all life is the adaptive "at homeness" of the creature within its environment, through movement.[7]

Evolutionary anthropology underscores for us the fact that, as intensely social and altruistic creatures, we have been at home in the world through our bonding with other human beings. The face of the human other has been our immersive environment. But if we were able to relate richly to the "person" behind the face, then we could also— very distinctively—see "tools" hidden in the shapes of stones. Both of these point to an unparalleled creativity of the human imagination.[8] But we were creative in another way too. Our sociality and our technological skills meant that we were immersively open to the world around us, even coming over time to enter into our environment through symbolic representations. At the same time, the hospitality of the face-to-face of our sociality and the instrumentality of the tool in the hand of our technology actually constituted two different kinds of *cognitive orientation*. Over a period of some two million years, the contrary orientation of these two tendencies was held in creative tension in what has been called the "ratcheting effect," whereby each orientation in turn sustained and fostered the other.[9]

It is very likely it was this productive tension that played a key role finally in the emergence of advanced language. Here the creativity of face and hand combine in the generation of what is in itself an intrinsically creative system. Dating the arrival of advanced language has been a long-term problem, since many nonhuman species communicate very well in their respective environments. What is distinctive about advanced human language, however, is that it involves the internalization of thousands of material signs (of sound or shape) that have only an arbitrary relation to what they signify. Andy Clark has compared this to the internalization within the human body and brain of thousands of "micro-chips" that "push the mind from the biological flux" and "ground the neural wet-ware."[10] It is this internalization of elements from the environment that generates our high levels of self-possession and self-awareness. And here we return to the theme of freedom. The creativity of our advanced language lies in the fact that we experience a sense of freedom in how we *choose* our words: in speaking, we become responsible for what we say, with implications too, for the responsibility we feel in what we to do. It is our creativity, then, that makes us distinctive, shaping the construction of our human niche. Following our dreams or instincts, we have populated the globe (though in ways that have often compromised our natural environment). We dream of space travel. All this points to the power of our imagination and to our inventive technologies. And so in us, the evolutionary principle of being "at home" in our environment becomes the possibility of being "at home" in the whole world or universe. But there is a problem, for our linguistic consciousness is also the "observer" and perceives itself as being somehow "outside" our own embodiment. If we are "outside" our embodiment as a self-possessing "mind," how

---

[7]See Markus Mühling, *Resonances: Neurobiology, Evolution and Theology* (Göttingen: Vandenhoek and Ruprecht, 2014), for a good introduction to "niche construction theory," in the light of theology.
[8]Agustin Fuentes, *The Creative Spark: How Imagination Made Humans Exceptional* (New York: Penguin Random House, 2017).
[9]Claudio Tennie et al., "Ratcheting Up the Ratchet: On the Evolution of Cumulative Culture," *Philosophical Transactions of the Royal Society B: Biological Sciences* 364, no. 1528 (2009): 2405–15.
[10]Andy Clark, *Supersizing the Mind. Embodiment, Action and Cognitive Extension* (New York: Oxford University Press, 2011), 53–60.

can we ever be properly "at home" in our own bodies? If we want authentically to *belong* in the world, then somehow the mind must also learn to be fully "at home" in the body.[11]

Language and Evolution

It is our advanced modern language, then, that becomes key to our understanding of the human. But understanding language is by no means easy. We experience ourselves as subjects who sit at the center of our advanced linguistic consciousness and so see language everywhere. However, it is only very late in the archaeological record that we find hard evidence for the presence of the kind of modern language we have today, with its multiple and complex range of functions. Language acquisition is the extension of gestures together with late, sophisticated, tool manufacture and use (words are "social tools"[12]). The actual precipitation of advanced language is associated with such neolithic factors as the emergence of extended population size and social hierarchalization, as well as key cognitive elements such as the capacity to represent the face of the human other.[13] Advanced language is also associated with the development of mathematics, and with religion. All of these things came together when agriculture was introduced, spreading from the Caucasus to both East and West, from around fifteen thousand years ago. It is in this context too that we see the first occurrences of "massacres" and the indiscriminate killing of populations (as Vittorio Gallese has observed, such killings require advanced language in order to name other human beings as "non-human"[14]).[15] We also find for the first time higher levels of male violence, with the formation of patrilineal kin groups and intergroup competition among these populations.[16]

As long as we make a proper distinction between early or biological languages and our own modern advanced language with its thousands of random signs, we can see that language—as we understand it—is relatively very late. Linguistic consciousness appears to be an integrative system that is particularly adapted to quick decision making. This is an essential property for a mobile creature whose capacious brain lets in a good deal of the world's complexity. Words are incisive, like tools, and they carry our intentionalities into the world, again like tools. On the one hand, we can "groom" others with language and so enhance our sociality. But we can also depersonalize others, turning them into a means to an end, or into statistics.

Most crucially however, our advanced linguistic consciousness conceals from us the simple truth that we are "in the world" for the greater part through the pre-thematic, pre-linguistic or "unconscious" information we receive about the world, and particularly from the intensely high-speed and interactive exchanges we have through bodily engagement

---

[11]Oliver Davies, "Niche Construction, Social Cognition, and Language: Hypothesizing the Human as the Production of Place," *Culture and Brain* 4, no. 2 (2016): 87–112.

[12]D. Stout and T. Chaminade, "Stone Tools, Language and the Brain in Human Evolution," *Philosophical Transactions of the Royal Society B: Biological Sciences*, 367, no. 1585 (2012): 75–87. See also Peter Hiscock, "Learning in Lithic Landscapes: A Reconsideration of the Hominid 'Toolmaking' Niche," *Biological Theory* 9, no. 1 (2014): 27–41.

[13]Ian Kuijt, "The Regeneration of Life," *Current Anthropology* 49, no. 2 (2008): 171–97.

[14]"All Too Human," *New Scientist* 221, no. 2952 (January 18, 2014): 3.

[15]On the late origins of systemic violence (and refutation of Steven Pinker), see Fuentes, *The Creative Spark*, 129–61.

[16]Tian Chen Zeng et al., "Cultural Hitchhiking and Competition between Patrilineal Kin Groups Explain the Post-Neolithic Y-Chromosome Bottleneck," *Nature Communications* 9, no. 1 (2018): 2077.

with one another. We have tended to assume that this "hidden" part of ourselves is filled with drives and instincts and altogether lacks the properties of reason that we associate with advanced linguistic consciousness. In the light of this inheritance, new scientific understandings of the nature of our sociality, and of its relation to consciousness, can have an almost revolutionary force.

SOCIAL NEUROSCIENCE

As human beings, we are creatures who have long since evolved both to discern each other in depth and to bond in depth. Indeed, our lineage was so bereft of natural advantages on the African savannah (lacking large teeth, claws and physical strength) that our only possibility of survival was to form highly integrated groups in which we could maximize our problem-solving skills and the associated technologies. For some two million years we lived in relatively small, nomadic groups, with intensely reciprocal modes of unconditional social bonding, supporting empathetic engagement and collaboration. We stood or fell together.

It is only relatively recently, however, that we have begun to develop scientific understandings of this social system within us. In the first place, it seems to exhibit an unexpected ontology. The human "social cognition system" (or "in-between," as we can call it) appears to be grounded in a set of pre-thematic responses that, since they are "self-organizing," can be described as "world" as much as they are an "interaction" or "encounter" between two persons. This has been well summarized in the following terms:

> When we interact with another person, our brains and bodies are no longer isolated, but immersed in an environment with the other person, in which we become a coupled unit through a continuous moment-to-moment mutual adaptation of our own actions and the actions of the other.[17]

These multiple reflex interactions occur at speeds well below the threshold of conscious perception but communicate to consciousness as a sense of "rapport."[18] They sit within the early motor system, involving sets of mutual responses ranging from eye movement, facial expression, posture and gesture to the synchrony of brain waves, breathing and pulse: a subtle and pervasive "alignment of behaviour" that includes "synergies, co-ordination and phase attraction."[19] The character of this "complex, multi-layered, self-organizing" as "world" is captured by the "enactivist" school of social neuroscience:

> When I see the other's action or gesture, I see (I *immediately perceive*) the meaning in the action or gesture; and when I am in a process of interacting with the other, my own actions and reactions help to constitute that meaning. I not only see, but I resonate with (or against), and react to the joy or the anger, or the intention that is in the face or in the posture or in the gesture or action of the other.[20]

---

[17]I. Konvalinka and A. Roepstorff, "The Two-Brain Approach: How Can Mutually Interacting Brains Teach Us Something about Social Interaction?," *Frontiers in Human Neuroscience* 6, no. 215 (2012): 2.

[18]Linda Tickle-Degnen and Robert Rosenthal, 'The Nature of Rapport and Its Nonverbal Correlates', *Psychological Inquiry* 1, no. 4 (1990): 285–93.

[19]Enrique di Paolo and Hanna de Jaegher, "The Interactive Brain Hypothesis', *Frontiers in Human Neuroscience* 6, no. 163 (2012), 1–16; Leonhard Schilbach et al., "Toward a Second-Person Neuroscience," *Behavioral and Brain Sciences* 36, no. 4 (2013): 393–414.

[20]Shaun Gallagher, "Understanding Others: Embodied Social Cognition," in *Handbook of Cognitive Science: an Embodied Approach*, ed. Paco Calvo and Toni Gomila (San Diego: Elsevier, 2008), 449. Emphasis original.

If the individual human brain can be described as "the most complex system so far encountered anywhere in the universe,"[21] then two human brains extensively interacting point to the social cognition system as arguably the most dense and powerfully interactive system of information exchange that is conceivable. Its interactive structure has been defined as our "participatory sense-making" of the human other, which, as such, appears to suggest that this "participatory sense-making" is the form of our most fundamental participation in the world.[22] Our "in-between" offers potentially revolutionary new self-understandings in terms of how, as human beings, we can be more fully *in* our own body and so also more fully at home in the world.

But such a fullness is not easily within our grasp. In the in-between, the evaluative protocols of one are densely exposed to the evaluative protocols of the other, in a way that can be described as our *human option for the other*. Here we risk or invest our own embodiment as the primary instrument of a far-reaching, open and interactive connectivity. But this is in fact an *unconditional* option for the other (as we see in the young child), since the preconscious in-between naturally responds to the triggers of the human face and body. On the other hand, our self-possessing consciousness is deeply shaped by experience, memory and culture, and by an identity that may wish to prejudge and to exclude categories of the human, or individuals, from our body's inclusivity. This means to say that the body *evaluates* or "makes sense of" the other in pre-thematic and unconditionally inclusive ways and in terms of how "we get on," while, as conscious mind, we are more inclined to selfishness and prejudice and to prejudging the other.[23]

Our body then is fine-tuned to unconditional hospitality since it is our strong human sociality that has secured our survival, while our consciousness, which has also been shaped by sophisticated tool manufacture and use, is fine-tuned to mechanisms of ordering, decision making and control. At the center of the "participative sense-making" of the social cognition system, however, there is a highly sophisticated, high-speed system of *evaluation*, of the human other and of our relating. It is this powerful and defining capacity that reappears in what we might call our "social reasoning." We can reason theoretically, as "observer," and we can reason practically, as "agent." But where we reason theoretically as "observer," we exercise a freedom *from*, while in practical reason the "agent" exercises a freedom *to*. Social reasoning is neither of these since it does not involve mechanisms of control that reduce the reality of a complex world. Social reasoning rather is characterized by the openness of the pre-thematic social cognition system with its unconditional "participatory sense-making." Where we openly accept the other, in all their complexity, our freedom is fulfilled as a freedom *in*. Through the relationship with the other, we gain a new level of our belonging in the world.

Social reasoning is not easy, however, since it involves the open acceptance of complexity (the personal complexity of the other) in a complex world. We depend upon cultural practices in order to learn how to exercise such freedom *in*. Among these, ritual is the most prominent. Religious ritual originates in the neolithic period where the sudden growth in population size called for the need to extend and magnify the bonding power of our social cognition. The freedom of choice that emerged with advanced language

[21]Adam Zeman, *A Portrait of the Brain* (New Haven, CT: Yale University Press, 2009), 1. The science of social cognition has arisen from within the field of "autism studies."
[22]Di Paolo and de Jaegher, "The Interactive Brain Hypothesis," 2.
[23]Chris D. Frith and Uta Frith, "Implicit and Explicit Processes in Social Cognition," *Neuron* 60, no. 3 (2008): 503–10.

(since words uttered, or what de Saussure called *parole*, are chosen from the system of language, or *langue*[24]) allows us to set aside the tool-based, cognitive control of language through deliberately highlighting the materiality of the sign. The ritual use of language, with its repetitions, serves to separate advanced language with its apparatus of control, from its utilitarian foundations. When we freely assent to the rhythms and sounds of chant, recitation, song, rhyme or cantillation, or to the flow of written forms of words as calligraphy, then we are in a sense "offering" advanced language on the altar of community rather than control. These all entail a degree of *nonemphatic* repetition and are ways of using or adapting language in an original celebratory way. With the help also of the universalist ethics of mutual recognition and love that we find in religions, ritual lays a strong cultural foundation for the practice of social reasoning with its freedom *in*.

THE PHYSICS OF SYMMETRY

This brings us to the science of physics and the theme of "symmetry." Symmetry denotes repeating patterns in which the same figures and proportions occur (such as the wings of a butterfly, or the two, almost identical halves of a human face). Physicists distinguish between two forms of stability or continuity: "translational symmetry" (the laws of physics are the same everywhere and do not change with time) and "rotational symmetry," (for instance, the kettle does not cease to be a kettle, when it is turned around). The strangest and most direct kind of translational symmetry is found in the speed of light, which is a constant. It always remains the same for us regardless of the speed at which we may ourselves be traveling when we measure it. This insight is a key element in Albert Einstein's 1905 paper on "special relativity." We can see the effects of this translational symmetry (or "translational invariance" as it also called) in the case of a car engine, following Andrew Steane, who states, "The workings of the engine do not change—they are invariant—when the location of the car is changed or 'translated' from one place to another."[25]

The image of a car engine working in more than one place may seem entirely normal to us. Of course, the engine will not work when the ambient temperature drops below a certain degree or above another. But within these limits, the car does work and so we can say that its status as a harmonious system, which accords with the laws of physics, is preserved. In other words, the car is free to be a car. Individual car engines are harmonic systems that accord with physical laws and their mathematical expressions, and for as long as this system can be preserved, they will work. But as Steane stresses, such a system can only be produced since we live in a universe *which allows such systems, or symmetries, to occur*.

It is often said that cause and effect, or efficient causation, is the dominant logic of the universe: how one thing affects another. But in addition to efficient causation, we need also to take account of the second, much more interesting, phenomenon, which is symmetry:

> The symmetry principle already makes its contribution before we ever write or discover the formulas and equations, because it places conditions on what sorts of equations

[24]Ferdinand de Saussure, *Course in general linguistics*, 3rd ed. (trans. R. Harris; Chicago: Open Court, 1986), 9–10, 15.
[25]Andrew Steane, *Science and Humanity: A Humane Philosophy of Science and Religion* (Oxford: Oxford University Press, 2018), 24.

could make sense. And science is all about making sense, or finding the sense that can be made. Symmetry principles in fact play an important role, because they amount to meta-laws which express higher-level principles that basic laws of motion must respect if they are to make certain types of sense.[26]

Steane quotes the Nobel laureate Philip Anderson to the effect that "it is only slightly overstating the case to say that physics is the study of symmetry,"[27] and he continues,

> The symmetry principle is first a guide, and then, in a certain hard-to-express but beautiful sense, it "inhabits" the equations of physics. The concrete phenomena that are in the world are a sort of physical embodiment of the symmetry principles. By moulding our mathematical notation, such insights shape the very way we "see" the world.[28]

Steane concludes that symmetry "is rather a fundamental law of the universe: the primary law even which conditions all else, making 'world' itself possible, and all the things that are within it. And we see that symmetry as simplicity and beauty."

Human Identity and "Translational Invariance"

Since we are materially embodied forms in a material universe, the rules of translational invariance will apply to us too, though now in distinctively "human" ways. However many times the millions of cells that make up my body are renewed, I nevertheless appear to remain the same person. But since we live in a constantly changing world, we must ourselves undergo change, if we are to remain the same person. Living entails growing. I am not like the car designer who updates their vehicles. Rather, I have to update myself. And I can only do this when I realize that I am in a new situation, confronted by choices about how I will treat others and so also, by implication, who I shall be. Whether I can act with integrity will depend to a large degree on whether I can be constant within change. In each new demanding situation in life, I need to learn how to be "me" in ways that preserve relationships, integrity and constancy within growth.

The neuroscience of free will and decision making suggests that harmony (which presupposes symmetry) is a key factor in how we change, grow or "become." Robert Kane, a leading scholar in this field, describes the "hot" conditions of conflicting possibilities of identity that exist when we are confronted with a significant ethical challenge. These represent "movement away from thermal equilibrium—in short a kind of stirring up of chaos in the brain that makes it sensitive to micro-indeterminacies at the neuronal level."[29] The human brain is "a parallel processor ... which can simultaneously process different kinds of information relevant to tasks such as perception or recognition through different neural pathways." This processing capacity is "essential to the exercise of free will."[30]

But there are two complementary systems in play here. The first is "bottom-up" and conflicted, with competing possibilities of response, action and therefore identity, while

---

[26]Ibid., 25.
[27]Ibid., 28.
[28]Ibid.
[29]Robert Kane, "Rethinking Free Will: New Perspectives on an Ancient Problem," in *The Oxford Handbook of Free Will*, 2nd ed. (Oxford: Oxford University Press, 2011), 387.
[30]Ibid., 390.

the second is "top-down," leading to harmonization, integration and the global unity of the self.[31] We make such ethical decisions by inhabiting the different competing images of the self as these combine and recombine in the brain. These inform our ethical decision making as inherent possibilities that can subtly be explored.[32] The key to difficult ethical decision making, in which none of the initial possibilities appear to allow resolution, is time, effort and, finally, the formation of new neural pathways in the brain through the top-down effect. These create the possibility of a refreshed identity and a new future: they constitute "growth."

To be human therefore is to be repeatedly challenged by the need to change in the face of a changing world, but in ways that show that what deeply identifies "me" for others (and for myself), remains a constant. Here translational invariance is in play in the human person: indeed, it is at the core of knowing who we are and our sense of being at home in the world. In such key moments of decision making, most of us will seek the advice of those close to us. This deeply rooted pursuit of the "right thing to do" marks us out as social creatures who are capable of attaining high levels of harmonization in the brain.

Compared with cars, such levels of harmonization within human translational invariance point to a cosmic relation in human beings with the principle of symmetry as defined in contemporary physics. Perhaps symmetry goes beyond the individual human and even shapes the way we form community? Can we say that the role of symmetry is to draw us all toward each other, in community and equality, and to do so in a way that will lay the foundation for a new planetary future? The human person may be the focus for this struggle between order and disorder at the point of our critical decision making, which determines the kind of person I am. But why would the symmetry that informs this possibility of growth in constancy not in fact be part of a much greater "plan"? Perhaps the subtle power of symmetry draws us as individuals toward a common future that transcends the individual or even the community, in its universal scope that we can feel and follow but scarcely understand?

CHRISTIAN THEOLOGY AND THE PROXIMITY OF JESUS

The primary message of the resurrection concerns the living proximity of Jesus. In early Christianity, the Church's experience of his proximity to us within space-time was configured in a certain way, on the grounds of an ancient cosmology, which then fell from grace with the rise of Enlightenment science. For premodern Christians, the ubiquity of Christ was matched by his proximity, and the intelligibility of his proximity was extensively supported by the scriptural cosmology of the day with its emphasis upon the place of heaven. For at least four hundred years, however, we have not been able to *represent* Christ's proximity to us as modern Christians in terms of space-time, despite the intimate connection between Jesus and where we are: in the Church and in the world. Of course, tradition, sacraments and preaching have all supported our sense of the presence of Christ in the modern world. But in fact, these too are all modes of proximity, which sit within space-time.

---

[31]Nancey Murphy and Warren S. Brown, *Did My Neurons Make Me Do It? Philosophical and Neurobiological Perspectives on Moral Responsibility and Free Will* (Oxford: Oxford University Press, 2007).
[32]Robert Kane, "Libertarianism," in *Four Views on Free Will*, ed. John Martin Fischer, Robert Kane, Dirk Pereboom and Manuel Vargas (Oxford: Blackwell, 2007), 5–43; Kane, "Rethinking Free Will," 384–401.

There are four elements in our contemporary science that seem in particular to draw out the active presence of Christ to us as *mystery*, in Henri de Lubac's definition, rather than just something not understood.[33] The first of these is the quantum perspective. The capacity of Jesus to pass through solid walls prior to the ascension recalls the phenomenon of "quantum tunneling" (whereby matter passes through matter at micro-levels). Without quantum tunneling, in the heart of stars and in living cells, our universe could not support life.[34] This is not to reduce the pre-ascension body of Christ to a quantum tunneling effect. It is rather to point to the signature of his living body, which is simultaneously at the extreme "edge" of the universe and at its heart.

The second element lies in the nature of our human language as performance, and the fact that to speak is always potentially a free, historical act. If Jesus spoke in the ways recorded in Scripture, then for us to repeat his words in prayer is in some sense for us to encounter him through "following." Jesus speaks as risen outside or beyond time and can in some sense be present too in our own prayer. For Pope Benedict, prayer is the Spirit's work in us, and it is the voice of Jesus that "goes ahead of us, and our mind must adapt to it."[35]

Neurologists think of the human brain as "the most complex system so far encountered anywhere in the universe."[36] The third area of scientific resonance is bound up with the "social cognition system" in which there is a large-scale interaction between two human brains in an unparalleled density of information. Deep human interactions in which all our faculties are engaged at every level of the human may constitute foci of information exchange that are exceptional in this universe. It is here too that mathematical modelers turn to deep quantum structures for parallels to how the interactive brain works, with its tolerance of simultaneous and multiple "worlds." It is appropriate then that Jesus should have stated that he would be present "where two or three gather in my name."[37] But we need to note also the role played by the Holy Spirit in terms of an *interactive* and *participatory* "sense-making" of the other. It is the Holy Spirit who communicates to us the *meaning* of the body of Jesus and does so in a way that is transformative. Saul requires the laying on of hands in order to be able to *read* the body of Jesus, and it is in his learning to read that risen body that he transitions from Saul to Paul.

But there seems to be a particular resonance between Christian doctrine and the physics of symmetry, with its translational invariance. Christians believe that Jesus enjoys eternal life through his free sacrifice and can be anywhere and everywhere. It was the role of the premodern, traditional heaven to underpin this belief. After a hiatus of several centuries, it is now the concept of cosmic symmetry or harmony that supports this function. Christian belief in the resurrection of Christ can now be taken as the assertion that in him the limits of translational invariance have been overcome in ways that have profound implications for both human and cosmic life.

---

[33]Henri de Lubac, *Corpus Mysticum. The Eucharist and the Church in the Middle Ages*, trans. Gemma Symonds CJ; ed. Laurence Paul Hemming and Susan Frank Parsons (London: SCM Press, 2006), 37–54.
[34]Jim Al-Khalili and Johnjoe Mcfadden, *Life on the Edge: The Coming of Age of Quantum Biology* (London: Penguin Random House, 2014), 10–23, 89–100.
[35]Pope Benedict XVI, *Jesus of Nazareth*, trans. Adrian J. Walker (London: Bloomsbury, 2007), 131. For a radical, contemporary account of prayer as a form of freedom that supports a "postmetaphysical doxology" and resists "certain structures of violence through counterviolent spirituality," see Andrew Prevot, *Thinking Prayer: Theology and Spirituality amid the Crises of Modernity* (Notre Dame, IN: University of Notre Dame Press, 2015), 326.
[36]Zeman, *A Portrait of the Brain*, 1.
[37]Mt. 18:20 (NIV).

This new science then brings the possibility of overcoming the "transcendental" or "metaphysical" basis of modern Christology with a material or physiological one. This does not serve to impose reductive limits upon Christian faith however. Rather it invites us to think of Christ in terms of de Lubac's sense of ancient mystery, as active presence, which transcends conceptualization and yet still fills the horizon of our situatedness and experience. In fact, it points to encounter with the risen Christ in space and time, not on our terms however, but on his.

SUGGESTED FURTHER READING

Al-Khalili, Jim, and Johnjoe Mcfadden, *Life on the Edge: The Coming of Age of Quantum Biology* (London: Penguin Random House, 2014).

Deane-Drummond, Celia, and Agustín Fuentes (eds.), *Theology and Evolutionary Anthropology: Dialogues in Wisdom, Humility and Grace* (New York: Routledge, 2020).

Gaine, Simon Francis, OP, *Did the Saviour See the Father? Christ, Salvation and the Vision of God* (London: Bloomsbury, 2015).

Lewis, Geraint F., and Luke A. Barnes, *A Fortunate Universe: Life in a Finely Tuned Cosmos* (Cambridge: Cambridge University Press, 2016).

Steane, Andrew, *Science and Humanity: A Humane Philosophy of Science and Religion* (Oxford: Oxford University Press, 2018).

van Huyssteen, J. Wentzel, *Alone in the World? Human Uniqueness in Science and Technology* (Grand Rapids, MI: Eerdmans, 2006).

CONTRIBUTORS

Susan Abraham (ThD, Harvard Divinity School) is Professor of Theology and Postcolonial Cultures and Dean at Pacific School of Religion, Berkeley, CA. Her recent publications include *Blessed are Those who Mourn: Depression, Anxiety and Pain on the Path of an Incarnational Spirituality* (2020).

Amey Victoria Adkins-Jones (PhD, Duke University) is Assistant Professor of Theology and African and African Diaspora Studies at Boston College. Her research focuses on Mariology and black feminist and womanist thought. She is completing her first monograph, a theological account of the rise of the global sex trade.

Jennifer Bader (PhD, The Catholic University of America) is Associate Dean for Academic Affairs at Boston College School of Theology and Ministry. Her research focuses on theological anthropology and fundamental moral theology.

Rosemary P. Carbine (PhD University of Chicago Divinity School) is Associate Professor of Religious Studies at Whittier College. Beyond numerous scholarly journal articles and essays, she has coedited three books: *Women, Wisdom, and Witness* (2012), *Theological Perspectives for Life, Liberty, and the Pursuit of Happiness* (2013) and *The Gift of Theology* (2015). She specializes in feminist, womanist and Latina/*mujerista* theologies, theological anthropology, ecological and public theologies, and teaching and learning in theology and religion. She is currently writing a book that offers a constructive feminist public theology in conversation with US faith-based social justice movements.

Francine Cardman (PhD, Yale University) is Associate Professor of the History of Christianity at the Boston College School of Theology and Ministry. She is the translator of Augustine's commentary on the Sermon on the Mount, *The Preaching of Augustine: The Lord's Sermon on the Mount*, ed. with introduction by Jaroslav Pelikan (1973) and numerous articles on early Christian theology and history, most recently "Risen to Judgment: What Augustine Saw," in *The End of the World in Medieval Thought and Spirituality* (2019).

Carolyn Chau (PhD, Regis College at the University of Toronto) is Associate Professor of Theology at King's University College, Western University. She is the author of *Solidarity With the World: Charles Taylor and Hans Urs von Balthasar on Faith, Modernity, and Catholic Mission* (2016) and forthcoming book chapters on various aspects of von Balthasar's work, including his understanding of kenosis and his relationship with fellow Catholic theologian Joseph Ratzinger (in the forthcoming *Oxford Handbook of Hans Urs von Balthasar*). Her research focuses on dynamic Catholic witness and mission in contemporary secular cultures, and ethics.

Edmund Kee-Fook Chia (PhD, University of Nijmegen) is Senior Lecturer of Theology at the Australian Catholic University. He wrote his dissertation on Edward Schillebeeckx, who was personally present at his doctoral defense. He is the author of *World Christianity Encounters World Religions* (2018) and the forthcoming *Asian Christianity and Theology*, and the editor of *Confucianism and Christianity: Interreligious Dialogue on the Theology* *of Mission* (2021). He is also Honorary Fellow at the University of Divinity (Melbourne) and Visiting Researcher at Radboud University Nijmegen (Netherlands).

Shawn Colberg (PhD, University of Notre Dame) is Associate Professor of Theology at Saint John's University and the College of Saint Benedict. He is the author of *The Wayfarer's End Bonaventure and Aquinas on Divine Rewards in Scripture and Sacred Doctrine* (2020). Colberg's recent research focuses on medieval theologies of grace for their systematic and ecumenical influence on modern treatments of Christian salvation.

Lorraine Cuddeback-Gedeon (PhD, University of Notre Dame) is Director of Mission and Ministry at Mercy High School in Baltimore, MA. She has authored articles for the *Journal of Moral Theology, Practical Matters*, and the *Journal for the Society of Christian Ethics*. Her research areas include Catholic social teaching, disability theology, fieldwork in ethics and feminist ethics.

Oliver Davies (MA, DPhil University of Oxford) is Emeritus Professor of Christian Doctrine at King's College London and International Professor of Science, Ethics and Religion at Renmin University of China, Beijing. He is author of *Theology of Transformation. Faith, Freedom and the Christian Act* (2013). He is currently working on philosophy, science and ethics in global contexts, in the light of new science of human sociality and developing a Catholic theology based on *Lumen Gentium*, §1, 1, which explores "the innermost nature of the Church" and "the unity of the whole human race."

Dominic Doyle (PhD, Boston College) is Associate Professor of Systematic Theology at Boston College's School of Theology and Ministry. He is the author of *The Promise of Christian Humanism: Aquinas on Hope* (2012). His research focuses on theological virtues and theological anthropology.

Douglas Finn (PhD, Notre Dame) is an instructor in the Humanities Department at Saint Anselm College and a member of the Centre for the Study of Augustine, Augustianism and Jansenism at KU Leuven, Belgium. He is the author of *Life in the Spirit: Trinitarian Grammar and Pneumatic Community in Hegel and Augustine* (Notre Dame Press, 2016). His current research focuses on scriptural exegesis, preaching and exemplarity in the early church.

Anthony J. Godzieba (PhD, Catholic University of America) is Professor of Theology and Religious Studies at Villanova University. He specializes in fundamental theology, theology of God, Christology, and philosophical theology. The author of numerous essays, his most recent publications include *Beyond Dogmatism and Innocence: Hermeneutics, Critique, and Catholic Theology* (2017, coedited with Bradford Hinze) and *A Theology of the Presence and Absence of God* (2018). He is currently writing on the intersection of art, music, theology and spirituality in early modern Catholicism, as well as a small book on theological method.

Michelle A. Gonzalez (PhD, Graduate Theological Union) is Dean of the College of Arts and Sciences at the University of Scranton. She is the author of *Created in God's Image: An Introduction to Feminist Theological Anthropology* (2007), *Shopping: Christian Explorations of Daily Living* (2010) and *A Critical Introduction to Religion in the Americas: Bridging the Liberation Theology and Religious Studies Divide* (2014).

Tim Hartman (PhD, University of Virginia) is Associate Professor of Theology at Columbia Theological Seminary. He is the author of *Theology after Colonization: Bediako, Barth, and the Future of Theological Reflection* (2020).

Mary Ann Hinsdale, I.H.M. (PhD, in Systematic Theology, University of St. Michael's College) is Associate Professor of Theology at Boston College. She is the author of *Women Shaping Theology* (2006), and "Mutual Responsibility for the Gospel: Schillebeeckx's Later Theology of Ministry and Its Implications for Today," in the *T&T Clark Handbook of Edward Schillebeeckx*, ed. Stephan Van Erp and Daniel Minch (T&T Clark, 2020), 375–92. Her research centers on theological anthropology, feminist theologies and theories, and ecclesiology.

Daniel P. Horan, OFM (PhD, Boston College) is Assistant Professor of Systematic Theology and Spirituality at Catholic Theological Union in Chicago. He is the author of several books, the most recent include *Catholicity and Emerging Personhood: A Contemporary Theological Anthropology* (2019) and *All God's Creatures: A Theology of Creation* (2018).

Arnold Huijgen (PhD, Theological University of Apeldoorn) is Professor of Systematic Theology at the Theological University of Apeldoorn. He is the author of *Divine Accommodation in John Calvin's Theology: Analysis and Assessment* (Vandenhoeck & Ruprecht, 2011). His research focuses on hermeneutics, theological anthropology, the Trinity, Reformed confessions and Calvin's theology.

Veli-Matti Kärkkäinen (Dr. Theol. Habil., University of Helsinki) is Professor of Systematic Theology at Fuller Theological Seminary and Docent of Ecumenics at the University of Helsinki. He is the author of the five-volume *A Constructive Christian Theology for the Pluralistic World* (2013–17).

Candace L. Kohli (PhD, Northwestern University) is an independent scholar and Manager of Education at the Accreditation Council for Continuing Medical Education. She is author of "The Medieval Luther on Poenitentia: Good Works as the Completion of Faith in the Christian Life" in *The Medieval Luther* (2020) and "The Gift of the Indwelling Spirit: Anthropological Resources in Luther's Robust Pneumatology" in *Lutheran Theology and the Shaping of Society: The Danish Monarchy as Example* (2018).

Néstor Medina (PhD in Theology, St Michael's College, University of Toronto) is Assistant Professor of Religious Ethics and Culture at Emmanuel College of Victoria University in the University of Toronto. He is the author of *Mestizaje: Remapping Race, Culture, and Faith in Latina/o Catholicism* (2009) and *Christianity, Empire and the Spirit* (2018).

Vincent J. Miller (PhD, Notre Dame) is the Gudorf Chair in Catholic Theology and Culture at the University of Dayton. He is the editor of *The Theological and Ecological Vision of Laudato Si: Everything is Connected* (Bloomsbury, 2017) and *Consuming Religion: Christian Faith and Practice in a Consumer Culture* (Bloomsbury, 2005). His research seeks to bring the formative power of material structures into critical theological understanding to guide a more effective ecclesial response.

Stephen Okey (PhD, Boston College) is Associate Professor of Theology at Saint Leo University. He is the author of *A Theology of Conversation: An Introduction to David Tracy* (2018). His research focuses on public theology, ethics, and technology.

Susan A. Ross (PhD University of Chicago Divinity School) is Professor Emerita at Loyola University Chicago. She is the author of *Anthropology: Seeking Light and Beauty* (2012), "Feminist Theology and the Clergy Sex Abuse Crisis," *Theological Studies* 80, no. 3 (September 2019): 632–52, and "Aesthetics and Ethics: Women Religious as Aesthetic and Moral Educators," *Journal of the Society of Christian Ethics* 38, no. 2 (2018). Her research centers on feminist theology and ethics, sacramental theology and theological anthropology.

Philip Rossi, SJ (PhD, University of Texas at Austin) is Emeritus Professor of Theology at Marquette University, Milwaukee, Wisconsin. He is the author of *The Ethical Commonwealth in History: Peace-making as the Moral Vocation of Humanity, Elements in the Philosophy of Immanuel Kant* (2019) and "Plurality as 'the Grace of Secularity': Reform, God's Transcendence, and the Horizons of Otherness," *Ecclesia semper reformanda: Renewal and Reform Beyond Polemics* (2020).

Heidi Russell (PhD, Marquette University) is Associate Professor of Systematic Theology at the Institute of Pastoral Studies, Loyola University Chicago. She is author of *The Source of All Love: Catholicity and the Trinity* (2017) and *Quantum Shift: Theological and Pastoral Implications of Contemporary Developments in Science* (2015). Her research includes the theology of Karl Rahner and the intersection of science and theology, particularly in the areas of neuroscience, quantum physics and cosmology.

J. Warren Smith (PhD, Yale) is Associate Professor of Historical Theology at Duke Divinity School and Senior Fellow for the Duke Divinity School's Center for Reconciliation. He is recently the author of *The Lord's Prayer: Confessing the New Covenant* (2016) and *Ambrose, Augustine, and the Pursuit of Greatness* (2020).

Karen Teel (PhD, Boston College) is Professor of Theology at the University of San Diego. Her research focuses on theological engagement with the problems of racism and white supremacy. Dr. M. Shawn Copeland directed her dissertation, which became *Racism and the Image of God* (2010). More recently, Teel authored "Whiteness in Catholic Theological Method" (*Journal of the American Academy of Religion*, June 2019).

Linn Marie Tonstad (PhD Religious Studies, Yale University) is Associate Professor of Systematic Theology at Yale Divinity School and Professor II in Systematic Theology at the University of Oslo. She is the author of *Queer Theology: Beyond Apologetics* (2018) and *God and Difference: The Trinity, Sexuality, and the Transformation of Finitude* (2016).

Kevin M. Vander Schel (PhD, Boston College) is Assistant Professor of Religious Studies at Gonzaga University. He is the author of *Embedded Grace: Christ, History, and the Reign of God in Schleiermacher's Dogmatics* (2012), coeditor of *The Fragility of Consciousness: Faith, Reason, and the Human Good* (2017), and coeditor of *Beyond Tolerance: Schleiermacher on Friendship, Sociability, and Lived Religion* (2019). His research centers on questions of grace and history, theory and method in the academic study of religion and social and political understandings of sin.

Darlene Fozard Weaver (PhD, University of Chicago) is Associate Provost for Academic Affairs and Professor of Theology at Duquesne University in Pittsburgh, Pennsylvania. She is the author of *The Acting Person and Christian Moral Life* (2011) and "Human Dignity in Catholic Tradition," *Value and Vulnerability: An Interfaith Dialogue on Human Dignity*, ed. Jonathan Rothchild and Matthew Petrusek (2020).

Jeremy D. Wilkins (PhD, Boston College) is Associate Professor of Systematic Theology in the Morissey College of Arts and Sciences at Boston College. He is author of *Before Truth: Lonergan, Aquinas, and the Problem of Wisdom* (2018), and coeditor of the Christology and Redemption volumes in the *Collected Works of Bernard Lonergan* (2016 and 2018).

BIBLIOGRAPHY

Acolaste, Esther, *For Freedom or Bondage?: A Critique of African Pastoral Practices* (Grand Rapids, MI: Eerdmans, 2014).

Acosta, Miguel, and Adrian J. Reimers, *Karol Wojtyła's Personalist Philosophy: Understanding Person and Act* (Washington, DC: Catholic University of American Press, 2016).

Adams, Marilyn McCord, "Genuine Agency, Somehow Shared? The Holy Spirit and Other Gifts," in *Oxford Studies in Medieval Philosophy* (Oxford: Oxford University Press, 2013), 1:23–60.

Agamben, Giorgio, *The Open: Man and Animal* (trans. Kevin Attell; Stanford: Stanford University Press, 2004).

Ailon, Galit, "The Discursive Management of Financial Risk Scandals," *Qualitative Sociology* 35 (2012): 251–70.

Al-Khalili, Jim, and Johnjoe Mcfadden, *Life on the Edge. The Coming of Age of Quantum Biology* (London: Penguin Random House, 2014).

Alison, James, *The Joy of Being Wrong: Original Sin Through Easter Eyes* (New York: Crossroad, 1998).

"All Too Human," *New Scientist* 221, no. 2952 (January 18, 2014).

Altintas, Merih, and Mustafa Bilici, "Evaluation of Childhood Trauma with Respect to Criminal Behavior, Dissociative Experiences, Adverse Family Experiences and Psychiatric Backgrounds among Prison Inmates," *Comprehensive Psychiatry* 82 (2018): 100–7.

Americans with Disabilities Act of 1990. Public Law 101–336. § 12102. 108th Congress, 2nd session (July 26, 1990).

Andolsen, Barbara Hilkert, "Agape in Feminist Ethics," *Journal of Religious Ethics* 9 (Spring 1981): 69–83.

Aquinas, Thomas, *Faith, Reason, Theology: Questions I–IV of his Commentary on the De Trinitate of Boethius* (trans. Armand Maurer; Toronto: Pontifical Institute of Mediaeval Studies, 1987).

Aquinas, Thomas, *Summa contra gentiles: Book Two: Creation* (trans. James F. Anderson; Notre Dame, IN: University of Notre Dame Press, 1976).

Aquinas, Thomas, *Summa contra gentiles: Book Three: Providence. Part II* (trans. Vernon J. Bourke; Notre Dame, IN: University of Notre Dame Press, 1975).

Aquinas, Thomas, *Summa theologiae (5 Volumes)* (trans. the Fathers of the English Dominican Province; Allen, TX: Christian Classics, 1948).

Aquinas, Thomas, *De Veritate* (trans. Robert W. Mulligan, SJ; Indianapolis: Hackett, 1994).

Aquino, María Pilar, "Latina Feminist Theology: Central Features," in María Pilar Aquino, Daisy L. Machado and Jeanette Rodríguez (eds.), *A Reader in Latina Feminist Theology: Religion and Justice* (Austin: University of Texas Press, 2002), 133–60.

Aquino, María Pilar, *Our Cry for Life: Feminist Theology from Latin America* (Maryknoll, NY: Orbis Books, 1993).

Aristotle, *De Anima (On the Soul)* (trans. Hugh Lawson-Tancred; New York: Penguin Classics, 1987).

Athanasius, *On the Incarnation of the Word* (trans. A Religious of C.S.M.V.; Crestwood, NY: Saint Vladimir's Seminary Press, 1996).

Athenagoras, *Embassy for the Christians, The Resurrection of the Dead* (rev. ed., trans. Joseph Hugh Crehan, SJ; Ancient Christian Writers, vol. 23; New York: Paulist Press, 1956).

Augustine of Hippo, *Answer to the Pelagians II* (ed. John E. Rotelle, OSA; trans. Roland J. Teske, SJ; vol. I/25; Hyde Park, NY: New City Press, 1999).

Augustine of Hippo, *Augustine's Comentary on Galatians* (ed. Eric Plumer; trans. Eric Plumer; Oxford Early Christian Studies; New York: Oxford University Press, 2006).

Augustine of Hippo, *City of God (Books 1–10)* (ed. Boniface Ramsay; trans. William Babcock; Works of Saint Augustine, vol. I/6; Hyde Park, NY: New City Press, 2012).

Augustine of Hippo, *City of God (Books 11–20)* (ed. Boniface Ramsay; trans. William Babcock; Works of Saint Augustine, vol. I/7; Hyde Park, NY: New City Press, 2013).

Augustine of Hippo, *City of God. Vol. V: Books 16–18.35* (trans. Eva M. Sanford; Loeb Classical Library, 415; Cambridge: Harvard University Press, 1957).

Augustine of Hippo, *Confessions* (trans. Henry Chadwick; Oxford: Oxford University Press, 1992).

Augustine of Hippo, *Confessions* (ed. John E. Rotelle, OSA; trans. Maria Boulding, OSB; Vol. I/1; Hyde Park, NY: New City Press, 2012).

Augustine of Hippo, *Expositions of the Psalms: Vol. 1, Ps 1–31* (ed. John E. Rotelle, OSA; trans. Maria Boulding, OSB; vol. III/15; Hyde Park, NY: New City Press, 2000).

Augustine of Hippo, *Expositions of the Psalms: Vol. 3, Ps 51–72* (ed. John E. Rotelle, OSA; trans. Maria Boulding, OSB; vol. III/17; Hyde Park, NY: New City Press, 2001).

Augustine of Hippo, *Homilies on the Gospel of John (1–40)* (ed. Allan Fitzgerald, OSA; trans. Edmund Hill, OP; vol. III/12; Hyde Park, NY: New City Press, 2009).

Augustine of Hippo, *The Immortality of the Soul; The Magnitude of the Soul; On Music; The Advantage of Believing; On Faith in Things Unseen* (trans. Ludwig Schopp; The Fathers of the Church; Washington, DC: Catholic University of America Press, 1947).

Augustine of Hippo, *Letters: Vol. 1, No. 1–99* (ed. Boniface Ramsey; trans. Roland J. Teske, SJ; vol. II/1; Hyde Park, NY: New City Press, 2001).

Augustine of Hippo, *Letters: Vol. 2, No. 100–155* (ed. Boniface Ramsey; trans. Roland J. Teske, SJ; vol. II/2; Hyde Park, NY: New City Press, 2001).

Augustine of Hippo, *The Manichean Debate* (ed. Boniface Ramsey; trans. Roland J. Teske, SJ; Works of Saint Augustine, vol. I/19; Hyde Park, NY: New City Press, 2006).

Augustine of Hippo, *On Christian Belief* (ed. Boniface Ramsey; trans. Edmund Hill, OP, Ray Kearney, Michael G. Campbell and Bruce Harbert; Works of Saint Augustine, vol. I/8; Hyde Park, NY: New City Press, 2005).

Augustine of Hippo, *On Genesis* (ed. John E. Rotelle, OSA; trans. Edmund Hill, OP; Works of Saint Augustine, vol. I/13; Hyde Park, NY: New City Press, 2002).

Augustine of Hippo, *On Nature and Grace*, in *Four Anti-Pelagian Writings* (trans. John A. Mourant and William Collinge; The Fathers of the Church, vol. 86; Washington DC: Catholic University of America Press, 1992).

Augustine of Hippo, *On the Predestination of the Saints*, in *Four Anti-Pelagian Writings* (trans. John A. Mourant and William Collinge; The Fathers of the Church, vol. 86; Washington DC: Catholic University of America Press, 1992).

Augustine of Hippo, *Responses to Miscellaneous Questions* (ed. Raymond Canning; trans. Boniface Ramsey; Works of Saint Augustine, vol. I/2; Hyde Park, NY: New City Press, 2008).

Augustine of Hippo, *Revisions* (ed. Roland Teske, SJ; trans. Boniface Ramsey; Works of Saint Augustine, vol. I/2; Hyde Park, NY: New City Press, 1993).

Augustine of Hippo, *Sermons 230-272B* (ed. John E. Rotelle, OSA; trans. Edmund Hill, OP; Works of Saint Augustine, Vol. III/7; Hyde Park, NY: New City Press, 1993).

Augustine of Hippo, *The Soliloquies*, in J.H.S. Burleigh (ed. and trans.), *Earlier Writings* (Louisville, KY: Westminster John Knox, 2006), 17–63.

Augustine of Hippo, *The Trinity* (ed. John E. Rotelle, OSA; trans. Edmund Hill, OP; Works of Saint Augustine, vol. I/5; Hyde Park, NY: New City Press, 2012).

Avalos, Hector, Sarah J. Melcher and Jeremy Schipper, *This Abled Body: Rethinking Disabilities in Biblical Studies* (Atlanta: Society of Biblical Literature, 2007).

Ayala, Francisco J., "The Evolution of Life: An Overview," in Mary Kathleen Cunningham (ed.), *God and Evolution: A Reader* (London: Routledge, 2007), 58–67.

Ayres, Lewis, *Augustine and the Trinity* (Cambridge: Cambridge University Press, 2010).

Bader, Jennifer, "Engaging the Struggle: John Paul II on Personhood and Sexuality," in Kieran Scott and Harold Daly Horell (eds.), *Human Sexuality in the Catholic Tradition* (Lanham: Rowan & Littlefield, 2007), 91–110.

Bair-Merritt, M. H., P. F. Cronholm, M. B. Davis, R. Wade Jr., J. A. Fein, C. M. Forke, M. Harkins-Schwarz and L. M. Pachter, "Household and Community-Level Adverse Childhood Experiences and Adult Health Outcomes in a Diverse Urban Population," *Child Abuse and Neglect* 52 (2015): 135–45.

Balibar, Etienne, and Immanuel Wallerstein, *Race, Nation, Class: Ambiguous Identities* (New York: Verso, 2011).

Balthasar, Hans Urs von, *Bernanos: An Ecclesial Existence* (trans. Erasmo Leiva-Merikakis; San Francisco: Ignatius Press, 1996).

Balthasar, Hans Urs von, *Explorations in Theology V: Man Is Created* (San Francisco: Ignatius Press, 2014).

Balthasar, Hans Urs von, *The Office of Peter and the Structure of the Church* (trans. Andrée Emery; San Francisco: Ignatius Press, 1986).

Balthasar, Hans Urs von, "On the Concept of Person," *Communio* 13, no. 2 (Spring 1986): 18–26.

Balthasar, Hans Urs von, *Theo-drama, Volume II - Dramatis Personae: Man in God* (trans. Graham Harrison; San Francisco: Ignatius Press, 1990).

Balthasar, Hans Urs von, *Theo-drama, Volume III - Dramatis Personae: Persons in Christ* (trans. Graham Harrison; San Francisco: Ignatius Press, 1992).

Balthasar, Hans Urs von, *Theo-drama, Volume IV - The Action* (trans. Graham Harrison; San Francisco: Ignatius Press, 1994).

Balthasar, Hans Urs von, *A Theological Anthropology* (Eugene, OR: Wipf and Stock, 2010).

Balthasar, Hans Urs von, *Unless You Become like This Child* (trans. Erasmo Leiva-Merikakis; San Francisco: Ignatius Press, 1991).

Balthasar, Hans Urs von, *Who Is a Christian?* (trans. John Cumming; London: Burns and Oates, 1968).

Bantum, Brian, *Redeeming Mulatto: A Theology of Race and Christian Hybridity* (Waco: Baylor University Press, 2010).

Barbarin, Oscar A., "Halting African American Boys' Progression from Pre-K to Prison: What Families, Schools, and Communities Can Do!," *American Journal of Orthopsychiatry* 80, no. 1 (2010): 81–8.

Barbour, Ian G., "Neuroscience, Artificial Intelligence, and Human Nature: Theological and Philosophical Reflections," *Zygon* 34, no. 3 (September 1999): 361–98.

Barth, Karl, *Church Dogmatics*, 4 vols. (Edinburgh: T&T Clark, 1956–75).

Barth, Karl, *Dogmatics in Outline* (New York: Harper & Row, 1959).

Barth, Karl, *Die kirchliche Dogmatik*, vol. III, part 2 (Zürich: EVZ, 1948).

Barth, Karl, *Epistle to the Romans*, 2nd ed. (trans. Edwyn C. Hoskyns; London: Oxford University Press, [1933] 1968).

Barth, Karl, *Evangelical Theology* (Grand Rapids, MI: Eerdmans, 1963).

Barth, Karl, *Humanity of God* (Louisville: Westminster John Knox, 1960).

Barth, Karl, "The Humanity of God," in *The Humanity of God* (trans. John Newton Thomas; Atlanta: John Knox Press, 1960), 37–68.

Barth, Karl, *Protestant Theology in the Nineteenth Century* (Valley Forge: Judson, 1973).

Barth, Karl, *A Unique Time of God: Karl Barth's WWI Sermons* (ed. and trans. William Klempa; Louisville: Westminster John Knox, 2016).

Basil the Great, *On the Holy Spirit* (trans. Stephen Hildebrand; Yonkers, NY: St. Vladimir's Seminary Press, 2011).

Bauckham, Richard, *The Bible and Ecology: Rediscovering the Community of Creation* (Waco: Baylor University Press, 2011).

Baumgardner, Jennifer, and Amy Richards, *Manifesta: Young Women, Feminism, and the Future* (New York: Farrar, Straus and Giroux, 2010).

Van Bavel, Tarsicius Jan, "'No One Ever Hated His Own Flesh': Eph. 5:29 in Augustine," *Augustiniana* 45 (1995): 45–93.

Beattie, Tina, "Dignity, Difference and Rights—a Gendered Theological Analysis," *Louvain Studies* 40 (2017): 58–81.

Beattie, Tina, "Feminism, Vatican-Style," *The Tablet* 258, no. 8549 (August 7, 2004): 4–6.

Beattie, Tina, "A 'Frozen' Idea of the Feminine," *The Tablet* 274, no. 9340 (February 22, 2020): 4–6.

Beattie, Tina, "Gendering Genesis, Engendering Difference: A Catholic Theological Quest," *Svensk teologisk kvartalskrift* 92 (2016): 102–17.

Beattie, Tina, *New Catholic Feminism: Theology and Theory* (London: Routledge, 2006).

Becker, Gary S., *The Economic Approach to Human Behavior* (Chicago: University of Chicago Press, 1976).

Becker, Gary S., *Human Capital: A Theoretical and Empirical Analysis, with Special Reference to Education* (New York: National Bureau of Economic Research/Columbia University Press, 1975).

Bednarowski, Mary Farrell, *The Religious Imagination of American Women* (Bloomington: Indiana University Press, 1999).

Behe, Michael J., *Darwin's Black Box: The Biochemical Challenge to Evolution* (New York: The Free Press, 1996).

Behr, John, *Asceticism and Anthropology in Irenaeus and Clement* (Oxford: Oxford University Press, 2000).

Behr, John, *Irenaeus of Lyons: Identifying Christianity* (Oxford: Oxford University Press, 2013).

Behr, John, "The Rational Animal: A Rereading of Gregory of Nyssa's *De hominis opificio*," *Journal of Early Christian Studies* 7, no. 2 (1999): 219–47.

Bell, Daniel, *Liberation Theology After the End of History: The Refusal to Cease Suffering* (New York: Routledge, 2001).

Pope Benedict XVI, *Jesus of Nazareth* (trans. Adrian J. Walker; London: Bloomsbury, 2007).

Berkman, John, "Are Persons with Profound Intellectual Disabilities Sacramental Icons of Heavenly Life? Aquinas on Impairment," *Studies in Christian Ethics* 26, no. 1 (2013): 83–96.

Betcher, Sharon V., *Spirit and the Politics of Disablement* (Minneapolis, MN: Fortress Press, 2007).

Bevans, StephenB. and RogerP. Schroder, *Constants in Context: A Theology for Mission for Today* (Maryknoll, NY: Orbis, 2004).

Bjork, Russell C, "Artificial Intelligence and the Soul," *Perspectives on Science and Christian Faith* 60, no. 2 (June 2008): 95–102.

Black, Kathy *A Healing Homiletic: Preaching and Disability* (Nashville, TN: Abingdon Press, 1996).

Boersma, Gerald, *Augustine's Early Theology of Image: A Study in the Development of Pro-Nicene Theology* (Oxford: Oxford University Press, 2016).

Boersma, Hans, *Embodiment and Virtue in Gregory of Nyssa: An Anagogical Approach* (Oxford: Oxford University Press, 2013).

Boff, Leonardo, *Liberating Grace* (trans. John Drury; Maryknoll, NY: Orbis Books, 1979).

Boeve, Lieven, *Lyotard and Theology* (London/New York: Bloomsbury, 2014).

Borgman, Erik, *Edward Schillebeeckx: A Theologian in His History* (London: Continuum, 2004).

Boullier, Mary, and Mitch Blair, "Adverse Childhood Experiences," *Pediatrics and Child Health* 28, no. 3 (2018): 132–7.

Bowden, John, *Edward Schillebeeckx: Portrait of a Theologian* (London: SCM Press, 1983).

Boyer, Ann, *The Undying: Pain, Vulnerability, Mortality, Medicine, Art, Time, Dreams, Data, Exhaustion, Cancer, and Care* (New York: Farrar, Straus and Giroux, 2019).

Brakke, David, *The Gnostics: Myth, Ritual and Diversity in Early Christianity* (Cambridge, MA: Harvard University Press, 2010).

Bratsiotis, N. P., "Basar," in G. Johannes Botterweck and Helmer Ringgren (eds.), *Theological Dictionary of the Old Testament II* (Grand Rapids, MI: Eerdmans, 1975), 317–32.

Breckenridge, Gillian, "Looking for Likeness and Hope: Beyond Super- and Subordination in Barth's Discussion of Gender in *Church Dogmatics*§45.3," *Zeitschrift für Dialektische Theologie* 33, no. 2 (2017): 166–78.

Bremmer, Jan N., *The Early Greek Concept of the Soul* (Princeton: Princeton University Press, 1983).

Brett, Mark G., "Earthing the Human in Genesis 1–3," in Norman C. Habel and Shirley Wurst (eds.), *The Earth Story in Genesis* (Sheffield: Sheffield Academic Press, 2000), 73–86.

Briggman, Anthony, *Irenaeus of Lyons and the Theology of the Holy Spirit* (New York: Oxford University Press, 2012).

Brock, Brian, and John Swinton, *Disability in the Christian Tradition: A Reader* (Grand Rapids, MI: Eerdmans, 2012).

Brock, Rita Nakashima, "Cooking without Recipes: Interstitial Integrity," in Rita Nakashima Brock, Jung Ha Kim, Kwok Pui-lan, and Seung Ai Yang (eds.), *Off the Menu: Asian and Asian North American Women's Religion and Theology* (Louisville, KY: Westminster John Knox Press, 2007), 125–44.

Brown, Warren S., "Neurological Embodiment of Spirituality and Soul," in Malcolm Jeeves (ed.), *From Cells to Souls—and Beyond: Changing Portraits of Human Nature* (Grand Rapids, MI: Eerdmans, 2004), 58–76.

Brown, Warren S., Nancey C. Murphy and H. Newton Malony (eds.), *Whatever Happened to the Soul? Scientific and Theological Portraits of Human Nature* (Minneapolis, MN: Fortress, 1998).

Brown, Wendy, *Undoing the Demos: Neoliberalism's Stealth Revolution* (Cambridge, MA: Zone Books, 2015).

Brown, William P., *The Ethos of the Cosmos: The Genesis of Moral Imagination in the Bible* (Grand Rapids, MI: Eerdmans, 1999).

Brown, William P., *The Seven Pillars of Creation: The Bible, Science, and the Ecology of Wonder* (New York: Oxford University Press, 2010).

Buckley, Michael J., *At the Origins of Modern Atheism* (New Haven: Yale University Press, 1987).

Burnell, Peter, *The Augustinian Person* (Washington, DC: Catholic University of America Press, 2005).

Burrell, David B., "*Creatio ex Nihilo* Recovered," *Modern Theology* 29 (2013): 5–21.

Burrell, David B., *Freedom and Creation in Three Traditions* (Notre Dame, IN: University of Notre Dame Press, 1993).

Burrell, David B., "Creation as Original Grace," in Philip J. Rossi (ed.), *God, Grace, and Creation* (Maryknoll, NY: Orbis Books, 2010), 97–106.

Burrell, David B., *Knowing the Unknowable God* (Notre Dame, IN: University of Notre Dame Press, 1986).

Burrell, David B., *Towards a Jewish-Christian-Muslim Theology* (Chichester: Wiley-Blackwell, 2011).

Burrus, Virginia, and Karmen Mackendrick, "Bodies without Wholes: Apophatic Excess and Fragmentation in Augustine's *City of God*," in Chris Boesel and Catherine Keller (eds.), *Apophatic Bodies: Negative Theology, Incarnation, and Relationality* (New York: Fordham University Press, 2010), 79–93.

Busch, Eberhard, *Karl Barths Lebenslauf: Nach Seinen Briefen und Autobiograph Texten* (München: Kaiser, 1975).

Cacioppo, John T., and Gary G. Berntson, "Social Neuroscience," in R. Adolphs, G. G. Berntson, and J. T. Cacioppo (eds.), *Foundations in Social Neuroscience* (Social Neuroscience Series; Cambridge, MA.: Bradford Books, 2002), 3–10.

Cahill, Lisa, "Feminist Theology and a Participatory Church," in Stephen J. Pope (ed.), *Common Calling: The Laity & Governance in the Catholic Church* (Washington, DC: Georgetown University Press, 2004), 140–5.

Calvin, John, *The Bondage and Liberation of the Will: A Defence of the Orthodox Doctrine of Human Choice against Pighius* (ed. A. N. S. Lane; trans. G. I. Davies; Grand Rapids, MI: Baker, 1996).

Calvin, John, *Commentary on 1 Corinthians*, in Guilielmus Baum, Eduardus Cunitz and Eduardus Reuss (eds.), *Ioannis Calvini opera quae supersunt omnia* (vol. 49; Brunsvigae: C.A. Schwetschke, 1863).

Calvin, John, *Commentary on 1 John*, in Guilielmus Baum, Eduardus Cunitz and Eduardus Reuss (eds.), *Ioannis Calvini opera quae supersunt omnia* (vol. 55; Brunsvigae: C.A. Schwetschke, 1863).

Calvin, John, *Commentary on the Psalms*, in Guilielmus Baum, Eduardus Cunitz and Eduardus Reuss (eds.), *Ioannis Calvini opera quae supersunt omnia* (vol. 32; Brunsvigae: C.A. Schwetschke, 1863).

Calvin, John, *Defensio sanae et orthodoxae doctrinae de servitute et liberatione humani arbitrii contra Alberti Pighii Campensis* (Geneva: Joannes Gerardus, 1543), in Guilielmus Baum, Eduardus Cunitz and Eduardus Reuss (eds.), *Ioannis Calvini opera quae supersunt omnia* (Brunsvigae: C.A. Schwetschke, 1863), 6:225–404.

Calvin, John, *Genesis* (Geneva Series of Commentaries; Wheaton, IL: Crossway Books, 2001).

Calvin, John, *Institutes of the Christian Religion*, 2 vols. (trans. Ford Lewis Battles; Philadelphia: Westminster Press, 1960).

Calvin, John, *Psychopannychia* , in Guilielmus Baum, Eduardus Cunitz and Eduardus Reuss (eds.), *Ioannis Calvini opera quae supersunt omnia* (vol. 5; Brunsvigae: C.A. Schwetschke, 1863).

Calvin, John, *Sermons on Ephesians*, in Guilielmus Baum, Eduardus Cunitz and Eduardus Reuss (eds.), *Ioannis Calvini opera quae supersunt omnia* (vol. 51; Brunsvigae: C.A. Schwetschke, 1863).

Callahan, Allen Dwight, *The Talking Book: African Americans and the Bible* (New Haven: Yale University Press, 2006).

Camelot, P. Th., OP, "La Théologie de L'Image de Dieu," *Revue des Sciences Philosophiques et Théologiques* 40 (1956): 443–71.

Cameron, Michael, *Christ Meets Me Everywhere: Augustine's Early Figurative Exegesis* (Oxford: Oxford University Press, 2012).

Caputo, John D., *The Weakness of God: A Theology of the Event* (Bloomington: Indiana University Press, 2005).

Carbine, Rosemary P., "Turning to Narrative: Toward a Feminist Theological Understanding of Political Participation and Personhood," *Journal of the American Academy of Religion* 78, no. 2 (June 2010): 375–412.

Carey, Allison, *On the Margins of Citizenship* (Philadelphia: Temple University Press, 2009).

Carlson, Licia, *The Faces of Intellectual Disability Philosophical Reflections* (Bloomington: Indiana University Press, 2010).

Carter, J. Kameron, *Race: A Theological Account* (Oxford: Oxford University Press, 2008).

Case, Mary Anne, "The Role of the Popes in the Invention of Complementarity and the Vatican's Anathematization of Gender," *Religion & Gender* 6 (2016): 155–72.

Cauley, Kashana, "Erica Garner and How America Destroys Black Families," *New York Times*, January 2, 2018. Available online: https://www.nytimes.com/2018/01/02/opinion/erica-garner-black-families.html (accessed May 10, 2020).

Cavadini, John, "Ambrose and Augustine: *De bono mortis*," in William E. Klingshirn and Mark Vessey (eds.), *The Limits of Ancient Christianity: Essays on Late Antique Thought and Culture in Honor of R.A. Markus* (Ann Arbor: University of Michigan Press, 1999), 232–49.

Cavadini, John, "The Anatomy of Wonder: An Augustinian Taxonomy," *Augustinian Studies* 42, no. 2 (2011): 153–72.

Cavadini, John, "Feeling Right: Augustine on the Passions and Sexual Desire," *Augustinian Studies* 36, no. 1 (2005): 195–217.

Cavanaugh, William T., *Being Consumed: Economics and Christian Desire* (Grand Rapids, MI: Eerdmans, 2008).

"The Chapter of Expulsion of 1492," in Edward Peters (ed. and trans.), "Jewish History and Gentile Memory: The Expulsion of 1492," *Jewish History* 9, no. 1 (1995): 23–28.

Choi, Michael J., "Consciousness and Intentionality in AI and the *Imago Dei*," *Canon & Culture* 10, no. 2 (2016): 69–90.

Christian, Brian, *The Most Human Human: What Artificial Intelligence Teaches Us about Being Alive* (New York: Anchor Books, 2012).

Clark, Andy, *Supersizing the Mind. Embodiment, Action and Cognitive Extension* (New York: Oxford University Press, 2011).

Clarke, W. Norris, *Person and Being* (Milwaukee, WI: Marquette University Press, 1993).

Clayton, Philip, *Mind and Emergence: From Quantum to Consciousness* (New York: Oxford University Press, 2004).

Clayton, Philip, "Neuroscience, the Person, and God: An Emergentist Account," *Zygon* 35 (2000): 613–52.

Clifford, Catherine E. *Decoding Vatican II: Interpretation and Ongoing Reception* (New York: Paulist Press, 2014).

Clifford, Richard J., "*Creatio ex nihilo* in the Old Testament/Hebrew Bible," in Gary A. Anderson and Markus Bockmuehl (eds.), *Creation 'ex Nihilo': Origins, Development, Contemporary Challenges* (Notre Dame, IN: University of Notre Dame Press, 2017), 55–76.

Clough, David, "All God's Creatures: Reading Genesis on Human and Nonhuman Animals," in Stephen C. Barton and David Wilkinson (eds.), *Reading Genesis after Darwin* (New York: Oxford University Press, 2009), 145–61.

Clough, David, *On Animals: Systematic Theology, vol. 1* (New York: T&T Clark, 2012).

Coakley, Sarah, *God, Sexuality and the Self: An Essay "On the Trinity"* (Cambridge: Cambridge University Press, 2013).

Coates, Ta-Nehisi, *Between the World and Me* (New York: Spiegel & Grau, 2015).

Coates, Ta-Nehisi, "The Case for Reparations," *Atlantic Monthly*, May 21, 2014.

Coates, Ta-Nehisi, "This Town Needs a Better Class of Racist," *The Atlantic*, May 1, 2014. Available online: https://www.theatlantic.com/politics/archive/2014/05/This-Town-Needs-A-Better-Class-Of-Racist/361443/ (accessed July 17, 2019).

Cogliati, Carlo, "Introduction," in David B. Burrell, Carlo Cogliati, Janet M. Soskice and William R. Stoeger (eds.), *Creation and the God of Abraham* (New York: Cambridge University Press, 2010), 1–10.

Cole-Turner, Ronald, "Going beyond the Human: Christians and Other Transhumanists," *Dialog: A Journal of Theology* 54 (Spring 2015): 150–61.

Cole-Turner, Ronald, "Introduction: The Transhumanist Challenge," in Ronald Cole-Turner (ed.), *Transhumanism and Transcendence: Christian Hope in an Age of Technological Enhancement* (Washington, DC: Georgetown University Press, 2011), 1–18.

Cone, James, *Black Theology and Black Power* (Maryknoll, NY: Orbis Books, 1997).

Cone, James, *A Black Theology of Liberation: Twentieth Anniversary Edition* (Maryknoll, NY: Orbis, 1990).

Cone, James, *A Black Theology of Liberation: Fortieth Anniversary Edition* (Maryknoll, NY: Orbis Books, 2010).

Congregation for Catholic Education (for Educational Institutions), *"Male and Female He Created Them": Towards a Path of Dialogue on the Question of Gender Theory in Education* (Vatican City: Vatican Press, 2019).

Congregation for the Doctrine of the Faith, "Instruction on Certain Aspects of the Theology of Liberation," *Origins* 14, no. 15 (1984): 194–204.

Cooper, Melinda, *Family Values: Between Neoliberalism and the New Social Conservatism* (New York: Zone Books, 2017).

Copeland, M. Shawn, "The Cross of Christ and Discipleship," in Tatha Wiley (ed.), *Thinking of Christ: Proclamation, Explanation, Meaning* (New York: Continuum, 2003), 177–92.

Copeland, M. Shawn, *Enfleshing Freedom: Body, Race, and Being* (Minneapolis, MN: Fortress, 2010).

Copeland, M. Shawn, "God among the Ruins: Companion and Co-Sufferer," in Margaret R. Pfeil and Tobias L. Winright (eds.), *Violence, Transformation, and the Sacred: "They Shall Be Called Children of God"* (Maryknoll, NY: Orbis, 2012), 15–29.

Copeland, M. Shawn, "Memory, #BlackLivesMatter, and Theologians," *Political Theology* 17, no. 1 (January 2016): 1–3.

Copeland, M. Shawn, "Racism and the Vocation of the Theologian," *Spiritus* 2, no. 1 (Spring 2002): 15–29.

Copeland, M. Shawn, Dwight N. Hopkins, Charles T. Mathewes, Joy Ann McDougall, Ian A. McFarland and Michele Saracino, "Human Being," in Serene Jones and Paul Lakeland (eds.), *Constructive Theology: A Contemporary Approach to Classical Themes* (Minneapolis, MN: Fortress Press, 2005), 77–116.

Correll, Joshua, C. M. Judd and B. Park, "The Police Officer's Dilemma: Using Ethnicity to Disambiguate Potentially Threatening Individuals," *Journal of Personality and Social Psychology* 83, no. 6 (2002): 1314–29.

Cortez, Marc, *Embodied Souls, Ensouled Bodies: An Exercise in Christological Anthropology and Its Significance for the Mind/Body Debate* (London: T&T Clark, 2008).

Cotter, David W., *Genesis* (Berit Olam; Collegeville: Liturgical Press, 2003).

Couenhoven, Jesse, *Stricken by Sin, Cured by Christ: Agency, Necessity, and Culpability in Augustinian Theology* (Oxford: Oxford University Press, 2013).

Coyle, J. Kevin, "Mani, Manicheism," in Allan D. Fitzgerald (ed.), *Augustine through the Ages* (Grand Rapids, MI: Eerdmans, 2009), 520–4.

Cozolino, Louis J., and Erin N. Santos, "Why we Need Therapy—and Why It Works: A Neuroscientific Perspective," *Smith College Studies in Social Work* 84, no. 2–3 (2014): 157–77.

Crawford, Nicholas G., Derek E. Kelly, Matthew E. B. Hansen, Marcia H. Beltrame, Shaohua Fan, Shanna L. Bowman, Ethan Jewett, Alessia Ranciaro, Simon Thompson, Yancy Lo, Susanne P. Pfeifer, Jeffrey D. Jensen, Michael C. Campbell, William Beggs, Farhad Hormozdiari, Sununguko Wata Mpoloka, Gaonyadiwe George Mokone, Thomas Nyambo, Dawit Wolde Meskel, Gurja Belay, Jake Haut, NISC Comparative Sequencing Program; Harriet Rothschild, Leonard Zon, Yi Zhou, Michael A Kovacs, Mai Xu, Tongwu Zhang, Kevin Bishop, Jason Sinclair, Cecilia Rivas, Eugene Elliot, Jiyeon Choi, Shengchao A. Li, Belynda Hicks, Shawn Burgess, Christian Abnet, Dawn E. Watkins-Chow, Elena Oceana, Yun S. Song, Eleazar Eskin, Kevin M. Brown, Michael S. Marks, Stacie K. Loftus, William J. Pavan, Meredith Yeager, Stephen Chanock and Sarah A. Tishkoff, "Loci Associated with Skin Pigmentation Identified in African Populations," *Science* 358, no. 6365 (November 7, 2017). DOI: 10.1126/science. aan8433.

Creamer, Deborah Beth, *Disability and Christian Theology Embodied Limits and Constructive Possibilities* (American Academy of Religion Academy Series; Oxford: Oxford University Press, 2009).

Crowe, Frederick E., *Lonergan* (Outstanding Christian Thinkers; Collegeville, MN: Michael Glazier, 1992).

Crenshaw, Kimberlé, "Demarginalizing the Intersection of Race and Sex: A Black Feminist Critique of Antidiscrimination Doctrine, Feminist Theory and Antiracist Politics," *University of Chicago Legal Forum* (1989): 139–67.

Crysdale, Cynthia, and Neil Ormerod, *Creator God, Evolving World* (Minneapolis, MN: Fortress Press, 2013).

Culotta, C. M., P. A. Goff, M. C. Jackson, B. A. L. Di Lione and N. A. DiTomasso, "The Essence of Innocence: Consequences of Dehumanizing Black Children," *Journal of Personality and Social Psychology* 106, no. 4 (2014): 526–45.

Cunningham, David S., "The Way of All Flesh: Rethinking the *Imago Dei*," in Celia Deane-Drummond and David Clough (eds.), *Creaturely Theology: On God, Humans, and Other Animals* (London: SCM Press, 2009), 100–17.

Curran, Charles, *The Catholic Moral Tradition Today: A Synthesis* (Washington, DC: Georgetown University Press, 1999).

Daley, Brian, "Christology," in Allan D. Fitzgerald (ed.), *Augustine through the Ages* (Grand Rapids, MI: Eerdmans, 2009), 164–9.

Daley, Brian, *The Hope of the Early Church: A Handbook of Patristic Eschatology* (Cambridge: Cambridge University Press, 1991).

Dallavalle, Nancy, "Neither Idolatry nor Iconoclasm: A Critical Essentialism for Catholic Feminist Theology," *Horizons*, 25, no 1 (1998): 23–42.

Dalzell, Thomas, *The Dramatic Encounter of Divine and Human Freedom in the Theology of Hans Urs von Balthasar*, 2nd ed. (Bern: Peter Lang, 2000).

Darwin, Charles, *On the Origin of Species by Means of Natural Selection* (New York: Bantam Books, 2008).

Darr, Ryan, "Social Sin and Social Wrongs: Moral Responsibility in a Structurally Disordered World," *Journal of the Society of Christian Ethics* 37, no. 2 (2017): 21–37.

Davies, Oliver, "Niche Construction, Social Cognition, and Language: Hypothesizing the Human as the Production of Place," *Culture and Brain* 4, no. 2 (2016), 87–112.

Davis, Lennard J., *The Disability Studies Reader*, 4th ed. (New York: Routledge, 2013).

Davis, Lennard J., *Enabling Acts: The Hidden Story of How the Americans with Disabilities Act Gave the Largest US Minority Its Rights* (Boston: Beacon Press, 2015).

Davis, Lennard J., *Enforcing Normalcy: Disability, Deafness, and the Body* (New York: Verso, 1995).

de Beauvoir, Simone, *The Second Sex* (trans. and ed. H. M. Parshley; New York: Random House, 1953).

de Gruchy, John W., *Liberating Reformed Theology: A South African Contribution to an Ecumenical Debate* (Grand Rapids, MI: Eerdmans, 1991).

de Gruchy John W., and Charles Villa-Vicencio, *Apartheid is a Heresy* (Grand Rapids, MI: Eerdmans, 1983).

de Knijff, H. W., *Venus aan de leiband: Europa's erotische cultuur en christelijke sexuele ethiek* (Kampen: Kok, 1987).

de Lubac, Henri, *Corpus Mysticum. The Eucharist and the Church in the Middle Ages* (ed. Laurence Paul Hemming and Susan Frank Parsons; trans. Gemma Symonds CJ; London: SCM Press, 2006).

Deane-Drummond, Celia, *Christ and Evolution: Wonder and Wisdom* (Minneapolis, MN: Fortress Press, 2008).

Deane-Drummond, Celia, and Agustín Fuentes (eds.), *Theology and Evolutionary Anthropology: Dialogues in Wisdom, Humility and Grace* (New York: Routledge, 2020).

DeAngelo, Faye Bodley, *Sexual Difference, Gender, and Agency in Karl Barth's Church Dogmatics* (London: Bloomsbury Academic, 2019).

Delgado, Teresa, "This is My Body…Given for You: Theological Anthropology *Latina/mente*," in Susan Abraham and Elena Procario-Foley (eds.), *Frontiers in Catholic Feminist Theology: Shoulder to Shoulder* (Minneapolis, MN: Fortress Press, 2009), 25–47.

Delio, Ilia, *The Unbearable Wholeness of Being: God, Evolution, and the Power of Love* (Maryknoll, NY: Orbis Books, 2013).

Derrida, Jacques, *The Animal That Therefore I am* (ed. Marie-Louise Mallet; trans. David Wills; New York: Fordham University Press, 2008).

Derrida, Jacques, *The Beast & The Sovereign* (eds. Michel Lisse, Marie-Louise Mallet and Ginette Michaud; trans. Geoffrey Bennington; 2 vols; Chicago: University of Chicago Press, 2009–11).

Derrida, Jacques, "Différance," in Alan Bass (ed.), *Margins of Philosophy* (Chicago: University of Chicago Press, 1982), 3–27.

Derrida, Jacques, "Structure, Sign, and Play in the Discourse of the Human Sciences," in Jacques Derrida, *Writing and Difference* (trans. Alan Bass; Chicago: University of Chicago Press, 1978), 278–93.

Descartes, René, *The Method, Meditations and Philosophy of Descartes* (trans. John Veitch; Washington, DC: M. Walter Dunne, 1901).

di Paolo, Enrique, and Hanna de Jaegher, "The Interactive Brain Hypothesis," *Frontiers in Human Neuroscience* 6, no. 163 (2012): 1–16.

Doak, Mary, "Sex, Race, and Culture: Constructing Theological Anthropology for the Twenty-First Century," *Theological Studies* 80, no. 3 (2019), 508–29.

Dobbs, Michael, "The Inspiration for a Workers' Revolution," *Washington Post Sunday*, April 3, 2005, A37. Available online: http://www.washingtonpost.com/wp-dyn/articles/A22109-2005Apr2.html?noredirect=on.

Dodaro, Robert, "'Christus Iustus,' and Fear of Death in Augustine's Dispute with the Pelagians," in Adolar Zumkeller, OSA (ed.), *Signum Pietatis: Festgabe für Cornelius Petrus Mayer zum 60. Geburtstag* (Würzburg: Augustinus-Verlag, 1989), 341–61.

Douglas, Kelly Brown, *The Black Christ* (Maryknoll, NY: Orbis, 1994).

Douglas, Kelly Brown, *Sexuality and the Black Church: A Womanist Perspective* (Maryknoll, NY: Orbis, 1999).

Douglas, Kelly Brown, *What's Faith Got to Do with It? Black Bodies/Christian Souls* (Maryknoll, NY: Orbis, 2005).

Douglass, Jane Dempsey, *Woman, Freedom, and Calvin* (Philadelphia: Westminster, 1985).

Drever, Matthew, *Image, Identity, and the Forming of the Augustinian Soul* (Oxford: Oxford University Press, 2013).

Dreyer, Elizabeth, *Manifestations of Grace* (Collegeville, MN: Liturgical Press, 1990).

Drobner, Hubertus, *Person-Exegese und Christologie bei Augustinus: Zur Herkunft der Formel Una Persona* (Leiden: Brill, 1986).

Du Bois, W. E. B., *The Souls of Black Folk* (London: Penguin, 1989).

Duffy, Stephen, *The Dynamics of Grace: Perspectives in Theological Anthropology* (Collegeville, MN: Liturgical Press, 1993).

Dunn, Dana S., Erin E. Andrews and Norman Anderson, "Person-First and Identity-First Language," *American Psychologist* 70, no. 3 (2015): 255–64.

Dunn, James D. G., *The Theology of Paul the Apostle* (Grand Rapids, MI: Eerdmans, 1998).

Dupré, Louis, *Passage to Modernity: An Essay in the Hermeneutics of Nature and Culture* (New Haven, CT: Yale University Press, 1993).

Dych, William V., SJ, *Karl Rahner* (Collegeville, MN: Liturgical Press, 1992).

Eagleman, David, "What Makes Me Me?," Episode 2, *The Brain with David Eagleman* (Films Media Group, Public Broadcasting Corporation, 2016).

Eagleton, Terry, *The Illusions of Postmodernism* (Oxford/Cambridge, MA: Blackwell, 1996).

Eagleton, Terry, *Literary Theory: An Introduction*, 2nd ed. (Minneapolis: University of Minnesota Press, 1996).

Eaton, Matthew, "Theology and An-Archy: Deep Incarnation Christology Following Emmanuel Lévinas and the New Materialism," *Toronto Journal of Theology* 32 (2016): 3–15.

Ebeling, Gerhard, "Luthers Wirklichkeitsverständnis," *Zeitschrift für Theologie und Kirche* 90 (1993): 409–24.

Ebeling, Gerhard, *Lutherstudien: Disputatio de homine*, 3 vols. (Tübingen: Mohr Siebeck, 1977–89).

Edwards, Denis, *Christian Understandings of Creation: The Historical Trajectory* (Minneapolis, MN: Fortress Press, 2017).

Edwards, Denis, *How God Acts: Creation, Redemption, and Special Divine Action* (Minneapolis, MN: Fortress Press, 2010).

Eggemeier, Matthew T., and Peter Joseph Fritz, *Send Lazarus: Catholicism and the Crises of Neoliberalism* (New York: Fordham University Press, 2020).

Eiesland, Nancy L., *The Disabled God: Toward a Liberatory Theology of Disability* (Nashville: Abingdon Press, 1994).

Endean, Philip (ed.), *Karl Rahner: Spiritual Writings* (Maryknoll, NY: Orbis Books, 2004).

Engel, Mary Potter, "Gender Equality and Gender Hierarchy in Calvin's Theology," *Journal of Women in Culture and Society* 11 (1985): 725–39.

Engel, Mary Potter, *John Calvin's Perspectival Anthropology* (Atlanta: Scholars Press, 1988).

Erisman, Al, and Tripp Parker, "Artificial Intelligence: A Theological Perspective," *Perspectives on Science and Christian Faith* 71, no. 2 (June 2019): 95–106.

Ermarth, Elizabeth Deeds, "Postmodernism: 2. The Role of Language," in *Routledge Encyclopedia of Philosophy* (New York: Taylor and Francis, 2011), https://www.rep.routledge.com/articles/thematic/postmodernism/v-2/sections/the-role-of- language.

Ernst-Habib, Margit, "'Chosen by Grace': Reconsidering the Doctrine of Predestination," in Amy Plantinga Pauw and Serene Jones (eds.), *Feminist and Womanist Essays in Reformed Dogmatics* (Louisville: Westminster John Knox, 2006), 75–94.

Espín, Orlando O., *Disruptive Cartographers: Pneumatology* (Minneapolis, MN: Fortress Press, forthcoming).

Espín, Orlando O., "An Exploration into the Theology of Grace and Sin," in Orlando O. Espín and Miguel H. Díaz (eds.), *From the Heart of Our People: Latino/a Explorations in Catholic Systematic Theology* (Maryknoll, NY: Orbis Books, 1999), 121–52.

Espín, Orlando O., *The Faith of the People: Theological Reflections on Popular Catholicism* (Maryknoll, NY: Orbis Books, 1997).

Espín, Orlando O., "Grace and Humanness: A Hispanic Perspective," in Roberto S. Goizueta (ed.), *We Are a People! Initiatives in Hispanic American Theology* (Minneapolis, MN: Fortress Press, 1992), 133–64.

Espín, Orlando O., *Grace and Humanness: Theological Reflections Because of Culture* (Maryknoll, NY: Orbis Books, 2007).

Espín, Orlando O., *Idol & Grace: On Traditioning and Subversive Hope* (Maryknoll, NY: Orbis Books, 2014).

Espín, Orlando O., "Immigration, Territory, and Globalization: Theological Reflection," *Journal of Hispanic/Latino Theology* 7, no. 3 (Fall 2000): 46–59.

Espín, Orlando O., "Migration and Human Condition: Theological Considerations on Religious Identities and Unexpected Inter-Religious Dialogue," in Raúl Fornet-Betancourt (ed.), *Migration und Interkultiralität: Theologische und Philosophische Herausforderungen* (Aachen: Wissenschaftsverlag Mainz, 2004), 177–88.

Espín, Orlando O., "Pentecostalism and Popular Catholicism: The Poor and *Traditio*," *Journal of Hispanic/Latino Theology* 3, no. 2 (November 1995): 14–43.

Espín, Orlando O., "Popular Religion as an Epistemology (of Suffering)," *Journal of Hispanic/Latino Theology* 2, no. 2 (November 1994): 55–78.

Espín, Orlando O., "Tradition and Popular Religion: An Understanding of the *Sensus fidelium*," in Arturo J. Bañuelas (ed.), *Mestizo Christianity: Theology from the Latino Perspective* (Maryknoll, NY: Orbis Books, 1995), 146–74.

Espín, Orlando O., "Traditioning: Culture, Daily Life and Popular Religion, and Their Impact on Christian Tradition," in Orlando O. Espín and Gary Macy (eds.), *Futuring Our Past: Explorations in the Theology of Tradition* (Maryknoll, NY: Orbis Books, 2006), 1–22.

Eusebius of Caesarea, *The History of the Church from Christ to Constantine* (trans. G. A. Williamson; Harmondsworth: Penguin Books, 1965).

Eusterschulte, Anne, and Hannah Wälzholz (eds.), *Anthropological Reformations: Anthropology in the Era of the Reformation* (Göttingen: Vandenhoeck & Ruprecht, 2015).

Fanon, Frantz, *Black Skin, White Masks*, rev. ed. (trans. Richard Philcox; New York: Grove, 2008).

Farley, Margaret, *Just Love: A Framework for Christian Sexual Ethics* (New York: Continuum, 2008).

Felder, Cain Hope (ed.), *Stony the Road We Trod: African American Biblical Interpretation* (Minneapolis, MN: Augsburg Fortress, 1991).

Fergusson, David, *Creation* (Grand Rapids, MI: Eerdmans, 2014).

Fergusson, David, "Humans Created According to the *Imago Dei*: An Alternative Proposal," *Zygon* 48 (2013), 439–453.

Fields, Karen, and Barbara Fields, *Raceraft: The Soul of Inequality in American Life* (New York: Verso, 2012).

Fingelkurts, Alexander A., and Andrew A. Fingelkurts, "Is Our Brain Hardwired to Produce God, or Is Our Brain Hardwired to Perceive God? A Systematic Review on the Role of the Brain in Mediating Religious Experience," *Cognitive Processing* 10 (2009): 293–326.

Finkelhor, D., S. Hamby, A. Shattuck and H. Turner, "A Revised Inventory of Adverse Childhood Experiences," *Childhood Abuse and Neglect* 48 (2015): 13–21.

Flescher, Andrew Michael, *Moral Evil* (Washington, DC: Georgetown University Press, 2013).

Foerst, Anne, "Artificial Intelligence: Walking the Boundary," *Zygon* 31, no. 4 (December 1996): 681–93.

Foerst, Anne, "Cog, a Humanoid Robot, and the Question of the Image of God," *Zygon* 33, no. 1 (March 1998): 91–111.

Foerst, Anne, *God in the Machine: What Robots Teach Us about Humanity and God* (New York: Dutton Adult, 2004).

Foucault, Michel, *Birth of Biopolitics: Lectures at the College de France 1978–1979* (trans. Graham Burchell; New York: Picador, 2008).

Foucault, Michel, *The Order of Things: An Archaeology of the Human Sciences* (New York: Vintage/Random House, 1973).

Pope Francis, *The Joy of Love: On Love in the Family* (The Post-Synodal Apostolic Exhortation Amoris Laetitia; New York: Paulist Press, 2016).

Pope Francis, *Laudato Sí*, (Vatican City: Libreria Editrice Vaticana, 2015).

Pope Francis, *Querida Amazonia* ("Beloved Amazon"), Post-Synodal Apostolic Exhortation on the Synod on the Amazon, February 2, 2020. Available online: http://www.vatican.va/content/francesco/en/apost_exhortations/documents/papa-francesco_esortazione-ap_20200202_querida-amazonia.html.

Fredriksen, Paula, "Beyond the Body/Soul Dichotomy: Augustine on Paul against the Manichees and the Pelagians," *Recherches Augustiniennes* 23 (1988): 87–114.

Fredriksen, Paula, *Sin: The Early History of an Idea* (Princeton: Princeton University Press, 2012).

Friedman, Milton, "Nyliberalismen Og Dens Muligheter [Neoliberalism and its Prospects]," *Farmand* (February 17, 1951): 89–93.

Friedman, Milton, and Rose Friedman, *Capitalism and Freedom* (Chicago: University of Chicago Press, 1962).

Frith, Chris D., and Uta Frith, "Implicit and Explicit Processes in Social Cognition," *Neuron* 60, no. 3 (2008): 503–10.

Frykberg, Elizabeth, "Karl Barth's Theological Anthropology: An Analogical Critique Regarding Gender Relations," *Studies in Reformed Theology and History* 1, no. 3 (Summer 1993): 1–54.

Fuentes, Agustin, *The Creative Spark: How Imagination Made Humans Exceptional* (New York: Penguin Random House, 2017).

Fulkerson, Mary McClintock, "The Imago Dei and a Reformed Logic for Feminist-Womanist Critique," in Amy Plantinga Pauw and Serene Jones (eds.), *Feminist and Womanist Essays in Reformed Dogmatics* (Louisville: Westminster John Knox Press, 2006), 95–106.

Gaillardetz, Richard, *By What Authority*, rev. ed. (Collegeville MN: Liturgical Press, 2018).

Gaine, Simon Francis, OP, *Did the Saviour See the Father? Christ, Salvation and the Vision of God* (London: Bloomsbury, 2015).

Gallagher, Shaun, "Understanding Others: Embodied Social Cognition," in Paco Calvo and Toni Gomila (eds.), *Handbook of Cognitive Science: an Embodied Approach* (San Diego: Elsevier, 2008), 439–52.

Gandolfo, Elizabeth O'Donnell, *The Power and Vulnerability of Love: A Theological Anthropology* (Minneapolis, MN: Fortress Press, 2015).

García-Rivera, Alejandro, "Artificial Intelligence and De Las Casas: A 1492 Resonance," *Zygon* 28, no. 4 (December 1993): 543–50.

Gaventa, Beverly Roberts, "The Cosmic Power of Sin in Paul's Letter to the Romans: Toward a Widescreen Edition," *Interpretation* 58 (2004): 229–40.

Gawronski, Raymond, SJ, *Word and Silence: Han Urs von Balthasar and the Spiritual Encounter between East and West* (Edinburgh: T&T Clark, 1995).

Gebara, Ivone, *Out of the Depths: Women's Experience of Evil and Salvation* (trans. Ann Patrick Ware; Minneapolis, MN: Fortress Press, 2002).

Gerber, Chad Tyler, *The Spirit of Augustine's Early Theology: Contextualizing Augustine's Pneumatology* (Surrey: Ashgate, 2012).

Gerson, Lloyd P., George Boys-Stones, John M. Dillon, R. A. H. King, Andrew Smith and James Wilberding (trans.), *Plotinus: The Enneads*, repr. ed. (New York: Cambridge University Press, 2019).

Gijsbers, Alan, "The Dialogue between Neuroscience and Theology," Conference on Science and Christianity (COSAC) (Avondale College, Cooranbong, Australia, July 18–20, 2003; ISCAST Christians in Science and Technology), 1–14.

Gilmore, Ruth Wilson, *Golden Gulag: Prisons, Surplus, Crisis, and Opposition in Globalizing California* (Berkeley: University of California Press, 2007).

Godzieba, Anthony J., "Knowing Differently: Incarnation, Imagination, and the Body," *Louvain Studies* 32 (2007): 361–82.

Godzieba, Anthony J., "'Refuge of Sinners, Pray for Us': Augustine, Aquinas, and the Salvation of Modernity," in Lieven Boeve, Frederick Depoortere, and Martin Wisse (eds.), *Augustine and Postmodern Thought: A New Alliance against Modernity?* (BETL 219; Leuven: Peeters, 2009), 147–65.

Goetz, Rebecca Anne, *The Baptism of Early Virginia: How Christianity Created Race* (Baltimore: Johns Hopkins University Press, 2012).

Goizueta, Roberto S., *Caminemos con Jesús: A Hispanic/Latino Theology of Accompaniment* (Maryknoll, NY: Orbis Books, 1995).

Goizueta, Roberto S., "Fiesta: Life in the Subjunctive," in Orlando O. Espín and Miguel H. Diaz (eds.), *From the Heart of Our People: Latino/a Explorations in Catholic Systematic Theology* (Maryknoll, NY: Orbis Books, 1999), 84–99.

Goldenberg, David M., *The Curse of Ham: Race and Slavery in Early Judaism, Christianity, and Islam* (New Haven: Yale University Press, 2003).

Gonzalez, Michelle, *Created in God's Image: An Introduction to Feminist Theological Anthropology* (Maryknoll, NY: Orbis Books, 2007).

Gorringe, Timothy, *Karl Barth: Against Hegemony* (Oxford: Clarendon Press, 1999).

Grabowski, John, "The Luminous Excess of the Acting Person: Assessing the Impact of Pope John Paul II on American Catholic Moral Theology," *Journal of Moral Theology* 1, no. 1 (2012): 116–47.

Graff, Ann O'Hara, "The Struggle to Name Women's Experience," in Ann O'Hara Graff (ed.), *In the Embrace of God: Feminist Approaches to Theological Anthropology* (Maryknoll, NY: Orbis Books, 1995), 71–90.

Graham, Elaine, "Nietzsche Gets a Modem: Transhumanism and the Technological Sublime," *Literature and Theology*, 16 (2002): 65–80.

Graham, Elaine, *Representations of the Post/Human: Monsters, Aliens and Others in Popular Culture* (New Brunswick, NJ: Rutgers University Press, 2002).

Graham, Elaine, *Words Made Flesh: Writings in Pastoral and Practical Theology*, (London: SCM Press, 2009).

Grant, Jacquelyn, "'Come to My Help, Lord, for I'm In Trouble': Womanist Jesus as the Mutual Struggle for Liberation," in Maryanne Stevens (ed.), *Reconstructing the Christ Symbol: Essays in Feminist Christology* (New York: Paulist Press, 1993), 54–71.

Grant, Jacquelyn, "Subjectification as a Requirement for Christological Construction," in Susan Brooks Thistlethwaite and Mary Potter Engel (eds.), *Lift Every Voice: Constructing Christian Theologies From the Underside* (Maryknoll, NY: Orbis Books, 1998), 207–20.

Graves, Mark, "Gracing Neuroscientific Tendencies of the Embodied Soul," *Philosophy & Theology* 26 (2014): 97–129.

Graves, Mark, *Mind, Brain and the Elusive Soul: Human Systems of Cognitive Science and Religion* (Burlington, VT: Ashgate, 2008).

Gray, Alison J., "Whatever Happened to the Soul? Some Theological Implications of Neuroscience," *Mental Health, Religion & Culture* 13 (2010): 637–48.

Green, Joel B., *Body, Soul, and Human Life: The Nature of Humanity in the Bible* (Grand Rapids, MI: Baker Academic, 2008).

Green, Joel B., *Practicing Theological Interpretation: Engaging Biblical Texts for Faith and Formation* (Grand Rapids, MI: Baker Academic, 2011).

Greenaway, James, *The Differentiation of Authority: The Medieval Turn toward Existence* (Washington, DC: Catholic University of America Press, 2012).

Greer, Rowan A., *Christian Hope and Christian Life: Raids on the Inarticulate* (New York: Crossroad, 2001).

Gregersen, Niels Henrik (ed.), *Incarnation: On the Scope and Depth of Christology* (Minneapolis, MN: Fortress Press, 2015).

Gregory of Nyssa, *Address on Religious Instruction*, in *Christology of the Later Fathers* (trans. Edward R. Hardy; Philadelphia: Westminster Press, 1954), 268–326.

Gregory of Nyssa, *Against Eunomius*, in *Gregory of Nyssa: Contra Eunomium III: An English Translation with Commentary and Supporting Studies* (ed. Johan Leemans and Mattieu Cassin; trans. Stuart G. Hall; Leiden: Brill, 2014).

Gregory of Nyssa, "Concerning We Should Think of Saying That There Are Not Three Gods, To Ablabius," in William G. Rusch (ed.), *The Trinitarian Controversy* (trans. William G. Rusch; Minneapolis, MN: Fortress, 1980), 117–126.

Gregory of Nyssa, *Homilies on the Song of Songs* (trans. R. Norris; Atlanta: Society of Biblical Literature, 2012).

Gregory of Nyssa, "In Regard to Those Fallen Asleep," in *One Path for All: Gregory of Nyssa on the Christian Life and Human Destiny* (trans. Rowan A. Greer; Eugene, OR: Cascade Books, 2015), 94–117.

Gregory of Nyssa, *The Life of Moses*, in *Classics of Western Spirituality* (trans. Abraham Malherbe and Everett Ferguson; Mahwah, NJ: Paulist Press, 1978).

Gregory of Nyssa, *On the Making of Man*, in *Nicene and Post-Nicene Fathers* (ed. Philip Schaff; trans. W. Moore and H. A. Wilson; 2nd series 2, vol. 5; Edinburgh: T&T Clark, 1898).

Gregory of Nyssa, *On the Soul and Resurrection*, in *Macrina the Younger, Philosopher of God* (trans. Anna M. Silvas; Turnhout: Brepols, 2008).

Gregson, Vernon (ed.), *The Desires of the Human Heart: An Introduction to the Theology of Bernard Lonergan* (New York: Paulist Press, 1988).

Greig, Jason Reimer, *Reconsidering Intellectual Disability: L'Arche, Medical Ethics, and Christian Friendship* (Washington, DC: Georgetown University Press, 2016).

Grenz, Stanley J., *The Social God and Relational Self: A Trinitarian Theology of the Imago Dei* (Louisville: Westminster John Knox, 2001).

Griffin, David Ray, "Creation out of Nothing, Creation out of Chaos, and the Problem of Evil," in Stephen T. Davis (ed.), *Encountering Evil: Live Options in Theodicy* (Louisville: Westminster John Knox Press, 2001), 101–36.

Grimes, Katie Walker, *Christ Divided: Antiblackness as Corporate Vice* (Minneapolis, MN: Fortress Press, 2017).

Gross, Rita M., and Rosemary Radford Ruether, *Religious Feminism and the Future of the Planet* (London: Bloomsbury Academic, 2016).

Gudorf, Christine, "A New Moral Discourse on Sexuality," in Kieran Scott and Harold Daly Horell (eds.), *Human Sexuality in the Catholic Tradition* (Lanham: Rowan & Littlefield, 2007), 51–69.

Gustafson, James M., *Protestant and Roman Catholic Ethics* (Chicago: University of Chicago, Press 1978).

Gutkowska, J., M. Jankowski, S. Mukaddam-Daher and S. M. McCann, "Oxytocin Is a Cardiovascular Hormone," *Brazilian Journal of Medical and Biological Research* 33 (2000): 625–33.

Gutting, Gary, *French Philosophy in the Twentieth Century* (Cambridge: Cambridge University Press, 2001).

Hadhazy, Adam, "Think Twice: How the Gut's 'Second Brain' Influences Mood and Well-Being," *Scientific American*, February 12, 2010. Available online: https://www.scientificamerican.com/article/gut-second-brain/ (accessed August 13, 2018).

Haldane, John, *Reasonable Faith* (Abingdon: Routledge, 2010).

Hamilton, David, "Can Kindness Cut the Risk of Heart Disease?," *Huffington Post*, December 23, 2010, updated November 17, 2011. Available online: https://www.huffingtonpost.com/david-r-hamilton-phd/can-kindness-cut-the-risk_b_799562.html (accessed August 13, 2018).

Han, Byung-Chul, *Psychopolitics: Neoliberalism and New Technologies of Power* (trans. Erik Butler; London: Verso, 2017).

Han, Byung-Chul, *The Transparency Society* (trans. Erik Butler; Stanford, CA: Stanford University Press, 2015).

Haraway, Donna, "A Cyborg Manifesto: Science, Technology and Socialist Feminism in the Late Twentieth Century," in *Cyborgs, Simians and Women: The Reinvention of Nature* (London: Free Association Books, 1991), 149–82.

Harris, Malcolm, *Kids These Days* (New York: Little, Brown, 2017).

Harrison, Victoria, *The Apologetic Value of Human Holiness* (Dordrecht: Kluwer Academic, 2000).

Harrison, Victoria, "Personal Identity and Integration: Von Balthasar's Phenomenology of Human Holiness," *Heythrop Journal* 40 (1999): 429–30.

Hartman, Tim, "Humanity and Destiny: A Theological Comparison of Karl Barth and African Traditional Religions," in Christian Collins Winn and Martha Moore-Keish (eds.), *Karl Barth and Comparative Theologies* (New York: Fordham University Press, 2019), 228–47.

Hartman, Tim, *Theology after Colonization: Bediako, Barth, and the Future of Theological Reflection* (Notre Dame, IN: University of Notre Dame Press, 2020).

Harvey, David, *The Condition of Postmodernity: An Enquiry into the Origins of Cultural Change* (Oxford: Basil Blackwell, 1989).

Haslam, Molly Claire, *A Constructive Theology of Intellectual Disability: Human Being as Mutuality and Response* (New York: Fordham University Press, 2012).

Hauerwas, Stanley, *Suffering Presence: Theological Reflections on Medicine, the Mentally Handicapped, and the Church* (Notre Dame, IN: University of Notre Dame Press, 1986).

Haught, John F., *God after Darwin: A Theology of Evolution* (Boulder: Westview Press, 2nd edn, 2008).

Hawley, Scott H.; "Challenges for an Ontology of Artificial Intelligence," *Perspectives on Science and Christian Faith* 71, no. 2 (June 2019): 83–93.

Hayek, Friedrich A., *The Constitution of Liberty* (Chicago: University of Chicago Press, 1978).

Hayek, Friedrich A., "The Use of Knowledge in Society," *American Economic Review* 35, 4 (September 1945): 519–30.

Haynes, Stephen R., *Noah's Curse: The Biblical Justification of American Slavery* (New York: Oxford University Press, 2002).

Hebblethwaite, Peter, *The New Inquisition? Schillebeeckx and Kung* (London: Fount Paperbacks, 1980).

Heidegger, Martin, "The Onto-Theo-Logical Constitution of Metaphysics," in *Identity and Difference* (trans. Joan Stambaugh; New York: Harper and Row, 1969), 42–74.

Hellman, Ivy, *Women and the Vatican: An Exploration of Official Documents* (Maryknoll, NY: Orbis Books, 2012).

Helm, Paul, *John Calvin's Ideas* (Oxford: Oxford University Press, 2004).

Helmer, Christine, *The Trinity and Marin Luther: A Study on the Relationship between Genre, Language and the Trinity in Luther's Works (1523–1546)* (Mainz: Verlag Philipp von Zabern, 1999).

Henrich, Dieter, "The Moral Image of the World," in Eckart Förster (ed.), *Aesthetic Judgment and the Moral Image of the World: Studies in Kant* (Stanford: Stanford University Press, 1994), 3–28.

Henrich, Peter, "Hans Urs von Balthasar: A Sketch of His Life," in David L. Schindler (ed.), *Hans Urs von Balthasar: His Life and Work* (San Francisco: Ignatius, 1991).

Herzfeld, Noreen, *In Our Image: Artificial Intelligence and the Human Spirit* (Minneapolis, MN: Fortress Press, 2002).

Heyer, Kristin E., "Social Sin and Immigration: Good Fences Make Bad Neighbors," *Theological Studies* 71 (2010): 410–36.

Hill, Charles E., *From the Lost Teaching of Polycarp, Wissenschaftliche Untersuchungen zum Neuen Testament* 186 (Tübingen: Mohr Siebeck, 2006).

Hilkert, Mary Catherine, "Cry Beloved Image: Rethinking the Image of God," in Ann O'Hara Graff (ed.), *In the Embrace of God: Feminist Approaches to Theological Anthropology* (Maryknoll, NY: Orbis Books, 1995), 190–205.

Hilkert, Mary Catherine, and Robert Schreiter (eds.), *The Praxis of the Reign of God: An Introduction to the Theology of Edward Schillebeeckx* (New York: Fordham University Press, 2002).

Hill Fletcher, Jeannine, *Motherhood as Metaphor: Engendering Interreligious Dialogue* (New York: Fordham University Press, 2013).

Hill Fletcher, Jeannine , *The Sin of White Supremacy: Christianity, Racism, & Religious Diversity in America* (Maryknoll, NY: Orbis, 2017).

Hinsdale, Mary Ann, I.H.M., "A Feminist Reflection on Postconciliar Catholic Ecclesiology," in Richard Gaillardetz and Edward Hahnenberg (eds.), *A Church With Open Doors: Post-Conciliar Reflection on Ecclesiology* (Collegeville, MN: Liturgical Press, 2015), 112–37.

Hinsdale, Mary Ann, I.H.M., "Vatican II and Feminism: Recovered Memories and Refreshed Hopes," *Toronto Journal of Theology* 32, no.2 (2016): 251–72.

Hiscock, Peter, "Learning in Lithic Landscapes: A Reconsideration of the Hominid 'Toolmaking' Niche," *Biological Theory* 9, no. 1 (2014): 27–41.

Hochschild, Paige, *Memory in Augustine's Theological Anthropology* (Oxford: Oxford University Press, 2012).

Holbrook, Colin, Daniel M. T. Fessler and Carlos David Navarrete, "Looming Large in Others' Eyes: Racial Stereotypes Illuminate Dual Adaptations for Representing Threat Versus Prestige as Physical Size," *Evolution and Human Behavior* 37, no. 1 (2016): 67–78.

Horan, Daniel P., OFM, *All God's Creatures: A Theology of Creation* (Lanham: Lexington Books/ Fortress Academic, 2018).

Horan, Daniel P., OFM, *Catholicity & Emerging Personhood: A Contemporary Theological Anthropology* (Maryknoll, NY: Orbis Books, 2019).

Howard, Thomas A., *Protestant Theology and the Making of the Modern German University* (New York: Oxford University, 2006).

Huijgen, Arnold, "The Challenge of Heresy: Servetus, Stancaro, and Castellio," in R. Ward Holder (ed.), *John Calvin in Context* (Cambridge: Cambridge University Press, 2020), 258–66.

Huijgen, Arnold, *Divine Accommodation in John Calvin's Theology. Analysis and Assessment* (Göttingen: Vandenhoeck & Ruprecht, 2011).

Hull, John M., *In the Beginning There Was Darkness : A Blind Person's Conversations with the Bible*, 1st US ed. (Harrisburg, PA: Trinity Press International, 2002).

Hunsinger, George, "Barth on What It Means to Be Human: A Christian Scholar Confronts the Options," in Clifford B. Anderson and Bruce L. McCormack (eds.), *Karl Barth and the Making of Evangelical Theology: A Fifty-Year Perspective* (Grand Rapids, MI: Eerdmans, 2015), 139–55.

Hunsinger, George, "Karl Barth and Human Rights," in *Karl Barth and Radical Politics*, 2nd ed. (Eugene: Cascade, 2017), 181–92.

Hunter, David, "Augustine on the Body," in Mark Vessey (ed.), *A Companion to Augustine* (West Sussex: Wiley-Blackwell, 2012), 353–64.

Ignatius of Antioch, "Letter to Polycarp," in Andrew Louth (ed.), *Early Christian Writings* (London: Penguin, 1968), 107–12.

Irenaeus, *Against Heresies: Books I-V* (ed. A. Roussau et al.; Sources Chrétienne, 10 vols; Paris: Cerf, 1965–82).

Irenaeus, *Against Heresies Book I* (trans. Dominic J. Unger, OFM Cap; Ancient Christian Writers, vol. 55; New York: Paulist Press, 1992).

Irenaeus, *Against Heresies Book II* (trans. Dominic J. Unger, OFM Cap; Ancient Christian Writers, vol. 65; New York: Paulist Press, 2012).

Irenaeus, *Against Heresies Book III* (trans. Dominic J. Unger, OFM Cap; Ancient Christian Writers, vol. 64; New York: Paulist Press, 2012).

Irenaeus, *Against Heresies Books IV-V*, in Philip Schaff (ed.), *Apostolic Fathers with Justin Martyr and Irenaeus* (The Ante-Nicene Fathers, vol. 1; Grand Rapids, MI: Eerdmans, 1987).

Irenaeus, *Proof of the Apostolic Preaching* (trans. Joseph P. Smith, SJ; Ancient Christian Writers, vol. 16; New York: Paulist Press, 1978).

Isasi-Díaz, Ada María, "Defining Our *Proyecto Histórico: Mujerista* Strategies for Liberation," in Charles E. Curran, Margaret A. Farley and Richard A. McCormick, SJ (eds.), *Feminist Ethics and the Catholic Moral Tradition* (Readings in Moral Theology, vol. 9; New York: Paulist Press, 1996), 120–35.

Isasi-Díaz, Ada María, *La Lucha Continues: Mujerista Theology* (Maryknoll, NY: Orbis Books, 2004).

Isasi-Díaz, Ada María, *Mujerista Theology: A Theology for the Twenty-First Century* (Maryknoll, NY: Orbis Books, 1996).

Jackelén, Antje, "The Image of God as *Techno Sapiens*," *Zygon* 37, no. 2 (June 2002): 289–302.

Jacobs, Brianne, "An Alternative to Gender Complementarity: The Body as Existential Category in the Catholic Tradition," *Theological Studies* 80, no. 2 (2019): 328–45.

Jameson, Fredric, "Postmodernism and Consumer Society," in Hal Foster (ed.), *The Anti-Aesthetic: Essays on Postmodern Culture* (New York: The New Press, 1998), 111–25.

Jameson, Fredric, *Postmodernism, or, The Cultural Logic of Late Capitalism* (Durham, NC: Duke University Press, 1991).

Jeeves, Malcolm (ed.), *The Emergence of Personhood: A Quantum Leap?* (Grand Rapids, MI: Eerdmans, 2015).

Jeeves, Malcolm, *Minds, Brains, Souls, and Gods: A Conversation on Faith, Psychology, and Neuroscience* (Downers Grove, IL: InterVarsity Press, 2013).

Jennings, Willie James, *The Christian Imagination: Theology and the Origins of Race* (New Haven, CT: Yale University Press, 2010).

John Paul II, "Letter to George V. Coyne" (June 1, 1988; http://www.vatican.va/content/john-paul-ii/en/letters/1988/documents/hf_jp-ii_let_19880601_padre-coyne.html).

John Paul II, *Christifedeles Laici* (http://www.vatican.va/content/john-paul-ii/en/apost_exhortations/documents/hf_jp-ii_exh_30121988_christifideles-laici.html).

John Paul II, "Letter to Women" (June 29, 1995; http://www.vatican.va/content/john-paul-ii/en/letters/1995/documents/hf_jp-ii_let_29061995_women.html).

John Paul II, *Man and Woman He Created Them: A Theology of the Body*, 2nd ed. (trans. Michael Waldstein; Boston: Pauline Books & Media, 2006).

John Paul II, "Message to the Pontifical Academy of Sciences on Evolution," *Origins* 26, no. 22 (1996): 350–52.

John Paul II, *Mulieris Dignitatem* (August 15, 1988; http://w2.vatican.va/content/john-paul-ii/en/apost_letters/1988/documents/hf_jp-ii_apl_19880815_mulieris-dignitatem.html).

John Paul II, *Ordinatio Sacerdotalis* (May 22, 1994; http://www.vatican.va/content/john-paul-ii/en/apost_letters/1994/documents/hf_jp-ii_apl_19940522_ordinatio-sacerdotalis.html).

John Paul II, *Redemptor Hominis* (March 4, 1979; http://w2.vatican.va/content/john-paul-ii/en/encyclicals/documents/hf_jp-ii_enc_04031979_redemptor-hominis.html).

John Paul II, *Redemptoris Mater* (March 25, 1987; https://w2.vatican.va/content/john-paul-ii/en/encyclicals/documents/hf_jp-ii_enc_25031987_redemptoris-mater.html).

John Paul II, *Sollicitudo rei socialis* (December 30, 1987; http://www.vatican.va/content/john-paul-ii/en/encyclicals/documents/hf_jp-ii_enc_30121987_sollicitudo-rei-socialis.html).

Johnson, Elizabeth A., *Ask the Beasts: Darwin and the God of Love* (New York: Bloomsbury, 2014).

Johnson, Elizabeth A., *Creation and the Cross: The Mercy of God for a Planet in Peril* (Maryknoll, NY: Orbis Books, 2018).

Johnson, Elizabeth A., "Does God Play Dice? Divine Providence and Chance," *Theological Studies* 57 (1996): 3–18.

Johnson, Elizabeth A., "The Maleness of Christ," in Elisabeth Schüssler Fiorenza (ed.), *The Power of Naming: A Concilium Reader in Feminist Liberation Theology* (Maryknoll, NY: Orbis Books, 1996), 307–15.

Johnson, Elizabeth A., *Quest for Living God: Mapping Frontiers in the Theology of God* (New York: Continuum, 2007).

Johnson, Elizabeth A., "Redeeming the Name of Christ: Christology," in Catherine Mowry LaCugna (ed.), *Freeing Theology: The Essentials of Theology in Feminist Perspective* (San Francisco: HarperSanFrancisco, 1993), 120–7.

Johnson, Elizabeth A., *She Who Is: The Mystery of God in Feminist Theological Discourse* (New York: Crossroad, 1992).

Johnson, Keith L., *Karl Barth and the Analogia entis* (London: T&T Clark, 2010).

Jonas, Beth Felker (ed.), *The Image of God in an Image Driven Age: Explorations in Theological Anthropology* (Downers Grove, IL: Intervarsity Press, 2016).

Jones, Paul Dafydd, *The Humanity of Christ: Christology in Karl Barth's Church Dogmatics* (London: T&T Clark, 2008).

Jones, Paul Dafydd, "Liberation Theology and 'Democratic Futures' (by way of Karl Barth and Friedrich Schleiermacher)," *Political Theology* 10, no. 1 (2009): 261–85.

Jones, Serene, *Feminist Theory and Christian Theology: Cartographies of Grace* (Minneapolis, MN: Fortress Press, 2000).

Jung, Patrica Beattie, and Aana Marie Vigen, "Introduction," in Patricia Beattie Jung and Aana Marie Vigen (eds.), *God, Science, Sex, and Gender: An Interdisciplinary Approach to Christian Ethics* (Champaign: University of Illinois Press, 2010), 1–22.

Jüngel, Eberhard, "The Royal Man: A Christological Reflection on Human Dignity in Barth's Theology," in *Karl Barth: A Theological Legacy* (trans. Garrett E. Paul; Philadelphia: The Westminster Press, 1986), 127–38.

Justin Martyr, *The First Apology, The Second Apology, Dialogue with Trypho, Exhortation to the Greeks, Discourse to the Greeks, The Monarchy of the Rule of God* (trans. Thomas B. Falls; Washington, DC: Catholic University of America Press, 2008).

Kane, Robert, "Libertarianism," in John Martin Fischer, Robert Kane, Dirk Pereboom and Manuel Vargas (eds.), *Four Views on Free Will* (Oxford: Blackwell, 2007), 5–43.

Kane, Robert, "Rethinking Free Will: New Perspectives on an Ancient Problem', in Robert Kane (ed.), *The Oxford Handbook of Free Will*, 2nd ed. (Oxford: Oxford University Press, 2011), 381–404.

Kant, Immanuel, *The Conflict of the Faculties* (trans. M. J. Gregor; Lincoln: University of Nebraska, 1992).

Kant, Immanuel, *Critique of Pure Reason* (ed. and trans. Paul Guyer and Allen W. Wood; New York: Cambridge University, 1998).

Kant, Immanuel, "The Only Possible Argument in Support of a Demonstration of the Existence of God," in D. Walford and R. Meerbote (eds.), *Theoretical Philosophy 1755–1770* (Cambridge: Cambridge University Press, 2002), 107–201.

Kant, Immanuel, *Religion within the Limits of Reason Alone* (trans. T. M. Greene and H. H. Hudson; New York: Harper & Row, 1960

Kärkkäinen, Pekka, *Luthers trinitarische Theologie des Heiligen Geistes* (Mainz: Verlag Philipp von Zabern, 2005).

Kärkkäinen, Veli-Matti, *Creation and Humanity: A Constructive Christian Theology for the Pluralistic World*, vol. 3 (Grand Rapids, MI: Eerdmans, 2015).

Karle, Isolde, "Beyond Distinct Gender Identities: The Social Construction of the Human Body," in Michael Welker (ed.), *The Depth of the Human Person: A Multidisciplinary Approach* (Grand Rapids, MI: Eerdmans, 2014), 333–50.

Kasper, Walter, *The Christian Understanding of Freedom and the History of Freedom in the Modern Era* (The 1988 Père Marquette Lecture in Theology; Milwaukee: Marquette University Press, 1988).

Kasper, Walter, *The God of Jesus Christ* (trans. Matthew J. O'Connell; New York: Crossroad, 1994).

Kaufman, Gordon D., *In the Beginning…Creativity* (Minneapolis, MN: Fortress Press, 2004).

Kearney, Richard, "Ethics and the Postmodern Imagination," *Thought* 62 (1987): 39–58.

Kearney, Richard, *The Wake of Imagination: Towards a Postmodern Culture* (Minneapolis: University of Minnesota Press, 1988).

Keel, Terence, *Divine Variations: How Christian Thought Became Racial Science* (Palo Alto, CA: Stanford University Press, 2018).

Keller, Catherine, *Face of the Deep: A Theology of Becoming* (London: Routledge, 2003).

Keller, Catherine, *On the Mystery: Discerning Divinity in Process* (Minneapolis, MN: Fortress Press, 2008).

Kelly, J. N. D., *Early Christian Doctrines*, rev. ed. (New York: Harper & Row, 1978).

Kelsey, David H., *Eccentric Existence: A Theological Anthropology*, 2 vols. (Louisville: Westminster John Knox, 2009).

Kendi, Ibram X., *Stamped from the Beginning: The Definitive History of Racist Ideas in America* (New York: Nation Books, 2016).

Kennedy, Philip, *Deus Humanissimus: The Knowability of God in the Theology of Edward Schillebeeckx* (Fribourg: University Press, 1993).

Kennedy, Philip , "God and Creation," in Mary Catherine Hilkert and Robert Schreiter (eds.), *The Praxis of the Reign of God: An Introduction to the Theology of Edward Schillebeeckx* (New York: Fordham University Press, 2002), 37–58.

Kennedy, Philip, Schillebeeckx (London: Chapman, 1993).

Kilby, Karen, *Karl Rahner, A Brief Introduction* (New York: Crossroads, 2007).

Kim, Grace J-Sun, and Susan M. Shaw, *Intersectional Theology: An Introductory Guide* (Minneapolis, MN: Fortress Press, 2018).

Kim, Nami, "The 'Indigestible' Asian," in Rita Nakashima Brock, Jung Ha Kim, Kwok Pui-lan, and Seung Ai Yang (eds.), *Off the Menu: Asian and Asian North American Women's Religion and Theology* (Louisville, KY: Westminster John Knox Press, 2007), 23–44.

Kirk, J. R. Daniel, "Principalities and Powers," in Keith L. Johnson and David Lauber (eds.), *T&T Clark Companion to the Doctrine of Sin* (New York: Bloomsbury, 2016), 401–16.

Kohli, Candace, "Help for Moral Good: The Spirit, the Law, and Human Agency in Martin Luther's Antinomian Disputations (1537–40)" (PhD diss., Northwestern University, 2017).

Konings, Martijn, "Imagined Double Movements: Progressive Thought and the Specter of Neoliberal Populism," *Globalizations* 9, no. 4 (August 2012): 609–22.

Konvalinka, I., and A. Roepstorff, "The Two-Brain Approach: How Can Mutually Interacting Brains Teach Us Something about Social Interaction?," *Frontiers in Human Neuroscience* 6, no. 215 (2012): 1–10.

Koonz, Claudia, *The Nazi Conscience* (Cambridge: Belknap, 2003).

Krötke, Wolf, "The Humanity of the Human Person in Karl Barth's Anthropology," in John Webster (ed.), *Cambridge Companion to Karl Barth* (Cambridge: Cambridge University Press, 2000), 159–76.

Kuijt, Ian, "The Regeneration of Life," *Current Anthropology* 49, no. 2 (2008): 171–97.

LaCugna, Catherine Mowry, "God in Communion with Us: The Trinity," in Catherine Mowry LaCugna (ed.), *Freeing Theology* (San Francisco: HarperSanFrancisco, 1993), 83–114.

LaCugna, Catherine Mowry, *God for Us: The Trinity and Christian Life* (San Francisco: Harper, 1973).

Lai, Pan-chiu, "Barth and Universal Salvation: A Mahayana Buddhist Perspective," in Christian Collins Winn and Martha Moore-Keish (eds.), *Karl Barth and Comparative Theologies* (New York: Fordham University Press, 2019), 85–104.

Laird, Martin, *Gregory of Nyssa and the Grasp of Faith: Union, Knowledge, and Divine Presence* (Oxford: Oxford University Press, 2004).

Lambert, Pierrot, and Philip McShane, *Bernard Lonergan: His Life and Leading Ideas* (Halifax: Axial Press, 2010).

Lane, Anthony N. S., "Anthropology," in Herman J. Selderhuis (ed.), *The Calvin Handbook* (Grand Rapids, MI: Eerdmans, 2009), 275–85.

Lawson, D. M., "Understanding and Treating Children Who Experience Interpersonal Maltreatment: Empirical Findings," *Journal of Counseling and Development* 87 (2009): 204–15.

Lecky, William E. H., *The History of European Morals from Augustus to Charlemagne*, vol. 2 (New York: George Braziller, 1955).

Leftow, Brian, "Souls Dipped in Dust," in Kevin Corcoran (ed.), *Soul, Body, and Survival: Essays on the Metaphysics of Human Persons* (Ithaca, NY: Cornell University Press, 2001), 120–38.

Levy, Steven, "What Deep Blue Tells Us about AI in 2017," *Wired*, May 23, 2017. Available online: https://www.wired.com/2017/05/what-deep-blue-tells-us-about-ai-in-2017/ (accessed June 6, 2020).

Lewis, Geraint F., and Luke A. Barnes, *A Fortunate Universe: Life in a Finely Tuned Cosmos* (Cambridge: Cambridge University Press, 2016).

Lewis, Hannah, *Deaf Liberation Theology* (Explorations in Practical, Pastoral, and Empirical Theology; Burlington, VT: Ashgate Pub, 2007).

Libreria Editrice Vaticana, *Catechism of the Catholic Church* (Washington, DC: United States Conference of Catholic Bishops, 1997).

Lightsey, Pamela, *Our Lives Matter: A Womanist Queer Theology* (Eugene, OR: Pickwick, 2015).

Livingston, J. C., and F. S. Fiorenza (eds.), *Modern Christian Thought, vol. II: The Twentieth Century* (Saddle River, NJ: Prentice Hall, 2000).

Lloyd, Seth, *Programming The Universe: A Quantum Computer Scientist Takes on the Cosmos* (New York: Random House, 2007).

Lonergan, Bernard J. F., "Christ as Subject: A Reply," in Frederick E. Crowe and Robert M. Doran (eds.), *Collection* (Collected Works of Bernard Lonergan, vol. 4; New York: University of Toronto Press, 1993), 222–31.

Lonergan, Bernard J. F., "Dimensions of Meaning," in Frederick E. Crowe and Robert M. Doran (eds.), *Collection* (Collected Works of Bernard Lonergan, vol. 4; Toronto: University of Toronto Press, 1988), 232–45.

Lonergan, Bernard J. F., "*Existenz* and *Aggiornamento*," in Frederick E. Crowe and Robert M. Doran (eds.), *Collection* (Collected Works of Bernard Lonergan, vol. 4; Toronto: University of Toronto Press, 1993), 153–84.

Lonergan, Bernard J. F., "Healing and Creating in History," in John D. Dadosky and Robert M. Doran (eds.), *A Third Collection* (Collected Works of Bernard Lonergan, vol. 16; Toronto: University of Toronto Press, 2017), 94–103.

Lonergan, Bernard J. F., *The Incarnate Word* (ed. Robert Doran and Jeremy D. Wilkins; trans. Charles C. Hefling, Jr.; Collected Works of Bernard Lonergan, vol. 8; Toronto: University of Toronto Press, 2016).

Lonergan, Bernard J. F., *Insight: A Study of Human Understanding* (ed. Frederick E. Crowe and Robert M. Doran; Collected Works of Bernard Lonergan, vol. 3; Toronto: University of Toronto Press, 1992).

Lonergan, Bernard J. F., "An Interview with Fr Bernard Lonergan, S.J.," in John D. Dadosky and Robert M. Doran (eds.), *A Second Collection* (Collected Works of Bernard Lonergan, vol. 13; Toronto: University of Toronto Press, 2016), 176–94.

Lonergan, Bernard J. F., *Method in Theology* (Toronto: University of Toronto Press, 1971).

Lonergan, Bernard J. F., *Method in Theology*, 2nd ed. (Toronto: University of Toronto, 1994).

Lonergan, Bernard J. F., *Method in Theology* (ed. John D. Dadosky and Robert M. Doran; Collected Works of Bernard Lonergan, vol. 14; Toronto: University of Toronto Press, 2017).

Lonergan, Bernard J. F., "The Natural Desire to See God," in Frederick E. Crowe and Robert M. Doran (eds.), *Collection* (Collected Works of Bernard Lonergan, vol. 4; Toronto: University of Toronto Press, 1988), 81–91.

Lonergan, Bernard J. F., "Questionnaire on Philosophy: Response," in Robert C. Croken and Robert M. Doran (eds.), *Philosophical and Theological Papers, 1965–1980* (Collected Works of Bernard Lonergan, vol. 17; Toronto: University of Toronto Press, 2004), 352–83.

Lonergan, Bernard J. F., *The Redemption* (ed. Robert M. Doran, H. Daniel Monsour and Jeremy D. Wilkins; trans. Michael G. Shields; Collected Works of Bernard Lonergan, vol. 9; Toronto: University of Toronto Press, 2018).

Lonergan, Bernard J. F., "Sacralization and Secularization," in Robert C. Croken and Robert M. Doran (eds.), *Philosophical and Theological Papers, 1965–1980* (Collected Works of Bernard Lonergan, vol. 17; Toronto: University of Toronto Press, 2004), 259–81.

Lonergan, Bernard J. F., "Self-Transcendence: Intellectual, Moral, Religious," in Robert C. Croken and Robert M. Doran (eds.), *Philosophical and Theological Papers, 1965–1980* (Collected Works of Bernard Lonergan, vol. 17; Toronto: University of Toronto Press, 2004), 313–31.

Lonergan, Bernard J. F., "The Subject," in John D. Dadosky and Robert M. Doran (eds), *A Second Collection* (Collected Works of Bernard Lonergan, vol. 13; Toronto: University of Toronto Press, 2016), 60–74.

Lonergan, Bernard J. F., "Theology in Its New Context," in John D. Dadosky and Robert M. Doran (eds.), *A Second Collection* (Collected Works of Bernard Lonergan, vol. 13; Toronto: University of Toronto Press, 2016), 48–59.

Lonergan, Bernard J. F., *Verbum: Word and Idea in Aquinas* (ed. Frederick E. Crowe and Robert M. Doran; Collected Works of Bernard Lonergan, vol. 2; Toronto: University of Toronto Press, 1997).

Gabriela López-Zerón, Adrian Blow, "The Role of Relationships and Families in Healing from Trauma," *Journal of Family Therapy* 39, no. 4 (2017): 580–97.

Losinger, Anton, *The Anthropological Turn: The Human Orientation of the Theology of Karl Rahner* (New York: Fordham University Press, 2000).

Ludlow, Morwenna, *Gregory of Nyssa: Ancient and [Post]modern* (Oxford: Oxford University Press, 2007).

Luther, Martin, *Freedom of a Christian*, in John Dillenberger (ed.), *Martin Luther, Selections from His Writings* (New York: Anchor Books, 1962), 42–85.

Luther, Martin, *Luthers Werke: Kritische Gesamtausgabe [Schriften]*, 73 vols. (Weimar: H. Böhlau, 1883–2009).

Luther, Martin, *On the Bondage of the Will*, in *Luther and Erasmus: Free Will and Salvation* (ed. Gordon Rupp; Philadelphia: Westminster Press, 1969), 101–334.

The Lutheran World Federation and the Roman Catholic Church, "Joint Declaration on the Doctrine of Justification" (Grand Rapids, MI: Eerdmans, 2000).

Lyotard, Jean-François, "Answering the Question: What is Postmodernism?" (trans. Régis Durand), in Jean-François Lyotard, *The Postmodern Condition: A Report on Knowledge* (trans. Geoff Bennington and Brian Massumi; Theory and History of Literature, vol. 10; Minneapolis: University of Minnesota Press, 1984), 71–82.

Mackenzie, Adrian, and Celia Roberts, "Adopting Neuroscience: Parenting and Affective Indeterminacy," *Body & Society* 23 (2017): 130–55.

Malin, Shimon, *Nature Loves to Hide* (Oxford: Oxford University Press, 2001).

Mangu-Ward, Katherine, "Wikipedia and Beyond: Jimmy Wales' Sprawling Vision," *Reason* 39, no. 2 (June 2007): 18–29.

Mariña, Jaqueline, "Kant on Grace: A Reply to his Critics," *Religious Studies* 33 (1997): 379–400.

Markus, Robert A., *Conversion and Disenchantment in Augustine's Spiritual Career* (Villanova, PA: Villanova University Press, 1989).

Marmion, Declan, and Mary E. Hines (eds.), *The Cambridge Companion to Karl Rahner* (Cambridge: Cambridge University Press, 2005).

Martin, Raymond, and John Barresi, *The Rise and Fall of Soul and Self: An Intellectual History of Personal Identity* (New York: Columbia University Press, 2006).

Massa, Mark, SJ, *The Structure of Theological Revolutions: Models of Natural Law in American Catholic Theology* (New York: Oxford University Press, 2018).

Massingale, Bryan N., "The Erotic Life of Anti-Blackness," in Vincent W. Lloyd and Andrew Prevot (eds.), *Anti-Blackness and Christian Ethics* (Maryknoll, NY: Orbis, 2017), 173–94.

Massingale, Bryan N., "Has the Silence Been Broken? Catholic Theological Ethics and Racial Justice," *Theological Studies* 75, no. 1 (2014): 133–55.

Massingale, Bryan N., *Racial Justice and the Catholic Church* (Maryknoll, NY: Orbis, 2010).

Mateo-Seco, Lucas F., and Giulio Maspero (eds.), *The Brill Dictionary of Gregory of Nyssa* (Leiden: Brill, 2010).

May, Gehard, *Creatio Ex Nihilo: The Doctrine of 'Creation out of Nothing' in Early Christian Thought* (trans. A. S. Worrall; Edinburgh: T&T Clark, 1994).

Mayer, Emeran A., "Gut Feelings: The Emerging Biology of Gut–Brain Communication," *Nature Reviews Neuroscience* 12 (2011): 453–66.

McCabe, Herbert, *God, Christ, and Us* (ed. Brian Davies; New York: Continuum, 2003).

McCarthy, Michael H., *Authenticity as Self-Transcendence: The Enduring Insights of Bernard Lonergan* (Notre Dame, IN: University of Notre Dame Press, 2015).

McCormack, Bruce L., "Barth's Historicized Christology: How Chalcedonian Is It?," in *Orthodox and Modern: Studies in the Theology of Karl Barth* (Grand Rapids, MI: Baker Academic, 2008), 201–34.

McDade, John, SJ, "Von Balthasar and the Office of Peter in the Church," *The Way* 44 (2005): 97–114.

McDonough, Sean M., "Being and Nothingness in the Book of Revelation," in Gary A. Anderson and Markus Bockmuehl (eds.), *Creation ex Nihilo: Origins, Development, Contemporary Challenges*, (Notre Dame, IN: University of Notre Dame Press, 2017), 77–98.

McEnroy, M. Carmel, *Guests in Their Own House: The Women at Vatican II* (New York: Crossroad, 1996; repr. Eugene, OR: Wipf and Stock, 2011).

McFadyen, Alistair I., *Bound to Sin: Abuse, Holocaust and the Christian Doctrine of Sin* (Cambridge Studies in Christian Doctrine 6; Cambridge: Cambridge University Press, 2000).

McFarland, Ian, *Difference and Identity: A Theological Anthropology* (Cleveland, OH: Pilgrim Press, 2001).

McFarland, Ian, *The Divine Image: Envisioning the Invisible God* (Minneapolis, MN: Fortress Press, 2005).

McFarland, Ian, *From Nothing: A Theology of Creation* (Louisville: Westminster John Knox Press, 2014).

McGee, Timothy, "Against (White) Redemption: James Cone and the Christological Disruption of Racial Discourse and White Solidarity," *Political Theology* 18, no. 7 (2017): 542–59.

McIntosh, Mark, *Christology from Within: Incarnation and Spirituality* (Notre Dame, IN: University of Notre Dame Press, 2000).

McShane, Philip J., *Process: Introducing Themselves to Young (Christian) Minders* (Halifax: Mount Saint Vincent Press, 1990).

Meconi, David Vincent, SJ, *The One Christ: St. Augustine's Theology of Deification* (Washington, DC: Catholic University of America Press, 2013).

Medina, Néstor, *Christianity, Empire, and the Spirit: (Re)Configuring Faith and the Cultural* (Leiden: Brill, 2018).

Medina, Néstor, "The Pneumatological Dimension of Orlando Espín's Theological Work and Its Implications for Engagement with Pentecostal Communities," *Journal of Hispanic/Latino Theology*, September 16, 2010. Available online: http://www.latinotheology.org/node/96 (accessed October 12, 2010).

Menninger, Karl, *Whatever Became of Sin?* (New York: Hawthorn Books, 1973).

Mercer, Calvin, and Tracy J. Trothen (eds.), *Religion and Transhumanism: The Unknown future of Human Enhancement* (Santa Barbara, CA: Praeger, 2015).

Merriell, D. Juvenal, "Trinitarian Anthropology," in Rick van Nieuwenhove and Joseph Wawrykow (eds.), *The Theology of Thomas Aquinas* (Notre Dame, IN: University of Notre Dame Press, 2005), 123–42.

Middleton, J. Richard, *The Liberating Image: The* Imago Dei *in Genesis 1* (Grand Rapids, MI: Brazos Press, 2005).

Miles, Margaret, *Augustine on the Body* (Missoula, MT: Scholars Press, 1979).

Miller, Kenneth R., "Answering the Biochemical Argument from Design," in Mary Kathleen Cunningham (ed.), *God and Evolution: A Reader* (New York: Routledge, 2007), 159–174.

Miller, Mark T., *The Quest for God and the Good Life: Lonergan's Theological Anthropology* (Washington, DC: Catholic University of America Press, 2013).

Miller, Vincent, "The Common Good and the Market," *America Magazine* 220, no. 7 (April 1, 2019): 32–7.

Minns, Denis, *Irenaeus: An Introduction* (London: T&T Clark International, 2010).

Mirowski, Philip, *Never Let a Serious Crisis Go to Waste: How Neoliberalism Survived the Financial Meltdown* (London: Verso, 2013).

Mitchem, Stephanie Y., *Introducing Womanist Theology* (Maryknoll, NY: Orbis Books, 2002).

Molinario, Joel, "Human Fallibility and Neuroscience," in Thierry-Marie Courau, R. Ammicht-Quinn, H. Haker and Marie-Theres Wacker (eds.), *Theology, Anthropology and Neuroscience* (London: SCM Press, 2015), 87–99.

Moltmann, Jürgen, *God in Creation: A New Theology of Creation and the Spirit of God* (trans. Margaret Kohl; Minneapolis, MN: Fortress Press, 1993).

Mongrain, Kevin, *The Systematic Thought of Hans Urs von Balthasar: An Irenean Retrieval* (New York: Crossroad-Herder, 2002).

Moreland, J. P., and Scott B. Rae, *Body and Soul: Human Nature and the Crisis in Ethics* (Downers Grove, IL: InterVarsity Press, 2000).

Morrill, Bruce, *Divine Worship and Human Healing: Liturgical Theology at the Margins of Life and Death* (Collegeville, MN: Pueblo Books, 2009).

Morrison, Toni, *Beloved* (New York: Random House, 1987).

Moss, Candida R., "Heavenly Healing: Eschatological Cleansing and the Resurrection of the Dead in the Early Church," *Journal of the American Academy of Religion* 79, no. 4 (2011): 991–1017.

Moss, Candida R., and Jeremy Schipper, "Introduction," in Candida R. Moss and Jeremy Schipper (eds.), *Disability Studies and Biblical Literature* (New York: Palgrave McMillan, 2011), 1–13.

Mühling, Markus, *Resonances: Neurobiology, Evolution and Theology* (Göttingen: Vandenhoek and Ruprecht, 2014).

Muray, Leslie, "Human Uniqueness vs. Human Distinctiveness: The *Imago Dei* in the Kinship of All Creatures," *American Journal of Theology and Philosophy* 28 (2007): 299–310.

Murphy, Nancey C., *Bodies and Souls, Or Spirited Bodies?* (Cambridge: Cambridge University Press, 2006).

Murphy, Nancey C., "Human Nature: Historical, Scientific, and Religious Issues," in Warren S. Brown, Nancey C. Murphy, and H. Newton Malony (eds.), *Whatever Happened to the Soul? Scientific and Theological Portraits of Human Nature* (Minneapolis, MN: Fortress, 1998), 1–30.

Murphy, Nancey C., and Warren S. Brown, *Did My Neurons Make Me Do It?: Philosophical and Neurobiological Perspectives on Moral Responsibility* (Oxford: Oxford University Press, 2007).

Nelson, Derek R., *What's Wrong with Sin: Sin in Individual and Social Perspective from Schleiermacher to Theologies of Liberation* (London: T&T Clark, 2009).

Newberg, Andrew B., *Neurotheology: How Science Can Enlighten Us about Spirituality* (New York: Columbia University Press, 2018).

Niebuhr, H. Richard, *The Responsible Self* (New York: Harper & Row, 1966).

Nielsen, Kim E., *A Disability History of the United States* (Boston: Beacon Press, 2012).

Nietzsche, Friedrich, *Beyond Good and Evil* (trans. Walter Kaufmann; New York: Random House, 1966).

Nietzsche, Friedrich, *On Truth and Lies in the Nonmoral Sense,* in Daniel Breazeale (ed. and trans.), *Philosophy and Truth: Selections from Nietzsche's Notebooks of the Early 1870's* (Atlantic Highlands, NJ: Humanities Press International, 1979), 79–97.

Norris, Richard A. (ed.), *The Christological Controversy* (Minneapolis, MN: Fortress, 1980), 55.

Novak, Michael, "Introduction," in Jaroslaw Kupczak, OP, (ed.), *Destined for Liberty: The Human Person in the Philosophy of Karol Wojtyła/John Paul II* (Washington, DC: Catholic University of America Press, 2000), xi–xxiii.

Nowak, Kurt, *Schleiermacher: Leben, Werk und Wirkung* (Göttingen: Vandenhoeck & Ruprecht, 2001).

Oakes, Edward, *Pattern of Redemption: The Theology of Hans Urs von Balthasar* (New York: Continuum, 1994).

Oakes, Edward, *A Theology of Grace in Six Controversies* (Grand Rapids, MI: Eerdmans Publishing Company, 2016).

Oberman, Heiko A., *John Calvin and the Reformation of the Refugees* (Genève: Droz, 2009).

O'Hara, J. Martin (ed.), *Curiosity at the Center of One's Life: Statements and Questions of R. Eric O'Connor* (Montreal: Thomas More Institute, 1984).

O'Keefe, Mark, *What Are They Saying About Social Sin?* (New York: Paulist Press, 1990).

O'Malley, John, *What Happened at Vatican II* (Cambridge, MA: Harvard University Press, 2008).

Origen, *On First Principles* (trans. G. W. Butterworth; Notre Dame, IN: Christian Classics, 2013).

Ormerod, Neil, *Re-Visioning the Church: An Experiment in Systematic-Historical Ecclesiology* (Minneapolis, MN: Fortress, 2014).

Osborn, Eric, *Irenaeus of Lyons* (Cambridge: Cambridge University Press, 2001).

Painter, Nell Irvin, *The History of White People* (New York: W. W. Norton, 2010).

Panksepp, Jaak, R. Lane, M. Solms and R. Smith, "Reconciling Cognitive and Affective Neuroscience Perspectives on the Brain Basis of Emotional Experience," *Neuroscience & Biobehavioral Reviews* (2016): 1–29.

Pannenberg, Wolfhart, "Anthropology and the Question of God," in Wolfhart Pannenberg, *The Idea of God and Human Freedom* (trans. R.A. Wilson; Philadelphia: Fortress, 1973), 80–98.

Pannenberg, Wolfhart, *Anthropology in Theological Perspective* (trans. Matthew J. O'Connell; Philadelphia: Westminster Press, 1985).

Pannenberg, Wolfhart, *Systematic Theology: Vol. 2* (trans. Geoffrey W. Bromiley; Grand Rapids, MI: Eerdmans, 1994).

Papanikolaou, Aristotle, "Persons, Kenosis and Abuse: Hans Urs von Balthasar and Feminist Theologies in Conversation," *Modern Theology* 19 (January 2003): 41–65.

Parens, Erik, "Authenticity and Ambivalence: Toward Understanding the Enhancement Debate," *Hastings Center Report*, 35 (May–June 2005): 34–41.

Partee, Charles, *Calvin and Classical Philosophy* (Leiden: Brill, 1977).

Payne, Christopher, *Consumer, Credit and Neoliberalism: Governing the Modern Economy* (London: Routledge, 2012).

Peacocke, Arthur, "Biological Evolution—A Positive Theological Appraisal," in Mary Kathleen Cunningham (ed.), *God and Evolution: A Reader* (London: Routledge, 2007), 251–72.

Peck, Jamie, *Constructions of Neoliberal Reason* (Oxford: Oxford University Press, 2012).

Pelagius, "To Demetrias," in B. R. Rees (ed. and trans.), *The Letters of Pelagius and His Followers* (Woodbridge: Boydell Press, 1991), 29–70.

Pew Research Center, "83% Say Measles Vaccine Is Safe for Healthy Children," February 2015. Available online: https://www.people-press.org/2015/02/09/83-percent-say-measles-vaccine-is-safe-for-healthy-children/.

Phan, Peter, "Woman and the Last Things: A Feminist Eschatology," in Ann O'Hara Graff (ed.), *In the Embrace of God: Feminist Approaches to Theological Anthropology* (Maryknoll, NY: Orbis Books, 1995), 206–28.

Picard, Rosalind W., *Affective Computing* (Cambridge, MA: MIT Press, 2000).

Pinches, Charles, *Theology and Action: After Theory in Christian Ethics* (Grand Rapids, MI: Eerdmans, 2002).

Pitkin, Barbara, "Erasmus, Calvin, and the Faces of Stoicism in Renaissance and Reformation Thought," in John Sellars (ed.), *The Routledge Handbook of the Stoic Tradition* (London: Routledge, 2016), 145–59.

Pius XI, *Casti connubii* (http://www.vatican.va/content/pius-xi/en/encyclicals/documents/hf_p-xi_enc_19301231_casti-connubii.html).

Plato, *Phaedo* (trans. David Gallop; New York: Oxford University Press, 2009).

Plotinus, *The Enneads* (trans. Lloyd P. Gerson, George Boys-Stones, John M. Dillon, R. A. H. King, Andrew Smith, and James Wilberding; New York: Cambridge University Press, 2019).

Polkinghorne, John C., "*Creatio Continua* and Divine Action," *Science and Christian Belief* 7 (1995): 101–8.

Pontifical Council for Justice and Peace, *Compendium of the Social Doctrine of the Church* (Washington, DC: USCCB, 2005).

Post, Stephen G., "A Moral Case for Nonreductive Physicalism," in Warren Brown, Nancey Murphy, and H. Newton Malony (eds.), *Whatever Happened to the Soul?* (Minneapolis, MN: Fortress Press, 1998), 195–212.

Pothos, E. M., and J. R. Busemeyer, "Can Quantum Probability Provide a New Direction for Cognitive Modeling?," *Behavioral and Brain Sciences* 36, no. 3 (2013): 255–74.

Pramuk, Christopher, "Living in the Master's House: Race and Rhetoric in the Theology of M. Shawn Copeland," *Horizons* 32, no. 2 (2005): 295–331.

Prevot, Andrew, *Theology and Race: Black and Womanist Traditions in the United States* (Leiden: Brill, 2018).

Prevot, Andrew, *Thinking Prayer: Theology and Spirituality amid the Crises of Modernity* (Notre Dame, IN: University of Notre Dame Press, 2015).

Puffer, Matthew, "Taking Exception to the *Grenzfall*'s Reception: Revisiting Karl Barth's Ethics of War," *Modern Theology* 28 (2012): 478–502.

Pui-lan, Kwok, "Fishing the Asia Pacific: Transnationalism and Feminist Theology," in Rita Nakashima Brock, Jung Ha Kim, Kwok Pui-lan and Seung Ai Yang (eds.), *Off the Menu: Asian and Asian North American Women's Religion and Theology* (Louisville, KY: Westminster John Knox Press, 2007), 3–22.

Quash, Ben, *Theology and the Drama of History* (Cambridge: Cambridge University Press, 2005).

Rahner, Karl, *Foundations of Christian Faith: An Introduction to the Idea of Christianity* (trans. William Dych; New York: Seabury Press/Crossroad, 1978).

Rahner, Karl, "Man (Anthropology), III. Theological," in Karl Rahner (ed.), *Encyclopedia of Theology: The Concise* (Sacramentum Mundi; New York: Crossroad, 1984), 887–93.

Rahner, Karl, *On the Theology of Death* (trans. C. H. Henkey; New York: Seabury Press, 1973).

Rahner, Karl, "Theology and Anthropology," in Karl Rahner, *Theological Investigations, Vol. IX* (trans. Graham Harrison; New York: Herder and Herder, 1972), 28–45.

Rahner, Karl, "Thoughts on the Possibility of Belief Today," in Karl Rahner (ed.), *Theological Investigations V: Later Writings* (trans. Karl-H. Kruger; Baltimore: Helicon, 1966), 3–22.

Rahner, Karl, "Zur Theologie des Todes," *Zeitschrift für katholische Theologie* 79, no. 1 (1957): 1–44.

Rakoczy, Susan, I.H.M., "Mixed Messages: John Paul II's Writings on Women," in Gerard Mannion (ed.), *The Vision of John Paul II: Assessing His Thought and Influence* (Collegeville, MN: Liturgical Press, 2008), 159–83.

Reinders, Hans S., *The Future of the Disabled in Liberal Society : An Ethical Analysis*, (Notre Dame, IN: University of Notre Dame Press, 2000).

Reinders, Hans S., *Receiving the Gift of Friendship: Profound Disability, Theological Anthropology, and Ethics* (Grand Rapids, MI: Eerdmans, 2008).

Reno, R. R., "Rahner the Restorationist," *First Things* 233 (May 2013): 45–51.

Reynolds, Thomas E., *Vulnerable Communion: A Theology of Disability and Hospitality* (Grand Rapids, MI: Brazos Press, 2008).

Rickabaugh, Brandon L., "Responding to N.T. Wright's Rejection of the Soul: A Defense of Substance Dualism," an unpublished presentation at the Society of Vineyard Scholars Conference, Minnesota. http://www.academia.edu/1966881/ (accessed April 28, 2012).

Rist, John, *Augustine: Ancient Thought Baptized* (Cambridge: Cambridge University Press, 1994).

Robinette, Brian D., "The Difference Nothing Makes: *Creatio Ex Nihilo*, Resurrection, and Divine Gratuity," *Theological Studies* 72 (2011): 525–57.

Romero, Miguel J., "The Happiness of 'Those Who Lack the Use of Reason'," *The Thomist: A Speculative Quarterly Review* 80, no. 1 (2016): 49–96.

Ross, Susan A., *Anthropology: Seeking Light and Beauty* (Engaging Theology: Catholic Perspectives; Collegeville, MN: Liturgical Press, 2012).

Ross, Susan A., "The Bridegroom and the Bride: The Theological Anthropology of John Paul II and Its Relation to the Bible and Homosexuality," in Patricia Beattie Jung, with Joseph Andrew Coray (eds.), *Sexual Diversity and Catholicism: Toward the Development of Moral Theology* (Collegeville, MN: Liturgical Press, 2001), 39–49.

Rossi, Philip J., "Reading Kant from a Catholic Horizon: Ethics and the Anthropology of Grace," *Theological Studies*, vol. 71 (2010), 79–100.

Roughgarden, Joan, "Evolutionary Biology and Sexual Diversity," in Patricia Beattie Jung and Aana Marie Vigen (eds.), *God, Science, Sex, Gender: An Interdisciplinary Approach to Christian Ethics* (Urbana: University of Illinois Press, 2010), 89–104.

Rovelli, Carlo, *Seven Brief Lessons on Physics* (London: Alan Lane, 2015).

Rubenstein, Mary-Jane, "Cosmic Singularities: On the Nothing and the Sovereign," *Journal of the American Academy of Religion* 80 (2012): 485–517.

Rubio, Julie Hanlon, "Moral Cooperation with Evil and Social Ethics," *Journal of the Society of Christian Ethics* 31, no. 1 (Spring/Summer 2011): 103–22.

Ruether, Rosemary Radford, "The Collision of History and Doctrine: The Brothers of Jesus and the Virginity of Mary," *Continuum* 7, no. 1 (Winter 1969): 93–105.

Ruether, Rosemary Radford, "Conference Report: The World Parliament and Religious Diversity," *Feminist Theology* 26 (January 2001): 121–8.

Ruether, Rosemary Radford, "Consciousness-Raising at Puebla: Women Speak to the Latin Church," *Christianity and Crisis* (April 1, 1979): 77–80.

Ruether, Rosemary Radford, *Disputed Questions: On Being a Christian* (Nashville, TN: Abingdon, 1982).

Ruether, Rosemary Radford, *Gaia and God: An Ecofeminist Theology of Earth Healing* (San Francisco: Harper Collins, 1992).

Ruether, Rosemary Radford, *Introducing Redemption in Christian Feminism* (Sheffield: Sheffield Academic Press, 1998).

Ruether, Rosemary Radford, "My Ecumenical and Interfaith Journey," *Journal of Ecumenical Studies* 49, no. 1 (2014): 159–65.

Ruether, Rosemary Radford, *New Woman New Earth: Sexist Ideologies & Human Liberation* (New York: Seabury Press, 1975).

Ruether, Rosemary Radford (ed.), *Religion and Sexism: Images of Woman in the Jewish and Christian Traditions* (New York: Simon and Schuster, 1974).

Ruether, Rosemary Radford, *Sexism and God-Talk: Toward a Feminist Theology* (Boston: Beacon Press, 1993).

Ruether, Rosemary Radford, *To Change the World: Christology and Cultural Criticism* (New York: Crossroad, 1981).

Ruether, Rosemary Radford, *Women and Redemption: A Theological History* (Minneapolis, MN: Fortress Press, 1998).

Ruether, Rosemary Radford, *Women-Church: Theology and Practice* (San Francisco: Harper and Row, 1985).

Ruether, Rosemary Radford, and Eleanor McLaughlin (eds.), *Women of Spirit: Female Leadership in the Jewish and Christian Traditions* (New York: Simon and Schuster, 1979).

Ruether, Rosemary Radford, and Rosemary Skinner Keller (eds.), *Women and Religion in America* (San Francisco: Harper & Row, 1981).

Russell, Heidi, "Quantum Anthropology: Reimaging the Human Person as Body/Spirit," *Theological Studies* 74 (2013): 934–59.

Russell, Heidi, *Quantum Shift: Theological and Pastoral Implications of Contemporary Developments in Science* (Collegeville, MN: Liturgical Press, 2015).

Russell, Norman, *The Doctrine of Deification in the Greek Patristic Tradition* (Oxford: Oxford University Press, 2006).

Salomon, Daniel Aaron, *Confessions of an Autistic Theologian: A Contextual, Liberation Theology* (CreateSpace Independent Publishing Platform, 2013).

Salzman, Todd A., and Michael G. Lawler, "Theology, Science, and Sexual Anthropology: A Methodological Investigation," *Journal of Religion and Society: Supplement* 11 (2015): 46–72.

Saracino, Michele, *Being about Borders: A Christian Anthropology of Difference* (Collegeville, MN: Liturgical Press, 2011).

Saracino, Michele, *Christian Anthropology: An Introduction to the Human Person* (Mahwah, NY: Paulist Press, 2015).

Saracino, Michele, and Robert J. Rivera (eds.), *Enfleshing Theology: Embodiment, Discipleship, and Politics in the Work of M. Shawn Copeland* (Lanham, MD: Lexington, 2018).

Sarna, Nahum, *Genesis* (JPS Torah Commentary; Philadelphia: Jewish Publication Society, 1989).

Saussure, Ferdinand de, *Course in General Linguistics*, 3rd ed. (trans. R. Harris; Chicago: Open Court, 1986).

Schilbach, Leonhard, Bert Timmermans, Vasudevi Reddy, Alan Costall, Gary Bente, Tobias
    Schlicht, and Kai Vogeley, "Toward a Second-Person Neuroscience," *Behavioral and Brain
    Sciences*, 36, no. 4 (2013): 393–414.

Schillebeeckx, Edward, *Christ: The Christian Experience in the Modern World* (trans. John
    Bowden; London: SCM, 1980).

Schillebeeckx, Edward, *Christ: The Christian Experience in the Modern World* (trans. John
    Bowden, Marcelle Manley and Ted Schoof; Edward Schillebeeckx Collected Works, vol. 7;
    New York: Bloomsbury, 2014).

Schillebeeckx, Edward, "The Church as the Sacrament of Dialogue," in *God the Future of Man*
    (New York: Sheed & Ward, 1968), 119–142.

Schillebeeckx, Edward, *Church: The Human Story of God* (trans. John Bowden;
    New York: Crossroad, 1990).

Schillebeeckx, Edward, *Church: The Human Story of God* (trans. John Bowden and Ted Schoof;
    Edward Schillebeeckx Collected Works, vol. 10; New York: Bloomsbury, 2014).

Schillebeeckx, Edward, *God Is New Each Moment: Edward Schillebeeckx in Conversation with
    Huub Oosterhuis and Piet Hoogeveen* (trans. David Smith; New York: Seabury, 1983).

Schillebeeckx, Edward, *I am a Happy Theologian: Conversations with Francesco Strazzari* (trans.
    John Bowden; New York: Crossroad, 1994).

Schillebeeckx, Edward, *Interim Report on the Books Jesus and Christ* (trans. John Bowden;
    London: SCM Press, 1980).

Schillebeeckx, Edward, *Interim Report on the Books Jesus and Christ* (trans. John Bowden;
    Edward Schillebeeckx Collected Works, vol. 8; New York: Bloomsbury, 2014).

Schillebeeckx, Edward, *Jesus: An Experiment in Christology* (New York: Collins and
    Crossroad, 1979).

Schillebeeckx, Edward, *Jesus: An Experiment in Christology* (trans. John Bowden and Marcelle
    Manley; Edward Schillebeeckx Collected Works, Vol. 6; New York: Bloomsbury, 2014).

Schillebeeckx, Edward, "Plezier en woede beleven aan Gods schepping," *Tijdschrift voor
    Theologie* 33 (1993): 325–47.

Schillebeeckx, Edward, *The Understanding of Faith: Interpretation and Criticism* (trans. N. D.
    Smith; London: Sheed and Ward, 1974).

Schillebeeckx, Edward, *The Understanding of Faith: Interpretation and Criticism* (trans. N.D. Smith
    and Ted Schoof; Edward Schillebeeckx Collected Works, vol. 5; New York: Bloomsbury, 2014).

Schindler, David L., "Being, Gift, Self-Gift: A Reply to Waldstein on Relationality and John Paul
    II's Theology of the Body (Part One)," *Communio* 42 (2015): 221–51.

Schleiermacher, Friedrich, *Brief Outline of Theology as a Field of Study* (trans. Terrence N. Tice;
    Louisville: Westminster John Knox, 2011).

Schleiermacher, Friedrich, *Christian Faith: A New Translation and Critical Edition* (ed. Catherine
    L. Kelsey and Terrence N. Tice; trans. Terrence N. Tice, Catherine L. Kelsey and Edwina
    Lawler; Louisville: Westminster John Knox, 2016).

Schleiermacher, Friedrich, *On the Glaubenslehre: Two Letters to Dr. Lücke* (trans. J. Duke and F.
    Fiorenza; Atlanta: Scholars, 1981).

Schleiermacher, Friedrich, "Pentecost Sunday (May 1825), 1 Corinthians 2:10–12," in
    Schleiermacher: Christmas Dialogue, The Second Speech, and Other Selections (ed. and trans.
    Julia A. Lamm; New York: Paulist, 2014), 224–40.

Schleiermacher, Friedrich, "The Second Speech: 'On the Essence of Religion' (1806)," in
    Schleiermacher: Christmas Dialogue, The Second Speech, and Other Selections (ed. and trans.
    Julia A. Lamm; New York: Paulist, 2014), 152–223.

Schleiermacher, Friedrich, "To F.H. Jacobi. Berlin, March 30, 1818," in *Schleiermacher: Christmas Dialogue, The Second Speech, and Other Selections* (ed. and trans. Julia A. Lamm; New York: Paulist, 2014), 262.

Schneiders, Sandra M., *With Oil in Their Lamps: Faith, Feminism, and the Future* (New York: Paulist Press, 2000).

Schoof, Ted, "E. Schillebeeckx: 25 years in Nijmegen," *Theology Digest* 37, no. 4 (Winter, 1990): 313–31.

Schore, Allan N., "Effects of a Secure Attachment Relationship on Right Brain Development, Affect Regulation, and Infant Mental Health," *Infant Mental Health Journal* 22 (2001): 7–66.

Schore, Allan N., "The Effects of Early Relational Trauma on Right Brain Development, Affect Regulation, and Infant Mental Health," *Infant Mental Health Journal* 22 (2001): 201–69.

Schreiter, Robert (ed.), *The Schillebeeckx Reader* (New York: Crossroad, 1984).

Schreiter, Robert, "Edward Schillebeeckx: An Orientation to His Thought," in Robert Schreiter (ed.), *The Schillebeeckx Reader* (New York: Crossroad, 1984), 1–24.

Schüssler Fiorenza, Elisabeth, "Between Movement and Academy: Feminist Biblical Studies in the Twentieth Century," in Elisabeth Schüssler Fiorenza (ed.) *Feminist Biblical Studies in the Twentieth Century: Scholarship and Movement* (Atlanta: Society of Biblical Literature, 2014), 1–18.

Schüssler Fiorenza, Elisabeth, *But She Said: Feminist Practices of Biblical Interpretation* (Boston: Beacon Press, 1992).

Schüssler Fiorenza. Francis, "Method in Theology," in Declan Marmion and Mary Hines (eds.), *The Cambridge Companion to Karl Rahner* (Cambridge: Cambridge University Press, 2005), 65–82.

Schweizer, Eduard, "*Soma*," in Gerhard Friedrich and Geoffrey W. Bromiley (eds.), *Theological Dictionary of the New Testament Theology, Volume 7* (trans. Geoffrey W. Bromiley; Grand Rapids, MI: Eerdmans, 1971), 1024–94.

Searle, John R., *Consciousness and Language* (New York: Cambridge University Press, 2002).

Searle, John R., *The Rediscovery of the Mind* (Cambridge: MIT Press, 1992).

Sewell, Alida Leni, *Calvin and the Body: An Inquiry into his Anthropology* (Amsterdam: VU University Press, 2011).

Shanley, Brian, "Divine Causation and Human Freedom in Aquinas," *American Catholic Philosophical Quarterly* 72 (1998): 99–122.

Sheehan, James J., *German History, 1770–1866* (New York: Oxford University, 1989).

Sheveland, John, "Do Not Grieve: Reconciliation in Barth and Vedanta Desika," in Christian Collins Winn and Martha Moore-Keish (eds.), *Karl Barth and Comparative Theologies* (New York: Fordham University Press, 2019), 184–202.

Siebers, Tobin, *Disability Theory* (Ann Arbor: University of Michigan Press, 2008).

Siegel, Daniel J., *The Developing Mind: How Relationships and the Brain Interact to Shape Who We Are*, 2nd ed. (New York: Guilford, 2012).

Sikorski, John, "Towards a Conjugal Spirituality: Karol Wojtyła's Vision of Marriage Before, During, and After Vatican II," *Journal of Moral Theology* 6, no. 2 (2017): 103–29.

Silverman, Emily Leah, Dirk Von Der Horst and Whitney Bauman (eds.), *Voices of Feminist Liberation: Writings in Celebration of Rosemary Radford Ruether* (London: Taylor & Francis Group, 2014).

Singler, Beth, "An Introduction to Artificial Intelligence and Religion for the Religious Studies Scholar," *Implicit Religion* 20, no. 3 (2017): 215–31.

Slenczka, Notger, "Luther's Anthropology," in Robert Kolb, Irene Dingel, and L'Ubomir Batka (eds.), *The Oxford Handbook of Martin Luther's Theology* (Oxford: Oxford University Press, 2014), 212–32.

Smit, Dirk J., "On Reading Karl Barth in South Africa Today," in Robert R. Vosloo (ed.), *Essays on Being Reformed: Collected Essays 3* (Stellenbosch: Sun Press, 2009), 275–92.

Smith, J. Warren, "The Body of Paradise and the Body of the Resurrection: Gender and the Angelic Life in Gregory of Nyssa's *De hominis opificio*," *Harvard Theological Review* 92, no. 2 (2006): 207–28.

Smith, J. Warren, *Passion and Paradise: Human and Divine Emotion in the Thought of Gregory of Nyssa* (New York: Crossroad, 2004).

Sokolowski, Robert, "The Method of Philosophy: Making Distinctions," *Review of Metaphysics* 51 (1998): 515–32.

Soskice, Janet, "Why *Creatio ex nihilo* for Theology Today?," in Gary A. Anderson and Markus Bockmuehl (eds.), *Creation ex Nihilo: Origins, Development, Contemporary Challenges* (Notre Dame: University of Notre Dame Press, 2018), 37–54.

Spezio, Michael L., "Social Neuroscience and Theistic Evolution: Intersubjectivity, Love, and the Social Sphere," *Zygon* 48 (2013): 428–38.

Spezzano, Daria, *The Glory of God's Grace: Deification According to Saint Thomas Aquinas* (Ave Maria, FL: Sapientia Press, 2015).

Spinello, Richard A., "Karol Wojtyla on Artificial Moral Agency and Moral Accountability," *National Catholic Bioethics Quarterly* 11, no. 3 (2011): 479–501.

Stapp, Henry P., *Quantum Theory and Free Will* (New York: Springer International, 2017).

Stauffer, Richard, *Dieu, la création et la Providence dans la prédication de Calvin* (Bern: Peter Lang, 1978).

Steane, Andrew, *Science and Humanity: A Humane Philosophy of Science and Religion* (Oxford: Oxford University Press, 2018).

Steele, Diane Marie, *Creation and Cross in the Later Soteriology of Edward Schillebeeckx* (PhD diss., University of Notre Dame, 2000), 303.

Steenberg, M. C., "Children in Paradise: Adam and Eve as 'Infants' in Irenaeus of Lyons," *Journal of Early Christian Studies*, vol. 12, n. 1 (2004): 1–22.

Steenberg, M. C., *Irenaeus on Creation: The Cosmic Christ and the Saga of Redemption* (Leiden: Brill Academic Publishers, 2008).

Stegman, Thomas D., SJ, "'Actualization': How John Paul II Utilizes Scripture in the Theology of the Body," in John M. McDermott and John Gavin (eds.), *Pope John Paul II on the Body: Human, Eucharistic, Ecclesial* (Festschrift Avery Cardinal Dulles, SJ; Philadelphia: Saint Joseph's University Press, 2007), 47–64.

Steiner, George, *Real Presences* (Chicago: University of Chicago Press, 1989).

Stoeger, William, "The Mind-Brain Problem, the Laws of Nature, and Constitutive Relationships," in Robert John Russell, Nancey Murphy, Theo C. Meyering and Michael A. Arbib (eds.), *Neuroscience and the Person: Scientific Perspectives on Divine Action* (Series on Scientific Perspectives on Divine Action; Vatican City State: Vatican Observatory Publications and The Center for Theology and the Natural Sciences, 1999), 129–46.

Stout, D., and T. Chaminade, "Stone Tools, Language and the Brain in Human Evolution," *Philosophical Transactions of the Royal Society B: Biological Sciences* 367, no. 1585 (2012): 75–87.

Stump, Eleonore, "Non-Cartesian Substance Dualism and Materialism without Reductionism," *Faith and Philosophy* 12, no. 4 (1995): 505–31.

Swidler, Leonard, and Arlene Swidler (eds.), *Women Priests: A Catholic Commentary on the Vatican Declaration* (New York: Paulist Press, 1977).

Swiezawski, Stefan, "Introduction," in Karol Wojtyła, *Person and Community: Selected Essays* (trans. Theresa Sandok, OSM; New York: Peter Lang, 1993), ix–xvi.

Swinton, John, "From Inclusion to Belonging: A Practical Theology of Community, Disability and Humanness," *Journal of Religion, Disability & Health* 16, no. 2 (April 1, 2012): 172–90.

Swinton, John, "Who Is the God We Worship? Theologies of Disability; Challenges and New Possibilities," *International Journal of Practical Theology* 14, no. 2 (2011): 273–307.

Tanner, Kathryn, *Christ the Key* (New York: Cambridge University Press, 2010).

Tanner, Kathryn, *God and Creation in Christian Theology* (Minneapolis, MN: Fortress Press, 2005).

Tanner, Kathryn, *Jesus, Humanity, and the Trinity: A Brief Systematic Theology* (Minneapolis, MN: Fortress Press, 2001).

Taylor, Charles, *Hegel and Modern Society* (Cambridge: Cambridge University Press, 1979).

Taylor, Charles, *Modern Social Imaginaries* (Durham: Duke University Press, 2004).

Taylor, Charles, *A Secular Age* (Cambridge, MA: The Belknap Press of Harvard University, 2007).

Taylor, Charles, *Sources of the Self: The Making of the Modern Identity* (Cambridge, MA: Cambridge University Press, 1989).

Taylor, Laura, "Redeeming Christ: Imitation or (Re)citation?," in Susan Abraham and Elena Procario-Foley (eds.), *Frontiers in Catholic Feminist Theology: Shoulder to Shoulder* (Minneapolis, MN: Fortress Press, 2009), 119–40.

te Velde, Rudi, *Aquinas on God: The 'Divine Science' of the Summa Theologiae* (Burlington, VT: Ashgate, 2006).

te Velde, Rudi, "Evil, Sin, and Death: Thomas Aquinas on Original Sin," in Rick van Nieuwenhove and Joseph Wawrykow (eds.), *The Theology of Thomas Aquinas* (Notre Dame, IN: University of Notre Dame Press, 2005), 143–66.

Teel, Karen, *Racism and the Image of God* (New York: Palgrave Macmillan, 2010).

Tennie, Claudio, Josep Call, and Michael Tomasello, "Ratcheting Up the Ratchet: On the Evolution of Cumulative Culture," *Philosophical Transactions of the Royal Society B: Biological Sciences* 364, no. 1528 (2009): 2405–15.

Teske, Roland, "Soul," in Allan Fitzgerald (ed.), *Augustine through the Ages* (Grand Rapids, MI: Eerdmans, 1999), 807–12.

Thatcher, Adrian (ed.), *The Oxford Handbook of Theology, Sexuality and Gender* (Oxford Handbooks Online, 2014), DOI:10.1093/oxfordhb/9780199664153.013.33.

Theophilus of Antioch, *To Autolycus*, in Alexander Roberts and James Donaldson (eds.), *The Ante-Nicene Fathers: Vol. 2* (Peabody: Hendrickson, 1994), 89–122.

Thompson, John, "Barth and Balthasar: An Ecumenical Dialogue," in Bede McGregor, OP, and Thomas Norris (eds.), *The Beauty of Christ: An Introduction to the Theology of Hans Urs von Balthasar* (Edinburgh: T & T Clark, 1994), 171–92.

Thompson, John L., "*Creata ad imagem dei, licet secundo gradu*: Woman as the Image of God according to John Calvin," *Harvard Theological Review* 81 (1988): 125–43.

Thurman, Howard, *Jesus and the Disinherited* (Boston: Beacon Press, 1976).

Tickle-Degnen, Linda, and Robert Rosenthal, "The Nature of Rapport and Its Nonverbal Correlates," *Psychological Inquiry* 1, no. 4 (1990): 285–93.

Tonstad, Linn Marie, *God and Difference: The Trinity, Sexuality, and the Transformation of Finitude* (New York: Routledge, 2017).

Torrance, Thomas F., *Calvin's Doctrine of Man* (London: Lutterworth Press, 1949).

Torrell, Jean–Pierre, *Saint Thomas Aquinas. Vol. 2, Spiritual Master* (trans. Robert Royal; Washington, DC: Catholic University of America Press, 2003).

Traina, Cristina L. H., "Whose *Sensus*? Which *Fidelium*?," in Bradford E. Hinze and Peter C. Phan (eds.), *Learning from All the Faithful* (Eugene, OR: Pickwick), 155–69.

Trent, "Decree on Justification," in H. J. Schroeder (trans.), *The Canons and Decrees of the Council of Trent* (Charlotte, NC: TAN Books, 1978), 29–45.

Trible, Phyllis, "Depatriarchalizing in Biblical Interpretation," *Journal of the American Academy of Religion* 41, no. 1 (March 1973): 30–48.

Trible, Phyllis, *God and the Rhetoric of Sexuality* (Minneapolis, MN: Fortress Press, 1978).

Turek, Margaret, *Towards a Theology of God the Father: Hans Urs von Balthasar's Theodramatic Approach* (New York: Peter Lang, 2001).

Turing, Alan M., "I.—Computing Machinery and Intelligence," *Mind* LIX, no. 236 (October 1950): 433–60.

Turkle, Sherry, *Alone Together: Why We Expect More from Technology and Less from Each Other* (New York: Basic Books, 2011).

Turner, Bryan S., *Religion and Social Theory*, 2nd ed. (London: SAGE, 1991).

UN Women, "Gender Equality: Where Are We Today?," September 2020. Available online: http://www.unwomen.org/en/digital-library/multimedia/2015/9/infographic-gender-equality-where-are-we-today (accessed September 12, 2020).

van der Kooi, Cornelis, "Christology," in Herman J. Selderhuis (ed.), *The Calvin Handbook* (Grand Rapids, MI: Eerdmans, 2009), 257–67.

Van Erp, Stephan and Daniel Minch (eds.), *The T & T Clark Handbook of Edward Schillebeeckx* (London: Bloomsbury, 2019).

van Huyssteen, J. Wentzel, *Alone in the World? Human Uniqueness in Science and Technology* (Grand Rapids, MI: Eerdmans, 2006).

van Nieuwenhove, Rick. and Joseph Wawrykow (eds.), *The Theology of Thomas Aquinas* (Notre Dame, IN: University of Notre Dame Press, 2005).

Van Vliet, Jason, *Children of God: The Imago Dei in John Calvin and His Context* (Göttingen: Vandenhoeck & Ruprecht, 2009).

Vander Schel, Kevin, *Embedded Grace: Christ, History, and the Reign of God in Schleiermacher's Dogmatics* (Minneapolis, MN: Fortress, 2013).

Vannier, Marie-Anne, "L'Anthropologie de S. Augustin," in Barbara Feichtinger, Stephen Lake and Helmut Seng (eds.), *Körper und Seele: Aspekte spätantiker Anthropologie* (Munich: K.G. Saur, 2006), 207–36.

Vasko, Elisabeth, *Beyond Apathy: A Theology for Bystanders* (Minneapolis, MN: Fortress, 2015).

Vatican Council II, *Gaudium et spes*, in Walter M. Abbot (ed.), *The Documents of Vatican II* (New York: Guild Press, 1966).

Vatican Council II, *Gaudium et spes*, in Austin Flannery, OP (ed.), *Vatican II: The Conciliar and Post-Conciliar Documents* (Northrup, NY: Costello, 1992).

Vatican Council II, *Lumen Gentium*, in Austin Flannery, OP (ed.), *Vatican II: The Conciliar and Post-Conciliar Documents* (Northrup, NY: Costello, 1992).

Verhees, Jacques, "Heiliger Geist und Inkarnation: Unlöslicher Zusammenhang zwischen Theologie und Ökonomie," *Revue des études Augustiniennes* 22 (1976): 234–53.

Vial, Theodore, *Modern Religion, Modern Race* (New York: Oxford University, 2016).

Vicini, Andrea, and Agnes Brazal, "Longing for Transcendence: Cyborgs and Trans- and Posthumans," *Theological Studies*, 76 (2015): 148–65.

Vienne, "Decree 1," http://www.ewtn.com/library/councils/vienne.htm (accessed May 14, 2018).

Villa-Vicencio, Charles (ed.), *On Reading Karl Barth in South Africa* (Grand Rapids, MI: Eerdmans, 1988).

Vind, Anna, "The Human Being According to Luther," in Anne Eusterschulte and Hannah Wälzholz (eds.), *Anthropological Reformations-Anthropology in the Era of Reformation* (Refo500 Academic Studies; Göttingen: Vandenhoeck & Ruprecht, 2015), 69–86.

Von Rad, Gerhard, *Genesis*, rev. ed. (trans. John H. Marks; Old Testament Library; Louisville: Westminster John Knox Press, 1973).

Vos, Antonie, "John Duns Scotus: An Anthropology of Dignity and Love," in Joseph Chinnici (ed.), *Words Made Flesh: Essays Honoring Kenan B. Osborne, OFM* (St. Bonvaventure, NY: Franciscan Institute, 2011).

Voss Roberts, Michelle, *Body Parts: A Theological Anthropology* (Minneapolis, MN: Fortress Press, 2017).

Waldstein, Michael, "Introduction," in John Paul II, *Man and Woman He Created Them: A Theology of the Body*, 2nd ed. (trans. Michael Waldstein; Boston: Pauline Books & Media, 2006), 1–128.

Walker, Alice, *In Search of Our Mothers' Gardens* (Orlando, FL: Harcourt, 1983).

Wall, Glenda, "'Love Builds Brains': Representations of Attachment and Children's Brain Development in Parenting Education Material," *Sociology of Health & Illness* 40 (2018): 395–409.

Wannenwetsch, Bernd, "A Love Formed by Faith: Relating Theological Virtues in Augustine and Luther," in Robert Song and Brent Waters (eds.), *The Authority of the Gospel: Explorations in Moral and Political Theology in Honor of Oliver O'Donovan* (Grand Rapids, MI: Eerdmans, 2015), 1–32.

Ward, Keith, *Defending the Soul* (Oxford: Oneworld, 1992).

Ward, Keith, *More than Matter: Is There More to Life than Molecules?* (Grand Rapids, MI: Eerdmans, 2011).

Waters, B., "Whose Salvation, Whose Eschatology?," in Ronald Cole-Turner (ed.), *Transhumanism and Transcendence: Christian Hope in an Age of Technological Enhancement* (Washington DC: Georgetown University Press, 2011), 163–76.

Wawrykow, Joseph, "Grace," in Rick van Nieuwenhove and Joseph Wawrykow (eds.), *The Theology of Thomas Aquinas* (Notre Dame, IN: University of Notre Dame Press, 2005), 192–221.

Waytz, Adam, "Psychology beyond the Brain: What Scientists Are Discovering by Measuring the Beating of the Heart," *Scientific American*, October 5, 2010 Avaiable online: https://www.scientificamerican.com/article/the-neuroscience-of-heart/ (accessed August 13, 2018).

Weaver, Darlene Fozard, *The Acting Person and Christian Moral Life* (Washington, DC: Georgetown University Press, 2011).

Weaver, Darlene Fozard, "Death," in Gilbert Meilaender and William Werpehowski (eds.), *Oxford Handbook of Theological Ethics* (Oxford: Oxford University Press, 2005), 254–70.

Weber, Max, *The Protestant Ethic and the Spirit of Capitalism* (trans. Talcott Parsons; New York: Routledge, 2001).

Weigel, George, *Witness to Hope: The Biography of John Paul II* (New York: Harper Collins, 2001).

Welker, Michael, "Introduction," in *The Depth of the Human Person: A Multidisciplinary Approach* (Grand Rapids, MI: Eerdmans, 2014), 1–14.

Wendell, Susan, *The Rejected Body: Feminist Philosophical Reflections on Disability* (New York: Routledge, 1996).

West, Traci C., *Disruptive Christian Ethics: When Racism and Women's Lives Matter* (Louisville, KY: Westminster John Knox Press, 2006).

White, Andrea C., "The Political Theology of Karl Barth: Why a Womanist Theologian Should Care," *Karl Barth Society of North America Newsletter* No. 52 (November 2016).

White, Graham, *Luther as Nominalist: A Study of the Logical Methods Used in Martin Luther's Disputations in the Light of Their Medieval Background* (Schriften der Luther-Agricola-Gesellschaft 30; Helsinki: Luther-Agricola-Society, 1994).

White, Jr., Lynn, "The Historical Roots of our Ecologic Crisis," *Science* 155 (1968): 1203–7.

White, Stephen K., *Political Theory and Postmodernism* (Modern European Philosophy; Cambridge: Cambridge University Press, 1991).

Whitmore, Todd, "Catholic Social Teaching: Starting with the Common Good," in Kathleen Mass Weigert and Alexia K. Kelley (eds.), *Living the Catholic Social Tradition: Cases and Commentary* (Lanham: Rowman & Littlefield, 2005).

Wilken, Robert Louis, "Biblical Humanism: The Patristic Convictions," in Richard Lints, Michael S. Horton and Mark R. Talbot (eds.), *Personal Identity in Theological Perspective* (Grand Rapids, MI: Eerdmans, 2006), 13–28.

Wilkins, Jeremy D., *Before Truth: Lonergan, Aquinas, and the Problem of Wisdom* (Washington, DC: Catholic University of America Press, 2018).

Williams, Delores, *Sisters in the Wilderness: The Challenge of Womanist God-Talk* (Maryknoll, NY: Orbis, 1993).

Williams, Rowan, "Balthasar and Difference," in Rowan Williams, *Wrestling With Angels: Conversations in Modern Theology* (ed. Mike Higton; Grand Rapids, MI: Eerdmans, 2007), 77–85.

Williams, Rowan, "Balthasar and Rahner", in John Riches (ed.), *The Analogy of Beauty: The Theology of Hans Urs von Balthasar* (Edinburgh: T&T Clark, 1996), 11–34.

Williams, Rowan, "On Being Creatures," in Rowan Williams, *On Christian Theology* (Oxford: Blackwell Publishing, 2000), 63–78.

Williams, Rowan, "The Paradoxes of Self-Knowledge in the *De trinitate*," in Joseph Lienhard, Earl Muller, and Roland Teske (eds.), *Augustine: Presbyter Factus Sum* (New York: Peter Lang, 1993), 121–34.

Willimon, William H., *Pastor: The Theology and Practice of Ordained Ministry* (Nashville: Abingdon Press, 2010).

Wilson, John Paul, Kurt Hugenberg and Nicholas O. Rule, "Racial Bias in Judgments of Physical Size and Formidability: From Size to Threat," *Journal of Personality and Social Psychology* 113, no. 1 (2017): 59–80.

Winn, Christian Collins, and Martha Moore-Keish (eds.), *Karl Barth and Comparative Theologies* (New York: Fordham University Press, 2019).

Wojtyła, Karol, *The Acting Person* (trans. Andrzej Potocki; Dordrecht: D. Reidel, 1979).

Wojtyła, Karol, *The Collected Plays and Writings on Theater* (trans. Boleslaw Toberski; Oakland: University of California Press, 1987).

Wojtyła, Karol, "From *The Controversy about Man*," in Alfred Bloch and George T. Czuczka (eds.), *Toward a Philosophy of Praxis* (trans. George Czuczka; New York: Crossroad, 1981).

Wojtyła, Karol, *Love and Responsibility* (trans. H. T. Willetts; San Francisco: Ignatius Press, 1993).

Wojtyła, Karol, *Miłość i Odpowiedzialność* (Cracow: TN KUL, 1960).

Wojtyła, Karol, "The Personal Structure of Self-Determination," in Karol Wojtyła, *Person and Community: Selected Essays* (trans. Theresa Sandok, OSM; New York: Peter Lang, 1993), 187–95.

Wolf, Miroslav, *Exclusion and Embrace: A Theological Exploration of Identity, Otherness, and Reconciliation* (Nashville: Abingdon, 1996), 24.

Wolff, Hans Walter, *Anthropology of the Old Testament* (trans. Margaret Kohl; Philadelphia: Augsburg/Fortress, 1974).

Wright, N. T., "Mind, Spirit, Soul and Body: All for One and One for All; Reflections on Paul's Anthropology in his Complex Contexts," paper presented at Society of Christian Philosophers Eastern Meeting, March 18, 2011. http://ntwrightpage.com/2016/07/12/mind-spirit-soul-and-body/ (accessed May 14, 2018).

Wynn, Kerry H., "The Normate Hermeneutic and Interpretations within the Yahwistic Narratives," in Hector Avalos, Sarah J. Melcher and Jeremy Schipper (eds.), *This Abled Body: Rethinking Disabilities in Biblical Studies* (Atlanta: Society of Biblical Literature, 2007), 91–102.

Yancy, George, *Black Bodies, White Gazes: The Continuing Significance of Race* (Lanham, MD: Rowman & Littlefield, 2008).

Yee, Gale A., "'She Stood in Tears amid the Alien Corn': Ruth, the Perpetual Foreigner and Model Minority," in Rita Nakashima Brock, Jung Ha Kim, Kwok Pui-lan and Seung Ai Yang (eds), *Off the Menu: Asian and Asian North American Women's Religion and Theology* (Louisville, KY: Westminster John Knox Press, 2007), 45–65.

Yenson, Mark, *Existence as Prayer: The Consciousness of Christ in the Theology of Hans Urs von Balthasar* (New York: Peter Lang, 2014).

Yong, Amos, *The Bible, Disability, and the Church: A New Vision of the People of God* (Grand Rapids, MI: Eerdmans, 2011).

Yong, Amos, "Disability Theology of the Resurrection: Persisting Questions and Additional Considerations–A Response to Ryan Mullins," *Ars Disputandi* 12 (2012): 4–10.

Yong, Amos, *Theology and Down Syndrome: Reimagining Disability in Late Modernity* (Waco, TX: Baylor University Press, 2007).

Zachhuber, Johannes, *Human Nature in Gregory of Nyssa: Philosophical Background and Theological Significance* (Leiden: Brill, 1999).

Zeman, Adam, *A Portrait of the Brain* (New Haven, CT: Yale University Press, 2009).

Zeng, Tian Chen, Alan J. Aw and Marcus W. Feldman, "Cultural Hitchhiking and Competition between Patrilineal Kin Groups Explain the Post-Neolithic Y-Chromosome Bottleneck," *Nature Communications* 9, no. 1 (2018): 2077.

Zizioulas, John D., *Communion and Otherness* (London: T&T Clark, 2006).

INDEX

Made in United States
North Haven, CT
14 January 2024

47439374R00259